UNIX® AND WINDOWS 2000 HANDBOOK

Planning, Integration, and Administration

LONNIE HARVEL
DAVID WEBB
STEVEN FLYNN
TODD WHITEHURST

ISBN 0-13-025493-2

9 780130 254931

90000

Prentice Hall PTR, Upper Saddle River, NJ 07458
www.phptr.com

Library of Congress Cataloging-in-Publication Data

Harvel, Lonnie et al
   Unix and Windows 2000 handbook : planning, integration, and administration/ Lonnie Harvel...
   [et al.].
      p. cm.
   ISBN 0-13-025493-2 (alk. paper)
     1. UNIX (Computer file)   2. Microsoft Windows (Computer file)   3. Operating Systems
   (Computers)   I. Harvel, Lonnie.
   QA76.76.O63 U58 2000
   005.4'476--dc21
                                               00-029831
                                                      CIP

Editorial/Production Supervision: *Wil Mara*
Acquisitions Editor: *Tim Moore*
Developmental Editor: *Jim Markham*
Technical Editors: *Jim Keogh & Frank Schmidt*
Marketing Manager: *Bryan Gambrel*
Manufacturing Manager: *Alexis R. Heydt*
Buyer: *Maura Goldstaub*
Cover Design Director: *Jerry Votta*
Cover Designer: *Anthony Gemmellaro*
Art Director: *Gail Cocker-Bogusz*

© 2000 Prentice Hall PTR
Prentice-Hall, Inc.
Upper Saddle River, New Jersey 07458

Prentice Hall books are widely used by corporations and government agencies for training, marketing, and resale. The publisher offers discounts on this book when ordered in bulk quantities. For more information, contact Prentice Hall's Corporate Sales Department—phone: 1-800-382-3419; fax: 1-201-236-7141; email: corpsales@prenhall.com; address: Corp. Sales Dept., Prentice Hall PTR, 1 Lake Street, Upper Saddle River, NJ 07458.

Printed in the United States of America
10 9 8 7 6 5 4 3 2 1

ISBN 0-13-025493-2

Prentice-Hall International (UK) Limited, *London*
Prentice-Hall of Australia Pty. Limited, *Sydney*
Prentice-Hall Canada Inc., *Toronto*
Prentice-Hall Hispanoamericana, S.A., *Mexico*
Prentice-Hall of India Private Limited, *New Delhi*
Prentice-Hall of Japan, Inc., *Tokyo*
Pearson Education Asia P.T.E., Ltd.
Editora Prentice-Hall do Brasil, Ltda., *Rio de Janeiro*

TRADEMARKS

All product names mentioned in this book are the trademarks or service marks of their respective companies, organizations or, owners—

- AIX is a registered trademark of International Business Machines Corporation
- Apache is a trademark of the Apache Group
- AT&T is a registered trademark of American Telephone and Telegraph
- BSD is a trademark of University of California, Berkeley
- Ethernet is a trademark of Xerox Corporation
- HP is a trademark of Hewlett-Packard Company
- HP-UX is a trademark of Hewlett-Packard Company
- HPFS is a trademark of Microsoft Corporation
- IBM is a registered trademark of International Business Machines Corporation
- Innosoft is a trademark of Innosoft International, Inc.
- InterNIC is a registered service mark of the U.S. Department of Commerce
- Intel is a registered trademark of Intel Corporation
- Internet is a registered trademark of Internet, Inc.
- Kerberos is a trademark of Massachusetts Institute of Technology
- Linux is a Registered Trademark of Linus Torvalds
- Motif is a trademark of Open Software Foundation
- MS-Dosis registered trademark of Microsoft Corporation
- Network File System, and NIS/NIS+ are trademarks and NFS is a registered trademark of Sun Microsystems, Inc.
- NFS Maestro is a registered trademark of Hummingbird, Inc.
- Novell is a trademark of Novell, Inc.
- Netscape is a registered trademark of Netscape Communications Corporation
- NetWare is a trademark of Novell, Inc.
- OSF is registered trademark of Open Software Foundation
- OS/2 is a trademark of International Business Machines Corporation
- PADL Software is a trademark of PADL Software Pty Ltd, Austraila
- PostScript is a registered trademark of Adobe Systems, Inc.
- RedHat Linux is a registered trademark of RedHat, Inc.
- SNA is a trademark of International Business Machines Corporation
- Sun and Sun Microsystems are registered trademarks of Sun Microsystems
- Solaris and Sun OS are registered trademarks of Sun Microsystems
- UNIX is a registered trademark in the United States and other countries, licensed exclusively through X/Open Company Limited
- Windows is a registered trademark of Microsoft Corporation
- Windows NT is a trademark of Microsoft Corporation
- Windows 2000 is a trademark of Microsoft Corporation
- X11 is a trademark of Massachusetts Institute of Technology
- X Window System is a registered trademark of Mass. Institute ofTechnology
- Yellow Pages is a registered trademark of British Telecommunications, plc. in the United Kingdom

The authors dedicate this book to their parents and families,
with thanks for their love and support.

CONTENTS AT A GLANCE

CONTENTS

PART TWO : INTEGRATION   185

INTRODUCTION

A few years ago, while teaching a course in UNIX system administration, a student approached me at the end of the day. He was concerned about implementing backup strategies for the systems he would soon have to manage. I was surprised. The gentleman had been an NT administrator for quite a while, managing a rather large infrastructure. When I took the time to explain how the concepts of backups were the same, only the commands differed, he was greatly relieved. That and many similar experiences over the last several years inspired this book. Our intent is to convey the fundamentals of system administration as an independent skill set, with the specific operating system as the application.

This book is an introduction to the complexity of supporting the user environment in a multi-vendor installation. *UNIX and Windows 2000 Handbook: Planning, Integration & Administration* is designed to assist system administrators of all levels in creating and maintaining a productive environment for their users. This book includes a discussion of the issues, guidelines for solving the related problems, technical examples where applicable, and a more philosophical discussion of the nature of support and the policy issues involved in planning and administering a heterogeneous environment.

Over the years, the separation among UNIX variants, and the resulting advocacy of administrators and programmers has resulted in a lack of commonality within the administrative functions of the systems. The inclusion of Windows NT/2000 and the increased capabilities of the personal computer have further complicated the issue of administration. Applications exist to span this diversity; implementations of DNS, NIS, and NFS are three notable examples.

Throughout this book, we present the tasks of System Administration and how they are implemented in the UNIX and Windows 2000 environments. The intent is to view system administration tasks as independent concepts and the support of a specific operating system as an application of those concepts.

Who is This Book For

This book is intended for individuals who are competent users of one or more of the operating systems, but not necessarily a system administrator in any. The basic concepts are provided, as well as moderate to advanced discussions on topics related to creating an integrated user environment.

How this Book is Organized

The book is structured to serve as a tutor as well as a reference. The fundamental issues of installation planning and the role of the system administrator will be thoroughly discussed. The book has been divided into three parts: Planning, Integration, and Administration. As the book progresses, the overlapping nature of these areas will become increasingly evident. We placed individual administration tasks in a particular area based on our perception of the task constraints. For example, upgrades and patches are administrative tasks, but careful planning is required for efficiency and stability. The latter constraint outweighs the former, and we placed the chapter in the Planning part of the book.

PART 1: PLANNING

The first section of this book relates to the foundational concepts required to begin system administration. In presenting these concepts, we introduce and explain the need for planning carefully. Planning is always good, but it becomes essential when attempting to integrate diverse operating systems in to a stable heterogeneous infrastructure. Though the material may be review for some readers, we recommend that you take the time to refresh your knowledge of these fundamentals.

PART 2: INTEGRATION

Networking, file sharing, information services, host recognition, and resource sharing are where the true work of integration begins. In this section we present chapters which introduce the tools and concepts necessary to create a distributed environment, including those tools and techniques which can be used to bridge the chasm between the Windows 2000 and UNIX worlds.

PART 3: ADMINISTRATION

Though not the most exciting section of the book, administration and maintenance of the heterogeneous infrastructure is necessary to maintain a stable environment for users. In this section we cover the tasks necessary to support a distributed environment and, where possible, ways to save time and resources.

Conventions Used in This Book

This book uses different features to help highlight key information.

CHAPTER HIGHLIGHTS

Major topics covered in the chapters are listed in tables at the beginning. Though more material is often covered. These topics are considered essential. The topics are divided into Windows 2000 and UNIX categories.

ICONS

Icons represent called-out material that is of significance and that you should be alerted to. Icons include:

Note

This icon is used to call out information that deserves special attention; one that the reader may otherwise run a highlight marker through.

Tip

This icon is used to flag particularly useful information that will save the reader time, highlight a valuable technique, or offer specific advice.

Warning

This icon flags information that may cause unexpected results or serious frustration.

Command

This icon calls out system commands used in the previous section. A summary of these commands can be found in the appendix.

We hope that this book will prove useful. There is a great deal of information presented here, but it is not possible to include everything. If you have any questions or comments, please send them to questions@system-administration.com or comments@system-administration.com You can also visit our website at www.system-administration.com for updates and internet-based resources.

ACKNOWLEDGEMENTS

A *notre estimé collègue:*

We would like to thank Didier Contis for his work on Chapter 11, Security. Mr. Contis is a Research Engineer at the Georgia Institute of Technology and has developed networking and security strategies for corporate, financial and educational institutions in Europe and the United States.

Throughout this project, we have had the good fortune to work with an astounding team of editors at Prentice Hall. We especially wish to thank Tim Moore for his assistance in creating the vision for this book, Jim Markham for his constant support in the creation of the text, and Wil Mara for his work in producing the final manuscript. Likewise, the knowledge and guidance of our technical editors, Frank Schmidt and Jim Keogh, greatly enriched the substance of this book.

Many thanks to Peter Flur and John Lockhart for the use of their domain, sniglets.com.

We would also like to thank our colleagues at Georgia Tech and the Southern Company for their patience with us during this endeavor.

PLANNING

In the next few chapters, we will discuss the fundamental concepts of installation, system startup and shutdown, the filesystem, and upgrades and patches. Along with these topics, we will discuss the need for careful planning in your system and infrastructure design. Through planning, you can create a more stable environment for your users while reducing your overall workload. To plan well, you must understand the basics. In the next five chapters, we will explain the underlying concepts of system administration. These will form the foundation upon which the remainder of the book will build.

"Being busy does not always mean real work. The object of all work is production or accomplishment and to either of these ends there must be forethought, system, planning, intelligence, and honest purpose, as well as perspiration. Seeming to do is not doing."

Thomas Edison (1847–1931)

THE ART AND SCIENCE OF SYSTEM ADMINISTRATION

Way back at the beginning of the information age, when computers were enormous and data storage was tiny, system administrators were created. They were chosen for their unique ability to arbitrate between the often-petulant operating systems and the equally unique group of people trying to program them. A mystique grew up around those selected few. To most users, it appeared that only system administrators could wring compliance from the early electronic tormentors. Each machine had its own idiosyncrasies, and its own cadre of conjurors to keep it entertained. As the mechanized wonders became more powerful, they paradoxically shrank and replicated. As computers shrank in size, their capabilities, and the job of the system administrator, grew. Networking, file sharing, databases, email, Web servers, printing, and users all added to the job description. System administrators must now juggle the *science* of operating systems, their resources, and the *art* of user support and administration.

The support of computers and users in the face of ever-changing operating systems continues to challenge even the most experienced of administrators. Price wars, as well as diverse system features like application requirements and other market forces within the computer industry have created a wide range of multi-vendor environments. In particular, the mingling of UNIX and the Windows family of operating systems has become common. The combination of these factors has resulted in a shifting morass, upon which the system administrator must build a stable environment for the users. The following chapters will guide you through the labyrinth of supporting the ever-changing needs of users and the ever-growing complexity of the infrastructure.

Understanding the Job

In this chapter, and throughout this book, we present system administration as a concept, independent of the operating system. The true basis of integrating a heterogeneous environment is understanding that system administration is a skill set that exists regardless of operating system. If you learn system administration, then you can apply the concepts to whatever operating system you are working with. Understanding the basic building blocks makes it possible to provide similar or identical services across operating systems. This book will weave this concept in with another one as *leveraged learning*. Operating systems are tools, incredibly complex, but still only tools. The understanding of how and when to use those tools is the foundation of good administration.

Most problems can be divided in multiple ways. This is certainly true with system administration. We have chosen to divide the administrator's job into three parts: *planning, integration,* and *administration.* These parts are not completely distinct. They are more like three intersecting circles. The most complex tasks exist where the three circles intersect, as shown in Figure 1.1. This book, therefore, is divided into three parts, to coincide with this grouping.

Figure 1.1
System administration areas.

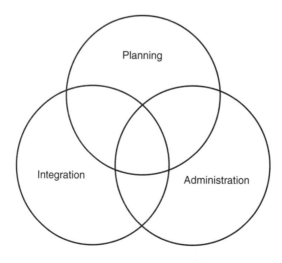

PLANNING

The adage, "A stitch in time saves nine," is certainly true when applied to system administration. Regretfully, a significant amount of your work as an administrator is done under tremendous time constraints, with anxious users standing in the wings, if not actually in your office. Planning is often sacrificed in these circumstances. In the next few chapters, we discuss the fundamental concepts of installation, system startup and shutdown, the filesystem, upgrades, and patches.

INTEGRATION

Integration, with respect to this book, is the sharing of resources between diverse operating systems. For clarity, we need to compare this with *interoperability* and *coexistence*. The three are ascending levels of the same concept. Coexistence is simply the state of cohabitation on a network. There are often applications provided to facilitate the transfer of information between diverse systems, but not without direct manipulation by the user. Integration is the next level, providing shared resources among constituent systems. The most commonly shared resources are filesystems, email, information and domain services, printing, and networking. Interoperability is the highest level of interaction, with identical application resources made available regardless of the operating system. A common example of interoperability is a database application, which must be distributed throughout a heterogeneous environment.

Our focus will be on integration, the middle ground between coexistence and interoperability. Specifically, we will be concerned with creating a stable environment for the user to work with. Network address resolution, user and system identification, shared filesystems, email, printing, networking, and security are the key issues in creating an integrated infrastructure. We will discuss tools and strategies for accomplishing these goals between Windows 2000 and a variety of UNIX operating systems.

ADMINISTRATION

The administrative tasks are, simply put, the most boring. However, they are easily the most critical to the users. Tasks in this part of the book deal directly with the users, or with the tools necessary to support them. Creating user accounts (and deleting them) is of obvious importance. Backups, performance-tuning, and developing user interfaces also affect the quality of the user environment. Many of the tools necessary to accomplish these tasks, and others in this book, are discussed here as well.

It is extremely easy to forget that the reason most systems and networks exist is to support some set of activities performed by users. We believe that the ultimate test of an integrated infrastructure is its ability to meet the needs of the people who use it. No matter how nice it looks on paper, or how well it is designed in theory, if the users are not happy, then it is not right, period.

LEVERAGED LEARNING

It is amazing the number of people who believe that variations in tasks and tools constitute a unique job. For example, there is a popular misconception that Solaris administration, HPUX administration, or even Windows 2000 administration are disparate skill sets. While it is certainly true that each UNIX variant, Windows 2000, and other operating systems require specific knowledge to manage correctly, the underlying fundamentals for each are extremely similar. Accountants move from job to job regardless of the unique nature of each position. Likewise, CEOs move from company to company with no concern for the actual nature of the company. The common belief in many fields is that once you have mastered a core set of concepts, they can be applied to a wide variety of different tasks. We believe that this is the case for system administration. Continuous changes in the field have also made it an absolute necessity. Without the ability to adapt, a system administrator will rapidly become obsolete and unemployed.

The understanding of basic networking principles, account management, file management, security issues, printing, and many more of our tasks is not dependent on the specific commands used to implement them. If necessary, you can always look them up in a manual if you know what you are trying to accomplish. In this book, we have attempted to *leverage* the reader's knowledge of one operating system against the task of learning a new one. In each chapter, we present fundamental concepts first, followed by specific examples. This structure is intended to emphasize the concepts you need to master and provide substantial examples of how they are used in practice. By this process, we intend to create a mental model of how system administration is done. The danger lies in incorrectly mapping the model when applying it to a specific operating system. For this reason, we have included notes, tips, and warnings that are related to places where the mapping fails throughout the chapters.

Explaining the Job

One of the most challenging roles of the system administrator is providing sound business reasons for what they do. The advantages of adding to your infrastructure may seem obvious to you; but those same advantages might not be clear to the person with the checkbook. Maintaining network throughput, licensing software, and adding faster hardware to cope with increased demand can easily be lost in the bottom line if your management team has a variety of responsibilities to juggle. Selling management on the pluses of new technologies and additional infrastructure can be one of the most difficult and frustrating tasks of system administration.

Managers speak the language of budgets, cost savings, value add, and customer satisfaction. These concepts are their primary responsibility. The language of the system administrator can be confusing, unless you learn to translate from bits and bytes to dollars and cents. Performing this translation does not take a business degree, just some common sense and the resolve to do some paperwork.

Information is key to helping the manager understand the business reasons for your recommendations. Organizing this information and presenting it in a clear and comprehensive way is the key to successful communication. This information, when presented in such a way as to clarify the requirements, the costs, and the pluses and minuses, is called a *business case*. A solid business case not only explains the technical needs and situation to the management, but also will provide the system administrator with peace of mind that the best solution has been found.

UNDERSTANDING THE SITUATION

Before any technical documentation is read, or any vendors are called, it is imperative that the system administrator thoroughly understands all the aspects, requirements, and underlying needs for a given project. These aspects, called *business drivers*, are the motivations for a new piece of hardware, a new software package, or the birth of a new, complicated project that may cost big dollars. Sometimes, the business driver is as simple as replacing a dead server. Other times, the business driver is very complex, such as the need to implement a new human resources management system for a global, multi-billion dollar company.

While these two examples may seem quite different, arriving at the correct answer will follow the same path. The first and sometimes most important step is to understand the requirements surrounding the business need. All too often, when there is some requirement for a new technological gizmo, administrators and bosses focus more on using the latest technology instead of finding the best solution. It is all too easy to be mesmerized by the latest technological gizmos, causing you to overlook issues related to the problem at hand. Staying focused on the problem, and not the technology of the solution, is the key to a successful project.

Staying focused on the problem, and not the technology of the solution, is the key to a successful project.

Sound advice is to create some sort of form, or procedure, to document exactly what the business drivers are, who is affected, and what the expectations are *before* you begin to look at any type of technological solution. Don't let your exuberance to find a solution cause you to overlook or undervalue minute details, for those details may come back and bite you later.

While everyone hates meetings, it is better to meet early in a project and determine the requirements than to meet later in the project and discuss the problems. Try to bring all the necessary parties to the table early and solicit input from a broad spectrum. This means including more than just your own team. If the project is far-reaching, try to assemble all affected parties, as their inputs may help clarify which technological path to take. Not only does this help you gather information, but it also helps the users feel like they are stakeholders in the project and part of the team. The more support you have, the easier it is to cross hurdles later in the project.

Once you have gathered all the key players and have defined the needs and requirements of the project, try to document what you have gathered. Having the business needs on paper, along with the input of the team members, can help you later in the project if you begin to lose your way (it's also a great way to cover yourself).

RESEARCHING ALTERNATIVES

Now that you have gathered and documented the business need, you should begin to look for the technological solution. Even if you believe you know the solution, you need to invest in some research. Learning the proper way to conduct this research is not difficult, if you know what resources are available to you.

- **Use the Internet**—One of the best places to research problems is on the Internet. With the thousands of newsgroups and hundreds of sites dedicated to technology, there is a high probability that another administrator has already investigated your problem and developed a solution. Most likely, you'll be able to find multiple solutions. Use this data to help form some opinions; but remember, it is best not to believe everything you find on the Internet.

- **Communicate with peers**—Isolation is one of the administrator's worst enemies. In many organizations, the administrator may be a one-person shop, managing everything including the network, servers, and user workstations. Even if you are in a large shop, don't let yourself fall into the trap of working in a vacuum. Administrators need to get our of their environment and breed new ideas. Joining local user groups and attending large conferences help lend perspective, and generally will yield a few new ideas. At worst, the administrator has a new forum in which to vent about their day-to-day problems.

■ **Read trade magazines and journals**—Everyone hates receiving junk mail; but the fact is, mountains of unsolicited paper is an occupational hazard. However, in the computing world, there are a lot of magazines and email digests you can subscribe to that only cost the few minutes it takes for you to fill out a questionnaire. While the information you provide will result in tons of vendor-related mailings, the information you receive from the publications will be highly valuable. Examples include *InfoWorld* and *PC Week*, just to name a few. Once you've visited a conference, or subscribed to one of these magazines, you will be solicited to join others. While you may only read one or two, the effort is worth the few nuggets of information you will find that hit the spot.

■ **Solicit vendor input**—Vendors are those people and organizations you deal with to acquire new technology and resources. Vendors can run the gamut from being very helpful, to being very annoying and downright unlikable. One of the things you should work on is developing relationships with vendors you like. These vendors have resources that you can call on when you need help. One of the benefits of having a good vendor relationship is that vendors are all too happy to loan you equipment or software licenses, especially when you are in the process of evaluating new technology. Don't abuse this avenue, but also don't be afraid to ask for help. Vendors are out to make money, and they know that if they don't help you, there's a good chance their competition will.

■ **Conduct your own evaluation**—While talking to other administrators, doing your homework, and obtaining help from vendors can help you come to the right conclusion, *you* are still your best avenue for evaluating the right solution to a problem. If you have the resources, create a test lab where you can evaluate new technology, tinker with configurations, and re-create your environments. Bottom line is: No one knows your environment better than you do, so do as much leg work as you can yourself so you are confident with the solution you present to your users. Remember, your neck is on the line, so make sure you have all the information before you decide on which path to take.

Using these resources should help you find the right technical solution to almost any problem. Yet most problems require more than just technology. Once you come to the right decision, you'll need to implement the solution, train the users, and provide ongoing support to make the project successful. Choosing a technological solution that is inexpensive, but that requires many hours of training and countless long nights of support, may not be the correct solution. You need to weigh all the alternatives, comparing not just the technology, but the dollar and human costs involved, before implementing a new technology.

DELIVERING A BUSINESS CASE

So, you have looked at all the technological possibilities and you're ready to go to the boss and share your conclusions. Before you make that visit, you might want to create a document that supports your conclusions, as many a good solution has been brushed aside when the value of the technology was not made clear. You need to present a concise list of all the costs, benefits, and limitations of the solutions you investigated.

Determining Product Costs

When building a business case, if you can create a comparison that encompasses the following six elements, you will have captured the major costs, and hopefully, give the boss all the information necessary to give you the green light on your project.

- **Hardware**—While this may seem simple enough, you would be surprised at how many items in this category get overlooked when attaching cost to hardware. Few administrators will miss the cost of the server, monitor, printer, and scanner, yet many will overlook the cost of network ports, uninterruptable power supplies, and cables to tie it all together. Most commonly, administrators will overlook shared or commodity resources, such as network equipment, power strips, and cables. If you are only configuring one server, this may not be an issue. But, if you are working on a large project with a number of systems, these items can add up fast. Try to develop set formulas for recovering these costs, and make sure your manager understands the issues.
- **Software**—Software encompasses everything installed on your systems, including the operating system, virus software, system utilities, and user applications. These costs can be overlooked as customers focus on the usually larger hardware costs. While a single

missed application may only cause a small increase in overall cost, it is bad form to repeatedly ask management for more money so that you can install a critical piece of software down the line.

- **Installation**—Once you have all the parts in hand, how much time will be needed to assemble them into a working, breathing system. Is the installation straightforward, or is it a special case that will require added time or even outside resources? Determining the cost of time will be discussed in the next section,"Determining Labor Costs."

- **Ongoing support**—Now that you have the system installed, what will the day-to-day management of the solution require. Is it a simple system that will run almost by itself, or is it a complex configuration of components that will require the full-time attention of a single person? While estimating this is not an exact science, failure to ballpark this number correctly will greatly impact the lifespan of the project. Make sure your management team understands that systems require maintenance, upgrades, patches, and *backups*, and that these things cost time and money. If these costs are not favorable to your operation, then maybe you need to find a cheaper hardware or software solution, as skimping on support is always a recipe for failure.

- **Maintenance contracts**—These are the costs for ongoing support of software, or the ability to replace a piece of hardware in a short period of time. For software, maintenance is required to keep licenses intact and provide upgrades and bug fixes as the software package matures and changes over time. On the other hand, hardware contracts are akin to insurance in that they generally are not required, but if not utilized, can result in very high costs when a hardware component goes belly-up unexpectedly. Selling hardware contracts can be difficult, and the best way to explain them is to give replacement costs for key components. If they choose not to sign up, make sure they understand that you cannot guarantee that parts will be available if a failure occurs, and that you can't commit to have the system back on-line in a defined period of time.

- **Training**—Training is about the hardest cost/benefit to capture. While almost all technical types understand the benefits of a well-focused week of training, their management may have the attitude of "Go buy a book and learn all about it." Always try to include training costs when you're looking at implementing new hardware and software that doesn't fit into your current skill set, or those of your users.

Determining Labor Costs

Now that you've survived Accounting 101, and you've learned to capture all the piece-wise cost of a new project, you may ask,"How do I capture the cost of the time and effort that is put into making the project a success?"As the saying goes,"Time is money,"and as long as you're not donating your time for free Internet access, whenever you are working on a project, it is costing someone money.

If you are a contractor, determining cost is easy, as your consulting company charges a fixed hourly rate that is easy to factor into your business case. However, if you are paid a salary, plus benefits in some shape or form, try a formula like the following:

Hourly cost = Salary + Benefits/(Number of working hours)

Simple enough, but now you must calculate benefits and hours worked. If you work for a large corporation or organization, your human resources representative may be able to provide you with a good working number. Otherwise, a good approximation for benefits is to take half of your salary, or 50%. For number of hours worked, a good starting point is:

*52 – Number of weeks vacation * 40 Hours per week*

Of course, no administrator works only 40 hours per week, but why advertise that you are a workaholic? For an administrator that makes $60,000 per year, with 3 weeks vacation, an hourly cost would be:

Hourly Cost = $60,000 + $30,000/((52 – 3)*40)
= $90,000/1960
= $45.91 per hour

While these are not the world's most accurate numbers, they are in the ballpark, and when used consistently across all comparisons in a business case, will yield the result desired, which is finding the best solution.

Now that you have your information gathered, you need to create the actual business case. We provide a simple example here. You will need to create your own format that matches the needs of your operation. If you discuss this with your management team, they may provide you with specific guidelines for what to present and how to present it.

A Sample Business Case

Acme Widget Corporation needs a new email infrastructure. While their current email system works fine, they have money in the budget to either upgrade the existing email system or purchase a totally new solution. The boss would like to see a business case that documents the three-year cost of implementation and ownership for each choice. The boss doesn't care what technology is implemented, but wants the cheapest overall solution, with no surprises lurking in the future. While the budget is tight, the boss will shell out the cash for the right email system.

Given this information, you as the administrator can now begin your research by reading magazines, surfing the Internet, communicating with your peers, and calling in vendors to give you demos of prospective technological solutions. For the sake of space and sanity, let's assume that you do your research and are able to find all the necessary information for upgrading the current system or replacing it with a state-of-the-art, new gadget. Let's assume that the administrator makes $59,0000 per year, for a $45 per hour rate.

Table 1.1 shows the cost for upgrading the existing email system. As you can see, the up-front costs of this option are low, since you can reuse the existing server with only an inexpensive upgrade. The major cost here is the four hours of support per week required to keep the system running, coupled with the $3000 to keep the hardware and software maintenance contracts in place.

Table 1.1	Costs for Upgrading Existing Email System
Upgrade Existing Email System	Cost
Hardware: Upgrade existing server	$2000
Software: Stay with old package	$0
Installation: 4 hrs to install new hardware	$180
Ongoing Support: 4 hrs per week for 156 weeks	$28080
Maintenance Costs: $1000/year for 3 years	$3000
Training: None	$0
Total 3-Year Cost	$34880

Table 1.2 shows the costs for implementing a new email system. While the start-up costs are high because a new server and new software package are required, what stands out is that now the administrator is only spending two hours per week over the next three years supporting the new application. As you can see, this is a significant saving over the old system. Also note that the training costs for both the administrator and the users is captured under "Training". This item is often overlooked, and can bring signifi-

Table 1.2	**Costs for Implementing New Email System**	
Implement New Email System		Cost
Hardware: Purchase new server		$6000
Software: Purchase new software		$2000
Installation: 16 hrs to install server and software		$720
Ongoing Support: 2 hrs per week for 156 weeks		$14040
Maintenance Costs: $500 /year for 3 years		$1500
Training: $1200 for the administrator, $50/user for 100 users		$7200
Total 3-Year Cost		$31460

cant cost to a given solution. If the training cost per user had doubled, or the number of users was higher, the tables could have been turned, and the older email system would have been more cost-efficient.

So, you now have the solutions and the costs. Package up your results to include an easy-to-read summary and a short explanation of how you arrived at your numbers. The boss will love this, and may even give you a raise! (Don't go back and revise your hourly cost, as you could start a vicious circle!) Hopefully, your boss is reasonable and will agree with your assessment, thereby giving you the green light to start your project. Nothing is better than embarking on a new project knowing the boss, as well as any other involved parties, are in agreement from the outset, giving you time to focus on producing a high-quality product, on time and on budget.

Summary

The following chapters provide the concepts, skills, and tools necessary to create a stable environment for the user across a multi-vendor infrastructure. The most important thing to take from this book is an understanding of the fundamental principles that form the foundation of system administration. In each chapter, we discuss concepts, provide examples, and discuss policies and procedures where applicable.

As you use this book, focus on the similarities among the operating systems. Differences will always exist, but they are easier to identify and handle when recognized as exceptions to the functional model, and not the definition of our occupation.

SYSTEM PLANNING, INSTALLATION, AND CONFIGURATION

UNIX

Installation Planning

Installation Steps

Linux Example

Creating a Standard Installation

WINDOWS 2000

Installation Planning

Blue Screen Setup

GUI Mode Setup

Network Configuration

The acquisition of hardware immediately creates a demand on a system administrator's time. New hardware creates the natural and instantaneous desire for people to use it. This desire always seems more pressing than the need for a stable and supportable infrastructure. How can you overcome the demands of the needy masses and win the battle? Your best weapon is good planning. This chapter will help you develop a procedure for planning and deploying well-configured, standardized workstations and servers into a heterogeneous computing environment. We'll show you what questions to ask, point out what information is important, and finally, give you an installation checklist for UNIX and Windows that will help you to produce well-configured, standard systems that will keep your clients happy and your systems stable.

Just like any other user, one of the hardest things for an administrator to resist is the call of a shiny new piece of technology. The urge is to open the box and install the system. The administrator rationalizes by thinking, "I'll just install it to test it." They test the hardware, the software, and install an application or two. Being proud of their new toy, they invite their co-workers over for a test drive. They are then compelled to test the software, or borrow the system for a week or two to performance-test their application. They expound the system's virtues to anyone that will listen, even the boss. Of course, now the boss wants to play with the shiny new system; and why not, the boss paid for it. Life is good, and everyone is excited, that is, until the next new system arrives.

Now you, as the administrator, are left with a system that has slipped into production because your co-workers were so impressed by its performance that they moved their production application to the new machine. The new system has half a hard drive full of test material, but is not configured anywhere near the way you had intended. You have just lost your first major battle, and your system is still brand new!

Winning the war of system administration begins with formulating a strong battle plan, even before you acquire a single piece of hardware. Spending some time up-front talking with your clients, carefully designing your infrastructure, and discussing your decisions with your peers will pay off over time. A well-thought-out network of systems will:

- Generate fewer user complaints and problems.
- Require a smaller infrastructure (printers, DNS servers, file servers).
- Need fewer system re-installations.
- Provide higher reliability, stability, and flexibility.
- Allow you to increase the ratio of systems to system administration staff.

While spending three weeks in meetings to discuss the installation of a new system may or may not give you the world's best configured computer, experience tells us that in many cases, the administrator will need to install a new system as fast as possible. Many clients demand immediate service, without regard for the other critical projects you're working on, your family, or that it is three o'clock in the afternoon and you haven't eaten lunch.

Good Planning is Half the Battle

Good planning is more of a mindset than a tangible substance, and it differs for everyone. If, after reading this chapter, you can tailor an installation plan that works for you, then you have won half the battle of system administration. Good planning is highly dependent on *your* situation. An administrator working for a bank has a completely different set of priorities than an administrator working for a university.

While many of the core tools for installation are the same, in most cases, individualized requirements will choose your path for you. However, as the administrator, if you spend some time up-front to develop a plan, you will find that your environment will lead you to a sound installation process. To accomplish this, you need to gather information about your environment. If you know your environment, then you have all the information you need to install your systems.

KNOWING YOUR CLIENT

If possible, you should know about new computer orders in advance. Before the first system is ordered, you should thoroughly understand the tasks each system will perform. Most people dread receiving a call from a customer with a new system, without any prior knowledge that the customer *had* ordered a system. Oftentimes and too late, you find out the purpose for the computer, that the hardware is too small or too large, or worse, that it has the wrong operating system. Now you are forced to squeeze this system into your framework regardless of whatever standards you have set. Heading this problem off at the pass takes time, planning, and a lot of face time with your customers.

Knowing your users and their needs is probably the most important thing you can do to ensure a stable environment. By taking the time to discuss new systems before they are purchased, you can save time and money, and in most cases, provide a better system than the user could have ordered on their own. While small mistakes, like ordering too little memory or too large a disk can usually be solved with a phone call, larger mistakes, like ordering a system that runs a different operating system than the application requires, are harder to solve.

Do everything you can to help guide your users to the right system. Remind them that you, as a system administrator, spend countless hours a day working on computers, and that makes you uniquely qualified to help them find the right fit. Beg, plead, and if you have to, yell and scream, if that's what it takes to make your clients aware that part of your job is to make sure each and every system fits into the overall puzzle. Setting up standards means nothing if people who do not know the standards can introduce new pieces of equipment into your infrastructure.

Once you've made it known that you're available to help configure new systems, through word of mouth, the company intranet, or stalking newly delivered systems until they reach their destination, what do you do next?

Treat each new installation like a criminal investigation. You need to ask the right questions so that you are sure that beyond a reasonable doubt you have all the evidence you need to choose the right computer for your client. Questions you should ask are listed in Table 2.1.

While you may be the expert, the user knows what they need. Use this opportunity to steer your user toward your standards, but never tell the user they are wrong. Give good, solid reasons why they should choose a configuration that fits your model. Reliability, stability, and the ability for you to support the system are always good places to start. Drop names of other users you have been successful with, and let them talk. Success breeds success!

Table 2.1	Questions to Ask Before and During a New Installation
Pre-Purchase	Installation
Who will be the main user of the system? If the system is a multi-user server, who will be the contact for the system?	Who should have administrator/root rights?
Who will be the contact in case of problems?	Who will need access to the system?
What will the primary purpose for this system be?	What version of the operating system is needed?
What are the budgetary restraints?	What are the virtual memory (swap) requirements for this system?
What platform preference does the customer have for hardware and	What infrastructure services will the system require (DNS, NIS, WINS, DHCP, NFS, DFS)?
What are the hardware and soft ware requirements for the application?	What is the system's IP address, net-mask, hostname, and default router IP address?
What, if any, special requirements exist, such as dual network connections, high-resolution graphics, or specialty interface cards?	
What third-party software needs to be ordered in addition to the base system?	What license keys need to be acquired to install third-party software?
Where will the system be located?	Where are the power and network connections located?
Where is the system being delivered?	Where are the best infrastructure servers that will provide the fastest response time (DNS, NFS, DFS, WINS, LDAP) located?
When can you order the system?	When is a convenient time for the customer to have the new system installed?
When is the system needed in production?	
How would you like the disks laid out?	When should the disks be partitioned and software installed?

Make sure you listen carefully to what your user is telling you. While you may be the expert, the user knows what they need.

KNOWING YOUR INFRASTRUCTURE

While infrastructure in many cases refers to the network, for our purposes, infrastructure refers to the support systems you have in place to make your day-to-day operations run smoothly. Infrastructure can include:

- Mail servers.
- NIS, DNS, and LDAP servers.
- File and print servers.
- Network infrastructure, including routers, switches, and bridges.

By understanding how your infrastructure is designed, you can architect your systems correctly from the start. Be aware of how many DNS, NIS+, and LDAP servers you have on each network segment. Use redundant services where possible. Be aware that multi-user systems require more resources than a stand-alone workstation, and may require you to install additional servers. If installing more servers is not an option, attempt to balance the load through proactive means instead of waiting for problems. DNS and NIS+ problems can be some of the hardest to debug, so kill the bugs early for best results. Configuring systems to use redundant services will be discussed in Chapter 6, "Name Resolution and Registration."

Understand how user groups work and what servers they use. Try to group or *cluster* users' filesystems with the workstations and servers they use most. Employ switches where users require high bandwidth. Don't be afraid to move servers around when you can take advantage of new network equipment. Faster routers and switches lose their purpose if they are under-utilized

Be sure a user doesn't order the wrong network card if you don't support a particular speed or medium. Ordering the wrong network card can delay installation for days, and cost you big dollars if you cannot return the incorrect card. Be sure to order the right cables, too!

PLANNING SUMMARY

As has been discussed, the first step in creating a successful system is asking the right questions. Use the information in Table 2.1 to help plan the installation of all new systems. By addressing these questions early in the planning process, your chances of success greatly increase. In heterogeneous environments that mix Windows and UNIX, the right questions not only help you mange the system, but they can help undecided users choose the best operating system and hardware for their desired application. Don't allow yourself to favor one operating system over another. Each operating system has strengths and weaknesses, and if you can learn to tell the differences, you can help steer your clients to the best possible platform.

UNIX Installation Steps

Once you've worked to determine the right systems to install, you need to tackle the actual installation of the operating system. Installation doesn't have to be a long, drawn-out process. With available GUI installation tools, super-fast hardware, and some knowledge of the system, installing the operating system can in many cases be a one-hour operation. However, for the novice administrator, installing UNIX can become a nightmare if GUI tools aren't available or if special configurations are required.

What follows is not an attempt to give you step-by-step instructions for installing every available flavor of UNIX. Each UNIX derivative has its own styles, interfaces, and rules for being successful. However, understanding the building blocks of a UNIX system is universal, and the next sections will give you some essential information, techniques, and tips that you can use to organize and complete successful UNIX installations.

PREPARING THE DISK

While it may be hard to believe today, there once was a time when disk sizes were small and disk costs were high. In the 1980s, a 100MB hard disk was considered large, and at a cost of thousands of dollars, it was also considered cost-effective. Because disk space was scare and expensive, it was important to manage disk resources effectively and waste as little space as possible. One way to manage disk space effectively was to subdivide the given resources at the operating system level, giving certain system functions a slice, or partition, of the available disk. This disk rationing, or partitioning, allowed the administrator to dole out this scarce resource fairly, as well as make sure that each operating system function received enough space to work efficiently.

Changes in technology have created larger and larger disks, to the point where having enough disk space for any given piece of the operating system is no longer a crisis. However, while rationing disk space is no longer necessary, there are still cases where subdividing disk drives is useful, and in some cases, necessary to provide proper system function and optimal system efficiency. Preparing your disk drive to receive the operating system is the first of many functions, but as with building a house, building a strong foundation is essential to overall structural integrity.

Disk layouts can be as simple as a single internal drive or as complicated as a large system with terabytes for external disk storage. What is important in all cases is choosing the right disk configuration before installation, and setting a standard for partition sizes and names across your UNIX platforms. Making a mistake early can cost you a great deal of anxiety, hours of moving files, or even a complete re-installation of the filesystem.

Be careful to allocate enough disk space in your partitions. Changing the partition size later is a difficult process that usually requires a complete re-install of either the operating system or the data on that partition.

THE `format` COMMAND

Most UNIX flavors have GUI installation tools that make the task of disk management as easy as point-and-click. However, if you don't have access to GUI tools, or if you enjoy command-line UNIX hacking, then you need to know how to manipulate partitions on your disk media. Disks are partitioned by using the `format` command. In most cases, your installation program will run `format` for you; your job is to provide the necessary information used to subdivide the disks. However, running `format` from the command line is a common occurrence, used when adding new or reconfiguring existing drives. While the `format` command contains many options, if you master a core few, you will be able to properly manage your environment. The `format` command is discussed in more detail in Chapter 4, "The Filesystem."

Partitioning disks is a little bit different in each version of UNIX. Table 2.2 contains a listing of commands by operating system to manipulate disk partitions. Disk partitioning is not a trivial chore. Disks are cheap, but user data is valuable. Invest in an external SCSI drive that you can hook up to any of your UNIX systems. Attach this disk to a non-production UNIX machine and "beat" on this disk until you become proficient with the disk partitioning commands. Once you have mastered one operating system, you can move the disk to other platforms.

`Format` is used to partition, label, and prepare a new or existing disk to be recognized by the system. Once a disk device is selected, use the `print` option to display the current partition table. The partition command is used to subdivide a disk into multiple sections. For standardization, always use `partition a` (slice 0) for root and `partition b` (slice 1) for swap.

Table 2.2	**Disk Partitioning Commands**
OS	Command
AIX	Diag SMIT
HPUX	Mediainit SAM
Linux	Cfdisk Fdisk
Solaris X86	fdisk

SETTING A PARTITION STANDARD

Partitions, as defined at the disk level, physically split a disk into distinct slices, or partitions, which help define different functions, including filesystems, swap space, and log areas for high-performance filesystems. In almost all cases, the partition layout, or *partition table*, can be split into eight different areas, or partitions.

As time has passed, disks have grown allowing larger disk partitions. For this reason, the requirement to subdivide a disk past eight slices has never been needed, and as time has progressed, administrators have generally chosen to have fewer partitions, and in many cases, just a single partition that covers the complete disk. Developing a standard for disk partitions will be a benefit by simplifying new installations and reducing time needed for additions to and upgrades of existing systems. Table 2.3 shows a chart of multiple partitions. Actual disk partitions will vary, based on how your system will be used.

In ancient times, when disks were small, it was necessary and to your advantage to partition your disks into multiple volumes, or distribute the operating system over multiple disks. While different flavors of UNIX may have their own variations, the partition layout in Table 2.3 provides a model that encompasses a number of different operating system pieces that at some point in UNIX evolution have been allocated their own slice of the disk. The most compelling reason to partition a disk is to isolate different system functions so that each function is guaranteed a certain amount of disk space for its functions to operate.

A good example of partitioning a disk is the control of spooling areas for mail and printer queues. While spooling will be discussed in Chapters 9 and 10, understanding spool areas in relation to disk space is an important issue.

Table 2.3	Multiple Partitions	
Partition	Name	Contents
0	root	System kernel, binaries, and configuration files.
1	swap	Virtual memory.
2	overlap	Don't modify this partition unless you plan to use the complete disk for a special use recommended by your operating system or application software vendor.
3	var	System logs, spooling areas for system programs such as mail and printing.
4	usr	Operating system programs and utilities for users.
5	home	User files and application directories.
6	log	Logging for high-performance filesystems.
7	unused	All partitions do not have to be used.

A spool area acts as temporary storage that holds data while the operating system performs its functions on a file. For example, if a user submits a 200MB file to be printed, it would first be moved to the spool area in /var, and from there, the printing program would execute the print operation and then delete this temporary copy of the file.

While printing seems like a simple operation, consider the amount of spool space needed if 100 print jobs were submitted at the same time, and the printer device was slow in rendering the printed item. It is easy to see that you would need a lot of space in /var to accommodate temporary files. If /var was not separated from the rest of the operating system, the print requests could easily overrun all of the available disk space, causing the system to run slowly, or not at all. For reasons such as this, subdividing the operating system disk such that no one area could cause a disk crash was chosen as the standard, and partition tables as in Table 2.3 were adopted as a standard as well.

During the mid-1990s, magnetic media technology advanced to the point where the price of a large, multiple gigabyte disk was about the same as a decent mouse and keyboard. Coupled with the ever-increasing size of the operating system, the partition listed in Table 2.4 has replaced the older partition table model presented in Table 2.3. With the ability to give multiple gigabytes to the operating system, it is no longer necessary to subdivide the disk to reduce the risk of one subsystem of the operating system overrunning all of the available resources.

Having larger disks also makes the job of system administration easier. With smaller disks, the amount of space for the system binaries was limited. While the initial installation of the operating system was not a problem, problems occurred further down the line when it came time to upgrade or patch the system. Over time, operating systems grow in both size and functionality. While this is a good thing in general, it is impossible to predict future operating system size. Subsequently, a partition that fits one operating system version usually doesn't work for subsequent revisions, causing administrators much work down the road in re-partitioning and re-installing the operating system when a simple upgrade would have been possible if the disk was larger to start with.

 A patch is an interim addition to a piece of code, generally used as a quick but temporary solution to a bug or glitch.

Table 2.4 illustrates the simplified disk partition that is recommended if you plan to only use the disk to support the operating system. In essence, choose the amount of swap space you need and then allocate the remaining disk space to the root partition. While the remaining partitions on the disk are still available, they remain unused, or can be considered to be of zero size.

The partition model in Table 2.4 works well in systems where providing maximum space for system operations is primary. File, print, and general-purpose servers fit this model. By providing maximum disk space for these functions, you limit the possibility of disk resource problems, and increase the reliability, stability, and maintainability of your system. While this is a very stable solution, one may wonder if a "One size fits all approach" is always the best, especially in situations where the operating system is not acting as a server. Table 2.5 shows a hybrid partition model that pools disk space to make system administration simple, yet provides file space for user and application files.

As you can see, the partition for /home has been added to allow space for user files as well as applications. A logging area is designed to be used by high-performance filesystems. The advantage of this partition model is that with large disks, you can provide ample space for operating system functions, patches, and future upgrades, while providing sufficient disk space for users and applications. The model also isolates the operating systems from application and user space, which guarantees that the users of the system

Table 2.4	Root-Only Partition	
Partition	Name	Comments
0	root	Operating system uses entire disk less swap space in partition 1.
1	swap	Virtual memory.
2	overlap	Don't modify this partition!
3	unused	
4	unused	
5	unused	
6	unused	

can't, either through use or mistake, fill up the entire disk, causing system problems. This hybrid partition standard will serve you well in systems where only one disk is available, but the system has to serve multiple purposes.

This section has presented three different partition models from which you may choose to build your partition standard. In these models, we have attempted to provide a foundation for building a partition standard. The important lesson to learn is to develop a partition standard that works for you, one that you can replicate throughout your environment. This may require some experimentation and refinement over time, but the payoff will emerge

Table 2.5	Hybrid Partition Model	
Partition	Name	Comments
0	root	Operating system.
1	swap	To increase swap space.
2	overlap	Don't modify this partition!
3	home	User and application files.
4	unused	
5	unused	
6	logging	Logging for high-performance filesystems.

when future upgrades and installations take only an hour or two, instead of turning into all-day events.

CONFIGURING SWAP SPACE

Knowing *how much* swap space to allocate is just as important as knowing *what partition to place* swap space on. Ten different UNIX administrators, could provide ten different solutions. To help you make the right decision, here are a few rules of thumb to use when planning for your installation:

- Double memory for swap is a good starting point. Once the system is up and running, if you determine more swap space is needed, it can easily be added then. For more information on how to determine if additional swap space is needed, see Chapter 14, "Performance Monitoring". If the system is dedicated to supporting a single application, check the software release notes or contact the vendor or developer for internally developed applications. They should give you a recommended configuration. However, if you are unable to determine your application needs directly, using the "double the system memory" rule is a good place to start.
- If you have multiple disk drives and have access to multiple controllers or channels, divide swap space evenly across these resources to increase performance.
- Plan with growth in mind. If you think additional real memory will be added to the system in the near future, add the swap space now. This will save you time and keep you from having to add swap files on regular filesystems.

 Swap memory is always significantly slower than real memory. Always try to configure your systems with as much real memory as possible, and only rely on swap memory for small periods of increased system demand.

Chapter 14, "Performance Monitoring," covers the connection between swap space and system performance. However, by following the rules just provided, your swap space should provide sufficient resources for awhile.

IP, DNS, NIS, AND NETWORKING

In today's environments, it is assumed that any new device is going to be attached to a LAN, WAN, an intranet, extranet, and of course, the Internet. With all the possible networks, it is no wonder that the most difficult part about installing a computer is the ability to make the network services for that system work on the first try. Couple the complexity of physical networks with the magic of naming services and any administrator will develop a few gray hairs installing a new system.

Any worthy administrator can install an operating system, but even the most seasoned guru won't be able to properly install a new system without some knowledge of the network infrastructure. Knowing the physical network layout along with the addresses of naming services is an absolute requirement before attempting to install an operating system. Before you attempt an install, make sure you take the time to gather the necessary network information, or prepare to suffer the consequences.

Table 2.6 defines the data you should gather before you attempt to install your system. Most GUI installation tools will prompt you for most if not all of this information, so before you start the install program, have this information on hand.

Table 2.6	Necessary Elements to Gather Prior to Installation	
You Need	Function of	Comments
Hostname	Networking	Good practice is to fully qualify your hostname.
System IP Address	Networking	Not needed if you use DHCP.
Default Router	Networking	Not needed if using a router.
Subnet Mask	Networking	In most cases, this is `255.255.255.0`.
Domain Name	DNS	For example, `mycompany.com` or `department.yourschool.edu`.
Search Domains	DNS	Optional, but useful in larger networks.
Domain Name Servers	DNS	You will want at least two for redundancy.
NIS Domain Name	NIS	Only needed if using NIS; for simplicity, can be the same as Domain Name.
NIS Server IP Addresses	NIS	Optional, not needed if you broadcast.

HOSTNAME

When beginning your installation, choosing a name for your system is a logical place to start. The hostname of a system helps define the identity of the computer for both the outside world as well as the system itself. In

UNIX, the hostname is tied into many services, including the Domain Name Service (DNS), Network Information Service (NIS), and Network Filesystem (NFS). Choose your hostnames wisely, as changing the hostname later can be a difficult and highly unrewarding exercise.

Choosing a hostname, and at a higher level a hostname scheme, can sometimes be as difficult as installing the system. You can choose a rigid scheme such as `f2r3c5.yourdomain.com` (for Floor 2, Room 3, and Cube 5), or something more fun such as `animals.yourdomain.edu` (and then choose the world's most obscure creatures). Be creative, but be consistent. Also try to choose hostnames that are easy to remember and spell. Nothing is more frustrating than attempting to telnet to an obscure server when you are blessed with poor spelling skills.

Your hostname will appear in a number of different places depending on your flavor of UNIX. In `/etc/hosts`, the hostname will appear on the line with the host IP address.

```
#

# Internet host table

#

127.0.0.1      localhost

10.1.1.15  mars.somedomain.com loghost
```

It is wise to always fully qualify your hostname. What this means is that your system knows itself as `host.yourdomain.com`, and not just a host, as we see from the output of the `hostname` command:

```
mars#hostname

mars.somedomain.com
```

This helps avoid confusion when your system is interacting with network services such as DNS, LDAP, and NFS. More confusion can arise when you have to manage systems in multiple domains that share resources. While fully qualifying your hostname may cause you a bit of extra effort if you move your system to a new domain or subnet, the problems you eliminate easily outweigh any extra work you may have to do down the line.

If you have multiple domains, don't duplicate hostnames in different domains, such as `rover.ourdomain.com` and `rover.yourdomain.com`. While there is nothing technically wrong with this, what happens when your boss tells you to move all your systems into `ourdomain.com`?

If you want your system to respond to short names also, you can add additional entries such as:

```
mars#cat /etc/hosts

#

# Internet host table

#

127.0.0.1       localhost

10.1.1.15 mars.somedomain.com mars redplanet loghost
```

This system will respond to the fully-qualified hostname as well the short names mars and redplanet. The `loghost` entry directs the system to use itself for logging through `syslogd`. If you want to use a different host, you can add another entry in the `/etc/hosts` file to direct logging to another system.

```
sflynn@duchess.sniglets.com>cat /etc/hosts

#

# Internet host table

#

127.0.0.1       localhost

192.168.3.13 duchess.sniglets.com duchess rover

192.168.3.15 logger.sniglets.com loghost
```

Here, `syslogd` on your system will direct all log entries to `logger.yourdomain.edu`. This is useful if you have multiple systems and you want to create a master system you can use to explore log entries.

 `hostname` determines the hostname of a given system. This command gives the true name (not aliases) and can be useful in scripting. Licensed software may also use this command to unlock the software.

SYSTEM IP ADDRESS

Obtain a new IP address from the proper authorities (or possibly yourself). If you are not the network administrator, make sure you have your hostname chosen prior to visiting your network guru's cubicle. Also remember to have any other information required by your network staff, including the port number and/or location where the machine will be installed, machine model, the network card's MAC address, and most importantly, a charge account if necessary.

Once you have the IP address in hand, remember to give the network administrator time to propagate the IP address throughout the network. Be sure to verify that your system has propagated to network services such as DNS and NIS+ before you begin your installation.

DEFAULT ROUTER

If you have a simple network mode, where each subnet has only one interface into a router, then make sure you know the IP address of the default router for your particular network. Most systems will define the default router as part of bringing up the network interface at boot time.

However, if your network has redundant routers or router interfaces, then you may not need to define the default router. Daemons such as `routed` will broadcast onto your network segment and find the appropriate router interfaces. This helps to provide redundancy and possible performance gains depending on the size of your network. A downside to using `routed` is that your system will be susceptible to problems caused by devices advertising themselves as routing devices. This occurs frequently in less secure networks where less than knowledgeable users have access to install their own systems, such as Linux.

Running `routed` can be a problem on a network that is not tightly controlled. If you have a network with many users who have the opportunity to configure systems, you will at some time have a user who configures a system that advertises itself as a router.

SUBNET MASK

The subnet mask is needed to properly route network information from your system onto your network, and is used when your system configures its network interface. While subnets and subnet masks will be discussed in Chapter 11, "Networking and Security," it is very important that you understand how to correctly configure your subnet mask during installation.

There are three common IP network classes shown in Table 2.7. A large company such as AT&T will have a class A network, a university or

Table 2.7	Network Classes			
Class	IP Address Range		Hosts Per Network	Default Netmask
A	`001.X.X.X` to `126.X.X.X`		16387064	`255.0.0`
B	`128.0.X.X` to `191.255.X.X`		64516	`255.255.0.0`
C	`192.0.0.X` to `233.255.255.X`		254	`255.255.255.0`

medium-sized company will have one or more class B networks, while small companies or individuals will have class C networks.

The netmask determines how you have decided to subnet, or partition, your network. Using the default netmask on a class B network ties all 64 thousand possible systems together. While this may seem ideal, the network delays would be quite large.

For large networks, your network administrators will decide how to partition your network. In practice, small portions of a class A or B network will be grouped together; for example, if you have a class B network and want to merge two networks with the address range `130.207.232` and `130.207.233`. This will give you 508 possible hosts on one network.

The binary representation of those networks when translated using the 1's in the subnet mask and a netmask of `255.255.254` gives the same value, which shows that the subnets have been concatenated.

```
10000010.11001111.11101000.X
11111111.11111111.11111111.00000000
10000010.11001111.11101000.00000000
```

```
10000010.11001111.11101001.X          (130.207.233)
11111111.11111111.11111111.00000000
10000010.11001111.11101000.00000000
```

If we now use use the 0's, the operation gives a unique host address with 508 different binary combinations (where X can be any binary value from 1 to 254).

```
10000010.11001111.11101000.X          (130.207.232)
11111111.11111111.11111111.00000000
00000000.00000000.00000000.X
```

```
10000010.11001111.11101001.X        (130.207.233)
11111111.11111111.11111111.00000000
00000000.00000000.00000001.X
```

 Incorrect subnet masks are a common mistake that is difficult to debug. If you are experiencing strange and unexplained network problems on a system, always make sure to check the subnet masks.

Make sure you have the correct subnet mask for your network. Never assume that your network uses a common netmask like 255.255.255.0 (for a fully subnetted class B network). Using the work subnet mask can cause unexpected results, and while your system may be able to perform some operations on the network, if you don't identify the netmask as the problem, you may spend hours looking for problems in other areas.

DOMAIN NAME

Your domain name is simply the extension that, when concatenated with the hostname, gives you the fully-qualified system name. For instance, if your system is `rover.yourdomain.edu`, then your domain is `yourdomain.edu`. This is important for DNS and NIS+.

 Do not confuse this with your NIS+ domain name and the output of the `domainname` command.

DOMAIN NAME SERVERS

If you plan to use DNS to resolve hostnames, you'll need to know the proper name servers to put into your `/etc/resolv.conf`. This file defines the servers and the order in which they should be contacted.

```
mars:> cat /etc/resolv.conf

domain yourdomain.edu

nameserver 192.168.3.49

nameserver 192.168.3.74
```

The first line defines the domain name to append to form a complete hostname to pass to the DNS server. The next two lines define the IP address of the DNS server to use for hostname resolution. Only IP addresses are valid here; never use the hostname of the DNS server. You add redundancy to your system by adding multiple DNS servers. DNS servers will be queried in the order in which you place *nameserver* entries. If the first server doesn't respond, your system will query the second server, and so on.

SEARCH DOMAINS

The addition of search domains to your `/etc/resolve.conf` file allows you to integrate additional domains into hostname resolution. Search domains provide an option to name resolution that is unnecessary if your system will live within a single domain. However, if your system will be part of a large network with multiple domains, using the search domain option can ease your administrative tasks as well as make navigating the network easier for your users.

```
mars:> cat /etc/resolv.conf

domain yourdomain.edu

search domain1,domain2,domain3,domain4

nameserver 192.168.3.49

nameserver 192.168.3.74
```

By adding the `search` line, hostname lookups will append each domain in the `search` line to the hostname you are attempting to resolve. For example, if you were trying to resolve the name `rover`, the system would request from the DNS server the address of `rover.yourdomain.edu`, `rover.domain1`, `rover.domain2`, etc. until the DNS server returned a valid IP address, or returned an error message that the host doesn't exist.

Be careful. Adding a large number of search domains can slow down hostname resolution. Also, attempt to optimize the `search` line so that more popular names come first.

NIS+ DOMAIN NAME

If you are using Network Information Services (NIS+) for name services, make sure you know your NIS+ domain *before* you begin your installation. While NIS+ will be discussed in more detail in Chapter 7, "Directory Services" in many cases you will be asked at install time if you are going to use NIS+ for naming services. Double-check that you have the correct domain and triple-check that your NIS+ domain is spelled correctly. Incorrectly configured NIS+ domains can cause your system to hang when you reboot at the end of installation.

Most UNIX systems support NIS+ as well as NIS, or they will shortly. For the purpose of this discussion, they can be used interchangeably.

Many flavors of UNIX will choose to install or not to install NIS+ compatibility based on your choices at install time. So, choosing not to use NIS+ at install time can be a problem if you choose to move your system into NIS+ at a later date. At minimum, adding NIS+ later will require at least one or two hours for you to find your installation CD that you haven't used since the initial installation.

Conversely, removing a system from NIS+ after installation can be very difficult. Unless you are a seasoned UNIX pro, you may wish to attempt a complete re-install if your flavor of UNIX doesn't react well to having NIS+ turned off.

The command `domainname` will give you the NIS+ domain name for your system. This is useful as an argument to scripting, or if you have multiple NIS+ domains.

`domainname` displays the domain name for the system. Generally this is used to determine the NIS+ domain to which the system is attached.

NIS SERVER IP ADDRESSES

For some installations of NIS+, you will need to know the IP address of your NIS+ replica. (A replica is a copy of your NIS+ database and functions as a slave NIS+ server. For more information on NIS+, see Chapter 7). This will allow your system to connect to the NIS+ domain after the system is installed. By defining an NIS+ replica(s) at install time, the system will always attempt to connect to that NIS+ replica, and only that NIS+ replica.

Defining static NIS+ replicas has two useful functions. First, it allows you to define NIS+ replicas on different subnets than where your system is installed. This is particularly useful if you have a limited number (or only one) of systems that can function as NIS+ replicas. Second, it provides additional security, as you know what machine(s) your systems will attempt to receive NIS+ information from, making it almost impossible for hackers to use a dummy NIS+ master to gain access to your systems. The downside is that if your defined NIS+ replicas are unavailable, your system may hang, or function in a degraded state.

 When given the opportunity, always choose to find your NIS+ server using the broadcast option. This gives you the most fault-tolerant configuration and allows seamless infrastructure changes.

If you are given the choice, *always* choose the broadcast option of NIS+. By using a broadcast, your system will ask to be serviced by any NIS+ replicas on the network, and the first system to respond will become the NIS+ server for the system. In an environment where you can place one or more NIS+ replicas on each network, broadcasting allows for greater flexibility and fault tolerance. As long as one NIS+ replica is available, your system will be able to connect and receive NIS+ data. The downside is that NIS+ broadcasts generally don't flow off of your network segment; so, if the NIS+ replica(s) on your network is unavailable, your system will be unable to use NIS+.

Linux Installation Example

The following sections provide Red Hat Linux 6.0 installation instructions. Red Hat supports installation from CD-ROM, hard drive (local), NFS, and FTP. This example utilizes a CD-ROM. Make sure your BIOS is set up to allow booting from the CD. Additional information required by the Red Hat installation process is contained at the end of this section in Table 2.8.

INITIAL SETUP

1. Booting from the Red Hat CD, you will be presented with the screen shown in Figure 2.1. To install a new distribution, press <ENTER>. The machine will actually boot and the next screen will instruct you to read the *Official Red Hat Linux Installation Guide* and to register your purchase.
2. The next screen allows you to select a language for the installation process. Selection is accomplished with the arrow keys, while the <TAB> key allows you to switch between elements. Make your selection.
3. Select your keyboard.
4. The next screen requires you to select the type of media from which you will be installing Red Hat.
5. The next screen gives you the choice of installing or upgrading. Select `installing`.
6. Select one of three different types of machines to install (`Worksta-tion`, `Server`, or `Custom`), as shown in Figure 2.2. In this case,

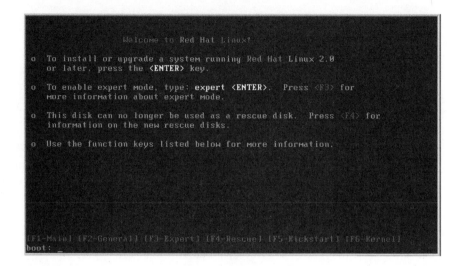

Figure 2.1
Red Hat initial installation screen.

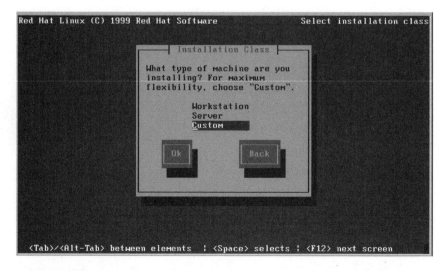

Figure 2.2
Selecting a machine type.

choose `Custom` and click `OK` (selecting `Workstation` may leave out certain packages, while selecting `Server` may include packages not needed).

SELECTING SCSI AND RAID ADAPTERS

1. Select the `Adaptec 152x` driver as shown in Figure 2.3. Next, select your manufacturer and model number from the available drivers (Figure 2.4). Unless you are well-versed in SCSI options, select `Autoprobe`. You should get a confirmation for your adapter and a query for any more SCSI adapters. Once you have completed installing all of your SCSI adapters, you get to partition the disks as shown in Figure 2.5.

2. There are two choices when partitioning disks. The *user-friendly* `Disk Druid` and the more traditional command-line `fdisk`. Select `Disk Druid` (Figure 2.5). The screen is divided into two portions (Figure 2.6). The top half is a listing of your current disk partitions and the lower half is a listing of your disk drives. Since this is a new installation, there aren't any current disk partitions.

3. The first thing to add is a partition for the root directory. Select `Add` as in Figure 2.7. Enter a slash (/) in the `Mount Point` field. Subtract

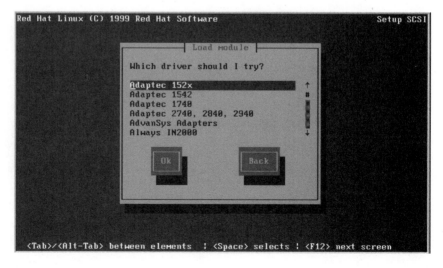

Figure 2.3
SCSI adapter drivers.

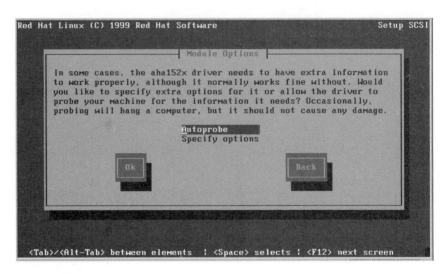

Figure 2.4
SCSI make and model.

Figure 2.5
Disk partition setup.

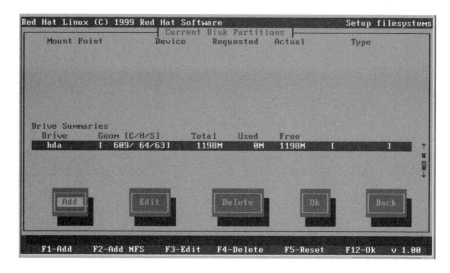

Figure 2.6
Disk Druid interface.

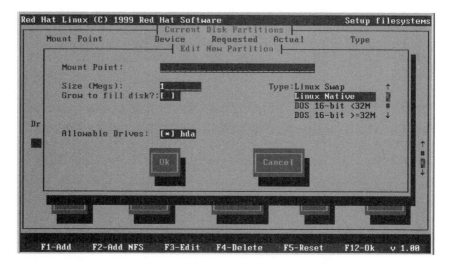

Figure 2.7
Disk Druid's `Edit New Partition` window.

the number of megabytes required for your swap partition from the total and enter the result in the `Size` field. The `Grow to fill disk` field will ensure that you use all of the available space. We will select this field when we set up the swap partition. Next, go to `Type` and select `Linux Native` and then <TAB> to `OK`. <TAB> to `Add icon`.

SETTING UP A SWAP PARTITION

1. For the swap partition, you do not need to enter a mount point. Enter a value of `40 Megs` for the `Size` field, select the `Grow to fill disk` field, and specify a `Type` of `Linux Swap` (Figure 2.8).

2. Select `OK`. Note that the second partition (`Linux Swap`) has a requested size of `40 Megs`, but an actual size of `127 Megs`, as shown in Figure 2.9. This is a result of selecting `Grow to fill disk` for the swap partition. Select `OK`.

3. This completes disk partitioning for this installation. For multiple disk drives, you will need to go through the same steps for each disk. (Remember, the disk highlighted in the bottom half of the screen is the current disk.) Use the practices outlined previously in this chapter to get the best performance from your disks. Finally, you will be given the option of specifying which swap partitions should be active. Select the `Check for bad blocks during format` field (Figure 2.10), and then select `OK`.

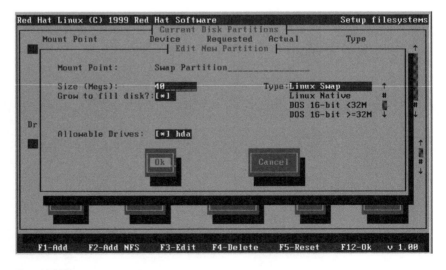

Figure 2.8
Disk Druid edit swap partition.

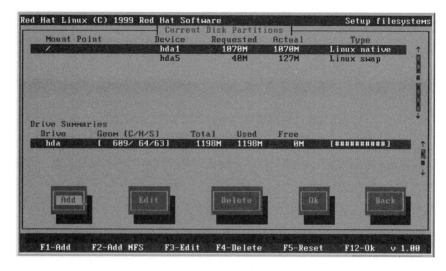

Figure 2.9
Disk Druid swap partition actual size.

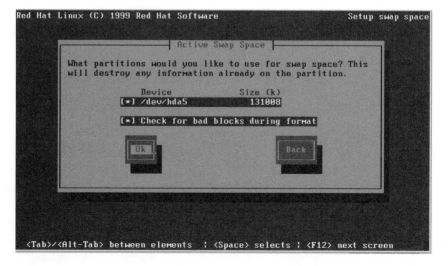

Figure 2.10
Disk Druid Active Swap Space window.

4. The screen provides a progress bar for the formatting process for swap and then requests you to select all the other partitions you specified above for formatting. Select all of the partitions and then select the `Check for bad blocks during format` field.

SELECTING COMPONENTS

1. The Red Hat installation program will pre-select the components that are necessary for a fully functional system (Figure 2.11). Items not selected include the alternative X Windows environment (KDE), development tools, printer support, and different server components. The `Everything` component is at the end of the list and is included for those with tons of disk space and problems making decisions. The `Select individual packages` field allows you to examine components on a package level (Figure 2.12). Just highlight a component, press the <SPACE BAR>, and you will get a list of the different packages. Pressing the <F1> key will provide you with a description for that package. <TAB> to `Done` once you have selected your packages.

2. The information screen will tell you that a complete log of the installation will be in `/tmp/install.log` after you reboot the system. Click `OK` and the installation will format and copy the packages to the partitions you previously created. This portion will take from 10 to 45 minutes, depending on the number of packages and the speed of the hard drive and CD-ROM drive (Figure 2.13).

Figure 2.11
Components.

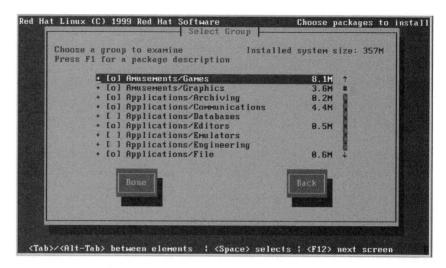

Figure 2.12
Packages.

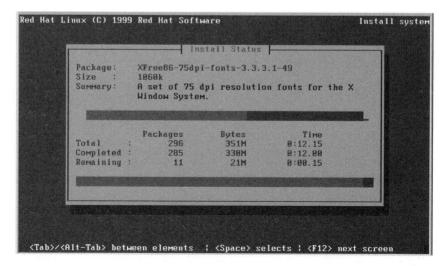

Figure 2.13
`Install Status` window.

3. Upon completion, the installation program (Figure 2.14) will probe for a mouse. Next, select the type of mouse (default selection will be based on what was detected in the previous probe screen (Figure 2.15). This is no problem since you obtained all the information in Table 2-8 before beginning the installation.

4. Next, configure the network interface card (Figure 2.16). Select your card as in Figure 2.17, then select `Autoprobe`. You will get a confirmation screen indicating your NIC was found. You can set up the NIC now or configure it later. However, it is easier to configure it now.

5. Configure the correct time zone and click `OK`. In the next screen (Figure 2.18), you will be requested to select the services that should be automatically started at boot. Pre-selected services will provide you with a functioning system, and other services can be configured after installation.

6. We will not configure a printer in this installation. It is more important at this point to pick a good root password and remember it. Type your password as in Figure 2.19. Entries for this page depend on your network (Figure 2.20). If you are running NIS, then you will want to enable NIS, enter the NIS domain name, and broadcast on the subnet or bind to an NIS server. Selecting different password parameters will depend on your site. You should select to make a bootdisk (Figure 2.21). Lilo allows Linux to boot from the hard drive (Figure 2.22). Select the `Master Boot Record` and don't provide any options (Figure 2.23).

Table 2.8 **Key Red Hat installation information**	
Item	Information Required
SCSI or RAID Adapters	Manufacturer and model.
	Optional Linux device driver.
Network Interface Card (NIC)	Manufacturer and model.
Display Card	Manufacturer, model, and amount of on-board video memory.
Monitor	Manufacturer and model.
Keyboard	Type.
Mouse	Type (Serial, PS2,..).

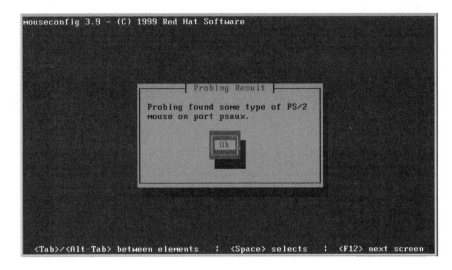

Figure 2.14
Mouse probe.

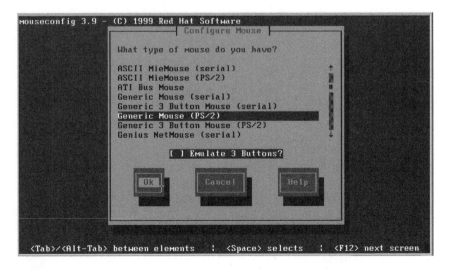

Figure 2.15
Mouse selection.

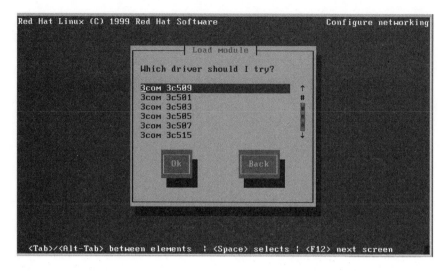

Figure 2.16
Select network interface card.

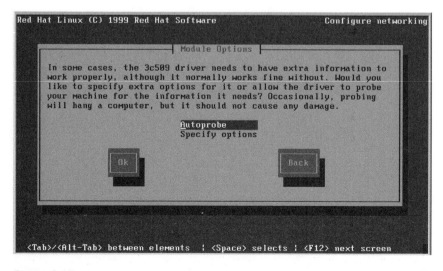

Figure 2.17
NIC Autoprobe selected.

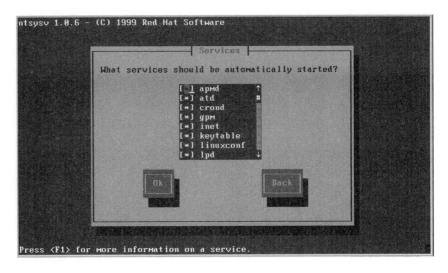

Figure 2.18
Services started at boot.

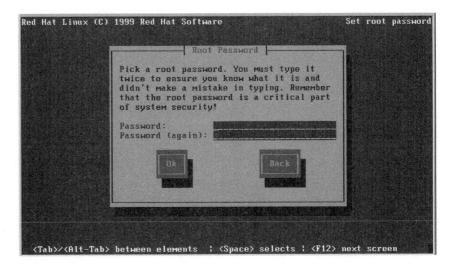

Figure 2.19
Root password selection.

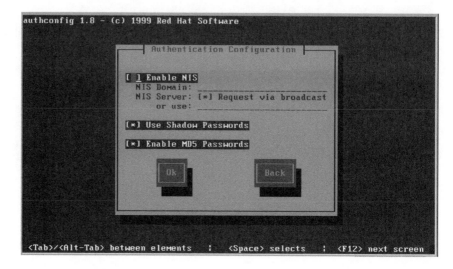

Figure 2.20
NIS configuration.

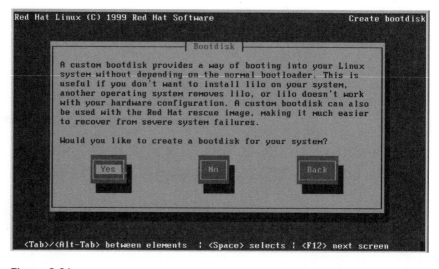

Figure 2.21
Boot floppy creation.

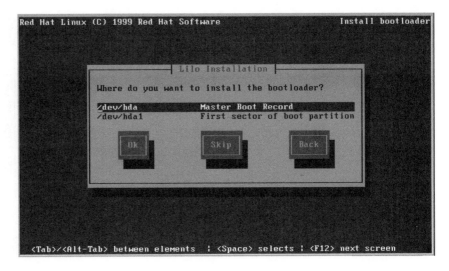

Figure 2.22
Lilo.

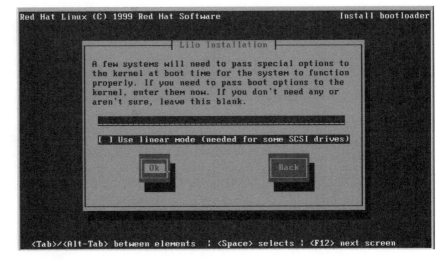

Figure 2.23
Lilo configuration.

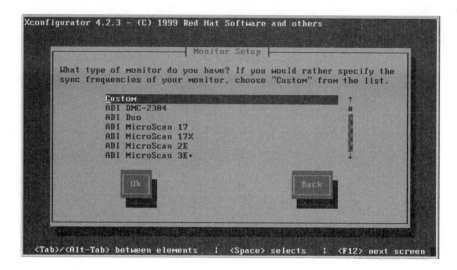

Figure 2.24
Monitor selection.

7. The installation program will try and detect your video card for X Windows configuration. Next, you will be prompted for your type of monitor (Figure 2.24). The last two screens require you to select the amount of video memory on your display card and select video modes (Figure 2.25). You can select multiple video modes. The installation program will configure and start X. The screen will change and ask you to confirm that you can read a box. Confirm and you reach the final screen, Figure 2.26. The X Windows package does not have to be successfully installed for you to complete the Red Hat installation. You can continue the installation and then log in to your Red Hat system and run the Xconfigurator program.

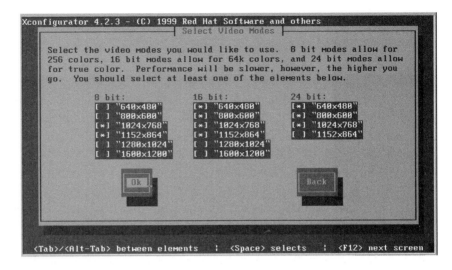

Figure 2.25
Video modes.

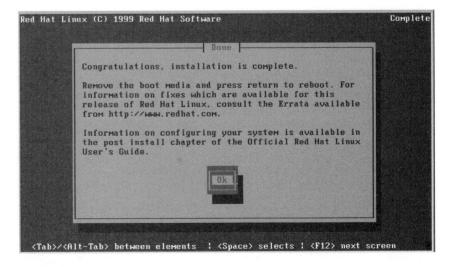

Figure 2.26
Installation complete.

Windows 2000 Installation

There are several ways to begin the Windows 2000 installation process. Some of the options available to you are:

- Upgrading from Windows 95, Windows 98, or Windows NT 4.0.
- Booting from the Windows 2000 CD-ROM.
- Booting from the Windows 2000 boot floppies.

Each of the available options has a little bit different process, at least until the first reboot. The main thing to remember is that when upgrading from an existing operating system, you should plan to install Windows 2000 into a different partition than the current operating system. Installing on top of the current operating system is not recommended, but is possible. The best way to install Windows 2000 is to use one of the two boot methods.

BOOTING AND BEGINNING INSTALLATION

The easiest way to begin the installation is to boot from the Windows 2000 CD-ROM. If your CD-ROM reader does not support booting (most modern CD-ROM readers support bootable CD-ROMs), then you can boot from the Windows 2000 floppies. Either way, the process is the same, just slower with the floppies.

 One thing to keep in mind is that you must press <F6> during the setup initialization phase if you have both SCSI and IDE devices in your system (only if booting from the CD-ROM). Pressing <F6> will allow you to load all of the necessary drivers to complete the setup successfully. After basic files are copied, you will be presented with Figure 2.27 in response to pressing <F6>. This screen allows you to load device drivers from the manufacturers support disks.

Once the system has begun to boot from either the CD-ROM or the floppies, you should be presented with relatively few screens that require a response.

BLUE SCREEN SETUP

1. When the system is booting (Figure 2.28), you will be presented with a series of blue information screens. Some of the screens will ask you to confirm system settings such as keyboard and mouse types. Other

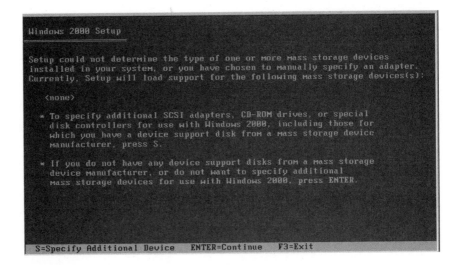

Figure 2.27
Load device drivers.

Figure 2.28
Initial boot screen.

screens will pose questions about the type of installation you wish to perform. For our purposes, we will be performing a fresh install, so you should answer No to questions regarding upgrading and repairing previously installed operating systems.

2. Perhaps the most important portion of the blue screen phase of installation is the partitioning menu (Figure 2.29). From here you can add and delete partitions on any of your disks. If this is a fresh install, you should create a new 2GB (2048MB) partition following the on-screen instructions. If you are installing for dual-boot or onto a system that has been partitioned by other operating systems, you should either select a pre-existing partition or manipulate the existing partitions to suit your needs. Once you have selected your installation partition, you will be asked to format it with either NTFS or FAT (you can also leave the partition intact if it was previously formatted). You should select NTFS and continue with the format. NTFS and FAT are discussed in Chapter 4.

3. Once the disk has been formatted, you will be asked where to install the Windows 2000 files. The default location of /WINNT is recommended. From here, the installation program will copy files and reboot when complete.

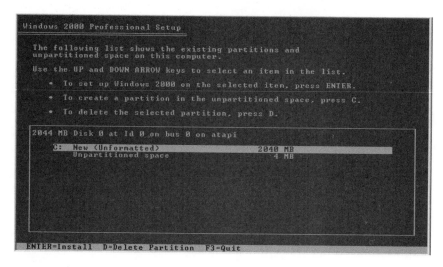

Figure 2.29
The partitioning menu is a key step.

GUI MODE SETUP

Once the blue screen portion of setup is complete, the system will be re-booted and Windows 2000 will continue the setup process in GUI mode. The GUI mode is controlled by the `Windows 2000 Setup Wizard`, which will guide you through completing the rest of the installation steps. The information you collected while planning your installation should be used here. Throughout the GUI phase, you will be able to use the mouse to navigate from screen to screen using familiar pushbuttons (Next, Back, Finish, etc.).

1. The next dialog box (Figure 2.30) does nothing more than ask you to click `Next` to continue with the setup process. You should do that to allow the Windows 2000 setup utility to begin installing devices. This process can take several minutes and you can check on the progress by viewing the progress bar located in the middle of the dialog box. If your disk stops responding, or if you are unable to move the mouse cursor, there may be a problem with one of the hardware devices in your system. Once the device installation process is complete, you should click `Next` to continue.

Figure 2.30
Windows 2000 Setup Wizard.

2. Next you will be presented with the `Regional Settings` dialog box, Figure 2.31. Here you can customize the Windows 2000 installation for different regions and languages. The default options should be sufficient. Click `Next` to continue.

3. Next you are asked to enter your name and organizational information. Enter the information you desire and click the `Next` button to continue on to the `Computer Name and Administration` dialog box (Figure 2.32). Here you should enter the `Computer name` for your Windows 2000 system and also choose the `Administrator password`. Once you have done this, click the `Next` button to continue.

4. The next dialog box you are presented with allows you to set the date, time, and time zone for your Windows 2000 system (Figure 2.33). You should adjust the settings to the appropriate values for your region and click `Next` to continue.

5. The next portion of the setup program allows you to configure the `Networking Settings` for your Windows 2000 installation. The setup program will automatically detect and configure most network interfaces. Once the detection and installation processes are complete, you are asked to choose between typical and custom configurations (Figure 2.34). The `Typical settings` are usually sufficient, but you can fine-tune your setup by choosing the `Custom Settings` option. Make your choice and click `Next` to continue.

6. If you chose to customize your settings, you will be presented with a dialog that will allow you to add and remove different network components (Figure 2.35).

7. You are now presented with the `Workgroup or Computer Domain` dialog. You can choose to remain in a standalone configuration, or join a Windows 2000 domain. Your choice will depend on your network infrastructure. If you select to join a domain, then you will be prompted for an account and password with authority to join the machine to that domain (Figure 2.36). Make the appropriate selections and click `Next` to continue.

8. The next dialog displays the progress of Windows 2000 component installation (Figure 2.37). The component installation process will take several minutes.

9. Once it is complete, the setup process will display the `Performing Final Tasks` dialog (Figure 2.38), where setup will install `Start` menu items, register components, save settings, and remove temporary files.

10. Once the setup program has completed its final installation tasks, you will be presented with the last dialog box (Figure 2.39). At this

Figure 2.31
Regional
Settings dialog.

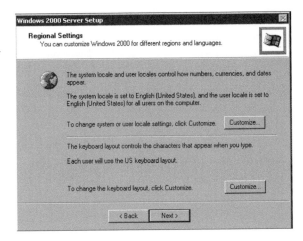

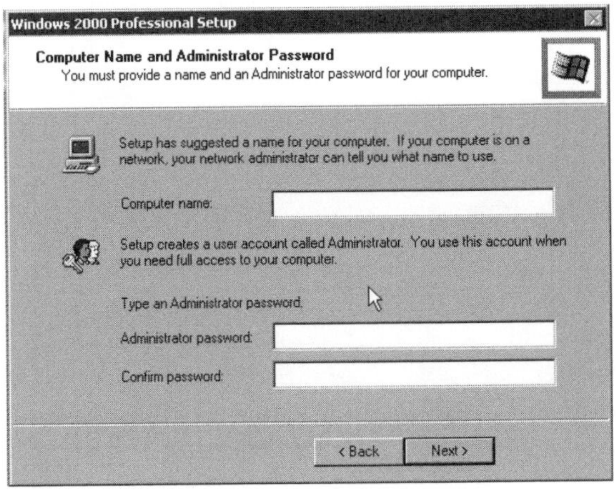

Figure 2.32
Computer
Name and
Administrator
Password dialog.

Figure 2.33
Date and time
settings
dialog.

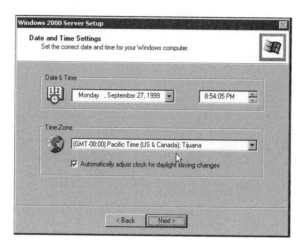

Figure 2.34
Network selection.

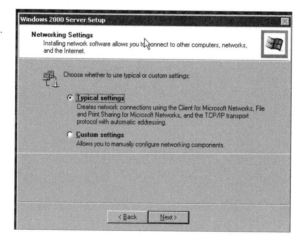

Figure 2.35
Customize
networking.

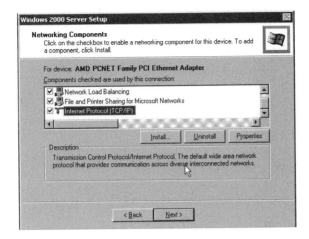

Figure 2.36
Workgroup or
Computer
Domain dialog.

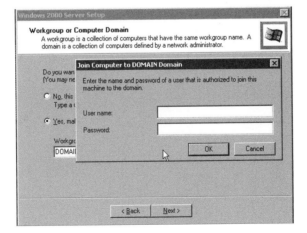

Figure 2.37
Installation
progress.

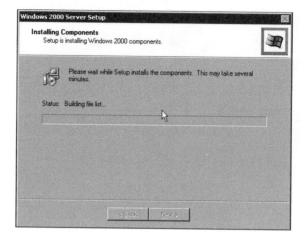

Figure 2.38
Final tasks.

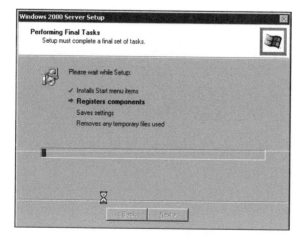

Figure 2.39
Completing
setup.

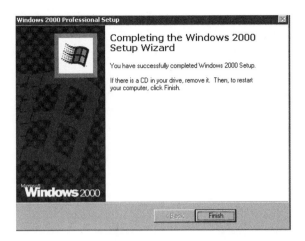

point, you should remove the floppy diskettes and CDs from the system and click the Finish button. The system will reboot and start Windows 2000 for the first time.

NETWORK CONFIGURATION

After Windows 2000 has started for the first time, you will need to configure the TCP/IP network setting (assuming you are running in a TCP/IP environment). Please note that these same steps can be carried out during the GUI mode setup if you chose to configure your network components manually. The first thing you will see after logging on after installation is the familiar desktop in Figure 2.40.

1. To begin configuring the network, click My Network Places, and then select Properties from the menu. You will see the Network and Dial-up Connections window in Figure 2.41.
2. Click the Local Area Connection icon, and then select Properties from the menu. The Local Area Connection Properties window appears as shown in Figure 2.42.
3. Select Internet Protocol (TCP/IP) and click the Properties button. You should now see the window in Figure 2.43.
4. Now enter the appropriate information for your network in the following fields:

Figure 2.40
Windows 2000
desktop.

Figure 2.41
Network and
Dial-up
Connections
screen.

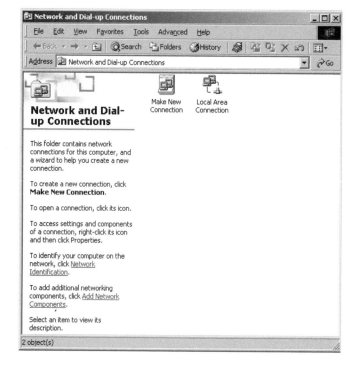

Figure 2.42
Local Area
Connection
Properties
screen.

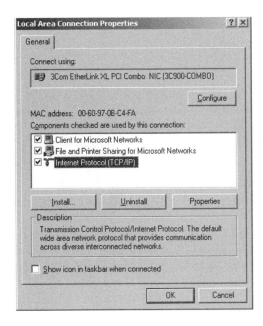

- IP address
- Subnet mask
- Default gateway
- Preferred DNS server
- Alternate DNS server

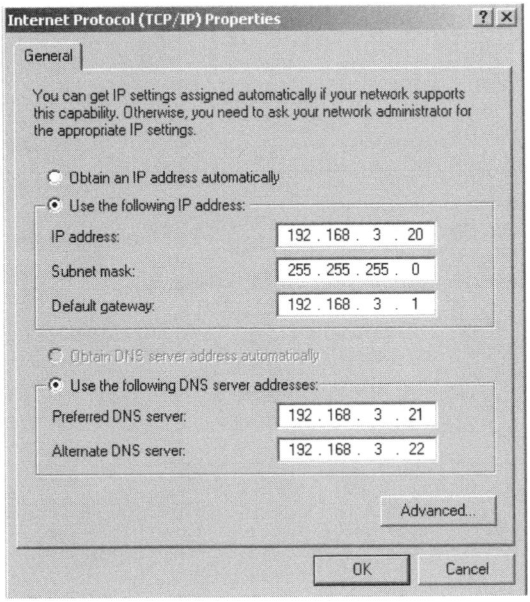

Figure 2.43
Internet
Protocol
(TCP/IP)
Properties
screen.

The default settings obtain all of this information automatically from a DHCP server. Using and configuring DHCP will be discussed in Chapter 6.

5. Once your date is entered, click OK to save the settings, or you can fine-tune your settings by clicking the Advanced button. If you need to fine-tune your IP and DNS settings, or if you are using WINS on your network, you can view the advanced settings by clicking the Advanced button, which will bring up the window in Figure 2.44.

6. The Advanced TCP/IP Settings window allows you to add multiple IP and gateway addresses to you machine. In most cases, you will not make any changes to the settings displayed here. If you wish to view the advanced DNS settings, click the DNS tab at the top of the window, as shown in Figure 2.45.

7. The Advanced TCP/IP Settings—DNS window allows you to specify more than two DNS servers to use, as well as initiate customized domain search orders. In most cases, you will not need to

Figure 2.44
Advanced
TCP/IP
Settings
screen.

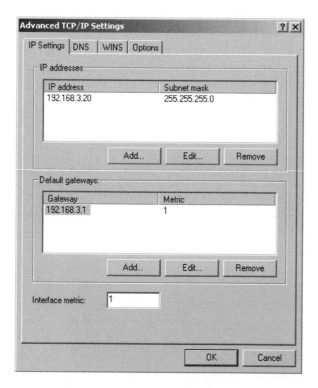

Figure 2.45
Advanced
TCP/IP
Settings
screen—DNS.

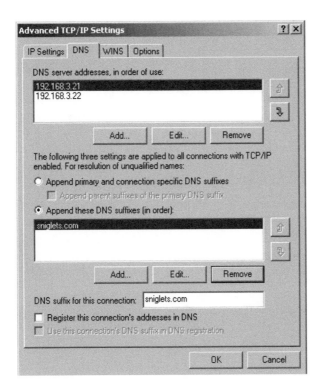

modify these settings unless you are in a large, heterogeneous environment. If you are using WINS to support NT, 95, and/or 98, click
the WINS tab at the top of the window to display the screen in Figure
2.46.

8. The Advanced TCP/IP Settings—WINS screen allows you to
configure your WINS information. WINS services work the same in
Windows 2000 as they did in Windows 95 and NT 4.0.

9. Once you have configured all of your network components, click OK
on all the open dialog boxes to save the settings. You may be asked to
reboot the machine and should do so when asked. Once the machine reboots, you should be able to access your network.

The Default Installation Quandary

While creating a standard installation for NT, UNIX, or both may seem an
easy task, you are confronted with a chicken and egg problem in creating
your initial process. Today, most administrators don't have the opportunity

Figure 2.46

Advanced
TCP/IP
Settings
screen—WINS

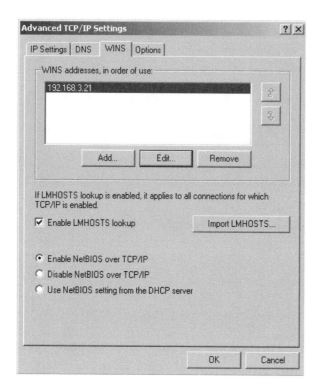

to create a computer infrastructure from scratch. You are brought into a living, evolving ecosystem of computers, and if you are lucky, your predecessors have created some sort of standard installation. If they haven't, you are faced with the problem of where to start, how to define the standard model, and where to begin implementing your model.

Using the default installation from a vendor can seem like a quick and easy way to install your systems. Why not, a vendor created the software, so they probably know the best way to install it. Yet, the default installation was probably tailored to suit the largest audience, and in many cases, will deny the majority of specific benefits from a custom installation. Your goal is to not cause administrative nightmares down the road because you don't want each system wildly different from every other system in your infrastructure. So now you have a *default installation problem*.

How do you combat the default installation problem? First, you need to realize when to use the default installation. It is usually better to create an installation model to suit your own needs. Don't assume the vendor knows best, as you are the most qualified person to determine the needs of your clients. Then, work to create a *standard installation model*.

STANDARD INSTALLATION MODEL

If your management doesn't believe that a standard installation is worth the time and effort, present them with the following benefits, and see if they change their answer:

- Reduced time and cost to install new systems.
- Increased stability.
- Ability to quickly re-install systems after a catastrophic failure.
- Decreased time to identify and solve problems.
- Increased ability to manage patch installation and system upgrades.

There is a saying, "It takes money to make money." If you twist this a bit for our purposes, you get, "It takes time to save time, create stability, and save your sanity." Investing the time and effort to create a standard installation model is worth the journey, and once you reach your destination, you will be richly rewarded.

CREATING A STANDARD INSTALLATION

Creating a default installation can be as easy as collecting a set of files that when added to a default operating system install gives you a standard system. On the other hand, you may wish to create a default installation server that contains multiple versions of the operating system to install along with patch clusters, system software, and third-party packages. What process you choose is entirely dependent on your environment, and what benefits you can attain from creating a standard installation.

 If you are in a new environment, don't try to create a standard installation immediately.

Spend some time installing new servers from scratch so you can begin to understand the requirements of your users, what software they generally require, and what modifications to make to the operating system. Pay close attention to what network information is static across your infrastructure (i.e., DNS and NIS+) so that you can include that in your model. Also, take the time to investigate already installed systems to see if you can find some commonality that can be incorporated into the standard model.

WHAT TO INCLUDE IN THE STANDARD INSTALLATION

What to include in your standard installation model is a difficult question. However, a simpler question might be what not to include. When building a system to function as your standard model, you want to exclude anything that is specific to a particular system. The standard installation should be as generic as possible.

The goal is to have minimal information to add after the system has received the new operating system. Things you want to include on the standard server include:

- The core OS installed on a standard disk layout.
- A formula for virtual memory.
- Patches and updated drivers.
- Security enhancements.
- DNS, NIS+, and WINS information.
- Messaging components (`sendmail` and Outlook server information).

You want to add anything to the standard installation server that you would have added to the majority of your systems after the operating system install. By doing this, you help create a standard environment, save time and effort, and avoid forgetting key components that you'll have to go back and install later.

What you don't want to have installed to each new server is:

- Hostname.
- IP address.
- Router information.
- Specific user information.

MANAGING THE STANDARD INSTALLATION SERVER

Take the time to create a process to manage your standard installation server. Remember that all changes you make to this system will be replicated to every new system you install and all old systems you upgrade. A mistake that goes undetected for weeks or months will create a great deal of work down the road.

Make sure you have enough disk space to store all of your patches and driver updates. This doesn't mean that the installation server has to be larger than your largest system. Just be sure that you give the system enough resources to hold all your data, and on the UNIX side, you may have multiple versions of the operating system that you are supporting at the same time. Limit access to the system so you can be sure changes aren't made without your knowledge, and to ensure security, don't use the system for purposes other than the standard model. Once you make an investment in an installation server, protect your investment, and do all you can to maintain its integrity.

 Once you make an investment in an installation server, protect your investment, and do all you can to maintain its integrity.

Installation Checklist and Logs

Two valuable tools for the system administrator are checklists and logs. These are extremely important in maintaining continuity in your installations. An installation checklist will help you remember what you need to know before installing a system, and provide a record of that information. It is also wise to maintain a log of each installation. This should be the initial log created for the system; you will add more as you go. The installation log will be extremely useful during upgrades and disaster recovery. Table 2.9 gives an example of a basic installation checklist that you will want to modify to fit your needs.

Summary

This chapter provided the framework for installing new systems. While installing Windows 2000 is rather straightforward with a minimum of options, each UNIX flavor has a myriad of different installation options. Hopefully this chapter gave you some tips, procedures, and guidelines so that you can streamline and standardize your environment.

For specific installation concerns and available options, refer to your installation documentation or your favorite UNIX-specific manual. For some flavors of UNIX, books are available that completely cover what was presented in this chapter. If your environment contains a large number of systems, invest the time in reading one of these books to gain a more in-depth understanding of standardizing your installations.

Table 2.9	Generic Installation Checklist

Hardware
Processors
Memory
Graphics adapters
Network interface cards
Cables
Power cords and adapters
Third-party cards
Software
Operating System
Version
Patch cluster level
Special patches needed
Drivers
Third-party software
Distribution CD
License keys (if necessary)
Infrastructure Information
Hostname
Domain name
IP address
Subnet mask
Default router
DNS server IP addresses
DNS search domains
NIS+ domain
NIS+ server IP
Primary domain controller
WINS server
LDAP server

PLANNING YOUR INSTALLATION

The computer installation process has come a long way from the early years when it would take an entire day or more to configure a new system. GUI tools exist for almost every operating system. In the "good ol' days," however, you were forced to plan your installations carefully, given the amount of time you expected it to take. The advantages of nice installation interfaces has brought the disadvantage of pop-and-go setups which cause administration problems later.

If you take only one piece of information from this chapter, learn to carefully plan your installations. Use the information in Table 2.1 and the installation checklist in Table 2.9 to gather all the necessary information about a system before you install the operating system. The time you spend collecting this information up-front will save you many hours of headaches, problems, and unpleasant conversations with your clients.

UNIX INSTALLATION

Since UNIX is a "networked" operating system, you must have complete and accurate information about the overall infrastructure before installing a new system. Specifically, you must know:

- Hostname.
- Domain name.
- IP address.
- Subnet mask.
- Default router.
- DNS server IP addresses.
- DNS search domains.
- NIS/NIS+ domain.
- NIS/NIS+ server IP.

Before starting an installation, you must also know how the disks should be partitioned. Of all the initial decisions, this is the hardest to change, and will often require a complete re-installation to correct.

WINDOWS 2000 INSTALLATION

There are several ways to begin the Windows 2000 installation process. Some of the options available to you are:

- Upgrading from Windows 95, Windows 98, or Windows NT 4.0.
- Booting from the Windows 2000 CD-ROM.
- Booting from the Windows 2000 boot floppies.

The easiest way to begin the installation is to boot from the Windows 2000 CD-ROM. After Windows 2000 has started for the first time, you will need to configure the TCP/IP network setting.

SYSTEM BOOT AND SHUTDOWN

UNIX

BSD Startup

`rc` Scripts in BSD

SysV Startup

SysV Startup Script Structure

Shutdown, Reboot, and Halt

WINDOWS 2000

Booting Windows 2000

System vs. Boot Partition

Advanced Boot Options

`boot.ini`

System Shutdown

For most people, the simple act of flipping on the power *is* the whole boot process. In this chapter, we will take you through the steps performed by the system while you are waiting for the login screen. We call this process "booting" (short for bootstrapping) the system.

The booting sequence involves both hardware and software components. Understanding this process is essential to a system administrator. There are very few things in this field more frustrating than a system that will not boot, often for no apparent reason, and usually in the presence of a user. Knowledge of these steps (from powering up the system to getting a login) is essential to properly diagnose and correct problems that occur when the system is most vulnerable.

The Physical Boot Sequence

Booting a computer system is somewhat similar to waking up in the morning. Once the alarm goes off, a small, although not necessarily, functional part of our subconsciousness acknowledges the signal and begins the process of loading the rest of our conscious faculties. At some point, we perform a physical inventory; we stretch and begin to move.

Likewise, when you power on traditional UNIX hardware, a physical component called *firmware* instructs the system to access a section of the disk drive known as the *boot block*. The boot block provides basic instructions for loading the operating system. One important piece of information is the location of the secondary boot file, called `ufsboot` in some systems. The secondary boot file handles the loading of the *kernel* into the system memory. The kernel is the core of the UNIX operating system. Once it is loaded, the system is a UNIX system and the process of waking up begins. Figure 3.1 shows the physical boot sequence for a traditional UNIX system.

The boot sequence of a PC is very similar. Instead of the firmware, we have the *BIOS* (Basic Input Output System; same thing as firmware, different name). The BIOS performs a basic system diagnostic, gathering information about the system architecture. The BIOS will provide information on the CPU, memory, and hardware. Then, based on how your system is configured, the BIOS will launch either a *boot manager* or the actual operating

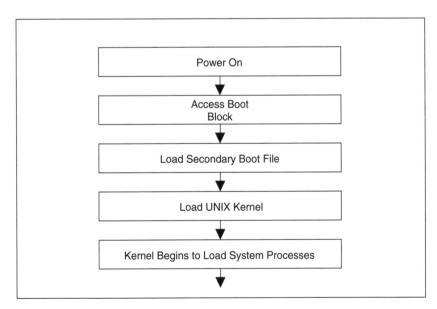

Figure 3.1
Physical boot sequence—traditional UNIX.

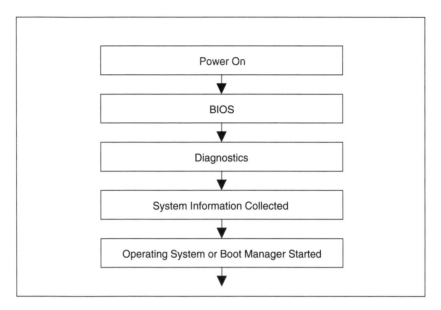

Figure 3.2
Physical boot sequence—PC.

system for the system. In Figure 3.2, you can see the similarity between the UNIX and PC physical boot sequence.

Whereas the UNIX firmware and boot block are completely vendor-dependent, the PC world has standardized on a few BIOS configurations. Linux and other PC-based UNIX operating systems follow the PC boot sequence using the boot manager to load the kernel.

Loading the Operating System

A computer without an operating system is like a human without a brain. The operating system provides the fundamental communications between the software and hardware components. The operating system is itself software, but it serves as the mediator between other applications and the physical layer. UNIX and NT use different approaches in this process of obtaining a higher level of consciousness.

Once the UNIX kernel is loaded, the ability to become conscious is there, but it is not entirely awake. A UNIX system can be brought up in two main operating modes, commonly called *single-user* and *multi-user*. Single-user mode is a state in which many but not all of the system functions are alive. This state is used primarily for administrative purposes, allowing a system administrator to perform corrective functions on disks or startup scripts.

Table 3.1	BSD System States
State	Use
Halted	Halted.
Single-User	Single-user mode for administration and diagnostics. Only console logins are allowed; networking is not yet active. User filesystems are not mounted.
Multi-user	Multi-user mode with networking; common default operating state.

In single-user mode, user functions are usually not available, including friendly interfaces, networking, or printing. Single-user mode is the state many of us are in prior to a shower and a large dose of caffeine. A system in this mode usually offers the system administrator a *root* prompt. For that reason, this mode is often password-protected, requiring the root password before allowing access.

Multi-user mode is the normal functioning state of the system. All system processes are running and the system is ready for network communication and user services. This is the state of being fully awake and ready.

There are two major ways of handling system startup in the UNIX environment: BSD (Table 3.1) and SysV (Table 3.2). Though every vendor has its variations, most fall at least close to these two.

Following the BSD Startup Sequence

The BSD startup sequence is shown in Figure 3.3. The first full-fledged process started by a BSD kernel, often called the *spontaneous process,* is init. This is the mother of all UNIX processeses, literally. init reads a series of scripts that provide instructions on which processes to launch, and in what order. The BSD startup scripts are called rc scripts, which stands for "run commands". All rc scripts are found in the /etc directory and are plain text files. The following rc scripts are the ones read by init, in the order listed:

```
/etc/rc.boot
```

```
/etc/rc.single
```

```
/etc/rc
```

```
/etc/rc.local
```

These scripts are simple Bourne shell scripts that execute a series of commands. The rc.boot script performs these basic functions:

- Set hostname.
- Enables IP networking.
- Mounts / and /usr filesystems in read-only mode.
- Checks filesystems.

If all filesystems are clean, rc.boot runs rc.single. The first thing rc.single does is remount / and /usr in read-write mode. The rc.single script cleans up the mount table, shared library cache, and other system files. It also sets the time based on your local time zone. The loadkeys command is used to set the system keyboard mapping to match your system. When rc.single exits, rc.boot returns a system prompt if you are entering single-user mode.

If the system is going into multi-user mode, /etc/rc is run immediately after /etc/rc.boot (remember, rc.boot executed rc.single). /etc/rc

Figure 3.3
BSD boot
sequence.

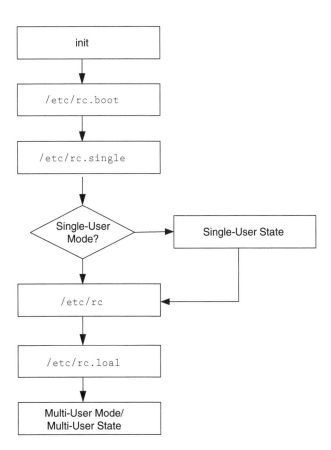

first checks the work done by `rc.boot` and `rc.single`. Once it is satisfied that its cousins have done their jobs, it checks to be sure that the `passwd` file was not open if the system crashed. If it was, the `passwd` file is recovered from `/etc/ptmp`. `/etc/rc` then mounts all of the local filesystems.

`loadkeys`, and `dumpkeys` (SysV and BSD) load and dump keyboard translation tables, respectively.

Changing the System Startup

Changing system startup scripts is something you should do with caution. It is extremely rare that you would need to make changes to either startup script used in the single-user startup. Likewise, `/etc/rc` should not be tampered with under normal circumstances. `/etc/rc.local`, as the name implies, is the place to make changes needed in your local system configuration. However, keep in mind that most vendors have cluttered the rc.local script with startup calls relevant to their particular flavor, so you must use caution in editing this script as well. DNS, NFS, and other local background processes called daemons, like `sendmail`, are often started from this script. Typical additions to the `rc.local` script include:

- License managers.
- Third-party application start scripts.
- Special print drivers or managers.

RC.LOCAL

When making changes to the startup script, always try to add them near the bottom of the file. Here is an example of starting a third-party license file from `rc.local`:

```
#

# Matlab license manager.

#

if [ -f /etc/lmboot ]; then

        sh /etc/lmboot && echo -n ' Matlab'

fi
```

The # symbol denotes a comment and everything to the right of it is ignored. In this case, we are calling the Matlab license manager, /etc/lmboot. The logic call if ends with the close call fi. The test [-f /etc/lmboot] is important. It checks to see if the file exists, then executes it and displays a line confirming that you have executed the script. When adding your own additions, always use the -f predicate to confirm that the file is there before executing; printing the confirmation makes it much easier to debug if the startup script is hanging.

As mentioned before, these scripts are just Bourne shell scripts, so any of the logic available to a Bourne script is available in the rc scripts. A major rule of thumb is to keep it simple. Another rule is never to remove code from an rc script. If you wish to disable lines, use the # symbol to make them comments. A great deal of the code found in an rc script is system-dependent, and re-creating it would be very difficult. Do not edit these scripts unless it is absolutely necessary.

Following the System V Startup Scripts

The System V (SysV) startup process is more complicated, and likewise offers more options. Instead of the three run levels found in BSD, the SysV startup has eight. The run levels are 0-6 and s (or S) for single-user. Each run level has a different functionality. The run levels are defined by a series of scripts that are called by init. The relationship between run levels and scripts is contained in the system file, inittab. The run levels are shown in Table 3.2.

INITTAB

The run levels above are controlled by a file named /etc/inittab. This file controls the operation of the init process. Following is a sample inittab file from a Solaris 2.6 system:

```
mars# cat /etc/inittab

ap::sysinit:/sbin/autopush -f /etc/iu.ap

ap::sysinit:/sbin/soconfig -f /etc/sock2path

fs::sysinit:/sbin/rcS            >/dev/console 2<>/dev/console </dev/console

is:3:initdefault:
```

Table 3.2	SysV Run Levels
Run Level	Use
0	Halted.
S, s	Single-user mode for administration and diagnostics. Only console logins are allowed; networking is not yet active. User filesystems are not mounted if the system is coming up, but are left if coming down to this state. `init`-spawned processes are killed.
1	Another single-user mode. All filesystems remain mounted, many scripts are left running, and only console logins are allowed.
2	Multi-user mode with limited networking.
3	Multi-user mode with networking; common default operating state.
4	Unused state on most systems.
5	Halt and reboot.
6	Halt and reboot to default state.

```
p3:s1234:powerfail:/usr/sbin/shutdown -y -i5 -g0 >/dev/console 2<>/dev/
console

s0:0:wait:/sbin/rc0             >/dev/console 2<>/dev/console </dev/console

s1:1:wait:/usr/sbin/shutdown -y -iS -g0 >/dev/console 2<>/dev/console
</dev/console

s2:23:wait:/sbin/rc2            >/dev/console 2<>/dev/console </dev/console

s3:3:wait:/sbin/rc3             >/dev/console 2<>/dev/console </dev/console

s5:5:wait:/sbin/rc5             >/dev/console 2<>/dev/console </dev/console

s6:6:wait:/sbin/rc6             >/dev/console 2<>/dev/console </dev/console

fw:0:wait:/sbin/uadmin 2 0      >/dev/console 2<>/dev/console </dev/console

of:5:wait:/sbin/uadmin 2 6      >/dev/console 2<>/dev/console </dev/console

rb:6:wait:/sbin/uadmin 2 1      >/dev/console 2<>/dev/console </dev/console
```

```
sc:234:respawn:/usr/lib/saf/sac -t 300
```

```
co:234:respawn:/usr/lib/saf/ttymon -g -h -p "'uname -n' console login: " -T
   sun -d /dev/console -1 console -m ldterm,ttcompat
```

The structure of the file is:

```
label : run-level : action : process
```

The `label` is a mnemonic: for states, it is usually the letter `s` and the number of the state; for terminals, it is usually the terminal number. The `run-level` is a numeric (or `s`) that represents the state in which the action and command should be performed. If the field is blank, then the `action` applies to all `run-levels`. If it has multiple numbers, like `234`, it means that the `action` applies to `run-levels` 2, 3, and 4. The action describes how the following `process` is to be handled.

There are many `actions` that can be assigned. They vary slightly from one UNIX operating system flavor to another. Here is an explanation of the ones in the `inittab` just shown:

- `sysinit`: Perform this process before trying to access the console.
- `initdefault`: Set the default run-level.
- `powerfail`: Perform this process when init receives a power fail signal.
- `wait`: Wait for this action before continuing.
- `respawn`: Restart this process when necessary.

Two more useful actions are:

- `bootwait`: Wait for this action only during bootup.
- `off`: Do not perform this process.

 The final action is used to comment out run level actions that are no longer in use. Like the rc scripts of the BSD, you should never remove code from the `inittab`; just use the `off` action to disable them.

So, the following line would tell us that in states 2 and 3, you should run `/sbin/rc2` and wait until the script has completed before progressing:

```
s2:23:wait:/sbin/rc2>/dev/console
2<>/dev/console </dev/console
```

RC SCRIPTS

Most work is done in the processes run in what are often called the run-level scripts (/sbin/rc2 or /sbin/rc3, etc.). These scripts work on a hiearchy of directories that is found in /etc/rc2.d and /etc/rc3.d, respectively. If you look at part of /sbin/rc2, you will see how the basic process works.

The first thing the script does is to determine the state of the system using the who -r command.

```
set '/usr/bin/who -r'
```

If the system is booting up, it sets the boot variable to yes.

```
if [ x$9 = "xS" -o x$9 = "x1" ]

then

        echo 'The system is coming up.  Please wait.'

        BOOT=yes
```

The next test is to determine if the system is coming up to level 2, or going down. In other words, is the current state of the sytem higher or lower than level 2?

```
elif [ x$7 = "x2" ]

then

        echo 'Changing to state 2.'

        if [ -d /etc/rc2.d ]

        then

                for f in /etc/rc2.d/K*

                {

                        if [ -s ${f} ]

                        then

                                case ${f} in

                                    *.sh)   . ${f} ;;
```

```
                                        *) /sbin/sh ${f} stop ;;

                              esac

                    fi

          }

     fi

fi
```

This code reveals how the run-level hierarchy works in SysV. If the conditional state resolves to this case, then the system is at a higher run level than level 2. In that case, several processes or resources must be removed to reduce the state to level 2. The script first checks to be sure that /etc/rc2.d exists. Next, it finds all files in /etc/rc2.d that begin with the letter "K" and executes them in order. Note that it gives the script the "stop" argument.

```
ls -l K*

K20spc

K60nfs.server

K76snmpdx

K77dmi
```

The next section of /sbin/rc2 handles starting the processes necessary to come up to level 2:

```
if [ x$9 != "x2" -a x$9 != "x3" -a -d /etc/rc2.d ]

then

          for f in /etc/rc2.d/S*

          {

                    if [ -s ${f} ]

                    then

                              case ${f} in

                                        *.sh) . ${f}

                                        *) /sbin/sh ${f} start ;;

                              esac
```

```
                                            fi

                           }

        fi
```

In this case, it finds all the files in `/etc/rc2.d` that start with the letter "S" and executes them with the `start` command. There are many more S files in this run level than K files. These files are often called start files and kill files, respectively.

who **(SysV and BSD)** exists on both flavors, but has far more functionality in its SysV incarnation. In its basic state, the `who` command returns a list of users currently logged onto the system. On SysV systems, `who -r` returns the current run level of the `init` process. `ls` also exists in all variations of UNIX. It provides a directory listing. `ls-l` provides a detailed listing.

INIT.D

Now, here is the sneaky part. The start and kill files are actually the hard links to the same file that resides in `/etc/init.d`. The files function differently based on whether they are called with the `start` or `stop` argument. This is important to remember if you are going to change the existing scripts or add your own. If you edit a hard link, you actually edit all of the other links that share the same inode. (We will go over inodes in the next chapter.) If you plan to add a script, you must place it in `/etc/init.d` and create the appropriate S or K link in the corresponding `/etc/rc#.d` directory in which you wish it to run. Most of these scripts are added in `/etc/rc2.d` or `/etc/rc3.d` based on whether or not they are network-dependent. In Figure 3.4, the start script `S99dtlogin`, which launches a graphics-based login program, is actually a hard link to the script `dtlogin` in the `init.d` directory. Likewise, `S15nfs.server` links to `nfs.server`.

This may seem needlessly complicated, but it provides a standardized way to handle the addition of scripts to the startup process. Before you decide to ignore this convention, remember that you should try to keep a system as "standard" as possible. Always leave a system in the state in which you would like to inherit it. You never know when you will be the one to try to fix a system set up by a different administrator. You know what you call someone who has left you with an eccentric system; do you want to be called the same?

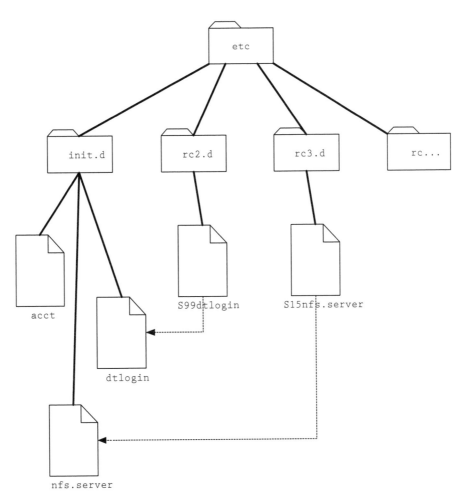

Figure 3.4
init/rc directory structure.

UNIX Logins

Once the system has completed the boot process, it provides a login prompt for the user. The init process launches the getty daemon, or ttymon in Solaris. Console or terminal style logins are not used often anymore. However, the underlying process is still used by graphical login systems. The getty daemon produces the login: prompt. When a user enters a login and presses ENTER, getty spawns the actual login program that prompts for a password. The login program verifies the login and password and spawns whichever login shell is specified by the passwd table. Most

UNIX systems now use X Windows-based interfaces, like CDE's `dtlogin`, which are launched by `init` and intercede between the user and the `getty`/`login` cycle.

Shutting Down a UNIX System

Shutting down a UNIX system is equally important. For a UNIX system to shut down correctly, the administrator must bring it to a halt state (state 0 in SysV). The most commonly used command for shutdown is, of course, `shutdown`. The options vary from one variety of UNIX to another. The two most common are again BSD and SysV as follows:

```
BSD:     shutdown   -h +10
```

This will bring the system to a halt state after giving 10 minutes of warning messages to the users.

```
SysV:    shutdown -i0 -g600 -y
```

This will do the same as the BSD command, bringing the system to run level 0 with a grace period of 600 seconds. The –y option answers all the pesky "Are you sure?" questions with "Yes." You should check the man pages on `shutdown` commands before trying these.

Beyond shutting down, SysV has the `init` command, which can move the system between states. To change a system from run level 3 to run level 2, you can issue the following command:

```
init 2
```

Likewise, the command `init 6` will halt and reboot the system without any warnings to the user. This will not harm the system, but it may harm your reputation in the eyes of the users if you use it on a system in production. During the shutdown process, the system asks all processes to terminate by means of the TERM signal. If that fails, it kills them off with the KILL signal. In addition, the sync primitive synchronizes the disk with the buffers so that no data is lost.

Once a system has been brought to a halt state, it is safe to turn off the power. There will be times when the system will not respond to the console, or to any remote connections. In these cases, it may be necessary to cycle the power to regain access. On some systems, there is a special button for this labeled TOC. On many modern UNIX systems, the power switch activates a firmware version of the disk synchronization program before removing power from the system. This addition greatly improves the likelihood of recovery from a manual shutdown.

UNIX BOOT AND SHUTDOWN POLICIES

In most circumstances, you should not allow general users to boot, reboot, or shut down systems. For one reason, users cannot run the `reboot`, `init`, or `shutdown` commands; only the *super-user* can execute them. In addition, in cases where security is important, a system in the process of rebooting can be vulnerable. If you ban rebooting from the user, you can consider a rebooted system with suspicion. Finally, and most importantly, it is unlikely that a user will be certain of the role an individual workstation may play within the overall network. The system they shut down may have the print servers for the accounting office's printers, the boss's filesystem, or it may have other users working remotely. Since in UNIX the network is the machine, you should use caution with the shutdown or reboot process.

Of course, the need for caution applies to the system administrator as well. A policy should exist to cover when, why, and who may bring down a system. The possession of root privileges does not confer omniscience. The following should be checked before a shutdown:

- What filesystems are being exported?
- Do those filesystems contain users?
- Do those filesystems contain shared programs?
- Are users logged on?
- Are processes running in the background?
- Is this system a printer or license server?
- Is this system a mail, database, or Web server?
- Is this an emergency, or can the shutdown/reboot be done later?

Once you have the answers to these questions, you must use good judgement. In some cases, consigning reboots and shutdowns to off-peak hours is the best approach. The use of `shutdown` instead of `reboot`, `init`, or `halt` to halt or reboot a system is also wise. The options in `shutdown` to provide users warning and time to logout is just good manners, and will be less of an impact on productivity.

Only a system administrator should physically turn off a system if a shutdown has not been performed. The "it was hung" argument should not be accepted. The console could be locked up, but the rest of the system might be functioning fine.

shutdown (SysV and BSD) is used to halt or reboot the system. It has options (many unique to individual versions of UNIX) that allow a grace period to be provided, user warnings to be broadcast, and boot options to be provided.

halt (SysV and BSD) halts the system. If given the `-q` option, it will do so without any attempt at a graceful shutdown. With the `-n` option, it prevents the `sync` command. Use caution with this command; if used unwisely, it could result in damage to the filesystems and loss of data. On some systems, it is linked to `poweroff`.

reboot (SysV and BSD) performs a shutdown and then a restart of the operating system. You can pass boot arguments to the system with this command. It does not warn users of its actions.

sync (SysV and BSD) updates the super-block and writes all system buffers to disk. This is necessary for filesystem integrity. `Shutdown`, `reboot`, and `init` call the `sync` primitive.

init (SysV and BSD) is a BSD command but it is only called by the system and should not be called by users. The SysV version of the command allows the super-user to change the run level of the `init` process.

Booting Windows 2000

One might assume that Windows 2000 is a simple operating system, since Microsoft designed it to run primarily on x86-class machines. On the contrary; Windows 2000 is a powerful operating system, which, like UNIX, has a complex boot sequence. In fact, Windows 2000 is capable of running on both x86 and RISC (Reduced Instruction Set Computer, an alternative CPU architecture to X86) architectures, although there is much more software support for the x86 version of the operating system.

THE BASICS—UNDERSTANDING PARTITIONS AND THEIR FILES

The first lesson that must be learned is the difference between the SYSTEM partition and the BOOT partition. The SYSTEM partition contains the Master Boot Record (MBR) and the core files for loading Windows 2000, such as NTLDR and boot.ini. The BOOT partition contains the rest of the operating system, such as the \WINNT directory and its associated contents. Most often, the SYSTEM and BOOT partitions are one and the same, since they are physically located on the same physical disk partition. However, the SYSTEM and BOOT partitions can be located on different partitions, and it

Table 3.3	Windows 2000 Boot Files	
File	X86 Location	RISC Location
NTLDR	System Partition Root	-
boot.ini	System Partition Root	-
BOOTSECT.DOS	System Partition Root	-
NTDETECT.COM	System Partition Root	-
NTBOOTDD.SYS	System Partition Root	-
NTOSKRNL.EXE	*SystemRoot*\System32	*SystemRoot*\System32
OSLOADER.EXE	-	OS\nt40
HAL.DLL	*SystemRoot*\System32	OS\nt40
*.pal (ALPHA)	-	OS\nt40
System	*SystemRoot*\System32\Config	*SystemRoot*\System32\Config
Device Drivers	*SystemRoot*\System32\Drivers	*SystemRoot*\System32\Drivers

is in this case where it becomes important that you understand the content and function of each.

Table 3.3 lists the files required to successfully boot Windows 2000, and the appropriate location of each.

NTLDR

NTLDR is located at the root of the system partition and is automatically loaded by the boot sector on the boot drive. NTLDR controls the boot process of the Windows 2000 system. This program is not required on RISC-based systems. The firmware of a RISC-based system performs the function of NTLDR.

BOOT.INI

boot.ini is the first file accessed by NTLDR. It is a simple text file that provides a listing of the available operating systems. A more detailed description of boot.ini will be included later in this chapter. This file is neither required nor included on RISC-based systems.

BOOTSECT.DOS

BOOTSECT.DOS contains a copy of the DOS boot sector, which previously resided on the boot drive. This file is only present if the machine contains both a Windows 2000 and a DOS installation, and will dual-boot between the two. If the user chooses to boot DOS, NTLDR will access this file. This file is neither required nor included on RISC-based systems.

NTDETECT.COM

NTLDR uses NTDETECT.COM to detect the hardware present on a Windows 2000 system. NTDETECT.COM is only required on x86-based systems; it is not included on RISC-based systems.

NTBOOTDD.SYS

NTBOOTDD.SYS is required on x86-based systems that boot from a SCSI controller that *does not* have an on-board BIOS, or whose on-board BIOS has been disabled. NTBOOTDD.SYS is simply a copy of the appropriate driver for the system's SCSI controller. This file is neither required nor included on RISC-based systems.

NTOSKRNL.EXE

NTOSKRNL.EXE is the Windows 2000 kernel. The Windows 2000 kernel is the heart and soul of the operating system (as is the kernel of all operating systems). It is located on the boot partition of both x86- and RISC-based systems. NTOSKRNL.EXE loads the Hardware Abstraction Layer (known as the HAL), and begins the process of loading device drivers and system services.

OSLOADER.EXE

OSLOADER.EXE is required only on RISC-based systems. It performs all functions up to the loading of the kernel, as well as loading the HAL and any *.pal files needed.

HAL.DLL

NT uses the HAL to conceal platform-specific issues from Windows 2000. The HAL allows Windows 2000 to communicate with a variety of hardware platforms using the same system calls. The HAL translates these *high-level* system calls into *low-level* hardware routines. Windows 2000 includes HALs for most systems right out of the box. However, some proprietary systems may require a customized HAL file, which will be provided by the hardware vendor. If Windows 2000 cannot locate a suitable HAL for your hardware during system setup, you will be prompted to provide a proprietary HAL via diskette.

*.PAL FILES

`*.pal` files contain hardware-specific code for use only on ALPHA-based RISC platforms.

SYSTEM

The `System` file contains the System Hive of the Windows 2000 Registry. The System Hive contains driver and service information required to complete the boot process.

DRIVERS

The `Drivers` folder contains all of the driver files necessary to support the hardware installed on the Windows 2000 system.

THE WINDOWS 2000 PRE-BOOT PROCESS

Before Windows 2000 can even begin to boot, the system must start up and execute its own set of routines. The main player in this *pre-boot* process is the BIOS, or Basic Input Output System. The BIOS is a very simple operating system stored in flash memory on the system board. The BIOS is responsible for providing a rudimentary communications channel between the system hardware and operating system.

The first phase of the *pre-boot* process is the Power On Self Test, or POST routine. The BIOS executes this routine and performs functions such as memory tests, interrupt tests, and tests of basic hardware, such as keyboard and mouse controllers and built-in disk controllers. If the POST routine fails for any reason, the system will fail to boot until you take corrective action.

Upon the successful completion of the POST routine, the BIOS locates the boot device (typically a fixed disk). It loads the Master Boot Record (MBR) into memory and executes the program contained in the MBR. The active partition is located by the MBR program's scan of the Partition Boot Record table.

At this point, the boot sector from the active partition is loaded into memory. In the case of Windows 2000, the boot sector contains NTLDR, which is loaded and initialized. This is where the boot process really begins.

THE WINDOWS 2000 BOOT PROCESS

The NTLDR program is the first step of the *boot* process. We will focus in this section on booting x86 systems. If you would like to know more about booting RISC systems, we suggest you acquire one of the Microsoft Press reference guides, such as the *Windows 2000 Beta Training Kit*.

NTLDR first switches the processor into 32-bit flat memory mode (386 mode). Next, NTLDR starts built-in simple filesystem drivers to access the operating system. At this point, NTLDR may access NTBOOTDD.SYS (in the unlikely event you are using a SCSI controller without a BIOS) to boot from a SCSI device. Once NTLDR has access to the filesystem, it examines the boot.ini file to determine which operating systems are on the system. The boot.ini file contains an entry for each operating system, specifying where it is located on the system. A detailed description of the boot.ini file and instructions on modifying it are included later in this chapter. The following sample boot.ini includes entries for Windows 2000 and DOS:

```
[boot loader]

timeout=30

default=multi(0)disk(0)rdisk(0)partition(1)\WINNT

[operating systems]

multi(0)disk(0)rdisk(0)partition(1)\WINNT="Microsoft Windows
2000 Server" /fastdetect

C:\="Microsoft MS-DOS 6.22"
```

Once NTLDR has examined the boot.ini file, it presents the user with a screen allowing the selection of one of the installed operating systems. If Windows 2000 is the only installed operating system, the selection screen is not displayed. If the user does not select an operating system within the specified timeout period (30 seconds by default), NTLDR selects the default. If the user selects an operating system other than Windows 2000, NTLDR loads and runs BOOTSECT.DOS and relinquishes control to that operating system.

After selecting Windows 2000, NTLDR executes NTDETECT.COM. At this point, NTDETECT.COM will display the Starting Windows screen shown in Figure 3.5.

NTDETECT.COM is used to examine your system's hardware and returns a list of what hardware was found to NTLDR. The list of hardware located by

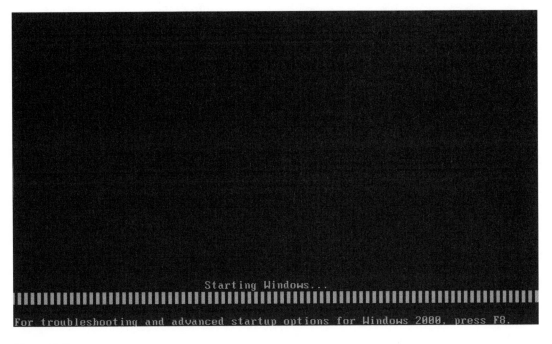

Figure 3.5
`Starting Windows` screen.

`NTDETECT` is included in the Registry under `HKEY_LOCAL_MACHINE\`
`HARDWARE`. `NTDETECT` looks for the following on your system:

- CPU ID.
- BUS type.
- Video board.
- Keyboard and mouse (if present).
- Serial and parallel ports.
- Floppy drives.

Next, once `NTDETECT` has successfully completed, `NTLDR` passes control of the system to `NTOSKRNL.EXE`. We can divide the rest of the boot
process into five phases: loading the kernel, initializing the kernel, loading
system services, starting the Win32 subsystem, and user logon.

LOADING THE KERNEL

As soon as `NTLDR` passes control to `NTOSKRNL.EXE`, the kernel is
loaded. While the `Starting Windows` screen from Figure 3.5 is displayed,
you can press the <F8> key to display the `Advanced Options Menu`,

which provides advanced boot and recovery options. This menu provides the ability to start your system after experiencing problems during a normal boot. We will discuss the `Advanced Options Menu` later in this chapter.

Once the kernel is loaded, the system HAL is loaded from HAL.DLL. Once the HAL has been loaded, the kernel loads the System Hive from *System-Root*\System32\Config\System and scans it to determine which drivers and services should be loaded. The drivers and services set to start at *boot* (this setting can be viewed/changed from the services and devices applets in the `Control Panel`) are loaded based on the order in which they appear in the `HKEY_LOCAL_MACHINE\SYSTEM\CurrentControlSet\Control\ServiceGroupOrder\List` Registry value. As we mentioned previously, device driver files are accessed from the *SystemRoot*\System32\ `Drivers` folder. While this phase is executing, the system displays a series of progress dots (....) across the top of the display. If you wish to have a more detailed progress display, you can add the `ShowOnScreen` (`/sos`) switch to the `Operating System` entry in `boot.ini`.

INITIALIZING THE KERNEL

After the kernel has been successfully loaded into memory (NTOSKRNL.EXE, HAL, and all drivers and services), the system must initialize the loaded components. If you are familiar with the Windows NT 4.0 boot sequence, then you can immediately recognize this phase when the screen has been painted blue and the following (or something similar) is displayed at the top of the screen:

```
Microsoft ® Windows NT ® Version 4.00 (Build 1381)

2 System Processors MultiProcessor Kernel [512 MB Memory]
```

Windows 2000, however, greets you with a "modernized" splash screen. This splash screen is shown in Figure 3.6.

During this phase, the following operations are completed:

1. The current control set is saved and used to create the clone control set, which is stored under the `HKEY_LOCAL_MACHINE\SYSTEM\Clone` Registry key.
2. The services and drivers loaded into memory during the kernel load phase are initialized.
3. The `HKEY_LOCAL_MACHINE\HARDWARE` key is built using the information collected by `NTDETECT` (x86) or `OSLOADER` (RISC) earlier in the boot process.
4. The System Hive is again scanned to locate, initialize, and start the services and drivers set to be started by the *system*.

Figure 3.6
Windows 2000 boot splash screen.

LOADING SYSTEM SERVICES

Once the kernel initialization phase has been successfully completed, the Services Manager (`SMSS.EXE`) is loaded. In this phase, the following tasks are completed:

1. The Services Manager completes the specified operations under the `HKEY_LOCAL_MACHINE\SYSTEM\CurrentControlSet\Control\SessionManager\BootExecute` Registry value. By default, the only entry under `BootExecute` is *autocheck autochk* *. Autocheck is the boot-time version of `chkdsk` and is used to examine all of the available partitions.

2. The system paging files are set up based on the entries defined in HKEY_LOCAL_MACHINE\SYSTEM\CurrentControlSet\Control\Session Manager\Memory Management\Paging-Files.

3. The HKEY_LOCAL_MACHINE\SYSTEM\CurrentControlSet\Control\Session Manager\DosDevices Registry value is examined and the specified filesystem links are created.

4. The HKEY_LOCAL_MACHINE\SYSTEM\CurrentControlSet\Control\Session Manager\Subsystems\Required value is examined and the required subsystems are loaded. By default, only the Win32 subsystem is required.

STARTING THE WIN32 SUBSYSTEM

If all of the previous phases have completed, the Win32 subsystem is loaded and performs the following tasks:

1. The WINLOGON.EXE program starts, which in turn starts the Local Security Authority (LSASS.EXE). When this is completed, the familiar Ctrl+Alt+Del message is displayed, indicating that the system is ready for a user to begin the logon process. This message box is shown in Figure 3.7.

2. The Service Controller (SCREG.EXE) is executed and makes one last pass through the Registry to locate and start any devices and services set to start *automatically*. This includes starting the workstation and server services, which are required for network access. Services and drivers are loaded based on the dependencies specified in the Registry. It is a good idea not to attempt a logon (especially if you are in a networked environment) until all of the services and drivers have been loaded (i.e., the disk has stopped chattering).

Figure 3.7
Windows 2000
logon message.

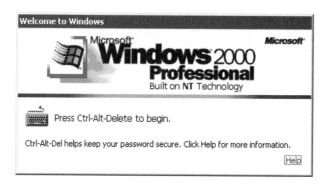

USER LOGON

The last, and potentially most important, phase of the boot process is the user logon phase. You cannot consider a boot to be good until a user has successfully logged on to the Windows 2000 system. The user begins the logon process by pressing CTRL+ALT+DEL to display the logon dialog box shown in Figure 3.8. Once you have entered your user name and password, as well as selected the appropriate domain (if applicable), you can begin the logon by clicking the OK button. It is in this phase that the system creates the LastKnownGood control set from the clone control set. At this point, the system should be stable and usable.

DUAL-BOOT SYSTEMS

Dual-boot and multi-boot systems are becoming more prevalent. The ability to have both UNIX and NT operating systems available has certain attractions. Likewise, the ability to have Windows 98 or other systems available makes the ability to run certain programs a lot easier.

"The Windows 2000 Boot Process" section provided an example of a dual-boot system. The wide range of options in a dual-boot system makes it impossible to discuss all of the different permutations here.

Advanced Windows 2000 Boot Options

As we stated earlier, pressing the <F8> key during the display of the Starting Windows screen will display the Advanced Options Menu, which is shown in Figure 3.9.

Figure 3.8
Windows 2000
logon dialog box.

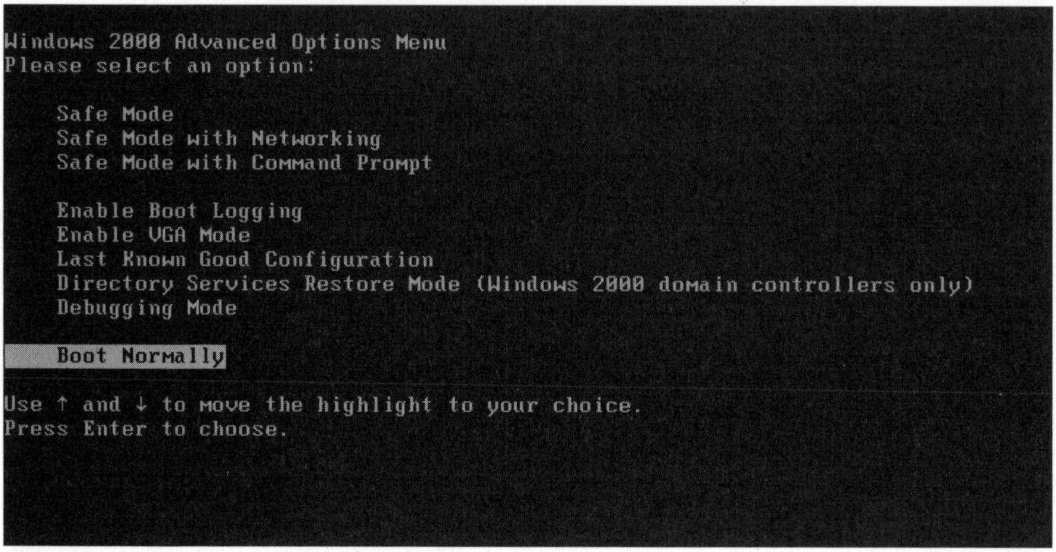

```
Windows 2000 Advanced Options Menu
Please select an option:

    Safe Mode
    Safe Mode with Networking
    Safe Mode with Command Prompt

    Enable Boot Logging
    Enable VGA Mode
    Last Known Good Configuration
    Directory Services Restore Mode (Windows 2000 domain controllers only)
    Debugging Mode

    Boot Normally

Use ↑ and ↓ to move the highlight to your choice.
Press Enter to choose.
```

Figure 3.9
Windows 2000 Advanced Options Menu.

The Advanced Options Menu provides several different recovery and troubleshooting options for booting Windows 2000. This section will explain these options and the situations in which you might want to use them.

SAFE MODE

If you are having difficulty booting your system normally, then selecting Safe Mode may help. When you select Safe Mode, Windows 2000 loads only the bare minimum of drivers and services necessary for the system to start. When you boot into Safe Mode, your normal Windows 2000 desktop is replaced with the special Safe Mode desktop, a black screen with Safe Mode displayed in all four corners. If your system still fails to start in Safe Mode, you will need to perform a system recovery.

There are three flavors of Safe Mode: the standard Safe Mode, as discussed above, Safe Mode with Networking, and Safe Mode with Command Prompt. All three variations are basically the same, but have minor variations. If you select Safe Mode with Networking, Windows 2000 will attempt to load the networking drivers and services in addition to the drivers and services loaded under the standard Safe Mode option. If your system will boot in standard Safe Mode, but not in Safe Mode with Networking, then your system is probably suffering from an incompatible or corrupt network driver. Removing the driver while running in Safe Mode should allow you to boot normally and re-install the networking components. If you select `Safe Mode with Command Prompt,` your computer will start Safe Mode with a command prompt interface instead of the GUI desktop.

ENABLE BOOT LOGGING

When you select `Enable Boot Logging,` Windows 2000 will record information about the loading and initialization of drivers and services in the `%windir%\ntbtlog.txt` file. This file can be useful in troubleshooting and diagnosing boot problems. All three flavors of Safe Mode automatically create this file.

ENABLE VGA MODE

If you are having trouble with your display driver, you can select `Enable VGA Mode` to force Windows 2000 to load only the basic VGA driver.

LAST KNOWN GOOD CONFIGURATION

The `Last Known Good Configuration` option can be used to boot Windows 2000 using Registry information saved during the last shutdown. This option is useful when you have added or modified a service or driver and the system will not boot. The `Last Known Good Configuration` command should revert to the configuration in place prior to the changes you made.

DIRECTORY SERVICES RESTORE MODE

The `Directory Services Restore Mode` option is reserved for Windows 2000 Server Systems running Active Directory. In the event that your Active Directory database is lost or corrupted, you can use this option to recover it.

DEBUGGING MODE

The `Debugging Mode` command turns on debugging for Windows 2000 Server systems. It is not used on Windows 2000 Professional systems.

BOOT NORMALLY

As you might have suspected, this will invoke the normal boot process.

boot.ini and You

The *boot.ini* file provides a list of installed operating systems and their locations to the Windows 2000 boot loader. Our previous example showed Windows 2000 and MS-DOS in the *boot.ini* file. The *boot.ini* file is shown here:

```
[boot loader]

timeout=30

default=multi(0)disk(0)rdisk(0)partition(1)\WINNT

[operating systems]

multi(0)disk(0)rdisk(0)partition(1)\WINNT="Microsoft Windows
2000 Server" /fastdetect

C:\="Microsoft MS-DOS 6.22"
```

This section will provide an overview of the two boot.ini sections, a description of available switches for Windows 2000, and a brief explanation of how to modify boot.ini.

BOOT.INI SECTIONS

The `boot.ini` file has two sections: the `[boot loader]` section and the `[operating systems]` section. Each section is independent of the other. The following discusses the role of these sections, as well as provides an overview on how to construct an entry.

The [boot loader] Section

The `[boot loader]` section has two purposes: to specify a timeout period before the default operating system is loaded and to specify the location of the default operating system. The default value for the timeout parameter is 30 seconds, but it can be any number you specify, including 0. The default parameter is typically the same as your first entry in the `[operating systems]` section discussed below, but can point to any valid operating system location.

The [operating systems] Section

The `[operating systems]` section lists the locations and descriptions of the different operating systems installed. You can have more than one entry for a single OS if, for instance, you wish to have different switches specified for different situations. The location of an operating system is specified using an ARC (Advanced RISC Computing) path, which is discussed below.

Understanding the ARC Path

ARC, or Advanced RISC Computing, paths are used to tell NTLDR where to find an installed operating system. In the simplest of terms, the ARC path provides a roadmap for NTLDR to follow, which should lead to a valid installation of Windows 2000. A simple ARC path is shown below:

```
multi(0)disk(0)rdisk(0)partition(1)\WINNT
```

The ARC path from above is described in detail in Table 3.4.

The most important piece of information in the ARC path is the use of $multi(x)$ or $scsi(x)$. When using the $multi(x)$ option, the $rdisk(z)$ parameter specifies which disk is being accessed. When using the $scsi(x)$

Table 3.4	ARC Path Components
Switch	Description
$multi(x)$ or $scsi(x)$	Specifies the adapter or disk controller to which the boot disk is connected. The scsi option is used when a SCSI controller without a BIOS is installed. The multi option is used for all non-SCSI controllers and SCSI controllers with a BIOS installed. The value x represents the load order for the controller. As each controller is initialized, it is assigned a number beginning with 0. You must specify the correct controller or the system will fail to boot.
$disk(y)$	This specifies the SCSI ID when the scsi option is used. The value y is always 0 if the multi option is used.
$rdisk(z)$	This identifies the disk(s) connected to non-SCSI disk controllers.
$partition(a)$	This specifies which partition is to be searched. The value a starts with 1 and specifies which disk partition is to be booted from. Disk partitions are numbered in order, beginning with primary partitions and then logical drives in an extended partition.
\WINNT	Specifies the subdirectory in the partition that contains the operating system.

option, the `disk(y)` parameter specifies which disk is being accessed. Incorrect ARC paths will prevent the system from booting and can force you to perform a system recovery.

BOOT.INI SWITCHES

There are a few switches available for your use in the `boot.ini` file. These switches provide additional functionality to suit your personal preference. They have some troubleshooting value as well. Table 3.5 describes the available switches in detail.

Table 3.5	`boot.ini` **Switches**
Switch	Description
`/basevideo`	You can add this switch to an entry in your `boot.ini` file to force Windows 2000 to load the default VGA driver instead of an adapter-specific driver. This is useful when you are having problems with your display driver. This switch performs the same function as the `Enable VGA Mode` option on the `Advanced Options Menu`.
`/fastdetect = [comx | comx,y,z]`	This switch disables the detection of serial mice on the specified port(s). If no ports are specified, then serial mouse detection is disabled on all ports. This option is added to the `boot.ini` file by default during Windows 2000 setup.
`/maxmem:n`	This switch specifies the maximum amount of memory Windows 2000 can use. This switch is useful if you have or suspect that you have a bad memory module.
`/noguiboot`	Specifying this switch disables the Windows 2000 splash screen normally displayed during the boot process.
`/sos`	This switch causes the names of device drivers to be displayed on-screen as they are loaded. This switch is very useful when attempting to determine which driver is failing to load during boot.

MODIFYING BOOT.INI

You can use your favorite text editor to make changes to the `boot.ini` file. By default, Windows 2000 sets the `boot.ini` file to be read-only. To successfully edit and save the `boot.ini` file, you will need to remove the read-only attribute. Once you are done modifying the file, add the read-only attribute to prevent the file from being accidentally deleted or modified.

Shutting Down Windows 2000

Well, if you've made it this far, then you probably haven't done too bad setting up and configuring your system. This section will round out the chapter by describing how to shut down a Windows 2000 system. In the past, many people assumed that shutting down a Windows-based system was as simple as turning off the power. Well, times have changed, and it is just as important that a Windows 2000 system be shut down correctly as it is that a UNIX system be shut down correctly.

Earlier you read about the UNIX shutdown process. You may have been a bit overwhelmed by the complexity of the shutdown process. Fortunately, Windows 2000 shutdown is as simple as point and click. The operating system itself conveniently hides all of the steps necessary to safely shut down the system. The following steps detail how to properly shut down your Windows 2000 system:

1. Open the `Shut Down Windows` dialog box by choosing `Shut Down...` from the `Start` menu. The dialog box is displayed in Figure 3.10.
2. Select `Shut down` from the drop-down list.

Figure 3.10
`Shut Down Windows` dialog box.

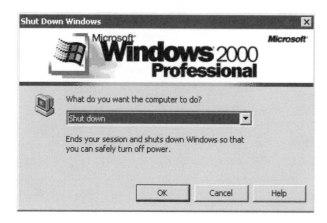

3. Click the OK button.

4. The system will close all applications and shut down cleanly.

5. A message box will be displayed when a safe shutdown has been completed.

WINDOWS 2000 SHUTDOWN POLICIES

Windows 2000 is far more resilient to unfriendly starting and stopping. However, since they are becoming more interconnected, users should still be cautioned against restarting systems that are not theirs. The guidelines suggested for UNIX earlier in the chapter also apply to Windows 2000, especially in an integrated infrastructure. File and application sharing are becoming as prevalent in the NT/2000 community as they are in UNIX.

Summary

THE PHYSICAL BOOT SEQUENCE

The UNIX and Windows 2000 boot sequences are very similar. Actually, the x86-based UNIX operating systems share the same physical boot sequence as the Windows 2000 operating system. Once the power switch is turned on, the `firmware` or `BIOS` perform low-level diagnostics and begin the initial processes of loading the operating system. The firmware used in RISC-based architectures of traditional UNIX computers is completely vendor-dependent. The firmware supplied by Sun is different than that provided by HP or SGI. There are also a variety of BIOS chips on the market, but a few standard configurations dominate.

LOADING THE OPERATING SYSTEM

The operating system can be viewed as a complex interface between the physical capabilities of the hardware: memory, CPU, and disk, and the resource demands of the software applications. In reality, it is also a software application that uses low-level I/O and computational routines embedded in system components. UNIX and Windows 2000 take different approaches to the process of creating this interpretation layer. Within the UNIX family of operating systems, there are two major groups, BSD and SysV. Differences between the two are apparent in the early stages of loading the operating system. Though they both use `rc` scripts, the BSD variants use them in a sequential chain and the SysV variants use them in a directory structure. SysV also has more *run levels* than BSD, using the `inittab` file to control the `rc` scripts used for each run level.

In Windows 2000, the MBR, and core files for loading the operating system are contained in the SYSTEM partition. The remainder of the operating system is stored in the BOOT partition. NTLDR, from the SYSTEM partition, is similar in function to the *ufsboot* type programs in UNIX. It is important to understand that in all of these operating systems, the actual operating system is loaded in layers. Each layer provides more system functionality than previous layers.

CHANGING THE SYSTEM STARTUP

Extreme caution should be used in modifying the system startup process. It is always possible to modify this process so that the system is no longer functional. Be sure you have a good system backup before changing boot scripts!

In the BSD family of UNIX operating systems, the scripts that control the startup process are rc.boot, rc.single, rc, and rc.local. These scripts are Bourne shell scripts. Editing them is straightforward, but remember never to delete information from the files. Re-creating the vendor-supplied code would be rather difficult. The SysV family of UNIX also uses Bourne shell scripts, but the scripts are stored in the init.d hierarchy. Changes in the startup can be made either in the inittab file or by adding start (S) or kill (K) scripts to the correct rc directory.

The Advanced Options Menu in Windows 2000 can be used to modify system startup, primarily for system recovery and troubleshooting. The boot.ini file is used to configure the system startup to allow for dual-boot or multi-boot systems. Like the UNIX startup scripts, boot.ini is a plain text file.

SHUTTING DOWN A SYSTEM

It is important, in both UNIX and Windows 2000, for the system to be shut down correctly. Data integrity is the primary reason for this. The UNIX shutdown process is obviously intended for system administrators only. The Windows 2000 shutdown, however, is simple and can be performed by any user. If file or application sharing is used, in either or both operating systems, policies and procedures should be set to control when and by whom systems may be shut down. The days of just "hitting the power" are gone.

THE FILESYSTEM

UNIX

UNIX Filesystems

Inodes

UNIX File Types

Disk Formatting

Creating Filesystems

WINDOWS 2000

NTFS Features

NTFS Structure

Logging and Recovery

NTFS Fault Tolerance

Adding Disks

The filesystem is the lifeblood of the modern operating system. The filesystem is a cohesive, structured organism that contains the data required and created by the operating system and applications. This chapter will discuss the features, structures, and use of the UNIX and Windows 2000 filesystems. While we will avoid discussing the low-level details of how the filesystems work, we will provide the framework necessary for you to use them effectively.

The UNIX Filesystems

Files in the UNIX universe reside within a *filesystem,* which in turn makes up the *file tree.* The file tree on a UNIX system can contain filesystems from multiple disks or even multiple machines. The basic tree consists of a *root* filesystem and subsequent directories or branches. Figure 4.1 shows a local-only file tree.

Some of the subdirectories shown in the tree are on the same physical partition as the root directory, and others are on different partitions. Add local partitions to the file tree with the mount command as follows.

```
mount -F ufs /dev/dsk/c0t0d0s3 /var
```

The mount command associates the block device specified with the directory name given, using the filesystem type provided. There are many filesystem types available. Usually, the -F option can be omitted and the system's default filesystem will be used. A commonly used filesystem type is

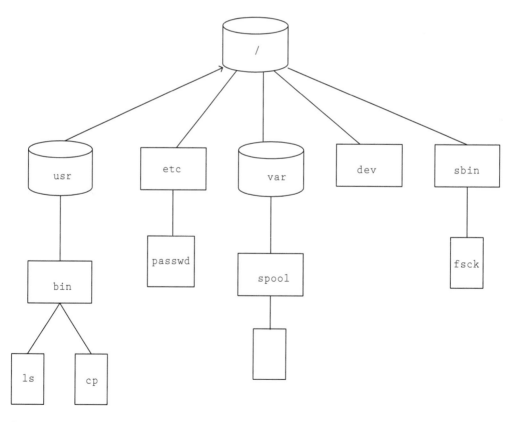

Figure 4.1
Local file tree.

hsfs(commonly know as ISO9660), which is the High-Sierra filesystem. This is the most widely used format for CDs.

Once a filesystem has been mounted, all of its subdirectories become part of the file tree in which it resides. Files within a tree can be addressed either by an absolute pathname, starting from the root (or /) directory, or by a relative pathname, which starts from your current (or `dot`) directory. Table 4.1 shows three different ways in which you can address with the `ls` command.

Like NT, a UNIX filesystem resides on a physical partition. There are two major filesystem formats currently used in UNIX: the original *s5* filesystem from the AT&T System V release, and the BSD-based *ufs (UNIX File-system)*. The s5 format is flat, using four specific sections. The ufs filesystem uses a set of sections that repeats across the physical partition based on size and configuration.

The s5 filesystem, shown in Figure 4.2, begins with the *boot block*, which contains the bootstrapping programs discussed in Chapter 3, "System Boot and Shutdown". In the s5 filesystem, the boot block exists on non-bootable partitions, but it remains empty. The second section is the *super-block*, which contains administrative information, like free-blocks, for the entire filesystem. The third section is for the *inode list*. We will discuss *inodes* later in this chapter. The final section is the *data block*, which contains the actual data blocks used in files.

Like the s5 filesystem, ufs has a *boot block* and a *super-block*. However, Figure 4.3 shows that ufs has multiple copies of the super-block to provide better data integrity. If the super-block is lost, the partition is lost, hence multiple copies provide more stability. The *cylinder group block* is another feature of ufs. The file-system is divided, based on the size of the partition, into cylinder groups. Each cylinder group contains the copy of the super-block mentioned previously, a cylinder group block which contains a subset of the inode list, and a subset of the data blocks. By attempting to assign inodes and data blocks within a geographic region on the physical partition, disk efficiency is increased.

Table 4.1	Absolute and Relative Paths	
Address Used	Explanation of Address
/usr/bin/ls	Absolute path to `ls`.
./bin/ls	Relative path to `ls`, assuming you were in the /usr directory.
ls	Relative path to `ls`, assuming you were in the /usr/bin directory.

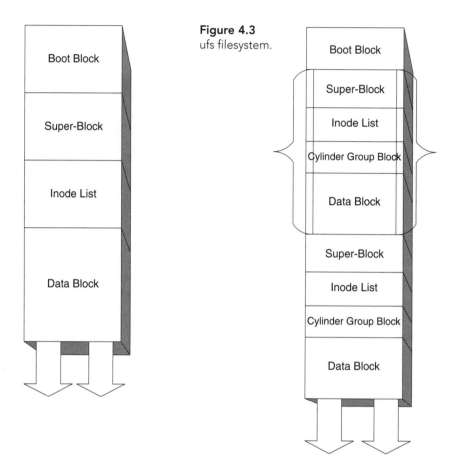

Figure 4.2
5 Filesystem.

Figure 4.3
ufs filesystem.

Linux began by using the MINIX filesystem, which was one of the first UNIX filesystems designed for x86 systems. Most Linux variants are now distributed with the EXT2 filesystem, which is a variant of ufs. Specifically, EXT2 has added an *inode bitmap* and a *block bitmap* to better handle the allocation of resources.

mount allows you to attach file systems into your directory structure from either your local machine or a remote NFS server. mount is covered in more detail in Chapter 8.

INODES

Inodes are the file descriptors of UNIX. Each inode contains information about the owner of a file, its creation and modification times, and the location of the data blocks in which data is stored. Actually, the kernel uses another file abstraction called the *vnode,* which is handled by the VFS. The VFS, or Virtual Filesystem, and the vnode abstraction are out of the scope of this book. The inode, which is the physical abstraction, is the concept that is necessary for a system administrator to understand.

As you saw earlier, each cylinder group has an `inode` list. Each entry in a `ufs inode` table is structured like Figure 4.4.

The administrative information includes creation time, modification and access times, ownership information, and link count. This is followed by a series of 15 data slots. The first 12 slots (0 – 11) hold pointers to 12 data blocks located on the disk. If the files are too large to fit into these 12 data blocks, known as direct data blocks, then there are three indirect blocks. The single indirect block creates links to 2048 data blocks. The double indirect block creates links to 2048 blocks, each of which points to 2048 other data blocks. And, as you can guess, the triple indirect block points to 2048 blocks, each of which points to 2048 other blocks, each of which points to 2048 other blocks of data. (If you think that was hard to read, you should try writing it.) If a file required all of the data blocks its size, on an 8K data block system, this would be:

Figure 4.4
ufs inode.

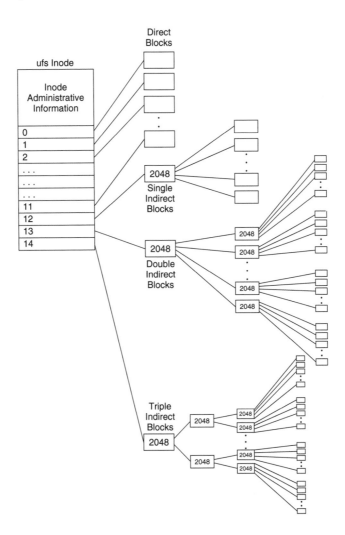

$$8192*(12 + 2048 + 2048^2 + 2048^3) = 7.0403^{13} \ bytes$$

Thus, 70 trillion bytes should handle most users' needs.

File permissions are also contained in the inode information. We will cover the use of file permissions in our discussion of security in Chapter 11, "Networking and Security".

DIRECTORIES AND LINKS

Each inode is a pointer to a set of data. This concept is expressed as a link. A directory in UNIX is a file that contains a table of couplets. Each couplet is made up of an inode number and an identification string. The inode number points to an inode listing in the inode table, which in turn points to the data. The identification string is the filename associated with that set of data accessed via the inode. The pointers are shown in Figure 4.5.

One of the most powerful features in UNIX is the concept of file links. There are two types of links: hard and soft. For a hard link, you have an entry in a directory file where the inode component of the couplet has the same inode number as another entry in that directory, or another directory on the same partition. By doing this, you have created two names that point to the same data. Once a hard link has been created, one name cannot have

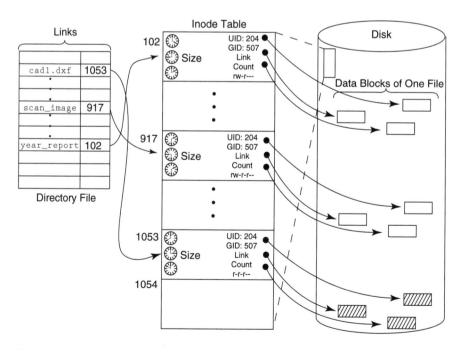

Figure 4.5
Directory.

a greater ownership than any other name. Regardless of which name you use to modify a file, all the links point to the same data, so all the names associated with the inode will reflect the same data. Since each partition has a unique inode table, hard links cannot span partitions.

The second kind of link is a soft link, which is shown in Figure 4.6. In a soft link, the inode component of the directory couplet points to a unique inode in the inode table. It, in turn, has a reference to another inode stored in its first associated data block. The reference inode can be on any partition accessible to the file tree, regardless of what system it is located on. With symbolic links, the inode that points directly to the actual data block is the only official inode associated with the files; the other links are only references.

It does not matter how many hard links a data set accumulates; as long as one exists, the file exists. By contrast, if the original file/inode that is referenced by a symbolic link is removed, the symbolic link will now be pointing to nothing. Links are created with the `ln` command.

`ln` creates a hard link to a file

`ln -s` creates a soft link to a file

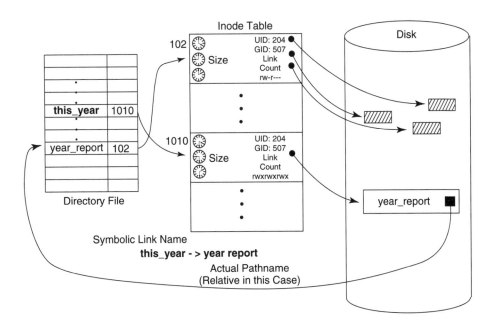

Figure 4.6
Symbolic links.

There is a wonderful in-depth discussion of the `ufs` and `s5` filesystems in *The Magic Garden Explained* by Berny Goodheart and James Cox.

FILE TYPES

The link structure means that everything in UNIX is actually a file. A directory is just a file that contains information relating to the filenames and inodes listed in the directory table. Likewise, a disk partition is represented in UNIX as a special file that contains information relating to the device drivers and disk information necessary to access the physical device. There are six major types of files in UNIX:

- Ordinary files.
- Directories.
- Links.
- Symbolic links.
- Named pipes.
- Special files.

Ordinary files can be anything from flat text documents to compressed archives. They can be considered as the leaves on the file tree. To be more specific, they are files that contain data in zero or more data blocks, not including addressing or redirection data. We discussed directories in the previous section. They are files in which the data is composed of inode-filename couplets. Links and symbolic links were also discussed. In the first case, the directory couplet is a direct reference to the inode table. In the latter case, the data block associated with the reference inode, in turn, references another inode entry.

Named pipes are FIFO (First In, First Out) structures. A named pipe makes it possible for one application to be writing data to a file while another application is reading the file. Special files do not contain any data. Instead, they provide an interface between physical devices and the filesystem. There are two types of special files: *block* and *character* files. A block file passes the data blocks received from a physical device, usually a disk, through the system buffer cache. The `mount` command requires block files. A character file transfers data directly from a device driver to a process without passing through the buffer cache. The `fsck` and `newfs` commands require character, or *raw,* files.

Formatting in UNIX

Disks are partitioned by using the `format` command. In most cases, your installation program will run `format` for you, where your job is to provide the necessary information used to subdivide the disks. However, running `format` from the command line is a common occurrence; it is used when adding new or reconfiguring existing drives. While the `format` command contains many options, if you master a core few, you will be able to properly manage your environment. The `format` command varies some among the UNIX flavors, but the fundamental concepts are the same. Linux uses the `fdisk` command instead. Here we show an example of the Solaris version of `format`:

```
# format
Searching for disks...done

AVAILABLE DISK SELECTIONS:
       0. c0t0d0 <Seagate 34342A cyl 8892 alt 2 hd 15 sec
63>
          /pci@1f,0/pci@1,1/ide@3/dad@0,0
Specify disk (enter its number):
```

The initial `format` screen shows a list of available disks, along with detailed disk information including the device name. Choose a disk to modify and you'll see:

```
Specify disk (enter its number): 0
selecting c0t0d0
No defect list found
[disk formatted, no defect list found]
Warning: Current Disk has mounted partitions.

FORMAT MENU:
        disk       - select a disk
        type       - select (define) a disk type
        partition  - select (define) a partition table
        current    - describe the current disk
        format     - format and analyze the disk
        repair     - repair a defective sector
        show       - translate a disk address
        label      - write label to the disk
        analyze    - surface analysis
        defect     - defect list management
        backup     - search for backup labels
        verify     - read and display labels
        save       - save new disk/partition definitions
        volname    - set 8-character volume name
        !<cmd>     - execute <cmd>, then return
        quit
format>
```

You will never use many of these selections unless you have disk problems and need to analyze and/or repair a disk. The most common use of `format` is to set up the partition table on a disk. While at the `format` prompt, type *partition* and you will see:

```
format> partition

PARTITION MENU:
        0       - change '0' partition
        1       - change '1' partition
        2       - change '2' partition
        3       - change '3' partition
        4       - change '4' partition
        5       - change '5' partition
        6       - change '6' partition
        7       - change '7' partition
        select  - select a predefined table
        modify  - modify a predefined partition table
        name    - name the current table
        print   - display the current table
        label   - write partition map and label to the disk
        !<cmd>  - execute <cmd>, then return
        quit
partition>
```

The selections 0 through 7 (or a through h on SunOS systems) allow you to modify individual partitions, or slices. However, before you begin modifying the partition table, always use the `print` option to view the current partition table:

```
partition> print
Current partition table (original):
Total disk cylinders available: 8892 + 2 (reserved cylinders)

Part    Tag         Flag    Cylinders       Size        Blocks
  0    root         wm       0 - 7807      3.52GB     (7808/0/0) 7378560
  1    swap         wu    7808 - 8891    500.19MB     (1084/0/0) 1024380
  2    backup       wm       0 - 8891      4.01GB     (8892/0/0) 8402940
  3   unassigned    wm       0               0        (0/0/0)          0
  4   unassigned    wm       0               0        (0/0/0)          0
  5   unassigned    wm       0               0        (0/0/0)          0
  6   unassigned    wm       0               0        (0/0/0)          0
  7   unassigned    wm       0               0        (0/0/0)          0
partition>
```

Each line gives you information about a partition, including its size, number of blocks, and the cylinder range. Cylinder range is very important, as you want to make sure as you partition a disk that you don't allow cylinders to be owned by multiple partitions. While this may seem unusual, UNIX will allow you to overlap cylinders, and if this situation goes undetected, it can cause some strange behavior which is difficult to debug.

By entering the number corresponding to the partition you want to modify, you are then prompted to change the partition. The current value is displayed in brackets ([ ]). If no new information is entered, the partition keeps its current value.

```
partition> 0
Part   Tag    Flag    Cylinders       Size            Blocks
  0    root    wm      0 - 7807        3.52GB      (7808/0/0) 7378560

Enter partition id tag[root]:
Enter partition permission flags[wm]:
Enter new starting cyl[0]:
Enter partition size[7378560b, 7808c, 3602.81mb, 3.52gb]:
partition>
```

The best way to avoid making a mistake when partitioning a system is to size each partition using number of cylinders, as in our example, 7808c. Checking that your total number of cylinders equals the total, as shown in partition 2, will keep you from overlapping partitions.

Table 2.2 gives a listing of commands used to format disks in other UNIX variants. The concepts are similar, but the command names differ greatly.

Never modify partition 2, as this is the overlap partition that defines the complete disk. Partition 2 will always give you the total number of cylinders and space available on your disk.

`format` is a disk partitioning and maintenance utility. Options vary throughout the UNIX family. Linux uses the `fdisk` command.

Creating Filesystems

The UNIX `format` command does not create a filesystem like the NT command. There are many options in creating a filesystem, so it must be done after formatting. The raw command for creating a filesystem is `mkfs`. However, most administrators use the easier and more intuitive `newfs`.

The `newfs` command can only be run on a raw partition. The basic command is straightforward:

```
# newfs /dev/rdsk/c0t0d0s04
```

The default filesystem will be created with the number of bytes per inode set to 2048. Raising the number will decrease the number of available inodes, and lowering the number will increase the number of inodes. Back at the dawn of time, when disk space was expensive, limiting the space used in filesystem overhead was crucial, so adjusting the inode-to-byte ratio was important. To change the ratio, you would use:

```
# newfs -i 4096 /dev/rdsk/c0t0d0s4  to create one inode for
every 4096 bytes.
```

The default filesystem also provides a ten percent buffer, or free space, on the actual file space available. If you have 8GB of space, the system will automatically reserve 800MB as a buffer against overwriting. You can change this percentage with:

```
# newfs -m 5 /dev/rdsk/c0t0d0s4
```

which will lower the percentage to 5. The free space can be adjusted later using the `tunefs` command.

You should be careful in adjusting the parameters to `newfs`. In most cases, you will not need to change them, and can use the default. The free space parameter is the only one that can be changed after the creation of a new filesystem. Be sure to choose wisely.

`newfs` constructs a new UNIX filesystem. It is a friendly front-end to the `mkfs` program.

The Windows 2000 Filesystem

In this section, we discuss many aspects of the Windows 2000 filesystem, or NTFS, focusing on a description of the filesystem structure, and an introduction to NTFS logging, recovery, and fault tolerance. This section deals mainly with how to use NTFS effectively, as opposed to how NTFS has been implemented.

NTFS OVERVIEW AND FEATURES

When Microsoft began designing Windows NT in the late 1980's, it became apparent that none of the available filesystems (particularly FAT and

HPFS) fulfilled the requirements that had been set forth. The File Allocation Table (FAT) filesystem had been around since the early 1980's and was designed to meet the needs of the original IBM PC. The FAT filesystem was designed to support small disks, such as floppy disks and small hard drives. The original version of FAT did not support disks larger than 500MB and, in theory, the FAT structure could not support any disk larger than 4GB. Over the years, FAT has been extended to support large disk sizes, and now, the FAT32 filesystem can support much larger disks than the original FAT filesystem. Still, FAT lacks the advanced features Microsoft was looking for in the filesystem to be used in Windows NT.

IBM developed the High Performance Filesystem (HPFS) for use with OS/2 about the same time Microsoft began development on Windows NT. While HPFS provided better performance and supported larger disks than the FAT filesystem, it still fell short of Microsoft's requirements for Windows NT's filesystem.

Microsoft decided that it would develop a completely new filesystem with the following general guidelines in mind:

- Large disk support.
- High performance.
- Security.
- Recoverability.
- Data redundancy.
- Fault tolerance.

Although NTFS was a new design, much of the filesystem was influenced by FAT and HPFS, as well as by properties of POSIX (loosely translated as the Portable Operating System Interface based on UNIX), which would be supported under NT. You have already read about FAT and HPFS; POSIX is one of Windows NT's many subsystems that can be exploited by developers. Microsoft felt that Windows NT would be more attractive to the developer community if it supported a familiar interface. When Microsoft was done with NTFS, all of the major goals had been accomplished and NTFS surpassed both FAT and HPFS in every area. Table 4.2 shows a comparison of the three filesystems.

When Windows NT 3.1 shipped in 1993, NTFS was in the box and ready to go. The NTFS filesystem has been revised with every release of Windows NT, including updates included with some of the Service Packs. Windows 2000 will ship with NTFS version 5.0, which includes all of the features of the current version of NTFS (version 4.0), as well as support for disk quotas, disk defragmentation, file encryption, and improved filesystem structures.

Table 4.2	Overview of FAT, HPFS, and NTFS	
Filesystem	Maximum File and Volume Sizes	Performance Characteristics
FAT	4 gigabytes	Best for partitions smaller than 500 megabytes.
HPFS	4 gigabytes	Better than FAT, but worse than NTFS.
NTFS	16 exabytes (theoretical) 2 terabytes (realistic)	Best for partitions larger than 500 megabytes.

Large Disk Support

NTFS supports very large disks, theoretically up to 16 exabytes. Current physical limitations place the actual limit at 2 terabytes. While it is not possible to have such a large disk volume or logical partition today, we must remember that it was nearly inconceivable to have 1-gigabyte disks in personal computers just 10 years ago. Since we cannot predict the future, Microsoft designed NTFS as a 64-bit filesystem capable of adapting to whatever the future may bring. Another notable and related feature is that NTFS also supports a maximum theoretical file size of 16 exabytes, so it is possible to have a single file occupying the maximum volume size in NTFS. This may prove to be very useful in the future, as databases continue to grow in size.

Security

NTFS supports file-level security; that is, access permissions can be set on individual files, directories, and volumes. This feature gives system administrators nearly unlimited control over access permissions. The amount of control is really only limited by the amount of time the administrator wants to spend configuring the system (and by the imagination, of course).

The security structure is stored as an Access Control List (ACL), along with the other file attributes in the file record. Access Control Lists will be discussed in greater detail in Chapter 11. Access permissions can be both granted and denied in NTFS on both user and group levels. Permissions can be adjusted by system administrators, the designated owner of a file or directory, and those users and groups granted permission to change the access permissions by the administrator or owner. It should be clear by now that NTFS provides a high level of access control.

Although we will be discussing ACLs in greater detail later in the book, you should use care when editing an ACL to avoid making very costly mistakes. A simple mistake in modifying an ACL can actually prevent even the administrator from accessing a file or other object (that is, not without a lot of extra work).

Compression

NTFS, unlike FAT and HPFS, natively supports file compression. It is possible under NTFS to achieve a 2:1 compression ratio. NTFS compression is enabled on a per-directory basis and will affect all files and subdirectories. It is important to remember that enabling compression on a directory does not automatically compress the current data. Only new data written to the directory will be compressed. If you want to compress the current data, you must explicitly do so in the `Advanced Directory Properties` window. To modify the compression settings for a directory, follow these steps:

1. Open the `Directory Properties` window by right-clicking a directory in Windows Explorer and selecting `Properties` from the list that appears. The window in Figure 4.7 should appear.
2. Click the `Advanced` button to display the `Advanced Attributes` window shown in Figure 4.8.

Figure 4.7
The `Download` directory's `Properties` window.

Download Properties	? X

General | Sharing | Security |

Download

Type:	File Folder
Location:	C:\
Size:	21.2 MB (22,276,190 bytes)
Size on disk:	21.2 MB (22,286,336 bytes)
Contains:	4 Files, 2 Folders
Created:	Tuesday, September 28, 1999, 12:13:04 PM
Attributes:	☐ Read-only Advanced...
	☐ Hidden

OK | Cancel | Apply

Figure 4.8
Selecting
`Compress`
`contents to`
`save disk`
`space` in the
`Advanced`
`Attributes`
window.

3. Select or deselect (depending on whether you are applying or removing compression) the `Compress contents to save disk space` under the `Compress or Encrypt attributes` section.

4. Click the `OK` button when you are finished making changes.

5. Click the `OK` button to close the `Download Properties` window and apply your changes.

6. You will be prompted to confirm your changes and select the level of compression (whether or not compression will apply to subdirectories). The `Confirm Attribute Changes` window is shown in Figure 4.9.

7. Select the level of compression you desire and click the `OK` button.

8. Depending on how much data is already in the directory, it may take a few minutes to complete the compression operation.

Figure 4.9
Confirming your
compression
changes.

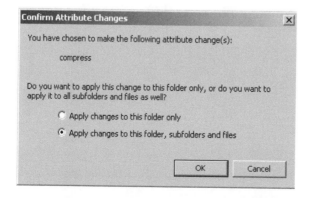

One unique aspect of NTFS compression is that it is possible (but not rec-ommended) to compress the operating system files. In many cases, you will find that access to compressed data is faster than access to uncompressed data. You should not compress your operating system files to avoid the situa-tion where you cannot access those files because of a missing or corrupt file system driver. Remember, the operating system files are accessed during the boot process.

Encryption

One of the significant new features in Windows 2000 is the Encrypting Filesystem (EFS). EFS extends the capabilities of NTFS by encrypting your data using a combination of encryption methods, including public-key and the Data Encryption Standard (DES). With EFS enabled, only allowed users will be able to access the encrypted data. Additionally, EFS does not produce a noticeable degradation in filesystem performance. To enable or disable en-cryption for a folder, use the following procedure:

1. Open the `Directory Properties` window by right-clicking a folder in Windows Explorer and selecting `Properties` from the list that appears. (See Figure 4.7.)
2. Click the `Advanced` button to display the `Advanced Attributes` window (Figure 4.10).
3. Select or deselect (depending on whether you are applying or remov-ing encryption) the `Encrypt contents to secure data` under the `Compress or Encrypt attributes` section.
4. Click the `OK` button when you are finished making changes.

Figure 4.10
Selecting
`Encrypt`
`contents to`
`secure data` in
the `Advanced`
`Attributes`
window.

5. Click the OK button to close the `Directory Properties` window and apply your changes.

6. You will be prompted to confirm your changes and select the level of encryption (whether or not compression will apply to subdirectories). The `Confirm Attribute Changes` window appears (Figure 4.11).

7. The data in your folder should now be encrypted.

The EFS now makes it possible for users to safely store data on their systems, with the added security many people require. There are a few features of EFS that you should keep in mind:

■ Data cannot be both encrypted and compressed. You can only do one or the other.

■ Encrypted data sent over the network is still vulnerable while in transit. You should use caution when transmitting sensitive material over the network.

Disk Quotas

Another new feature provided by Windows 2000 is disk quotas. While UNIX has always provided the ability to track and limit a user's disk space, it has been a long time coming for Windows. Windows 2000 provides the ability to set a default quota on new users via the following steps:

1. In Windows Explorer, right-click the volume you wish to apply the quota on and select `Properties` from the list that appears. You can only apply quotas to volumes, not individual files and folders. The `Local Disk Properties` screen shown in Figure 4.12 should appear.

Figure 4.11
Confirming your encryption changes.

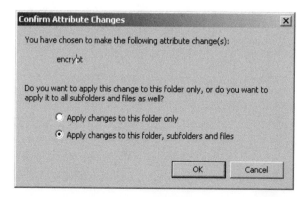

2. Select the `Quota` tab. The window should change and display the quota settings, similar to those shown in Figure 4.13.
3. Set your default quota options to your liking. I have chosen basic settings in Figure 4.14.
4. Click the `OK` button to apply your quota settings. You will be prompted to confirm your selection; do so by clicking the `OK` button. It may take a few minutes for the filesystem to be scanned. Quotas are now active on your volume.

The `Quota Entries` button on the `Quota Settings` window will allow you to view the usage of individual users. You can use this advanced menu to adjust the settings for individual users. Figure 4.14 shows the `Quota Entries` screen.

Quotas in Windows 2000 are based on file and directory ownership. You should make sure that individual users are the owners of their files and directories, otherwise the quota settings will be useless. We will discuss file and directory ownership in Chapter 11.

Figure 4.12
`Local Disk`
`Properties`
window.

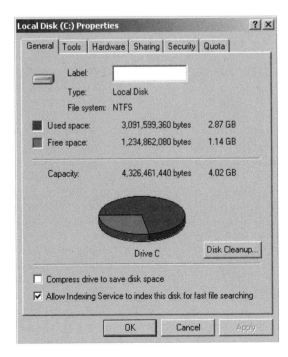

Figure 4.13
Local disk quota
settings.

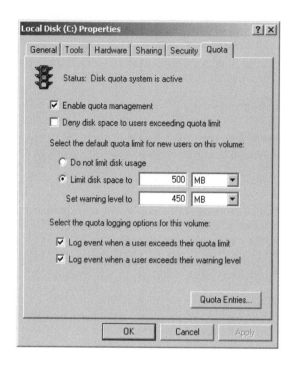

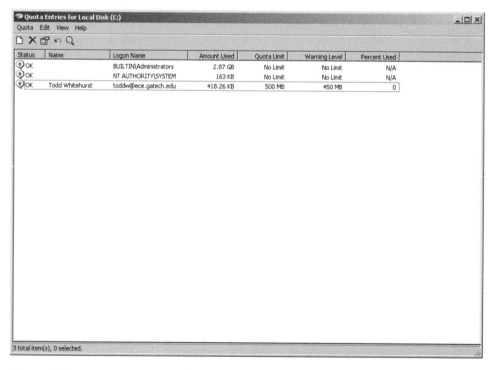

Figure 4.14
Quota entries for the local disk.

Disk Defragmentation

A final, and much welcomed, addition to Windows 2000 is the ability to defragment hard disks. In previous versions of Windows NT, this was only possible using third-party utilities. Today, we can use the following procedure to defragment our disk:

1. Open the `Computer Management` MMC snap-in from the `Administrative Tools` folder, which is contained in the `Control Panel` and/or the `Start` menu. You should see the window shown in Figure 4.15.
2. Select the `Disk Defragmenter` entry under the `Storage` menu. You will see a screen similar to the one in Figure 4.16.
3. Each of your local disks will be listed, and you can select to `Analyze` and/or `Defragment` each disk. We suggest you analyze a disk and defragment it only if the analysis operation recommends for you to do so.

Windows 2000 can defragment any supported filesystem. We recommend that you only defragment your system when the demand on your worksta-

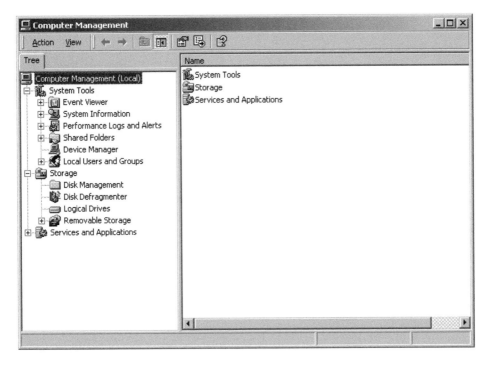

Figure 4.15
`Computer Management` MMC snap-in.

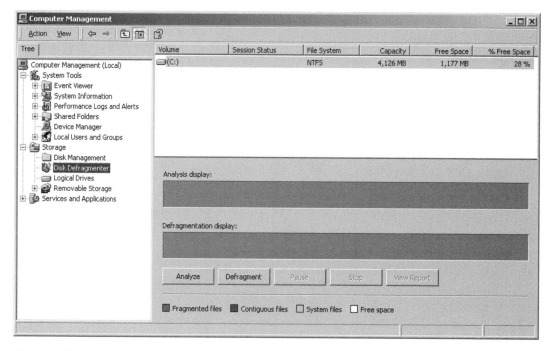

Figure 4.16
Disk defragmenter utility.

tion or server is at a minimum. Disk defragmentation is very disk-intensive and will make your disks unavailable during the defragmentation process.

Logging and Recovery

NTFS contains built-in logging and recovery functions to maintain a high level of reliability. All disk access is considered transactional by NTFS, and is written to logs to recover from any failed or interrupted disk I/O operation. Recovery is automatic in NTFS; there is no user interaction required. A more detailed discussion of logging and recovery is included later in this chapter.

Fault Tolerance

NTFS offers four disk configuration options: two non-fault-tolerant options and two fault-tolerant options. `Volume Sets` and `Stripe Sets` provide the ability to create large disk partitions without fault tolerance. `Mirror Sets` and `Stripe Sets with Parity` provide the ability to create large disk partitions with fault tolerance. Each option has advantages and disadvantages, which will be discussed later in this chapter.

NTFS STRUCTURE

This book is not intended to provide a development-level discussion of the filesystem structure. Rather, it is geared to provide system administrators with a functional understanding of how NTFS is structured so that they can effectively use and support NTFS on a server or workstation. With that in mind, this section will cover the basic NTFS on-disk structure, Master File Tables (MFTs), files, and compression.

Volumes

As is the case with most filesystems, NTFS is structured in logical volumes. A volume can consist of an entire physical disk, a portion of a physical disk, or a combination of two or more physical disks. Each logical volume is handled independently of the other volumes, regardless of which physical disk they are contained on. To view and manage NTFS volumes, you should use the `Computer Management` MMC snap-in provided in the Administrative Tools folder (contained in the `Control Panel` or on the `Start` menu). The Computer Management snap-in is shown in Figure 4.17.

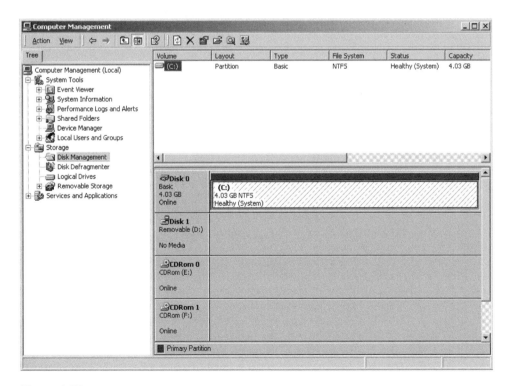

Figure 4.17
`Computer Management` snap-in displaying the disk configuration.

Clusters

NTFS is not aware of the physical disk structure; this functionality is left to the disk driver. NTFS, instead, is only aware of disk clusters. A disk cluster consists of one or more disk sectors, but the number of sectors is always a power of two.

A cluster on an NTFS volume may be as small as 512 bytes or as large as 64 kilobytes, depending on the size of the volume. It is recommended that you always use the default cluster size when formatting a volume, but it is possible to override the default value.

Master File Table

NTFS stores all filesystem data as files on the disk volume. These special filenames all begin with a dollar sign ($) and are normally hidden. Table 4.3 describes each of these files and their relation to the Master File Table (MFT).

The MFT is constructed as an array of file records, which makes searching for and locating files very fast. The MFT is the heart of the NTFS volume and contains information on every file and directory contained in the volume. A single MFT record represents each file, except in cases where the file is highly fragmented or contains many attributes. In these cases, the *base file record* contains pointers to one or more additional file records, which contain the actual file information.

Files

As mentioned earlier, everything stored on an NTFS volume is a file, even the MFT. Files are identified by reference numbers, described by records and attributes, and are visible to the user as simple filenames. This section will attempt to demystify NTFS files.

Reference Numbers A 64-bit reference number identifies all files on an NTFS volume. There are two parts to the file reference number. The lower 48 bits correspond to the position of the file's file record in the MFT. The upper 16 bits correspond to a sequence number, which is incremented each time the file record position in the MFT is reused. The sequence number allows NTFS to perform internal consistency checks.

Records Unlike many filesystems, NTFS stores files as attribute/value pairs. Each attribute (or item) in the file record has a value associated with it. For example, `Filename` is an attribute and `myfile.txt` is the value associated with the attribute. The data contained within a file is just an attribute contained in the file record. The NTFS routines for

Table 4.3	NTFS MFTs and System Files		
System File	Filename	MFT Record	Purpose
Master File Table volume.	$MFT	0	A list of the contents on the NTFS
Master File Table Mirror	$MftMirr	1	A mirror of the MFT's first three records. The mirror is used to guarantee access to the MFT in the event of a single-sector disk failure.
Log File	$LogFile	2	The list of NTFS transactions used for recovery.
Volume	$Volume	3	Contains the volume name, NTFS version, and other volume-specific information.
Attribute Definition Table	$AttrDef	4	A table of available attribute names, numbers, and descriptions.
Root Filename Index	$.	5	Root folder.
Cluster Bitmap	$Bitmap	6	Represents the clusters on the volume in use.
Partition Boot Sector	$Boot	7	Contains the bootstrap code for bootable volumes.
Bad Cluster File	$BadClus	8	Lists the locations of all of the bad clusters found on the volume.
Quota Table	$Quota	9	Index of disk quota usage for each user on the volume. This is not utilized on NTFS versions previous to NTFS 5.0.
Upcase Table	$Upcase	10	Used to convert lowercase characters to the matching Unicode uppercase characters.

accessing/modifying files normally operate on the data portion, but can modify any attribute in the file record. Table 4.4 describes the standard NTFS file attributes.

Filenames NTFS supports filenames up to 255 characters long. Filenames can contain Unicode characters, embedded spaces, and multiple periods. By default, NTFS will also generate an MS-DOS-compatible 8.3

Table 4.4	Standard NTFS File Attributes
Attribute Name	Attribute Description
Standard Information	Contains timestamps, link counts, and standard attributes such as system, hidden, read-only, archive, etc.
Attribute List	Lists the location of all the attribute records when they do not all fit in the MFT record.
Filename	This contains one or more filename attributes for the file. The long Unicode name, short MS-DOS name, and POSIX hard links can be contained in this record.
Security Descriptor	Contains the security information that specifies who owns the file and who can access the file.
Data	Contains the file data. NTFS allows files to have multiple data attributes. Each file usually has one unnamed data attribute and one or more named data attributes. Directories do not have an unnamed data attribute, but can have optional named data attributes.
Index Root	Used to implement folders.
Index Allocation	Used to implement folders.
Volume Information	Used only in the $Volume system file and includes information such as the version and name of the volume.
Bitmap	Provides a map representing records in use on the MFT or folder.
Extended Attribute Information	Used by file servers that are linked with OS/2 systems and is not used by Windows NT or Windows 2000.
Extended Attributes	Used by file servers that are linked with OS/2 systems and are not used by Windows NT or Windows 2000.

filename (you know, the old FAT limitation on filename lengths) that is stored in the file record. However, NTFS does not generate 8.3 filenames for POSIX-based applications.

POSIX files cannot be viewed by MS-DOS- and Windows-based applications unless they are created in compliance with the 8.3 format (i.e., you must give the file an 8.3 name and not a long filename).

Compression

NTFS supports per-file, per-directory, or per-volume compression. The compression occurs in real time and is transparent to the user. While the compression process does slow file access a bit, the NTFS driver does it automatically and you should experience minimal impact.

Once compression has been enabled for a directory or volume, all new directories and files written are compressed by default. However, existing directories and files must be manually compressed if compression was not enabled before they were written.

NTFS LOGGING AND RECOVERY

NTFS provides two very important functions: logging and recovery. The functions are, in fact, dependent upon one another to provide a highly recoverable volume.

Logging

The NTFS filesystem provides a built-in logging function. Since all disk accesses are processed as transactions, it is possible to log and monitor transactions and use this information in the event of a failure. The best part about NTFS logging is that it requires no user intervention. All logging operations are handled by the Log File Service (LFS), which is embedded in the NTFS driver. NTFS uses the LFS to create two main types of records, update records and checkpoint records.

Update Records Update records are the most common ones used by NTFS. Each update record consists of two pieces of information:

- **Redo information** is used to reapply one sub-operation (a single action that is part of a full transaction) of a fully logged transaction in the event of a system error prior to the transaction being flushed from the cache.
- **Undo information** is used to reverse one sub-operation of a partially logged transaction in the event of a system failure.

Checkpoint Records Checkpoint records are created periodically to provide information so that NTFS could recover from an immediate failure. Checkpoint records tell the filesystem where the log file processing should begin to repair the volume after a failure.

Recovery

NTFS performs disk recovery automatically the first time a volume is accessed after a system has been booted. As you might be wondering, this means recovery is performed every time you boot Windows NT or Windows 2000. However, if no recovery is necessary, the process will exit without performing any operations. NTFS recovery relies on the following two tables maintained in memory:

- **Transaction table:** Keeps track of active transactions that have not yet been committed. During recovery, the sub-operations of these transactions must be removed from the disk.
- **Dirty Page table:** Records which cache pages have been modified, but not yet written to the disk. During recovery, this data must be flushed to the disk to maintain a consistent volume.

NTFS creates a checkpoint record and stores the Transaction and Dirty Page tables once every five seconds. When recovery is initiated after a failure, NTFS opens the log file and locates the most recent checkpoint records and copies of the Transaction and Dirty Page tables. In most cases, update records are present after the most recent checkpoint records. At this point, the log file is loaded into memory and the recovery operation is completed in three passes:

Analysis Pass During the analysis pass, NTFS scans the log file from the beginning of the last checkpoint operation to the end of the file. During this pass, the information contained in additional update records is used to update the copies of the Transaction table and Dirty Page table. At the end of the analysis pass, the Transaction and Dirty Page tables should be accurate up to the time of failure.

Redo Pass During the redo pass, NTFS scans forward in the log file starting at the oldest record found in the analysis pass. The redo pass is used to locate *page-update* records that completed before the failure occurred, but may not have been flushed from the cache in time. Each operation found is re-committed to the cache for completion.

Undo Pass The undo pass is used to roll back any un-committed operations at the time of the system failure. After the undo pass has completed, the volume should be stable and coherent up to the time of failure.

chkdsk

Although NTFS includes built-in recovery functions, it is sometimes useful to manually check a volume for errors. chkdsk is the NTFS equivalent of the UNIX fsck utility. chkdsk has the ability to scan a volume for filesystem errors, and for physical disk errors as well. You should not have to run `chkdsk` unless you are experiencing unusual file system problems. There are two common ways to run `chkdsk`:

- ■ To have `chkdsk` scan and repair drive C: for filesystem errors, use the following syntax:

  `chkdsk C: /f`

- ■ To have `chkdsk` scan and repair drive C: for filesystem and physical media errors, use the following syntax:

  `chkdsk C: /f /r`

Keep in mind that `chkdsk` cannot operate on volumes that are currently in use. If you need to run `chkdsk` on a volume currently in use (i.e. the System partition), you should execute one of the above commands, answer yes when prompted to run `chkdsk` during the next reboot, and then reboot the system. `chkdsk` will run at the time of the next reboot.

`chkdsk` scans a volume for filesystem errors and for physical errors.

NTFS FAULT TOLERANCE

NTFS is one of the few filesystems that supports advanced volume configuration and fault tolerance. NTFS is compliant with the Redundant Array of Inexpensive Disks (RAID) standard. All of the advanced volumes, except volume sets, are RAID-compliant. There are two non-fault-tolerant configurations: volume sets and stripe sets. NTFS also provides two fault-tolerant configurations: mirror sets and stripe sets with parity. This section will discuss the attributes of all four configurations. In every case, the Disk Administrator is used to manage the various disk configurations. The different RAID levels are described in Table 4.5.

Volume Sets

Volume sets are created from up to 32 areas of free space of varying size located on one or more physical volumes. Data is written to volume sets sequentially and a volume set performs almost identically to a single partition on a single disk. Volume sets are useful because they can be expanded without losing any of the data contained on them. However, volume sets do not provide any fault tolerance and if one of the disks contained in the volume set is damaged, the entire volume set is corrupted.

Stripe Sets

Stripe sets are created from two or more areas of identically-sized free space on one or more physical volumes. Stripe sets are typically created from two or more identically-sized disks. When data is written to a stripe

Table 4.5	**RAID Levels Supported on Windows 2000**
RAID Level	Description
0: (Striping)	RAID Level 0 allows you to combine two or more disks of equal size into a larger logical volume. Data is written in equal-sized chunks to each disk in the volume. There is no redundancy in this configuration, but disk reads and writes are faster because multiple disks are being accessed concurrently.
1: (Mirroring)	RAID Level 1 allows data from one physical disk to be duplicated to a second physical disk. In the event that the primary disk fails, the secondary disk can take the place of the primary disk with no data loss.
5: (Striping with Parity)	RAID Level 5 provides similar functionality to RAID Level 0. However, this level provides redundancy when a single disk fails. A RAID 5 volume can be established using three or more disks of equal size. The actual size of the volume will be the number of disks minus one multiplied by the size of the disk. The reason for the "loss" of one disk is to store parity information so data can be regenerated if a disk fails. While read performance is better with RAID 5, write performance is slower that RAID 0 because parity information is generated and stored with each write.

set, it is broken into equal-sized chunks and one chunk is written to each of the disks in the stripe set. Read and write accesses to a stripe set are very fast because the data is being streamed from multiple disks (and possibly multiple disk controllers). Stripe sets cannot be expanded without losing the data contained in the set. Stripe sets do not provide any fault tolerance, so a single disk failure will cause all of the data to be lost. A stripe set corresponds to RAID Level 0.

Mirror Sets

A mirror set is created from two identically-sized disks. In a mirror set, both disks contain the exact same data. In the event of a disk failure, the mirror set can be broken and the good disk can be brought on-line as if nothing had ever happened. Once the damaged disk is replaced, the mirror set can be re-created from the remaining good disk. While read performance from a mirror set is unaffected, write performance slows because the data must be written twice. However, a mirror set provides a highly redundant configuration and is most commonly used for high-availability servers and database applications. A mirror set corresponds to RAID Level 1.

Stripe Sets with Parity

A stripe set with parity is constructed the same as a standard stripe set, except three disks must be used. Parity information is written along with the data so that a single disk failure will not result in data loss. In a stripe set with parity, a single disk can be replaced and the data regenerated automatically. Stripe sets with parity enjoy the same read performance as stripe sets, but take a hit on write performance because parity information must be written with each piece of data. Stripe sets with parity are one of the most common fault-tolerant configurations and are typically used for large data storage. It must be noted that a stripe set with parity is as large as the number of disks minus one multiplied by the size of the smallest disk. This is due to the parity requirement. A stripe set with parity corresponds to RAID Level 5.

ADDING DISKS IN WINDOWS 2000

Well, this chapter just wouldn't be complete if we didn't discuss adding and preparing a new disk. This section will describe how to correctly add a new disk to your system and make it available to your users.

Installing a New Disk

Once you have purchased a new disk for your system, you should install it according to the manufacturer's recommendations. Always work on your system in a static-free environment with the power disconnected. Once you have installed the new disk in your system, you can turn the power on and let Windows 2000 boot.

Preparing the Disk for Use

Once you have powered up your system and Windows 2000 has started, go ahead and log on as a local administrator; this is where the fun really begins. Follow the procedure below to create a partition on your disk and assign a drive letter:

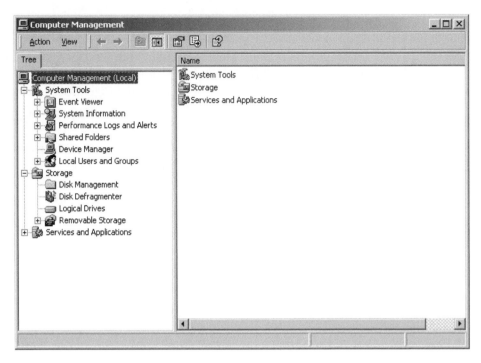

Figure 4.18
`Computer Management` MMC snap-in.

1. Open the `Computer Management` MMC snap-in from the `Admin-istrative Tools` folder, which is contained in the `Control Panel` and/or the `Start` menu. You should see the window in Figure 4.18.

2. Select the `Disk Management` entry under the `Storage` menu. If you installed a brand new disk (one with no pre-defined partitions), you will be greeted by the `Write Signature and Upgrade Disk Wizard`. Go through the wizard to begin the installation of your new disk. Once you have completed the wizard, you will see a screen similar to the one in Figure 4.19.

3. Right-click the unallocated disk and select the `Create Volume` option to start the `Create Volume Wizard`. Answer the questions to complete the steps necessary to create a partition, assign a drive letter, and then format the new volume. The default options should be sufficient.

4. Once the wizard is complete and the format operation is finished, your new disk will be ready for use.

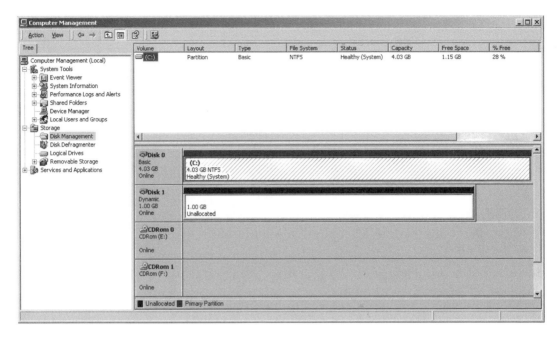

Figure 4.19
Disk management utility.

Summary

UNIX FILESYSTEMS

The UNIX filesystem is structured as a tree, starting at the *root* and branching out into individual files. It is both simple and complicated at the same time. The entire structure is created by pointers. A directory is a set of couplets containing a pointer to an *inode* in the *inode list.* The inode contains all of the information connected with a file, like the owner, modification times, and most importantly, pointers to the actual data blocks on the disk.

Everything in UNIX is considered to be a file, so there are several file types. There are six major file types in UNIX:

- Ordinary files.
- Directories.
- Links.
- Symbolic links.

- Named pipes.
- Special files.

Hard links and *symbolic* (soft) *links* are powerful features in UNIX. For a hard link, you have an entry in a directory file where the inode component of the couplet is the same inode number as another entry in that directory, or another directory on the same partition. In a soft link, the inode component of the directory couplet points to a unique inode in the inode table. It, in turn, has a reference to another inode stored in its first associated data block.

To add a disk to a UNIX system, you must first *format* the disk. Different flavors of UNIX use different commands to perform this operation. In this chapter, we showed you an example of the Solaris `format` command. Regardless of the operating system or command, the *slices* or *partitions* must be defined and configured. Once this is done, you can use `newfs` or the relevant program for your flavor of UNIX to create the actual filesystem.

WINDOWS 2000 FILESYSTEMS

NTFS is a robust, powerful filesystem. The security model is extremely powerful and provides almost unlimited control to the administrator. The built-in recovery features of NTFS are indispensable and help guarantee a highly available, fault-tolerant disk configuration. Microsoft developed NTFS with the following general guidelines in mind:

- Large disk support.
- High performance.
- Security.
- Recoverability.
- Data redundancy.
- Fault tolerance.

NTFS was influenced by FAT and HPFS, as well as by properties of POSIX. NTFS is not aware of the physical disk structure; this functionality is left to the *disk driver*. NTFS instead is only aware of disk clusters. Like UNIX, everything stored on an NTFS volume is a file, even the *Master File Table*. Files are identified by reference numbers, described by records and attributes, and are visible to the user as simple filenames. NTFS provides two very important functions: *logging* and *recovery*. Logging operations are handled by the *Log File Service* (LFS), which is embedded in the NTFS driver. NTFS uses the LFS to create two main types of records: *update records* and *checkpoint records*. Recovery is performed every time you boot Windows NT or

Windows 2000. If no recovery is necessary, the process will exit without performing any operations.

NTFS supports advanced volume configuration and fault tolerance. NTFS is also compliant with the RAID standard. There are two non-fault-tolerant configurations: *volume sets* and *stripe sets*. NTFS also provides two fault-tolerant configurations: *mirror sets* and *stripe sets with parity.*

UPGRADES, PATCHES, SERVICE PACKS, AND HOT FIXES

UNIX

Upgrade Techniques

Pre-Patch Planning

Patching AIX: SMIT

Patching HPUX: SAM

Patching Linux: GNOrpm

Patching Solaris: Installpatch

WINDOWS

Upgrade Techniques

Installing Service Packs

Installing Hot Fixes

Owning a computer system is similar to owning a car, though computers depreciate in value faster. With a car, you are expected to perform maintenance at regular intervals to ensure that the vehicle runs smoothly and lasts a long time. Sometimes the maintenance is simple, such as checking the oil or rotating the tires, while other times a full tune-up or even a complete engine rebuild is required. Depending on the model of your vehicle, you may receive notice from the manufacturer in the form of a recall that informs you of a defect that needs to be fixed.

Managing your computer's operating system is like managing maintenance on your vehicle. After installing a new operating system, you will periodically need to do general maintenance to keep the operating system running smoothly. Sometimes the work will be simple, sometimes complex. In some instances, you will discover or be informed of vulnerabilities and problems with your operating system. In many cases, you will receive updates to your operating system that will provide better performance, stability, and security.

The periodic improvements you add to your operating system are defined as upgrades and patches. Upgrades are any addition to your operating system that provides new functionality or introduces better performance over the older operating system. Generally, upgrades to an operating system come in the form of releases, where the new release is an increment to the older version of the operating system; for example, the difference between HPUX 10 and HPUX 11. Big changes in number indicate a large amount of improvement, while small increments in number, for example HPUX 10.0 to HPUX 10.01, usually indicate minimal changes and enhancements. Patches are pieces of code that fix a problem, usually related to performance, security, or stability. Each operating system version will have hundreds of patches as users, developers, and system administrators discover weaknesses in the operating system code.

What is important is that over time you will spend significant resources researching, managing, and installing patches and system upgrades. This chapter will help you learn how to effectively manage this enormous task by taking a structured approach to managing this mountain of information. Managing patches and upgrades is very similar for Windows and UNIX. Installing patches and upgrades is very specific to each operating system, and this chapter will present you with the information you need to perform upgrades and patches for your favorite UNIX operating system, as well as Windows 2000.

Upgrading an Operating System

Depending on what type of system administrator you've aspired to be, the term "upgrade" can have different meanings. If you are a hardware nut, when your boss mentions an upgrade, you get all excited and check the product catalog for the price of the super-fast, new processor, or the cost of another stick of memory. Hardware upgrades can be exciting times. If your focus is on the operating system and software, the term "upgrade" can be enough to cause ticks, twitches, and uncontrolled speech. If this is you, then you've survived your share of software upgrades and have experienced some of the "benefits" they bring.

An operating system *upgrade* is any post-installation modification you make to the core operating system to enhance flexibility, remedy flaws, or add functionality. Generally, upgrades are generated by the operating system vendor and provide new programs or options, fix bugs, and generally give you something better than you had before. Upgrades can come in the form of a new operating system version or as updates to the current system. Regardless of how they are packaged, upgrades are an important way to keep your systems running over the long haul.

 An operating system *upgrade* is any post-installation modification you make to the core operating system to enhance flexibility, remedy flaws, or add functionality

Operating system upgrades need not invoke nightmares and late-night trips to the local copy center to update your resume. Upgrades are generally a useful and productive way to improve system performance. Operating system developers have designed upgrades to add functionality, eliminate bugs and quirks, and increase performance and reliability. While many of us may question the value of past upgrades, in general, operating system programmers don't start out to be sadistic people who only want to make your life unbearable.

Upgrading in an integrated environment adds the complexity of cross-operating system dependency. Various integration tools, like SAMBA and LDAP, require the administrator to confirm compatibility after the upgrade. Something that works fine with Red Hat Linux 6.0 and NT 4.0 may not work with Linux 5.1 and Windows 2000, or vice versa.

An informed administrator will understand the key elements of an operating system upgrade, and will develop a plan for successful implementation. In the sections that follow, we will give the tips and tools necessary to evaluate, plan, and install your next operating system upgrade. With these tools, your chance of success should increase, while your stress and blood pressure levels should decrease.

UPGRADING VS. RE-INSTALLING

If you are an experienced administrator, you are most likely the survivor of many system upgrades and re-installations. However, the terms "upgrade" and "re-installation" may not be the words you have used to describe your processes. It is important to understand the difference, as your strategies for maintaining your systems change based on which method you choose to use.

Upgrading an operating system is the act of adding and deleting elements from the existing system to create a new operating system. A good example of this is when you upgraded from Windows 95 to Windows 98. Once you finished, you had a new operating system (Windows 98), but many core elements from the previous operating system were still intact (from Windows 95). You also didn't have to re-install any of your programs or hardware, and once you completed the upgrade, your task was finished.

Re-installation consists of taking the new version of the operating system and installing it as if the data on your hard drive didn't exist. Basically, you are installing the operating system from scratch, with the outcome of a complete new and virgin operating system when you are finished. However, after the installation is complete, you still have a lot of work to do. Sometimes re-installing is the only way to get to the new operating system version (Windows 95 to Windows 2000, or SunOS to Solaris), so in some cases, you may not have a choice.

Table 5.1	Pros of Upgrading and Re-installing
Advantages of Upgrading	Advantages of Re-installing
System files remain intact; little or no post-upgrade work is necessary.	New installation is much faster than upgrade process.
Upgrades provide finer granularity when modifying the operating system as less changes are required per upgrade compared to a complete re-installation.	Allows the administrator to reconfigure hardware without affecting the system configuration.
In many cases, it is possible to back out of an upgrade and revert to the old operating system.	Clean, virgin copy of new operating system.

Cases can be made for both upgrading and re-installing, as seen in Table 5.1. By completing an upgrade, you have little post-upgrade work to do, as upgrading generally does not disturb application software or operating system modifications. Also, in many cases, you get the added peace of mind that you can back out, and uninstall the upgrade, and revert to your previous operating system level. With a new installation, you'll find that the amount of time needed to install a new operating system is two to three times faster then attempting an upgrade. Also, you get a fresh, new copy of the operating system, so you are sure what you are working with.

While upgrading and re-installing each have positives, looking at the negatives of each choice is just as important. Table 5.2 shows some of the negatives for each procedure.

Re-installing a system has relatively few drawbacks. The most time-consuming task is that you need to spend time after the operating system has been transferred to disk. Basically, re-installing the OS is the same as installing the system from scratch—a new install. Given that you have a solid installation procedure, re-installation should be a piece of cake. The only other issue with a re-installation is that you don't have an on-line backout path if the new operating system has problems. However, as long as you have good backups, you should be able to recover from any disaster.

When choosing an upgrade route, you must install each new version of the new operating system if you wish to progress to the future version. For operating systems that don't change very often, this isn't an issue, but if your operating system changes two or three times a year, do you really want the

Table 5.2	**Cons of Upgrading and Re-installing**
Disadvantages of Upgrading	Disadvantages of Re-installing
Requires upgrading each operating system version. You can't skip ahead or fail to install one of a series of versions.	Requires post-installation reconfiguration, which can be time-consuming for systems with a large number of installed applications or complicated configurations.
Time-consuming process, especially on older hardware.	Can't back out upgrade; must recover from tape.
Requires more disk space as copies of older components are archived.	
May modify system files that you have customized.	
New version may be too large to fit in current disk configuration.	

hassle of performing that many upgrades, especially if the new version doesn't directly benefit your installation?

Upgrades are also a time-consuming process. While the average clean install of an operating system can take anywhere from 30 minutes to two hours, an upgrade can take four or five hours or more depending on the speed of your hardware. It takes a great deal of time to check the version level of each operating system component, archive it, and then replace it with the newer version. Upgrades also require more disk space because of the archiving feature, and subsequently may not fit into your current configuration. Nothing is more frustrating than progressing halfway through an upgrade only to realize that it won't fit on the disk.

The final and possibly most frustrating drawback to upgrading is that the upgrade process in many cases replaces or modifies system configuration files in ways that you may not expect. Windows `INI` and UNIX files such as `sendmail.cf` are often replaced as part of the upgrade process. Unless you know where and what to look for, you may introduce inconsistencies into your environment that can cause hours of work later.

 Whenever possible, choose to re-install the operating system over choosing to upgrade. The small amount of time spent reconfiguring after a re-install will be greatly outweighed by the many problems an upgrade can present.

With the information from Tables 5.1 and Table 5.2 firmly implanted in your mind, we hope you come to the conclusion that choosing the upgrade option is something to be avoided if and whenever possible. Experienced administrators each have their own horror stories of upgrades gone bad. That is why developing a sound installation procedure, as described in Chapter 2, "System Planning, Installation, and Configuration," is so important. If you have a well-developed and organized installation scheme, moving your system to the latest operating system should be as easy as a new installation.

UPGRADING: MAKING THE RIGHT CHOICE

In the past, new operating system versions were something that happened very infrequently, and subsequently were greatly anticipated and cheerfully received. As technology and programming techniques began to change more quickly, the frequency of new operating system versions kept pace. In today's work, an administrator can count on a new operating system version every year, with minor revisions to the operating system available two and sometime three times each year. Multiply the number of operating system releases times the number of systems you manage and it's easy to see that for even an environment of moderate proportions, keeping up with each and every release may not be physically, or mentally, possible.

So, given that you probably don't want to install every new operating system version on each system you manage, how do you decide which new versions make the cut? If you were hoping for a quick and easy answer, you might want to close your book and check back later. Choosing when to upgrade is an involved process that will produce unique answers depending on who is asking the question. However, here are some points to consider when deciding to upgrade your operating system:

- **Availability of new features and enhancements**—New operating system versions usually contain features and enhancements that were not available in older versions. These new features can include upgraded performance, increased security, and newer administration tools.
- **Bug fixes and corrections to past deficiencies**—New releases incorporate bug fixes (patches) from earlier releases, and may fix deficiencies that patches can't correct. Often your operating system manufacturer may not take the time to generate patches for the older release, thereby encouraging you to upgrade to obtain the benefits.

■ **Application requirements**—New applications may require that you have the latest and greatest operating system.

■ **Hardware requirements**—In some cases, new hardware may only be supported by a newer operating system, depending on your hardware and software vendors.

If your reason for upgrading doesn't fit one of these categories, you may want to re-evaluate your decision. If your system is running fine, users are happy, and you have no major problems, your best bet is to just leave the system as it is and consider upgrading after the next operating system release.

> As a lesson we hope you learned in Chapter 2, taking the time to plan your installation up-front should save you hours of work later. Planning an upgrade is no different, and many of the techniques for installing an operating system are the procedures you should use when upgrading the operating system.

Modifying your Backup Plan in Case of Disaster

It is important to learn how to do a complete backup of your system before you start an upgrade. Performing a complete backup is more than just running your daily or weekly full backup. For both UNIX and Windows 2000, verify that your backups are valid. Almost every administrator of worth will have a story about how they completed a backup before some failed system maintenance, only to find that the backup was corrupted, the tape was bad, or the backup software was configured incorrectly and didn't back up what they had expected. The time spent validating your backups is a fair exchange for the time you would have to spend groveling for your life in front of one of your most important users.

> Perform and *verify* backups before you initiate an upgrade. Nothing is worse than having to explain why data was lost when you performed a backup that did not work.

Another technique that can save you time in the event of disaster is to perform your pre-upgrade backup in a way that is easily accessible. With the huge amount of data in today's environments, many administrators use backup packages that are more complicated than the basic backup tools available from within the operating system. If you use a third-party backup tool, re-creating the environment so that your failed system can be restored quickly may present a problem. Whenever possible, attach a backup device directly to the system being upgraded and perform the backup to that medium. This way, if disaster strikes, you can restore the data quickly and efficiently without worrying about network configurations or re-installing the client part of your backup software.

 Whenever possible, attach a backup device directly to the machine and perform a backup using tools that are part of the operating system. If disaster strikes it is much easier to restore key operating system elements using operating system tools and local files than it is to restore from complicated network backup tools.

Upgrading UNIX

With the vast number of different UNIX flavors, it is very likely that if you have a mixed environment, you will spend more time upgrading your UNIX systems than you will upgrading your Windows-based computers. As a rule of thumb, UNIX manufacturers generally release a new version of their operating system once every two years, with a minor version being released maybe once a year. With releases being spread a year apart, it may seem, to the novice administrator, a simple task to keep up with the latest version. This, however, is not always the case.

While software vendors receive pre-releases and beta copies of new operating systems, sometimes vendor software support of a new operating system can lag six months or more behind the operating system release. Also, new operating systems tend to have more than their share of bugs, and even a wide beta release may not catch or provide enough time to fix all the deficiencies in a new operating system. For these reasons, it is a very good idea not to ride on the leading edge of operating system technology unless you have a very good reason to do so.

 In most cases, it is best to wait four to six months after a new release before you introduce a new operating system into your production environment.

When dealing with new releases, always find an out-of-the-way, non-production system on which to deploy your initial copy of the new operating system. Use this environment to familiarize yourself with any new features that the new operating system may bear. If you have specialized hardware in your production environment, you may want to take this opportunity to test the new operating system, on a similarly configured non-production system if one is available.

Test the new operating system with the pieces of your environment, including NFS, NIS, Windows-UNIX file sharing, backups, and security. Until you are comfortable with all the pieces, don't be pressured to release the new operating system too early. Pay attention to what patches are being released, especially those that relate to kernel and security. If you see too many patches being released in a short period of time, you might want to wait before you make the new operating system part of your environment.

Up to now, our discussions of upgrading techniques have been generic. While upgrading to a new UNIX version is not usually a difficult operation, there are a few things that are specific to UNIX you can do to improve your success. Effectively managing your disk space and /etc directory will help you walk away from your UNIX upgrade with happy users and your sanity. You will also want to unmount any non-operating system filesystems to ensure that you don't accidentally overwrite them. Murphy's Law dictates that if you skip this step, something bad will happen.

EFFECTIVE DISK ADMINISTRATION

The best time to think about how you are going to upgrade to the next operating system release is during the initial installation of your new system. You want to do this now, as the choices you make during installation will affect how difficult it will be to upgrade the system down the road.

Usually, the biggest obstacle to future upgrades is lack of disk space.

Over time, the size of future releases increases while the amount of free space on your hard drive decreases. Installations of patches, the growth of log files, and software and drivers eat up what you thought was plenty of hard disk space during initial installation. Pay close attention to the filesystems /, /var, and /usr, as these areas will need to have adequate space during subsequent upgrades. Some tips for ensuring adequate disk space down the road are:

- If possible, specify a single disk drive to be used for only the operating system. Partition the disk such that you only have two partitions: one for / and one for swap. By dividing your disk in this manner, you will have the greatest available space. If you only have a single disk, keep /, /var, and /usr together on the / partition, and give this partition as much space as possible.

- Don't install non-operating system hardware on the root disk. If you have additional disks, place user and user software there.
- Be careful about the number of patches and drivers you install. Only install what you need, and remove any obsolete drivers and patches. You'll be surprised how much disk space three years' worth of patches can devour.
- Manage your log files aggressively. Don't leave months of log files in /var. Periodically go through your log files and remove files older than a couple of months. If you need to retain your log files, compress them, or migrate them to a log server or another partition.

By taking the time to manage the space on your root partition, you will be rewarded at upgrade time when you are able to upgrade to the new version of the operating system on the first try.

MAKING A COPY OF THE /ETC DIRECTORY

An effective technique that many administrators discover with time is making a copy of the files in the /etc directory and moving them to a safe, yet easily accessible place prior to an upgrade. After an upgrade, especially if you perform a new installation, the majority of your time is spent restoring the original identity of the system. This usually includes modifying the /etc/hosts file, mount locations, sendmail configurations, default routers, and other network, NIS, and DNS configurations. By archiving the /etc directory, you can quickly recover this information without having to employ the backup tape or manual re-creation method. However, make sure the syntax of these files has not changed from the previous operating system.

UNMOUNTING DATA FILESYSTEMS

One final step before you begin your upgrade is to unmount any non-operating system filesystems. If you followed the guidelines for system configuration in Chapter 2, you should have all of your data files located on filesystems that are not part of the root operating system partition. Removing them from vfstab or fstab will ensure that during the upgrade, the installation program won't accidentally choose these areas to grow the root filesystem. Some upgrade utilities allow you to grow a filesystem in place, and these utilities may go looking for additional places to add new operating system files. Unmounting data directories does not excuse you from backing up your data directories before the upgrade. Make sure any and all filesystems are backed up and verified to avoid problems later.

PERFORMING THE UPGRADE

Once you have completed all your pre-upgrade tasks, you are ready to perform your upgrade. The simplest way to initiate the upgrade is to boot from the CD-ROM with the new version of the operating system. During the installation process, you will be given the choice to perform an initial install or an upgrade. *Make sure you perform the upgrade or you will overwrite all of the data on your root disk.* Each flavor of UNIX will have different choices, but read each set of instructions carefully so that you don't damage what you are planning to save by performing an upgrade. Be especially careful that you don't modify the disk parameters or grow your filesystems onto non-root disk partitions that may contain user data.

POST-UPGRADE INSPECTION

One you have completed your upgrade, you need to perform a post-upgrade inspection. During the upgrade process, the installation program may have replaced system files that you may have modified for your environment. You should check any configuration files that are related to system-level utilities, such as `sendmail`. Other files to check include `/etc/hosts`, `/etc/system`, and other places where you can modify system parameters. Most upgrade packages provide upgrade logs, and it is good practice to review the logs to see if any unexpected modifications took place.

Upgrading Windows 2000

Unlike a typical UNIX installation, Windows 2000 does not split your physical disk into different partitions that will eventually prove to be too small to allow for future upgrades. Instead, you need only concern yourself with ensuring that the physical disk is large enough to hold the operating system itself, plus a page file that is twice the size of your physical memory. Once this requirement has been met, the general issues surrounding upgrades to Windows 2000 are very similar to the issues surrounding upgrades to UNIX systems.

Some tips for making your upgrade to Windows 2000 easy are:

- Always install software that is not specifically related to the operating system itself on a separate partition/disk from the operating system installation. This will ensure that your operating system disk contains only operating system-related drivers and files, making upgrading very simple.

- Always keep a record of everything you have installed on your system, and where it was installed. Not all software is compatible with future operating system releases, and knowing this ahead of time can save countless hours of troubleshooting after performing an upgrade.

- Keep an *archive* of any drivers and utilities you need for your hardware and user environment. Although most upgrades will either include an appropriate driver or will require a new driver from a vendor, knowing what drivers you need is half the battle of keeping your system up after an upgrade.

- Last, but certainly not least, make sure the new operating system supports the upgrade you wish to perform. In other words, make certain that you *can* upgrade from your current operating system to the new operating system. In many cases, you must perform a complete re-install, or patch your current operating system for the upgrade to complete successfully. All of this information can be found in the documentation included with your new operating system.

Performing an actual upgrade on a Windows 2000 system is quite simple. In most cases, the new operating system will be accessible from a CD-ROM or network drive. In the case of the CD-ROM media, you should be prompted to perform an upgrade when inserting the disk in the drive. In both cases, there will be a setup program included on the media. This program will be either `winnt32.exe` or `setup.exe`, depending on what operating system you are upgrading to. Once you have executed the setup program, the upgrade will perform very similarly to a base installation. The main difference will be the copying of files before your system reboots, and the setup program will ask few, if any, questions requiring your input.

Always perform a test upgrade on a non-critical system before deploying a new operating system in your production environment. Remember that there will *always* be problems after upgrading to a new operating system. The problems are usually simple to solve and are of a non-critical nature, but knowing what to expect when deploying the upgrade in your production environment will make everyone's life a lot easier.

The most common scenario you will encounter in the months ahead is upgrading your existing systems to Windows 2000. In our experience with the pre-release builds of Windows 2000, we found it to be relatively painless. Use the following as a guideline for upgrading to Windows 2000:

1. When you insert your Windows 2000 CD into your CD-ROM drive, the AutoRun feature should kick in and you will be greeted with a pleasant-looking splash screen, such as the one shown in Figure 5.1.

Figure 5.1
Windows 2000
AutoRun splash
screen.

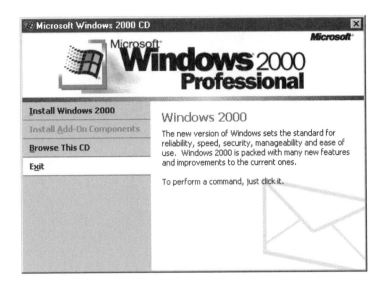

2. If your current operating system can be upgraded to Windows 2000, you will be asked if you want to upgrade. Immediately after the splash screen appears, you will see the dialog box in Figure 5.2.

3. If you are ready to upgrade, click the Yes button, otherwise click the No button.

4. If you chose to upgrade, Windows 2000 setup will start and you will see the window in Figure 5.3.

5. It is up to you to determine if upgrading or performing a clean install is the best solution for your system. Make your choice and click the Next button.

6. Once you select to upgrade, you will be asked to approve the license agreement. Select the appropriate option to agree and click the Next button.

7. Windows 2000 setup will inspect your current system and warn you if anything is incompatible with Windows 2000. Assuming you do not have any problems, setup will begin the upgrade procedure.

8. You should refer to Chapter 2 for assistance with installation once you get to this point. You will be prompted for very little input when performing an upgrade.

Figure 5.2
Upgrade dialog
box.

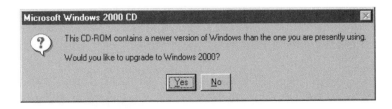

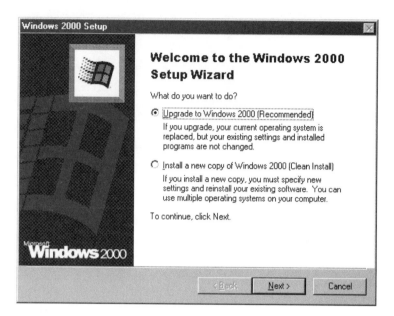

Figure 5.3
`Windows 2000 Setup` window.

 Before beginning any upgrade, always consult the `Read1st` and `Readme.doc` files on the Windows 2000 CD. These files will contain the latest information regarding hardware and software compatibility.

Patching

Patches are those little "upgrades" that every operating system is blessed with. They add stability, compatibility, or new functionality to your system without having to do a full upgrade. In the past, system patches were chunks of operating system code to be added to the current operating system. After installation, a recompilation of the kernel was required. Recompiling the code wasn't always so easy, and on older, slower systems, it sometimes took a long time. As operating systems evolved, vendors modularized their code such that patches generally contained new binaries for system programs, or configuration file replacements contained new information. By providing new binaries instead of new code, patches were usually more stable and required less time to implement.

Between version releases, every operating system has literally hundreds of "additions." In some cases, patches are free and available for download from the vendor's Web site. Most vendors provide core kernel and security patches without cost, but all other patches require a service contract. If your users are demanding, get a contract, or run Linux. However, do not underestimate the advantages of having a software contract with your vendor. Operating system contracts generally give you access to patches, as well as upgrades and phone support. Nothing is more work than having an operating system problem and nobody to call.

WHEN SHOULD I PATCH MY SYSTEM?

Once you have access to the many hundreds of patches, how do you decide when and what patches to apply to your system? A good rule of thumb is to apply patches using the adage, *"If it ain't broke, don't fix it!"* Attempting to install all the possible patches is a bad idea because:

- Patches can eat up a great deal of disk space.
- Some patches will actually break more then they fix.
- Attempting to apply all available patches on just one system could become a full-time job.

 When considering applying patches, remember, *"If it ain't broke, don't fix it!"*

A good strategy is to apply all recommended kernel (usually performance- and stability-related) and security patches. After that, only install patches if you have a system that is exhibiting a problem that a patch specifically claims to correct. If you have mission-critical systems, patch a non-critical system first just to make sure the patch doesn't have any unexpected consequences. While patches are released to fix problems, it isn't uncommon for a patch to break something else, or even disable a system.

Windows 2000 is no exception to the rule. Microsoft's patch mechanism comes in two flavors: Service Packs and Hot Fixes. There is one big difference between the two. Service Packs contain ALL previously released fixes, as well as any new fixes since the last Service Pack. Service Packs are also regression-tested to ensure that, in most cases, the application of the Service Pack will not break anything. Hot Fixes are interim patches released between Service Packs and typically fix a single problem, which occurs in a given environment. Hot Fixes are not regression-tested and should only be applied if it is necessary to fix a problem you are actually experiencing. With that said, it should be clear that it is safe to apply Service Packs once you have tested them on a non-production system to ensure that nothing breaks.

Managing and Installing UNIX Patches

Managing your patch installation should be a reflection of your infrastructure. If you are managing mission-critical, highly available systems, then you should investigate new patches on a weekly, if not daily, basis. However, if your systems are stand-alone, single-user workstations, then you will probably benefit from a quarterly or bi-yearly patch schedule. However, don't overlook security, performance, and patches that target a known problem that has affected your systems.

If you stay three to six months behind the releases of the latest operating system, patch clusters should be available that you can use at install time, which will provide a very stable system. In many cases, the creators of your operating system will give you a list of patches that they recommend that you install on every system. Gathering these patches into a cluster and making sure you install them at install and upgrade time will help you provide a stable environment out of the box.

While you may provide a well-patched system upon installation, how do you manage patches after systems have left the comfort of your office and reached the harsh environment of the user's desktop? If we remove point patches, which are installed to solve specific problems, some tips for patch installation management include:

- Build a patch cluster that includes all security, stability, and performance patches.
- Install the cluster on a test system to ensure that the patches you are testing don't have unexpected interactions with your installed hardware and software.
- Once you have test-certified the patches, begin installing them on all new systems and older systems during operating system upgrades.
- Set and follow a schedule for distributing patches to all other existing systems—monthly, quarterly and bi-yearly are all good patch schemes, depending on the criticality of your systems and the stability of your operating system.
- You now have a consistent environment; go to Step 1.

As you can see, like system administration, patching is a never-ending cycle. However, don't be daunted by the mountain of available patches you have to install on all the systems in your infrastructure. If you carefully select only the patches you need and set a reasonable patch schedule, you can turn the mountain into a molehill.

WHERE TO FIND UNIX PATCHES

When looking for patches, one of the best places to start is on the installation CD for your operating system. If your CD isn't the first revision level of the operating system, many performance, security and stability patches may already be part of the distribution.

Many vendors also distribute supplemental CDs that contain all patches available at the time of release with their core operating systems. These patch CDs can be particularly helpful when you are attempting to solve a particular problem and you don't want to spend a lot of time searching the Internet and downloading patches. Some useful sites for downloading patches are:

- http://sunsolve.sun.com
- http://hp.com
- http://service.software.ibm.com
- http://redhat.com/support

AIX: SMIT and FixDist

The System Management Interface Tool (SMIT) is AIX's menu-driven system administration and management tool. SMIT will automatically detect a user's environment variables and run in either an X11 display (Figure 5.4) or a character mode interface (Figure 5.5). To ensure a character interface, utilize the following:

#smit -C

or

#smitty,

smit menu-driven system administration and management tool for AIX

smitty character based version of *smit*

SMIT can be invoked with the FastPath switch install to immediately place you in the software installation and maintenance portion of SMIT. Here, the character interface provides quicker response.

SMIT automatically creates two files in the user's home directory ($HOME) during each session. The smit.log file contains the sequence of submenus visited during the session. The smit.script file contains the AIX commands that SMIT invoked in response to your selections. The script file is a great resource for understanding the switches and inputs required in command-line software maintenance. This file can also be used to automate redundant software installs.

FixDist is a tool developed by IBM to aid the system administrator in downloading fixes for AIX. The tool does not install fixes. It has the capability to download all requisite fixes to a directory on your home system. It can run interactively or be scheduled to download at a later time. You can search

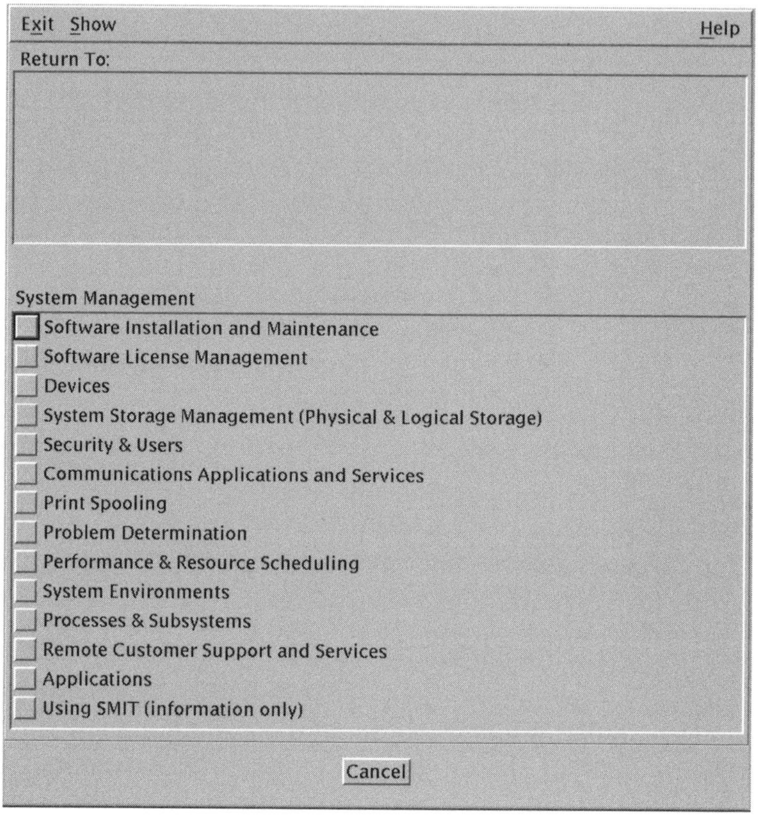

Figure 5.4
X11 SMIT.

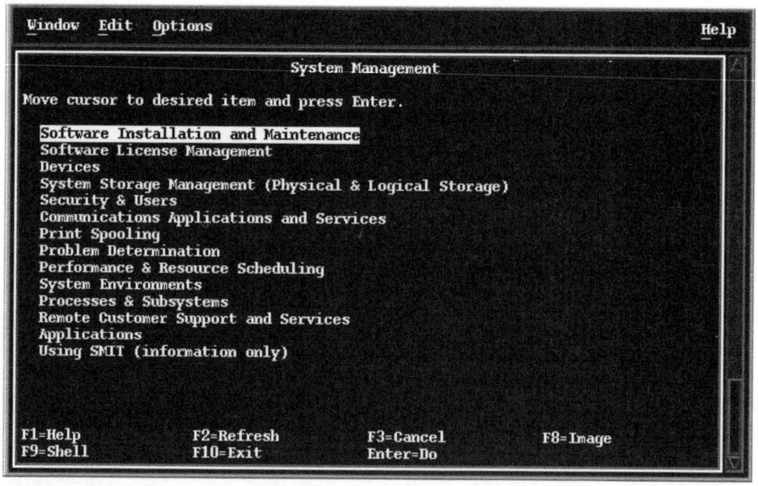

Figure 5.5
ASCII SMIT.

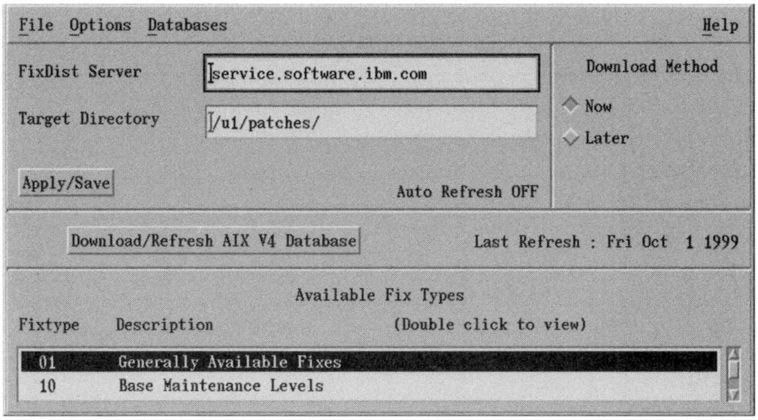

Figure 5.6
X11 FixDist.

for fixes either by Authorized Problem Analysis Report (APAR) or Program Temporary Fix (PTF) views. The FixDist package can be obtained from `http://service.software.ibm.com`.

The FixDist distribution includes a text file that contains instructions and a list of anonymous AIX FTP servers. FixDist runs in ASCII or X11 mode (Figure 5.6). Configuration is very simple. The `FixDist Server` can be obtained from the list included with the distribution. The `Target Directory` is the local directory you will use to download the FixDist database. `Download Method Later` actually generates an FTP script, `.netrc`, that can be implemented with a `cron` job. Double-clicking one of the `Available`

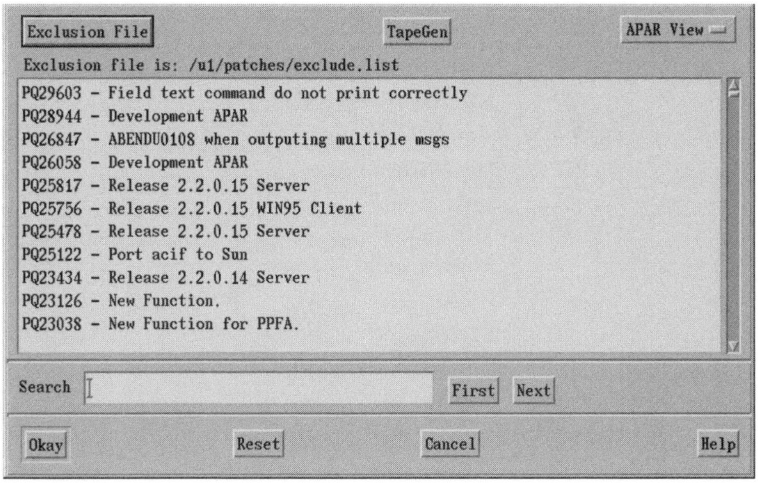

Figure 5.7
X11 Fix listing.

`Fix Types` generates a separate screen listing all current fixes for that database (Figure 5.7). This screen allows searching of the database, creating an exclusion file, and selecting fixes to download. FixDist is a valuable tool when trying to "tame" the patch "beast".

The HPUX: System Administration Manager (SAM) is a menu-driven system administration package for HP-UX. SAM examines the user's environment variables and starts in either an X11 display, which is shown in Figure 5.8, or in the current terminal window in character mode, as shown in Figure 5.9.

The X11 display is nice, but the character mode is a little faster. SAM can be configured to allow non-root users to execute a subset of commands. SAM logs all actions taken to the file `/var/sam/log/samlog`. The `samlog` file is best viewed with `/usr/sam/bin/samlog_viewer`, and the size of the `samlog` file can be controlled under the `Options` header on the main page of SAM.

Now, let's go through the procedures of installing a package using the character mode of SAM. The arrow and <TAB> keys provide cursor movement in the window. Keyboard help can be obtained via CTRL-K.

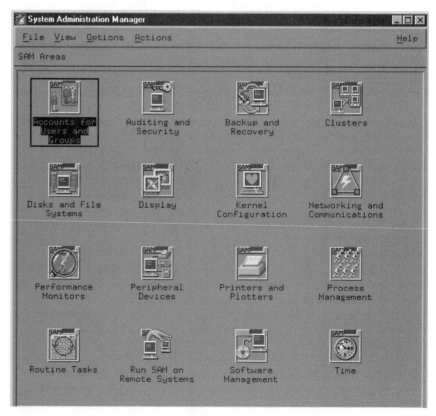

Figure 5.8
Main X11 SAM screen.

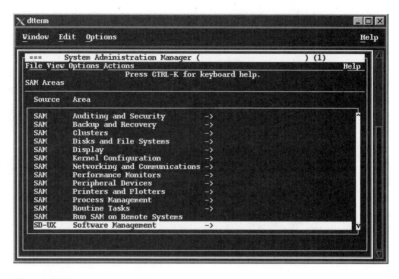

Figure 5.9
Main character-based SAM screen.

1. Selecting `Software Management` takes you to a menu that will allow you to install, list, and remove software from the local client or copy software to a depot, as shown in Figure 5.10.

2. Next, select `Install Software to Local Host`. Figure 5.11 shows the screen that requires you to designate the software depot you will be using for this package.

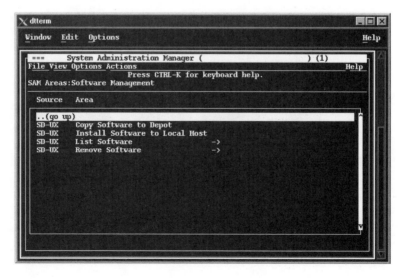

Figure 5.10
Software management.

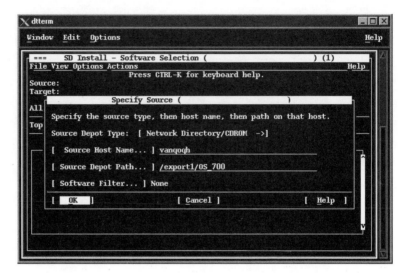

Figure 5.11
Software depot source.

3. Normally you will set up a network software depot that is available to all of your workstations. Select `Network Directory/CDROM` for the `Source Depot Type`.

4. Next, enter the name of the server containing the software depot on the `Source Host Name` line. You can now highlight `Source Depot Path`, press <ENTER> and you will be presented with a list of all registered software depots on that host (Figure 5.12).

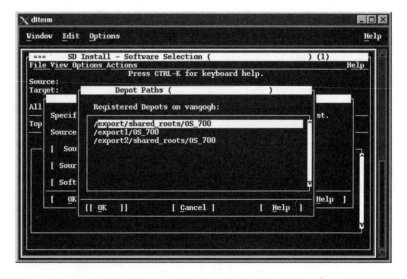

Figure 5.12
Registered depot.

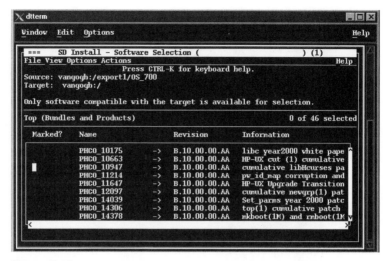

Figure 5.13
Available patches.

5. Select the correct depot from the list. You will now be presented with a listing of all the products that can be applied to that local workstation (Figure 5.13).

6. Next, highlight products using the <SPACEBAR>, <TAB> to the Actions menu and select Mark for Install m. Repeat this procedure until all of the required products are marked. <TAB> to the Actions menu and select Install Analysis. Assuming the analysis was completed successfully, you will be presented with the screen in Figure 5.14.

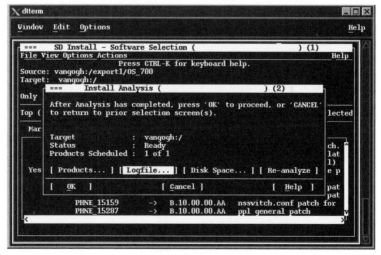

Figure 5.14
Install Analysis screen.

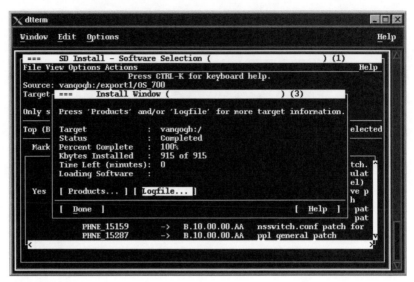

Figure 5.15
Install Window.

7. <TAB> to the OK button and select it. You will be presented with a few screens of information about the install that will require you to accept or cancel the installation. After accepting the installation, you will see the information shown in Figure 5.15, indicating that the product has been installed successfully.

This has been a very simple example of installing software on an HPUX machine. For a more in-depth and detailed explanation, see *HP-UX 11.X System Administration* by Marty Poniatowski.

Command Line

The Software Distributor HPUX commands (SD-UX) manage software on the local host only. SAM utilizes this command set in the `Software Management` menu. A list of the SD-UX commands and a brief explanation of the actions they perform are provided in Table 5.3. The first three commands in the table, invoked without any arguments, will run interactively in an X11 window or in character mode. You should recognize the look and feel from the SAM interface.

You can establish a software depot with the `swcopy` command. The first step is to download a patch from the Hewlett Packard Electronic Support Center.

Table 5.3	HPUX Software Configuration Programs
Command	Action
swinstall	Install and configure software.
swcopy	Copy software for subsequent installation.
swremove	Unconfigure and remove software.
swlist	Display information about software products.
swacl	View or modify Access Control Lists (ACLs).
swcluster	Install or remove software from a diskless server.
swconfig	Configure, unconfigure, or reconfigure installed software.
swmodify	Modify definitions of software objects.
swpackage	Package software products into target depot or tape.
swreg	Register or unregister depots or roots.
swverify	Verify software products.

Download patch `PHKL_19235.html`. Patches are shell archives that contain `.depot` and `.text` files. Run the command `sh PHKL_19235.html` and you will now have three files in the directory:

`PHKL_19235.html`

`PHKL_19235.depot`

`PHKL_19235.text`

The `.text` file contains all kinds of information regarding this patch with respect to the problems it fixes, previous patches it incorporates, files included, dependencies, and even installation instructions. We are going to install this patch to our software depot, so we are not going to install it to the local system now.

1. Enter the command swcopy. You will be prompted for the location of your software depot (Figure 5.16).
2. Click the `Target Depot Path` button and select the correct location of your software depot. Next, enter the location of the `PHKL_19235.depot` file (Figure 5.17).
3. Now you have the name of the product, revision, and information about the package on the screen (Figure 5.18).

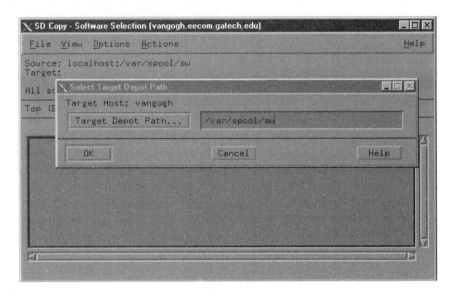

Figure 5.16
Select Target Depot Path.

4. Highlight the package and then go to the Actions menu and choose Copy Analysis. The window will show the target directory and status of the product to be copied to the depot (Figure 5.19).
5. Click OK and the software will be copied to the depot (Figure 5.20).
6. Click Done and you will return to the Main Menu. At this point, you can quit or add more software to the depot.

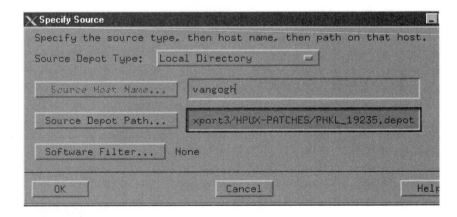

Figure 5.17
Select Source Depot Path.

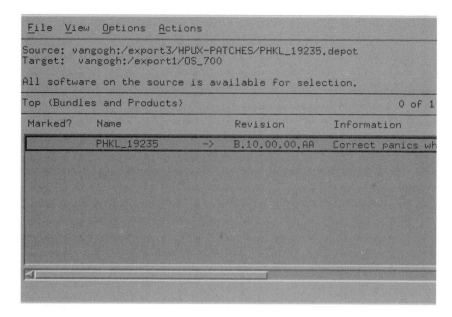

Figure 5.18
Available patches.

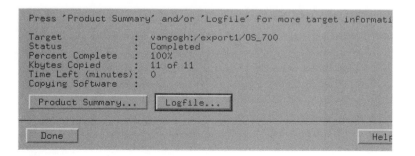

Figure 5.19
Copy Analysis.

```
Press 'Product Summary' and/or 'Logfile' for more target informati

    Target              :  vangogh:/export1/OS_700
    Status              :  Completed
    Percent Complete    :  100%
    Kbytes Copied       :  11 of 11
    Time Left (minutes):   0
    Copying Software    :

    Product Summary...       Logfile...


    Done                                                     Help
```

Figure 5.20
Copy status.

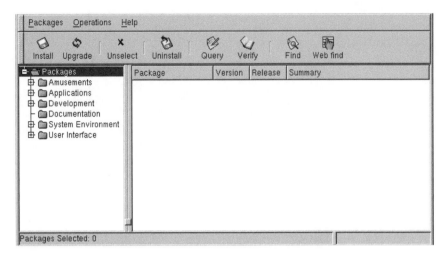

Figure 5.21
Gnome RPM main page.

Red Hat Linux: GNOrpm

Gnorpm is an X Windows front-end to the Red Hat Package Manager (RPM). The main window displays a tree of currently installed software on the machine. Opening a package in the tree produces a listing in the right portion of the display of all packages installed on the local machine (Figure 5.21). Gnorpm can be utilized to install, upgrade, uninstall, query, and verify packages. We are going to install a new package using the Web Find utility in Gnorpm.

1. Click `Web Find` to produce the window shown in Figure 5.22.

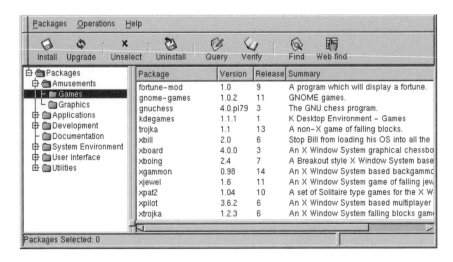

Figure 5.22
Package list.

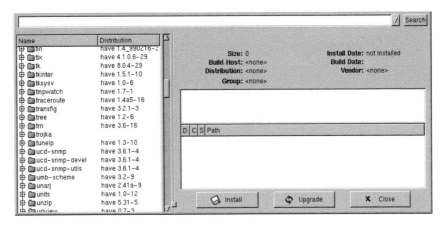

Figure 5.23
Installed packages.

2. The left portion of the screen lists packages found on the metadata server specified in the `Operations->Preferences->Rpmfind->Metadata Server` field. The `Distribution` column indicates which version of the package is currently installed on the local machine. An empty `Distribution` column indicates that the package is not installed on the local machine. Our list indicates that we do not have the `trojka` package loaded (Figure 5.23).

3. Open the `trojka` package (Figure 5.24) and highlight the package to provide the appropriate data.

4. Click `Install` to request a confirmation of the download. Once the package successfully downloads, a new `Install` screen with the package highlighted appears (Figure 5.25).

5. Select `Install` and the package is loaded onto the local system.

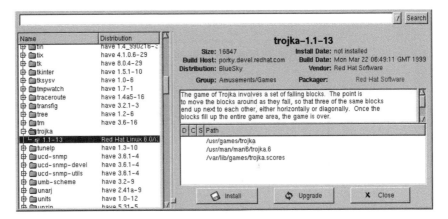

Figure 5.24
Package data.

Figure 5.25
RPM install.

RPM Command Line

RPM is a powerful utility that can be used to install, uninstall, query, and verify software. The format of the rpm command is:

```
rpm [options] [packages]
```

The basic modes of RPM that we will cover are summarized in Table 5.4. The mode is included in [options] when invoking `rpm`. Options can be utilized with all `rpm` modes, and Table 5.5 contains the major options.

Options preceded by -- cannot be combined with other options.

We are going to install, query, verify, and then remove the `zsh-3.0.5-10` package. We are going to use the FTP server `ftp.sniglets.com`. The command to install from the FTP server is:

```
rpm -i --quiet
```

```
ftp://ftp.sniglets.com/pub/Linux/distributions/redhat/
```

Table 5.4	RPM Basic Modes
Mode	Action
-U	Upgrade.
-i	Install.
-q	Query.
-e	Remove.
-V	Verify.

Table 5.5	**Major RPM Options**
Option	Definition
`-vv`	Prints a lot of debugging information.
`--quiet`	Does very little printing—normally just error messages.
`--help`	Prints a longer usage message than normal.
`--version`	Prints the version number of RPM in use.
`--rcfile <filelist>`	Colon-separated list of files that is read sequentially for configuration information.

```
redhat6.0/i386/RedHat \
```

```
/RPMs/xpuzzles-5.4.1-7.i386.rpm
```

The above command retrieved the package `xpuzzles-5.4.1-7.i386.rpm` from `ftp.sniglets.com`. It then installed the package on the local machine. The package is comprised of the name `xpuzzles`, the version `5.4.1`, the release `7`, the architecture `i386`, and the default extension identifier `rpm`.

Next we want to query the local machine via RPM to make sure that the `xpuzzles` package was installed.

We issue the command:

```
Rpm -q xpuzzles
```

```
The workstation returns:
```

```
xpuzzles-5.4.1-7
```

The RPM query mode can also print out more detailed information about a package. Table 5.6 contains the major query options.

Now we want to verify the `xpuzzles` package. To verify the package, we enter:

```
Rpm -V xpuzzles
```

The result is nothing. Nothing is good, and indicates that we have a good package. If a package has a problem, the query will produce an eight-character string that can be decrypted with Table 5.7.

The last action we want to take on our `xpuzzles` package is to remove it. However, if you are a little worried that maybe some files you really need will be deleted with the `xpuzzles` package, have no worry, mate—just utilize the `--test` option with the `--vv` option.

Table 5.6	**Query Mode Options**
Option	Definition
`-I`	Displays name, version, and description of package.
`-R, --requires`	Gives packages this package depends on.
`-l, --list`	Lists files in the package.
`-s, --state`	Supplies state of files in package:
	Normal, Not Installed, Replaced.
`-d, --docfiles`	Provides documentation files.
`-c, --configfiles`	Lists only configuration files.

```
rpm -e --test -vv xpuzzles
```

The result is a listing of every file that will be deleted when the `xpuzzles` package is deleted. Now that you are sure there aren't any files that you need, you can do the dirty deed:

```
Rpm -e xpuzzles
```

Check your work by entering:

```
Rpm -q xpuzzles
```

```
Package xpuzzles is not installed
```

Table 5.7	**Verifying String Codes**
Character	Test Failed
`5`	`MD5 sum`
`S`	`File size`
`L`	`Symlink`
`T`	`Mtime`
`D`	`Device`
`U`	`User`
`G`	`Group`
`M`	`M` (Includes permissions and file type.)

We did not cover the upgrade option for RPM. The upgrade option will uninstall and then install the package. If the package is not already installed on the system, then RPM will just do an install of the package.

SOLARIS: INSTALLPATCH

Patches for the Solaris system are obtained from Sun's Web site, or from a patch CD. Sun Microsystems provides kernel and security patches at their publicly accessible site if you do not have access to the CD. Sun provides patch clusters, which are conglomerations of patches for a specific Solaris version and hardware platform (Sun or x86). These patch clusters are available as far back as Solaris 2.3. It is highly recommended that you occasionally install the latest patch cluster onto your system to provide a high level of reliability, performance, and security.

To install a patch cluster, download the appropriate patch cluster and follow the instructions from the `README` file. For individual patches, Sun identifies each patch with a patch number and revision, in the form `<patch number>-<revision>`. For example, the patch `104945-02` is the second revision of patch `104945`. The `README` files will usually provide information on how to apply a patch to different revisions of the operating systems that are currently supported.

`rpm` is a powerful utility that can be used to install, uninstall, query, and verify software.

Windows 2000 Service Packs

A Service Pack is a periodic update to the Windows 2000 operating system. It is analogous to recommended patches for UNIX systems. A Service Pack contains all previously released fixes (from previous Service Packs), as well as any new fixes since the last Service Pack. All Service Packs have undergone regression testing to ensure, in most situations, that the Service Pack itself will not break the system. However, you should *always* perform your own tests on non-production systems before deploying any Service Pack on a production system.

In the past, some Service Packs have actually upgraded the operating system to a new revision. This can cause major problems with some software, so Microsoft has agreed not to use Service Packs as a means to upgrade Windows 2000. Service Packs for Windows 2000 will only contain bug fixes and will not introduce any new features or functionality, as was the case with some Windows NT 4.0 Service Packs.

WHEN DO YOU NEED THEM?

Service Packs are typically essential to keeping your operating system up-to-date and secure. Although it is not always necessary to immediately apply a new Service Pack, you should intend to deploy a new Service Pack within a month or two of its release. Service Packs usually contain fixes that are essential for system security and stability and will generally not cause problems.

WHERE DO YOU GET THEM?

Service Packs can be obtained, primarily, from two places. The first is from Microsoft's Web site, `http://www.microsoft.com/windows`. The second, and often faster, location is from Microsoft's FTP site, `ftp.microsoft.com` in `/bussys/winnt/winnt-public/fixes/usa/nt40/usspn`, where *n* is the number of the Service Pack you wish to download. You should also note that `nt40` can be different depending on which operating system you are running.

HOW DO YOU INSTALL THEM?

Service Packs are extremely easy to install. If you download a Service Pack from Microsoft's Web or FTP site, then simply running the executable will start the installation process. If you obtain a Service Pack on CD, then you will need to run `update.exe`, which is usually located under the `/update` directory. You will typically be asked about backing up current files and about reading a license agreement. The following guidelines will help you answer any questions posed during the application of the Service Pack:

- Always back up your current files. You will not be able to uninstall the Service Pack if you do not back up the current files.
- Never overwrite newer files. Although this situation is rare, it is possible that the installation of some applications will actually include files that are newer than those included in the Service Pack. The only situation we have seen this in is when Internet Explorer 5 was installed before Service Pack 5 for NT 4.0.
- It is generally a good idea to replace OEM-installed files with the versions included in the Service Pack. The Service Pack files have all been tested together, whereas an OEM-provided file might behave unpredictably when not replaced with the Service Pack version.

Once the application is complete, you will need to reboot your system. If all goes as intended, your system will reboot without much fanfare and you will generally not see any obvious differences.

Windows 2000 Hot Fixes

A Hot Fix is an interim patch released between Service Packs that is intended to immediately fix a specific problem. The most common problem a Hot Fix corrects is one relating to system security, especially in networked environments. Hot Fixes are not regression tested like Service Packs and can cause a system to become unstable.

WHEN DO YOU NEED A HOT FIX?

You should only apply Hot Fixes when you are experiencing the problem the Hot Fix purports to correct. As I stated earlier, Hot Fixes are not regression-tested and can cause your system to become unstable. As always, you should test a Hot Fix on a non-production system before deploying it on your "live" systems.

WHERE DO YOU GET THEM?

Hot Fixes cannot be obtained from Microsoft's Web site. They are only available from the Web site `ftp.microsoft.com` in the `/bussys/winnt/winnt-public/fixes/usa/nt40/hotfix-postSP`n directory, where n should be replaced with the number of the Service Pack you are currently running. Also note that `nt40` can be replaced with whatever operating system you are actually running; see the directory listing for the available operating systems.

HOW DO YOU INSTALL THEM?

When you download a Hot Fix, it is typically a self-extracting file that will install when you execute it from the command line or double-click it in the Explorer. If for some reason you wish to extract the Hot Fix files but not install them immediately, you can specify the `/x` command-line option. This will bring up a dialog box asking you to provide a location in which to store the extracted files. Among the files extracted will be one named `hotfix.exe`, which can be run to install the Hot Fix. Table 5.8 lists several command-line options that can be appended to `hotfix.exe` to customize the installation.

Table 5.8	`Hotfix.exe` **Command-Line Options**
Option	Function
`-y`	Performs uninstall (only with `-m` or `-q`).
`-f`	Forces applications to close at shutdown.
`-n`	Does not create uninstall directory.
`-z`	Does not reboot when update completes.
`-q`	Initiates Quiet mode – no user interface.
`-m`	Initiates Unattended mode.
`-l`	Lists installed Hot Fixes.

Be careful when modifying the default functionality of `hotfix.exe` to avoid putting your system in an unstable state.

Summary

This chapter has attempted to give you a framework for managing patches and upgrades. While upgrading and reinstalling systems can be a tedious and time-consuming process, it is important to understand the motivations behind these tasks, as well as create a solid process to perform them. Each operating system has its own set of tools and commands to install patches, and the information presented here should provide value to experienced as well as inexperienced administrators on a given platform.

UPGRADING VS. RE-INSTALLING

Upgrading and re-installation are the two methods you can use to move your systems from one operating system version to another. Over the course of one to two years, you should expect to upgrade or re-install each server in your environment. If you have only a few servers, or if a given server has a very complex set of software and configurations, you may opt for upgrading over reinstalling. Upgrades generally retain system information and allow you to back out of the upgrade if problems arise. However, upgrades can require more resources, and may require longer periods of time to complete.

If you have a large number of servers that are similarly configured, or if you are concerned about the amount of time an upgrade may take, then re-installation may be the best option for you. Re-installations are generally faster and cleaner than upgrades. Re-installations also give you the opportunity to reconfigure the hardware, such as disk layouts, whereas upgrades must rely on the current configuration of the system. Use the information in Tables 5.1 and 5.2 to help you determine which course of action is right for you.

PATCH, HOT FIX, AND SERVICE PACK MANAGEMENT

Over time, users, administrators, and developers discover performance, stability, and security problems with their operating systems. Patches, Hot Fixes and Service Packs are the vehicles that vendors use to relay operating system fixes to users. Literally hundreds of different patches can be made available for any one version of an operating system, so it is important to understand how to choose and manage those patches that you plan to introduce into your environment.

Patches can quickly get out of hand if you have a large installation or a mix of different operating systems. Developing a strategy and schedule for testing and deploying patches is crucial to your overall patch management scheme. Poor patch management not only leads to poor systems performance, but may lead to patch apathy, where the administrator is so frustrated with patches that they are not even deployed. Don't let this happen to you.

Develop a schedule and a procedure, and stick with them. Only deploy those patches that are absolutely necessary to avoid bloating your servers, as well as to avoid possibly introducing more problems than you can solve. Use the GUI and command-line tools available to properly install patches, and whenever possible, have software contracts with your vendors so that you are assured to always have access to the latest available patches.

## PART TWO

INTEGRATION

Integration is the middle ground between coexistence and interoperability. It involves the use of tools and strategies for sharing resources and information throughout your infrastructure. Network address resolution, user and system identification, shared filesystems, email, and printing are the key issues in creating an integrated infrastructure. Specifically, we will be concerned with creating a stable environment within which the user can work. As the number of systems grows and the infrastructure becomes more complex, the functions the administrator needs to perform can soon become overwhelming. Through the use of DNS, WINS, and DHCP, addressing and naming services are quite manageable. NIS/NIS+ and Windows Active Directory provide the ability to share user account information among systems. Likewise, distributed filesystems make it possible to share file data between systems and platforms. Finally, we will discuss the essential resources of electronic mail and printing, providing strategies for integrating these throughout a heterogeneous infrastructure.

NAME RESOLUTION AND REGISTRATION

UNIX

The UNIX HOSTS File

DNS Setup

BIND 4 DNS Server Configuration

BIND 8 DNS Server Configuration

nslookup

WINDOWS

The Windows HOSTS File

DNS Setup

LMHOSTS

WINS

DHCP

You cannot open a technical magazine or turn on the TV without hearing about the Internet. To have access to the Internet, computer systems need to know how to communicate with each other. Every system on the Internet must have a unique identifier. Name resolution and registration are integral parts of any network operating system. Name resolution is the ability to convert a system name, or hostname, into a network IP address, while name registration is the ability to manipulate a database that maps machine names to network addresses, as well as the ability to dynamically assign network addresses. Name resolution is the address book of the Internet, giving computer systems the ability to translate human-readable names into Internet addresses and conversely translate network addresses into names that have some meaning. Without this resolution, addresses on the Internet would be as difficult to understand as the white pages in the phone book, that is, if all the names were removed.

Because of these needs, the industry created the Domain Name System (DNS), Windows Internet Name Service (WINS), and Dynamic Host Configuration Protocol (DHCP) tools to facilitate and administer this information. In this chapter, we will discuss how to use and configure DNS, WINS, and DHCP. Each of these tools is essential to helping your operating systems determine their network information, and sometimes more importantly, what else is out there in the vast land of the Internet.

DNS and WINS provide the foundation for name registration to address mapping, and DHCP provides the ability to dynamically assign addresses. It gets interesting when the ability to dynamically register a machine name is added to network address mapping. Traditional DNS servers rely on static address tables, while WINS is purely dynamic, meaning the client machine provides the registration information to the WINS server. Recently, Dynamic DNS has emerged with the introduction of Windows 2000. With this new version of DNS, it will be possible to have a completely dynamic name registration system.

At the conclusion of this chapter, you should have a good understanding of DNS, WINS, and DHCP. With the tips and tools contained here, you will be able to manage most of the day-to-day name resolution services of your network.

Name Resolution Using DNS

During the infancy of the Internet, keeping track of all the attached systems was easy. A single file contained the list of all IP addresses and hostnames associated with each address. As a system administrator, if you were lucky enough to have one of the few connected systems, all you needed to do was to FTP the list once every two or three weeks to keep up-to-date with the latest new systems that came on-line. Life was simple when the growth of the Internet was slow.

However, as the Internet grew, new systems were added at an ever-increasing rate. The master list of Internet IP hostnames became more and more difficult to maintain, and system administrators needed to update their copy of the file daily to keep up. Due to the difficulty in managing this simple file, DNS was born.

DNS is a conglomeration of all the possible domain namespaces that are currently recognized. In the beginning, the domain namespaces consisted of simple domains such as `.com`, `.gov`, `.edu` and `.org`. However, with the huge growth of the Internet, many new namespaces were added, including `.net`, `.mil`, and a namespace for each country on the planet. While not a simple process to manage, the fine folks at the Network Information Center, commonly know as the *Internic*, have taken responsibility for assigning and maintaining the data and conventions that make up the top level, or the root of DNS. For more information about the Internic, you can visit them at `www.internic.net`.

UNIX NAME RESOLUTION

Translating IP addresses into hostnames and vice versa in UNIX is accomplished by using one or more of the following techniques:

- `/etc/hosts`.
- NIS.
- DNS.

Resolving Hostnames Through Use of the /etc/hosts File

UNIX systems were running long before tools such as DNS were created. Before the advent of the Internet, systems tended to work in isolation, as stand-alone systems. However, with the advent of networking, which gave systems the ability to intercommunicate, it was now necessary for each computer to understand its unique network address, as well as the network addresses of other systems. To facilitate this process, the use of the `/etc/hosts` file was employed. Using `/etc/hosts` provides a fast and simple, yet static, name resolution process. Each `/etc/hosts` entry is local to that system, and is only used by that system. The example is a rather standard `/etc/hosts` file.

The first entry in the `/etc/hosts` file is common to all systems. The *localhost* value of `127.0.0.1` is a convention used by the local system to communicate with its own Ethernet device. It is important for UNIX systems to have this in place to test the local interface. The second IP address, `192.168.3.13`, defines the network IP address of `duchess.sniglets.com`. In general, the first IP address listed in the `/etc/hosts` file, other than the local host address, refers to the local system. However, this is only a convention, and most flavors of UNIX have some other mechanism to define the hostname of the system. In most cases, the `/etc/hosts` file is referenced to define this value.

Note that for both systems, each is configured so that the local system understands multiple permutations of the same name. This is useful if you are not using NIS or DNS, and want to make sure names are resolved, regardless if the domain is fully-specified. In this example, we have also defined `duchess` as a `loghost`. The *loghost* entry in `/etc/hosts` instructs `syslogd` to send all log messages to the defined system. If the `loghost` is defined to be another system, `syslogd` would transmit all logs to the remote system.

```
#
# Internet host table
#
127.0.0.1       localhost
192.168.3.13  duchess.sniglets.com duchess loghost
192.168.3.14      mars.sniglets.com venus.sniglets.com earth
```

The IP address `192.168.3.14` is configured so that it responds to multiple hostnames, with `mars` and `venus` having their names and domains defined, or fully-qualified. Assigning multiple hostnames to a single IP address can be very useful, especially if you have one system performing multiple functions, as shown in the following `/etc/hosts` file:

```
# Internet host table for a multi-function system

#

127.0.0.1   localhost   192.168.3.2   mail.sniglets.com
news.sniglets.com www.sniglets.com
```

While using the `/etc/hosts` file can be a quick way to modify hostnames and IP addresses on a single system or a small group of machines, it is easy to see that as the number of systems increase, using `/etc/hosts` as a means to maintain IP data becomes increasingly difficult. What makes this even more difficult is that the hostname entry for each system is different, making distribution of a standard `/etc/hosts` file impossible. For these reasons `/etc/hosts` files should only be used for defining local aliases, log hosts, and for debugging localized name resolution problems.

Using NIS

Another common method for name resolution is using NIS (Network Information Service). NIS, formally known as Yellow Pages or YP, provides the ability to create a central file of IP addresses and hostnames that are shared with all systems on your network using NIS. NIS uses the same general format as the `/etc/hosts` file, but doesn't have machine-specific information, so it doesn't interfere with the function of the `/etc/hosts` file.

Before the invention of DNS, NIS was a popular way to distribute hostname information. By using NIS, only one file containing host address information needed to be modified. This allowed the system administrator to add addresses, both local and on the Internet, and in a matter of minutes, replicate this information to the infrastructure. While this works well when the number of systems the clients need to know about is static and manageable, think how difficult it would be to have to enter every system on the Internet into a file.

The downside of just using NIS is that your systems only know about systems in the NIS host's file, and have no knowledge of the outside world.

While using NIS may not seem practical by today's standards, you may find yourself managing systems that still share host address information through NIS. Using this method is still popular in situations where clusters of machines do not need to know about the Internet, and only care about a static group of machines. This can provide a more stable environment, as these clients don't rely on the availability of DNS servers or the infrastructure to connect to DNS servers.

Use and configuration of NIS will be discussed in greater detail in Chapter 7, "Directory Services."

Using Client DNS in UNIX

For the majority of UNIX variants, using DNS is as simple as creating a single file. The /etc/resolv.conf file acts as a configuration file, instructing the operating system on how to use DNS. Following is a standard /etc/resolv.conf file that contains information on what name servers to use, what domain the current system is part of, and information on how to search for names in other domains.

```
mars:> cat /etc/resolv.conf

domain sniglets.com

nameserver 192.168.3.49

nameserver 192.168.3.30
```

domain The domain entry defines the DNS domain in which your system lives. This value is added to hostname queries to form a fully-qualified hostname if the host being queried is not a fully-qualified hostname.

nameserver The nameserver entries identify the IP addresses of the nameserver(s) you want your system to use for DNS name resolution. You need at least one nameserver entry, but don't list more than three as additional entries will not be recognized. The nameservers are queried in the order in which they appear in the file, so if 192.168.3.49 doesn't respond to a DNS request, 192.168.3.30 will then be queried with the same request.

There is no comment mechanism, so refrain from adding UNIX-like comment fields to /etc/resolv.conf, as they cause strange results.

If you decide to use a generic or static /etc/resolv.conf for your installations, make sure to rotate the nameserver lines. While DNS queries in general do not generate a great deal of network traffic, having too many client DNS systems using a single DNS server could cause performance problems on the server. Having multiple server entries in your `/etc/re-solv.conf` does nothing to load-balance your DNS queries. Your client system will always start by querying the first server in `/etc/resolv.conf`. If that query fails, the next server will be queried. As long as your network and DNS server are functioning properly, the subsequent servers in `/etc/resolv.conf` will not be contacted.

Having multiple DNS servers is an effective way to handle failure in your infrastructure. In our `/etc/resolv.conf` example, a failure of DNS server `192.168.3.49` will cause DNS queries to be handled by server `192.168.3.30`. Yet, what happens if the `192.168.3` network has a problem and none of the servers there are available? If a system on another network is running fine, but can't contact the `192.168.3` network, your network failure now has a larger impact on your infrastructure. An effective way to combat this problem is to have your client systems use DNS servers on multiple networks, as seen here:

```
domain sniglets.com

nameserver 192.168.3.49

nameserver 192.168.4.34
```

Your choices for DNS servers will be driven by your network design. Try to design your DNS infrastructure to take advantage of redundancy in your network. Seek your network manager's input when creating your DNS architecture.

While having these other DNS servers defined provides fault tolerance if the first DNS server fails, it is not an effective way to utilize the resources of all your DNS servers. Assume you have 100 computer systems in your infrastructure that function as DNS client systems. On every system, you have installed the following `/etc/resolv.conf` file:

```
domain sniglets.com

nameserver 192.168.3.49

nameserver 192.168.4.34
```

As long as your network is reliable and DNS server `192.168.3.49` performs well, DNS server `192.168.4.34` will never be contacted. While it is good that your primary DNS server and network are running well, you are under-utilizing the DNS services on `192.168.4.34`. For fault tolerance, you still need to keep `192.168.4.34`. So, how can you better utilize your DNS resources? A very effective way is to create the `/etc/resolv.conf` file and distribute this file to half, or in our example 50, client DNS systems:

```
domain sniglets.com

search domain1,domain2,domain3,domain4

nameserver 192.168.4.34

nameserver 192.168.3.49
```

By swapping, or rotating, the DNS server entries, you have effectively load-balanced your DNS queries, as each system is now taking DNS queries from half of your infrastructure. If you use more then two `nameserver` entries, then you can continue to rotate the entries to equally distribute the load. Be aware that DNS load varies greatly from system to system, depending on the user and load characteristics of the system. Don't take the top 50 of your systems and point them to one server and then expect the DNS load to be balanced. Try to divide your systems based on load and network topology so that you have a balanced distribution of systems pointing to each DNS server.

Configure `nameserver` entries differently on multiple systems so they help to load-balance DNS queries on your DNS servers.

Search Domains The addition of search domains to your `/etc/resolv.conf` file allows you to integrate additional domains into host-name resolution. Search domains are unnecessary, however, if your system lives within a single domain. But, if your system is part of a large network with multiple domains, using the search domain option can ease your administration, as well as make navigating the network easier for your users.

```
domain sniglets.com

search domain1,domain2,domain3,domain4

nameserver 192.168.4.34

nameserver 192.168.3.49
```

By adding the `search` line, hostname lookups will append each domain in the `search` line to the hostname you are attempting to resolve. For example, if you were trying to resolve the name `rover`, the system would request from the DNS server the addresses of `rover.sniglets.com`, `rover.domain1`, `rover.domain2`, etc. until the DNS server returned a valid IP address or an error message that the host doesn't exist.

Be careful. Adding a large number of search domains can slow down hostname resolution. Also attempt to optimize the search line so that more popular domains appear first.

WINDOWS 2000 NAME RESOLUTION

Windows 2000 supports several name resolution methods. The most common methods are the `HOSTS` file and/or DNS. Windows 2000 also supports the mapping of NetBIOS names to IP addresses through the use of the `LMHOSTS` file and/or WINS. A discussion of these different methods is provided in this section.

A more detailed discussion of WINS is included in the "WINS Overview" section later in this chapter.

Using the HOSTS File

The `HOSTS` file used by Windows 2000 is strikingly similar to the `HOSTS` files used on UNIX systems. In fact, the only difference is the location of the file. On UNIX systems, the `HOSTS` file can be found under `/etc`, while on Windows 2000, the `HOSTS` file is located under `%SystemRoot%\System32\Drivers\etc`. The format of the file is the same as that of the UNIX variants; to illustrate, a sample of the `HOSTS` file is shown here:

```
# Copyright (c) 1993-1999 Microsoft Corp.

#

# This is a sample HOSTS file used by Microsoft TCP/IP for Windows.

#

# This file contains the mappings of IP addresses to host names. Each

# entry should be kept on an individual line. The IP address should

# be placed in the first column followed by the corresponding host name.

# The IP address and the host name should be separated by at least one
```

```
# space.

#

# Additionally, comments (such as these) may be inserted on individual

# lines or following the machine name denoted by a '#' symbol.

#

# For example:

#

#     102.54.94.97      rhino.acme.com        # source server

#      38.25.63.10      x.acme.com            # x client host

Localhost

192.168.3.2 mail.sniglets.com
```

Windows 2000 relies primarily on DNS for IP name and address resolution. The HOSTS file is rarely used, but is readily available and queried prior to any DNS server.

Using DNS in Windows 2000

Windows 2000 DNS functions in a manner that is nearly identical to DNS on a UNIX system. The main difference is in how DNS is configured. As you now know, DNS on a UNIX system can be configured by creating or editing a single file called /etc/resolv.conf. Windows 2000 DNS is configured through a GUI; configuration can be easily accomplished through the following steps:

1. Log on as Administrator.
2. Right-click the My Network Places icon and select Properties. You should now see the window in Figure 6.1.
3. Next, right-click the Local Area Connection icon and select Properties. You should now see the window in Figure 6.2.

Figure 6.1
Network and
Dial-up
Connections
properties
window.

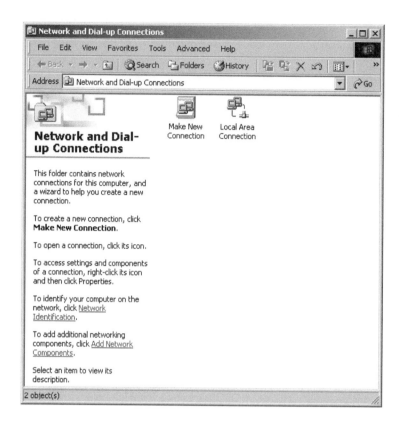

Figure 6.2
Local Area
Connection
Properties
window.

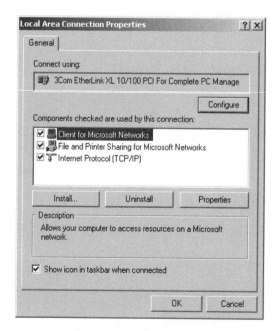

4. Select (highlight) `Internet Protocol (TCP/IP)` from the list and click the `Properties` button. The `Internet Protocol (TCP/IP) Properties` window will be displayed, as shown in Figure 6.3.

5. Click the `Advanced` button to display the `Advanced TCP/IP Settings` window, as shown in Figure 6.4.

6. Click the DNS tab and you will see the window shown in Figure 6.5.

7. In the `DNS server addresses` box, click the `Add` button to add each of your DNS servers to the list in the order you wish the servers to be used.

8. Select the `Append these DNS suffixes` option and add the DNS suffixes you wish to query when an unqualified hostname is being searched (i.e., `mypc` instead of `mypc.mycompany.com`).

The DNS suffix order should always be configured to have your local domain as the first domain in the list. You should order your domains so that the most common ones are searched after the local domain.

9. Enter your machine's DNS suffix in the `DNS suffix for this connection` box.

10. If you are using Dynamic DNS, place a check mark next to `Register this connection's addresses in DNS`; otherwise, uncheck the box.

Figure 6.3
TCP/IP properties window

Internet Protocol (TCP/IP) Properties	? X

General

You can get IP settings assigned automatically if your network supports this capability. Otherwise, you need to ask your network administrator for the appropriate IP settings.

○ Obtain an IP address automatically
● Use the following IP address:

IP address:	192 . 168 . 3 . 254
Subnet mask:	255 . 255 . 255 . 0
Default gateway:	192 . 168 . 3 . 1

○ Obtain DNS server address automatically
● Use the following DNS server addresses:

| Preferred DNS server: | 192 . 168 . 3 . 21 |
| Alternate DNS server: | 192 . 168 . 3 . 22 |

Advanced...

OK   Cancel

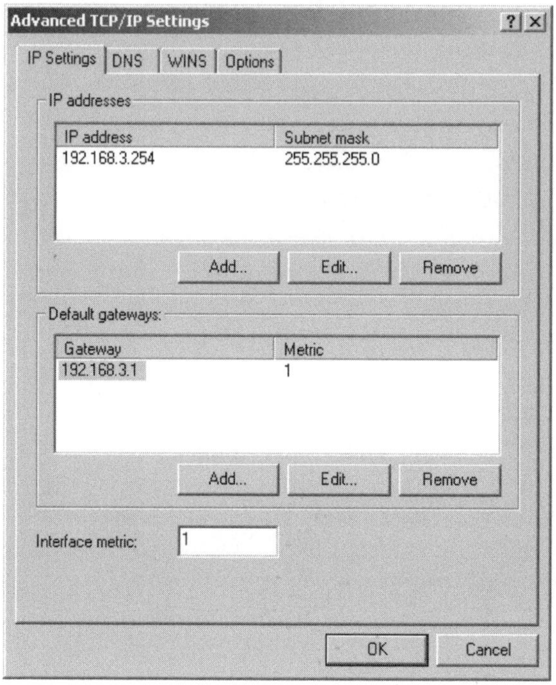

Figure 6.4
Advanced
TCP/IP
Settings
window

Figure 6.5
DNS properties
window.

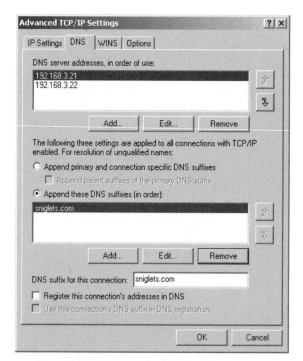

11. Click the OK button to commit your changes to the DNS settings.
12. Click the OK button to close the TCP/IP properties window, and also click OK to close the Local Area Connection Properties window.

Most changes to the TCP/IP settings in Windows 2000 do not require a reboot of the system. However, if you are prompted to reboot the system, you should do so at this point.

Using LMHOSTS

Windows 2000 provides the ability to resolve NetBIOS names to IP addresses using a text file very similar to the HOSTS file discussed earlier. Instead of mapping hostnames to IP addresses like the HOSTS file, the LMHOSTS file is used to map a NetBIOS name to an IP address when necessary, such as when trying to locate a computer or resource using Universal Naming Convention (UNC) pathnames (i.e., \\MYSERVER\myshare).

The LMHOSTS file is stored in %SystemRoot%\System32\Drivers\etc, and it allows you to specify the IP address that corresponds to a specific NetBIOS name. It also provides the ability to specify domain controllers and whether or not the entries should be pre-loaded into the system name cache. For all intents and purposes though, LMHOSTS is out-dated and should not be used. Instead, you should implement WINS on your network, which is discussed later in the chapter.

Server DNS

Any mix of UNIX and Windows systems can handle server DNS. If you plan to manage your own DNS domains, you'll probably want to choose the platform with which you are most comfortable. DNS is a hierarchical process, where you have one master DNS server and as many slave DNS servers as you like. DNS entries are managed on the master server, and they are passed along to the slave DNS servers at regular intervals.

Since UNIX and Windows DNS are compatible, you can choose to have a mix of UNIX and Windows systems serve DNS in a heterogeneous environment. A UNIX system can't tell it is receiving information from a Windows DNS server, and vice versa. What you choose for your design depends on your administration ability, your budget, and most likely what system the previous administrator decided to use for your DNS server.

UNIX SERVER DNS

Building a UNIX DNS infrastructure is a highly reliable, efficient way to provide DNS for your environment. The DNS process, `named` or `in.named`, requires very few physical resources such as memory or disk. You can install a DNS server on just about any system without impacting performance. For servers that rely heavily on DNS, such as SMTP and Web servers, you will probably see a performance increase by installing a local DNS server.

Since UNIX relies heavily on the services DNS provides, a poor-performing or overloaded DNS server can severely impact your infrastructure. In almost any infrastructure that contains multiple systems and networks, it is good practice to place at least one slave DNS server on each subnet. By having a localized DNS server, you help reduce the delay time of DNS queries and you build in fault tolerance by distributing your servers on different networks, as explained in the previous section, "Client DNS." Of course, this requires you to have one or two UNIX systems on each subnet with the resources available to serve DNS.

DNS Master Server

Setting up a new master DNS server from scratch is a straightforward process given that you have an understanding of the structure and processes involved. The master server only has a small number of files that need to be configured to have a simple, running system. They include:

- Host database.
- Reverse lookup database.
- Localhost database.
- Root cache.
- Named configuration.

Probably the most difficult part of creating a new master DNS server is determining the naming convention you want to use to organize your DNS host files, called *zone files*. Standard conventions that you will come across will suggest that you name your zone files something like `db.`*`yourdomain`* for forward lookups and `db.`*`yournetwork`* for reverse lookups. The `.db` extension signifies a DNS data file containing hostname information. While this convention is simple, it is not a requirement. You can name your files in any manner you wish, as long as you follow a consistent naming scheme and create your configuration files accordingly.

Host Database File For our examples, we have assumed a simple configuration with only one subnet and one domain name to configure. For our naming convention, our files will be of the form `db.domain`, i.e., `db.sniglets`. Our primary zone will be `sniglets.com`. The primary zone host database file for our DNS master is `/var/named/db.sniglets`.

```
;

; db.sniglets

;

@        in     SOA     dns.sniglets.com.
hostperson.sniglets.com (

                        19990610 ; Serial - date & revision
                        YYYYMMREV

                        21600    ; Refresh (6 hours)

                        3600     ; Retry (15 minutes)

                        604800   ; Expire (7 days)

                        86400    ; Minimum

                        )


             IN     NS            dns1.sniglets.com

             IN     NS            dns.sniglets.com


pilots       IN A          192.168.3.4

drivers      IN     CNAME         pilots.sniglets.com

             IN     MX            10 mail.sniglets.com.

             IN     MX            20 sniglets.com.

             IN     HINFO         HP HP/UX


$INCLUDE hosts.sniglets.4

;end of primary zone file
```

The host database file includes the critical information needed to identify your DNS domains. Usually the first entry in the file is the Start Of Authority (`SOA`) record. Primarily what the SOA record does is tell other DNS servers that this server is the best, or authoritative, server for the domain. The first line of the entry,

```
@      in      SOA     dns.sniglets.com.
hostperson.sniglets.com.
```

states that system `dns.sniglets.com` is the authoritative server for domain `sniglets.com` and any associated domains, and that `hostperson.sniglets.com` is the email address for any inquiries you need to direct to a human for those domains. The next entry,

```
19990610 ; Serial - date & revision YYYYMMREV
```

is the `SOA` serial number. This number acts as a flag to DNS slave servers that information has changed on the DNS master server. In this example, we use a concatenation of the year, month, and a revision number to form the serial number. Here we see the 10th revision in June of 1999.

One of the most frequent mistakes made when managing master DNS records is incorrectly modifying or forgetting to increment the serial number. Always double-check that your serial number is correct.

Be extremely careful when modifying or creating a script to modify your DNS records. One of the most frequently made mistakes when managing master DNS records is incorrectly modifying or forgetting to increment the serial number. Always double-check that your serial number is correct.

The final pieces of the `SOA` record are:

```
21600   ; Refresh (6 hours)

                 3600    ; Retry (15 minutes)

                 604800  ; Expire (7 days)

                 86400   ; Minimum TTL ( 1 day)
```

The `Refresh` interval is the number of seconds between attempts by each DNS slave server to download the zone files. A short interval will cause a great deal of load on your master server, while too long an interval may cause DNS changes to propagate too slowly. The `Retry` interval is the amount of time the DNS slave should wait after a failed attempt to connect to the DNS master (possibly due to network traffic or a system problem). The `Expire` interval tells the DNS slaves to stop answering queries and expire their data after the specified number of seconds. This is to keep slave servers from handing out data indefinitely if the master server has changed or has been out of service for a long period of time. The `Minimum TTL` (Time To Live) is the amount of time other name servers can cache data for this domain. The ability to cache data helps distribute the load from the master server to slave servers, but too long a TTL can cause slave servers to cache data that is out-of-date.

There is no right answer when determining the values for your `SOA` record. An ISP that has thousands of DNS changes per day will need to have short values so that new DNS changes will take effect quickly. However, this ISP will also need to have the resources to handle the increased traffic that this will generate. Conversely, a small business with only a hundred DNS entries can have values that are rather large since their data will rarely change. A DNS server running on the company server will function well here, but new entries could take days to reach out into the Internet.

The next entries in our `hosts.sniglets` file are:

```
    IN      NS              dns1.sniglets.com

    IN      NS              dns.sniglets.com
```

There are two important entries that are defined in these records. The `IN` entry is the class of the record, with `IN` representing Internet. For all of our examples in this chapter, we will deal with Internet classes. If the class identifier is omitted, `IN` is assumed. The next field is the resource entry, which contains an example of the `NS` entry. The `NS` resource identifies name servers for the domain. In our example, `dns1.sniglets.com` and `dns.sniglets.com` are defined name servers for the domain `ee.gatech.edu`. While `NS` records are not required, this information may be useful for debugging. If you are a security nut, you may wish to omit the `NS` entries so as not to "advertise" your DNS servers to the world.

 If you are security conscious, you may wish to omit the `NS` entries so as not to "advertise" your DNS servers to the world.

The next entry in our file is the A record, which maps hostnames to host IP addresses:

```
pilots      IN      A               192.168.3.4
```

The A record tells us that hostname `pilots.sniglets.com` is associated with IP address `192.168.3.4`. A CNAME record, such as

```
drivers     IN      CNAME           pilots.sniglets.com
```

creates an alias, or a duplicate mapping from one host entry to another. In this example, `drivers.sniglets.com` is mapped to `pilots.sniglets.com`. You can have as many `CNAME` entries as you would like mapped to a single `A` record. You can even have `CNAME` entries mapped to other `CNAME` entries. However, be aware that you can only have one `A` record for each distinct IP address.

A records are a one-to-one mapping, with only one A record for each distinct IP address. You may have as many CNAME entries as you like associated with a single A record. You may also associate CNAME entries with other CNAME entries.

With an understanding of the `SOA`, `NS`, `A`, and `CNAME` records, you can build a functional zone. However, there are two more resource records that you will find useful when creating your master DNS information. If we look back to our entry for `pilots.sniglets.com`, you first see the MX resource defined:

```
pilots          IN    A         192.168.3.4

drivers         IN    CNAME     pilots.sniglets.com

                IN    MX        10 mail.sniglets.com.

                IN    MX        20 sniglets.com.

                IN    HINFO     HP710 HP/UX
```

The `MX` resource defines the SMTP mail exchanger for the entry. Mail exchangers are useful when you want to redirect incoming SMTP mail to a single or well-defined set of SMTP mail servers. In large networks, it is unwise to have each UNIX system function as its own mail server. By using MX records, you provide a mechanism to inform remote SMTP servers where to attempt to deliver mail destined for users at the defined system.

In this example, `mail.sniglets.com` is the primary SMTP system for `pilots.sniglets.com`, with system `sniglets.com` acting as a backup mail server should `mail.sniglets.com` fail to respond. The integer values in front of the SMTP servers represent a weight, with smaller numbers representing the most preferred SMTP server. For more information on configuring your SMTP mail servers, see Chapter 9, "Electronic Mail and Messaging."

The final resource record you'll find useful is the `HINFO` resource. `HINFO` provides a way to insert comment information into DNS. The `HINFO` record is defined as a two-field text record separated by a space. You can use these two fields to insert information about the system, such as system type, operating system level, system owner, or location. This can be very useful if you have a large installation, or if you want to share information through DNS.

Reverse Lookup Database File Now that you can go from hostname to IP address, you need to be able to do the inverse, IP address to hostname. This is called a reverse lookup, and the reverse lookup file is the complement to the host database file that assigns hostnames to IP addresses. The reverse lookup file takes a similar form as the host database file:

```
;

; db.3.168.192.in-addr.arpa

;

@       IN      SOA     dns.sniglets.com. hostperson.sniglets.com. (

                        19990604 ; Serial   year month . revision (yymm.rr)

                        10800    ; Refresh (15 minutes)

                        3600     ; Retry (15 minutes)

                        604800   ; Expire (5 days)

                        86400 )  ; Minimum TTL(4 hours)

        IN      NS      dns.sniglets.com.

        IN      NS      duchess.sniglets.com.


4       IN      PTR     pilots.sniglets.com.
```

You can see that the same `SOA` record information is present, as well as the name server information. While the `SOA` record is of the same form, the data entries can be different. In most instances, you'll want to keep your `Refresh`, `Retry`, `Expire`, and `TTL` values consistent; but, your serial number will most likely be different as day-to-day management of DNS may cause you to touch database files at different intervals.

The entries in the reverse lookup file that are different are the values that relate the IP address to the hostname. The record type for entries in the reverse lookup file are type `PTR`, which relates IP addresses to hostnames.

```
4       IN      PTR     pilots.sniglets.com.
```

This entry associates the IP address `192.168.3.4` with the hostname `pilots.sniglets.com`. When creating `PTR` records, be sure only to associate the IP address with the `A` record that you have set up in the forward database file. While you can create multiple `PTR` records, most systems don't take advantage of this feature. Also, make sure each `PTR` record ends with a period. Failure to include the period can and will cause problems with your DNS server.

 Failure to include a period at the end of a `PTR` record will cause inconsistencies in your DNS server and may be difficult to debug.

Localhost Database File With your forward and reverse files complete, you have enough host information to have a useful and functional DNS server. However, you as the astute reader at this point may ask, "How do I handle the loopback IP address of `127.0.0.1`?" Since network `127.0.0` isn't directly owned by anyone, you have to define this network yourself. While omitting this file may not cause problems, it is always best to take the time to define file `db.127.0.0`.

```
;

;          db.127.0.0.in-addr.arpa

;

@          IN     SOA       dns.sniglets.com.   host-
person.ee.gatech.edu.  (

                           19970701          ;Serial

                           10800     ; Refresh

                           3600      ; Retry

                           604800  ; Expire

                           86400 )   ; Minimum



           IN     NS    dns.sniglets.com.

IN      NS            duchess.sniglets.com.



1          IN     PTR       localhost.
```

As you can see, the only difference in the `db.127.0.0` file is the following entry:

```
      1          IN      PTR           localhost.
```

This entry directs the reverse lookup of `127.0.0.` to resolve to `local-host`, which is the desired result. With the implementation of this file, you have now completed the data configuration portion of your DNS server.

The Root Cache File With all your local data now configured, the next question is: How does the name server know where to go to get information from the Internet? The `db.cache` file defines a list of name servers for your master server to use to get information from the Internet.

```
;      This file holds the information on root name servers needed to

;      initialize cache of Internet domain name servers

;      (e.g. reference this file in the "cache  .  <file>"

;      configuration file of BIND domain name servers).

;

;      This file is made available by InterNIC registration services

;      under anonymous FTP as

;          file                  /domain/named.root

;          on server             FTP.RS.INTERNIC.NET

;      -OR- under Gopher at     RS.INTERNIC.NET

;            under menu          InterNIC Registration Services (NSI)

;              submenu           InterNIC Registration Archives

;          file                  named.root

;

;      last update:    May 19, 1997

;      related version of root zone:   1997051700

;

;

; formerly NS.INTERNIC.NET

;
```

```
.                       3600000  IN  NS    A.ROOT-SERVERS.NET.

A.ROOT-SERVERS.NET.     3600000      A     198.41.0.4

;

; formerly NS1.ISI.EDU

;

.                       3600000      NS    B.ROOT-SERVERS.NET.

B.ROOT-SERVERS.NET.     3600000      A     128.9.0.107

;

; formerly C.PSI.NET

;

.                       3600000      NS    C.ROOT-SERVERS.NET.

C.ROOT-SERVERS.NET.     3600000      A     192.33.4.12

;

; formerly TERP.UMD.EDU

;

.                       3600000      NS    D.ROOT-SERVERS.NET.

D.ROOT-SERVERS.NET.     3600000      A     128.8.10.90

;

; formerly NS.NASA.GOV

;

.                       3600000      NS    E.ROOT-SERVERS.NET.

E.ROOT-SERVERS.NET.     3600000      A     192.203.230.10

;

; formerly NS.ISC.ORG

;

.                       3600000      NS    F.ROOT-SERVERS.NET.
```

```
F.ROOT-SERVERS.NET.        3600000        A      192.5.5.241

;

; formerly NS.NIC.DDN.MIL

;

.                          3600000        NS     G.ROOT-SERVERS.NET.

G.ROOT-SERVERS.NET.        3600000        A      192.112.36.4

;

; formerly AOS.ARL.ARMY.MIL

;

.                          3600000        NS     H.ROOT-SERVERS.NET.

H.ROOT-SERVERS.NET.        3600000        A      128.63.2.53

;

; formerly NIC.NORDU.NET

;

.                          3600000        NS     I.ROOT-SERVERS.NET.

I.ROOT-SERVERS.NET.        3600000        A      192.36.148.17

;

; temporarily housed at NSI (InterNIC)

;

.                          3600000        NS     J.ROOT-SERVERS.NET.

J.ROOT-SERVERS.NET.        3600000        A      198.41.0.10

;

; housed in LINX, operated by RIPE NCC

;

.                          3600000        NS     K.ROOT-SERVERS.NET.

K.ROOT-SERVERS.NET.        3600000        A      193.0.14.129
```

```
;

; temporarily housed at ISI (IANA)

;

.                          3600000      NS     L.ROOT-SERVERS.NET.

L.ROOT-SERVERS.NET.        3600000      A      198.32.64.12

;

; temporarily housed at ISI (IANA)

;

.                          3600000      NS     M.ROOT-SERVERS.NET.

M.ROOT-SERVERS.NET.        3600000      A      198.32.65.12

; End of File
```

The cache file is available for `ftp` from `ftp.rs.internic.net` through anonymous FTP. You should grab this file on a regular basis. Even though it may change infrequently, you want to always have the latest version. This list of name servers is stored upon initialization of `named`, and never discarded or reloaded. In older versions of `bind`, this data was truly cache data, and was reloaded over the Internet after some very long interval. The largest timeout value available was `9999999`, which is a very long time. Once `named` was rewritten to make the cache data static, timeouts were no longer necessary. Somewhere along the line, the timeout value of `3600000` was introduced. Feel free to make up your own story as to what this number means, as its true meaning has been lost to antiquity.

The DNS Configuration File Up to this point, there were no differences between the BIND version 4 and 8 instances of DNS. While BIND 8 has many new features, for our discussion, the only major difference is the configuration file that `named` reads during initialization. In BIND 4, the configuration file was `/etc/named.boot`, while in BIND 8, the initial configuration file is `/etc/named.conf`. We'll start by investigating the BIND 4 `/etc/named.boot` file.

```
;

; BIND 4 named.boot

;

directory         /var/named
```

```
cache              .                         db.cache


;

; type         domain                     source host/file

;

primary        0.0.127.in-addr.arpa         db.0.0.127.in-addr.arpa

;

; domain maps

;

primary          sniglets.com                  db.sniglets
primary          3.168.192.in-addr.arpa   db.3.168.192.in-addr.arpa
;end of named.boot
```

The `directory` directive tells `named` to look in the directory
`/var/named` for data files. The `cache` directive defines the cache file, in
this instance, `/var/named/db.cache`. The `primary` directives tell
`named` that it is the authoritative server for the following domains. In this
case, named is the authoritative server for the loopback address, as well as
for the domain `sniglets.com` (with data file `/var/named/db.snig-
lets`) and the class B network `192.168.3` (with data file `db.3.168.192
.in-addr.arpa`). This is all the necessary information you need to config-
ure BIND 4 `named` to run.

Now, if we compare the BIND 4 `/etc/named.boot` file to the BIND 8
`/etc/named.conf` file, at first we realize that the form is drastically
different. However, once you take a moment to analyze the `named.conf`
file, you realize that the information is the same, just the directives are different.

```
; BIND 8 named.conf

;

options {

          directory "/var/named";

          };
```

```
zone "." in {

        type hint;

        file "db.cache"

        };


zone "0.0.127.in-addr.arpa" in {

        type master;

        file "db.0.0.127.in-addr.arpa"

        };


zone "sniglets.com"      in {

        type master;

        file "db.sniglets";

        };


zone "3.168.192.in-addr.arpa" in {

        type master;

        file "db.3.168.192.in-addr.arpa"

        };

; end for named.boot
```

The `options` directive provides a single entry to specify program options to `named`. For our example, the only option we have specified is database directory `/var/named`. The `zone` directive, coupled with the `type`
`master`, replaces the `primary` directive in the BIND 4 `named.boot`.
While in this case the migration from BIND 4 to BIND 8 is rather straightforward and obvious, for complicated BIND 4 DNS installations, porting the
`named.boot` file by hand is quite difficult. Programs are available to automatically convert BIND 4 to BIND 8, so be sure to do your homework before
you attempt a major DNS upgrade.

DNS Slave Servers

Once you have grasped the concept of DNS master servers, creating DNS slave servers is almost trivial. DNS slave servers are replications of your master server, created to distribute the DNS load across multiple machines, and yet allowing the administrator to only have to manage the master server on a day-to-day basis.

DNS Slave Files To create a DNS slave server, you only need to configure the /etc/named.boot (or named.conf) file, and have a localized copy of the db.cache and 127.0.0.in-addr.arpa files. For the BIND 4 named.boot file, the only difference between the slave server and master server is that domain maps are defined as secondary.

```
;

;

; BIND 4 named.boot

;

directory          /var/named

cache              .                                db.cache


;

; type          domain                     source
host/file

;

primary         0.0.127.in-addr.arpa
db.0.0.127.in-addr.arpa

;

; domain maps

;

secondary         sniglets.com                    db.sniglets

secondary               3.168.192.in-addr.arpa
db.3.168.192.in-addr.arpa

;end of named.boot
```

Defining `domain maps` as `secondary` instructs `named` to perform a zone transfer for these domains. You'll notice that the `0.0.127.in-addr.arpa` file is still defined as `primary`. Since the `0.0.127.in-addr.arpa` file never changes, it makes little sense to have to reload it every time you reload your other files. For this reason, you'll want to make sure to install a copy of your `0.0.127.in-addr.arpa` file.

For BIND 8, the only change in the `named.conf` file is the `type` change from `master` to `slave`. Otherwise, the `named.conf` file is exactly the same as the `named.conf` file on the master server.

```
; BIND 8 named.conf

;

options {

    directory "/var/named";

    };


zone "." in {

    type hint;

    file "db.cache"

    };


zone "0.0.127.in-addr.arpa" in {

    type master;

    file "db.0.0.127.in-addr.arpa"

    };


zone "sniglets.com"       in {

    type slave;

    file "db.sniglets.com";

    };
```

```
zone "3.168.192.in-addr.arpa" in {

    type slave;

    file "db.3.168.192.in-addr.arpa"

    };

; end for named.boot
```

Once you have your files in place, you can start the `named` process in same way you start `named` on your master server.

Updating Slave Server DNS Information The DNS slave server obtains its zone information by doing a zone transfer from the DNS master server, or a peer DNS slave server. The domain databases are reloaded after the time defined by the `Refresh` directive for a given database has expired. Be aware of your `Refresh` value, as longer `Refresh` intervals will cause delays in propagating new DNS information outside the master DNS server.

There will be times when you don't want to wait for DNS information to propagate through the normal zone transfer mechanism. The simplest way to refresh a DNS slave server is to remove the replicated zone file, and restart the `named` process. The `named` program will automatically initiate a zone transfer at start time for any zone file that is not present in the defined

```
#ps -ef | egrep named
    root    152      1  0 17:58:38 ?         0:14 /usr/sbin/in.nam
    root   7458   7342  0 20:08:19 pts/4     0:00 egrep named
#
# kill -9 152
#
#ls
db.0.0.127.in-addr.arpa        db.cache
db.3.168.130.in-addr.arpa   db.ee
#
#rm db.ee
#rm db.3.168.192.in-addr.arpa
#
#ls
db.0.0.127.in-addr.arpa db.cache
#
#/usr/sbin/in.named
#
#ps -ef | egrep named
    root   7832      1  0 20:17:30 pts/4     0:01 /usr/sbin/in.nam
    root   7857   7857  0 20:18:13 pts/4     0:00 egrep named
#
```

Figure 6.6 Restarting a DNS slave server.

named directory. If the file is present, named will look at the file time, calculate the refresh interval, and then decide whether or not to reload the file. Deleting the proper database files will guarantee that fresh copies of the files will be downloaded.

If you choose to use this method to restart your DNS slave servers, you might want to rename your db.cache and db.0.0.127.in-addr .arpa files to something unique. For example, you may change the cache file to named.cache and the 0.0.127.in-addr.arpa file to named.loopback. To make this take effect, all you need to do is modify your named.boot or named.conf file. Now, all you have to do to restart your DNS slave servers is kill the named process, remove the database files, and restart named, as shown in Figure 6.6.

WINDOWS 2000 SERVER DNS

Windows 2000 Server ships with a built-in DNS server. If you did not install the DNS server during the initial installation, it can be added through the Add/Remove Programs applet in the Control Panel. The Microsoft DNS server functions much like any UNIX DNS server, and although it is an independent implementation, it is very similar to BIND version 8. There is one notable exception: By default, the Windows 2000 DNS server boots from either the Registry or the Active Directory. However, the Windows 2000 DNS server can be configured to boot from a file just like the UNIX DNS server. DNS data files are stored in %SystemRoot%\System32\DNS. All of the zone and reverse lookup files are formatted identically to those used in the UNIX DNS server. The boot file (%SystemRoot%\System32\DNS\boot) is also formatted the same as named.boot under UNIX. So, for those of you familiar with DNS on UNIX, start by simply manipulating the files and then learn the GUI. You will find it much easier to approach Microsoft DNS this way, as opposed to jumping in with both feet. Eventually, you will find that the GUI can help simplify many tasks and prevent you from making common mistakes.

Creating a DNS Zone in Windows 2000

If you have not already installed the DNS server service on your Windows 2000 server, do so now using the Add/Remove Programs applet in the Control Panel. You will need this service to host a primary DNS zone, which we will create here. We are assuming you have all of the relevant information, such as domain name, IP ranges, etc. for your network. If you don't have this information, now is a good time to obtain it. Assuming you are ready, let's create our new zone:

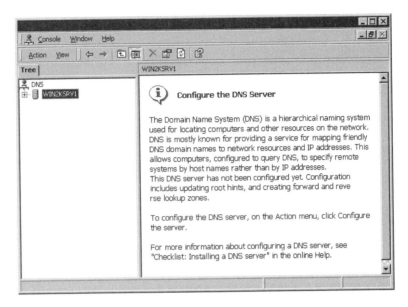

Figure 6.7 DNS MMC snap-in.

1. Open the DNS MMC snap-in from the `Administrative Tools` folder, which is opened from the `Start` menu. You will see a screen similar to Figure 6.7.
2. Select the server (there should be only one listed), and then select `Configure the DNS server...` from the `Action` menu. The `Configure DNS Server Wizard` shown in Figure 6.8 will appear.

Figure 6.8
`Configure DNS Server Wizard.`

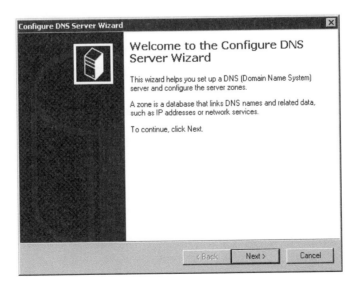

Figure 6.9
Forward Lookup
Zone **selection
screen.**

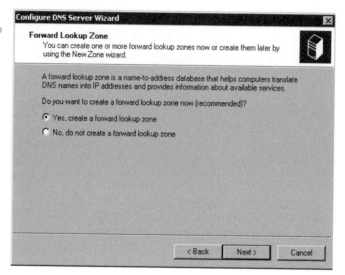

Figure 6.9
Forward Lookup
Zone **selection
screen.**

3. Click Next to display the Forward Lookup Zone selection screen shown in Figure 6.9.

4. Select Yes, create a forward lookup zone and click Next to continue. The Zone Type selection screen in Figure 6.10 will be displayed.

5. Select Standard primary and click Next to continue. The Zone Name configuration screen in Figure 6.11 will be displayed.

6. Enter the name of your zone, such as ece.gatech.edu, and click Next to continue. The Zone File configuration screen in Figure 6.12 will be displayed.

Figure 6.10
Zone Type
selection screen.

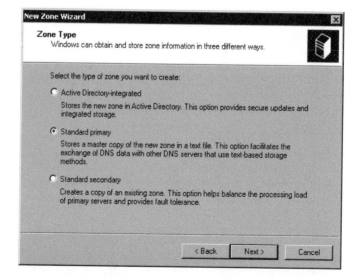

Figure 6.11
Zone Name
configuration
screen.

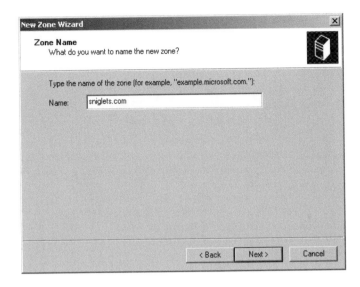

7. Accept the default values and click Next to continue. The Reverse Lookup Zone selection screen in Figure 6.13 will be displayed.

8. Accept the default selection of Yes, create a reverse lookup zone, and then click Next to continue. The Zone Type selection screen previously shown in Figure 6.10 will be displayed again. Select the same zone type as you did in Step 5, Standard primary. Click Next to continue. The Reverse Lookup Zone configuration screen in Figure 6.14 will be displayed.

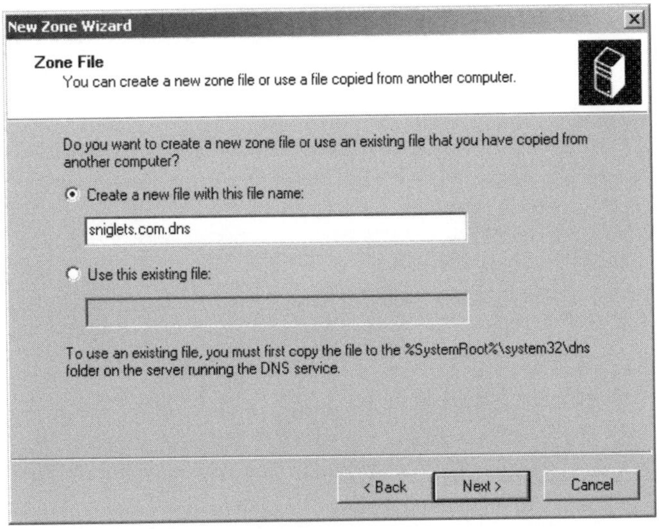

Figure 6.12
Zone File
configuration
screen.

Figure 6.13
Reverse
Lookup Zone
selection screen.

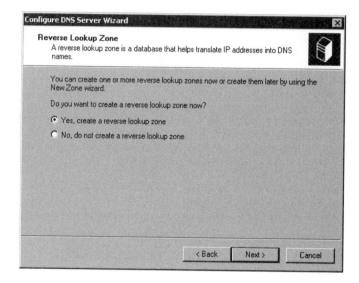

9. Enter your Network ID and subnet mask in the spaces provided. In our case, we entered *192.168.3.0* as the Network ID and *255.255.255.0* as the Subnet mask. Click Next to continue. The Zone File configuration screen in Figure 6.15 will be displayed.

10. Accept the default configuration and click Next to continue. The Completing the Configure DNS Server Wizard screen in Figure 6.16 will be displayed.

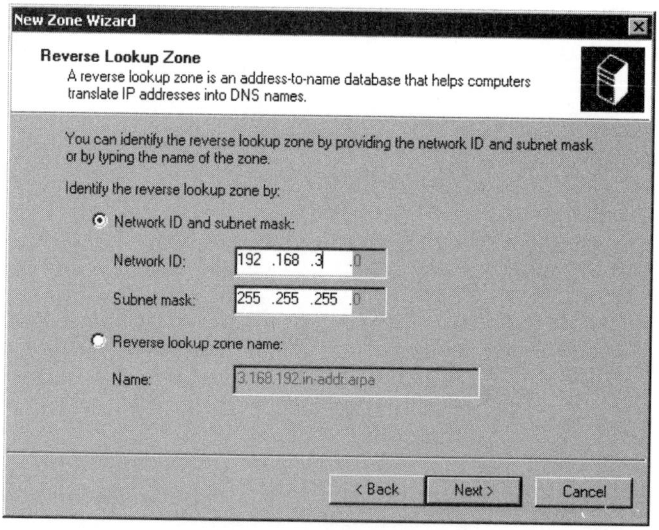

Figure 6.14
Reverse
Lookup Zone
configuration
screen.

Figure 6.15
`Zone File`
configuration
screen.

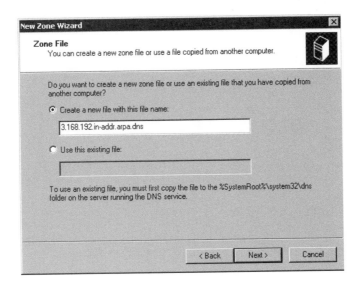

Figure 6.15
`Zone File`
configuration
screen.

11. Click `Finish` to complete the configuration. If you expand the server entry in the MMC and then expand the two zone entries, you will see the screen in Figure 6.17.

Now that you have created your new zones, let's add a record for your machine. You will notice, if you select a zone, that a record for your server was automatically added to the zone. Let's add a record for another client machine:

Figure 6.16
Configuration
completion
screen.

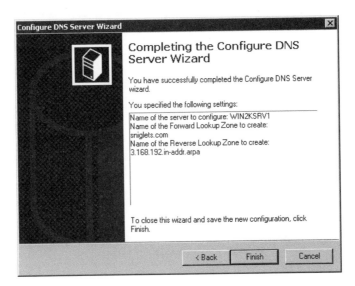

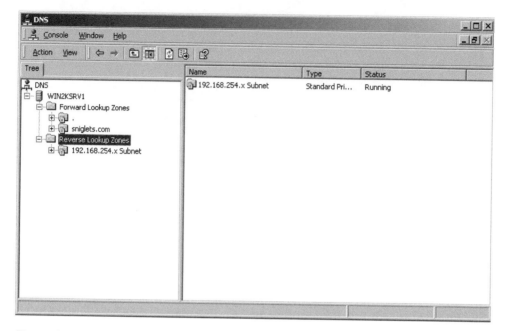

Figure 6.17 DNS MMC snap-in showing new zones.

1. Select a zone entry you previously created. In this case, use *sniglets.com*. From the Action menu, choose the "New Host" option. The New Host configuration window in Figure 6.18 will be displayed.

2. Enter the hostname and IP address in the spaces provided. Make sure that you check the Create associated pointer (PTR) record option.

Figure 6.18
New Host
configuration
screen.

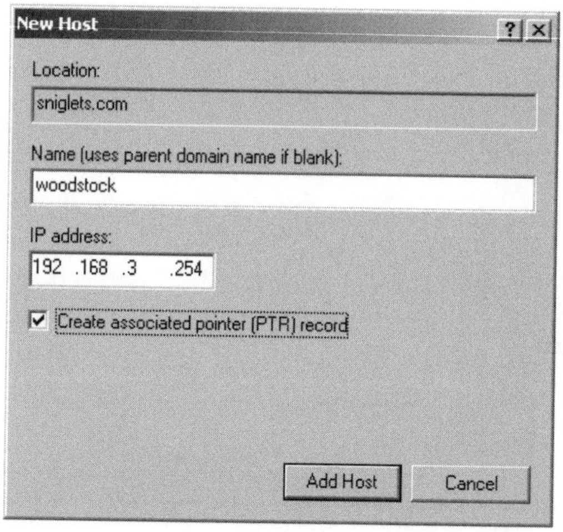

Figure 6.19
Add host
confirmation
window.

3. Click the Add Host button to create the records. You will be prompted to confirm the creation, as shown in Figure 6.19. Click OK to continue.

4. You can continue to add hosts in this manner. When you are done, click the Done button.

Your DNS server is now ready for action. If you need to further customize your server, consult the Windows 2000 documentation for advanced configuration options.

Dynamic DNS

Dynamic DNS (DDNS) is a new Internet Engineering Task Force (IETF) standard for automatic DNS record updates. Basically, DDNS functions in a similar manner to WINS in that the client machine registers with the DNS server and the DNS entry is updated if necessary. DDNS is also fully integrated with the Windows 2000 Active Directory and DHCP service. The DNS server can also be linked with the WINS server to provide continuity across all Windows 2000 name resolution and registration services. With DDNS, the need to manually edit DNS configuration files is reduced significantly. DDNS also allows services such as LDAP to be registered with the DNS server. With this addition, it is now possible for clients to locate a server providing a specific service simply by querying the DNS server. A sample DDNS session is explained here:

1. A client, *mycomputer*, requests an IP address from the DHCP server.
2. The DHCP server assigns an available IP address from the address pool to *mycomputer*.
3. The DHCP server registers the PTR record for *mycomputer* with the DNS server.
4. The client *mycomputer* registers its own A record with the DNS server.

When a lease for an IP address expires, the DHCP server will remove the appropriate PTR and A records from the DNS server.

You must use the DHCP Manager MMC snap-in to configure the DHCP server to send DDNS updates to the DNS server.

Your DNS server must be configured to accept DDNS updates from the DHCP server and/or client workstations. Follow these steps to enable DDNS for the zone we created earlier:

1. Open the DNS MMC snap-in from the `Administrative Tools` folder and expand the zone folders.
2. Select the zone for which you wish to enable DDNS from `the Forward Lookup Zones` section. For our server, we selected `sniglets.com`.
3. Select `Properties` from the `Action` menu. The zone is properties window is shown in Figure 6.20.
4. On the General tab, change the `Allow dynamic updates` option to Yes.
5. Click the OK button to apply the changes.
6. Use the same procedure for your reverse lookup zone and any other zones for which you wish to enable DDNS.

Figure 6.20
DNS zone
properties
window.

sniglets.com Properties   ? X

| General | Start of Authority (SOA) | Name Servers | WINS | Zone Transfers |

Status: Running   [Pause]

Type: Primary   [Change...]

Zone file name:

sniglets.com.dns

Allow dynamic updates? | Yes   ▼ |

To set aging/scavenging properties, click Aging.   [Aging...]

[OK]   [Cancel]   [Apply]

Figure 6.21
Using `nslookup`.

```
#nslookup mars.sniglets.com
Server:  earth.sniglets.com
Address:  192.168.0.2

Name:    mars.sniglets.com
Address:  192.168.0.1

#nslookup
Default Server:  earth.sniglets.com
Address:  192.168.0.2

> mars.sniglets.com
Server:  earth.sniglets.com
Address:  192.168.0.2

Name:    mars.sniglets.com
Address:  192.168.0.1

> exit
#
```

DDNS is now enabled and you can start using it from your clients and/or DHCP and WINS servers.

DDNS is also supported in the latest version of the Berkeley Internet Name Daemon (BIND).

Using nslookup in UNIX and Windows 2000

One common need when debugging DNS information is checking if the DNS server is functioning, or if the server is handing out incorrect information. The `nslookup` program, can be invoked from the command line, or by using the interactive shell interface, as shown in Figure 6.21

Figure 6.22
Using nslookup
to query multiple
name servers.

```
#nslookup
Default Server: localhost
Address:  127.0.0.1

> mars.sniglets.com
Server: localhost
Address:  127.0.0.1

Name:    mars.sniglets.com
Address:  192.168.0.1

> server earth.sniglets.com
Default Server: earch.sniglets.com
Address:  192.168.0.2

> mars.sniglets.com
Server: earth.sniglets.com
Address:  192.168.0.2

Name:    mars.sniglets.com
Address:  192.168.0.1

>quit
```

Figure 6.23
Using `nslookup` to determine the SOA for a given zone.

```
#nslookup
Default Server:  localhost
Address:  127.0.0.1

> set q=soa
> sniglets.com
Server:  localhost
Address:  127.0.0.1

sniglets.com
        origin = earth.sniglets.com
        mail addr = hostperson.sniglets.com
        serial = 20000111
        refresh = 21600 (6 hours)
        retry   = 3600 (1 hour)
        expire  = 604800 (7 days)
        minimum ttl = 86400 (1 day)
sniglets.com    nameserver = earth.sniglets.com
sniglets.com    nameserver = moon.sniglets.com
earth.sniglets.com      internet address = 192.168.0.2
moon.sniglets.com       internet address = 192.168.0.3
> exit
#
```

Using the server command allows you to point the `nslookup` command at a different server than the first name server defined in the `/etc/resolv.conf` file. As we can see in Figure 6.22, the first server gives different results than a query to the second server.

Unless you know something about the DNS structure, you won't know which server is giving the correct information. However, if you know the SOA for a zone, you should trust the results of a DNS response from the SOA system over any other DNS server. Since DNS changes take a nontrivial amount of time to propagate, there will be times when local DNS servers have old cached information that may be incorrect until the cached entry times out.

```
#nslookup
Default Server:  earth.sniglets.com
Address:  192.168.0.2

> set q=mx
> mars.sniglets.com
Server:  earth.sniglets.com
Address:  192.168.0.2

mars.sniglets.com       preference = 20, mail exchanger = moon.sniglets.com
mars.sniglets.com       preference = 10, mail exchanger = mail.sniglets.com
sniglets.com    nameserver = earth.sniglets.com
sniglets.com    nameserver = moon.sniglets.com
moon.sniglets.com       internet address = 192.168.0.3
earth.sniglets.com      internet address = 192.168.0.1
> exit
#exit
```

Figure 6.24 Using `nslookup` to determine MX records for a given host or domain.

```
#nslookup
Default Server: earth.sniglets.com
Address:  192.168.0.2

> set q=any
> mars.sniglets.com
Server:  earth.sniglets.com
Address:  192.168.0.2

mars.sniglets.com        CPU = HP        OS = HP/UX
mars.sniglets.com        preference = 20, mail exchanger = moon.sniglets.com
mars.sniglets.com        internet address = 192.168.0.1
mars.sniglets.com        preference = 10, mail exchanger = mail.sniglets.com
sniglets.com     nameserver = earth.sniglets.com
sniglets.com     nameserver = moon.sniglets.com
mail.sniglets.com        internet address = 192.168.0.5
earth.sniglets.com       internet address = 192.168.0.2
> exit
#
```

Figure 6.25
Using set q = any to see all possible DNS information for a given host or
domain.

Using the set q = value command (or query) is another way to extract
information from DNS using nslookup. While there are many different
types of queries, knowing a few can help you gather important information
quickly. Using the set q=soa query in nslookup will give you the SOA
information for a given domain, as seen in Figure 6.23.

Another useful feature is the ability to determine the mail exchanger (MX)
values for a given system. This is highly useful when debugging SMTP problems. Using the set q=mx query, as in Figure 6.24, you will see the MX values for the domain or host, as well as the preference values.

Finally, if you're not quite sure what information you are looking for, you
can generate a query to give you as much information as is available by
using the set q = any query, as shown in Figure 6.25.

nslookup allows users to contact DNS servers for information about
various hosts and domains.

WINS Overview

Windows 2000 provides the ability to map NetBIOS names to IP addresses
using WINS servers. WINS stands for Windows Internet Name Service. The
unique aspect of WINS, as compared to DNS, is that each client machine
registers its own name and IP address with the server. This provides the
ability to implement an (almost) hands-off name resolution service. WINS
can be used (and it is recommended to do so) to replace the functionality of
the local LMHOSTS file.

Using WINS

Let's walk through configuring the client in this section, while leaving the details of the server implementation to the next section. Use the following steps to configure WINS:

1. Follow Steps 1-5 of the procedure in the "Using DNS in Windows 2000" section.
2. Click the "WINS" tab and you should see the window displayed in Figure 6.26.
3. Leave all of the settings at their default values and only change the WINS addresses list. Enter your WINS servers, in the order in which you wish them to be used, by clicking the Add button for each server and entering the address when prompted.
4. Click OK to commit your changes and close the window.
5. You should also click the OK button to close the TCP/IP properties window, and then click OK to close the Local Area Connection Properties window.
6. Most changes to the TCP/IP settings in Windows 2000 do not require a reboot of the system. However, if you are prompted to reboot the system, you should do so at this point.

Figure 6.26
WINS properties window.

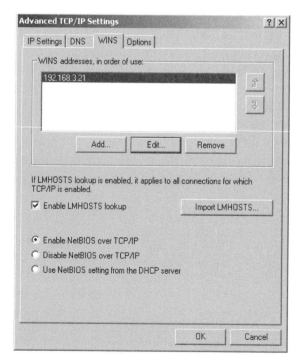

Once you have configured your machine to use a WINS server(s) you should be able to make network connections using \\YOURMACHINE\ YOURSHARE syntax. If you browse the local and remote networks in My Network Places, you should notice that there are many more domains, workgroups, and machines than before you implemented WINS. This is good, because you can now see everything on your network that is WINS-enabled.

As we stated earlier, WINS provides IP address to NetBIOS name mapping. This can be accomplished using static LMHOSTS files or by querying WINS servers. As you have already discovered, for any network bigger than a few machines, LMHOSTS is not practical to employ. WINS, on the other hand, works well in networks of all sizes.

WINS CLIENTS

WINS clients are machines that perform two primary functions:

- Upon boot, they register their name and IP address with the WINS server.
- They query the WINS server to resolve NetBIOS names to IP addresses.

The important thing to understand in relation to WINS clients is *how* they perform these two functions. The first is rather simple. When a WINS client boots up, it contacts the specified WINS server and attempts to register its hostname and IP address. If no other WINS client has already registered the specified hostname, the WINS server acknowledges the request and other WINS clients can now resolve the new hostname to an IP address. When a WINS client wishes to resolve a NetBIOS name to an IP address, one or more of the methods described in Table 6.1 are used to do so.

Depending on your network infrastructure, you may wish to customize the way your clients attempt to resolve NetBIOS names to IP addresses. Fortunately, there is an easy way to do this – the NetBIOS Node Type setting. There are two ways to set the NetBIOS node type:

- Modify the Registry key: HKEY_LOCAL_MACHINE\SYSTEM\ CurrentControlSet\Services\NetBT\Parameters\ NodeType.

Table 6.1	NetBIOS Name Resolution Methods
Name Resolution Method	Description
Local NetBIOS Name Cache	The NetBios name cache is stored in memory and keeps a list of recently accessed NetBIOS names and their IP addresses.
Local `LMHOSTS` File	The `LMHOSTS` file , stored in `%System-Root%\System32\Drivers\etc`, can be parsed to resolve a NetBIOS name to an IP address. Some `LMHOSTS` entries can be pre-loaded into the NetBIOS name cache for faster access.
Local `HOSTS` File	The local `HOSTS` file, stored in %System-Root%\System32\Drivers\etc, can be parsed in a similar fashion to the `LMHOSTS` file.
NetBIOS Name Server (WINS Server)	The NetBIOS name server (a.k.a. WINS Server) can be queried, via the network, for the mapping.
DNS Server	A DNS server can be queried just like a WINS server to return a mapping, although it is not as reliable as a WINS server.
Network Broadcast	Usually used as a last-ditch effort, the client can broadcast a request for a specific NetBIOS name to the local network. If the destination host is on-line and "hears" the broadcast, it will respond. Broadcasts are only useful on the local subnet.

■ If you are using DHCP, you can specify the NetBIOS node type as one of the DHCP parameters and the `NodeType` key will be set automatically.

Be very careful when manipulating the Windows 2000 Registry. Modifying settings incorrectly can leave your system in an unusable state.

Table 6.2 outlines the different node types and their values, and gives a description of how they affect name resolution.

Table 6.2	NBT Node Type Settings	
Node Type	Description	NodeType Registry Setting
B-Node	Uses broadcasts to find a NetBIOS name. This can create a lot of network traffic and will be limited to the local subnet.	0x00000001 (0x1)
Enhanced B-Node	This is a Microsoft enhancement to the traditional B-Node method and name resolution is attempted in the following order: • Local NetBIOS name cache is checked. • NetBIOS name query is broadcasted. • Local LMHOSTS file is checked. • Local HOSTS file is checked. • DNS server is queried. This is an improvement over the traditional B-Node method, but can still generate a lot of network traffic.	0x00000001 (0x1)
P-Node	This method does not rely on any broadcasts and name resolution is attempted in the following order: • Local NetBIOS name cache is checked. • NetBIOS name server is queried. • Local HOSTS file is checked. • DNS server is queried. This method eliminates broadcast traffic, but if no name server can service the request and mapping is not available locally, name resolution will fail.	0x00000002 (0x2)
M-Node	This method is a "mixed" implementation of B-Node and P-Node. Name resolution is attempted in the following order: • Local NetBIOS name cache is checked. • NetBIOS name query is broadcasted. • Local LMHOSTS file is checked. • NetBIOS name server is queried. • Local HOSTS file is checked. • DNS server is queried. This method allows the client to perform a broadcast if necessary, but it is not suitable for large, modern networks.	0x00000004 (0x4)

(continued)

Table 6.2	NBT Node Type Settings (continued)	
Node Type	Description	NodeType Registry Setting
H-Node	This method is a "hybrid" implementation of M-Node. Name resolution is attempted in the following order: • Local NetBIOS name cache is checked. • NetBIOS name server is queried. • NetBIOS name query is broadcasted. • Local LMHOSTS file is checked. • Local HOSTS file is checked. • DNS server is queried. This method is currently the default when a WINS server is configured on the client. H-Node provides the most efficient name resolution of all the options.	0x00000008 (0x8)

As you might have guessed, we recommend the H-Node method for NetBIOS name resolution on WINS-enabled networks. The only other component necessary for successful name resolution is the WINS server itself, which is discussed in the next section.

WINS SERVERS

A WINS server is simply a Windows NT or Windows 2000 server with the WINS server service installed. If you did not install the WINS server service during your initial installation, you can do so using the Add/Remove Programs applet in the Control Panel.

In actuality, a WINS server is one of the simplest servers to install and configure. Once the server is up and running, it requires very little administrative attention. There are two things that you must remember when configuring your WINS servers:

■ Always configure master/slave servers as push/pull partners on both ends. This will ensure that the database is completely replicated.

■ Always have a master and slave server in each domain, and maintain a single master for your entire enterprise.

Use the following procedure to configure your WINS server service:

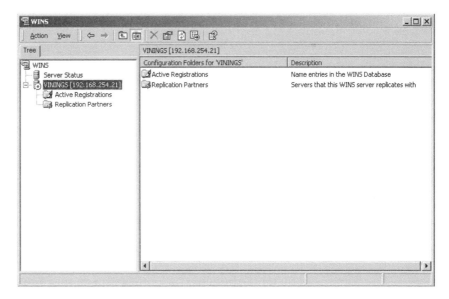

Figure 6.27 WINS Manager MMC snap-in.

1. If you did not do so during the initial installation, add the WINS server service from the `Add/Remove Programs` applet in the `Control Panel`.
2. Launch the WINS Manager MMC snap-in from the `Administrative Tools` folder in the `Start` menu. You will see a window similar to the one in Figure 6.27.
3. Once WINS has been installed, it is ready for use right away. The only thing left to do is to configure the new WINS server to replicate with an existing WINS server. `Select Replication Partners` and then choose `New Replication Partner` from the `Action` menu. The `New Replication Partner` configuration window in Figure 6.28 will appear.

Figure 6.28
New
Replication
Partner
configuration
window.

4. Enter the name of another WINS server in the space provided. Here, vanntleer.ee.gatech.edu has been chosen. Click OK to add the new replication partner.

A master WINS server is no different from any other WINS server; it is just one that replicates with all other WINS servers, either directly or through a tree of WINS servers.

That's it; WINS is now ready to go. For more advanced options, see the Windows 2000 documentation.

WINS AND UNIX

If you are running SAMBA or some other SMB service on your UNIX systems, you should create static mappings to those UNIX systems in the WINS database. You can do this using the WINS Manager MMC snap-in. UNIX systems cannot dynamically register with the WINS server. You should consult the SAMBA documentation for more information on WINS and registering with the WINS server. Follow the steps below to create a static mapping for a UNIX system:

1. Launch the WINS Manager MMC snap-in from the Administrative Tools group in the Start menu. You will see a window similar to the one in Figure 6.27.
2. Select Active Registrations, and then choose New Static Mapping from the Action menu. The New Static Mapping configuration window in Figure 6.29 appears.
3. Enter the name of your UNIX system in the Computer name field, leave the NetBIOS Scope field blank (it is no longer required), set the Type option to Unique, and enter the machines IP address in the IP address field. Click OK to continue.

You can also add static mappings for domains, groups, and multi-homed systems. The process is the same as the one described above, only you need to set the Type field appropriately.

Figure 6.29
New Static
Mapping
configuration
window.

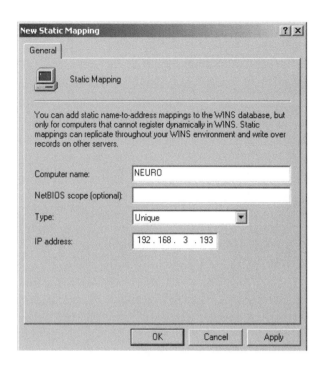

Using DHCP

DHCP can be used to assign IP addresses to networked client machines. In addition to the IP address, the DHCP server can also assign the default router, DNS servers, WINS servers, and the NBT node type. With DHCP, the only parameter that must be set locally on the client machines is the host-name and (optionally) the domain name and domain search order. DHCP can be integrated with DDNS and WINS to provide a seamless name reso-lution and registration infrastructure. Suffice it to say, the scope of this book does not lend itself to cover every aspect of DHCP, so we will focus on the most common implementation.

WINDOWS 2000 DHCP CLIENTS

A DHCP client is nothing more than a standard Windows NT or Win-dows 2000 workstation enabled to query a DHCP server. To enable your client to support DHCP, do the following:

1. Follow Steps 1–4 of the procedure in the "Using DNS in Windows 2000" section.

2. On the General page, select the Obtain an IP address automatically option, as shown in Figure 6.30.

3. On the General page, select the Obtain DNS server addresses automatically option. Figure 6.30 also shows this option selected.

4. Click the OK to close the TCP/IP properties window, and then click OK to close the Local Area Connection Properties window.

5. Most changes to the TCP/IP settings in Windows 2000 do not require a reboot of the system. However, if you are prompted to reboot the system, you should do so at this point.

Make sure you remove all of the DNS and WINS server settings from the DNS and WINS pages. The local settings will override anything assigned by the DHCP server.

Figure 6.30
DNS client configuration.

Internet Protocol (TCP/IP) Properties   ？ ✕

General

You can get IP settings assigned automatically if your network supports this capability. Otherwise, you need to ask your network administrator for the appropriate IP settings.

◉ Obtain an IP address automatically

○ Use the following IP address:

IP address:

Subnet mask:

Default gateway:

◉ Obtain DNS server address automatically

○ Use the following DNS server addresses:

Preferred DNS server:

Alternate DNS server:

Advanced...

OK   Cancel

WINDOWS 2000 DHCP SERVERS

Windows 2000 Server ships with a DHCP server. If you did not install the DHCP server during installation, you can add it using the `Add/Remove Programs` applet in the `Control Panel`. The DHCP server that ships with Windows 2000 is more than adequate for most networks. However, if you require special functionality (such as access restrictions), then you should investigate commercial packages, which are available for both UNIX and Windows platforms. The DHCP server service will allow you to dynamically configure your clients and can also be integrated with your WINS and DHCP servers. This section will walk you through a typical DHCP scope configuration.

Setting up the Scope

When you first install the DHCP server service, a sample scope will be created for you. You will need to delete the sample scope and create a brand new scope. Use the following procedure to bring your new scope on-line:

1. Start the DHCP Manager MMC snap-in from the `Administra-tive Tools` group in the `Start` menu. You will see a window similar to the one shown in Figure 6.31.

2. The first step is to "authorize" the DHCP server to service clients; this is a new security feature included with Active Directory. Select your server and then choose `Authorize` from the `Action` menu. (It may take a few moments for the authorization to complete. If several

Figure 6.31
DHCP Manager
MMC snap-in.

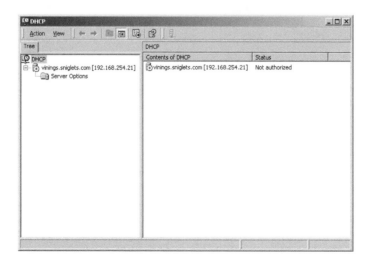

Figure 6.32
DHCP Manager
MMC snap-in
shown with
sample scope.

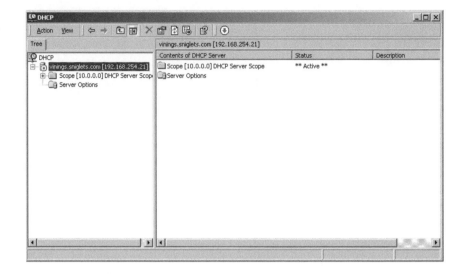

minutes pass and your server is still listed as Not Authorized,
close the DHCP Manager snap-in and then open it again.)

3. Expand your server by clicking the (+) to the left of it and you will see
the sample scope as shown in Figure 6.32.

4. Select the sample scope and then choose Delete from the Action
menu. You will be prompted to confirm the deletion. Confirm the
deletion to continue.

5. Select your server again and choose New Scope from the Action
menu. The New Scope Wizard in Figure 6.33 will be displayed.

Figure 6.33
New Scope
Wizard window.

Figure 6.34
Scope Name configuration screen.

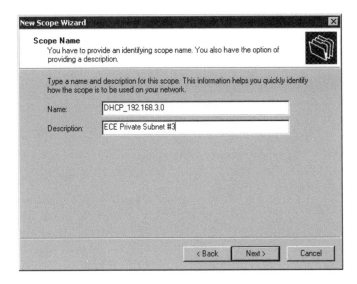

6. Click Next to display the Scope Name configuration screen in Figure 6.34.

7. Enter a Name and Description in the spaces provided; anything you choose is acceptable. Click Next to display the IP Address Range configuration screen in Figure 6.35.

8. Enter the IP address range in the spaces provided. The Subnet mask will default to the standard subnet mask for the IP range you entered. If you have a different subnet mask, you can modify it here. Click Next to display the Add Exclusions configuration screen in Figure 6.36.

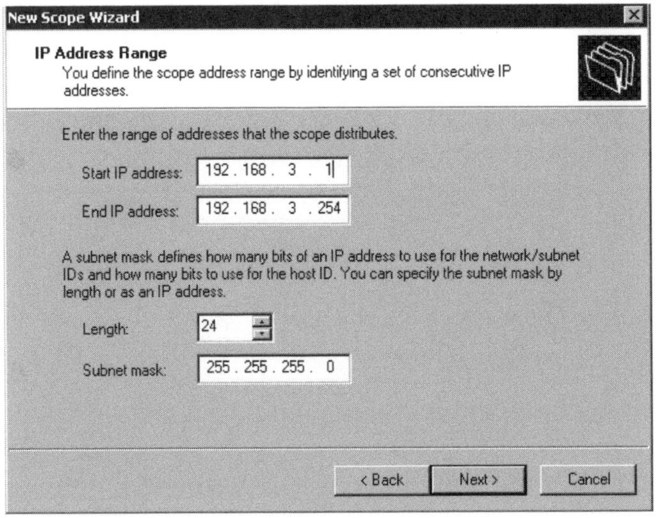

Figure 6.35
IP Address Range configuration screen.

Figure 6.36
`Add Exclu-sions` config-uration screen.

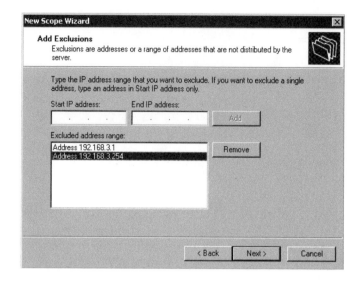

9. You can enter individual IP addresses or an entire range to be excluded. You will probably want to exclude those IPs and IP ranges that include your network equipment and server systems. Add the entries you want to exclude and click `Next` to display the `Lease Duration` configuration screen shown in Figure 6.37.

10. Set the lease duration to a value that will work well in your environment. If you have a large number of machines and a small number of IP addresses, use a smaller number, such as one day, or even just a few minutes. If you intend for machines to keep their IP addresses for a long time, make the duration longer. When you are finished,

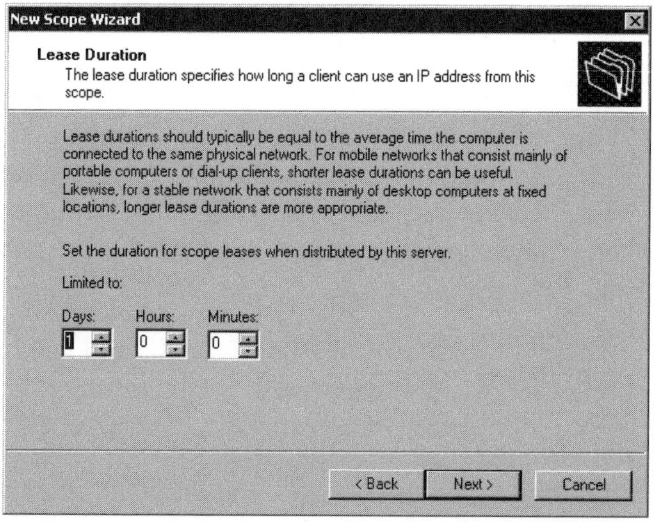

Figure 6.37
`Lease Duration` configuration screen.

Figure 6.38
`Configure`
`DHCP Options`
selection screen.

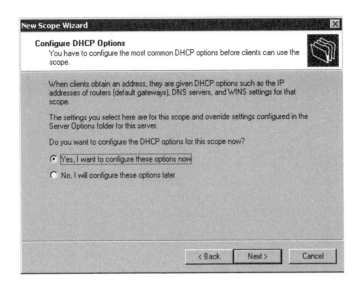

click Next to display the `Configure DHCP Options` selection screen in Figure 6.38.

11. We recommend that you go ahead and configure these options now, so select `Yes, I want to configure these options now` and click Next to display the `Router (Default Gateway)` configuration screen in Figure 6.39.

12. Enter your router's `IP address` in the space provided and click the `Add` button. You can add more than one entry if you have multiple routers. When you are finished, click Next to display the `Domain Name and DNS Servers` configuration screen in Figure 6.40.

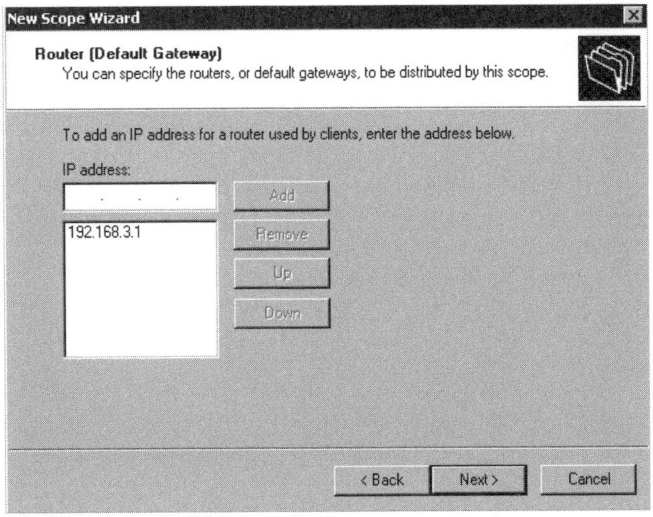

Figure 6.39
`Router`
`(Default`
`Gateway)`
configuration
screen.

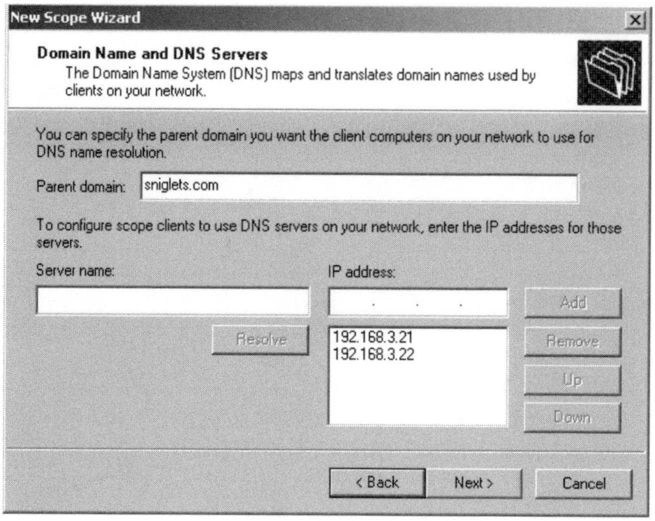

Figure 6.40
Domain Name
and DNS
Servers
configuration
screen.

13. Enter your domain name (ece.gatech.edu, in our case) and add one or more DNS servers to the list.

14. When you are finished, click Next to display the WINS Servers configuration screen in Figure 6.41.

15. Enter your WINS servers in the space provided and click Next to display the Activate Scope selection screen in Figure 6.42.

16. We suggest you accept the default action to activate the scope immediately. Click Next to continue.

17. Click the Finish button on the confirmation screen to complete the scope setup.

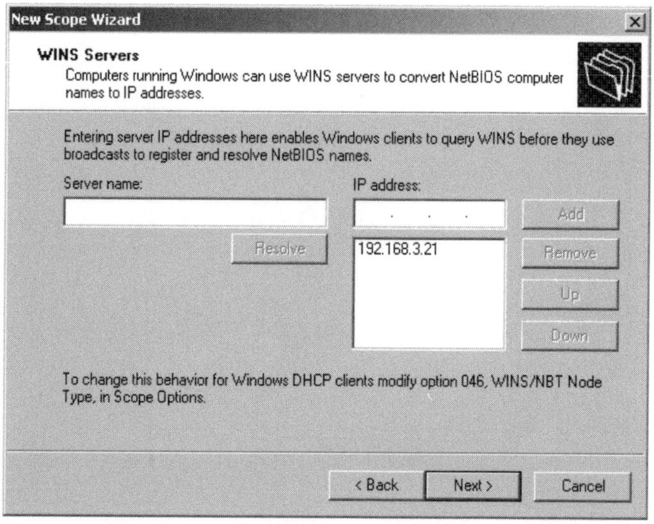

Figure 6.41
WINS Servers
configuration
screen.

Figure 6.42
Activate
Scope selection
screen.

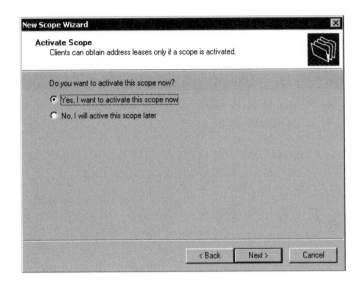

DHCP TIPS

An excellent way to centralize IP addressing while maintaining access control on your network is to use DHCP reservations. We like to refer to this as *static DHCP*. At first this seems like a contradiction in terms, since DHCP was designed to be dynamic. In reality, what you are doing is making everyone use DHCP and are ensuring that the same address is always assigned to the same network card. This allows you, as a system administrator, to change any of the key TCP/IP settings without ever having to sit down at a

Figure 6.43
DHCP Manager
MMC snap-in
with new scope
expanded into
view.

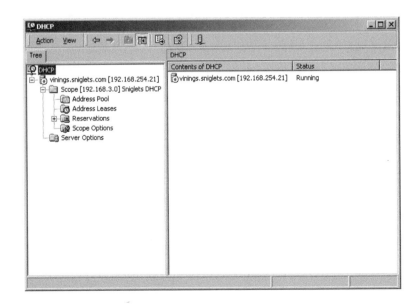

Figure 6.44
New Reserva-
tion configur-
ation screen.

user's machine. In large organizations, this can be an indispensable resource. Use the following procedure to add a DHCP reservation:

1. Open the DHCP Manager MMC snap-in from the Administrative Tools group in the Start menu.
2. Expand your server and expand the scope we just created to display
   the sub-categories of the scope, as shown in Figure 6.43.
3. Select the Reservations category and then choose New Reservation from the Action menu. The New Reservation configuration screen in Figure 6.44 will be displayed.
4. Enter the information requested in the spaces provided. Make sure
   the MAC address is 12 characters long and consists only of numbers
   and the letters A-F. Leave the Supported Types option set to
   Both and click the Add button. To create additional reservations,
   continue in this manner until you are done.
5. Click the Close button when you are finished.

You now have an active DHCP scope with reservations. If you want to modify the more advanced options, consult the Windows 2000 documentation.

Summary

This chapter showed three major ways of handling name resolution and
registration. These three methods, DNS, WINS, and DHCP, are not mutually

exclusive. In most integrated networks, they are used together to provide efficient and reliable addressing. DNS and WINS provide the foundation for name registration to address mappings, and DHCP provides the ability to dynamically assign addresses.

NAME RESOLUTION USING DNS

DNS is something that almost every computer hooked up to the Internet uses everyday. While `/etc/host` and the Network Information Service (NIS) can provide address resolution, the most widely used method for resolving Internet names is DNS. On UNIX systems, the `/etc/resolv.conf` file is used to define how your client system will communicate with servers that contain DNS information. For Windows 2000, setting up DNS is as simple as adding the appropriate server name in the `DNS` tab under the `TCP/IP Protocols` section of the `Network Neighborhood` icon. Client DNS is a robust service that allows for fault tolerance by permitting client systems to define a list of DNS servers to query. By tailoring your /etc/resolv.conf file to fit your network architecture, you can design a DNS scheme that is tolerant of server and network failures, and can compensate for overloaded DNS servers.

Managing a DNS server, while more difficult than managing DNS clients, is not an overwhelming chore. Both Windows 2000 and UNIX are a valid selection to function as a DNS server. Your best option is to choose the platform you are most comfortable with, as this choice will come in handy when you need to debug DNS problems. For UNIX platforms, possibly the most important choice when installing BIND (DNS server software) is deciding between BIND version 4 or BIND version 8. If you have inherited an infrastructure, most likely your DNS server software is BIND 4. If you are setting up a new infrastructure, you will probably want to invest in BIND 8. In either case, the concepts are very similar, with only the file structure being different. If you have the choice and the time, you'll be best served to chose BIND 8, as it has additional security features you can benefit from.

USING WINS

Windows 2000 provides the ability to map NetBIOS names to IP addresses using WINS servers. Unlike DNS, each WINS client machine registers its own name and IP address with the server. This provides the ability to implement an (almost) hands-off name resolution service. WINS should be used as the replacement for the local `LMHOSTS` file. `LMHOSTS` is not practical to employ for any network bigger than a few machines. WINS, on the other hand, works well in networks of all sizes.

USING DHCP

DHCP dynamically assigns IP addresses to networked client machines. In addition to the IP address, the DHCP server also assigns the default router, DNS servers, WINS servers, and the NBT node type. With DHCP, the only parameter that must be set locally on the client machines is the host name and (optionally) the domain name and domain search order. DHCP, DNS, and WINS can provide a seamless name resolution and registration infrastructure.

DIRECTORY SERVICES

UNIX

NIS/NIS+

Migrating NIS to NIS+

LDAP

WINDOWS

Active Directory

Password Synchronization

LDAP

Managing computer systems is a non-linear function. As the number of systems grows and the infrastructure becomes more complex, the functions the administrator needs to perform can soon become overwhelming. Chapter 6, "Name Resolution and Registration," presented tools and procedures to manage the IP address and host naming spaces in your infrastructure through the use of DNS, WINS, and DHCP. Through the use of these tools, the administrator has an efficient and effective way to change IP addresses, assign IP addresses and hostnames to systems, and advertise systems to the Internet through the use of a client/server hierarchy. For example, managing a DNS infrastructure provides a mechanism for managing IP addresses and names such that the administrator need only configure DNS on a client system at the time of system installation. After installation, all DNS information is managed at the server level.

Through the use of DNS, WINS, and DHCP, addressing and naming services are quite manageable. However, what can we do to manage user information and other systems' configurations? For example, consider user management. If you only have one computer system, adding or removing a user is simple. Edit one file, or traverse one set of GUI windows, and you have accomplished your task. Now, what if you have two systems. If both systems are exactly the same, then you perform the same set of tasks on each system, and you are done. This work is quite linear in that if you have 100 systems, all exactly the same, then you can perform the same task 100 times. It is easy to see how tedious and time-consuming managing information in this manner can become, but at least the operation is exactly the same each time, and through the use of scripts and other tools, you'll probably be able to find ways to automate this task.

Now, say you go back to only having two systems, but they are different. Maybe they are different in configuration, or possibly they have totally different operating systems. For this example, assume you want to modify your Network File System, or NFS, definitions (see Chapter 8, "Distributed System," for more information on NFS). If the systems are different, you cannot assume that the task of modifying the NFS definitions is exactly the same. You now have two sets of tasks. If your infrastructure grows, you may end up with as many different NFS definitions as you do systems. You're now faced with the task of touching every system each time you add a new NFS definition. If your infrastructure is constantly changing, you can see how difficult this would be to manage.

However, all is not lost, and you as the administrator are not doomed to an existence of editing files for hours each time a user modifies a password. Both UNIX and Windows 2000 provide *Directory Services*, which are tool sets that provide mechanisms for distributing system information using the client/server architecture. In the UNIX area, Network Information Services (NIS) are used to distribute information such as password files and NFS configurations. For Windows 2000, the Active Directory feature allows you to distribute information about users and file shares. Through the use of NIS and Active Directory, an administrator can significantly reduce the amount of work necessary to keep their infrastructure running well.

In this chapter, we discuss the tools you need to set up, manage, and troubleshoot an NIS/NIS+ infrastructure. NIS+ is the second generation of NIS. It has significant performance and security enhancements over NIS. We will provide the information you need to create an NIS/NIS+ database from scratch, merge multiple databases together, and maintain your infrastructure. However, due to the flexibility and complexity of NIS+, a book solely dedicated to NIS+, such as *All About Administering NIS+* by Rick Ramsey, may be useful.

Similarly, Windows 2000 Active Directory is a complex and powerful tool. While it is not possible to cover all of the complexities of Active Directory, this chapter will give you the basics you need to use Active Directory in your Windows 2000 infrastructure. You will learn how to design and implement an Active Directory installation, including integrating DNS into your Windows 2000 Active Directory structure. You will also learn how to create replicas of your Active Directory data to provide redundancy and enhance performance. Finally, the chapter will conclude with a brief discussion of the

Lightweight Directory Access Protocol (LDAP), which can be used to tie together the directory services of both Windows 2000 and UNIX.

Planning and Managing an NIS/NIS+ Installation

NIS/NIS+ is a powerful and useful tool when managing an infrastructure with more than just a few UNIX systems. It allows you to modify a single file and propagate that information throughout your environment with only a few commands. Planning your installation is similar to DNS in that you install a distributed information service. An early consideration should be to make sure you provide redundancy as well as load balancing. When used correctly, NIS/NIS+ drastically reduces administration time; but, if managed poorly, it can cause even your best system administrator to have nightmares.

WHEN TO USE NIS/NIS+

When to use NIS/NIS+ can be a difficult decision to make. The benefits of using NIS+ include:

- It drastically decreases administration overhead, as only one set of system files needs to be managed. Changes to these files are made in one place, but can then be propagated to hundreds or even thousands of clients with a few commands.
- Administration time stays relatively stable as the number of systems increases. The majority of your NIS/NIS+ work will be on the NIS/NIS+ server systems, whose numbers should remain small in relation to the number of client systems.
- It simplifies cross-platform administration, as the NIS/NIS+ protocol is platform-independent. You need to understand how to configure NIS/NIS+ for each type of UNIX client; the server architecture is platform-non-specific.
- It reduces the chance of human error in editing multiple files, as only one set of files is manipulated. If access to these files is securely managed, the chances for typographical or human errors are reduced.

DESIGNING YOUR INFRASTRUCTURE

Installing NIS/NIS+ is not as simple as installing a master server and making a few client system modifications. Designing your NIS/NIS+ installation is similar to planning your DNS infrastructure. You need to identify a master server and secondary servers, and then design with performance and fault tolerance in mind. Choose a system that is highly secure and stable. Systems that have many users, or systems that have unreliable hardware, can lead to unwanted information outages, through system failure or user "accidents" such as deleting files by mistake. Having your DNS and NIS/NIS+ master servers on the same machine is a good idea, as you can justify designating a single system for these services. Make sure to limit access to your NIS/NIS+ server by not allowing user accounts, or by having strict access policies. Remember, any user with root on the system can modify any information in your NIS+ domain, and essentially have the keys to your kingdom.

Once you have chosen a stable and secure master, you may want to look at your infrastructure and decide which systems you can designate as secondary, or replica, NIS/NIS+ servers. Replica NIS/NIS+ servers provide copies of the database information provided by the NIS/NIS+ master. This is useful for two reasons. First, replicas allow you to distribute the NIS/NIS+ load among multiple systems. Having too many clients pointing at one NIS/NIS+ server can cause the server to overload, run slowly, or even fail altogether. Second, by having multiple NIS/NIS+ servers, you can provide redundancy if another NIS/NIS+ server goes off-line, either for maintenance, or because of a failure.

Replica NIS/NIS+ servers provide copies of the database information provided by the NIS/NIS+ master.

NIS/NIS+ does not require that you have any more servers than the master server, so if your NIS/NIS+ master runs well while servicing all of your NIS+ clients, and you don't feel the need for a redundant server, you may not want to have replica servers. However, a good reason to have at least one replica is so that when you take your master server off-line for maintenance, your users and systems can continue to do their work. NIS/NIS+ servers don't require a great deal of system resources, so almost any of your client systems can be configured to be a replica server.

Make sure you have at minimum two NIS+ servers on each subnet to provide redundancy. Design your NIS+ infrastructure with failures in mind, and do everything you can to minimize NIS+ outages.

DNS VS. NIS/NIS+ FOR HOSTNAME RESOLUTION

Before DNS was the preferred method for hostname resolution, many administrators managed their hostname resolutions using NIS or NIS+. This allowed the administrator to enter new hostname information into the `/etc/hosts` file managed by NIS, and then distribute the information to all of the NIS clients in the infrastructure. This was highly effective in managing smaller installations, or infrastructures that were not yet connected to the Internet. However, while this was once a valuable method of managing hostnames, as DNS became more popular and almost every infrastructure was connected to the Internet, managing hostnames through NIS developed the following drawbacks:

- The hostname information for the infrastructure was limited to the entries in the `/etc/hosts` file managed by NIS. Without access to DNS, users needed to rely on the knowledge of the administrator to populate the /etc/hosts file with important information.
- Unless DNS was also in use, systems in the infrastructure were not advertised to the Internet. Even if the client systems were connected to the Internet, IP addresses had to be used unless administrators from other sites entered information into their `/etc/hosts` files.

As you can see, managing hostname information in NIS is a very manual process, and with the thousands of changes per day on the Internet, NIS management of host information is highly impractical. About the only use of NIS-managed host information is if you have systems that are on an isolated network that do not have access to DNS servers. In this case, managing host information in NIS is highly useful.

 One use of NIS-managed host information is if you have systems that are on isolated networks that do not have access to DNS servers. In this case, managing host information in NIS is highly useful.

GATHERING YOUR FILES

Once you have your installation plan in place, you need to bring together the files you need to create the master NIS+ database. For most NIS+ installations, the number of files you need to keep track of is relatively small. However, while the number of files that comprise your setup is small, their importance is great. Treat your NIS/NIS+ files with the utmost respect. Any mistake you make here will be quickly and efficiently replicated to every system in your domain. For example, if you accidentally delete a user from the /etc/password file on your master server, within minutes the user will cease to exist in your entire infrastructure.

Treat your NIS+ files with respect. Any mistake you make here will be quickly and efficiently replicated to every system in your domain.

Almost exclusively, the files you will serve using NIS+ will reside in the /etc directory. While it may be tempting to build your NIS+ distribution in the /etc directory, remember that while all of your systems are running NIS+, when running NIS+, the master server becomes your most important system. If NIS+ fails on the master server, then it is possible that every system in your environment will fail also. Additionally, you may end up locked out of your NIS+ master, which may cause you to have to reboot the system or even reinstall the operating system to obtain access. A valuable tool when managing your NIS+ files is a *version control system.* Version control software keeps track of changes you make to a file, and allows you to restore to any of the previous versions of the file. This is useful if you introduce a problem by editing files, as you can "back out" your changes without having to remember exactly what you modified in the file.

Whenever possible, use a version control system such as RCS or SCCS to maintain the integrity of the NIS/NIS+ files and reduce the chance of errors, especially if you have multiple administrators managing your NIS/NIS+ installation.

You will need to create a directory in which to store your NIS+ information, such as /var/nis or /usr/nis/etc. NIS+ is very configurable and will prompt you to define your install directory. However, it is highly recommended that you put the files in a safe and stable place such as the local disk on your NIS+ server, which should be a secure system with limited user access. Another advantage of having the NIS+ directory on a disk local to the NIS+ master is that you prevent the chance of NFS-related failures. The important part is that you want to store your files in a safe place, and whenever possible, use a version control system to maintain the integrity of the NIS+ files.

For our purposes, we will create the directory /var/nis to house our installation. Once you've created the directory, you should bring in a copy of each file you wish to share through NIS+. Again, for purposes of discussion, we will serve the /etc/hosts, /etc/passwd, and /etc/shadow files.

Network Information System

The Network Information System (NIS) was developed by Sun Microsystems to aid in the administration of distributed networks. NIS provides centralized control of configuration files utilized by UNIX workstations. It was later followed by NIS+, which has more functionality. NIS+, however, does not run on all of the major UNIX operating systems, so NIS is still widely used. We will begin by covering NIS, and then provide information on NIS+.

The configuration files used in NIS are grouped together into domains. A simple rule to follow in NIS domain name selection is to use your DNS domain. The most common configuration files distributed by NIS are summarized in Table 7.1.

Table 7.1	NIS Files and Maps		
File	Information	Maps	DBM Files
/etc/passwd	User ID, Group ID, Password, Name, Shell, Home directory	Passwd.byname Passwd.byuid	Passwd.byname.dir Passwd.byname.pag Passwd.byuid.dir Passwd.byuid.pag
/etc/group	Groups and members by user ID	Group.bygid Group.byname	Group.bygid Group.bygid.pag Group.byname.dir Group.byname.pag
/etc/hosts	Hostnames and IP addresses	Hosts.byaddr Hosts.byname	Hosts.byaddr.dir Hosts.byaddr.pag Hosts.byname.dir Hosts.byname.pag
/etc/networks	Name and IP address	Networks.byaddr Networks.byname	Networks.byaddr.dir Networks.byaddr.pag Networks.byname.dir Networks.byname.pag
/etc/services	Service names, port numbers/protocol	Services.byname	Services.byname.dir Services.byname.pag
/etc/protocols	Official protocol name, protocol number, and aliases	Protocols.byname Protocols.bynumber	Protocols.byname.dir Protocols.byname.pag Protocols.bynumber.dir Protocols.bynumber.pag
netgroup	Hostname, username, and domain name	Netgroup.byhost Netgroup.byuser	Netgroup.byhost Netgroup.byuser

NIS converts the information contained in text files into NIS maps. The maps are derived from DBM database files. DBM database files consist of a key value and information associated with the key. Information lookup is accomplished by matching the key value. Some configuration files contain information requiring the generation of multiple maps with different key values. The `passwd` file is a good example. UNIX provides two functions to look up information about a user. One function utilizes the user's login name and the other utilizes the user's ID (UID). NIS generates two maps with key values of the login name (`passwd.byname`) and the UID (`passwd.byuid`) for the `passwd` file. DBM database files are actually comprised of two files. The hashed index file has a `.dir` extension and the data file has a `.pag` extension. This allows much faster lookup of information than a sequential scan of an ASCII file.

NIS uses the client/server model to distribute information. There is one master server that maintains the master configuration files for the domain (the master server can serve multiple domains) on a local filesystem. The NIS maps are located under the `/var/yp` directory on the master server. Changes are made to the configuration files, a make is performed in the `/var/yp` directory, and new maps are built and pushed to slave servers for all changed files. Slave servers have the domain maps "pushed" from the master server, or they can "pull" the maps from the master server. Clients "bind" to a server (master or slave) and query the server for information contained in a map.

The next few sections will cover the important basics of NIS administration. We will assume that NIS is not running on our example network. The first section will cover the steps required to set up the NIS master server. The second section will cover creation of a slave server. The third section will cover the set up of an NIS client and explain the process of binding. The final section will cover important NIS commands.

NIS MASTER SERVER CREATION

The installation of an NIS master server will be covered in three steps. The first step will be the initialization of the master server's NIS maps. The second step will be enabling the `rpc.yppasswdd` daemon. The final step will be to ensure that the NIS services will start automatically at boot.

Initialization

The first step is to carefully select your master server. This process was covered earlier in the chapter. You also need to have the slave server names. The NIS maps are based on configuration files utilized by UNIX to aid in the boot process and limit access to a workstation. The man pages of `ypinit` or `ypfiles` contain a listing of the files that will generate NIS maps for

your version of UNIX. Edit the configuration files that will be part of the NIS
domain maps. Make sure to delete any lines containing +::0:0:: (This
notation will be explained in the "NIS Client" section). It is important that
only valid information is contained in these files. These files control access to
your NIS domain.

NIS adds a special file, called a netgroup file, to aid in the administration
of the domain. The netgroup file must be created by the administrator and is
only accessible via NIS. Create a simple netgroup file in the /etc directory.
A netgroup is composed of the following values:

```
(hostname, username, domain name)
```

A blank in a field indicates a wildcard, and a dash (-) means the field
can take no value. Netgroups are used primarily in /etc/passwd and
/etc/exports(/etc/dfs/dfstab). The hostname field is ignored
when utilized in the /etc/passwd file. The username field is ignored
when used in the /etc/exports or /etc/dfs/dfstab file. The domain name field is useful when multiple NIS domains exist on the network.
We will examine the following examples of netgroups.

- ```
  accounting (-, asmith, sniglets.com),
  (-,bjones,sniglets.com), (-,dwebb,sniglets.com)
  ```
- ```
  accounting-hosts
  (pencil.sniglets.com,,sniglets.com),
  (pen.sniglets.com,,sniglets.com)
  ```
- ```
  systems (pencil.sniglets.com,dwebb,),
  (pen.sniglets.com,ldh,)
  ```
- ```
  accountsys accounting, systems
  ```

The first netgroup, accounting, would be used in the passwd file.
The netgroup accounting would grant login permission to usernames
asmith, bjones and dwebb. The second netgroup, accounting-hosts,
would be used to grant NFS permissions to machines pencil.sniglets.
com and pen.sniglets.com by adding the netgroup to the /etc/ex-
ports (/etc/dfs/dfstab) file. The final netgroup, systems, could be
utilized in the passwd or exports(dfstab) file. NIS ignores the hostname
field in the passwd file and the username field in the exports/dfstab
file. A netgroup can incorporate other netgroups. The final netgroup, ac-
countsys, consists of the accounting and systems netgroups.

The domain name must be set to configure NIS. We recommend
using the DNS domain name for your NIS domain name. We will use
sniglets.com as our domain name and the master server will be
called master.sniglets.com. Set the domain name with the following
command:

```
#domainname sniglets.com
```

The `ypinit` command initializes a machine to become a master or slave server. To set up a master server, enter

```
#ypinit -m
```

You will be prompted for the names of additional slave servers. The slave servers do not have to be running NIS. Upon completion of the `ypinit` command, you should have a set of NIS maps for the `sniglets.com` domain under the `/var/yp/sniglets.com` directory.

The configuration files that build the NIS maps are currently located in the default location (`/etc` directory) on the master server. This allows any user in the NIS domain to be able to log in to the master server. This is not a good idea. The master server should be a secure workstation with only administrators having login privileges. Fixing this problem requires moving the NIS domain's password file (`/etc/passwd`) to a different location. For consistency and ease of use, copy all of the text configuration files to a new directory (`/var/yp/files`). This allows configuration of the NIS master server using local configuration files and maintains the NIS database in a separate location. Moving the configuration files to the `/var/yp/files` directory requires modification of the `Makefile` in the `/var/yp` directory. The following example contains a portion of `/var/yp/Makefile` for a Linux NIS master server. Skip down to the lines that begin with the following:

```
GROUP      = $ (YPPWDDIR)/group
```

This is the portion of the `Makefile` that determines which text configuration files will be utilized to construct the NIS maps. All of the configuration files are preceded with either the `YPPWDDIR` or `YPSRCDIR` variables. Since we have copied all of the configuration files to `/var/yp/files`, we need to change each one of these variables to point to the new location. To do this, we edit the `Makefile` and change the entries as depicted in Table 7.2.

Table 7.2	Changing the Location of NIS Configuration Files	
Current Line	Replacement Lines
`YPSRCDIR = /etc`	`#YPSRCDIR = /etc` `YPSRCDIR = /var/yp/files`
`YPPWDDIR = /etc`	`#YPPWDDIR = /var/yp/files`

`domainname` used without an argument will display the domain name of the system. If an argument is used, the domain name is set to that. `ypinit` initializes a system to be an NIS server.

```
#
# Makefile for the NIS databases
#
# This Makefile should only be run on the NIS master server of a domain.
# All updated maps will be pushed to all NIS slave servers listed in the
# /var/yp/ypservers file. Please make sure that the hostnames of all
# NIS servers in your domain are listed in /var/yp/ypservers.
#
# This Makefile can be modified to support more NIS maps if desired.
#

#
# These are the source directories for the NIS files; normally
# that is /etc, but you may want to move the source for the passwd
# and group files to (for example) /var/yp/ypfiles. The directory
# for passwd, group, and shadow is defined by YPPWDDIR; the rest is
# taken from YPSRCDIR.
#
YPSRCDIR = /etc
YPPWDDIR = /etc
YPBINDIR = /usr/lib/yp
YPSBINDIR = /usr/sbin
YPDIR = /var/yp
YPMAPDIR = $(YPDIR)/$(DOMAIN)


# These are the files from which the NIS databases are built. You may edit
# these to taste in the event that you wish to keep your NIS source files
# separate from your NIS server's actual configuration files.
#
GROUP       = $(YPPWDDIR)/group
PASSWD      = $(YPPWDDIR)/passwd
SHADOW      = $(YPPWDDIR)/shadow
GSHADOW     = $(YPPWDDIR)/gshadow
ADJUNCT     = $(YPPWDDIR)/passwd.adjunct
ALIASES     = $(YPSRCDIR)/aliases  # aliases could be in /etc or /etc/mail
#ALIASES     = /etc/aliases
ETHERS      = $(YPSRCDIR)/ethers      # ethernet addresses (for rarpd)
BOOTPARAMS  = $(YPSRCDIR)/bootparams # for booting Sun boxes (bootparamd)
HOSTS       = $(YPSRCDIR)/hosts
NETWORKS    = $(YPSRCDIR)/networks
PROTOCOLS   = $(YPSRCDIR)/protocols
PUBLICKEYS  = $(YPSRCDIR)/publickey
RPC         = $(YPSRCDIR)/rpc
SERVICES    = $(YPSRCDIR)/services
NETGROUP    = $(YPSRCDIR)/netgroup
NETID       = $(YPSRCDIR)/netid
AMD_HOME    = $(YPSRCDIR)/amd.home
AUTO_MASTER = $(YPSRCDIR)/auto.master
```

```
AUTO_HOME    = $(YPSRCDIR)/auto.home


YPSERVERS = $(YPDIR)/ypservers # List of all NIS servers for a domain
```

rpc.yppasswdd

Users must be able to change their passwords on any NIS client. The master NIS server must be running the `rpc.yppasswdd` deamon to allow users to change their passwords. This daemon accepts command-line options that allow you to specify the location of the `passwd` file and to execute the `make` command in the `/var/yp` directory. The format for passing options to `rpc.yppasswdd` is different for the different versions of UNIX and should be confirmed by examining the man pages. Table 7.3 contains the locations of the scripts to update to specify the location of the `passwd` file (`/var/yp/files`, in our example) for the `rpc.yppasswdd` daemon.

Startup Scripts

Each version of UNIX has a different startup script file. Table 7.4 contains startup files to edit for the `domain name`, `ypserv`, and `ypbind` daemons.

We will use a Red Hat Linux 6.1 system to examine the startup scripts to ensure the start of NIS services at boot.

1. Change directory (`cd`) to `/etc/rc.d/init.d` and do a directory listing (`ls`), as shown in Figure 7.1.
2. Confirm that a startup script exists for `ypserv`, `ypbind`, and `yppasswdd`. If a script is missing you will have to reinstall the module with RPM.
3. `cd` to `/etc/rc.d/rc.3` and do an `ls` (Figure 7.2). This directory contains scripts for services that must be started for full multi-user

Table 7.3	**Startup Scripts for** `rpc.yppasswdd`
Version	File
AIX	`/etc/rc.nfs`
HPUX	`/etc/rc.config.d/namesrvs`
Linux	`/etc/rc.d/init.d/yppasswdd`
Solaris	`/etc/init.d/rpc`

Table 7.4	**Domain Name Startup Scripts**	
UNIX Version	Startup Script File	Action Required
AIX	`/etc/rc.nfs`	Insert domain name and uncomment the `domain name`, `ypbind`, and `ypserv` lines.
HPUX	`/etc/rc.config.d/namesvrs`	Set following variables: `NIS_MASTER_SERVER=1` `NIS_DOMAIN="sniglets.com"` `NIS_CLIENT=1`
Linux	`/etc/sysconfig/network` `/etc/yp.conf` `/etc/ypserv.conf`	Set variables: `NISDOMAIN=sniglets.com` Set for broadcast or `hostname`. Configuration file for `ypser`.
SOLARIS	`/etc/defaultdomain`	Create the file and enter your domain name (`sniglets.com`).

mode. Files beginning with an S are start process files; K files are kill process files. The files are processed in ASCII sequence.

4. Create an S file to start `ypbind`, `ypserv`, and `yppasswdd`. The startup scripts already exist in `/etc/rc.d/init.d`. Now create a symbolic link back to `/etc/rc.d/init.d` for each of the services. If S files already exist, skip to Step 6.

5. The startup order should be `ypserv`, `ypbind`, and `yppasswdd`. NIS uses the RPC protocol. The `portmapper` daemon must be running for NIS to work properly. The file `S11portmap` starts the

apmd	gpm	killall	netfs	portmap	rwhod	xfs
arpwatch	halt	kudzu	network	random	sendmail	ypbind
atd	identd	linuxconf	nfs	routed	single	yppasswdd
crond	inet	lpd	nfslock	rstatd	smb	ypserv
	functions	keytable	named	pcmcia	rusersd	syslog

Figure 7.1 `ls` of `/etc/rc.d/init.d` directory.

K05innd	K20rwalld	K45arpwatch	K80nscd	S20random	S75keytable
K08autofs	K20rwhod	K45named	K88ypserv	S30syslog	S85gpm
K10xntpd	K25squid	K50snmpd	K92apmd	S40atd	S85httpd
K15postgresql	K30mcserv	K55routed	K96pcmcia	S40crond	S90xfs
K15sound conf	K30sendmail	K601pd	S10network	S50inet	S991inux-
K20bootparamd	K34yppasswdd	K60mars-nwe	S11portmap	S60nfs	S991ocal
K20rstatd	K35dhcpd	K68ipsec	S60nfslock		
K20rusersd	K35smb	K75gated	S15netfs	S72amd	

Figure 7.2 ls of /etc/rc.d/rc3.d directory.

portmapper daemon. A selection of 12 ensures that the portmap-per is running and there isn't a conflict with any other service.

6. As root in the /etc/rc.d/rc3.d directory, execute the following commands:

ln -s /etc/rc.d/init.d/ypserv S12ypserv

ln -s /etc/rc.d/init.d/ypbind S13ypbind

ln -s /etc/rc.d/init.d/yppasswdd S12yppasswdd

7. Next, cd to /etc/rc.d/rc.1 and do an ls (Figure 7.3). This is the single-user mode run level; NIS services should not be running at this run level.

8. Create links back to startup scripts in /etc/rc.d/init.d using a K prefix. Reverse the order of shutdown, and stop before the portmapper daemon.

ln -s /etc/rc.d/init.d/ypserv K87ypserv

ln -s /etc/rc.d/init.d/ypbind K86ypbind

ln -s /etc/rc.d/init.d/yppasswdd K85yppasswdd

9. The final acid test of your NIS master server installation is a reboot. Reboot the machine and check to see that the ypserv, ypbind, and rpc.yppasswdd daemons are running. Check the server by using the commands ypwhich, ypcat, and ypmatch, which are re-viewed in the "NIS Commands" section.

K001linuxconf	K20rstatd	K35smb	K60crond	K90network	S20random
K05keytable	K20rusersd	K45named	K601pd	K95kudzu	
K10xfs	K20rwhod	K50inet	K75netfs	K96pcmcia	
K15gpm	K30sendmail	K55routed	K84apmd	K99syslog	
K20nfs	K34yppasswdd	K60atd	K89portmap	S00single	

Figure 7.3 `ls` of `/etc/rc.d/rc3.d` directory.

It is very probable that one of your NIS servers may be performing multiple functions on the network. A function like email requires access to the `passwd` file for successful delivery to all accounts. It is much easier and more efficient to have all of the NIS servers be clients. Actions outlined in Table 7.4 will start the `ypbind` daemon at boot.

For those who are command-line challenged, AIX and HPUX offer a GUI alternative to the above procedures. AIX allows you to create an NIS master with the `smit mkmaster` command, which is a graphical front-end to set up the NIS master server. HPUX allows you to create a master server in SAM under the "Networking and Communications" area. All of the above steps can be accomplished in these GUI tools.

NIS SLAVE SERVER CREATION

The first step is to ensure that the NIS master server is up and running NIS for this domain.

1. Set the domain name on the host to be a slave server as outlined in the "Startup Scripts" section.
2. Execute the following command:

   ```
   # ypinit -s master.sniglets.com
   ```

3. The `ypinit` command will copy the complete set of NIS maps for this domain from the master server (`master.sniglets.com`) and place them in the `/var/yp/sniglets.com` directory.
4. Linux slave servers will require the same startup script modifications as outlined in the "Startup Scripts" section. HPUX will require a slight modification to the actions required in Table 7.4. Leave `NIS_MAS-TER_SERVER=0` and change `NIS_SLAVE_SERVER=1`.
5. Do not start the `rpc.yppasswdd` daemon on the slave server.

NIS CLIENT

The process of making a machine part of an NIS domain requires these steps:

1. Set the domain name on the local machine with the `domainname` command.

2. Start the `ypbind` daemon as follows:

   ```
   # ypbind
   ```

3. Now enable the changing of passwords for users. Go to the directory (`cd`) that contains the `passwd` program. Execute the following:

   ```
   # mv passwd passwd.orig
   ```

   ```
   # chmod 0700 passwd.orig
   ```

   ```
   # ln -s yppasswd passwd
   ```

Now a user can invoke either `passwd` or `yppasswd` and their changes will be passed to the NIS system.

The procedures to set the domain name at boot are covered in the "Startup Scripts" section. Do not enable the `ypserv` or `rpc.yppasswdd` daemon.

Binding is the association of an NIS server with a domain. This binding information is stored in the `/var/yp/binding` directory in a file utilizing the domain name. The `ypbind` daemon provides all client processes requiring NIS services on the workstation with the address of the NIS server. The `ypbind` daemon will attempt to bind to another NIS server on the network when an NIS server crashes or a timeout occurs on an NIS RPC request (usually two or three minutes).

The `/etc/nsswitch.conf` file controls the use of NIS maps on Solaris, HPUX, and Linux machines. The following example is the `nss-witch.conf` file from a Red Hat 6.1 workstation. Each line contains the name of the file, order of search, and optional actions. The `compat` entry is valid only for the `passwd` and `group` lines. The `compat` entry enables the +/- syntax (covered in the next paragraph) in the local configuration files.

Table 7.5	Lookup Action Results	
Result	Definition	Default Action
Success	Requested entry returned.	Return
Notfound	Lookup OK; item not found.	Continue
Unavail	Lookup service is unavailable.	Continue
Tryagain	Lookup service temporarily unavailable.	Continue

The dns entry is only valid for hosts. Table 7.5 contains the four results that can occur for a lookup action. The entry for hosts indicates that if the lookup process cannot find the request through dns or nis, it will return and not check the local /etc/hosts file. AIX uses the +/- syntax to access NIS map information.

```
passwd:      compat
group:       compat

# consult /etc "files" only if nis is down.
hosts:        dns nis [NOTFOUND=return] files
networks:    nis [NOTFOUND=return] files
protocols:   nis [NOTFOUND=return] files
rpc:         nis [NOTFOUND=return] files
ethers:      nis [NOTFOUND=return] files
netmasks:    nis [NOTFOUND=return] files
bootparams:     files nis
publickey:   nis [NOTFOUND=return] files


netgroup:    nis

automount:   files nis
aliases:     files

# for efficient getservbyname() avoid nis
services:    files nis
sendmailvars:   files
```

Setting up clients to use NIS maps is very simple. The following example is an /etc/passwd file that has been NIS-enabled. The lines beginning with a + or − refer to the NIS maps. The +@sysadmin line will allow all user-names in the netgroup sysadmin to log in to this workstation. Conversely, the -@badpeople line will not allow any username in the badpeople net-group to log in to this workstation. The line +metasoft grants login privi-leges to username metasoft and -asmith prevents username asmith from logging in. If you want everyone in the NIS passwd file to have access to a workstation, you would use the line:

```
+::0:0:::

root:Wv92xdAiDu1dY:0:3::/:/sbin/sh
daemon:*:1:5::/:/sbin/sh
bin:*:2:2::/usr/bin:/sbin/sh
sys:*:3:3::/:
adm:*:4:4::/var/adm:/sbin/sh
lp:*:9:7::/var/spool/lp:/sbin/sh
nuucp:*:11:11::/var/spool/uucppublic:/usr/lbin/uucp/uucico
```

```
hpdb:*:27:1:ALLBASE:/:/sbin/sh
nobody:*:-2:60001::/:
tftp:*:10:1:TFTP user:/usr/tftpdir:/bin/false
+@sysadmin::0:0:::
+@banned:*:0:0:::/bin/no_such_shell
+@lab_tas::0:0:::
-@badpeople::0:0:::
+metasoft::0:0:::
-asmith::0:0:::
```

 The `passwd` file is read sequentially and returns a result from the first match.

NIS COMMANDS

NIS commands can be broken into two groups. The first group, consisting of `ypwhich`, `ypcat`, and `ypmatch` contains good commands to use in troubleshooting the NIS domain. The second group, consisting of `ypxfr` and `yppush`, is utilized by the NIS servers to move maps from the master to the slave servers.

 `ypwhich` returns the name of the server to which a client is bound. The -m option provides a listing of available maps.

`ypcat` provides a listing of an NIS map.

`ypmatch` returns the match of a search key within a map, if any exist.

`ypxfr` transfers NIS maps from the master server to one slave.

`yppush` is used only on the server to transfer files to a slave.

Troubleshooting NIS

The first step in troubleshooting NIS problems is determining if the client is bound to a server. The `ypwhich` command, without any options, will return the name of the server the client is bound to or a message stating that the workstation is not bound. If the workstation is not bound, check for functional NIS servers on the network. If the workstation is bound to a valid server, enter `ypwhich` with the `-m` option. This provides a listing of all the available maps and the name of the NIS master server for each map. Missing maps will require a `ypxfr` on the server, determined with the initial `ypwhich` command. If all maps are present, you will need to move to the `ypcat` or `ypmatch` commands.

The `ypcat` and `ypmatch` commands are useful for examining the contents of NIS maps. The `ypcat` command provides a complete listing of an NIS map. The output can be "piped" to `grep` or `awk` to locate specific information related to a problem. The `ypcat` command is useful for searching the whole map for information. The `ypmatch` command provides more specific information, but requires a key and the map name to return the information associated with the key. The `ypmatch` command is very useful in debugging netgroup problems or specific username problems in the `passwd` file.

Map Transfers The master server utilizes the `yppush` command to transfer NIS maps to slave servers. The `yppush` command is used only on the master server. The command constructs a list of machines (slave servers) from the `ypservers` map for the domain. The master provides information to the slave for the transfer, and the slave server provides status back to the master on the success of the transfer. The `yppush` command is invoked when a `make` is performed in the `/var/yp` directory.

The `ypxfr` command transfers NIS maps from the master to the slave. The command is run on the slave server. It should be run periodically to ensure that all NIS maps are consistent between master and slave. All versions of UNIX provide scripts that can be run from the `crontab` to keep the maps consistent (the man page for `ypxfr` will have the location of these maps). `ypxfr` can also transfer maps from machines other than the server.

CREATING THE NIS+ MASTER

Once you've gathered your files, you are ready to begin your NIS+ installation. The two commands you need to build the NIS+ master are:

```
nisserver -r -d  sniglets.com.

nispopulate -F -p /var/nis -d sniglets.com.
```

The `nisserver` command initializes your system as an NIS+ server, creates your NIS+ file structure, and prepares you to populate your NIS+ database by using the `nispopulate` command. You will need to log in as root to execute these commands, and it is highly recommended that you work at the console of your system during the install. If you encounter problems during your NIS+ installation, you may place the system in such a state that only a root login from the console is possible.

`nisserver` initiates a system to be an NIS+ server. `nispopulate` populates the database of an NIS+ server.

Figure 7.4 shows the initiation of the `nisserver` command. Make sure that the information shown is correct, and type y. You will then be read the riot act and given an escape clause if you encounter problems. Once you are sure you're ready to proceed, type y again.

Once you've chosen to continue, your NIS+ skeleton database will be created. When this process is finished, you will be prompted for the password that you will use as the administration password for the NIS+ server, which is shown in Figure 7.5. Unless you are in a situation where users that are not part of your administration team need to access NIS+, you will probably want to use your standard root password for the server. This will help to avoid confusion later.

Once you have entered the NIS+ password, you are finished, as shown in Figure 7.6.

With the NIS+ database configured, you are now ready to insert your data into NIS+ using the `nispopulate` command. If you've been following along, you should have your files located in a directory such as `/var/nis` or `/usr/nis/etc`. For this example, we will load the files `/etc/passwd`, `/etc/shadow`, and `/etc/hosts` into our `nistest` database, using the `/nistest` directory as our depot for files.

Figure 7.4
Running
`nisserver`.

```
 Window   Edit   Options                                                  Help

 # nisserver -r -d sniglets.com
 This script sets up this machine "nisserver" as an NIS+
 root master server for domain sniglets.com..

 Domain name              : sniglets.com.
 NIS+ group               : admin.sniglets.com.
 NIS (YP) compatibility   : OFF
 Security level           : 2=DES

 Is this information correct? (type 'y' to accept, 'n' to change) y
 This script will set up your machine as a root master server for
 domain sniglets.com. without NIS compatibility at security level 2.

 WARNING: this script removes directories and files
 related to NIS+ under /var/nis directory with the
 exception of the client_info NIS_COLD_START file which
 will be renamed to <file>.no_nisplus.  If you want to save
 these files, you should abort from this script now to
 save these files first.

 WARNING: once this script is executed, you will not be able to
 restore the existing NIS+ server environment.  However, you can
 restore your NIS+ client environment using "nisclient -r"
 with the proper domain name and server information.

 Do you want to continue? (type 'y' to continue, 'n' to exit this script) y
```

Figure 7.5
Running
`nisserver`,
continued.

```
Window   Edit   Options                                            Help

setting up domain information "sniglets.com." ...

setting up switch information ...

running nisinit ...
This machine is in the "sniglets.com." NIS+ domain.
Setting up root server ...
All done.

starting root server at security level 0 to create credentials...

running nissetup to create standard directories and tables ...
org_dir.sniglets.com. created
groups_dir.sniglets.com. created
passwd.org_dir.sniglets.com. created
group.org_dir.sniglets.com. created
auto_master.org_dir.sniglets.com. created
auto_home.org_dir.sniglets.com. created
bootparams.org_dir.sniglets.com. created
cred.org_dir.sniglets.com. created
ethers.org_dir.sniglets.com. created
hosts.org_dir.sniglets.com. created
mail_aliases.org_dir.sniglets.com. created
sendmailvars.org_dir.sniglets.com. created
netmasks.org_dir.sniglets.com. created
netgroup.org_dir.sniglets.com. created
networks.org_dir.sniglets.com. created
protocols.org_dir.sniglets.com. created
rpc.org_dir.sniglets.com. created
services.org_dir.sniglets.com. created
timezone.org_dir.sniglets.com. created
client_info.org_dir.sniglets.com. created

adding credential for nisserver.sniglets.com...
Enter login password:
```

Figure 7.6
Completing
`nisserver`
installation.

```
Window   Edit   Options                                            Help

creating NIS+ administration group: admin.sniglets.com. ...
adding principal nisserver.sniglets.com. to admin.sniglets.com. ...

restarting NIS+ root master server at security level 2 ...
starting NIS+ password daemon ...
starting NIS+ cache manager ...
$ cat nisserver3
creating NIS+ administration group: admin.sniglets.com. ...
adding principal nisserver.sniglets.com. to admin.sniglets.com. ...

restarting NIS+ root master server at security level 2 ...
starting NIS+ password daemon ...
starting NIS+ cache manager ...

This system is now configured as a root server for domain sniglets.com.
You can now populate the standard NIS+ tables by using the
nispopulate script or /usr/lib/nis/nisaddent command.
#
```

The proper syntax for `nispopulate` is shown in Figure 7.7. The `-F` flag indicates we are using files to populate the database, `-p` designates our depot directory, and `-d` defines the NIS+ domain.

Once you have confirmed that you are sure and are ready to go, you will see the population process take place. For our example, we see a number of warning messages since we have chosen only to populate a small number of files. Figure 7.8 shows us the messages we should see during a successful NIS+ population process.

Once `nispopulate` completes, your root master is finished and you're ready to connect your first client.

 Be careful. Don't just install a root master and begin connecting clients. Before deploying NIS+ throughout your network, test it first using a single test client.

CONNECTING CLIENT SYSTEMS TO NIS+

Once you have your NIS+ server in place, adding clients is a rather simple operation, as shown in Figure 7.9.

The key pieces of information you need to know to attach your NIS+ client are your domain name, your NIS+ root password, and the name or IP address of your NIS+ root server. If you are using only NIS+ to resolve host-

Figure 7.7
Using
`nispopulate`.

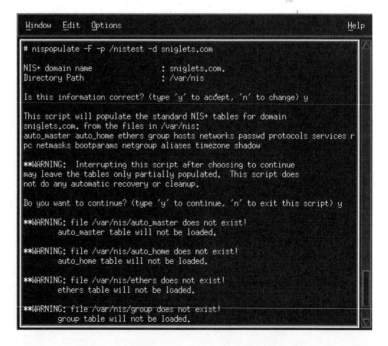

```
Window   Edit   Options                                          Help

# nispopulate -F -p /nistest -d sniglets.com

NIS+ domain name                : sniglets.com.
Directory Path                  : /var/nis

Is this information correct? (type 'y' to accept, 'n' to change) y

This script will populate the standard NIS+ tables for domain
sniglets.com. from the files in /var/nis:
auto_master auto_home ethers group hosts networks passwd protocols services r
pc netmasks bootparams netgroup aliases timezone shadow

**WARNING:  Interrupting this script after choosing to continue
may leave the tables only partially populated.  This script does
not do any automatic recovery or cleanup.

Do you want to continue? (type 'y' to continue, 'n' to exit this script) y

**WARNING: file /var/nis/auto_master does not exist!
        auto_master table will not be loaded.

**WARNING: file /var/nis/auto_home does not exist!
        auto_home table will not be loaded.

**WARNING: file /var/nis/ethers does not exist!
        ethers table will not be loaded.

**WARNING: file /var/nis/group does not exist!
        group table will not be loaded.
```

Figure 7.8
Completing
nispopulate.

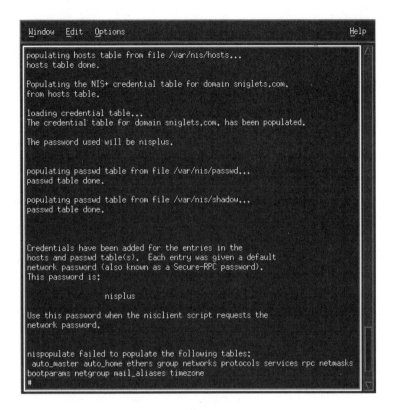

```
Window   Edit   Options                                          Help

populating hosts table from file /var/nis/hosts...
hosts table done.

Populating the NIS+ credential table for domain sniglets.com.
from hosts table.

loading credential table...
The credential table for domain sniglets.com. has been populated.

The password used will be nisplus.


populating passwd table from file /var/nis/passwd...
passwd table done.

populating passwd table from file /var/nis/shadow...
passwd table done.


Credentials have been added for the entries in the
hosts and passwd table(s).  Each entry was given a default
network password (also known as a Secure-RPC password).
This password is:

                nisplus

Use this password when the nisclient script requests the
network password.


nispopulate failed to populate the following tables:
 auto_master auto_home ethers group networks protocols services rpc netmasks
bootparams netgroup mail_aliases timezone
#
```

Figure 7.9
Using nis-
client to
connect client
systems to NIS+
servers.

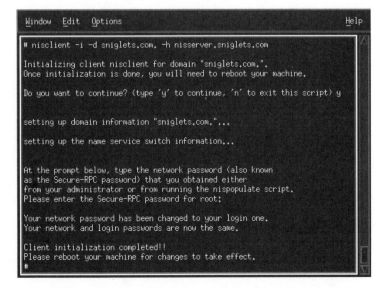

```
Window   Edit   Options                                          Help

# nisclient -i -d sniglets.com. -h nisserver.sniglets.com

Initializing client nisclient for domain "sniglets.com.".
Once initialization is done, you will need to reboot your machine.

Do you want to continue? (type 'y' to continue, 'n' to exit this script) y


setting up domain information "sniglets.com."...

setting up the name service switch information...


At the prompt below, type the network password (also known
as the Secure-RPC password) that you obtained either
from your administrator or from running the nispopulate script.
Please enter the Secure-RPC password for root:

Your network password has been changed to your login one.
Your network and login passwords are now the same.

Client initialization completed!!
Please reboot your machine for changes to take effect.
#
```

Figure 7.10
Using nisping.

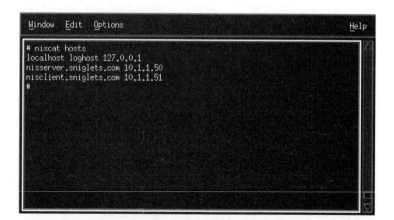

names, then you will need to use the IP address of your root master, as your
client system will not be able to resolve the root master hostname until after
your system is connected.

The first command you should execute after connecting a client system to
NIS+ is the nisping command. As shown in Figure 7.10, nisping gives
you information on your NIS+ root master, as well as the NIS+ replica (or
master if you have no replicas) you are currently using. This is a highly effective way to make sure your client is connected. This is also useful if you are
connected to an NIS+ server that is not completely broken, but performing
badly. nisping shows you which NIS+ server the client is using, allowing
the administrator to isolate a problem server.

Another useful command is niscat. As shown in Figure 7.11, niscat
will dump the contents of a NIS+ map. This is useful when you want to verify that certain information is stored in the NIS+ database. This is most useful after adding information, to determine that it has been accepted and
replicated to all servers.

Figure 7.11
Using niscat.

`nisping` provides information on the NIS+ root master you are using.

`niscat` similar to `ypcat` in NIS, it provides a listing of an NIS+ map.

Be aware that NIS+ stores its information in a non-ASCII form, so you'll need to redirect the output of `niscat` if you plan to view more than a few lines of text. For example:

```
niscat passwd | more
```

will allow you to use the `more` command to view the output. You can also redirect the output of `niscat` into a file using:

```
niscat shadow > shadow.file
```

Finally, one other nugget of wisdom that we can offer is restarting the `nis_cachemgr` daemon, which runs on every NIS+ client. This daemon stores information about your NIS+ infrastructure, including what servers to use and where they are located. If you have clients that are exhibiting strange behavior, such as hanging user logins or lack of NIS+ name resolution, or if you have experienced DNS problems or have moved NIS+ servers, stop and restart the `nis_cachemgr` daemon to see if the problem clears itself.

CREATING REPLICA NIS+ SERVERS

Like DNS, with NIS+ you want to distribute the load if you have a large environment or if your environment is geographically distributed. To do this, you need to set up secondary, or replica, NIS+ servers. Once your NIS+ root server is running, creating replica servers is a simple operation. Using the command shown in Figure 7.12, you can create a replica server running on the system `nisreplica.nistest.com`.

The -R flag to the `nisserver` command instructs the NIS+ root master on `nisserver.nistest.com` to install a replica of NIS+ on the server `nisreplica.nistest.com`, as designated by the -h flag. Answer the prompts and you're off and running. Later in this chapter, we will discuss the -Y flag and the NIS compatibility mode.

Migrating NIS Yellow Pages to NIS+

If you are currently managing a legacy Yellow Pages (YP), or simple NIS, environment, you may want to migrate to an NIS+-only infrastructure. If you can convert all of your systems to NIS+, here is a migration plan that will help you organize your move.

Figure 7.12
Creating
secondary NIS+
servers.

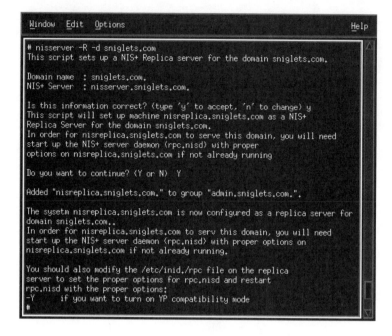

```
 Window   Edit   Options                                              Help

 # nisserver -R -d sniglets.com
 This script sets up a NIS+ Replica server for the domain sniglets.com.

 Domain name  : sniglets.com.
 NIS+ Server  : nisserver.sniglets.com.

 Is this information correct? (type 'y' to accept, 'n' to change) y
 This script will set up machine nisreplica.sniglets.com as a NIS+
 Replica Server for the domain sniglets.com.
 In order for nisreplica.sniglets.com to serve this domain, you will need
 start up the NIS+ server daemon (rpc.nisd) with proper
 options on nisreplica.sniglets.com if not already running

 Do you want to continue? (Y or N)  Y

 Added "nisreplica.sniglets.com." to group "admin.sniglets.com.".

 The sysetm nisreplica.sniglets.com is now configured as a replica server for
 domain sniglets.com..
 In order for nisreplica.sniglets.com to serv this domain, you will need
 start up the NIS+ server daemon (rpc.nisd) with proper options on
 nisreplica.sniglets.com if not already running.

 You should also modify the /etc/inid./rpc file on the replica
 server to set the proper options for rpc.nisd and restart
 rpc.nisd with the proper options:
 -Y     if you want to turn on YP compatibility mode
 #
```

1. Create an NIS+ master server. You can choose to create your new NIS+ master on its permanent home system, or on a test server. Creating the server on the permanent master server eliminates the need to re-install the master server later, but could cause problems during testing. If you are installing NIS+ for the first time, it would be more prudent to install the NIS+ master on a test server until you are more adept at handling NIS+. Also, use the same data for your NIS+ server that you are using for your NIS server.

2. Connect and test a single NIS+ client. Choose a non-critical system on which to test your NIS+ server. If you have multiple operating systems, try to connect test systems from each operating system, as different UNIX flavors may react differently to NIS+ depending on your configuration.

3. Create replica servers. Once you are sure your NIS+ installation is working, begin creating replicas, with at least two on each subnet if possible.

4. Migrate clients by subnet. Once your replica systems are up and running, begin migrating your clients systems, one subnet at a time. While migrating in this manner has no technical importance, it will help you focus on migrating all of your systems and help you make sure you don't leave any systems behind.

5. Don't turn off your old NIS systems too soon.

While it is ideal if you have a complete set of systems that can all run NIS+, it is quite possible that you will have a handful of machines with operating systems that don't support NIS+ services. Having to manage NIS and NIS+ just doubles the amount of work you have to do to maintain your environment. Fortunately, you have options when facing the NIS to NIS+ migration question.

Your first option is to upgrade all of your old non-NIS+ machines to an operating system that supports NIS+. Granted, if it were that easy, you would have probably already upgraded by now. However, make sure that if you have old operating systems in your environment that there is a good reason for them to be so far out-of-date. While NIS works very well, the security and management enhancements of NIS+ are worth the time and effort to upgrade those old systems. Given that you have decided to migrate to NIS+, plan a migration strategy that you can accomplish piecewise, maintaining your NIS infrastructure until you have completed building you new NIS+ infrastructure.

Using NIS Compatibility Mode in NIS+

If you have operating systems that don't support NIS+, or if you choose not to convert certain clients to use NIS+, you do have an option to allow you to manage only an NIS+ master server, and yet still serve NIS clients. This is through the use of *NIS compatibility mode* on your NIS+ server. While in our example we chose not to use compatibility, you may have an environment where it is required (if you have AIX or HPUX prior to version 11.0), or you may be in the process of converting from an NIS environment to NIS+. If you want NIS+ compatibility, you need to change your input to the `nis-server` command as follows:

```
#nisserver -R -Y sniglets.com
```

Running NIS+ in compatibility mode allows NIS clients to be serviced by an NIS+ server. This provides a smoother transition from NIS to NIS+. NIS clients can connect and receive all of their network information from an NIS+ server. To place an NIS+ server in compatibility mode requires the `rpc.nisd` daemon to be started with the command `rpc.nisd -Y`.

Compatibility mode has a few other limitations. There is no authentication, which allows any client to obtain information from the NIS+ tables. NIS clients will not be able to use the `yppasswd` command to change passwords. Also, NIS clients will not be able to perform any of the new functions added in NIS+ (forwarding through paths and links, security).

The NIS+ server can be configured to forward DNS queries for NIS clients. To enable this feature, the `rpc.nisd` daemon needs to be given the `-B` switch in addition to the `-Y` switch. This requires that you have a valid

`/etc/resolv.conf` file and that DNS is functioning correctly on the NIS+ server.

Merging NIS+ Domains

If you are in an older environment or you acquire other NIS+ domains, you may be asked to merge your NIS+ database with another already established domain. While on the surface this may sound simple, the process of merging NIS+ domains isn't as simple as it sounds. You can't just take all the files, concatenate them together, and expect to have a working NIS+ server!

 Merging two or more NIS+ databases is actually more difficult than creating one from scratch. You need to examine each database element to look for duplication.

Merging two or more NIS+ databases is actually exponentially more difficult than creating one from scratch. You need to examine each database element to look for duplication. You also may have stylistic differences that will require you to re-create information. When looking to merge NIS+ environments, make sure to:

- Check the `passwd` files for duplicate usernames and user IDs (UIDs). This is perhaps the most difficult part of merging NIS+ domains. Users are very protective of their identities, and if you have duplication, it may be difficult to coax one user to change their identity. Be courteous and understanding, and explain why the change is necessary. Of course, if understanding and compassion don't do the trick, make sure you let the person with the most authority keep their username unaltered!

- Given that you have to make UID changes, make sure you scan all filesystems on which that user may have owned files. Otherwise, you may leave files owned by a non-associated UID, or even worse, you may inadvertently grant ownership of files to another user.

- If you use NIS+ for hostname resolution, scan for duplicate hostnames. Just about every installation has a `mars.yourdomain.com` or `elvis.yourdomain.com`, so you'll need to motivate someone to change their hostname. This can be simple or difficult, depending on the complexity of the systems involved. Here it may not be wise to give the users a choice. You may just want to rename the server with the least amount of third-party software, network services, or user home directories. If you employ automounting, make sure you make the necessary changes there, as well as in any netgroup files.

Merging NIS+ domains is a highly administrative, manually-intensive task—something you may want to delegate to your co-ops!!! However, if you take the time to check and double-check UIDs, hostnames, netgroups, and automount points from every server and client host, you can help to make an NIS+ merger a seamless and painless process for you and your customers.

Windows 2000 Directory Services

Perhaps the most significant change between Windows NT 4.0 and Windows 2000 is the implementation of directory services. Even the most novice of Windows NT users is familiar with the concept of the Windows NT domain. The Windows NT domain provides directory services for authenticating user logons and managing access to network resources. In many respects the"flat" domain model was very limited and was not scalable. Microsoft has replaced the Windows NT 4.0 domain model with the Active Directory (AD) in Windows 2000. Active Directory essentially picks up where the Windows NT 4.0 domain stops and provides a highly scalable and intuitive directory service. This section will discuss the details of the AD in Windows 2000.

ACTIVE DIRECTORY OVERVIEW

Active Directory is an information store, or database, consisting of objects and object attributes. Everything is an object, including users, computers, and resources. Active Directory provides a consistent, reliable method of storing and accessing network information. This section will introduce you to Active Directory. While the details of *how* AD works are beyond the scope of this book, we will describe it from a functional perspective. Here, you will learn the basics of AD, a boot camp of sorts that will begin laying the tracks to understanding what is perhaps the most important new feature in Windows 2000. We will provide a framework that encompasses the structure, features, planning, and installation of AD.

ACTIVE DIRECTORY STRUCTURE

Perhaps the most significant change between Windows NT 4.0 and Windows 2000 is the directory service structure. The familiar flat domain model consisting of one or more independent domains linked via confusing trust relationships present in current Windows NT networks is almost completely gone in AD. Microsoft has morphed the NT 4.0 domain model into a robust, enterprise-level directory service. In this section, we will describe the AD hierarchy and schema, which are critical to understanding and exploiting AD.

Directory Hierarchy

In Windows NT 4.0, the domain hierarchy was built from a convoluted and complex web of multiple domains linked by confusing one- and two-way trust relationships. In AD, there is an inherent hierarchy that provides a means to create an organized, understandable, functional, and scalable domain model. The Active Directory hierarchy is shown in Figure 7.13.

This section will explain the different parts of the AD hierarchy. To understand the AD hierarchy, you must also understand the DNS naming system, as Active Directory employs the same naming scheme.

Organizational Unit The organizational unit, or OU, is the bottom-most member of the AD hierarchy. Of all the AD structures, the OU most resembles the familiar Windows NT 4.0 domain. Each OU can contain users, groups, systems, and resources, as well as other OUs. All objects in an OUs must have unique names. In our organization, $dsp.ece.gatech.edu$ would be an example of an OU. Here, user, system, and resource objects for the dsp group can be created and stored. As we begin to move up in the hierarchy, you will see the domain name shorten until we are simply at $.edu$.

Domains A domain can contain OUs and is itself contained within a tree. The domain is a logical grouping of OUs. All of the OUs within a domain trust each other and permissions can be granted across different OUs. In our organization, $ece.gatech.edu$ is an example of a domain. By now, you should begin to see how all of this is fitting together. The $ece.gatech$ $.edu$ domain provides a parent container for the more closely related OUs, such as $dsp.ece.gatech.edu$ and $cmpe.ece.gatech.edu$. In other words, it should be easy to see that the children of $ece.gatech.edu$ are much more closely related than $ece.gatech.edu$ and $me.gatech.edu$.

Figure 7.13
Active Directory
hierarchy.

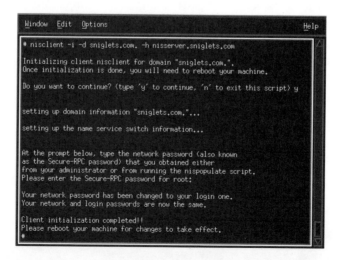

Trees A tree is a logical grouping of Windows 2000 domains. All of the domains in a tree share a common namespace. All of the child domains within a tree share a common schema and global catalog. The domain name of each child domain in the tree is equivalent to the relative name of the child domain appended with the name of the parent domain.

Forests A forest is a logical grouping of multiple domain trees that form a disjointed namespace. The different domain trees in the forest have different naming schemes, according to their domains. All of the domain trees contained in the forest share a common schema, and all domains in the forest share a common global catalog. The forest enables cross-domain communication, but each domain operates independently from the other domains.

Sites A site can be defined as a well-connected grouping of network resources. By "well-connected," we mean anything that is connected via network links of 512Kbps or higher. A site is not limited to a single geographical location. A site consists of one or more IP subnets. Sites can contain multiple domains, and a domain can span multiple sites. You should organize your site to provide the best network performance.

Schema

A schema is a set of attributes used to describe a particular object class in the AD. This section will explain objects and object classes, attributes, and how you can edit the schema to customize the directory.

Objects and Object Classes So, what is the difference between an object and an object class? Basically, an object is created from an object class, which contains all of the attributes that describe the object. The object inherits all of the properties of the object class. There are three standard object classes in AD: users, groups, and machine accounts.

User accounts in Windows 2000 are managed using the AD Users and Computers MMC snap-in shown in Figure 7.14. User accounts in the AD contain much more information than did user accounts in Windows NT 4.0, which only tracked user name, full name, description, password, and a few other pieces of information relating to profiles and rights. Most of the new attributes in Windows 2000 are optional.

Groups in Windows 2000 are very similar to groups under Windows NT 4.0. However, in keeping with the trend of expanding on Windows NT 4.0's feature set, Microsoft has provided a few new features for groups in the AD.

Groups can now be used as email lists in Microsoft Exchange 5.5. Groups can also contain the email addresses of users from different domain trees. Perhaps the most significant change is that groups can be nested within one another, reducing administrative overhead. Active Directory provides three distinct types of user groups. Universal groups can contain users and groups

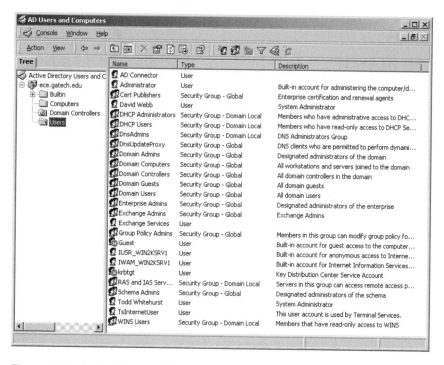

Figure 7.14 Active Directory Users and Computers MMC snap-in.

from any tree or domain in the forest, and are replicated outside of their parent domain. Universal groups appear in the global catalog, described later in this chapter. Global groups may only contain users and groups from the same domain, but are listed in the global catalog. The membership list of a global group is not published outside the domain. Last, but not least, domain local groups may contain users and groups from multiple domains, but can only be used in ACLs in the same domain. Domain local groups are not replicated outside of the domain and are not published in the global catalog. Windows 2000 also includes many built-in groups, as shown in Figure 7.15.

Machine accounts are created when any workstation joins a Windows 2000 domain. While this is very similar to the machine accounts created in Windows NT 4.0, Windows 2000 can contain machine accounts for tracking purposes, even if a machine does not participate in domain security.

Attributes Attributes are the individual pieces of information that describe the objects contained in object classes. A user object class requires attributes that are distinctly different from the attributes required by a printer object class or an application object class.

Editing the Schema   The attributes attached to an object class can be viewed and edited using the Active Directory Schema MMC snap-in shown

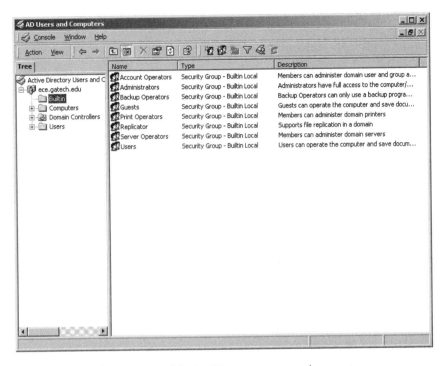

Figure 7.15 Built-in groups of Active Directory users and computers.

in Figure 7.16. Each object class includes a default set of attributes that should be more than sufficient for most organizations. However, there are situations where you may need to add a custom attribute to an object class, and you can accomplish this using the MMC snap-in.

You must manually add the Active Directory Schema snap-in to the MMC by launching the MMC interface and then adding the snap-in.

Before you can edit the schema, you must set the following Registry key:

```
HKEY_LOCAL_MACHINE\SYSTEM\CurrentControlSet\Services\NTDS\Pa
rameters\SchemaUpdateAllowed REG_DWORD = 1
```

When creating a new attribute, you will be presented with the dialog box in Figure 7.17. Schema attributes and classes cannot be deleted, so be careful when adding additional attributes to your schema.

As with all of Active Directory's objects, you can delegate control over the schema by modifying the permissions on the schema as shown in Figure 7.18.

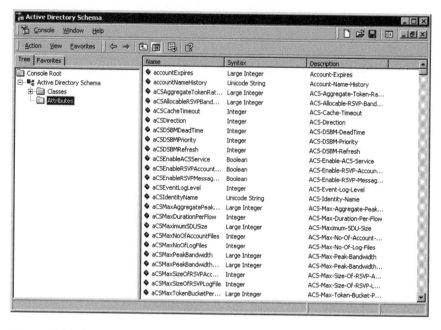

Figure 7.16 Active Directory Schema MMC snap-in.

Figure 7.17
Create New
Attribute
dialog.

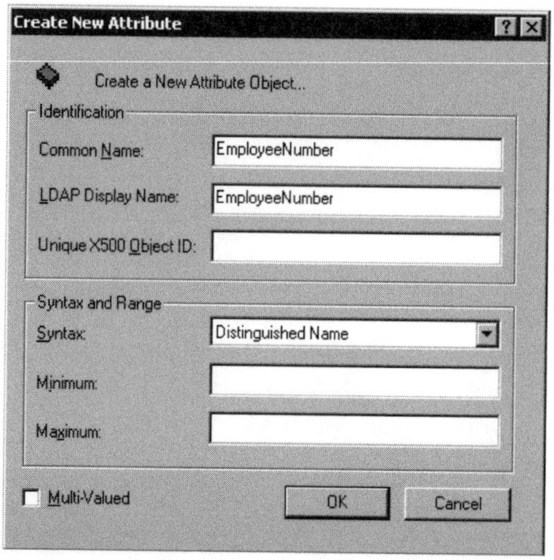

Figure 7.18
ACL editor for a
schema.

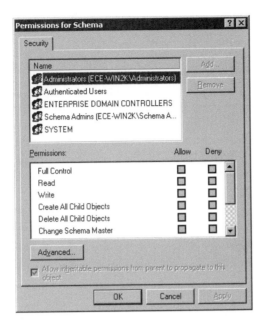

ACTIVE DIRECTORY FEATURES

Active Directory provides several new features over the traditional Windows NT domain model. Among the new features are integration with the domain name system, multi-master domain controller replication, enhanced domain security (including true parent-child relationships), a global catalog for quick searching, and the use of the industry standard Lightweight Directory Access Protocol (LDAP) for directory access. This section will provide a basic explanation of these features, which will help you to understand AD and effectively use it within your organization.

DNS Integration

Another important feature of AD is its integration with the Domain Name System (DNS). In previous versions of Windows, WINS or some other NetBIOS naming service was used to resolve Windows computer names to IP addresses. Previous versions of Windows also used WINS to locate Windows NT domain controllers on the network. Anyone who has managed a Windows NT network knows that WINS can be very tricky to bring on-line and that it doesn't always work properly. Active Directory uses the industry-standard DNS for all name resolution (WINS can be used for compatibility with older client systems), thus eliminating the need for WINS servers.

In the AD world, DNS is used for resolving Windows machine names to IP addresses, as well as for locating domain controllers and network services. Now, anyone who knows about DNS also knows that most current DNS servers do not have provisions for entries describing Windows domain controllers and network services. Of course, the DNS server packaged with Windows 2000 provides the necessary additions to support Dynamic Update (RFC 2136) and Service Resource Records (SRV RRs). DNS Dynamic Update allows servers and clients to publish DNS updates directly to the DNS server, without administrative intervention. Service Resource Records allow client workstations to locate network services (such as LDAP, which is used by AD and is discussed later in this chapter) by querying DNS for a `ser-vice.protocol.domain` record. For instance, to locate an AD server on our network, a DNS client would query DNS for `ldap.tcp.ece.gat-ech.edu`, which should point to the closest LDAP server on the network.

Fortunately, for those of us who prefer a UNIX-based DNS server, the latest version of the popular BIND server also supports DNS Dynamic Update and Service Resource Records. This allows both UNIX and Windows 2000 DNS servers to provide fully functional name resolution services for your UNIX and Windows 2000 systems.

Many of you are probably not running the latest version of BIND. If you wish to use a UNIX-based DNS system for Windows 2000, you must upgrade to the newer version of BIND to support Service Resource Records.

Domain Controllers and Partitioning

What you currently know about Windows NT domain controllers is about to drastically change. Currently, a Windows NT domain consists of a single Primary Domain Controller (PDC), one or more Backup Domain Controllers (BDCs), and member servers and workstations. The days of PDCs and BDCs are gone with the introduction of Active Directory.

In the AD world, all domain controllers are created equal; that is, there is no longer a master-slave relationship between domain controllers. Each domain controller in an AD domain can service logon requests, receive updates, and replicate those updates to other domain controllers in the domain. In large networks, there can be literally hundreds of thousands of objects in the AD. However, it doesn't make much sense for every domain controller to manage the entire AD database individually. Instead, you can partition your domain controllers such that each one manages a different section of the database. Not only does this reduce the load on any single domain controller, it also will allow you to logically assign "tasks" to each domain controller. While this is not necessary in small domains, the benefits become clear when we scale to domains that contain several thousand or even over a million objects.

Now that you know what a domain controller is, and how partitioning can be used, you can learn what domain controllers do. Active Directory domain controllers perform the following functions:

- All domain controllers store a copy of the AD database, can answer queries to the database, manage updates to the database, and replicate any updates to other domain controllers.
- Updates to the directory do not occur on all domain controllers at once. Instead, the update actually occurs on one domain controller and the updates are replicated to other domain controllers at intervals determined by the administrator. The administrator can also define how much information is replicated at each replication interval.
- Critical updates, such as user account deactivation, are immediately replicated to other AD domain controllers.
- Active Directory domain controllers all function as peers and there is no single master domain controller. Because of this multi-master replication, some domain controllers may contain different information until replication completes.
- Since every domain controller can serve as a master, the AD is truly fault-tolerant. In the event that one domain controller fails, it is not necessary to "promote" another domain controller to be the "master".
- Each domain controller can perform all required functions for users interacting with the domain, such as user logons and locating resource objects.

Replication

Replication is the means by which all of this information gets exchanged between domain controllers, and how multiple domain controllers receive updates and keep the databases synchronized.

Replication within an AD site is performed only by and among domain controllers. Replication between domain controllers in the same site and domain is carried out using a ring topology. The ring is structured such that each domain controller can directly replicate with two other domain controllers, thus minimizing the chances that replication will fail if one domain controller is temporarily down. The directory updates flow around the ring from one domain controller to another until each domain controller has received the updates. In the event that a domain controller is added to or removed from an AD domain, the replication ring is automatically reconfigured to account for the addition or removal.

Security

Like any other database, the AD database must have a security policy associated with it. Each object and object attribute in the AD has an Access Control List, or ACL, associated with it. The ACL specifies who has access to an object or attribute, and what level of access is granted. Permissions on AD objects can be managed using the `Delegation of Control Wizard` shown in Figures 7.19 and 7.20. The wizard allows different levels of permissions to be assigned to both groups and individual users.

Delegated Administration The AD security model provides the new and very useful concept of delegated administration. Delegated administration allows administrators to assign various administrative tasks to different users, while not granting more access than is necessary (such as granting Domain Admin status to a user in Windows NT 4.0). Delegated administration can be assigned over subtrees, or even individual objects in the directory. New objects added to the directory will inherit the ACL associated with their parent container.

Explicit Trusts In Windows NT 4.0, trusts between domains could be one-way or two-way, depending on the configuration desired by the administrator. Part of the parent-child relationship in AD is the concept of an *explicit trust*. Child domains explicitly trust their parent domains without any administrator intervention. Figure 7.21 details this concept.

As you can see from the figure, the child domains automatically trust the parent domain. In Windows NT 4.0 domains, this is where the buck stopped—but not in Active Directory.

Figure 7.19
Delegation of
Control
Wizard—Users
or Groups
page.

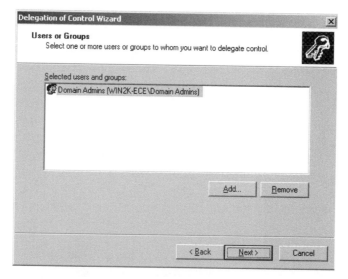

Figure 7.20

Delegation
of Control
Wizard—Tasks
to Delegate
page.

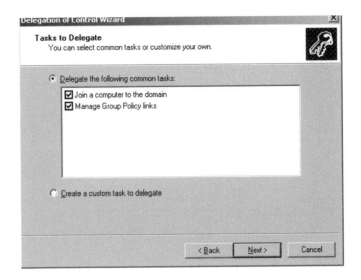

Implicit Trusts Windows 2000 supports another new concept called *implicit trusts*. Basically, this means that if Domain A trusts Domain B, and Domain A trusts Domain C, then there is an automatic *implicit trust* between Domain B and Domain C. Figure 7.25 extends the concept presented in Figure 7.22.

As you can see from Figure 7.22, `dsp.ece.gatech.edu` and `telecom.ece.gatech.edu` are both children of `ece.gatech.edu` and explicitly trust the parent domain. Because of this explicit trust relationship between parent and children, there is an implied or *implicit trust* between the `dsp.ece.gatech.edu` and `telecom.ece.gatech.edu` domains. This new trust model allows users from all three domains to access resources in any of the three domains, provided the administrator has granted the appropriate permissions.

Global Catalog

The global catalog is a central repository for information about all of the objects contained in a tree or forest. Perhaps the best feature of the global catalog is that Windows 2000 automatically generates its index through normal replication processes. The global catalog does not contain the entire di-

Figure 7.21

Explicit trusts in
Active Directory.

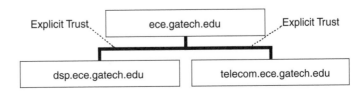

Figure 7.22
Implicit trusts in
Active Directory.

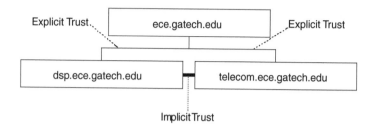

rectory—why do that when you could just query the individual domain controllers? Instead, the global catalog contains a subset of values, those most frequently used in search operations, to allow you to quickly search and locate objects anywhere in the tree or forest.

The global catalog is actually a service that can be provided by one of your domain controllers. By default, the first domain controller installed in a new forest is automatically designated as a global catalog server. You should keep in mind that the global catalog server needs to be capable of supporting from several hundred thousand to over one million objects. As your network grows, you can designate additional domain controllers to be global catalog servers, helping to distribute the load. You can use the Schema Manager MMC snap-in to configure what attributes are included in your global catalog. The Sites and Servers MMC snap-in can be used to designate additional global catalog servers.

Finding Network Resources The `Find Computer` command was commonly seen in previous versions of Windows. However, it is extremely limited and provides limited help in locating network resources such as printers, shares, applications, etc. With AD and the global catalog, any object can be located in the directory. Not only that, but the directory can be searched for objects with specific attributes, such as printers that allow printing at a given resolution. Figure 7.23 shows you an example of a search window for locating a network printer.

Managing the Index The global catalog index, as indicated above, contains a subset of all the possible attributes in the directory. The purpose behind this is to allow a user to quickly locate any network object, while not having to index all of the properties of each object. For this reason, only the most common attributes are included in the global catalog index. The Schema MMC snap-in can be used to customize which attributes are included in the global catalog.

Active Directory Services Interface

The Active Directory Services Interface (ADSI) allows applications to interact with a directory while remaining ignorant of the underlying protocols.

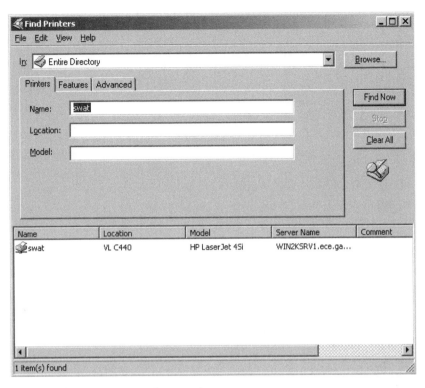

Figure 7.23 Resource search example.

This allows administrators to write programs that can access directories from Windows NT 4.0, NetWare, and LDAP-based directories. ADSI greatly eases the programming interface to the directory. For more information on using ADSI, download the ADSI documentation from Microsoft's Web site.

PLANNING FOR ACTIVE DIRECTORY

Planning for implementing AD can be a very exhausting task. Needless to say, it would be nearly impossible to discuss all of the different factors involved in the process. However, we can offer a set of general guidelines that will get you started. Keep in mind, however, that your implementation of AD will reflect your organizational structure. There are three general categories that you should look at when planning your AD implementation: namespace, site, and organizational units.

Namespace

Let's assume for a minute that your organization has a presence on the Internet. You must decide before implementing AD whether you wish to extend your existing namespace to your Windows 2000 domains, or if you wish to create a new internal namespace. There is no best way to choose which paradigm to use; it simply depends on your presence and your organization's needs. By extending your existing namespace, you will have consistent tree names for both internal and external resources, as well as the ability to use the same user names for both internal and external resources. You can request a second DNS namespace for internal use to separate your internal resources from your external resources. Using two namespaces will provide a clearer definition and ease the management of your internal and external resources, but you will have to reserve two DNS namespaces to accomplish this.

Site

Planning a good site is perhaps the most critical of the phases for planning your AD implementation. Remember that a site can be defined as a well-connected grouping of network resources. By "well connected," we mean anything that is connected via networks of 512Kbps or higher. Therefore, sites are not limited to physical locations, but can actually consist of multiple independent subnets linked by reliable network connections. Sites can include multiple domains, and domains can span multiple sites. It is important to include at least one AD domain controller on each subnet in a site. You should configure your domain to replicate at the times when it will cause the least amount of interruption to the network. One important point to remember is that intra-site replication occurs much more frequently than inter-site replication.

Organizational Units

Simply put, organizational units are logical groupings of objects that reflect the structure of your organization. For instance, you might want to place users in your domain into different OUs depending on the type of user they are. As an example, you could create an OU for faculty users and a separate OU for student users to control resource access individually.

INSTALLING ACTIVE DIRECTORY

Installing Active Directory is actually quite simple. One of the nice features of AD is the ability to add or remove the AD services on any Windows 2000 server. This allows you to change a server's role without having to perform a complete installation. This section will walk you through a basic AD installation.

1. After you have installed Windows 2000 Server, the `Configure Your Server` window will be displayed when you log on. If it is not displayed, you can launch it from the `Start` menu by selecting `Programs/`

Figure 7.24
Windows 2000
Configure Your
Server window.

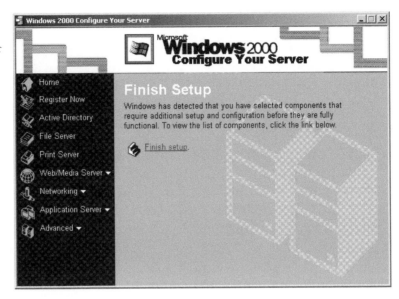

Administrative Tools/Configure Your Server. The Windows 2000 Configure Your Server window is shown in Figure 7.24.

2. Click the Active Directory item on the left side of the window and select Start the Active Directory Wizard. Once the Active Directory Installation Wizard is running, click the Next button to display the Domain Controller Type screen in Figure 7.25.

3. Select Domain controller for a new domain and click Next. The Create Tree or Child Domain selection screen is displayed. Select Create a new domain tree and click Next. The Create

Figure 7.25
Domain
Controller
Type selection
screen.

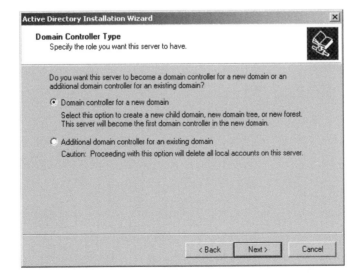

Figure 7.26
New Domain
Name
configuration
screen.

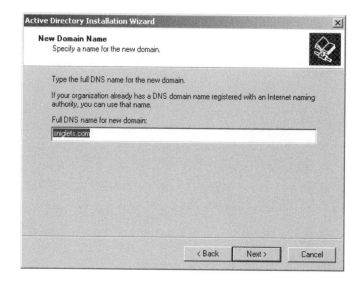

or Join Forest selection screen is displayed. Now select Create a new forest of domain trees and click Next. The
New Domain Name configuration screen in Figure 7.26 is displayed.

4. Enter your domain name in the space provided. This can be the same
as your DNS domain name, or another name of your choosing. We
chose ece-int.gatech.edu. Click Next when you are done and
the NetBIOS Domain Name configuration screen in Figure 7.27 will
be displayed.

5. Enter your desired NetBIOS name if you do not like the default. We
chose WIN2K-ECE. Click Next when you are done and the Database and Log Locations configuration screen will be displayed.

Figure 7.27
NetBIOS
Domain Name
configuration
screen.

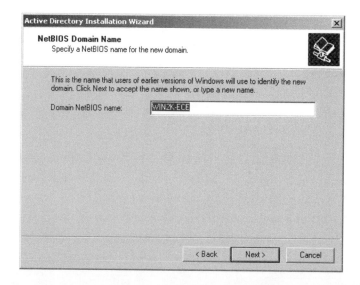

Figure 7.28
Directory
Services
Restore Mode
Administrator
Password
configuration
screen.

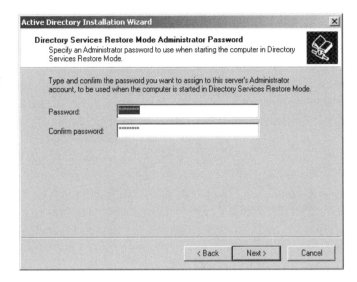

You should keep the default settings and click Next to continue. The Shared System Volume configuration screen is displayed. Again, you should keep the default settings and click Next to continue. The Permissions selection screen is displayed.

6. Select the permissions appropriate for your domain and click Next. The Directory Services Restore Mode Administrator Password configuration screen in Figure 7.28 is displayed.

7. Enter a password of your choice (we used the same password as the Administrator account, but it can be anything you want) and click Next. The Summary screen in Figure 7.29 is displayed.

Figure 7.29
Summary screen.

Active Directory Installation Wizard

Summary
Review and confirm the options you selected.

You chose to:

Configure this server as the first domain controller in a new forest of domain trees.

The new domain name is "ece-int.gatech.edu". This is also the name of the new forest.

The NetBIOS name of the domain is "WIN2K-ECE"

Database location: C:\WINNT\NTDS
Log file location: C:\WINNT\NTDS
Sysvol folder location: C:\WINNT\SYSVOL

Permissions compatible with pre-Windows 2000 servers will be used with this domain; this will allow anonymous access to domain information.

To change an option, click Back. To continue, click Next.

< Back   Next >   Cancel

Figure 7.30
Configuring
Active
Directory
status window.

8. Review the summary and click Next when you are ready to continue. The Configuring Active Directory status window in Figure 7.30 is displayed.

9. When the configuration process is complete, the Completing the Active Directory Installation window is displayed. Click Finish and reboot the system. Once your system reboots, Active Directory will be up and running. You can now add and remove users, as well as join other Windows 2000 systems to the Active Directory domain.

Integrating Windows 2000 and UNIX Directory Services

A single login and password in a heterogeneous environment is the Holy Grail for system administrators. This concept haunts system administrators the world over. Is it too much to ask for? Can't we all just get along? Maybe it is not such an unattainable concept anymore. We will take a look at two different ways of implementing a single login and password in a Windows 2000 and UNIX heterogeneous environment. Maybe the Holy Grail is within reach after all.

ONE-WAY PASSWORD SYNCHRONIZATION

Windows 2000 services for UNIX allow one-way password synchronization. These services allow passwords to be changed on a Windows 2000 system, and then the services will change the password on your designated UNIX workstation. This system requires the user to have the same login name on both systems and the password must adhere to the Windows 2000 password rules. The service must be running on all Windows 2000 servers running in the domain. Passwords must not be changed on the UNIX systems. This type of system can work well in an environment in which UNIX systems are utilized as backend servers with no interactive sessions for the unwashed (non-system administrators). Let's go through the procedure for setting up this service.

The first thing you will need to do is purchase the required number of licenses from Microsoft to run the services on all of your Windows 2000 domain controllers. Next you will need to configure your UNIX hosts that will be doing the synchronization. You have a choice of sending the password in clear or encrypted text. Root must be able to do an `rlogin` to the UNIX host for a clear text password. The encrypted text version requires FTPing the `SSOD` daemon and `ssod.config` files to the same directory on the UNIX host. You must then modify the ssod.config file. The `PASSWORD` variable is the encryption key that must be at least 12 characters long and contain characters from at least three of the groups in Table 7.6. You will need this encryption key when you set up the service on your Windows 2000 servers. After modifying the `ssod.config` file, you will need to start the `SSOD` daemon as root. Problems with the daemon will be reported on the system console or in the `syslog` file (depends on how your `/etc/syslog.conf` file is configured on the UNIX workstation). Automatically starting the services will require a simple shell script addition to the appropriate directory in the boot process (see Chapter 3, "System Boot and Shutdown").

Now that the UNIX workstation is ready and running, we need to install the software on all of the Windows 2000 domain controllers. Once it is installed, enter the following:

```
Start->Programs->Windows NT Services for UNIX->Password
Synchronization (Common)->Password Synchronization Adminis-
trator
```

You will then be presented with the screen shown in Figure 7.31 and should follow these steps:

Table 7.6	**Encryption Character Groups**	
Group	Characters	
1	A, B, C, … Z	
2	a, b, c, …. z	
3	0, 1,2, … 9	
4	(`~!@#$%^&*_-+=|\{}[] :;"'<>,.?)	

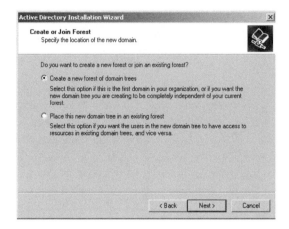

Figure 7.31

1. Click the Add button and you will be presented with the screen shown in Figure 7.32.
2. Type a meaningful name and click OK. The next screen (Figure 7.33) will require the configuration information that was previously completed for the UNIX workstation.
3. First select clear (Use Rlogin) or encrypted (Use encryption) text. If you are using encryption then you will need to click the Configure button and enter the encryption key you entered on the UNIX host.
4. Next you will need to add all the IP addresses of the fully-qualified domain names of the UNIX hosts configured to do synchronization with Windows 2000. Initially check Enable verbose logging; this will greatly enhance your ability to debug any problems that may arise.

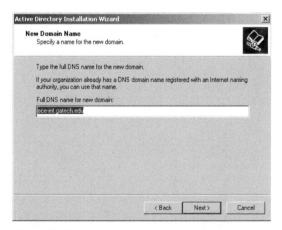

Figure 7.32

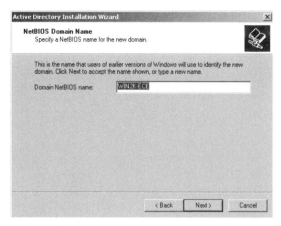

Figure 7.33

5. You can exclude accounts from being synchronized. Create a group in Windows 2000 called `PasswordPropDeny`. Add all user accounts to this group that should be excluded from the password synchronization process.

6. Finally, you will need to change the password on a test account and check the Event Viewer and logs on the UNIX workstation to ensure passwords are being changed in the UNIX domain.

 Beware of typos in the encryption key.

Lightweight Directory Access Protocol

Where do you go to find information on your users? How do you keep your accounts and passwords synchronized? Can you even locate all of the different databases you maintain in your UNIX and Windows 2000 worlds? Does adding a new user require updating multiple databases on Windows and UNIX systems? Is it a nightmare to delete accounts?

What you really want is a centralized database that allows you to enter information once about a new user. This new user would have a Windows 2000 account, a UNIX account, a single password, group privileges, email account, and be a member of all required mailing lists for the organization. The new user should also be included in the company's phone book and organizational charts. This database would also allow you to remove users from all of the above with just one simple action. Additionally this database would be a central repository for locating applications and devices available on the network.

Obviously, I have been dropped on my head late in life. There will never be anything that helpful and good to all system administration-kind. Wait, there is something out there that just might be all of that, and it is called LDAP.

LDAP is an Internet standard for directory services. LDAP runs over TCP/IP. The latest version (LDAP version 3) was specified in RFC 2252. Major vendors participating in the ratification process of LDAPv3 included Microsoft, Sun, Netscape, and Novell. This leaves us with an open standard that runs on top of a proven protocol available on every conceivable networking device, and it is supported by the major players in the workstation and networking fields.

Now that we have gotten through the hype, the reality of deploying and maintaining LDAP in a heterogeneous environment is formidable. The most important process in deploying LDAP is defining the information and services that this service should provide at your site. Remember, if it ain't broke, don't fix it! If you have services that are providing the level of support required by your users, then this is probably not something that needs to be incorporated in an LDAP server. The next few sections will review some of the top products available to implement LDAP servers and clients in Windows 2000 and UNIX systems.

WINDOWS 2000

Windows 2000 Server has replaced the Windows NT domain system with Active Directory. Active Directory utilizes LDAPv3 as its central protocol. Each object in AD has an LDAP distinguished name. On the development side AD can be accessed through the ADSI, which utilizes the Component Object Model (COM), the LDAP C API, and through MAPI. Active Directory provides a mechanism to replicate data between domain controllers, which provides a robust system of LDAP servers. Microsoft provides the command-line utility LDIFDE to import and export data in AD. Comma-separated variable (CSV) format files are also supported by the CSVDE command-line utility. It is important to understand two things about LDAP: distinguished names and user principal names.

Distinguished Names

Distinguished names are used by LDAP to describe individual objects and containers in the directory. For instance, the distinguished name for Todd Whitehurst is:

Table 7.7	Distinguished Name Identifiers
Identifier	Description
/O	Stands for Object.
/DC	Stands for DomainComponentName.
/CN	Stands for CommonName.

`/O=Internet/DC=com/DC=sniglets/CN=Users/CN=Todd Whitehurst`

The identifiers following each slash are described in Table 7.7.

You should now begin to understand what this all means. Represented graphically in Figure 7.34, it can be easily seen how the distinguished name described above describes the location of an object in a tree.

Obviously, as the tree becomes more complex and the number of objects grows, using the distinguished name to describe even a single user can become very cumbersome. This is where user principal names enter into the picture.

User Principal Names and Usernames

Because distinguished names are not easy for humans to remember, AD provides the user principal name to easily distinguish an object. In the case of a user, AD uses the email address to point to the full object name. In Figure 7.34, Todd Whitehurst is a user of the *sniglets.com* domain. The user principal name *toddw* has been created as a shortcut to the user account. Stored within the user account is the email address *toddw@*

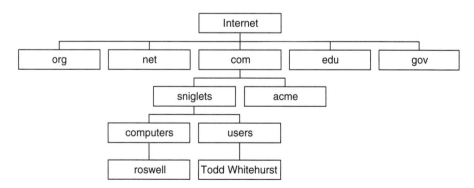

Figure 7.34 Object location in a tree.

sniglets.com. While it may seem that we have not simplified anything, suppose we extended our tree to include the *sales.sniglets.com* domain. If Todd Whitehurst were a user of that domain, the user principal name would remain toddw and the email address would still be *toddw@sniglets.com*, thus making it much simpler to access the user account.

User principle names will be used to log into both Windows 2000 and legacy Windows systems participating in a Windows 2000 domain. You might be wondering where User names and user principal names differ? The user name in Windows 2000 is the name assigned to the account by the administrator, and the user principle name is the name provided for logon and email purposes. The advantage here is that the administrator can change the user name, while the user principal name stays the same. The bottom line is that users have a simple, easy-to-remember way to access their account (without having to remember lengthy distinguished names), and administrators are given the flexibility of modifying accounts without impacting users.

NETSCAPE DIRECTORY SERVER

Netscape Directory Server supports LDAP versions 2 and 3. It is available for Solaris 2.6/7, HPUX 11.0, IBM AIX 4.3.2, Red Hat Linux 6.0, and Windows 2000. Directory Server provides LDAP client SDKs in C and Java for client development. Standard Netscape LDAP command-line tools work with the LDAP Data Interchange Format (LDIF), allowing importing and exporting of text from and to legacy systems. Sun and Netscape have announced that fully collaborative directory, security, and management servers based on Directory Server will be released in the first quarter of 2000.

UNIVERSITY OF MICHIGAN

The University of Michigan is the birthplace of LDAP. The server is free. It is primarily for UNIX platforms with command-line utilities. Development efforts for open source LDAP have been shifted to the OpenLDAP Project.

INNOSOFT

Innosoft Distributed Directory Server (IDDS) is an LDAP version 3 server. Platforms supported by IDDS include Windows 2000, AIX 4.3, HPUX 11.0, Red Hat Linux 6.0, and Solaris 2.6/7. Innosoft offerings include the LDAP Administrative Shell (ILASH) to manage LDAP servers and the LDAP Client SDK for organizations that want to develop their own applications.

OPENLDAP

The OpenLDAP Project is an open source initiative to provide a robust, commercial-grade set of LDAP applications and tools. The server is derived from the University of Michigan's LDAP distribution. It has been ported to AIX, HPUX, Linux, and Solaris.

SUN

Sun Directory Services is an LDAP version 3-compliant server. Sun Directory Services provides a replication service and an integrated NIS server for legacy systems. It includes a set of administration commands that allows conversion of text files for importing into the LDAP server. Sun should provide an upgrade path to convert from Sun Directory Services to the joint directory services based on the Netscape Directory Service.

YPLDAPD

`Ypldapd` is a gateway between legacy Network Information Services (NIS) and LDAP version 2 or 3 servers. `Ypldapd` is available for Solaris and Linux from Padl Software. It supports all commonly utilized NIS maps and includes tools for migrating NIS data to LDAP.

Summary

The management of user and system information is a monumental task. The use of directory services like NIS/NIS+ and Active Directory makes the task more manageable. As heterogeneous infrastructures proliferate, operating systems are creating ways to share information across operating systems. LDAP is a leading example of this kind of inter-operating system cooperation.

NIS/NIS+

NIS/NIS+ was developed by Sun and is a powerful tool for managing the sharing of information between UNIX systems. NIS is supported by all UNIX variants; however, NIS+ is only fully supported by Sun. NIS/NIS+ provides system and user data files to systems on the network via a client/server architecture. Redundancy can be created by using slave servers to replicate the information stored on the master NIS/NIS+ server. There is overlap between NIS/NIS+ and DNS for hostnames and IP addresses. A standard configuration is to use DNS as a primary source and NIS/NIS+ as a backup.

ACTIVE DIRECTORY

Active Directory is an information store consisting of objects and object attributes. The directory hierarchy inherent to Active Directory consists of organizational units, domains, trees, forests, and sites. A schema is a set of attributes used to describe a particular object class in the Active Directory. An important feature of Active Directory is its ability to integrate with DNS. Active Directory uses the industry-standard DNS for all name resolution.

LDAP

LDAP is an Internet standard for directory services. LDAP runs over TCP/IP. The standard was ratified by a group of industrial partners including Microsoft, Sun, Netscape, and Novell. LDAP is still new and deployment can be difficult within an existing infrastructure. However, it is an important concept that will be a major force in the future.

In the next chapter, we will expand the concept of system integration with the concept of distributed file-systems. The ability for users to share data between systems is essential to integrate diverse operating systems.

DISTRIBUTED FILESYSTEMS

UNIX

NFS Server

NFS Client

SAMBA

WINDOWS

MS Services for UNIX

SMB Server

SMB Client

D ata. Lots of it, and seemingly growing at a rate faster then junk email. As a system administrator, much of your time is spent creating, deleting, recovering, and organizing data. The more data you have to keep track of, the more user needs grow. Users demand fast, reliable, and simple access to their files, regardless of your infrastructure's architecture.

With this wealth of demands, you are faced with daily choices about how to manage your data efficiently as well as effectively. A simple answer to this is to just buy as much disk space as you need and place it directly on each user's system so they have fast, local access to their files. In a small environment, this is great, but as your environment grows, local disk space can be prohibitively expensive. In a large environment, you might suggest having a central server, with a large disk farm to fill all your users' data requirements. However, what if your users demand a mixed environment of servers? Maybe they just don't like to share. A mixed environment just may not be right for your situation. If you can't have local disks, and you can't have a central server, where does that leave you?

The solution is using a Distributed Filesystem (DFS). A DFS is any mechanism where data resides on one system, but can be shared over a network to other systems. By sharing data over a network, a server can provide data to other systems on the network (clients) in an efficient enough way that the client systems can perform well, but not have to incur the costs of having the disks locally.

This chapter provides a look at both the pros and cons of DFS (Table 8.1) as it relates to a pair of protocols, the UNIX Network Filesystem (NFS) and Windows Server Message Block (SMB). You'll also learn about the ways in which both UNIX and Windows systems can share data across a network.

UNIX and NFS

The NFS was developed by Sun Microsystems to allow different operating systems to exchange data transparently, and for it to appear as though the information resided locally. The major components of NFS are the remote procedure call (RPC) and the external data representation (XDR) language. RPCs allow a local machine to request that a remote machine perform a function and return the results of the request. XDR defines data structures in a machine-independent language so your Linux box can understand the results from a function performed on a Solaris workstation. This allows NFS to share directories and filesystems over the network between different operat-

Table 8.1 The Good and the Bad	
Pros	Cons
Partitions on client systems appear as local file-systems—There is no requirement to do things differently or learn new commands if you are a user on the client system.	**Impacts performance**—Distributed filesystems can negatively impact network performance if too much data is moving across your network.
Cross-platform interoperability—With proper configuration, it is possible to share data cross-platform, from Windows to UNIX, and vice versa, transparently.	**Decreased security**—Distributed filesystems are inherently less secure than local filesystems and require more vigilance to maintain and secure data.
Reduced cost—Storage and backup requirements are reduced by eliminating data duplication, as well as by allowing centralized backup strategies.	**Decreased system performance**—With data residing on the server, local system performance can be impacted if the client system is requesting data faster than the server can provide it to the client.
Simplified Maintenance—The job of data administration is made easier, as files can be centrally managed and updated, but be available globally, in real time.	

ing systems and make it appear as though the files are on the local machine. NFS has become the *de facto* standard in UNIX operating systems, but it is also available on many other operating systems, including Windows 2000, which is discussed later in the chapter.

PROCESSES

There are five main processes or daemons that NFS depends on for client and server functions.

- `Biod` asynchronous block I/O—Performs buffer cache read-ahead and write-behind.
- `Lockd` file locking.
- `Statd` status monitoring—Allows recovery of locks in the event of a crash.
- `Mountd`—Processes that mount requests.
- `Nfsd`—Services client requests.

Table 8.2 provides a mapping of daemons to client, server, and operating system.

The daemons are started during the boot process. Table 8.3 provides the location of the files for each operating system. All versions start the NFS client daemons. NFS server daemons are started if the `/etc/exports` file exists, or for Solaris, if the `/etc/dfs/dfstab` file exists. The `exports` and `dfstab` files contain the filessystems that are "exported" for remote access.

Table 8.2	Daemon Map						
Daemon	Client	Server	Solaris	Linux	HPUX	AIX	IRIX
Biod	Yes	N/A	N/A	N/A Rpciod	Yes	Yes	Yes
Lockd	Yes	Yes	Yes	Yes	Yes	Yes	Yes
Statd	Yes	Yes	Yes	Yes	Yes	Yes	Yes
Mountd	N/A	Yes	Yes	Yes	Yes	Yes	Yes
Nfsd	N/A	Yes	Yes	Yes	Yes	Yes	Yes

The first step in troubleshooting NFS problems is to make sure all the required processes are running. Use the `ps` command to make sure that the listed processes are running. If some are not starting, check the startup files in Table 8.3 for mistakes.

NFS SERVER

While building your NFS server, think about whom you want to access your data, that is, what users on which machines will be authorized to read and/or write data onto your NFS shared partitions. Security should be a main concern when implementing NFS. Since UNIX shares files based on UIDs, it is very easy for an unauthorized user to masquerade as one of your users, especially if you do not restrict what systems can connect to your NFS server. This can also happen by accident if you allow remote systems to mount your partitions, or you mount remote partitions on your local systems.

exportfs/share

To allow client systems to use NFS to connect to a server's partitions, you need a process for defining parameters to allow clients to connect to your NFS server. This process is called exporting. When you export a partition, you define the following:

Table 8.3	Startup Files
Operating System	File Location
AIX	`/etc/rc.nfs`
HPUX	`/sbin/init.d/nfs.client`
	`/sbin/init.d/nfs.server`
	`/etc/rc.config.d/nfsconf`
IRIX	`/etc/init.d/network`
	`/etc/config/network`
Linux	`/etc/rc.d/init.d/nfs`
	`/etc/sysconfig/network`
Solaris	`/etc/init.d/nfs.client`
	`/etc//init.d/nfs.server`

■ Which system or group of systems is allowed to access, or mount, the defined filesystem.
■ Whether or not the filesystem should be accessed read/write or read-only. Read/write states that remote users can read and modify any files for which they have permission. Read-only prevents files on the partition from being written to when mounted remotely.
■ What level of trust you give the root account on other systems.

The commands `exportfs` (BSD) and `share` (Sysv) are used to export filesystems. A typical export command can look like:

```
mars# exportfs -o rw=earth:saturn,root=earth /users/data
```

For this example, the NFS server `mars` exports the filesystem `/users/data` read/write to the systems `earth` and `saturn`. The `-o` defines a list of options for that given filesystem. For multiple `-o` options, a `(,)` is used to separate distinct parameters, as we can see with the `rw` and `root` options. In this example, the `rw` option defines that `saturn` and `earth` are allowed to NFS mount `/users/data` read/write.

The `root` option in this example defines that the root user on the machine `earth` can perform root functions on the shared filesystem as if the root user on `earth` were the root user on `mars`.

```
mars# exportfs -u /users/data
```

You should be very careful when allowing NFS client systems root access, and when the NFS client systems allow the root user on the client system full authority to add, remove, and change data on the filesystem. This can lead to security problems if you allow the creation of SUID (`setuid`) scripts. .

The `exportfs` command can also be used to remove, or unexport, a filesystem by using the `-u` option. This will unexport the filesystem, removing all rights for remote systems to access the data store there. This command can be used while NFS operations are underway, so be careful if you use this option when the system is operational. The `-u` option should only be used on idle or test systems, or for debugging NFS problems. For Sysv systems, the `share` command performs the function of exporting filesystems. An equivalent `share` command to our `exportfs` example would be:

```
mars# share -F NFS -o rw=earth:saturn,root=earth -d "User
Data" /users/data
```

As you can see, the differences are small, except for the introduction of the `-F` and `-d` options.

The `-F` option defines the filesystem type being exported. The `-d` option allows you to add an identifier to the export. The `-d` is optional, and can be

Table 8.4	Location of NFS Export Information
UNIX Flavor	File
AIX,HPUX,Linux	`/etc/exports`
Solaris	`/etc/dfs/dfstab`

excluded for simplicity. While the vast majority of filesystems are NFS, the `-F` option allows for other types of filesystems to be exported. Refer to your local man pages for a list of the types of filesystems your UNIX version supports.

While command-line exports are important tools for setting up and testing NFS environments, using the command line to export filesystems is not an efficient way to use NFS on a day-to-day basis. A mechanism exists that allows you to define NFS exports in such a way that the filesystem can be exported at boot time, as well as be manipulated more easily on the command line. The rest is done through the use of system files, most commonly the `/etc/exports` file, whose locations are defined Table 8.4.

For BSD-style systems, the `/etc/exports` file takes the form of (all of the following are partitions):

```
#
# Example BSD style /etc/exports
#
/usr/local
/user/stats         -ro
/usr                -access=earth:saturn
/users/homes        -access=plantes:stars
/users/data         -access=earth:saturn,root=saturn
```

The first line exports `/usr/local` to any client that can contact the NFS server, since there are no client definitions. While this is a feature, it is very insecure, and should not be used in general practice. The export of `/user/stats` is not much more secure, but the `-ro` option will export `/user/stats` to all possible systems read-only. Again, be very careful when exporting your NFS filesystems to the world. `/usr` is exported in a more normal fashion—with an access list. This is a colon-separated (:) list of machines or netgroups.

In the next example, `planets` and `stars` are netgroups, from either the `/etc/netgroups` file or NIS. Finally, `/users/data` shows how to mix multiple options. `/users/data` will be exported to the systems `earth` and `saturn`, with `saturn` having root privileges on the filesystem.

Sun Solaris uses the Sysv variation, which employs `share` commands. The `/usr/dfs/dfstab` file in Solaris will take the following form:

```
# place share(1M) commands here for automatic execution
#        on entering init state 3.
#
# share [-F fstype] [ -o options] [-d "<text>"] <pathname> [resource]
# .e.g,
# share  -F nfs  -o rw=engineering  -d "home dirs"  /export/home2
# note that netgroups cannot be used in rw to override an ro option
# also note the use of the root= option instead of anon=0 (which is less
# secure)

share -F nfs -o ro                              -d "CD-ROM"    /cdrom
share -F nfs -o rw=mars:saturn,root=mars  -d"/usr/local"   /users
share -F nfs -o rw=myclients              d "home dirs"    /user/home
```

The dfstab file follows the format of the share command, using the same options. It should be noted that Solaris supports the exportfs command. However, in Solaris the exportfs command is just a pass-through to the share command.

Some final options to consider with using exportfs and share are the -a and -ua options:

```
#mars> exportfs -a

#mars> exportfs -ua
```

The -a option allows you to export all of the defined filesystems in your /etc/exports or /etc/dfs/dfstab with one command. Conversely, the -ua option allows you to unexport all of your filesystems defined in /etc/exports or /etc/dfs/dfstab. These commands can be highly useful during initial system configuration and testing, as well as for debugging. Be careful when using the -ua option, as unexporting active filesystems can cause your users to lose data or remote systems to hang or crash.

exportfs (BSD) used export file systems to remote machines. share (SysV) similar to exportfs, used for SysV based systems.

NFS CLIENT

Now that you understand the technical workings via the NFS server, a discussion of using and configuring NFS clients is in order. In the UNIX world, one of the more useful features is sharing data via NFS regardless of the flavors of UNIX involved.

However, each UNIX variant has its own spin on using and configuring NFS. In this section, you will learn how to use the mount command and manage your `fstab/vfstab` files, as well as gain an introductory understanding to using `automount` to improve the performance and stability of your NFS systems.

mount

The `mount` command allows you to attach filesystems into your directory structure from either your local machine or a remote NFS server. While the `mount` command is necessary in mounting local filesystems as well as remote filesystems, for simplicity, we will only discuss the interaction of the `mount` command in an NFS environment. The command takes the form:

```
mount -o <options> <remote filesystem> <mount point>
```

The `remote filesystem` takes the form of `<remote machine name>:<NFS filesystem>`. The `remote machine` name can be resolved through DNS, NIS, or the HOSTS file, and the system IP address can also be used. However, there may be times when you are debugging NFS problems. In these situations, you'll want to use the IP address to determine if there are name resolution problems.

The `mount point` is the directory in your directory structure to which you want the remote filesystem to be attached. The `mount point` must be a directory, not a filename or symbolic link. The directory may not already have an NFS filesystem mounted on it. If the directory has subdirectories of files under it, when you mount the NFS filesystem, the NFS filesystem is in effect "mounted over" the existing subdirectory. While the data in the subdirectory isn't lost or damaged, mounting over active directories can cause confusion and/or system malfunction.

Be careful not to mount remote filesystems on top of local filesystems, as confusion or system malfunction may result. The files on the local filesystem will not be accessible, only the remotely mounted partition.

There are a number of options to the `mount` command, but for the majority of `mount` operations, you'll encounter only a few of them:

- ■ `rw` or `ro`—The read/write (`rw`) and read-only (`ro`) options allow you flexibility when mounting a remote filesystem. By default, the `mount` command attaches NFS filesystems with read/write. The read-only option is useful if you want to share data in such a way that it can't be modified, or if you are mounting read-only media such as CD-ROM devices.

- ■ `hard` or `soft`—By default, all mount operations are hard mounts, which means your client system will continue to ask the server for information until the server responds. This is important, for if you mount fileysystems with the `soft` option, you risk the potential for application or system failure if the client "gives up" asking for data if the NFS server is busy, down, or if you have network failures.

■ `bg`—This background option is most useful when incorporated into your `fstab/vfstab` file to be used at boot time. The background option instructs the `mount` command to run in the background, and continue running until the mount is successful. In the event of NFS server problems or network slowness, the `mount` command running in the background will allow your system to continue booting instead of waiting for the `mount` command to complete. The `fstab/vfstab` file will be discussed in more detail in the next section.

A good rule of thumb is to always use the `hard` and `bg` options.

For example, machine `mars` has a filesystem, `/users/data`, that it wants to share with machine `earth`. On `earth`, we want the information in directory `/users/data` to be visible to users on `earth` in `/remote/data`. The command should take the form:

```
earth# mount mars:/users/data /remote/data
```

As another example, on `earth` we have a local CD drive that resides in the directory `/devices/cdrom` and that we want to mount read-only into the directory `/local/cd`. The command looks like:

```
earth# mount -o ro /devices/cdrom /local/cd
```

The `mount` command is a simple, useful command for both attaching local data as well as sharing remote data. You may now ask the following question: What if I want to remove the mount filesystem? For once we have a simple and intuitive answer—use the `umount` command. The `umount` command unmounts the mounted filesystem when used in the form:

```
umount <filesystem>
```

Be careful not to unmount filesystems that are in use by users or the system.

In Figure 8.1, we have the home directory `/users/data/sjflynn` on the NFS server `saturn`, mounted on the local system `mars`, in `/home/sjflynn`. Note that an attempt to unmount the filesystem failed, most likely because the user `sjflynn` still had an active shell with `/home/sjflynn` as part of the current path.

Being sure you and your users are not actively manipulating the filesystem before you attempt a `umount` is a wise practice. The quickest way to determine which user or what program is causing `umount` to fail is to use the `fuser` command. In our previous example, the `umount` of `/home/sjflynn` failed. By using the `fuser` command, as shown in Figure 8.2, we can see what process ID numbers are currently operating in `/home/sjflynn`.

By using the `ps` and `grep` commands, we can determine which user and what program(s) are causing `umount` to fail. In this example, process number `360` is a shell (`ksh`) term belonging to user `sjflynn`. At this point, your own personal policies need to be put into effect. Killing user processes without warning the user is a poor system administration practice. So, if you have a busy system, you may need to wait until a less busy time to attempt the unmount again. Could you send a message to users before you kill the process? Of course, if the system is impaired or you are testing, use the `kill` command to terminate the process number and you're on your way. For more information on the `ps`, `grep`, and `kill` commands, consult your local man pages.

`mount` used to mount local or remote filesystems into the directory structure.

`umount` used to remove mounted filesystems.

`fuser` will show processes which are using a mounted filesystem.

Figure 8.1
Failed `umount` attempt.

```
 Window   Edit   Options                                                   Help

mars:# df -k
Filesystem              kbytes      used   avail capacity  Mounted on
/proc                        0         0       0      0%   /proc
/dev/dsk/c0t0d0s0      8219717    593393 7544127      8%   /
fd                           0         0       0      0%   /dev/fd
swap                    552888       392  552496      1%   /tmp
saturn:/users/home/sjflynn
                       7873338   5531668 1554340     79%   /home/sjflynn
mars# umount /home/sjflynn
nfs umount: /home/sjflynn: is busy
mars#
```

Figure 8.2
Using the `fuser`
command.

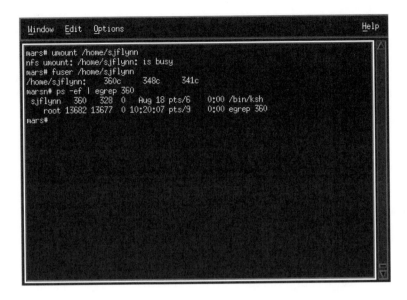

```
Window   Edit   Options                                        Help

mars# umount /home/sjflynn
nfs umount: /home/sjflynn: is busy
mars# fuser /home/sjflynn
/home/sjflynn:      360c      348c      341c
marsn# ps -ef | egrep 360
 sjflynn   360   328  0  Aug 18 pts/6     0:00 /bin/ksh
    root 13682 13677  0 10:20:07 pts/9    0:00 egrep 360
mars#
```

Fstab File

Now that you know how to mount remote filesystems, you may decide this is a great idea and want to distribute a large number of filesystems throughout your infrastructure. It would be a major problem if you had to mount every filesystem by hand, at the command line, every time you rebooted a system. However, fear not, for through the use of the `fstab` file, you can automate your remote mounts at boot time, or define remote mounts so that they can be executed at any time by the root user with a simple `mount` command.

Before we continue, it should be noted that `fstab` files are complex, vary from vendor to vendor, and if modified incorrectly, may cause your system to have problems, including failure to boot. As you should understand by now, the `fstab` file manages both local and remote mounts. While incorrect remote mounts may cause you some grief, incorrect local mounts, especially items like / and swap, will cause you great frustration.

The best way to understand the `fstab` file is by example. Here we have the `/etc/fstab` file from an HPUX system. The file is partitioned into two sections for simplicity, local and remote mounts. Local mounts are devices that are physically attached to our system, and that we want to mount at boot time. In this example, we see that we have local filesystems /, `/stand`, `/export1`, and `/export3`, as well as a swap area on device `/dev/vg00/lvol4`. Our HPUX system also mounts a remote system from `mars`, as was illustrated in the previous section.

```
# Sample HPUX 10 fstab file
#
# local mounts
#
#device           mount      FS     mount     backup fsck
#to mount         point             type      options    frequency    pass
#
/dev/vg00/lvol3  /          hfs    defaults  0                        1
/dev/vg00/lvol1  /stand     hfs    defaults  0                        1
/dev/vg00/lvol4  ...        swap   defaults    0                  0
/dev/dsk/c1t3d0  /export1   hfs    rw,suid   0                        1
/dev/dsk/c0t5d0  /export3   hfs    rw,suid   0                        1
#
# remote mounts
#
mars:/users/data /remote/data nfs  rw,hard,bg 0                       1
```

Having a remote NFS entry in the `fstab` file serves two purposes. First, it allows you to attach the remote NFS filesystem at boot time, so you don't have to worry about performing the mount manually. Second, if you need to mount and unmount the filesystem from the command line, you can do so using the abbreviated `mount` command:

```
mars# mount /remote/data
```

The `mount` command by design looks in the `fstab` file first, and if an entry exists, uses the information and options to execute the mount. This saves both time and effort, especially in cases where the mount points and options are long and complicated.

Automounter

Since system administration, including NFS, is difficult enough with all of its many processes to manage, there are some tools you can use to make your life easier. One of the most irksome problems in UNIX administration is the "stale NFS file handle" error. This error is registered whenever NFS clients and servers get in such a state that communication is no longer possible, and system administrator interaction is usually fruitless.

In most cases of stale NFS file handles, a client system reboot is usually the only remedy. If you manage a medium to large environment, chances are on average you'll end up rebooting two or three clients a week due to NFS file handle errors.

While rebooting a couple of systems a week may not seem much of a problem, remember what you as the administrator are working toward. Your goal should be to provide systems that are reliable and available, and if you have to reboot often, you fail at both. One way to improve your systems' uptime? is to use an automounter. Automounting is the process by which NFS filesystems are mounted on demand, and then unmounted after a specified period of inactivity. Automounting reduces the chance of NFS hangs, as only filesystems that are currently in use are mounted, thereby reducing the chance of an NFS problem.

Setup and use of the automounter are relatively simple operations, supported in most flavors of UNIX. In most cases the startup `rc` scripts of your client UNIX system will handle the start of the `automountd` daemon.

If you choose not to use the automounter, be sure to modify the `rc` script and comment out the automounter to reduce the number of processes running on your system.

If you don't use the automounter, be sure to modify the operating system's `rc` script that starts the automounter. Commenting out the line in the startup script is sufficient, and will save resources on your client machine.

If you choose to use the automounter, you need to configure your `/etc/auto_master` file to define how the automounter should work. `auto_home` is the master map for the automounter. In our example below, we have two entries in our `auto_master` file, one for `/net` and one for `/home`. The entry for `/home` refers to another automount map file, `auto_home`, which for this example resides in `/etc/auto_home`.

Note that you can distribute your maps through the use of NIS. The master file consists of three entries. The first entry is the mount point where NFS will mount the server filesystem. The second entry defines the mount point, or the subsequent map to use. The third entry is for any special mount options, such as read-only. In our example, we are using `-nosuid`, which causes the client system to not execute `setuid` programs.

```
#/etc/auto_master
#
# Master map for automounter
#
/net            -hosts          -nosuid
/home           auto_home
```

The first entry allows for mounting any NFS server that has granted the client system permission into the local directory. For example, to mount `earth:/usr/local` from `mars`, all we need to do is type:

```
mars# cd /net/earth/usr/local
```

The automounter will take care of the rest, mounting `earth:/usr/local` onto `/net/<remote host name>`. This is the beauty of the automounter—it allows us to quickly mount NFS directories. This is an espe-

cially useful feature for the system administrator when preforming maintenance and upgrading software. The second entry in the `auto_master` defines the mount parameters for `/home`. When attempting to mount
directories under `/home`, the automounter is directed to use the
`auto_home` map, which is shown here.

```
#
#/etc/auto_home
#
local            -bg     earth:/usr/local
*                -bg     saturn:/home/users/&
```

By directing `automountd` to `auto_home`, we can customize how the
automounter should act for the `/home` directory. In the example,
`/etc/auto_home`, the first entry, directs `automountd` to mount
`/home/local` from `earth:/usr/local` while running in the background. The second entry uses wildcard entries `*` and `&`. The `*` tells the automounter what to do with requests that are not explicitly defined in the
map. The `&` is an expansion wildcard that expands the current request into
the mount definition. For example, if user `harry` attempts to mount
`ralph`'s home directory using the command:

```
mars#  cd /home/ralph
```

The automounter looks in the `auto_home` map and sees that `ralph` is
not explicitly defined. All undefined requests are expanded using the `sat-`
`urn:/home/users/&` entry. By replacing the `&` with `ralph`, `mars` will attempt to mount the filesystem `/home/users/ralph` from the system
`saturn`.

If `/home/users/ralph` exists and is shared, it will be mounted; otherwise, `ralph` will see a "directory not found" error. As long as the filesystem
has activity, it will remain mounted. After some period of time (the default
time is generally five minutes), the automounter will attempt to unmount
the filesystem as long as there is no activity.

No user intervention is necessary, and better yet, no root user intervention is needed. By releasing the NFS file-system, there is less chance for an
NFS problem. You also reduce the resources necessary to manage NFS on
the client system.

Am-utils: 4.4BSD Automounter Utilities

The Am-utils comprise a suite of automounter tools that can be used in
place of Sun's automounter. The suite includes `amd`, the automounter daemon, and `amq`, the automounter query tool. Am-utils have been ported to
AIX, HPUX, Linux, and Solaris. They are available in source or binary form
for each platform. The source provides configuration tools that greatly sim-

plify the compilation and installation of the suite. The Am-utils suite provides greater support for diverse filesystem types, selector variables, and mount map types than the automounter.

Amd is the automounter daemon that mounts filesystems when a file or directory is accessed. The startup scripts discussed in Chapter 2, "System Planning, Installation, and Configuration," must be searched and modified to start amd in place of automountd. In the following example, amd reads configuration information from /etc/amd.conf on initialization. The file contains parameters and sections to govern the behavior of amd. Information is limited to one line and is case-sensitive. Parameters can be common to all sectors, or are only applicable to the global section. The man pages for amd.conf provide details on all valid parameters. There are two main sections: global and map.

Sections begin with the name of the section in square brackets and end when a new section begins or the file ends. The global section, which should be placed first in the file, applies to amd (in place of command-line switches) and all following map sections where applicable. The map section parameters apply only to a specific map entry. Parameters specified in the map section override parameters defined in the global section.

```
#
# amd default config file
#
# check amd.conf(5) man page for details about options in this file
#

# GLOBAL OPTIONS SECTION
[ global ]
normalize_hostnames =    no
print_pid =              yes
pid_file =               /var/run/amd.pid
restart_mounts =         yes
auto_dir =               /.automount
log_file =               /var/log/amd
#log_file =              syslog
log_options =            all
#debug_options =         all
plock =                  no
selectors_on_default =   yes
print_version =          no
# set map_type to "nis" for NIS maps, or comment it out to search for all
# types
map_type =               nis
```

```
search_path =                    /etc
browsable_dirs =                 yes
show_statfs_entries =            no
fully_qualified_hosts = no
cache_duration =                 300

# DEFINE AN AMD MOUNT POINT
[ /home ]
map_name =                       amd.home
[ /tools ]
map_name =                       amd.mf
[ /net ]
map_name =                               amd.net
```

The right-hand side of the equal sign (=) in the regular map section contains the name of the mount map. amd supports regular files, NDBM databases, NIS maps, NIS+ maps, LDAP maps, and a few other mount map forms. The map_type parameter in the global section of the example above specifies the use of NIS maps. A portion of the text file that will become the NIS mount map, amd.mf, is provided in the next example. To access the information in these directories, a user would only need to cd to /tools/solcad and /tools/cadence434. The actual mount points would be /a/yamacraw.company.com/export/home1/solaris/ic and /a/yamacraw.company.com/export/home1/cadence434 for machines other than yamacraw. The mount points for users on the yamacraw machine would be /export/home1/solaris/ic and /export/home1/cadence434.

This is just a simple example of the syntax for creating amd maps. This file requires further processing before it can become an NIS map. There are more than 20 selector variables that allow you to "tailor" your mount points for things such as machine architecture, operating system, or operating system version. You can also specify options used by the mount command for each map. The default option for each map is "rw,defaults". As you can see, Amd provides a lot of flexibility and features for mount maps that are not available in the automounter package.

```
solcad
     hostd!=yamacraw.company.com;
                type:=nfs;
                rfs:=/export/home1/solaris;
                sublink:=ic;
                rhost:=yamacraw.company.com
        hostd==yamacraw.company.com;
                type:=link;
                fs:=/export/home1/solaris;
                sublink:=ic;
```

```
#
cadence434
        hostd!=yamacraw.company.com;
                type:=nfs;
                rfs:=/export/home1;
                sublink:=cadence434;
                rhost:=yamacraw.company.com
        hostd==yamacraw.company.com;
                type:=link;
                fs:=/export/home1;
                sublink:=cadence434;
#
```

Monitoring the state of amd is accomplished with the amq command, which is RPC-based. The default output is a list of mount points and auto-mounted filesystems on the current system. Table 8.5 contains a listing of the more frequently used options for amq.

The following contains an example of the amq command with the -m option.

```
"root"     youdee:(pid157)    root    1    localhost is up
amd.home      /home toplvl  1    localhost is up
amd.mf        /tools toplvl  1    localhost is up
amd.net       /net     toplvl  1    localhost is up
duchess:/export/home1    /a/duchess/export/home1 nfs     1
duchess.company.com is up
mail:/var/mail                /a/mail/var/mail nfs     1
mail.company.com is up
```

nfsstat

It's easy to monitor the performance of NFS on a UNIX workstation—simply use the nfsstat command. This command is available on AIX,

Table 8.5	amq **Options**
Option	Definition
-h hostname	Query amd on a different host.
-m	Display information on mounted systems.
-p	Return the process ID of running amd.
-s	Display global statistics.
-u mount-point	Expires TTL interval of named mount points. Causes unmount attempt.

HPUX, Linux, and Solaris. nfsstat provides statistical data on NFS and RPC activity. To display NFS and RPC client information, use nfsstat -c (Figure 8.3). The primary indicator is the percentage of invalid NFS/RPC calls. This can be obtained from the calls and badcalls values for RPC and NFS. The following are some additional indicators you will want to examine:

- badxids—The number of acknowledgements from NFS servers with no corresponding outstanding call.
- timeouts—The number of times a call timed out waiting for a response from a server.

When the number of timeouts is greater than five percent of calls, you may have a problem in your network or server. If the badxids is approximately equal to the timeouts, then you probably have a server unable to meet NFS demands. If the badxids total is considerably less than timeouts, you probably have a network problem and you need to contact your network guru. Linux's nfsstat does not include badxids or timeouts indicators.

Display NFS server statistics by entering the command nfsstat -s (Figure 8.4). Solaris breaks the statistics into version 2 and 3 of NFS. Key indicators include:

- getattr—Get file attributes.
- null—The number of calls made by the automounter to locate a server for the requested file-system.

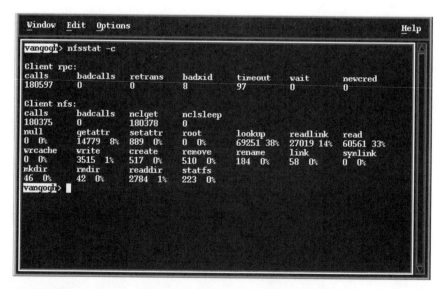

Figure 8.3 nfsstat -c output.

```
Window   Edit   Options                                      Help

Server rpc:
Connection oriented:
calls        badcalls    nullrecv    badlen      xdrcall     dupchecks  dupreqs
0            0           0           0           0           0          0
Connectionless:
calls        badcalls    nullrecv    badlen      xdrcall     dupchecks  dupreqs
81           0           0           0           0           0          0

Server nfs:
calls        badcalls
81           0
Version 2: (81 calls)
null         getattr     setattr     root        lookup      readlink   read
77 95%       2 2%        0 0%        0 0%        1 1%        0 0%       0 0%
wrcache      write       create      remove      rename      link       symlink
0 0%         0 0%        0 0%        0 0%        0 0%        0 0%       0 0%
mkdir        rmdir       readdir     statfs
0 0%         0 0%        0 0%        1 1%
Version 3: (0 calls)
null         getattr     setattr     lookup      access      readlink   read
0 0%         0 0%        0 0%        0 0%        0 0%        0 0%       0 0%
write        create      mkdir       symlink     mknod       remove     rmdir
0 0%         0 0%        0 0%        0 0%        0 0%        0 0%       0 0%
rename       link        readdir     readdir+    fsstat      fsinfo     pathconf
0 0%         0 0%        0 0%        0 0%        0 0%        0 0%       0 0%
commit
0 0%

Server nfs_acl:
Version 2: (0 calls)
null         getacl      setacl      getattr     access
0 0%         0 0%        0 0%        0 0%        0 0%
Version 3: (0 calls)
null         getacl      setacl
0 0%         0 0%        0 0%
youdee>
```

Figure 8.4 `nfsstat -s` output.

Each NFS client has an attribute cache. When `getattr` exceeds 50 percent of calls, then the attribute cache on the NFS clients accessing this server needs to be examined. Table 8.6 contains the commands to access the `actimeo` attribute for each UNIX version. If the `null` value is two or more percent, then the timeout value must be increased on the server. The attribute is `timeo` for HPUX, Linux and Solaris. The AIX attribute is `TimeOut`. Use the man page for specific instructions on how to use the commands in Table 8.6.

Table 8.6 **Setting** `actimeo` **and** `timeout`	
Version	Command
AIX	chnfsmnt
HPUX	mount_nfs
Linux	nfs
Solaris	mount_nfs

Setting `actimeo` will also set `acdirmax`, `acdirmin`, `acregmax`, and `acregmin` to the same value.

`nfsstat` provides statistical data on NFS and RPC activity.

Windows 2000 and NFS

Windows 2000 can, with a little help, export and mount NFS filesystems. There are currently three excellent add-ons that bring the NFS world and Windows 2000 together. Microsoft offers a complete NFS solution in the Microsoft Windows NT Services for UNIX add-on pack. The Microsoft package provides NFS mounting and NFS server support for the Windows 2000 Server and Professional editions.

WINDOWS NT SERVICES FOR UNIX

Windows Services for UNIX (SFU) version 2 is the one-stop package for NFS access on Windows 2000. SFUv2 provides an NFS server, NFS client, and a gateway for NFS. The gateway for NFS creates a gateway for SMB clients to access NFS file and print resources without the requirement of NFS client software. Table 8.7 contains a complete listing of packages and availability. In this section, we will cover the NFS server/client and gateway for NFS.

1. Inserting the CD automatically brings up the `Windows 2000 Installation Wizard` window. The wizard's screen is split into two parts. The left part of the screen shows your progress for the installation. The right side of the screen is where you will actually be entering information for the installation. The first page requires your name, organization, and CD key.

2. The second screen is the `End-User License Agreement` screen. The third screen is where you start earning your big bucks as a system administrator. Select `Customize` and you are presented with a listing of disk partitions and space available to install SFUv2. Select the appropriate partition and directory.

3. You will next be presented with the `Select Features` window (Figure 8.5). All features except `Client for NFS` will be installed. `Client for NFS` and `Gateway for NFS` are mutually exclusive features in Windows 2000 Advanced Server.

4. Click `Install Now`. Installation will be completed and a reboot of the workstation will be required.

Table 8.7	Windows Services for UNIX	
Component	Windows 2000 Advanced Server	Windows 2000 Professional
Telnet Client	Yes	Yes
Telnet Server	Yes	Yes
UNIX Utilities	Yes	Yes
Client for NFS	Yes	Yes
Gateway for NFS	Yes	No
Server for NIS	Yes	No
PCNFSD	Yes	Yes
Server for NFS	Yes	Yes
Server for NFS Authorization	Yes	Yes

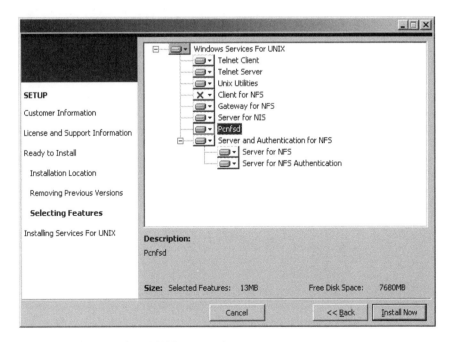

Figure 8.5 Services for UNIX feature selection.

Configuring the NFS Server

Once installed, the services must be configured. This configuration is a straightforward GUI operation.

1. Setup is accessed by the following progression: `Start->Programs->Windows Services for UNIX->Services For UNIX Administration`. The Microsoft Management Console (MMC) is the host for configuring all of the Windows Services for UNIX version 2. Highlight `Server for NFS` on the left side of the window and the configuration pages will appear on the right side of the window (Figure 8.6).

2. Click `Show User Maps`. You will need to enter the Windows 2000 domain and NIS domain/server. Next, check the box for `Set As Automatic Mapping Domain` to map identical user names between Windows 2000 and your UNIX NIS domain. Click `Download UNIX Usernames` UIDs and GIDs from the UNIX NIS domain to Windows 2000 accounts. To map groups, you will need to repeat the above procedures while `Show Group Maps` is highlighted. Microsoft also provides a manual procedure to map Windows 2000 login names to UNIX logins. Make sure you click the disk icon in the top right-hand corner to save your settings.

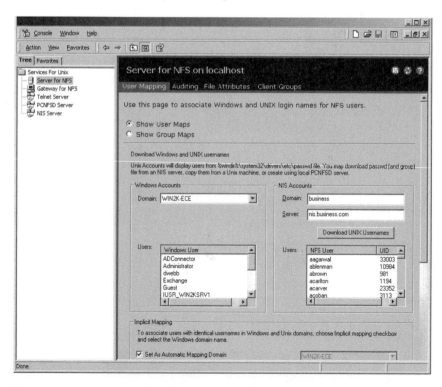

Figure 8.6 `Services for UNIX server for NFS.`

3. The `Auditing` tab allows you to specify a log file and operations to be logged. The `Files Attributes` tab allows you to configure the `lock` daemon and FAT filesystem.

Configuring the NFS Gateway

Setting up the gateway for NFS is very similar to the NFS server configuration procedure.

1. Click `Gateway for NFS` to configure the server as a gateway. You will need to enter the Windows domain and NIS domain information, check `Implicit Mapping` and `Display Implicit Maps`, and then click `Get UNIX Accounts`.

2. Now the `Windows Users` in the `Explicit Mapping` section should have UIDs and GIDs from the NIS domain. Like the server, there is also a manual procedure for mapping different user names between Windows and UNIX NIS domains. Next, click the `Sharing` tab, and then click the `Launch Sharing` utility. The `Gateway for NFS Shares` window pops up (Figure 8.7).

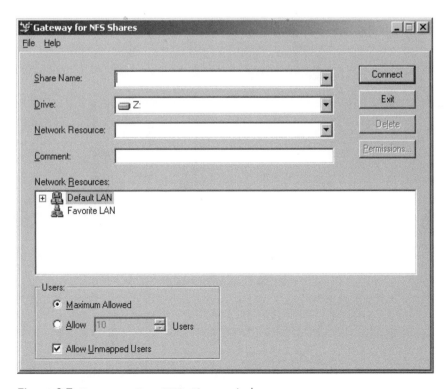

Figure 8.7 `Gateway for NFS Share` window.

3. Enter the share name and select the machine and NFS filesystem to mount from the `Network Resources` section. A network resource can also be entered manually using the universal naming convention. The final step is to create a share on the local machine to allow SMB clients to access this NFS directory via the SMB share on the Windows 2000 gateway.

 The `Gateway for NFS` service should be configured for client machines that have minimal NFS activity.

Configuring an NFS Client

Configuring a `client for NFS` is the easiest of the NFS configuration services.

1. Click `Client for NFS` in the left-hand portion of the window to access the configuration pages. The first page is the authentication page (Figure 8.8).

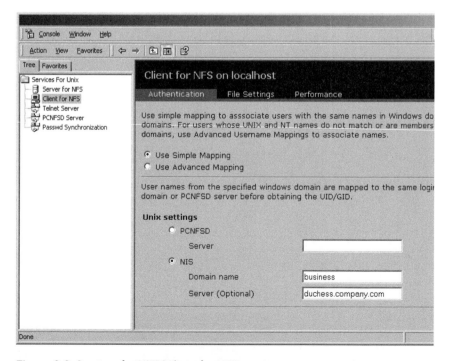

Figure 8.8 Services for UNIX client for NFS.

2. Click `Use Simple Mapping` and then enter your NIS domain information or your PCNFSD server. This will map logins that are identical between your Windows domain and specified UNIX NIS domain. If your Windows and UNIX logins are different, you need to click `Use Advanced Mapping`.

3. The `File Settings` tab allows you to set read, write, and execute permissions for new files or folders created.

4. The `Performance` tab contains parameters for buffer sizes, timeouts, retries, and mount types. Go with the defaults on the performance page unless you experience problems.

 Don't forget to save your settings by clicking the disk in the upper right-hand corner of each configuration page.

Now you are ready to mount NFS filesystems. Mounting an NFS filesystem is accomplished in Windows Explorer following the same procedures for a Windows 2000 share. You can also mount NFS filesystems from the command line with the `mount` command. The `mount` command is located in the common folder under the `Services for UNIX` directory. The `mount` command is invoked with the following switches/parameters:

```
mount [switches] [network path] [drive]  where

switches /u: username  /o options Table8mount Valid only for that filesystem

network path  =  server:/full/path/name or \\server\full\path\name

drive = drive:
```

A `mount` command invoked without any switches or parameters displays all currently NFS-mounted filesystems on the local machine. The specific options are listed in Table 8.8.

Table 8.8	Specific Options of the `mount` Command
Option	Definition
`Rsize=n`	Read buffer size in bytes.
`Wsize=n`	Write buffer size in bytes.
`Timeo=n`	NFS timeout in tenths of a second.
`Retrans=n`	NFS retransmissions; default is 5.
`Soft	hard`	Soft or hard mount.

To disconnect an NFS filesystem, right-click the filesystem in Windows Explorer and select `Disconnect`.

HUMMINGBIRD'S NFS MAESTRO SUITE FOR WINDOWS 2000

Hummingbird Communications' family of NFS Maestro products provides additional packages for NFS connectivity. Hummingbird's NFS Maestro products are native Microsoft 32-bit TCP/IP implementations. The Maestro Server installs as a Windows 2000 service and provides long filename support up to 255 characters. It supports NFS versions 2/3, WebNFS, and NFS via TCP. Hummingbird includes a utility to map UNIX user IDs (UIDs)/group IDs (GIDs) to Windows 2000 users and groups. The Maestro Suite is divided into four products:

- NFS Maestro Client, which enables PC desktops to access local and remote NFS filesystems and printers.
- NFS Maestro Solo, which provides the core NFS functionality of NFS Maestro Client to users while taking advantage of the existing and powerful multi-threaded 32-bit operating system.
- NFS Maestro Server, which enables UNIX workstations and network-attached NFS computers to access Windows-based resources such as Windows NT filesystems, directories, printers, and CD-ROMs across a network.
- NFS Maestro Gateway, which provides controlled, occasional NFS access to UNIX file-systems while offering centralized management for network administrators.

SMB: A Client/Server Protocol

SMB is the protocol primarily used by Windows 2000 for network connections to files, printers, and resources. The SMB protocol is designed to run on top of TCP/IP (commonly referred to as NetBIOS over TCP/IP), NetBEUI, and IPX/SPX. This versatility allows SMB to be deployed in almost any network environment.

There have been several variants to the base SMB protocol over the years, most notably the NTLM protocol used in Windows NT 4.0 and Windows 2000. The latest variant to the SMB protocol is CIFS, or the Common Internet Filesystem. CIFS is basically NTLM plus a few extras for optimizing performance over the Internet.

SMB is implemented as a client/server protocol, and is available for many platforms. In this chapter, we will discuss SMB clients, SMB servers, SMB security, SMB network browsing, how SMB is implemented in Windows 2000, and the SAMBA package for UNIX.

CLIENTS

An SMB client is any machine capable of connecting to an SMB resource, such as a file or printer share on an SMB server. As mentioned earlier, SMB is a client/server protocol; hence, the client initiates an SMB session with the server. The following is a typical sequence of events for connecting to an SMB share:

1. The client begins the session by sending a list of available protocol dialects to the server. The server will then respond with the dialect it wishes to use, or with an error code if none of the dialects are acceptable.
2. The client will begin a *session setup* by attempting to log on to the server, if required. The server will send a response indicating if valid logon credentials were supplied, and can provide additional information if necessary. Included in the response (assuming a successful logon) is the UID of the logged-on user, which is used for all subsequent SMBs on the current connection.
3. The client sends a command to connect to a specific network share. If everything is specified correctly, the server sends a response, including an ID, to be used for all subsequent SMBs in relation to the specified share.
4. The client can proceed with additional requests for performing operations on the share, such as opening, reading, writing, and closing.

An SMB client is provided with Windows 2000 (as well as most other versions of Windows), and with the SAMBA package for UNIX systems.

SERVERS

An SMB server is any machine capable of sharing an SMB resource, such as a file or printer, to SMB clients on the network. SMB servers listen for client requests, provide security for SMB shares, and may provide browsing capabilities. An SMB server is provided with both Windows 2000 Server and Windows 2000 Professional. The SAMBA package also includes an SMB server.

SECURITY

Security is critical in a networked environment. There are two levels of security provided by SMB: share-level and user-level. A potentially important aspect of SMB security is that user- and share-level security can be used concurrently. It is also important to understand the differences between domains and workgroups, and how they affect your SMB security. This section will explain domains and workgroups, as well as the two security models available.

Domains vs. Workgroups

Both domains and workgroups consist of machines connected via a LAN or WAN, typically for organizational purposes. Domains, however, provide a central security authority for users, groups, and resources. Workgroups do not provide any security beyond what is configured on each machine locally. In a domain, security can be managed from domain controllers, and each workstation that is a member of the domain can contact a domain controller to authenticate users when network connections are made.

Share-Level Security

With share-level security, a password is assigned to a resource itself. Any user who knows the password can access a given resource. In some cases, separate passwords can be set for read and write access, providing a bit more security.

User-Level Security

In user-level security, permissions for a share are set based on user accounts that can be local to the machine or domain accounts. To connect to a share on a machine participating in user-level security, a user must provide a user name and password, which will be authenticated against a local account database and/or a domain controller. Provided the user enters the correct password and the user has been granted the appropriate access to the share, they will be allowed to access the resource.

NETWORK BROWSING

There must be some way for clients to find servers on the network. This is where browsing comes into the picture. In "traditional" SMB networks, the servers broadcast information about their resources to the network and the clients build *browse lists* from these broadcasts. This works fine for small networks using non-routed protocols such as NetBEUI. In modern TCP/IP environments, however, broadcasts are not typically routed between individual subnets. Implementing a NetBIOS Name Server (NBNS), such as Microsoft's Windows Internet Name Service (WINS) or SAMBA server, solves this problem. An NBNS server is similar to a DNS server in that it maps NetBIOS names to IP addresses. Each subnet will have a *master browser*, and each domain will have a *domain master browser*. A *master browser* maintains the browse list for a domain/workgroup on each subnet. The clients on the subnet will obtain their *browse lists* from the *master browser*. The different master browsers in the domain/workgroup synchronize their browse lists with one another. Each domain in your network will also have a *domain master browser*, which maintains the list for the entire domain. The *domain master browser* receives updates from the master browsers and publishes these lists to other domain master browsers and its own master browsers.

Windows 2000 and SMB

Both the Server and Professional versions of Windows 2000 provide client and server SMB services. However, Windows 2000 Server is optimized to provide server services. With Windows 2000 SMB servers, you can share directories and printers to your network. There is, of course, the ability to mount SMB shares from Windows 2000 clients and servers. This section will describe how to create and mount shares, as well as explain the administrative and default shares. We will also introduce you to Microsoft's distributed Filesystem.

CREATING SHARES

Windows 2000 provides two direct methods for creating SMB shares. The first method is probably the most widely used, and is done using the Windows Explorer. Use the following steps to create a new folder and share it on your network:

1. Open Windows Explorer and expand the `My Computer` tree. Select `Drive C:` and you should see something similar to Figure 8.9.
2. Create a new folder, `C:\Data`. Right-click on `C:\Data` and select `Sharing`... from the menu that appears. You should see something similar to Figure 8.10.
3. Click the `Share this folder` radio button. Type `Data` in the `Share name` text box. Type `My Data` in the `Comment` text box. You should leave the `User limit` selections as they are.
4. Click the `Permissions` button and the window in Figure 8.11 will be displayed.

Figure 8. 9
Windows
Explorer.

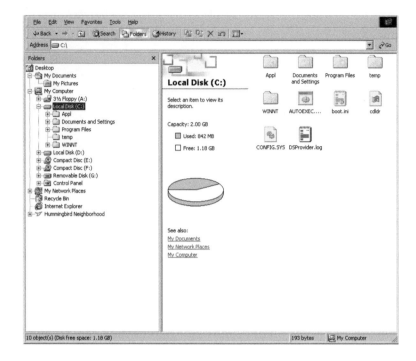

5. Click the `Allow Full Control` and `Change` under the `Permis-sions` heading. This will allow everyone read-only access. Next, click the `Add` button and the window in Figure 8.12 will be displayed.

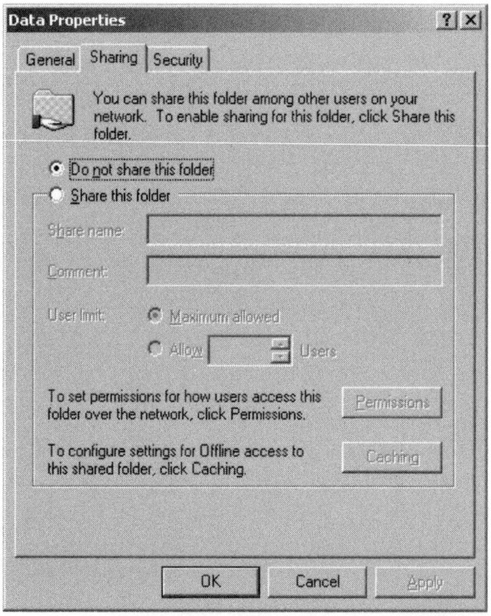

Figure 8.10
Sharing
properties for
`C:\Data`.

Figure 8.11
Permissions
for Data
window.

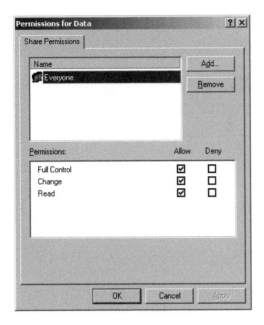

6. Scroll through the list until you find Administrators. Click Administrators, and then click the Add button. Next, click the OK
button. You should now be back to the Permissions for Data
window, as shown in Figure 8.13.

7. Click the Full Control to allow administrators full control to the
share. Click the OK button to apply your security changes. Now you
can click the OK button to create the share.

Figure 8.12
Adding a group to
the permissions
list.

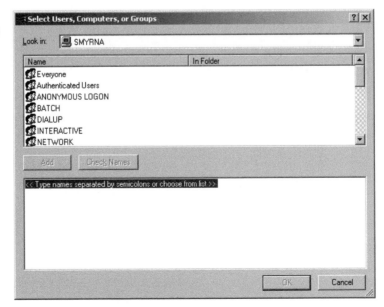

Figure 8.13
Permissions
showing
additional users.

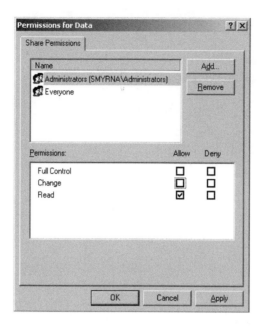

The second method for creating a share is through the MMC. The following steps will show you how to use the MMC to create the C:\Data share:

1. Follow Steps 1 and 2 from the previous method to create the C:\Data share.

2. Open the Computer Management console from the Administrative Tools folder in the Control Panel folder. You will see something similar to Figure 8.14.

Figure 8.14
Computer
Management
MMC snap-in.

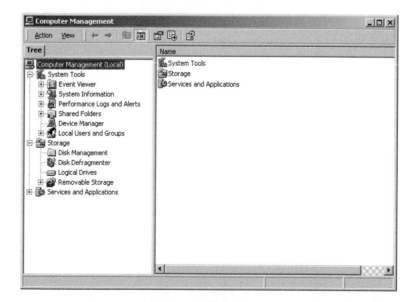

Figure 8.15
Shares menu.

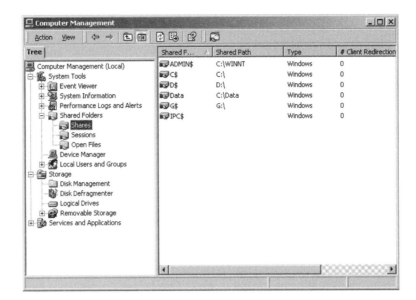

3. Select and then expand the Shared Folders item in the System Tools folder. Click the Shares item. The display should change to look similar to Figure 8.15.

4. Select New File Share from the Action menu. The Create Shared Folder window will appear. Fill in the fields as shown in Figure 8.16.

5. Click the Next button to continue. The window in Figure 8.17 will be displayed.

6. Click the Administrators have full control; other users have read-only access radio button. Click the Finish

Figure 8.16
Completed
Create Shared
Folder dialog
box.

Figure 8.17
Share
permissions
selection window.

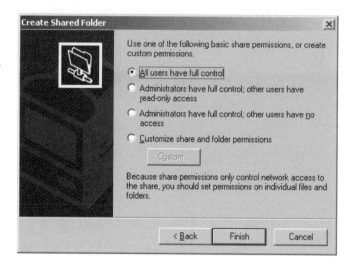

button. Answer No to the question about creating another shared folder. You can now close the MMC.

You should now have C:\Data shared. Next, we will move on to mounting SMB shares. Windows 2000 includes the ability to create hidden shares, which are not included in the browse list. You can create a hidden share by appending a $ to the end of the share name.

In addition to using the GUI to create shares, you can also use the *net* command-line utility to create shares. The following steps will guide you through using the *net* command to create a share:

1. Open a command prompt from the Start menu. You will see a window similar to the one shown in Figure 8.18.

Figure 8.18
Windows 2000
command
prompt.

Figure 8.19
Command prompt window with successful share creation.

```
D:\Users\toddw>net share Data=C:\Data /REMARK:"My Data"
Data was shared successfully.

D:\Users\toddw>
```

2. At the prompt, type the following (replacing *server* and *share* appropriately) and press <ENTER>:

   ```
   net share Data=C:\Data /REMARK:"My Data"
   ```

3. If all goes well, the share will be created successfully, as shown in Figure 8.19. Clients will now be able to connect to the new share.

MOUNTING SHARES

A network operating system would not be that good if you couldn't mount remote filesystems. Windows 2000 provides two direct methods for mounting a share on a network server. The first method is completed using the GUI interface, and the second is completed using the `net` command-line utility. The following steps will walk you through mounting a share using the GUI interface:

1. Open Windows Explorer from the `Start` menu. From the `Tools` menu, select the `Map Network Drive` option. You will see the dialog box in Figure 8.20.

2. The first available drive letter will appear in the `Drive` box. You can change this to any available letter. For fun, let's select drive `R:` In the `Folder` box, enter any valid share on your network, using the `\\`*server*`\`*share* syntax. If you want the share to be mounted every time you log on, leave the `Reconnect at logon` box checked; otherwise, clear the check box. Figure 8.20 shows the entries for connecting to the `C:\Data` share that was created earlier.

3. Once you have made your selections, click the `Finish` button to make the connection. Assuming you have the appropriate privileges,

Figure 8.20
Map Network
Drive dialog
box completed.

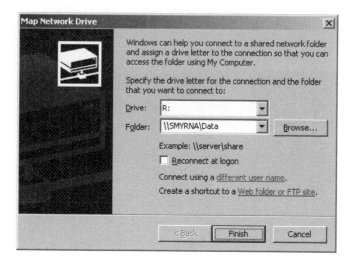

Figure 8.21
Explorer view of
mapped drive R:.

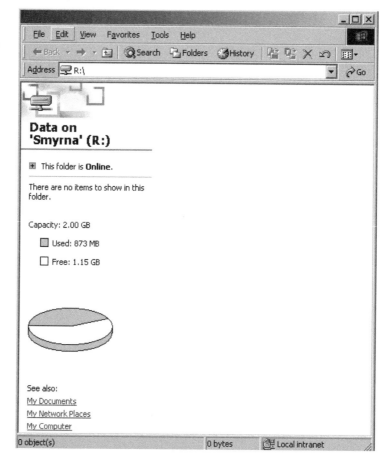

Figure 8.22 Command prompt window with successful drive mapping.

you will now have a drive R: in Explorer, and a new window should have opened displaying the contents of the new connection, similar to Figure 8.21.

If you're like me and prefer to use the command line to complete simple tasks such as these, then you can use the net command to connect. Follow the steps below to connect to our share using the net command:

1. Open a command prompt from the Start menu.
2. At the prompt, type the following (replacing *server* and *share* appropriately) and press <ENTER>:

   net use R: \\server\share

3. If all goes well, you should connect successfully, as shown in Figure 8.22. You can now interact with the share, just as before (see Figure 8.21).

UNMOUNTING SHARES

There are two methods to unmount a drive connected to a network share. The first method involves the GUI interface, and the second can be completed from the command prompt. To unmount our drive R:, created in the previous section using the GUI, follow these steps:

1. Open Windows Explorer from the Start menu. From the Tools menu, select the Disconnect Network Drive option. You will see the dialog box shown in Figure 8.23.

Figure 8.23
Drive R: has
been selected
from the list.

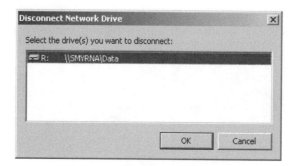

2. Select the drive to disconnect and click the OK button. If the operation completes successfully, you will see the drive disappear from the Explorer window. It may be necessary for you to refresh the Explorer display by pressing <F5> while the Windows Explorer window is the active window.

Again, you can use the command-line interface to disconnect from the network share. Use the following steps to disconnect using the command prompt:

1. Open a command prompt from the Start menu.

2. At the prompt, type the following and press, <ENTER>:

   `net use R: /delete`

3. If all goes well, you should disconnect successfully, as shown in Figure 8.24.

net—There are several commands beginning with net that provide command-line control on NT networking. net./? will provide a listing of the commands available.

```
Microsoft Windows 2000 [Version 5.00.2072]
(C) Copyright 1985-1999 Microsoft Corp.

D:\Users\toddw>net use R: /delete
R: was deleted successfully.

D:\Users\toddw>
```

Figure 8.24 Command prompt window with successful disconnection.

Table 8.9	Default Windows 2000 Shares
Share Name	Description
ADMIN$	Shared for administrative purposes, especially remote management of the server or workstation.
IPC$	Shared for inter-process communication. Connections to an SMB server share are initially negotiated over the IPC$ share.
C$, D$, etc.	The root of each logical drive is shared for administrative purposes, including remote management.

ADMINISTRATIVE AND DEFAULT SHARES

Windows 2000 includes several default shares for both administrative and system purposes. Various default shares are described in Table 8.9.

 Do not modify the default Windows 2000 shares to avoid leaving your system unstable.

UNIX SMB Services

In heterogeneous network environments, it is important to provide SMB services to and from UNIX systems. With the exception of Linux, none of the standard UNIX systems ship with any SMB service. Red Hat Linux includes a later build of SAMBA. SAMBA has quickly become the foremost SMB service for UNIX systems.

SAMBA

SAMBA provides both client and server SMB services for UNIX systems. The great advantage to this is having a unified filesystem for a user's UNIX and Windows 2000 home directories. SAMBA allows SMB connections to and from any supported UNIX platform. We will leave the actual installation of SAMBA as an exercise for the reader. SAMBA includes extensive documentation detailing the compilation and installation processes. Rather than regurgitate the SAMBA documentation, we will simply offer you what we feel to be the "best" configuration and describe the relevant features.

From here, we are assuming that you have compiled and installed SAMBA on your UNIX server. At this point, you will need to configure your smb.conf file. While reading this section, you may find it useful to have one of the SAMBA Web sites in front of you, so that you can access the

SAMBA documentation. The nearest SAMBA mirror site can be located by browsing to http://www.samba.org. You will find the following guidelines useful in configuring SAMBA:

- Keep it simple. Don't do more than is necessary, or you will just be wasting your time. Let Windows 2000 provide the services it was designed to provide. You should use Windows 2000 servers to provide WINS and browsing services; unless you are brave, don't use SAMBA to replace native Windows 2000 services.
- Use SAMBA's built-in sharing capabilities as much as possible. You don't want to be editing your smb.conf file every time you add/remove a user or printer. Use the *homes* and *shares* sections to make your UNIX home directories and printers available to your NetBIOS clients.

The following is an example *smb.conf* file:

```
#====================== Global Settings ===================
[global]
   netbios name = <SERVER_NAME>
   workgroup = <WORKGROUP/DOMAIN NAME>
   server string = Samba %v Server

   browseable = yes

   hosts allow = 192.168.1. 192.168.2.
   hosts deny = 192.168.3. 192.168.4.

   load printers = yes
   printcap name = /etc/printcap
   printing = bsd

   log file = /var/log/samba/log.%m
   max log size = 50

   security = server
   password server = <PDC_NAME>

   username map = /etc/smbusers
   domain group map = /etc/smbgroups

   encrypt passwords = no

   socket options = TCP_NODELAY SO_RCVBUF=8192 SO_SNDBUF=8192

   local master = no
   domain master = no
   preferred master = yes
   os level = 0
```

```
   name resolve order = wins lmhosts bcast
   wins support = no
   wins server = 192.168.1.10
   wins proxy = no

   lm announce = false

   dns proxy = no

#==================== Share Definitions =====================
[homes]
   comment = Home Directory for %U
   browseable = no
   guest ok = no
   writable = yes

[tmp]
   comment = Temporary file space
   path = /tmp
   read only = no
   public = yes

[printers]
   comment = All printers in /etc/printcap
   path = /var/spool/samba
   printable = yes
```

So what does all that mean? Well, if you set the names appropriately, you will be able to access all home directories and printers, as well as /tmp from any Windows machine on your domain. The SAMBA server will authenticate connections against your domain controller. Since this may seem a bit confusing taken all at once, we'll explain some of the various sections and the variables in those sections, so you'll better understand what we are doing here.

The [global] section contains settings that control the overall configuration of your SAMBA service. This section specifies the identity of your server and can set many defaults used in other sections. Table 8.10 describes some of the variables used in the [global] section.

The [homes] section, if defined, allows SAMBA to dynamically share users' home directories upon request, such as when an attempt is made to connect to \\server\username. This section sets defaults for all dynamically created home directory shares. Table 8.11 describes some of the variables used in the [homes] section.

The [printers] section, if defined, allows SAMBA to create printer shares from the local /etc/printcap configuration file. This section sets defaults for all dynamically created printer shares. Table 8.12 describes some of the variables used in the [printers] section.

Table 8.10 SAMBA `[global]` **Section Variables**

Variable	Value	Description
netbios name	*Text*	The name (no pun intended) really speaks for itself. This parameter specifies the name that the SAMBA server will advertise on the NetBIOS network. It is best to keep this name the same as your DNS hostname.
workgroup	*Text*	Indicates which NetBIOS network the SAMBA server will belong to. There is no option for domain name; this option covers both realms.
server string	*Text*	This is equivalent to the description of a Windows machine. Use this line to provide a more meaningful description of your SAMBA server.
browseable	*yes/no*	This sets the default browse option for all services. In a nutshell, this option determines whether or not a server is advertised to the network. We recommend setting this variable to *yes*.
hosts allow	*Comma-separated list*	Specifies a list of IP addresses (or subnets) that are allowed to access your SAMBA server.
hosts deny	*Comma-separated list*	Specifies a list of IP addresses (or subnets) that are *NOT* allowed to access your SAMBA server.
load printers	*yes/no*	Specifies whether or not the printers on your SAMBA server will be loaded when you start the SAMBA service.
printcap name	*Pathname*	Specifies where to find your `printcap` file to load the printers.
printing	*AIX	BSD	HPUX	LPRNG	PLP	QNX	SOFTQ	SYSV*	Specifies the type of printing system to use. The most common printing system is BSD.
log file	*Pathname*	Specifies a path to log Samba messages to. This is typically somewhere in the `/var/log` directory.
max log size	*Number*	Specifies how large the log file is allowed to be.

Table 8.10	SAMBA `[global]` Section Variables (continued)	
Variable	Value	Description
security	*Share	User	Server	domain*	Specifies the security level employed by the SAMBA sever. The values correspond to their Windows counterparts. Share-level security provides a password for each service/resource. User-level security requires that the user connecting be authenticated via the `passwd` file. Server- and domain-level security both use Windows NT servers to authenticate user connections. Domain-level security allows users from trusted domains to authenticate, while server-level security does not.
password server	*NetBIOS name*	Specifies the name of your server (typically the PDC) to use as the authentication server.
username map	*Pathname*	Specifies the file that maps UNIX user names to NT user names. This can be useful for users, such as root and administrator, which do not have identically named users on their respective systems.
domain group map	*Pathname*	This is the same as the `username map` variable, except it provides group mappings.
encrypt passwords	*yes/no*	Specifies whether passwords will be encrypted or passed as clear text. You should always specify `yes` when using server- or domain-level security.
socket options		Use the default values for this parameter, they work!
local master	*yes/no*	Specifies whether or not the SAMBA server will be a local master browser on the NetBIOS network. Unless an NT server is not available on the local subnet, you should always specify `no` for this parameter.
domain master	*yes/no*	Specifies whether or not the SAMBA server will be a domain master browser on the NetBIOS network. Unless an NT server is not available on the domain/workgroup, you should always specify `no` for this parameter.
preferred master	*yes/no*	Specifies whether the SAMBA server will be a preferred master browser on the NetBIOS network. Unless an NT server is not available anywhere, always specify *no* for this parameter.

(continued)

Table 8.10	**SAMBA** [global] **Section Variables (continued)**	
Variable	Value	Description
os level	*Number*	Specifies the priority the SAMBA server will have in winning browse master elections. The higher you set this number (max. 33), the more likely it is the SAMBA server will win the election. We recommend setting this parameter to 0, unless no NT server is available.
name resolve order	*String*	Specifies the order in which the SAMBA server will resolve NetBIOS names. The most common resolve order is *wins lmhosts bcast*.
wins support	*yes/no*	Specifies whether or not the SAMBA server will also provide NetBIOS name resolution capabilities. Unless an NT server is not available, do not enable this on your Windows NT network.
wins server	*IP address*	Specifies the server to query for WINS requests.
wins proxy	*yes/no*	Specifies whether or not the SAMBA server will serve as a WINS proxy for non-WINS-enabled clients, such as UNIX workstations not running SAMBA.
lm announce	*yes/no*	Specifies whether or not the SAMBA server will make LanManager announcements to the network. Unless you have legacy LanManager clients on your network, set this parameter to *no*.
dns proxy	*yes/no*	Specifies whether or not the SAMBA server will serve as a DNS proxy.

You can also explicitly create any share under a [<sharename>] section and configure it however you wish. You can use any of the allowed variables as specified in the SAMBA documentation. Following is a more complete version of the *smb.conf* file discussed earlier, including share and printer definitions:

Table 8.11	SAMBA [homes]	**Section Variables**
Variable	Value	Description
comment	*Text*	Used to describe the service being offered. When used in the [homes] section, you should specify a generic phrase.
browseable	*yes/no*	Specifies whether or not this service is browseable on the NetBIOS network.
guest ok	*yes/no*	Specifies whether or not guests are allowed to access this share. When used in the *homes* section, we recommend that you set this to *no*.
writeable	*yes/no*	Specifies whether or not the share can be written to. Unless you only want users to see their home directory and not use it, specify *yes* for this parameter.

Table 8.12	SAMBA [printers]	**Section Variables**
Variable	Value	Description
comment	*Text*	Used to describe the service being offered. When used in the [printers] section, you should specify a generic phrase.
browseable	*yes/no*	Specifies whether or not this service is browseable on the NetBIOS network.
path	*pathname*	Specifies the path to spool documents to. This is usually somewhere in the /var/spool directory.
printable	*yes/no*	Specifies whether or not the printers can be printed to. Why create the share and then say, "No, you can't print, ha, ha." Always set this parameter to *yes*.

```
#=============== Global Settings ===========================
[global]
    netbios name = LILDIPPER
    workgroup = COSMOS
    server string = Samba %v Server

    browseable = yes

    hosts allow = 192.168.
    hosts deny = 192.168.224.

    load printers = yes
    printcap name = /etc/printcap
    printing = bsd
```

```
      log file = /var/log/samba/log.%m
      max log size = 50

      security = server
      password server = ORION

      username map = /etc/smbusers
      domain group map = /etc/smbgroups

      encrypt passwords = no

      socket options = TCP_NODELAY SO_RCVBUF=8192 SO_SND-
      BUF=8192

      local master = no
      domain master = no
      preferred master = yes
      os level = 0

      name resolve order = wins lmhosts bcast
      wins support = no
      wins server = 192.168.1.10
      wins proxy = no

      lm announce = false

      dns proxy = no
#==================== Share Definitions =====================
[homes]
   comment = Home Directory for %U
   browseable = no
   guest ok = no
   writable = yes

[users]
   comment = Users file space
   path = /home/users
   read only = no
   public = yes

[tmp]
   comment = Temporary file space
   path = /tmp
   read only = no
   public = yes

[printers]
   comment = All printers in /etc/printcap
   path = /var/spool/samba
   printable = yes
```

Other Solaris Products

There are many other third-party products that have been developed to support data sharing between UNIX and the Windows family of operating systems. Though not as common as the packages covered in this chapter, the following two products are often found in Solaris/Windows 2000 environments.

SOLARIS PC NETLINK 1.1

Solaris PC Netlink 1.1 provides native Windows 2000 file, print, directory, and authentication services. PC Netlink is based on AT&T's Advanced Server for UNIX and runs under Solaris 7 on SPARC or Intel platforms. Solaris PC Netlink can act as a domain controller and interact with Windows 2000 domain controllers running Active Directory. This product is bundled with all new Sun servers equipped with from one to eight processors. There is no charge for client licenses.

SOLARIS EASY ACCESS SERVER 3.X

Solaris Easy Access Server is a suite of software allowing the integration of Solaris and Windows 2000 systems. The suite of software is divided into three areas, consisting of administration, network services, and interoper-

Table 8.13 Easy Access Server Administration

Package	Description
Solstice AdminSuite™ 3.0	Remote administration of users, groups, network information, and filesystems.
Solaris Administration Wizards	Perform administration tasks in Solaris such as changing passwords, configuring DNS, and making network settings.
Solaris Print Manager 1.0	Administer print services provided by Solaris.
Solaris Management Console 1.0.1	Administration console for Solaris on remote and local servers.
Solaris Web Start 2.0.2	Deployment of Solaris Easy Access Server 3.0.
AnswerBook2™ 1.4	Web-based help system for Easy Access Server components.

Table 8.14 **Easy Access Server Network Services**	
Package	Description
Sun Directory Services 3.1	LDAPv3 directory server.
Sun WebServer 2.1	HTTP server.
Solstice DiskSuite 4.2	Software RAID and disk administration utilities.
Solstice Internet Mail Server 2.0	Electronic mail and message server.
Solstice PPP 3.0.1	Remote dial-up connectivity.
Netscape Communicator 4.51	Solaris Netscape browser.
JDK 1.1.7-07	APIs and tools for developing Java programs.

ability. The Solaris Easy Access Server provides a complete package of services for all Windows 2000 workgroups.

The administration portion of Easy Access Server consists of six different packages. Table 8.13 contains a brief description of each package. These packages provide the foundation to administer Solaris machines on the network.

The network services portion consists of seven different packages that provide all the services required for an organization to participate in the Internet world. Table 8.14 contains a brief description of each package.

The interoperability package is the portion that provides the link between Solaris and Windows 2000 systems. Solaris PC Netlink 1.1 allows Windows 2000 clients to obtain file, print, naming, and authentication services from a Solaris server. The Sun Enterprise Authentication Mechanism 1.0 allows secure authentication between Solaris servers and Windows 2000 clients using the Kerberos V5 standard. Solaris WBEM Services 1.0 is a set of tools and services based on the Distributed Management Task Force's Web-Based Enterprise Management (WBEM) initiative, which allows applications to manage the Solaris operating environment.

Summary

In this chapter, we discussed protocols and services for sharing data between computers. NFS and SMB are both designed to run off TCP/IP and are used by their respective operating systems to allow for directory or filesystem sharing.

NFS

The Network Filesystem allows different operating systems the ability to exchange data transparently. The major components of NFS are the remote procedure call (RPC) and the external data representation (XDR) language. RPCs allow a local machine to request that a remote machine perform a function and return the results of that request. XDR defines data structures in a machine-independent manner. This allows NFS to share directories and filesystems over the network between different operating systems. NFS has become the *de facto* standard in UNIX operating systems, but it is also available on many other operating systems, including Windows 2000.

SMB

SMB is the protocol primarily used by Windows 2000 for network connections to files, printers, and resources. The SMB protocol runs on top of TCP/IP, NetBEUI, and IPX/SPX. This versatility allows SMB to function in almost any network environment. There have been several variants to the base SMB protocol over the years, most notably the NTLM protocol used in Windows NT 4.0 and Windows 2000. The latest variant to the SMB protocol is CIFS, or the Common Internet Filesystem. CIFS is NTLM plus a few extras for optimizing performance over the Internet. SMB is a client/server protocol, and is available for many platforms.

SAMBA

SAMBA provides both client and server SMB services for UNIX systems. SAMBA allows SMB connections to and from most UNIX platforms. With the exception of Linux, none of the standard UNIX systems ship with any SMB service. Red Hat Linux includes a later build of SAMBA. SAMBA has quickly become the foremost SMB service for UNIX systems. The nearest SAMBA mirror site is located at `http://www.samba.org`. SAMBA is free and not difficult to install.

This chapter explained the concepts, applications, and procedures necessary to share files and directories between computing systems. The next logical step, and an essential part of system administration, is to provide individuals the ability to share information with each other via the computer/network infrastructure. Thus, the next chapter will cover the installation and configuration of electronic mail services.

ELECTRONIC MAIL AND MESSAGING

UNIX

Electronic Mail Protocols

Sendmail Installing

Sendmail Configuring

Testing Sendmail

Running Sendmail

WINDOWS 2000

Microsoft Exchange Server

Installing Exchange Server 5.5

Creating Mailboxes

Creating Distribution Lists

Exchange 2000 Server

Electronic mail is quite possibly the most critical of all services provided on your network. In today's world, businesses depend on electronic mail as much as they to depend on electricity or telephones. This chapter provides an overview of Sendmail for UNIX systems and Microsoft Exchange Server for Windows 2000 systems. We intend to provide you with a basic framework that will help you to get started with electronic mail services. A fundamental difference between Sendmail and Exchange 5.5 is the way in which email accounts are created. Email is a direct by-product of a UNIX account. Once the account is created, email is available. In Exchange, however, an email account must be created separately. This difference is reflected in the material presented in this chapter.

Overview of Electronic Mail

Getting email to its destination requires three basic agents: the Mail Transfer Agent (MTA), the Mail Delivery Agent (MDA), and the Mail User Agent (MUA). These agents work together to send, route, and deliver email to its final destination. To successfully interact, agents must conform to standard protocols. The Internet Engineering Task Force (IETF) administers the official Internet protocol standards for electronic mail. We will briefly explain the agents and standards for electronic mail in the following two sections.

MAIL AGENTS

The MTA handles the routing of email on the Internet or within your local organization. The MTA performs three primary functions: it routes email to other MTAs, it delivers email to an MDA (Sendmail only) locally, and it accepts email from an MUA. Protocols utilized in the transfer of email are determined through negotiation. The main protocols are the Simple Mail Transfer Protocol (SMTP) and the Extended Simple Mail Transfer Protocol (ESMTP). Sendmail and Exchange are MTAs and will be reviewed later in this chapter.

The MDA handles local delivery of email. The MDA receives email from the MTA and delivers the email to a directory that can be accessed by the MUA. UNIX Sendmail frequently utilizes `/bin/mail` or `procmail` for its MDA. Exchange doesn't utilize an MDA.

The MUA is the user interface to email. It allows the user to edit, view, store, and manipulate email. The MUA is responsible for formatting email in accordance with the standard for the format of ARPA Internet text messages (RFC822). It also "talks" to SMTP/ESMTP with an MTA when it is sending email. The Post Office Protocol (POP) and Internet Message Access Protocol Version 4rev1 (IMAP4rev1) were developed to transfer email from the mail server to the client for manipulation. We cover the different types of MUAs for UNIX and Windows 2000 clients in the following sections.

STANDARDS

The official Internet protocol standards for email are contained in requests for comment (RFCs) that are administered by the Internet Engineering Task Force (IETF, `http://www.ietf.org`). The RFCs listed in Table 9.1 are the current Internet standards for email. Each of these RFCs contains detailed protocol specifications for the exchange of email on the Internet. The mail agents discussed above must conform to these standards to successfully send and receive electronic mail over the Internet. The RFCs dealing with Multipurpose Internet Mail Extensions (MIME, RFC1521 and

Table 9.1	Email RFCs
RFC Number	Title
RFC821	Simple Mail Transfer Protocol (SMTP)
RFC822	Format of Electronic Mail Messages
RFC1869	SMTP Service Extensions
RFC1870	SMTP Service Extensions for Message Size
RFC1939	Post Office Protocol, Version 3

RFC1522) are draft standards. RFC2060, Internet Message Access Protocol Version 4rev1(IMAP4rev1), is a proposed standard.

POP AND IMAP4REV1

POP and IMAP4rev1 utilize a client/server paradigm. The client contacts the server and is authenticated with a username and password. The server must have access to the maildrop directory, but is not necessarily an MTA. POP is older than IMAP4rev1. The majority of the newer email clients include both protocols.

POP is a very simple and effective protocol. Email is transferred from the server to the local client for manipulation. It is effective for users who utilize a single workstation for email.

IMAP4rev1 was developed for the user who utilizes multiple workstations for email. It incorporates all of the features of POP and adds the ability to access email/mailboxes on a remote server. IMAP4rev1 has the capability to manipulate mailboxes on a local machine or remote server. A mail client with IMAP4rev1 can be configured to download only message header or message body. These configuration options are utilized when accessing email remotely or when bandwidth is limited. The default configuration is to download a complete message when bandwidth is not a problem or the user requires attachments. By providing download options, IMAP4rev1 clients can be written to provide a quick email scanning capability, by allowing the client to only download certain message information. This is advantageous in situations where network connections are slow or client resources are limited (PDAs). There is also the capability to resynchronize an off-line client with the server. Information on IMAP4rev1 can be obtained at
`http://www.imap.org.`

A free version of the server daemon source code for IMAP4rev1 and POP can be obtained at `ftp://ftp.cac.washington.edu/imap/imap.tar.Z`. The installation is very easy and straightforward. The `makefile` contains configurations to allow easy compilation for all major versions of UNIX. The `/etc/services` file (updating the NIS or NIS+ master server database, which is covered in Chapter 7, "Directory Services") must be edited to contain the following lines:

```
pop2            109/tcp         pop-2           # Post Office
pop3            110/tcp         pop             # Post Office
imap            143/tcp                         # Pine IMAP protocol
```

The `/etc/inetd.conf` file on the server must have the following additional lines:

```
pop2    stream  tcp     nowait  root    /etc/local/etc/ipop2d    ipop2d
pop3    stream  tcp     nowait  root    /etc/local/etc/ipop3d    ipop3d
imap    stream  tcp     nowait  root    /etc/local/etc/imapd      imapd
```

The actual location of the daemons is dependent on your system. They do not have to be in the `/usr/local/etc` directory. Finally, send `inetd` a `SIGHUP`.

SECURE SOCKETS LAYER FOR POP AND IMAP4REV1

The Secure Sockets Layer (SSL) protocol can be layered on top of POP and IMAP4rev1 to provide an encrypted link between the UNIX server and client (UNIX or Windows 2000). The SSL protocol negotiates an encryption scheme and keys between the client and server. Upon completion of the negotiation, all data passed between the server and client is encrypted.

The OpenSSL Project has developed an open source toolkit that implements the SSL protocol. It is free and available for download at `http://www.openssl.org`. It is simple to install and recognizes all major UNIX versions. In addition, you will need to download `stunnel` at `http://mike.daewoo.com.pl/computer/stunnel/`. `stunnel` is a UNIX service that provides a "wrapper" for a TCP service (POP and IMAP4rev1). The "wrapper" encrypts the data connection using SSL. `stunnel` utilizes `include` files and libraries created by OpenSSL. The final step is obtaining a digital certificate, or secure server ID, from a certification authority. The client side just requires an email client that is SSL-enabled (like Netscape Communicator, Outlook Express, or Eudora).

Make sure you review the README file in the top level of the OpenSSL distribution directory. It contains an overview of what is included in the package. Make sure you read the information about patents. The RSA, RC5, and IDEA algorithms are patented and will require the permission of the patent holder in certain countries.

Sendmail

Sendmail is the most commonly used MTA in UNIX. Sendmail is provided in all UNIX distributions. However, it is a good idea to download the most recent version, which is usually more current than the one provided in your operating system release. Each version of Sendmail corrects known security problems and provides new options. Security issues related to electronic mail are discussed in Chapter 11, "Security."

INSTALLATION

To download the current version of Sendmail, point your browser at `http:\\www.sendmail.org`. This site is maintained by the Sendmail Consortium and has the latest freeware releases of Sendmail. There is a wealth of information at this site that will aid in your installation of Sendmail. Download the current release (Sendmail 8.9.3 for this example installation) of Sendmail. Once downloaded, you will have to uncompress (utilize GNU gunzip) and then extract the distribution using `tar`. Change into the directory created by `tar` (`sendmail-8.9.3`). The top-level directory for the distribution is provided here:

```
BuildTools    Makefile        contrib      makemap      src
FAQ           README          doc          praliases    test
KNOWNBUGS     RELEASE_NOTES   mail.local   rmail
LICENSE       cf              mailstats    smrsh
```

Compiling the source is performed in the `src` directory. Change into the `src` directory. This directory contains a `Build` shell script file that will automatically detect your operating system, compile the source, and leave the binaries in a subdirectory that reflects the operating system and architecture (e.g., `obj.Linux.2.2.12.i686`). The default values for installation of the binaries are contained in Table 9.2. To build and install the binaries with the default values, execute the following command:

```
#./Build install
```

Table 9.2	Default Location of Sendmail Binaries
Binary	Location
Sendmail	/usr/sbin
Sendmail.hf	/usr/lib
Sendmail.st	/etc
Man pages	/usr/man

For special configurations, the `Build` script will process command-line options. Consult the `README` file in the `src` directory for valid options. The subdirectory created by the build process contains a file named `Makefile`. `Makefile` controls the compilation and installation processes. Special options and switches can be added to `Makefile` before compiling the source. Be careful and always make a backup of the original `Makefile` before modifying the file.

CONFIGURATION

The successful implementation of Sendmail depends on the `send-mail.cf` file. `sendmail.cf` is a text file with a unique syntax. The syntax Sendmail uses makes it very difficult to edit the `sendmail.cf` file with a simple text editor. A small portion of `sendmail.cf` is provided here:

```
#     Trusted users     #
########################

# this is equivalent to setting class "t"
#Ft/etc/sendmail.ct
Troot
Tdaemon


###############################
#     Format of headers     #
###############################

H?P?Return-Path: <$g>
HReceived: $?sfrom $s $.$?_($?s$|from $.$_)
        $.by $j ($v/$Z)$?r with $r$. id $i$?u
        for $u; $|;
        $.$b
H?D?Resent-Date: $a
H?D?Date: $a
H?F?Resent-From: $?x$x <$g>$|$g$.
H?F?From: $?x$x <$g>$|$g$.
H?x?Full-Name: $x
```

This file is read every time Sendmail starts. It determines the location of important configuration files, Sendmail options, and rules for determining how email will be processed. The next few paragraphs take you through the procedures of developing a `sendmail.cf` file for a mail server.

The developers of Sendmail have included powerful m4 macros to provide a less painful way of generating the `sendmail.cf` file. The m4 utility is a macro processor used as a preprocessor for C, assembler, and other languages. The macros are located in the `cf` directory shown in the previous "Installation" section. The following `cf` directory contains the master configuration file that will call other macro files from the `domain`, `feature`, `hack`, `mailer`, and `ostype` directories:

README	domain	hack	mailer	sh
cf	feature	m4	ostype	siteconfig

We will create files in the `cf` and `domain` directories to generate an example `sendmail.cf` file. The first step is to change into the `domain` directory. This directory will contain files with the `m4` suffix. Copy the `generic.m4` file, changing its name to your domain, `sniglets.com.m4`. The new file is displayed in Listing 9.1. We will now examine the file we have just created.

`divert(-1)` (minus one) line signals `m4` to suppress output, which excludes comments from being added to the `sendmail.cf` file. `divert(0)` signals `m4` to resume regular output. The next few lines contain macros and definitions that will be added to the `sendmail.cf` file. This file should be used to specify macros, options, and definitions that may be required for this particular mail host. The `define` line configures the search path that Sendmail will traverse for a user's `.forward` file.

The next line, `FEATURE(redirect)dnl`, bounces mail back to the sender with the message `551 User not local ; please try <newaddress>` when the `REDIRECT` option is used in the alias file. The flexibility of `m4` allows `FEATURE` lines to be included in the master configuration file or the domain configuration file. There are approximately 30 features that can be specified. The `README` file, located in the `cf` directory, contains a complete listing of these features and their definitions. Best practice is to place all of the `FEATURE` lines in one configuration file.

The final line instructs Sendmail to read the `/etc/sendmail.cw` file. The `sendmail.cw` file contains hostnames that the local mail machine will interpret as its own name. The `sendmail.cw` file performs a mail alias function. The `README` file in the top level of the `cf` directory provides a complete listing of all macros, options, and definitions valid for the .m4 domain file.

Listing 9.1 Domain Configuration File for `sniglets.com`

```
divert(-1)
#
# Copyright (c) 1998 Sendmail, Inc.  All rights reserved.
# Copyright (c) 1983 Eric P. Allman.  All rights reserved.
# Copyright (c) 1988, 1993
#       The Regents of the University of California.  All rights reserved.
#
# By using this file, you agree to the terms and conditions set
divert(-1)
#
```

```
#
#  The following is a generic domain file.  You should be able to
#  use it anywhere.  If you want to customize it, copy it to a file
#  named with your domain and make the edits; then, copy the appropriate
#  .mc files and change 'DOMAIN(generic)' to reference your updated domain
#  files.
#
divert(0)
VERSIONID('@(#)generic.m4       8.9 (Berkeley) 5/19/1998')
define('confFORWARD_PATH',
'$z/.forward.$w+$h:$z/.forward+$h:$z/.forward.$w:$z/.
forward')dnl
FEATURE(redirect)dnl
FEATURE(use_cw_file)dnl
```

The master configuration file for `sendmail.cf` is located in the `cf` directory (`cf/cf`). This directory contains generic text configuration files named according to the type of UNIX version you have (e.g., `generic-hpux10.mc`, `generic-solaris2.mc`, etc.). Try to select a generic file that most closely matches your workstation/server. Make a copy of this file and give it your domain name.

We will configure a Linux workstation to be the main mail server for `sniglets.com`. The `tcpproto.mc` file is selected to serve as a template for developing our configuration file. Make a copy of the `tcpproto.mc` file, but change the name to your domain (`sniglets.com.mc`, Listing 9.2).

The master configuration file, `sniglets.com.mc`, must have an `OS-TYPE` line. The locations of files and queues are controlled by this macro. The `ostype` directory contains a file for each supported operating system. Locate your operating system and change `unknown` to the applicable operating system (`linux`).

The `OSTYPE` line should be the first line after the `VERSIONID` line.

Previously, we created a `sniglets.com.m4` file in the `domain` directory. To include the macros and features defined in this file, we need to add a `DOMAIN` line to our configuration file. This line should be placed after the `OSTYPE` line. Enter the following line in `sniglets.com.mc`:

```
DOMAIN(sniglets.com)
```

The final two lines specify the mailer type. The line `MAILER(local)` configures the local and prog MDAs. The local MDA delivers mail to users on the local machine. The prog MDA allows mail to be delivered by "piping" it through a program. This is not required if all of the mail is simply being relayed.

Listing 9.2   **Master Configuration File for** `sniglets.com`

```
divert(-1)
#
# Copyright (c) 1998 Sendmail, Inc.  All rights reserved.
# Copyright (c) 1983 Eric P. Allman.  All rights reserved.
# Copyright (c) 1988, 1993
#      The Regents of the University of California.  All rights reserved.
#
# By using this file, you agree to the terms and conditions set
# forth in the LICENSE file which can be found at the top level of
# the sendmail distribution.
#
#


#
# This is the prototype file for a configuration that supports nothing
# but basic SMTP connections via TCP.
#
# You MUST change the 'OSTYPE' macro to specify the operating system
# on which this will run; this will set the location of various
# support files for your operating system environment.  You MAY
# create a domain file in ../domain and reference it by adding a
# 'DOMAIN' macro after the 'OSTYPE' macro.  I recommend that you
# first copy this to another file name so that new sendmail releases
# will not trash your changes.
#

divert(0)dnl
VERSIONID('@(#)tcpproto.mc      8.10 (Berkeley) 5/19/1998')
OSTYPE(unknown)
MAILER(local)
MAILER(smtp)
```

The final line, `MAILER(smtp)`, enables the Simple Mail Transport Protocol (SMTP). This line activates SMTP, extended SMTP, SMTP8 (SMTP without converting 8-bit data to MIME), and the relay function. This line enables our Linux mail server to exchange mail with the rest of the Internet. This line assumes that all mailers are running DNS.

Listing 9.3 **Abbreviated Master Configuration File,** `sniglets.com.mc`

```
divert(0)dnl
VERSIONID('@(#)tcpproto.mc        8.10 (Berkeley) 5/19/1998')
OSTYPE(linux)
DOMAIN(sniglets.com)
MAILER(local)
MAILER(smtp)
```

The master configuration file is now complete and an abbreviated version is in Listing 9.3. The next step is to generate the `sendmail.cf` file utilizing m4. The Sendmail distribution includes a pre-processing file under the m4 (`cf.m4`) directory that must be part of the input for the m4 processor. The command to generate the `sendmail.cf` file for `sniglets.com` is:

```
#m4 ../m4/cf.m4 sniglets-com.mc > sniglets-com.cf
```

After you verify that the `sniglets-com.cf` file forwards email properly, copy it to `/etc/sendmail.cf`. The `Testing` section will review the procedures to validate your Sendmail binaries and configuration.

Configuring a `sendmail.cf` file for a client UNIX workstation that forwards email to a mail server is a much simpler process. Go directly to the `cf` directory and use the `clientproto.mc` file as the template for a UNIX relaying host. The `OSTYPE` line will require substituting the operating system type (`linux`) for the placeholder `unknown` (check the `ostype` directory for a list of known operating system types). The `FEATURE` line will require changing `mailhost.$m` to the name of your mail server (`mail.sniglets.com`, in our case). Run this file through the m4 processor like the example above for a mail server.

TESTING

The Sendmail configuration file must be tested before using it in a production environment. Running Sendmail in test mode allows you to confirm that the configuration file is processing email correctly.

The Sendmail binary is already in place in `/usr/sbin` as a result of our previous `Build install` command. The Sendmail configuration file is still in the configuration directory of the Sendmail distribution. For this example, we will assume a top-level directory of `/tmp/sendmail-8.9.3`. A good test consists of a mixture of local and remote addresses. To place Sendmail in test mode, execute the following command:

```
#/usr/sbin/sendmail -bt -C/tmp/sendmail-8.9.3/cf/cf/
sniglets-com.cf
```

The `-bt` option tells Sendmail to go into address test mode, and the `-C` option sets the configuration file (without the `-C` option, Sendmail will use `/etc/sendmail.cf`). The result is the following prompt:

```
ADDRESS TEST MODE (ruleset 3 NOT automatically invoked)
Enter <ruleset> <address>
>
```

Every message is processed by Sendmail using the options, configurations, and rulesets contained in the `sendmail.cf` file. Rulesets consist of an S# configuration command, which signifies the start of a rule (a number is inserted for the # sign). Lines beginning with an R signify a rule line and become part of the previous S# ruleset. An example of Ruleset 3 is provided below:

```
##################################################
###  Ruleset 3 — Name Canonicalization  ###
##################################################
S3

# handle null input (translate to <@> special case)
R$@                     $@ <@>

# strip group: syntax (not inside angle brackets!) and trailing semicolon
R$*                     $: $1 <@>                    mark addresses
R$* < $* > $* <@>       $: $1 < $2 > $3              unmark <addr>
R@ $* <@>               $: @ $1                      unmark @host:...
R$* :: $* <@>           $: $1 :: $2                  unmark node::addr
R:include: $* <@>       $: :include: $1              unmark :include:...
R$* [ $* : $* ] <@>     $: $1 [ $2 : $3 ]            unmark IPv6 addrs
R$* : $* [ $* ]         $: $1 : $2 [ $3 ] <@>        remark if leading colon
R$* : $* <@>            $: $2                        strip colon if marked
R$* <@>                 $: $1                        unmark
R$* ;                      $1                        strip trailing sem
S10
```

There are three values contained on the rule line. The first field, or left-hand side (lhs), is matched against the sender/recipient address on the message. The second field, or right-hand side (rhs), is expanded if the lhs matches the address. The final field is optional and contains comments. The rules are processed in order until a match is found.

Next you will need to enter rulesets and addresses. The following brief description of rulesets is in order of processing by Sendmail. Ruleset 3 performs pre-processing on the sender and recipient addresses to make them legible to the Sendmail program. Ruleset 0 determines which MDA will be utilized for each recipient address. Ruleset 1 processes the sender address, and Ruleset 2 processes all recipient addresses. Ruleset 4 processes all addresses and converts them from internal to external representations. Finally, Ruleset 5 processes all local addresses that have not been aliased to allow for selection of a different delivery agent (examples include forwarding to other types of networks or using a firewall as a mail exchanger to protect "interior" machines).

Ruleset 0 does the most important work of determining how the message will be sent. Ruleset 0 returns a tuple that is made up of the keys in Table 9.3. The first key determines the delivery agent. Email addresses not local to your domain in the recipient field should return ESMTP. For recipients local to your domain, Ruleset 0 will return the local delivery agent. We will use Rulesets 3 and 0 in all of our examples. You can enter a single ruleset or multiple rulesets (separate with commas), but only one address.

The first example (Listing 9.4) tests the address of local user `joe`.

Table 9.3	Ruleset 0 Output Fields
Key	**Definition** (Value is all text following the key, ignoring spaces and not including the next key.)
$##	Delivery agent
$@	Host
$:	User

Listing 9.4   **Ruleset Output for Local User**

```
> 3,0 joe
rewrite: ruleset   3    input: joe
rewrite: ruleset  96    input: joe
rewrite: ruleset  96 returns: joe
rewrite: ruleset   3 returns: joe
rewrite: ruleset   0    input: joe
rewrite: ruleset 199    input: joe
rewrite: ruleset 199 returns: joe
rewrite: ruleset  98    input: joe
rewrite: ruleset  98 returns: joe
rewrite: ruleset 198    input: joe
rewrite: ruleset 198 returns: $# local $: joe
rewrite: ruleset   0 returns: $# local $: joe
>
```

Rulesets can internally call other rulesets. In our example, Rulesets 3 and 0 both call other rulesets. The important information for this example is what Ruleset 3 and 0 return. Ruleset 3 returns `joe`, which is what you want for a local user. Ruleset 0 returns only two pieces of information: The delivery agent of `local` and the user `joe`. Since this is a local delivery, there is no requirement for a host. This output indicates that your `sendmail.cf` file is configured correctly for local deliveries.

The second example tests a remote recipient address. Listing 9.5 contains the output from Rulesets 3 and 0.

Listing 9.5   Ruleset Output for Remote User

```
> 3,0 dsw@anyxyz.com
rewrite: ruleset   3   input: dsw @ anyxyz . com
rewrite: ruleset  96   input: dsw < @ anyxyz . com >
rewrite: ruleset  96 returns: dsw < @ anyxyz . com >
rewrite: ruleset   3 returns: dsw < @ anyxyz . com >
rewrite: ruleset   0   input: dsw < @ anyxyz . com >
rewrite: ruleset 199   input: dsw < @ anyxyz . com >
rewrite: ruleset 199 returns: dsw < @ anyxyz . com >
rewrite: ruleset  98   input: dsw < @ anyxyz . com >
rewrite: ruleset  98 returns: dsw < @ anyxyz . com >
rewrite: ruleset 198   input: dsw < @ anyxyz . com >
rewrite: ruleset  95   input: < > dsw < @ anyxyz . com >
rewrite: ruleset  95 returns: dsw < @ anyxyz . com >
rewrite: ruleset 198 returns: $# esmtp $@ anyxyz . com $: dsw < @ anyxyz . com >
rewrite: ruleset   0 returns: $# esmtp $@ anyxyz . com $: dsw < @ anyxyz . com >
>
```

The return from Ruleset 3 rewrites the address into a format that can be processed internally by Sendmail. Ruleset 0 returns a tuple that includes the delivery agent of ESMTP (Extended SMTP), the host of `anyxyz.com`, and the user of `dsw`. This indicates that Sendmail will connect to the mail server for machine `anyzyx.com` to deliver this message. This result indicates that your `sendmail.cf` will handle sending email to remote users. Once you have tested a representative sample of remote and local addresses, you will need to copy the configuration file (in our example, `sniglets.com.cf`) to `/etc/sendmail.cf`. Next, edit the startup scripts (covered in Chapter 3, "System Boot and Shutdown") to automatically start the Sendmail daemon.

The client `sendmail.cf` configuration file should result in all email being forwarded to the mail server as specified in the master configuration file.

STARTING SENDMAIL

A mail server should run Sendmail as a daemon in the background. This allows Sendmail to listen for incoming connections from other mail servers. Sendmail must also be instructed to process the pending queue over a certain time interval. In the event the Sendmail daemon cannot contact the recipient's mail server, the message is placed in a queue. The queue needs to be processed periodically to attempt delivery of all queued messages. This is accomplished with the following command:

```
#/usr/sbin/sendmail -bd -q30m
```

The `-bd` option causes Sendmail to run as a daemon, and `-q30m` requires Sendmail to process the pending queue every 30 minutes. Other options include `-d` for debugging and `-v` for verbose mode.

Client UNIX workstations (not mail servers) do not require Sendmail running in the background as a daemon. Email from a client workstation is delivered to the mail server immediately. If the mail server is not available, the message will be queued.

QUEUE

Sendmail will attempt to deliver mail immediately. When immediate delivery is not possible, Sendmail will hold the message and attempt to deliver it at a later time (`-q60m` option). Queued messages are placed in a holding directory (`/var/spool/mqueue`) and are referred to as queued. A message is broken into separate files in the queue directory. Each filename begins with a single character identifier (Table 9.4), followed by the letter `f`, and then a unique identifier for each separate message. Sendmail accepts a command-line option to process the queue. In the example in the "Starting Sendmail" section, we used `-q30m`. This option instructs Sendmail to attempt delivery of all messages in the queue every 30 minutes.

Email queued on client UNIX workstations must also be processed. Queued email on a client is the result of the client not being able to contact the mail server. Since the client is not running the Sendmail daemon, another method of processing the queue must be utilized. On the client UNIX workstation, add the following line to root's `crontab`:

```
0 * * * * /usr/sbin/sendmail -q
```

This command ensures that the mail queue is processed every hour and that queued email will be delivered to the mail server when it is available.

The `mailq` command (`/usr/sbin/sendmail -bp`) prints out a summary of the mail queue. An example of its output is provided here:

```
                  Mail Queue (2 requests)
--Q-ID-- --Size-- -----Q-Time----- ------------Sender/Recipient---------
OAA14869     843 Tue Dec 28 14:57 <webb@sniglets.com>
                 (Deferred: Connection timed out with mail.nowhere.net.)
                              george@nowhere.net
OAA14794    1780 Tue Dec 28 14:53 <anyone@sniglets.com>
                 (Deferred: Connection timed out with mail.somewhere.com.)
                              user@somewhere.com
```

The first line provides a total number of email messages in the queue. The remaining lines provide information on each message in the queue. The first line for each message contains the identifier (ID), size of the message, date/time the message was placed in the queue, and the sender of the

Table 9.4	**Mail Queue Identifiers**
Identifier	Meaning
d	Message body
q	Queue control file and message header
t	Temporary file
x	Transcript

message. The second line for each message contains the error message describing the reason the message was queued and the recipient of the message.

LOGGING AND STATISTICS

The logging level is an option that is set in the `sendmail.cf` file (do a `grep -I loglevel sendmail.cf` to examine the value). The *Sendmail Installation and Operation Guide* contains a list of all logging levels. The default is Log Level 9, which provides useful information. Each level includes logging for all the levels below it (e.g., Level 2 logs all Level 0, 1, and 2 messages). The Sendmail daemon opens a connection to the `syslog` daemon for all logging messages. The `syslog` daemon reads the `/etc/syslog.conf` file on startup to determine where messages generated by sendmail should be directed . Messages can be directed to a local log file, the console of a machine, or they can be sent to another host. The `syslog` facility is covered in Chapter 15 "Software Administration."

The `mailstats` command provides current mail statistics for the local machine. Listing 9.6 is sample output from a medium-sized mail server.

Listing 9.6 `mailstats` **Output**

```
Statistics from Tue Jul 27 13:32:02 1999
 M   msgsfr  bytes_from    msgsto    bytes_to  msgsrej msgsdis  Mailer
 0        0          0K     31415      186235K        0       0  prog
 1        0          0K       120         493K        0       0  *file*
 3   225562  11305229K    634958    17348085K      592       0  local
 4      219       9772K      2296       12902K        0       0  smtp
 5   368708   9017330K    290406    15666563K     3488       0  esmtp
 7        1          1K        37        6910K        0       0  relay
================================================================
 T   594490  20332332K    959232    33221188K     4080       0
```

The first line gives the time and date when the statistics started. The output is separated by mailer program and can be used as an aid in determining email load.

ALIASES

Aliasing allows Sendmail to perform the following tasks:

- Send mail to a program or shell script.
- Append mail to a file.
- Distribute to a list.
- Allow a single username to receive mail for multiple usernames.

The `/etc/aliases` file is a text file that contains lines consisting of a local account name, followed by a colon in the first field, and an alias in the second field. A line beginning with a space or tab is considered to be part of the line above it. Lines beginning with # are comments, and empty lines are ignored. All other lines are viewed as alias lines and must have the following structure:

```
AccountName:      alias
```

`AccountName` must be a local username. The second field (`alias`) is defined as a username (local or remote), unless it has the characteristics described in Table 9.5. For performance purposes, the `/etc/aliases` file is converted to an `aliases.db` or `aliases.dir/aliases.pag` format. The conversion takes place when Sendmail starts or the `newaliases` command is executed.

 Always run the `newaliases` command after updating the `/etc/aliases` file.

Table 9.5	**Special Alias Cases**
Case	Interpretation
/	Append to file
|	Deliver to program with prog agent
\	Suppress all aliasing and deliver locally
:include:	Special case that allows an external file to contain a list of recipients

Listing 9.7 contains a sample /etc/aliases file. The first line is an example of aliasing a local account to a remote account. Lines 2 and 3 alias local usernames to different local usernames. Line 4 contains the :include: expression. The :include: expression must be followed by a full pathname to a list of recipients. The list referenced by the :include: statement contains lines of recipient addresses (more than one on a line requires commas between recipients), program names, filenames, or additional :include: lists. Line 5 is a list. Email sent to dsw is delivered to dweb, dws, and rand. Line 6 appends mail to a file. The last two lines deliver mail to the associated program. Programs that require options require the use of quotation marks. Sendmail requires two aliases: the MAILER-DAEMON and postmaster.

Listing 9.7   Sample /etc/aliases **File**

```
baude:             baude@research.busineess.com
bob:               bill
bcummings:             cummings
bo_list:                 :include:/tools/lists/lists/order_list
dsw:    dweb,dws,rand
joe:    /home/machine/joe/mailalways
rot:    | /tools/lists/process_this_mail
spyd:   |"/tools/lists/moreprocess -q -t"
MAILER-DAEMON:      postmaster
Postmaster:     root
```

Sendmail Pro

Sendmail Pro is a commercial offering that is based on the open source distribution from the Sendmail Consortium. The package includes compiled binaries, a setup wizard, and graphical configuration tools. There is a single management interface that allows administrators to install new configuration files, modify aliases, manage the mail queue, and analyze email traffic. Information for Sendmail Pro can be obtained at http://www.sendmail.com.

MAIL

Mail is one of the original MUAs in UNIX. Mail allows you to read incoming mail and send mail. Mail has a character interface and limited configuration options. The Mail program can be utilized to debug mail delivery programs on a UNIX client workstation. The Mail program has a command-line option, -v, that places the program in verbose mode. This option displays the details of the delivery process on the user's terminal. This allows the system administrator to determine that the client workstation is contacting the correct mail server.

ELM

Elm is a character screen-oriented UNIX mail system that supersedes Mail. It is included with most UNIX distributions (not AIX). Elm supports MIME-conformant mail, but does not support POP and IMAP. Development of Elm has recently been resumed by the Elm Development Group.

PROGRAM FOR INTERNET NEWS AND EMAIL

Program for Internet News and Mail (Pine) is a free utility for reading, sending, and manipulating email. The Office of Computing and Communications at the University of Washington designed Pine. The Pine distribution can be downloaded from http://www.washington.edu/pine/. Pine is available for UNIX and 32-bit Windows operating systems. Pine supports MIME, IMAP, Network News Transport Protocol (NNTP), and interfaces with Sendmail for outgoing mail on UNIX systems.

Pine is an ideal email utility for novice users, but can be extensively configured by experienced users. A user can view, save, delete, print, reply, to and forward messages. It has on-line, context-sensitive help screens. There is a simple editor (Pico) and an integrated spell checker (both can be changed via configuration files). It automatically checks for new mail and notifies the user. MIME attachments can be saved to a file, or with proper configuration, they can execute the appropriate program for the MIME object.

DTMAIL

dtmail is the Common Desktop Environment MUA. It uses a GUI for reading, sending, and managing email. It supports local and NFS mailboxes. It can be configured to access remote mailboxes with IMAP4. A user can view, save, delete, print, and reply to messages. dtmail periodically checks for new email and notifies the user.

`sendmail`—Is the email server in UNIX. `sendmail` does inter-network forwarding as necessary to deliver a message to its correct place. `sendmail` is commonly launched with `-bd -q30m` which puts the server in the background and processes the queue every 30 minutes.

`mailq`—Provides a listing of all messages in the mail queue.

`mailstats`—Provides current mail statistics for the local machine.

Microsoft Exchange Server for Windows 2000

Microsoft Exchange Server is Microsoft's native Windows 2000 messaging server. You might ask why we have referred to Exchange as a "messaging server" instead of a "mail server". Exchange provides much more than electronic mail service; Exchange supports enterprise calendaring, mailing lists, and on-line collaboration as well.

You should keep in mind that Exchange, unlike Sendmail, is not a public-domain product. You must purchase Exchange, either as a standalone product or as part of the Microsoft BackOffice Server package. Once you have purchased Exchange and enough licenses for the users who will connect to the server, you can begin your deployment and configuration. This section will help you set up Exchange Server 5.5 and begin providing messaging services for your users. We strongly urge you to purchase a book dedicated to Exchange Server before deploying it on your network, as this chapter cannot cover every aspect of deploying, configuring, and troubleshooting your Exchange installation.

INSTALLING EXCHANGE SERVER 5.5

As you have already experienced in previous chapters, software installation on Windows 2000 is largely GUI-based and tends to be a point-choose-click process. Installing Exchange Server 5.5 is no different. This section will help you choose and configure a server for the Exchange installation, prepare your DNS service for Exchange, perform the actual installation, configure the Exchange server for Internet mail, and configure the naming options for your Exchange server. This section assumes the following:

- This is the first Exchange server on your network.
- You are not using another mail server (such as Sendmail) on your network.
- You are directly connected to the Internet.

While Exchange can function perfectly well in environments that do not meet the above criteria, this book cannot cover all of the possible permutations you may encounter in non-standard network environments.

Configuring Name Resolution Services

For mail to be successfully delivered to your Exchange server, you must configure your DNS server correctly. This is accomplished using the DNS snap-in for the Microsoft Management Console to create a mail exchanger (MX) record for your domain.

This section assumes that you are using a Windows 2000 DNS server. If you are using a UNIX DNS server, you should create the MX record using the appropriate method for your server.

Complete the following steps to create the appropriate MX record on your Windows 2000 DNS server.

1. Launch the DNS snap-in from the `Administrative Tools'` `Start` menu program group. You will see a window similar to the one in Figure 9.1.

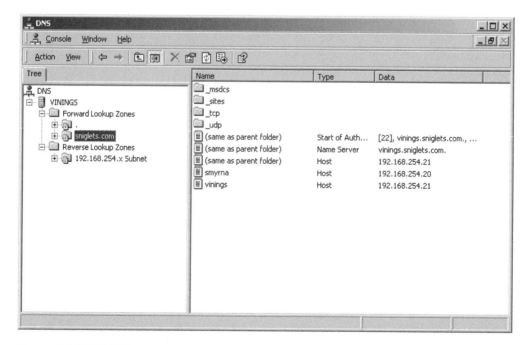

Figure 9.1 DNS MMC snap-in.

Figure 9.2
New mail
exchanger
configuration
screen

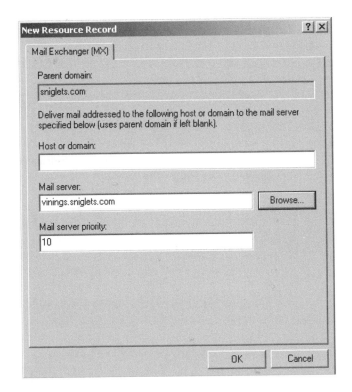

2. Expand the `Forward Lookup Zones` and right-click on your do-main. From the menu that appears, select `New Mail Exchanger`. You will see a window similar to the one in Figure 9.2.
3. To create the MX record for your domain, leave the `Host or domain` box empty and use the `Browse` button to select a server from your DNS zone. You should leave the `Mail server priority` setting alone.
4. Click `OK` to save the new record

Now that you have configured your name services, you can begin the instal-lation of Exchange Server.

Performing the Installation

Depending on whether you purchased Exchange Server separately or as part of Microsoft BackOffice Server, your installation will be a little different. We are going to install Exchange Server from the BackOffice Server media, which will also require that we install some core BackOffice Server components.

If you purchased Exchange Server separately, instructions for starting setup will be included in the documentation on the CD.

The following steps describe how to install Exchange Server from the Back-Office Server distribution:

1. Insert Disk 1 of the BackOffice Server distribution in your CD-ROM drive. Setup should start automatically. If it does not, run *setup.exe* from the CD. You will see the BackOffice Server splash screen.

 If a warning indicating that the program was not designed to run on Windows 2000 is displayed, you can ignore it and continue with setup.

2. Click BackOffice Server Setup to start the BackOffice Server installation wizard shown in Figure 9.3. Click the Next button to continue.

Figure 9.3
BackOffice Server Setup Installation Wizard.

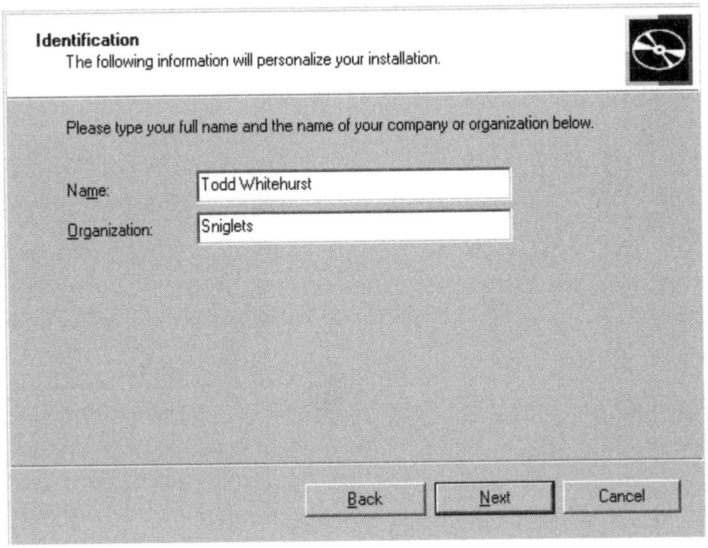

Figure 9.4
Identification
Setup Screen.

Identification
The following information will personalize your installation.

Please type your full name and the name of your company or organization below.

Name: Todd Whitehurst

Organization: Sniglets

Back	Next	Cancel

3. When the license agreement is displayed, you should read it, select I Agree, and click Next to continue.

4. Enter your Name and Organization information on the Identification configuration screen that is displayed (Figure 9.4) and click Next to continue.

5. The Autologon Password configuration screen in Figure 9.5 will appear. If you wish to have the system automatically log on after the final reboot, configure the settings appropriately. When you are done, click Next to continue.

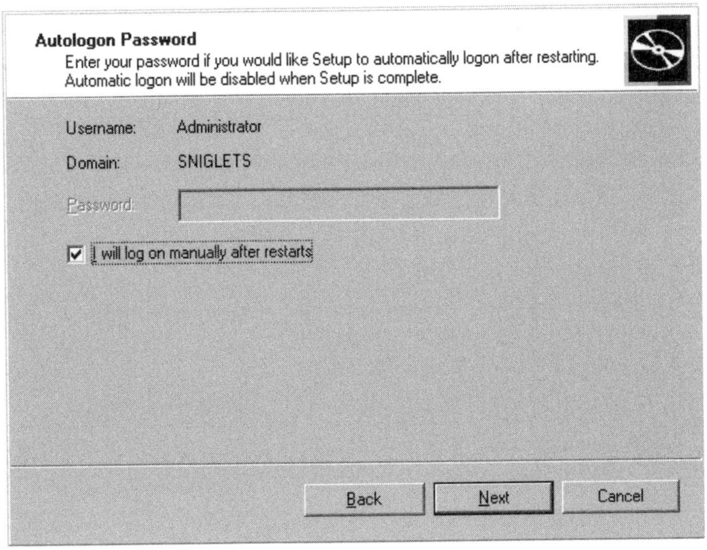

Figure 9.5
Autologon
Password
configuration
screen.

Autologon Password
Enter your password if you would like Setup to automatically logon after restarting.
Automatic logon will be disabled when Setup is complete.

Username: Administrator

Domain: SNIGLETS

Password:

☑ I will log on manually after restarts

Back	Next	Cancel

Figure 9.6
Installation type
selection screen.

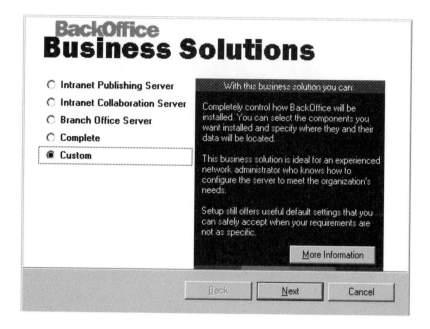

6. Setup will begin copying some required files to your system. When the file copy operation is complete, you will see the installation type selection screen shown in Figure 9.6.

7. Select Custom from the list and click Next to display the component selection screen in Figure 9.7.

Figure 9.7
Component
selection screen.

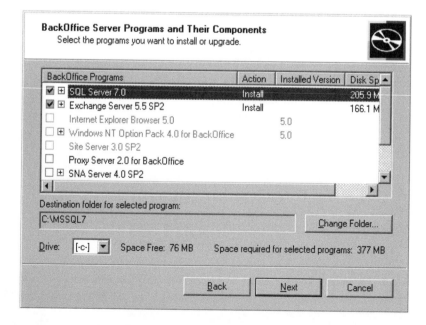

Figure 9.8
Service accounts
configuration
screen.

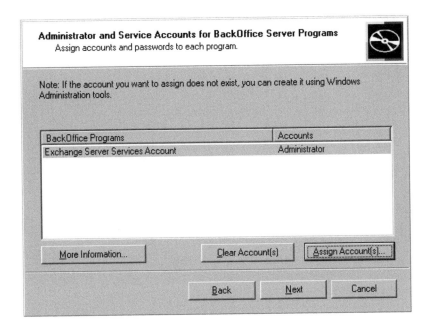

8. Use the following guidelines for selecting the appropriate components for your Exchange Server installation:

   ■ De-select the check box next to SQL Server 7.0.

   ■ Expand the Exchange Server 5.5 SP2 option, and then expand the Connectors option. If you do not intend to use *msmail*
   or *ccmail* on your network, remove the check marks next to their
   respective connectors.

   ■ Do not modify any other selections.

   ■ If you wish to change the installation location of Exchange Server,
   select Exchange Server 5.5 SP2 from the list, and then click
   the Change Folder button.

9. Click Next to continue. You will see the service accounts configuration screen in Figure 9.8.

10. Click the Assign Accounts button to specify an account for the
   Exchange Server services. You can use the Administrator account,
   which is the default. Click Next to continue.

You can create a separate service account for the Exchange Server services using the
Active Directory Users and Computers MMC snap-in. Creating user accounts is covered in detail in Chapter 12, "User Administration."

11. The site configuration screen in Figure 9.9 will appear. Complete the
   settings under Create a new site and click Next to continue.

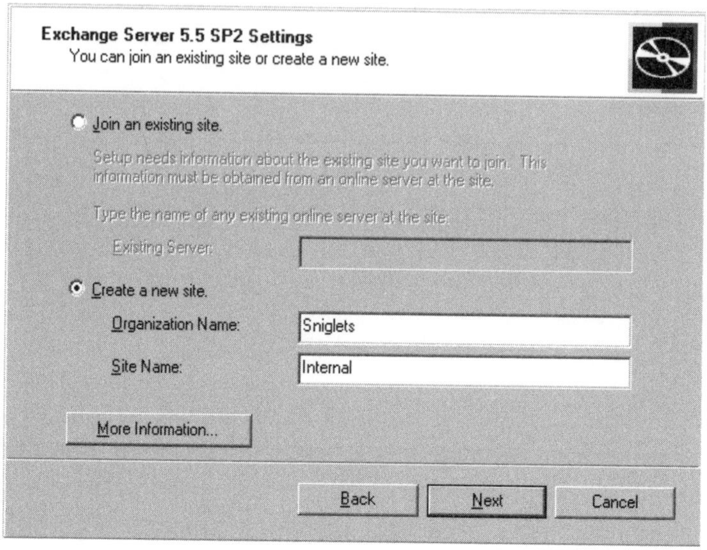

Figure 9.9
Site configuration
screen.

12. The installation choices confirmation screen will appear. Review your settings and click `Next` to continue.

13. The installation program will begin copying files. If you are asked for additional CDs, insert them when prompted.

14. When the file copy is complete, you will be prompted to run the Exchange Server Performance Optimizer. Click the `Next` button on the opening screen and you will see the configuration screen in Figure 9.10.

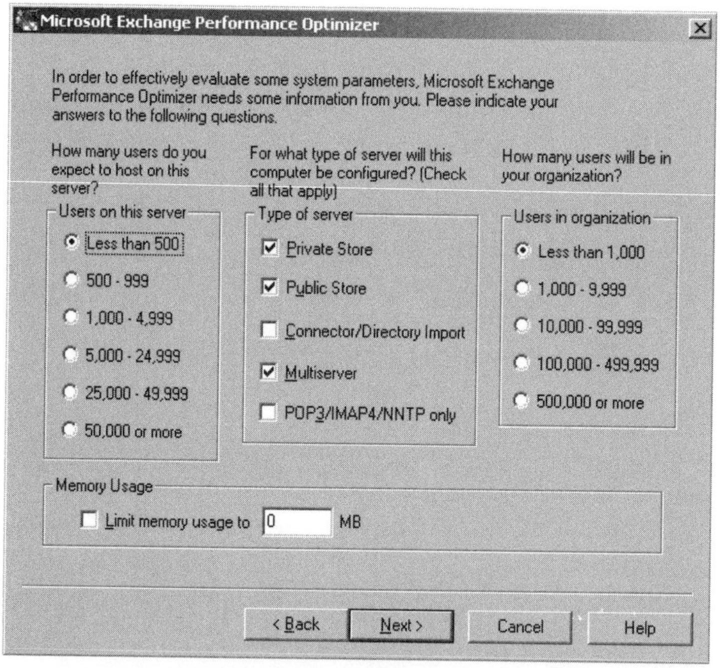

Figure 9.10
Microsoft
Exchange
Performance
Optimizer
configuration
screen.

15. Answer the questions as they pertain to your organization and click `Next` to continue.

16. The Optimizer will begin its analysis, which may take a few minutes to complete.

17. When the analysis is complete, click `Next` to continue. The results of the analysis will be displayed in a window similar to the one in Figure 9.11.

18. You should select the default settings, but you can make changes if you desire. When you are done reviewing and/or modifying the results, click `Next` to continue.

19. You will be prompted about moving the database files. You should accept the default settings and click `Next` to continue.

20. You will be prompted to restart any services that were stopped when the Performance Optimizer was started. Click `Finish` to restart those services and continue.

21. When the Performance Optimizer has completed its tasks, you should click `Finish` on the BackOffice Server setup wizard to complete the setup process.

22. You will be prompted to restart the system. Click `Yes` to do so now.

Figure 9.11
Microsoft
Exchange
Performance
Optimizer results
window.

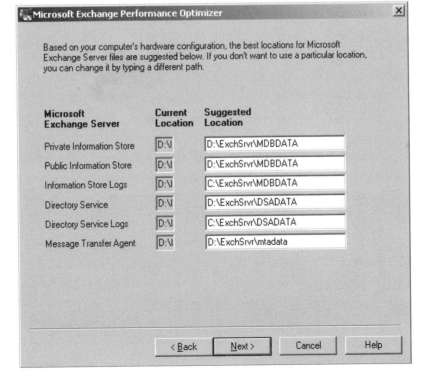

Once the system reboots, your Exchange Server services should be running. It is now time to configure the Internet Mail Service and fine-tune your Exchange Server.

Configuring Internet Mail Service

The Internet Mail Service is necessary to send or receive email messages over the Internet. If you do not intend to send or receive email messages over the Internet, you can ignore this section. The first step to configuring the Internet Mail Service is to install it as a connection in Exchange Server. To do this, complete the following steps:

1. Launch the `Exchange Server Administrator` from the Microsoft Exchange `Start` menu program group. You will be asked to select a server to administer, where you should select the current server. You will see a window similar to the one in Figure 9.12.

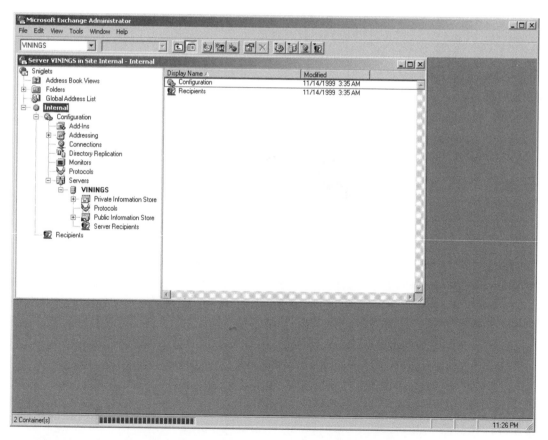

Figure 9.12 Microsoft Exchange Administrator.

2. Expand your site, and then expand the `Configuration` and `Servers` items.

3. Click on `Connections` under `Configuration` to highlight it. From the `File` menu, select `New Other`, and then choose `Internet Mail Service` to start the `Internet Mail Wizard`.

4. Click `Next` to begin the installation.

5. Click `Next` after reading the information presented. You should have already completed the tasks outlined. The Internet mail server selection screen in Figure 9.13 will be displayed.

6. Select your server from the list. Assuming this is your only Exchange server, there will only be one entry in the list. If you use a dial-up connection to access the Internet, check the appropriate box. Click the `Next` button to continue.

7. On the Internet mail routing selection screen in Figure 9.14, you should choose the option most appropriate for your organization. Selecting `Yes` is the most common configuration. When you are finished making your choice, click `Next` to continue.

8. The DNS configuration screen will appear. In most cases, you should accept the default selection. Click `Next` to continue.

9. The Internet address delivery selection screen will appear. You should accept the default setting, which allows delivery to all Internet addresses. Click `Next` to continue.

10. The email address configuration screen in Figure 9.15 will appear. You should configure the address to meet your site's configuration needs and click `Next` to continue.

Figure 9.13
Internet mail server selection screen.

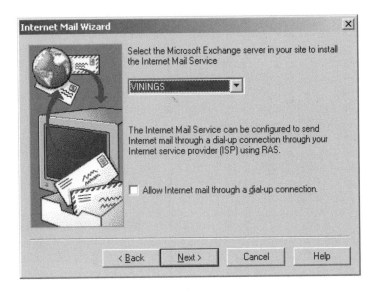

Figure 9.14
Internet mail
routing selection
screen.

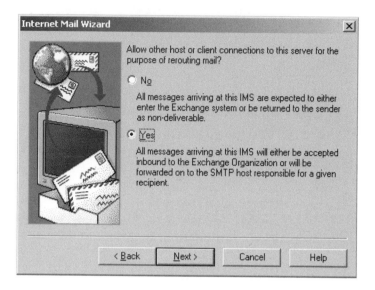

11. The administrator mailbox configuration screen in Figure 9.16 will appear. You should accept the default setting and click Next to continue.

12. The service account configuration screen requires that you enter the password for the account used as the service account for other Exchange services. Enter the appropriate password and click Next to continue.

13. Click the Finish button to complete the installation. The wizard will complete the installation tasks and inform you that email

Figure 9.15
Email address
configuration
screen.

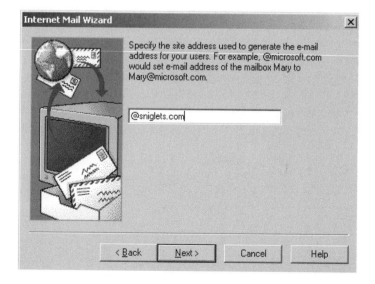

Figure 9.16
Administrator
mailbox
configuration
screen.

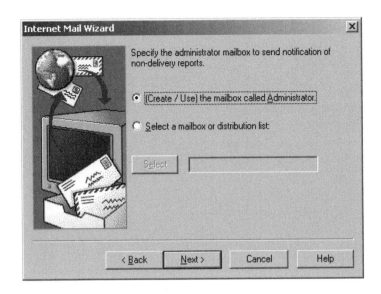

addresses for existing recipients will be updated. Confirm the message and the process should complete in a few minutes.

14. When installation is complete, the service will be started and the setup program will recommend that you run the Performance Optimizer again. Although running the Optimizer will not hurt anything on the server, we have found that settings rarely change and you do not need to complete this step immediately.

Now that the Internet Mail Service is installed and configured, your server is ready to send and receive messages between your organization and the Internet. The last step is to configure the Exchange Server naming options.

Exchange Server Naming Options

The naming options in Exchange Server are actually quite simple. In a nutshell, the naming options specify two things: 1) How a user's name is displayed, and 2) How each user's email address is generated. By default, each user's mailbox is created in a "firstname lastname" format and each user's email address is created in a "firstname+last initial@yourdomain" format. While this is probably acceptable for most installations, we felt it significant enough to mention how to change this option here. Follow the steps below to change the Exchange server's naming options:

1. Open the `Exchange Server Administrator` from the Microsoft Exchange `Start` menu program group. You will see a window similar to the one in Figure 9.12.

Figure 9.17
Exchange Server
Options window.

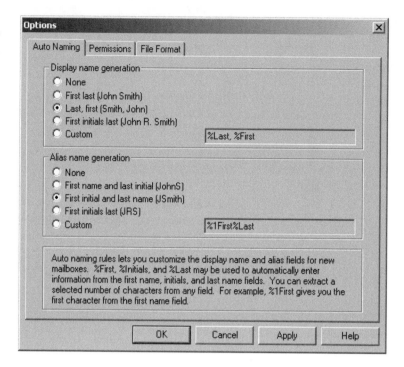

2. Select your site and then select `Options` from the `Tools` menu. You will see the window in Figure 9.17.

3. Make any changes to the naming option that you desire and then click `OK`. The changes will take effect immediately.

Your Exchange server is almost ready for action. All that is needed now are mailboxes, and if you desire, distribution lists. These are discussed in the next few sections.

CREATING MAILBOXES

Obviously, everything we have done up to now would be pointless if we didn't create some mailboxes for your users. Each mailbox is assigned to a user on your domain and stores all of that user's Exchange Server data. The mailboxes are contained in the Exchange Server's private information store. Only the user assigned to the mailbox can access the information contained in the mailbox. The steps below describe how to create a mailbox in Exchange Server:

1. Open the `Exchange Server Administrator` from the Microsoft Exchange `Start` menu program group. You will see a window similar to the one in Figure 9.12.

Figure 9.18
New mailbox
Properties
window.

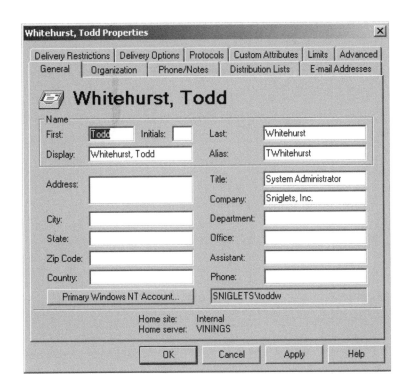

2. Expand your site, and then select the `Recipients` container at the bottom of the list.

3. Select `New Mailbox` from the `File` menu and the new mailbox `Properties` window in Figure 9.18 will be displayed.

4. Complete the `First` name and `Last` name fields and the `Display` and `Alias` fields will be completed automatically.

5. Click the `Primary Windows NT Account` button to assign an account to the new mailbox. You will be given the choice of choosing an existing account or creating a new account. Choose the option you desire to assign the new account to the mailbox.

6. Click `OK` to create the new mailbox.

At this point, the new mailbox is ready for use. However, you may have noticed that there were many options available in the mailbox `Properties` window that we did not configure.

Table 9.6 describes the different options available in the mailbox `Properties` window.

Table 9.6	**Mailbox** Properties **Window Options**
Tab Name	Description
General	Allows configuration of the user's name, address, office information, and Windows NT account information.
Organization	Allows you to configure the user's place in the organization, such as who he/she reports to and other users who are subordinates.
Phone/Notes	Allows you to specify additional phone numbers and make notes about the user or mailbox.
Distribution Lists	Allows you to view and modify the user's membership in distribution lists.
E-mail Addresses	Allows you to add, remove, and edit the email addresses assigned to the mailbox. The Exchange server will accept only mail sent to known email addresses.
Delivery Restrictions	Allows you to specify recipients who can and cannot send/receive mail to/from the current user.
Delivery Options	Allows you to configure options for users who can send mail on behalf of the current user, and to configure an alternate recipient.
Protocols	Allows you to customize Exchange Server protocols for the current mailbox. You should not have to modify the default settings.
Custom Attributes	Allows you to configure site-specific custom attributes for message tracking purposes.
Limits	Allows you to configure information store usage limits and message size restrictions.
Advanced	Allows you to customize some mailbox features. This option is rarely modified.

CREATING DISTRIBUTION LISTS

Distribution lists are Exchange Server's version of mailing lists. You can use distribution lists to send messages to multiple mailboxes using a single Exchange alias. Distribution lists can be stored in the recipients container, but for organizational purposes, it is desirable to create a separate recipients container for your distribution lists. This section will detail the procedures, for how to create a new recipients container for your distribution lists, and how to create a distribution list in the new container.

Creating a New Recipients Container

Use the procedure below to create a new recipients container:

1. Open the `Exchange Server Administrator` from the Microsoft Exchange `Start` menu program group. You will see a window similar to the one in Figure 9.12.
2. Select your site and then choose `New Other` and then `Recipients Container` from the `File` menu. The `Distribution Lists Properties` window in Figure 9.19 will appear.

Figure 9.19
Distribution Lists
Properties
window.

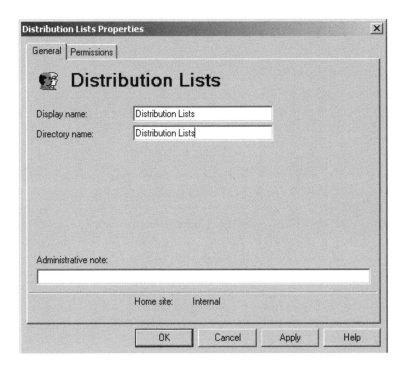

3. Enter `Distribution Lists` in both the `Display name` and `Directory name` boxes. You can call the new container anything you want, but for our purposes, let's use `Distribution Lists`.

4. Click `OK` to create the new container.

5. The new container will be created under your site.

Now that we have created the container, let's create the new distribution list.

Creating a New Distribution List

1. Select the new container you just created under your site.

2. From the `File` menu, choose `New Distribution List`. The `Support Properties` window in Figure 9.20 will be displayed.

3. Complete the fields in the `Support Properties` windows and click `OK` to create the new distribution list.

4. The new list will be created inside your new container.

Now that you have mailboxes and distribution lists, your server is ready for users to start accessing it. To access your Exchange server, you must use a messaging client, which is discussed in the next section.

Figure 9.20
Support
Properties
window.

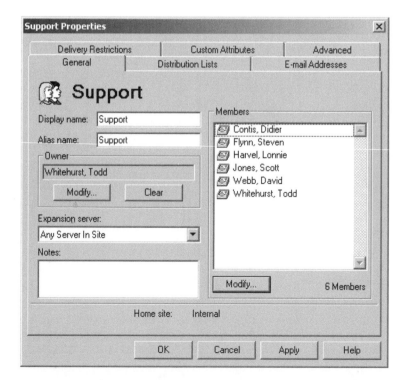

EMAIL CLIENTS FOR EXCHANGE SERVER

To access the Exchange server, your users will need to install and run any of several available email clients. Microsoft's native Exchange client is Microsoft Access, which is the preferred Exchange client. Microsoft Exchange Server 5.5 also supports the Internet standard POP3 and IMAP protocols. This section will provide a brief overview of the available clients.

Microsoft Outlook

Microsoft Outlook is Microsoft's native Exchange client. If you wish to take full advantage of Exchange Server's scheduling and collaboration features, as well as contact lists, you should deploy Microsoft Outlook to your users. Microsoft Outlook is available as part of the Microsoft Office package, or as a standalone product.

IMAP Clients

IMAP (Internet Mail Access Protocol) clients are compatible with Exchange Server 5.5. You can use any popular IMAP-compatible client such as Netscape Mail or Eudora to access the Exchange server. IMAP clients are not able to take advantage of Exchange Server's contact lists or scheduling and collaboration features.

POP3 Clients

POP3 (Post Office Protocol) clients are also compatible with Exchange Server 5.5. Again, any popular POP3 client such as Eudora, Netscape Mail, and Microsoft Outlook Express can be used to access the Exchange server. Like IMAP clients, POP3 clients cannot take advantage of Exchange Server's contact lists or scheduling and collaboration features.

EXCHANGE 2000 SERVER

Exchange 2000 Server is the next version of Exchange Server. It is due to be released in the first half of 2000. It is designed specifically for Windows 2000 Server and provides many new and enhanced features over Exchange Server 5.5. Complete details on Exchange 2000 Server can be found at `http://www.microsoft.com/exchange`. Table 9.7 details some of the key enhancements and added features in Exchange 2000 Server.

Table 9.7	Key Features of Exchange 2000 Server
Feature	Description
Active Directory integration	Exchange 2000 takes advantage of the Windows 2000 Active Directory by integrating the Exchange database with the Active Directory database. This provides a single point of administration for both user accounts and Exchange mailboxes.
Multiple message databases	The Exchange database can be split into multiple physical databases and accessed as a single logical database. This allows greater fault-tolerance and enhanced recovery features.
Windows 2000 security	The Windows 2000 security model is employed for securing access to the Exchange 2000 Server. This also simplifies the management of user and group permissions.
Outlook Web access	Outlook Web access has been significantly improved to provide a robust, scalable, and easy-to-use email client.
Data conferencing and application sharing	Data conferencing services based on the T.120 standard are provided for enterprise-ready client/server conferencing solutions.
Multicast video teleconferencing	Integrated scheduling and management for multicast video teleconferencing is now available.
Instant messaging	Messages can be sent directly to another user's screen for immediate delivery.
Chat services	Chat services support up to 20,000 users per server and are now integrated with Active Directory.

Email Resource Planning

It is important to choose the correct hardware and prepare it for your email server. Unless your organization receives thousands of emails per hour, email generally does not require a great deal of processing power or memory resources. The bulk of the needed resources center around the disk resources required to store email messages. Choose the largest disk possible for your users' inboxes, as a full inbox area can cause mail to be delivered slowly, or even worse, not at all.

Determining your email server needs for both UNIX and Windows 2000 is directly related to the amount of email your users receive and store. However, for most organizations, it is possible to maintain functional email with limited resources. For simplicity, you can assume that equivalent resources will work for both UNIX and Microsoft Exchange on Windows 2000. However, when installing Exchange, the system you choose must meet the minimum requirements for both Windows 2000 Server and Microsoft Exchange Server 5.5. The requirements for Windows 2000 Server were discussed earlier in this book and the requirements for Exchange Server 5.5 are outlined here:

- Pentium 60 or faster processor (Pentium 133 recommended).
- 24MB RAM (32MB recommended).
- 250MB hard disk space (500MB recommended).
- CD-ROM drive.

As a general rule, any system capable of running Windows 2000 Server should also be capable of running Exchange Server. There are a few additional guidelines you should follow:

- The Windows 2000 server you choose must be a member of a Windows 2000 or Windows NT 4.0 domain.
- The Windows 2000 server you choose should *not* be a domain controller. The Exchange Server LDAP service and Windows 2000 Server LDAP service should not be run on the same Windows 2000 server.
- The server you choose should have enough free disk space to store your users' data. The amount of disk space you need may vary based on your users' needs, but providing 20MB of space per user is a good starting point.

Email Policies

While email is a valuable tool for communication, there are times when using email can create problems in your organization. Email can be used inappropriately, incorrectly, or incoherently by your users, and can cause problems for your system administrator as well as business managers and leaders. Inappropriate email content, email harassment, and SPAM (unsolicited email sent to large groups of users) are just a few examples of where business and organizational issues, not technical problems, can arise through the use of email systems.

As a system administrator, your job is not to control the behavior of others in your organization. Managers and human resources personnel are generally responsible for making your workplace a safe and happy environment. However, as the system administrator, you will be called upon to help establish guidelines and acceptable use policies for your computing resources, and email is one topic that is high on everyone's list.

ACCEPTABLE USE

The first, and arguably the most important, email policy is the definition of when and how email is to be used in your organization. An acceptable use policy should clearly define what is allowed, and what is not allowed, when using email resources.

Acceptable use policies should cover incoming as well as outgoing email. Outgoing email is relatively easy to define, as this is email initiated by users within your organization. Incoming email is more difficult to police, as email received by your users may not be solicited, and therefore your users may not be able to control what they receive. Whatever policies you put in place, always try to err in the direction that gives your users the most privacy and flexibility so that you do not infringe on their ability to do their work.

While much of system administration is black and white, setting email policies is a gray area that can be difficult to define. Every organization has a different mission, as well as a different community of users. Depending on the demographics of your organization, you may choose to be more liberal or extremely restrictive in your email policies. The following three guidelines can be used as a starting point to create an acceptable use policy. They are presented in their most restrictive form.

- **Email is only to be used for organizational purposes**—This is a highly restrictive and conservative approach, but in organizations that have sensitive information or that monitor worker's activities, this policy is quite common. This also can be used to discourage personal use of email, especially in corporations where users are employees and should be working for the organization, not using corporate resources for their own gain.

- **Email is the property of the organization**—This policy gives the organization the ability to scan and read email that is stored or sent from within the organization. This is also a conservative policy. However, instituting policies such as this one raises issues of privacy, so be sure to consult senior members of your organization before instituting this policy.

- **Email with unacceptable content will not be tolerated**—This policy covers the range from sexual harassment to pornography being sent or received using organizational email resources. How different organizations define "unacceptable" will differ, but be sure to make the specifics of this policy very clear, as there is great latitude for interpretation.

While these three policies may seem simple, once you begin adding in the specific parameters of your organization, they can grow into a large and complex email policy that will help define the do's and don'ts in your email environment.

INBOX RETENTION

As the amount of email being sent across the Internet every year grows, the resources needed to maintain a functional email system grows also. As has already been discussed, the computational resources needed for email are not large, but the disk resources necessary to store email and its content can become very large. The majority of the disk resources needed are required to handle users' incoming mail, or their inbox. A user's inbox is where new mail is stored before it is read.

However, with many email systems, the inbox is also where old email is kept until it is either deleted or moved to another location. Over time, if a user does not perform housekeeping, their inbox will require more and more disk space. If a large number of users fail to keep their inboxes clean, additional disk may be necessary to provide resources for new incoming mail. This can present a problem if your mail resources, or your budget, are limited.

An effective way to manage email inboxes is to create inbox retention rules that govern how inboxes can be used. For example, a simple inbox retention rule could be: "All email more than two weeks old will be deleted from inboxes each night at midnight." This policy prevents users from storing email for vast periods of time, and forces them to move their email to other storage locations. Similar to acceptable use policies, there are some standard rules that can be used to model your organization's inbox policies:

■ **Email will be deleted from inboxes after a specific period—**
This prevents users from bypassing home directory disk quotas and
storing files in their email inbox.

■ **Once email is read, it is automatically moved to another location—**Many users will read an email message and mark it as un-
read. Some email systems will allow you to automatically move
email to another location once a user has read it.

■ **If an inbox exceeds a specific size, it will be archived—**This
policy is useful in organizations where deletion or movement of
email to a user's home directory are not viable options. In many organizations, users may abandon their accounts, but the administrator may not have the options to delete the user. If the user was a
member of mailing lists, their inbox could become quite large. By
archiving the inbox, email resources are conserved, and no email is
deleted.

INBOX BACKUP

One final policy to consider is if and how you choose to back up your
users' email in their inboxes. Current legal precedents have shown that
email is similar to other corporate documents in that a user's email corre-
spondence can be used as evidence during legal proceedings. If you work in
a corporation that is concerned about legal risks, you may consider not
backing up your email inbox filesystem.

There is a good reason for not backing up inboxes. Some users may feel
that once a message is deleted from their inbox, it is gone forever. However,
if you as the administrator had backed up that user's inbox, the message
will still exist on your backup media. If the authorities seize your corporate
records, you as the administrator may be asked to hand over all of your
backup media so the authorities can scan your backups for evidence. For this
reason, it is important to be sure that your user knows a message is deleted
when they delete it from their inbox.

Summary

There are three basic agents used to handle the flow of email: the Mail
Transfer Agent (MTA), the Mail Delivery Agent (MDA), and the Mail User
Agent (MUA). To successfully interact, these three agents must conform to
standard protocols. The IETF administers the official Internet protocol standards for electronic mail. In this chapter we briefly explained these agents

and the standards for electronic mail. We also discussed the two major electronic mail systems: Sendmail for UNIX and Exchange Server for Windows.

In this chapter, we provided the basic information necessary to install, configure, and run these applications. If the management of email will be one of your major responsibilities, you should invest in further resources that will explain these systems in greater detail.

PRINTING

UNIX

BSD Print Services

`printcap`

SysV Print Services

`lpadmin`

Commercial Print Servers

WINDOWS 2000

Windows 2000 Printer Server

Creating a Printer Port

Adding and Sharing a Printer

Print Services for UNIX

SAMBA

Perhaps one of the most time-consuming services you will provide to your users is a printing service.

Users will (maybe and maybe not, depending on the office environment and distribution of resources) place a tremendous burden on your printing resources, which in turn can place a tremendous burden on you. Printing problems are always emergencies and require immediate attention. In this chapter, we will discuss the creation and management of printing services for both UNIX and Windows 2000. We will then discuss how to share print services between operating systems.

UNIX Print Services

Print services are split into two primary flavors in the UNIX realm: Berkeley Software Distribution (BSD) and ATT System V (SysV). Table 10.1 contains a breakdown of the BSD and SysV camps. The overall method of printing for both flavors is very similar. They both have simple user programs (BSD `lpr` SysV `lp`) to submit jobs. Each job is queued in a spool directory. A spooler daemon monitors the printer queue and transfers jobs to the printer. In the following sections, we will provide an overview of the BSD and SysV versions of print services. The final part will review alternative ways of setting up printers on the four versions of UNIX included in Table 10.1.

Table 10.1 Versions of Print Services	
Operating System	Print Services Version
AIX	SysV, BSD extensions and extensive proprietary extensions (See section on AIX print services.)
HPUX	SysV
Linux	BSD
Solaris	SysV, BSD extensions

BSD PRINT SERVICES

The BSD version of print services consists of four major parts. The first part is the `lpr` program, which provides a command-line interface for the user to send a job to a printer. The second part is the `lpd` daemon. `lpd` is the spooler daemon responsible for controlling access to local printers, moving jobs from the spool directory to the printer, and transferring remote jobs. The third part is the `/etc/printcap` file. `/etc/printcap` is the configuration file for every printer recognized by the local machine. The `/etc/printcap` file is parsed by `lpd` and designates log files and filters for each printer. The administrative commands make up the final portion of the BSD system.

lpr

The `lpr` command is the command-line interface for submitting print jobs. Options can be entered with the `lpr` command to specify filters, change the parameters of a print job (specific printer destination or send mail on completion), and request multiple copies. `lpr` uses the

/etc/printcap file to determine the proper spool directory for a job. Two files are created in the spool directory for each job. A daemon control file (composed of cf and a control number, e.g., cf101) contains the username of the creator of the job and options provided on the command line. The data file (composed of df and the same control number as the cf file, e.g., df101) contains the actual data sent for printing. Upon completion of the creation of the files, lpr notifies lpd.

lpr is the command-line interface for sending jobs to a printer. Some of the options are listed here.

-P *printer*—Sends output to *printer*.

-h—Suppresses printing of the burst page.

-m—Sends mail upon completion.

-#*num*—Produces *num* copies for all files named.

lpd

lpd is the line printer daemon that is normally invoked at boot. The daemon is responsible for moving jobs from the spool directory to a local printer or remote machine. The daemon actually listens for requests and forks a child process to handle the actual work.

When a request is received, lpd determines whether the printer is local or remote from the /etc/printcap file. For local printers, lpd creates a series of pipes from the spool directory to the printer's /dev file. lpd also creates a process that sends data through the filters specified in the control file and /etc/printcap file for the selected printer. For a remote printer, lpd opens a connection to the remote machine to transfer the control and data files. Upon completion of a local or remote print job, lpd removes the control and data files from the spool directory.

/etc/printcap

The /etc/printcap file is the main configuration file for BSD print services. A printer has to be in this file for a user to submit jobs to it. /etc/printcap is a text file that contains configuration entries for printers. Entries for a printer must be defined on a single logical line, with (\) used for continuation onto the next line. Continuation lines must be indented one tab from the left margin. The fields are separated by (:). The first field of each entry must start at the left-hand margin and contain a list of names for the printer, separated by a (|). Listing 10.1 is a sample /etc/printcap file.

Listing 10.1   /etc/printcap **File**

```
line|line310|Lineprinter in 310:\
        :lp=:\
        :rm=server1.sniglets.com:\
         :rp=line1:\
        :sd=/var/spool/lp/line:\
         :lf=/var/spool/lp/errlog:


swat|lj440|Laserjet in 440:\
        lp=:\

        :rm=swat.sniglets.com:\
        :rp=swat:\
            :sd=/var/spool/lp/swat:\  :lf=/var/spool/lp/errlog:
```

The most commonly used field variables are listed in Table 10.2. The first entry in our sample printcap file is for a remote printer, line. The printer can also be referred to as line310 and "Lineprinter in 310". The

Table 10.2	printcap **Field Variables**
Name	Description
af	Accounting filename
If	Text filter
lf	Error logging filename
lp	Device name to open for output
mx	Maximum file size (in BUFSIZ blocks). zero=unlimited
rm	Machine name for remote printer
rp	Remote printer name
sd	Spool directory

first configuration entry (`:lp:\`) for `line` specifies the device name for this printer. Printer `line` is a remote printer, so we don't need to assign a value for `lp`. The second configuration entry for `line` specifies the remote machine name (`server1.sniglets.com`), that `lpd` connects to for transferring the control and data files. The third configuration entry (`:rp:line1:\`) specifies the name of this printer on the remote machine. The fourth configuration entry specifies the spool directory for this printer on the local machine. The final configuration entry specifies the error log file.

Notice that both printers share the same error logging file (`/var/spool/lp/errlog`). Each entry in the error log file contains the name of the printer that generated the error line. The error log file is important for troubleshooting problems with local printers and determining communication problems with remote printers. The error logging file can get quite large over time. A simple shell script to rotate the logs should be run weekly to limit the growth of this file. The following shell script should be run weekly by `cron` and will keep four weeks of compressed log files in the `/var/spool/lp` directory.

```
#! /bin/sh
# Rotate printer error logfile
#
SPOOLDIR=/var/spool/lp
if test -d $SPOOLDIR
then
        cd $SPOOLDIR
        if test -s $ERRLOG
        then
                test -f  $ERRLOG.1.gz && mv $ERRLOG.1.gz
$ERRLOG.2.gz
                test -f  $ERRLOG.0.gz && mv $ERRLOG.1.gz
$ERRLOG.1.gz
                mv $ERRLOG $ERRLOG.0
                /usr/local/bin/gzip -9 $ERRLOG.0
                cp /dev/null $ERRLOG
                chmod 644 $ERRLOG
        fi
    fi
```

Printers can share the same error log file, but should not share a spool directory. A spool directory must be created for all locally attached and remote printers. The control and data files for a print job are stored in this directory before being sent to a local printer or transferred to a remote machine. This directory must be created by the system administrator when a new printer is added. The steps in creating the spool directory are covered in the next paragraph.

Imagine that you have recently purchased a new Postscript printer and want to add it to your local UNIX workstation. The new printer will be connected to the parallel port (/dev/lp1) on the workstation, and it will be given the names laser and post. This printer will also make use of an input filter to convert text files to Postscript. The following lines need to be added to the /etc/printcap file:

```
Laser|post|Postscript printer in Rm 155:\
    :lp=/dev/lp1:\
    :sd=/var/spool/lp/laserjet:\
    :lf=/var/spool/lp/errlog:\
    :if=/usr/local/etc/filters/iflaser:
```

The next step is to create the spool directory /var/spool/lp/laser. The directory permissions should be 775 with owner and group set to daemon. To create the directory, enter the following command:

```
# mkdir /var/spool/lp/laser
```

To set the owner of this directory, enter the following:

```
#chown daemon /var/spool/lp/laser
```

Next, set the group of the directory to daemon:

```
#chgrp daemon /var/spool/lp/laser
```

Finally, change the permissions:

```
#chmod 775 /var/spool/lp/laser
```

Printers are quite commonly attached to most networks. They provide easy access and a faster link than printers attached by a serial or parallel port. An IP address will need to be assigned to each printer on a network. Check the documentation provided with the printer to configure the printer with the appropriate IP address.

The printcap entry for a network printer is the same as for a remote printer. The printer swat in Listing 10.1 is treated as a remote printer. The rm entry contains the fully-qualified domain name (FQDN) assigned to the printer. The FQDN should always be used when specifying a remote machine. The FQDN ensures that the print job will go to swat.sniglets .com. Specifying swat for the rm entry could result in the job being sent to swat.mark.sniglets.com instead of swat.sniglets .com.

Control Commands

The lpq command provides a snapshot of the print spool queue. Listing 10.2 contains the output of the lpq command. It includes the rank, owner, job number, file being printed, and size of the file before filtering. Job order is first in, first out. The job number is important when a specific job needs to be removed from the queue . By default, the `lpq` command examines the print spool queue of the default printer (printer with name `lp` in `/etc/printcap` file). To examine a specific printer queue, use the `-P printer` option.

Listing 10.2   `lpq` **Output**

```
laserjet is ready and printing

Rank      Owner         Job    Files          Total Size

Active    dws      1       /home/dws/ts    1298      bytes

1st       smg      300     resume.txt      4989      bytes

2nd       ldh            38        salary.txt     159456    bytes
```

The `lprm` command removes a job(s) from the queue. A user can delete jobs they submitted. The owner of a job is determined by the username and machine name on which the `lpr` command was invoked. Without any options, `lprm` will delete the currently active job if owned by the user invoking `lprm`.

`lprm`—Removes a job(s) from the queue.

`-Pprinter`—Specifies the queue associated with the printer, otherwise the default printer is used.

`-`—Removes all jobs for the user calling lprm; if it is the superuser, all jobs will be removed.

`User`—Removes all jobs for the user if a username is specified (superuser only).

`job#`—Removes the job number listed.

The `lpc` command enables the system administrator to control the actions of the printer system. The `lpc` command can enable/disable printers or queues. The order of pending print jobs can be changed with this command. `lpc` provides status on printers, daemons, and queues. `lpc` can only administer locally spooled printers. Be careful, however, because `lpc` does not always report valid information about the status of a printer/queue. Table 10.3 contains the options for `lpc`.

`lpc` will run interactively when no options are included on the command line. The user will be presented with an `lpc>` prompt that will accept any of the commands in Table 10.3. The most utilized options of `lpc` are the enable/disable and up/down commands. The enable/disable commands affect only the spooling of a job to a queue. Jobs already in the queue for a printer are not affected. The up/down commands affect the queue and printing. Sometimes the printing system gets in a state in which `lpc` has no effect. If `lpc` cannot fix a problem, you will need to stop and start the `lpc` daemon manually.

Table 10.3	`lpc` **Subcommands**
Command	Action
abort	Terminates active spooling daemon and then disables printing.
clean	Removes all temporary files, data files, and control files that cannot be printed.
disable	Turns off the specified printer queues.
down	Turns off the specified printer queue, disables printing, and puts message in printer status file.
enable	Enables spooling on local queue.
exit/quit	Exits from `lpc`.
restart	Attempts to start a new printer daemon.
start	Enables printing and starts a spooling daemon.
status	Displays status of daemons and queues.
stop	Stops spooling daemon after current job completes.
topq	Places jobs in order listed at top of queue.
up	Enables everything and starts a new printer daemon.
help or ?	Prints out help information.

The `lpc` command enables the system administrator to control the actions of the printer system.

SysV PRINT SERVICES

The SysV flavor of print services consists of four major components. The first component is the `lp` program, which provides a command-line user interface to send a job to a printer. The second component is the `lpsched` daemon. `lpsched` is the spooler daemon responsible for controlling access to local printers, moving jobs from the spool directory to the printer, and transferring remote jobs. The third component is the `lpadmin` command. `lpadmin` configures the local print system by defining printers and devices. Administrative commands make up the final component of the SysV print system.

lp

The `lp` command is the command-line interface for submitting print jobs. Multiple options can be entered with the `lp` command to specify destination, number of copies, and other options too numerous to mention. Check the man pages on lp to get the full story. In SysV, you can have printers or classes. A class is usually a group of printers with the same general characteristics (Postscript printers). If a job is sent to a class, the first printer available is given the job. `lp` copies the file to be printed to the spool directory, which is usually located at `/var/spool/lp/request/destination` (`destination` is a printer or class name).

lpsched

`lpsched` is the daemon that transfers print jobs from the spool directories to the printers. `lpsched` is invoked at boot from the startup scripts and runs in the background. `lpsched` keeps a log of all jobs processed and any errors that may occur. The log file is located at `/usr/spool/lp/log` and should be examined first when experiencing printing problems.

lpadmin

SysV uses the `lpadmin` command to configure printers. `lpadmin` configures spooling systems to describe printers and classes and to set the default printer. `lpadmin` can add and remove destinations (printers), change membership in classes, and change printer interface programs. The files it creates are placed in `/usr/spool/lp` and should never be edited.

Control Commands

SysV contains quite a few control commands. Table 10.4 contains the most frequently used commands. The `disable` command prevents `lp-sched` from sending jobs to the applicable printer. Printing jobs are accepted and placed in the queue by `lp` for a disabled printer. Print jobs placed in the queue while a printer is disabled will be printed after the printer is placed on-line with the `enable` command. The `reject/accept` commands affect the spooling of jobs in the print queue. The `reject` command does not allow print jobs to be added to the queue of the applicable printer. The `accept` command allows `lp` to spool print jobs to the applicable printer. The `accept` command must be executed after a new printer has been created with the `lpadmin` command.

Table 10.4	SysV **Control Commands**
Command	Definition
`accept destination`	Allows `lp` to accept printing requests for the named `destination`.
`cancel [id] [printer]`	Cancels requests made with `lp`. Jobs currently printing are stopped.
`disable printers`	Stops the named `printers` from printing requests taken by `lp`.
`enable printers`	Activates the named `printers` to print requests taken by `lp`.
`lpmove dest1 dest2`	Moves requests queued by `lp` between destinations. `lpsched` can not be running.
`lpshut`	Shuts down `lpsched`. All printers stop printing. Jobs printing at invocation will be reprinted when `lpsched` starts again. `lp` commands still function.
`lpstat`	Reports line printer status information (see man pages).
`reject -r reason destination.. -r reason destination...`	Allows `lp` command to reject subsequent printing requests for each named `destination`.

The `lp` command is the command-line interface for submitting print jobs. Multiple options can be entered with the `lp` command to specify destination, number of copies, and other options. `lpadmin` configures spooling systems to describe printers, classes, and set the default printer.

AIX

AIX provides a very robust set of print services. IBM has put a lot of time and effort into developing a robust print system. AIX is interoperable with BSD and SysV systems. It supports both the `lp` and `lpr` commands. The underlying structure, however, is quite different from BSD and SysV systems.

AIX print services utilize the `/etc/qdaemon` to schedule printing jobs. The starting and stopping of `qdaemon` is controlled in the `/etc/inittab` file. The `/etc/qconfig` file contains descriptions of the queues and devices available for print services. The `qdaemon` reads the `qconfig` file on startup and when `qdaemon` is refreshed. The `/usr/sbin/lpd` daemon is responsible for inbound TCP/IP remote printing requests. The `lpd` daemon can be started at system boot (add entry to `/etc/inittab` file) or via the command line.

Manipulation of print jobs and queues can be accomplished in many different ways in AIX. The `enq` command can start and stop queues and printers. It can also change the priority of a job, remove a job from a queue, and list the status of a printer's queue. `enq` is a very useful and powerful print services command.

AIX offers two GUIs to set up print services. Both GUIs are simple to use and do all of the hard work for you. `SMIT` provides a graphical interface that allows you to configure, start, stop, and manipulate all local printers and queues. All that is required is to enter the command `smit` and select the `Print Spooling` button under `System Management`. The other GUI is the Web-based System Manager (`WSM`). `WSM` is located at `/usr/bin/wsm`, and it provides a Web-based interface to manage an AIX system. Click the Printer Queues icon and you can perform all similar functions contained in `SMIT`.

`enq` can start and stop queues and printers. It can also change the priority of a job, remove a job from a queue, and list the status of a printer's queue.

HPUX

HPUX is based on SysV print services. It has enhanced the `lpsched` daemon to spool jobs to a remote BSD printer. HPUX can also accept remote jobs from a BSD system through `rlpdaemon`. The HP Distributed Print

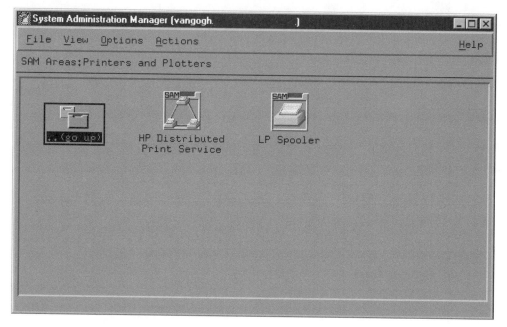

Figure 10.1 SAM printer administration.

Service (HPDPS) is a print administration and management product for distributed environments. It is compatible with the `lp` command, but provides extended administration capabilities. The System Administration Manager (SAM) provides a GUI interface that allows configuration of lp print services and HPDPS (Figure 10.1). We recommend using SAM to configure print services on HPUX.

RED HAT LINUX

Red Hat is based on BSD print services. The `printtool` command allows the system administrator to add, edit, and delete printers with a graphical interface on Red Hat systems (Figure 10.2). `printtool` provides tools to send test files and supports SMB printer servers on Windows 2000.

SOLARIS

Solaris print services are based on SysV. Configuration of print services can be accomplished with the commands outlined in the "SysV Print Services" section. Print services can also be configured using Admintool, which is a GUI system administration tool. Admintool can add or delete access to a printer (Figure 10.3). We recommend using Admintool for adding and deleting access to printers on Solaris systems.

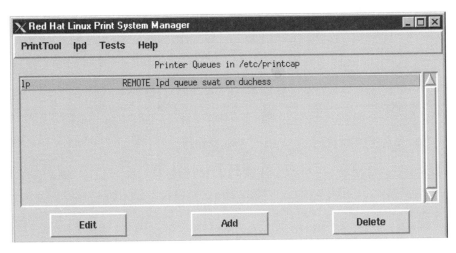

Figure 10.2 Red Hat Linux Print System Manager.

LPRng

LPRng is an enhanced print services package based on BSD. It includes the familiar `lpr`, `lpc`, and `lprm` commands. It also includes dynamic redirection of print queues, multiple printers serving a single queue, and greatly enhanced security checks. LPRng is compatible with remote printers using the BSD services, and it has been ported to HPUX, Solaris, Linux, and AIX.

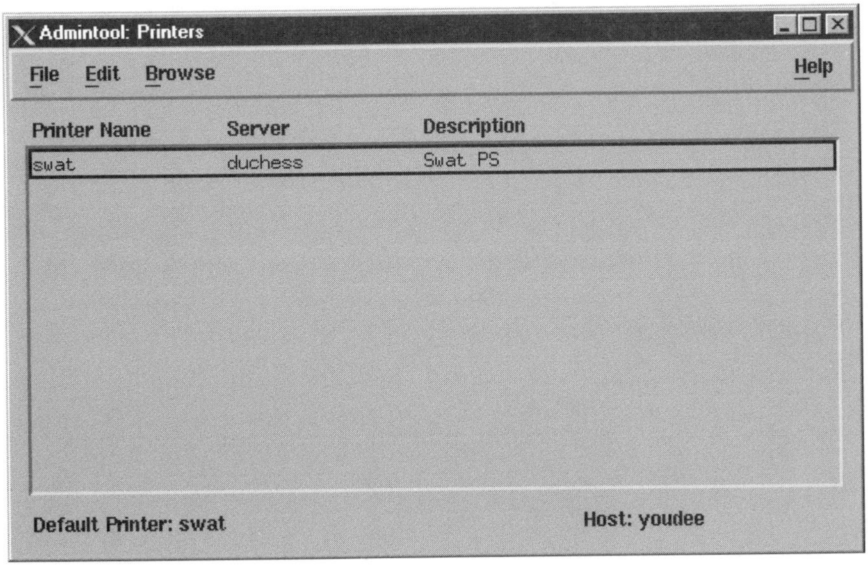

Figure 10.3 Admintool printer administration.

Source for the LPRng distribution can be obtained at `http://www.astart.com/lprng/`. The distribution contains a script that determines your type of system and sets options for compilation and installation. The distribution also contains detailed instructions on disabling the default print services for your version of UNIX. LPRng is a great choice for heterogeneous networks.

COMMON UNIX PRINTING SYSTEM

The Common UNIX Printing System (CUPS) is a portable printing layer for UNIX operating systems. It provides SysV and BSD command-line interfaces. The Internet Printing Protocol (IETF-IPP) is utilized as the basis for managing printers and queues. It also provides support for BSD and SMB protocols. The distribution can be obtained at `http://www.cups.org/`. Binary distributions for HPUX, Solaris, and Linux are available, in addition to the source code.

Windows 2000 Print Services

Windows 2000 makes for a very good print server, but you must deploy hardware that can handle the load you will place on the server. While you could simply have your users print directly to the printers themselves, it is more efficient to use a print server to process and queue the users' print requests. This section will discuss how to deploy a capable print server, connect that server to your printers, add the printer driver, and share the printer to your clients. You will also learn how to connect your clients to shared printers, as well as how to provide printing services to UNIX systems.

PRINT SERVER SYSTEM REQUIREMENTS

Any system you plan to deploy as a print server should meet the minimum requirements for installing Windows 2000 Server. This system must also be capable of processing print jobs effectively given the load you plan to put on the server. The following configuration should be considered a minimum for a print server running Windows 2000 Server:

- 256MB RAM.
- 9GB storage.
- 100 Mb/s network interface.

As your network grows, you may want to consider upgrading your server or deploying additional servers to distribute your printing load.

ADDING A PRINTER TO YOUR SERVER

The first step in providing print services to your clients is to connect your server to your printers. As always, you can connect your printers directly to the server via serial or parallel interfaces, but this requires that the server be located within 25 feet of the printers. In most modern networks, it is neither inconvenient to locate the server so close to your printers, or it is inconvenient to place all of your printers in one location. Many of today's high-end printers can be connected directly to your network via common network protocols.

We will assume in this section that you are connecting your printers to a TCP/IP Ethernet network. Other network topologies are supported and their configuration is very similar. This section will discuss both how to create a port on your server to communicate with a network printer and how to add the printer driver and share it to your network.

Creating a Printer Port

To communicate with network printers, you must create a printer port on your server for each printer with which you wish to communicate. Many printer manufacturers provide their own software for communicating with the printer, but most modern printers also support connecting via TCP/IP, which is described here:

1. Open the Printers folder using the following sequence: from the `Start` menu → `Settings` → `Printers`.
2. From the `File` menu, select `Server Properties`. From the window that is displayed, select the `Ports` tab. You will see a window similar to the one in Figure 10.4.
3. Click the `Add Port` button to display the `Printer Ports` selection window.
4. Select `Standard TCP/IP Port`, and then click the `New Port` button. The `Add Standard TCP/IP Printer Port Wizard` will be displayed.
5. Click `Next` to display the `Add Port` configuration window. Complete the `Printer name` and `Port name` fields, and then click `Next` to continue. The wizard will contact the printer and display a confirmation screen.
6. Click `Finish` to create the printer port.

Now that we have a port connected to our network printer, we need to add the printer driver and share the printer to the network.

Figure 10.4
The Ports tab of
the Print Server
Properties
window.

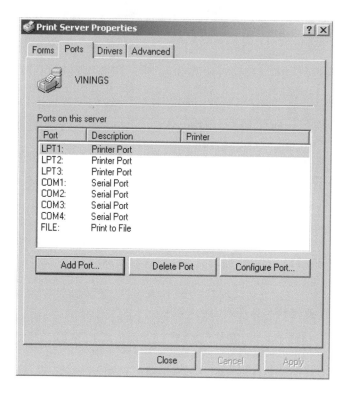

Adding and Sharing a Printer

Use the Add Printer Wizard to install and share the printer to the
network.

1. Open the Printers folder using the following sequence: from the
   Start menu → Settings → Printers.
2. Double-click Add Printer to launch the Add Printer Wizard.
3. Click Next to display the Local or Network Printer configuration screen in Figure 10.5.
4. Select Local printer and click Next to continue. The printer port
   selection screen in Figure 10.6 will be displayed.
5. Select the appropriate port from the list and click Next to continue.
   The printer type selection screen in Figure 10.7 will be displayed.
6. Select the correct manufacturer and model, and then click Next to
   continue. The printer name configuration screen will be displayed.

Figure 10.5
Local or Network
Printer
configuration
screen.

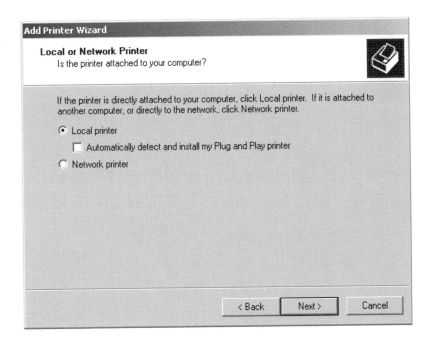

Figure 10.6
Printer port
selection screen.

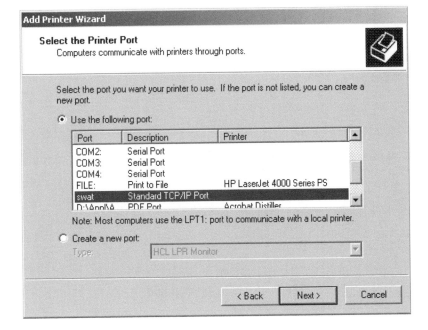

Figure 10.7
Printer type
selection screen.

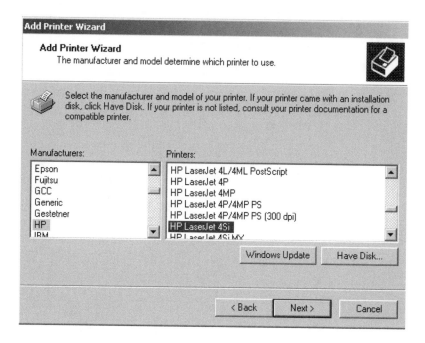

 If your printer is not on the list, you can use a vendor-supplied driver by clicking the Have Disk button and specifying the location of the alternate driver.

7. Type a name for your printer and click `Next` to continue. The `Printer Sharing` configuration screen in Figure 10.8 will be displayed.

8. Select `Share as` and give your printer a share name. Click `Next` to continue. The `Location and Comment` configuration screen in Figure 10.9 will be displayed.

9. Complete the fields as you desire and click `Next` to continue. The `Print Test Page` selection screen will be displayed.

10. To print a test page, select `Yes`, otherwise select `No` and click `Next` to continue. The `Add Printer Wizard Confirmation` screen will be displayed.

11. Review the settings and click `Finish` to install the printer.

12. The wizard will copy the necessary files and you will see your new printer appear in the Printers folder.

You are now ready to connect clients to your print server. We will discuss this in the next few sections.

Figure 10.8
Printer Sharing
configuration
screen.

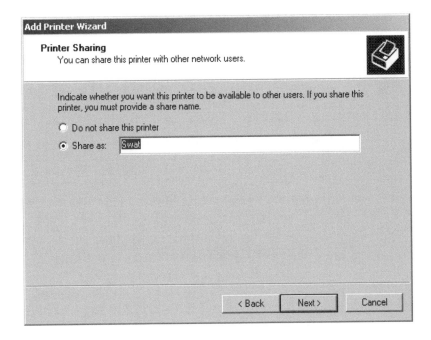

Figure 10.9
Location and
Comment
configuration
screen.

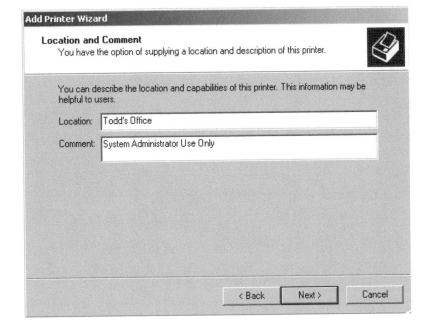

CONNECTING CLIENTS TO SHARED PRINTERS

Now that you have created and shared a new printer on your server, you can connect your Windows 2000 clients to it using a process similar to the one used to create the printer on the server.

1. Open the Printers folder using the following sequence: from the `Start` menu → `Settings` → `Printers`.
2. Double-click `Add Printer` to launch the `Add Printer Wizard`.
3. Click `Next` to display the `Local or Network Printer` configuration screen in Figure 10.5.
4. Select `Network Printer` and click `Next` to continue. The `Locate Your Printer` configuration screen in Figure 10.10 will be displayed.
5. You have three options here:
- You can find a printer in the Active Directory database.
- You can specify the location of the printer in `\\SERVER\share` format or browse the network to locate the share.
- You can specify a direct connection to the printer using a URL.
6. Make your selection and click `Next` to continue. We will use the Active Directory to locate our printer. The `Find Printers` dialog box in Figure 10.11 will appear.

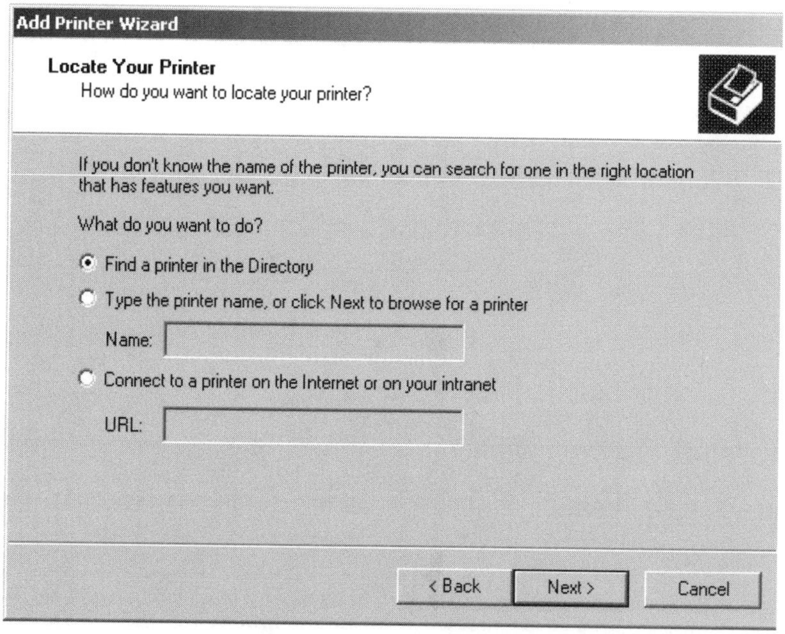

Figure 10.10
`Locate Your Printer` configuration screen.

Figure 10.11
Find Printers
dialog box.

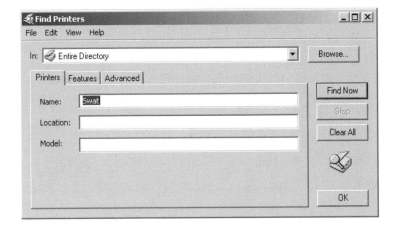

7. Fill in the fields as necessary to locate your printer. If you know the name of the printer, that is all you will need. When you are done, click the Find Now button to search the directory.

8. The result will be displayed in a window similar to the one shown in Figure 10.12.

9. Select your printer from the list and click OK to continue.

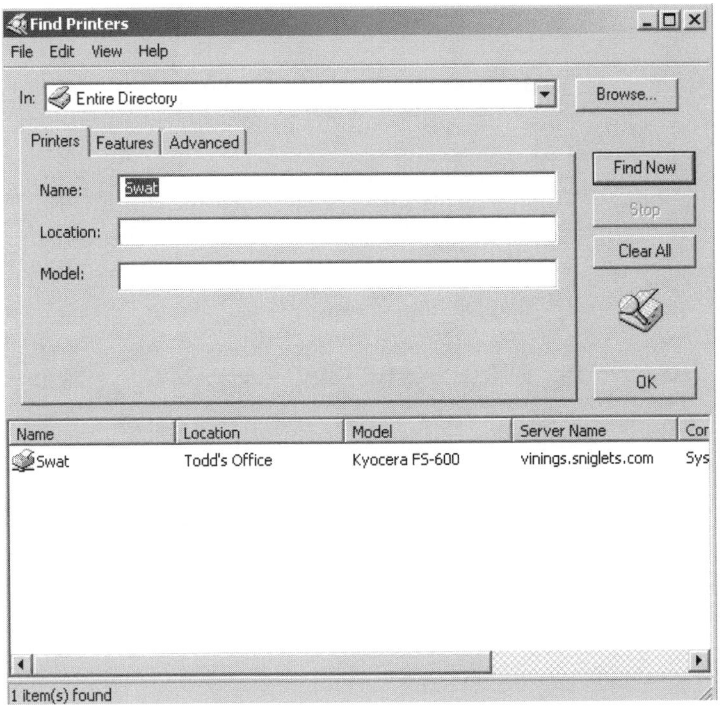

Figure 10.12
Find Printers
results window.

10. Complete the remaining steps in the wizard and your printer will be ready to use.

You can also connect Windows 95, Windows 98, and Windows NT clients to your network printer. To do this, follow the appropriate procedures for your client and use the \\SERVER\share syntax when specifying the printer to connect to.

Windows 2000 clients will automatically download the correct printer driver from the Windows 2000 server. Other Windows clients will need to have the correct driver installed locally. You will be prompted to select the appropriate driver if necessary.

PRINT SERVICES FOR UNIX

To allow UNIX clients to connect to printers shared from Windows 2000 servers, you must install the Windows 2000 print services for UNIX.

1. Open the Control Panel as follows: from the Start menu → Settings → Control Panel.
2. Double-click the Add/Remove Programs applet in the Control Panel. You will see a window similar to the one in Figure 10.13.
3. Click the Add/Remove Windows Components button on the left sidebar. The Windows Components Wizard in Figure 10.14 will be displayed.
4. Scroll down and select Other Network File and Print Services and click the Details button.
5. Select Print Services for UNIX from the list and click OK.
6. Click Next to continue.
7. The wizard will configure the components you have selected. You may need the Windows 2000 Server CD-ROM during this phase.
8. When the wizard is done, click Finish and then close the Add/Remove Programs window.
9. Open the Services MMC snap-in as follows: from the Start menu → Programs → Administrative Tools → Services. You will see a window similar to the one shown in Figure 10.15.
10. Scroll down to select TCP/IP Print Server.
11. Double-click TCP/IP Print Server to display the Properties window in Figure 10.16.

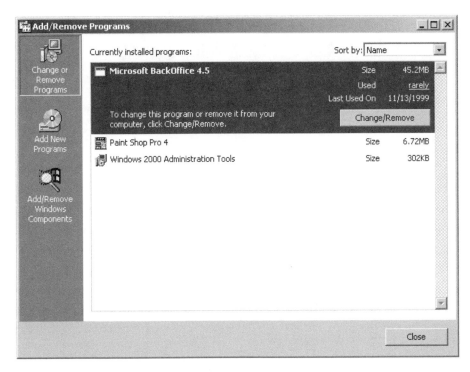

Figure 10.13
Add/Remove Programs Control Panel applet.

Figure 10.14
Windows
Components
Wizard.

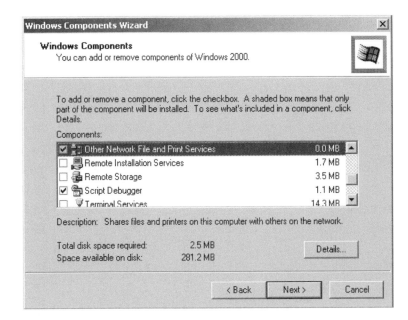

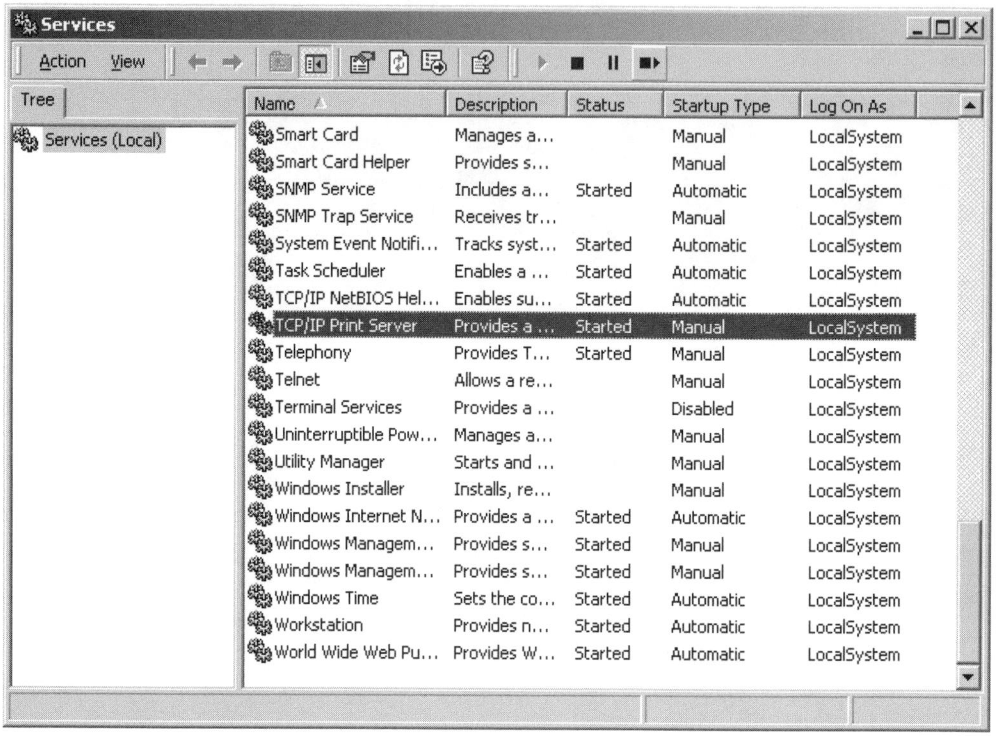

Figure 10.15 Services MMC snap-in.

12. Change `Startup type` to `Automatic` and click the `Start` button if the service is not already started.

13. Click `OK` to continue.

14. Close the Services MMC snap-in.

Now that you have installed print services for UNIX, you can connect your UNIX clients to the shared printers on your Windows 2000 server using the `lpr` protocol. Configuring and using the `lpr` protocol is discussed in the "UNIX Print Services" section earlier in this chapter.

For your UNIX users to print to Windows 2000 printers, they must have the same username on the Windows 2000 domain and UNIX clients.

MANAGING PRINTERS

Two important aspects of printing services is how to control access to your printers and how to manage documents spooled to your printers. This section will discuss both of these topics.

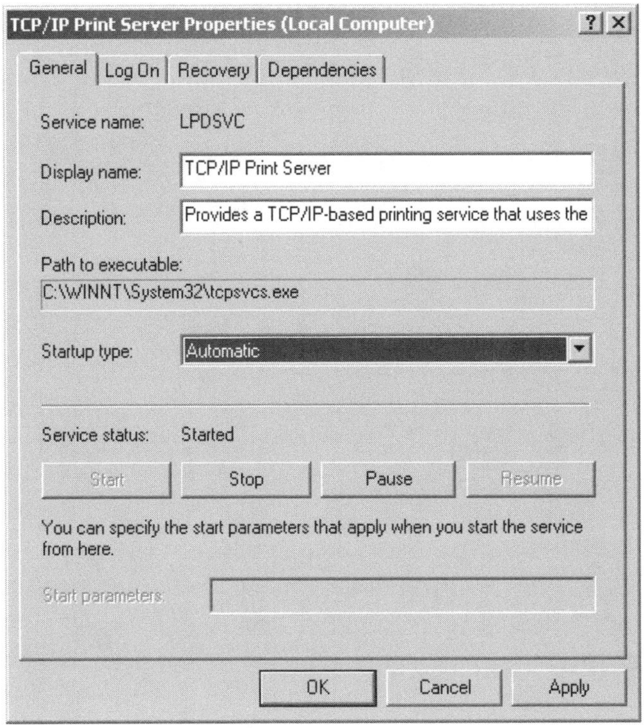

Figure 10.16
TCP/IP Print
Server Properties
window.

Controlling Access to Printers

It is often desirable to control who can access certain printers and/or when those printers can be accessed. All of this can be configured using the printer properties for each printer. Follow these steps to display and/or modify the users and groups that can access your printer:

1. Open the Printers folder using the following progression: from the Start Menu → Settings → Printers.
2. Right-click the printer you wish to modify and select Properties from the list. The printer's Properties window in Figure 10.17 will be displayed.
3. Select the Security tab to display the security settings for the printer. You should see a window similar to the one in Figure 10.18.
4. On this screen, you can add and remove users and groups to control who can access the printer on the network. You can also modify how much access each entry in the list has. Your options are outlined in Table 10.5.
5. Once you have made the desired modifications, click OK to apply the changes.

Figure 10.17
Printer Properties
window.

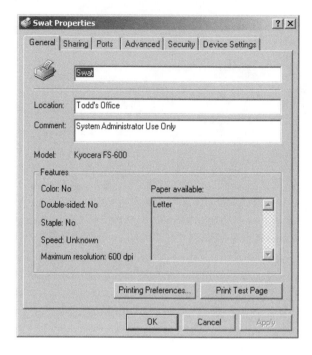

Figure 10.18
Printer security
settings window.

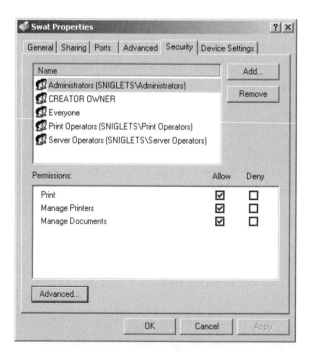

Table 10.5	**Printer Security Options**
Security Option	Description
Print	Allows/denies the user or group permission to print to the network printer.
Manager Printers	Allows/denies the user or group permission to modify printer settings.
Manage Documents	Allows/denies the user or group permission to pause, resume, restart, or cancel print jobs.

You can also modify the hours a particular printer is available. Use the following steps to modify the hours your printer is available:

1. Open the Printers folder as follows: from the `Start` menu → `Settings` → `Printers`.
2. Right-click the printer you wish to modify and select `Properties` from the list. The printer's Properties window in Figure 10.17 will be displayed.
3. Select the `Advanced` tab to display the advanced settings for the printer. You should see a window similar to the one in Figure 10.19.

Figure 10.19
Advanced printer properties window.

4. By default, the printer is always available. To make the printer available only between certain hours, Select the `Available from` option and modify the times to reflect the settings you desire.

5. When you are done making your changes, click `OK` to apply the changes.

Document Management

From time to time, it may become necessary to directly control a job in your printer queue. For example:

- The job is "stuck" and preventing other jobs from spooling. This can happen for any number of reasons, but is usually due to network problems or problems with the machine that sent the job.
- The job is a duplicate of another print job and does not need to be printed.
- The job has been paused for some reason and needs to be restarted.

To view the printer queue, follow these steps:

1. Open the Printers folder as follows: from the `Start` menu → `Settings` → `Printers`.

2. Double-click the printer you wish to control. You will see a window similar to the one shown in Figure 10.20.

Any active and pending jobs will be shown in this window.

To control a particular job, select it from the list and use the `Document` menu to perform any of the actions detailed in Table 10.6.

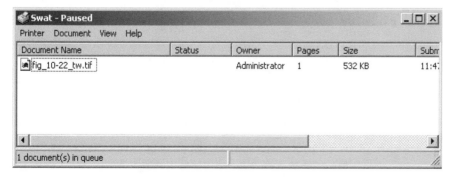

Figure 10.20 Printer queue.

Table 10.6	Document Management Options
Document Option	Description
Pause	Prevents the current job from printing until you select Resume from the Document menu.
Resume	Resumes the printing operation of a currently paused job.
Restart	Causes a job to be re-submitted by the client that spooled it.
Cancel	Cancels printing of the current document and removes it from the print queue

 By default, Windows 2000 Server allows users to manage their own documents. Administrators are also permitted to manage documents. You can specify additional users and groups who can manage documents with the printer's Security Properties page.

SAMBA Print Services

SAMBA has the ability to make printers spooled from a UNIX system available to Windows clients. This section assumes that you have read Chapter 8, "Distributed filesystem", and have already configured SAMBA on your UNIX system. We will discuss how to make printers available via SAMBA and the steps necessary to connect your Windows clients to those printers.

SHARING PRINTERS USING SAMBA

To make your UNIX printers available to Windows clients, you must modify the *smb.conf* file we discussed in Chapter 8. This is accomplished with two steps. First, the following lines must be present in the [global] section of the *smb.conf* file:

```
load printers = yes
printcap name = /etc/printcap
printing = bsd
```

Next, you must have the following section included below the [global] section:

```
[printers]
    comment = All printers in /etc/printcap
    path = /var/spool/samba
    printable = yes
```

As discussed in Chapter 8, the `printing` setting does not have to be set to `bsd`, but can be set to any valid option.

Once you have made these additions, you will need to restart the SAMBA service on your UNIX system. Once you have restarted the service, you should be able to print to any printer defined in the `/etc/printcap` file from a Windows client.

Refer to Chapter 8 for a more detailed description of the SAMBA options discussed here. You may also want to review the SAMBA documentation for additional information.

CONNECTING CLIENTS TO SAMBA SHARED PRINTERS

Connecting to SAMBA printers is nearly identical to connecting to Windows 2000 printers. Follow the steps described above to connect to a SAMBA printer, but keep the following in mind:

- You must install the printer driver locally, since it is not part of the share on SAMBA servers.
- You must be logged into Windows with a valid UNIX username and password to connect to the printer, or the SAMBA server must be able to authenticate against a Windows 2000 domain controller (this is the configuration we recommended in Chapter 8).
- You must connect to the printer share with the \\SERVER\share syntax.

Once you have connected to the SAMBA printer, it should behave just as if it were shared from a Windows 2000 server.

Summary

Though supporting printing is often frustrating, it is necessary. The paperless society predicted by the digital prognosticators has not yet materialized. In this chapter, we discussed the basics of printing for UNIX and Windows 2000.

BSD VS. SYSV

Print services in UNIX are divided into two camps: BSD and SysV. Generally speaking, BSD is easier to use, but SysV has more features. In recent years, individual UNIX vendors have produced print servers that are specific to their variant. These usually work well with a limited number of UNIX variants. AIX provides the most comprehensive print services package. Another option in UNIX is the third-party LPRng package. This is free and supports most UNIX variants.

MICROSOFT PRINT SERVICES

Printing in the Windows world is much better. The print services provided by Microsoft are efficient and easy to install. The ability to share printers is a transparent part of the service. Microsoft also provides print services for UNIX, which allow a UNIX system to use Windows 2000 print services.

SAMBA is a third-party package that allows UNIX systems to share their printers with Windows systems. SAMBA is widely used and is available for free.

## PART THREE

ADMINISTRATION

Though administration tasks are tedious, they are easily the most critical. Tasks described in this part of the book will deal directly with users, or with the tools necessary to support them. Creating user accounts (and deleting them) is of obvious importance. Backups and performance tuning also affect the quality of the user environment. It is extremely easy to forget that the reason most systems and networks exist is to support some set of activities performed by users. We believe that the ultimate test of an integrated infrastructure is its ability to meet the needs of the people who use it. Without proper administration, system stability cannot be maintained. Likewise, in a distributed environment, administration strategies are necessary to support software resources and security.

SECURITY

UNIX

WINDOWS 2000

Analysis of Security

Opponents and Attacks

Protection

Prevention

Detection

"In the ever-changing world of global data communications, inexpensive Internet connections, and fast-paced software development, security is becoming more and more of an issue. Security is now a basic requirement because global computing is inherently insecure. As your data goes from point A to point B on the Internet, for example, it may pass through several other points along the way, giving other users the opportunity to intercept, and even alter, your data. Even other users on your system may maliciously transform your data into something you did not intend. "

Dave Wreski, Linux Security Administrator's Guide, 1998

The format of this chapter differs a bit from earlier ones in that the UNIX and Windows discussions are interwoven.

Analysis of Security

There is no such thing as a totally secure system. Computer and network security is a balancing act between protection and usability. The more protected your system is, the harder it may be for your users to use it. The changing nature of system interaction, both hardware and software, also compounds the problem of maintaining a secure system. Security, therefore, is a destination and the journey is a difficult one. At the outset, you must understand how vulnerable computing systems are. Dave Wreski, in the on-line book quoted previously, uses the following points to illustrate the insecure nature of our computational environments:

- The Computer Emergency Response Team consistently reports an increase in computer vulnerabilities and exploits.
- TCP and UDP, the protocols that comprise the Internet, were not written with security as their first priority when it was created more than 30 years ago.
- A version of software on one host has the same vulnerabilities as the same version of software on another host. Using this information, an intruder can exploit multiple systems using the same attack method.
- Many administrators don't even take simple security measures necessary to protect their site, or don't understand the ramifications of implementing some services. Many administrators are not given the additional time necessary to integrate the necessary security measures.

Combining the balancing act with the inherent vulnerabilities, the security of an IT system can be defined as *the means deployed by an organization to preserve the state of the IT systems under which the same organization is able to access the IT systems in a predetermined and consistent manner.*

A more practical view of the security of an IT system is that security is the result of the combination of four actions:

Security = Protection + Prevention + Detection + Recovery

- **Protection** is the implementation of the security policy. This includes the procedures and technologies that are deployed into the infrastructure for the purpose of maintaining security.
- **Prevention** is any action that aims to reduce the level of security risk, that is, to increase the level of difficulty for an opponent to

break into the IT system. Such actions can have a direct effect on the protection and detection components.

- **Detection** is any action whose goal is to detect an intrusion and track down the opponent with the intent to prosecute.

- **Recovery** corresponds to the action to take when it is too late and how to recover when you have lost the race and have become the victim of an intrusion. Good methods and a minimum of action in the three areas of protection + prevention + detection are likely to protect your organization from 90-95% of all possible intrusions. However it is important not to neglect the last 5% as these are generally the most dangerous. The final 5% are those types of attacks that can only be attempted by an intruder with a high level of knowledge, and with that increased kno wledge, the amount of potential damage an intruder can inflict also increases.

Before going further into this journey, here are some thoughts that you may want to keep in mind while working with security:

- The security of an IT system can be addressed from a technical point of view (patching security holes, restricting access), but overall it has to be defined by a policy. The policy must define what a user can/cannot do inside the IT system (for example, what system(s) they can access, what commands they can execute, etc.).

- An analogy can be established between the concepts of quality and security of an IT system. Security represents a cost (loss) for the organization. Enforcing a security policy requires time and dedicated means, and it can have an indirect impact on productivity (users may have to follow some rules which may slow them down in their use of the IT system). But, not doing security can lead to greater costs, as will be explained later.

- The system administrator, when working on security, has to be paranoid by nature. Security is a way of life, and must be present in every action done by the system administrator. Doing something (like setting up a server) without paying attention to security or saying, "I have no time right now, I will secure the system later." is wrong, as "later" may become "too late".

Know Your Opponents and Types of Attacks

As generally stated by the military: The preparation of a good defense requires good knowledge of the opponent.

WHO IS THE INTRUDER?

Before going further, it is important to understand the jargon and slang used on the "dark side" of system administration. Speaking your enemy's language is the first step to understanding how they think. A good starting point is:

```
http://packetstorm.securify.com/docs/hack/jargon-4.1.2/jargon.html
```

Intruders can be classified from a defacto point of view into two main categories: *outsiders* and *insiders*.

Insiders

A statistic that is frequently quoted by security vendors and in articles is the rule of 80%–20%. It means that 80% of the intrusion attempts come from inside the organization, with the remaining 20% coming from outside the organization. Insiders can be:

- Angry employees seeking revenge.
- Employees trying to benefit by stealing private information and selling it or using it to their advantage.

Insiders break into IT systems through:

- **Physical intrusion**—They take advantage of special privileges that access to the physical console of the system can offer. For example, they reboot the system into single-user mode or from installation media in order to access data thereby bypassing the normal access control list. A physical intrusion can also include removing the hard drive from a system to read/write it more easily from another machine.
- **System intrusion**—The intruder uses existing low-privilege access and tries, by exploiting a security hole or by taking advantage of a system misconfiguration, to gain additional administrative privileges.

Outsiders

Outsiders try to break into your system remotely, from outside the network that is part of your infrastructure. It is possible to classify outsiders into four main categories:

- **Script kiddies**—Script kiddies are considered the least dangerous of the outsiders. They are generally teenagers, out to explore and create mischief using tools written by others without really understanding how and what they are attempting to exploit. More simply, script kiddies cause damage while having fun and without understanding what they are really doing.

- **Hackers**—A hacker does not act out of a search for profit or intent to cause physical damage to your systems. They do it for the challenge, to prove to themselves that they can do it, that they have defeated a new set of systems and administrators. Generally, the hacker will leave a note to the system administrator (anonymously, of course) on how they did it and how to fix it. However, hackers cause damage in an indirect way in that the organization attacked spends time detecting the intrusion, as well as spends additional time assessing the damage and verifying that systems have not been compromised.

- **Crackers**—Crackers are a malevolent form of hacker. Their intent is to compromise systems, causing physical damage to them through the loss of data, hardware damage, or denial of service that will directly affect the organization. Crackers are also called dark-side hackers, referring to their criminal or malicious side. Vandalism, such as defacing a Web site or denying access to an e-commerce site, is generally associated with crackers.

- **Profiteers**—A profiteer is potentially the most damaging type of outsider. A profiteer is a professional cracker whose goal is to profit by either stealing information or damaging your systems. Their intent is to gain benefit for themselves, or competitors of your organization.

To access your systems, outsiders first need a way to connect to the systems in your organization. Outsiders do not exclusively come in from the Internet. Basically, they can attempt to exploit any connection that your infrastructure has with the outside world. These connections include (but are not limited to):

- The Internet, by exploiting system flaws or stolen user identities.
- Dial-up lines, through the use of modems attached to computers or networking equipment.
- Direct connections with partners, where the outsider has gained access to the partner's infrastructure.

Given this simple profile of the outsider, it is important to understand how they will attempt to enter your systems and how they will plan to attack your infrastructure.

HOW DO THEY ENTER?

If a system administrator seeks to properly secure their systems, they must understand how their opponents think, and they must learn the strategies used to gain access. For years, attackers have written guides that explain what to look for and how to break into a system. These documents are available on the multiple hacking Web sites and exist for both Windows and UNIX. While the primary intent of such documents is to be guides to hacking, administrators can use them as a way to understand their opponents, as well as to fortify their infrastructure from the specified processes contained within. One of the best manuals to start with is at:
`http://www.nmrc.org/faqs/hackfaq/hackfaq.html`.

A typical scenario of intrusion by outsiders attempting to exploit a target system is:

- **Performing reconnaissance of the target system**—The initial goal of the intruder is to learn as much as they can about the system without being detected. It is very difficult to detect them at this stage, as the tools and information they are accessing have a low level of importance, and will look like normal activity to the administrator. Some typical ways to do reconnaissance is:
  - Use the `whois` database for accessing an organization's IP address information, Internet service provider, and system administrator contact information.
  - Analyze DNS tables with the conventional command `nslookup` or some advanced tools like `dig` or `dnswalk`.
  - The intruder can also use non-technical ways, like social engineering, to get information. As an example, they can pretend to be security vendors or firewall salespeople and through casual conversation learn the types of security software and hardware that is currently being used in the infrastructure.
- **Probing the target system**—In this second stage, the intruder starts to become more active on your system itself, which gives the administrator more opportunity to detect the intruder. At this point, their goal is to probe the infrastructure to find an entry point.
  - The first step is to see which machines can be reached from their location. For this, they can either use a command such as `ping` or some advanced scanning tools like `nmap`. In cases where a firewall is installed and is detected by the intruder, the intruder will try to determine its filtering rules using a tool like `firewalk`:
    - `firewalk: http://www.packetfactory.net/firewalk/`
    - `nmap: http://www.insecure.org/nmap/index.html`

- If the intruder can access your infrastructure, the next step is to try to determine what types of operating systems are running on the hosts that can be accessed. Operating systems each have a unique set of bugs and weaknesses that can be exploited if the intruder has knowledge of the operating system.

- If exploiting the operating systems is not possible, the intruder will then attempt to determine what types of applications and services are running on a system. Based on the applications and services available, the intruder will try to find weaknesses in those services. For example, if a service like SNMP is installed on a remote host and the community can be guessed, the intruder will use a tool like `snmpwalk` to gain as much information as possible.

The advanced intruder will use evasive techniques to minimize the risk of being detected. They will use a stealth scan rather than a direct `ping` to detect if a host is alive. Or, rather than scanning a set of hosts in sequential order and rapidly, they will do it in a random manner and slowly. Depending on the goal of the intruder, it is likely that hosts with a high presence on the Internet, such as Web, mail, or FTP servers, will be probed first, as they can provide the most "reward" for an intruder.

- **Gaining administrative privileges**—At this stage, the goal is not to study possible exploit, but to find a way to take advantage of it. As with any intrusion, the most dangerous to the infrastructure and most beneficial to the intruder is the ability to gain administrative privileges. All ways are good, and the intruder will try to gain advantage of vulnerable systems by:
  - System misconfiguration; for example, SNMP configured with easily guessed community names.
  - Login accounts with no or easily guessed passwords, such as guest accounts.
  - Exploits of security-related bugs, where patches may or may not be available or installed by the administrator.

The intruder will attempt some or all of these steps until they can finally reach the administrator level of privileges. The game is over at this point; the system administrator has lost the war!!!

- **Covering their tracks**—As soon as the intruder has succeeded in gaining administrative privilege, their goal shifts immediately in protecting themselves by hiding or destroying any evidence of their existence. The intruder does so by removing information from the system logging mechanism, either by editing the information, or by removing the complete logging infrastructure, including log files and even operating system programs. By removing this information, it makes the task of tracking and prosecuting the attacker more difficult, if not impossible. Some techniques that can be used by an intruder are described in one of the issues of *Phrack* magazine (`http://www.phrack.com/search.phtml?view&article =p43-14`).

 There is no guarantee that a URL taken from the "dark side" will always work!

- **Attaining the "prize"**—Once the intruder has gained access, they can begin to take advantage by:
  - Stealing confidential and valuable data and selling it to the highest bidder.
  - Shutting down pieces of your infrastructure to deny access to authorized users, removing data, or physically damaging systems.
  - Using system resources for their own advantage, either by gaining a higher stature among other hackers, or by reusing the organization's systems to attack other systems.
- **Keeping the account**—After having spent time and energy to gain administrative access, the intruder will try to keep the benefits of their efforts by taking action to preserve access. They may install some toolkit (commonly called Trojan horses), which will help them to hide their presence on the system. They may also set up a backdoor, a hidden access method such as a new user account, or a new program that will give them access whenever required. Replacing operating system-level programs with a similar program is a common attack. While users will still have the functionally they expect when they run the program, if the program is run a certain, undocumented way, the intruder can gain unauthorized access. The intruder will also fix, by installing patches, the security hole they have made in order to minimize the suspicion of the system administrator.

An insider intruder can also attempt:

- Password stealing, by taking the password database back home and trying to crack it. They can also do so by trying to sniff clear text passwords from the network if they can gain access to a system that can run network-level scanning tools.

- ■ Take advantage of a direct access to the console of hosts, if there is a device that is attached to the network that gives access to a group of system consoles.

ANALYSIS OF THE THREATS AND CONSEQUENCES

At first glance, some people may not be able to identify the direct benefits of implementing a good security policy. The management of a company may be reluctant to accept the costs of defining, implementing, and enforcing the security of the IT system. However, not doing so will sooner or later result in a loss for the organization and should be able to convince any CEO. Losses can be:

- ■ Direct:
  - ■ Confidential information being stolen.
  - ■ Downtime of the IT system (which means loss of direct revenue in most cases).
  - ■ Time and costs related to recovering from the intrusion.
- ■ Indirect, namely bad publicity. There is nothing worse for a big organization than to see their security breach discussed in the media. Organizations try to limit the publicity related to an intrusion. But, don't forget that nowadays, in our information-based society, word spreads quickly. The news of a Web site being compromised will be spread in the hacker world even before the organization realizes the problem. Some Web sites specialize in taking pictures of compromised sites, which can increase the publicity surrounding a break-in. For an example of such a Web site, see: `http://www.attrition.org/mirror/attrition`.

Protection

Protection is the first aspect of the security of an IT system that should be addressed; it is also the fastest line of defense that can be established.

SETTING UP A SECURITY POLICY

If attaining true security can be considered finding the Holy Grail, then the quest begins with the development of a security policy. Its definition is important since it is the fundamental principal, that will guide the system administrator in all of their security- related decisions.

There are two general types of security policies:

- Prohibitive—Everything, that is not expressly authorized is implicitly prohibited.
- Permissive—Everything, that is not expressly prohibited is implicitly authorized.

To design a security policy, the system administrator will have to make sure they understand how the organization's IT systems are used by the users, and for what activities. The components of the IT systems that are vital to normal activities of the organization must also be identified.

Do not forget that the security policy is going to limit the freedom of users in how they can access their systems. The policy must not prevent them from accomplishing their duties or they will find ways to circumvent the policy so they can complete their work. This trade-off can be balanced by using a detection component, rather than adding an extra layer of complexity in the security policy.

The design of the security policy will emphasize:

- Defining which systems should be servers.
- Defining the security requirements for a server and clients.
- Establishing the minimum trust relationship between the clients and server in terms of user access to data and services, in order for the users to perform their work and to limit the threat in case a client or server is compromised. These relationships must be classified into levels of access. Indeed, two users accessing the same server from two different clients do not necessarily access the same information in terms of confidentiality and sensibility. This leads to the definition of two separate trust relationships, belonging to two different levels of access.
- Defining per user or group of users the level of information that can be accessed. This definition will allow them to establish which authentication methods must be used per user or group of users regarding the sensibility and confidentiality of the data accessed.

PHYSICAL CONTROL

As has already been emphasized, the risk of an intrusion can come either from the outside or the inside. Therefore, it is important that a system administrator consider the physical security of a system. However, not all systems are created equal. In terms of physical security, servers and clients should not be treated the same. As you might guess, servers are generally the most important systems to secure, and when first implementing a security policy, should be secured first.

As a general rule, physical access to servers must be limited to system administrators only. Badge-controlled access to a secure room (equipped with a surveillance camera) is a good way to achieve this. Servers should be secured in such a way as to not allow easy access to the cabinet and its contents. Physical threats to the server include:

- The theft of information by stealing the server or just the hard drive.
- Damage to the physical system that renders the system unusable.

A lock on the case itself is a good way to protect a host.

The next step is to make sure the system will only run the operating system for which it was designed. This is to avoid having an insider reboot the host into a different operating system from which they can access the server's data. For example, with Linux or Solaris, it is possible to boot from a floppy or CD-ROM and have a minimum set of operating system utilities. At this point, the intruder can mount the root partition and re-initialize the administrator password. To prevent the boot of a system into an unknown operating system:

- In the case of a PC, deactivate the CD-ROM and floppy drive to eliminate the possibly of booting into an unknown operating system. Also, when possible, enable the password setting of your system BIOS.
- For a Sun Sparc system, you can set the variable `security-mode` under the `OpenBoot` prompt to full (use the following: `setenv security-mode full`). All `OpenBoot` commands except `go` will require you to enter the `OpenBoot` password. Note that the password must be setup under the `OpenBoot` first with the command `password` before changing the `security-mode`. Failure to do so leads to a dead-lock situation for the system administrator.

A final step is to make sure that the operating system on the host cannot be given special switches without a password.

Under UNIX, the single-user mode or booting from another filesystem can be selected during the boot process.

- Under Sun, the use of the key sequence STOP+A interrupts the boot process and allows the user on the console to either select the single-user mode by giving the switch `-s` to the `boot` command or to select another disk to boot from. The use of the `security-mode` variable as described before prevents this.

■ Under Linux, lilo, (the most common boot loader used, especially in cases of dedicated Linux servers), can also be told to boot the system in single-user mode, or to use a different root filesystem. For example, the user at the console can type `linux single` to access the single-user mode, or `linux root=/dev/hdb1` to boot using the filesystem located on partition 1 of the second IDE hard drive. This boot loader can be protected by editing its configuration file, `/etc/lilo.conf`, and by adding the lines highlighted below into the `common` section:

```
boot=/dev/sda
map=/boot/map
install=/boot/boot.b
message=/boot/message
compact
password = MyPassword
restricted
```

■ Under HPUX, the auto-boot process is interrupted by <ESC>. At this point, an ISL (Initial System Load) prompt is obtained. The command `hpux -iS` accesses the single-user mode. To our knowledge, there is no way to protect access to ISL.

■ In the case of AIX, the privileged access password is used to protect hardware configuration data and prevent a user from booting alternate disk images. This password can be set up under the `System Management's Utilities` SMS submenu, which is accessed by pressing F1 or 1 on the console during the POST (Power-On Self Test) sequence.

HOST ACCESS CONTROL

A major step in securing your environment is building and maintaining secure hosts. This section will discuss some useful processes for keeping your systems and the data on them safe from intruders while providing users the access they require.

User Authentication

User authentication is the process by which a server validates a user as they attempt to access a system. Each user is given a login name. This login name can be unique and valid on a single host or through the entire IT system. The most basic and widely used method to authenticate a user is to associate a simple password with the login name of the user. Only the user and system know this password. However, there are a number of more secure methods that can be used that provide better, or stronger, authentication methods. Some authentication schemes that are currently used are:

- Standard UNIX authentication and shadow password (UNIX).
- PAM : Pluggable Authentication Module (UNIX).
- Kerberos (UNIX and Windows).

Each authentication method has pros and cons. However, in each case, the security goal, which must be satisfied, is to prevent an intruder from impersonating a legitimate user, unless the latter has shared its authentication secret with the former. The purpose of a user authentication scheme is to make it impossible for an intruder to:

- Guess the password or token owned by a valid user and which is used in the authentication scheme.
- Reproduce the authentication password or token used by a valid user through other methods.

The initial authentication scheme used under UNIX is based on asking a user for their password and checking if the password entered, once encrypted, corresponds to the encrypted official password that is stored in the `/etc/passwd` file or an equivalent. The description of shadow passwords is done in the `protection` section, as it does not represent an authentication scheme, but a way to increase the level of security of this present scheme.

The immediate drawback of this system is that user passwords have to be sent in clear text over the network, when, for example, a remote user tries to access the system using a telnet session. The system becomes vulnerable if an intruder is able to capture the password in clear text by sniffing, i.e. listening to network traffic.

The immediate and recommended fix to this risk is to use encryption for all remote accesses to UNIX systems. Secure shell (SSH), which builds an encrypted channel between two systems, is one such way to provide a secure, encrypted session. In addition, SSH allows an advanced authentication scheme based on asymmetric cryptographic technology like public key (RSA or DSA). For more information on SSH, visit `http://www.ssh.org`.

PAM is not an authentication scheme by itself, but a flexible mechanism under UNIX which allows the system administrator to specify the authentication scheme (plain text, radius, Kerberos, LDAP) to use in the infrastructure. On the developer side, PAM presents the advantage to be able to develop programs without the burden of including all the possible authentication schemes. PAM was invented by Sun and was completely implemented for the first time in Solaris 2.6. A presentation of PAM by Sun can be found at `http://www.sun.com/software/solaris/pam`.

Today, PAM is used as the default authentication management scheme under Solaris, Linux, and HPUX (v11.x). The Linux implementation can be found at `http://www..kernel.org/pug/linux/libs/pam`.

Kerberos is a network authentication protocol developed at the Massachusetts Institute of Technology (more information can be found at `http://web.mit.edu/kerberos/www`). Kerberos' goal is to solve the issues left by the initial authentication scheme of UNIX. It provides strong authentication of both users and clients connected to the network against a server. Once authentication has been performed, the clients and server can encrypt their communication.

Under Windows 2000, Kerberos 5 is the default network authentication scheme used to authenticate users and computers as discussed in the Microsoft Windows Kerberos authentication white paper, which can be found at `http://www.microsoft.com/windows/server/Technical/security/kerberos.asp`.

Solaris 8.0 will also support Kerberos 5 as a possible authentication scheme. Currently, Solaris supports Kerberos 4 along with the PAM implementation. For Linux, the Kerberos module does not come by default with some distributions like Red Hat 6.0 and Red Hat 6.1. Indeed, it is not part of the standard PAM distribution either. AIX supports both Kerberos 4 and 5. Kerberos 5 is also supported under HPUX 11.x.

Restricting User Access

A well-restricted system is one in which access is denied even if an intruder has knowledge of an authorized user's login name and password. The first practice in restricting user access is to prohibit, or at least minimize, the access of users to servers. A user generally has no need to access a server with the primary function of serving the user's home directory. The underlying rule is: the fewer the number of users that have access to servers, the less the chance of an intruder finding a way onto the system.

A user must have access to the hosts they need and only those hosts. Under UNIX, the common practice to manage this using an NIS environment is to use the functionality of netgroups. The `/etc/passwd` file can then be edited in the following way:

```
root:x:0:1:Super-User:/:/bin/tcsh
daemon:x:1:1::/:
bin:x:2:2::/usr/bin:
```

```
sys:x:3:3::/:
adm:x:4:4:Admin:/var/adm:
lp:x:71:8:Line Printer Admin:/usr/spool/lp:
smtp:x:0:0:Mail Daemon User:/:
nuucp:x:9:9:uucp
Admin:/var/spool/uucppublic:/usr/lib/uucp/uucico
listen:x:37:4:Network Admin:/usr/net/nls:
nobody:x:60001:60001:Nobody:/:
noaccess:x:60002:60002:No Access User:/:
nobody4:x:65534:65534:SunOS 4.x Nobody:/:
+@systems::0:0:::
+@usergroup1::0:0:::
+@usergroup2::0:0:::
+user3::0:0:::
+::0:0:::/bin/false
```

Users whose login names belong to one of the three netgroups: `sys-tems`, `usergroup1`, and `usergroup2` are authorized to access the host (the @ sign designates an NIS netgroup). A single user, `user3`, is also given access.

The last line gives access to everyone. The user shell field is overridden by the local entry and replaced by `/bin/false`. Therefore, this last line acts as a "deny all" statement, as `/bin/false` is not a valid user shell.

In the future, host access restrictions will be performed using LDAP (as a replacement for NIS) and an equivalent of the netgroup structure. User authentication through LDAP now requires the use of a special PAM module. This module, supported as open source, is called `pam_ldap` and can be found at `http://www.padl.com/pam_ldap.html`.

A good practice for UNIX systems is to disable direct remote access by the root administrator account. This limits access to the console of the system to only the root account and to an already authenticated user via the use of `su`. The general scenario is that the system administrator logs on using their regular login name (corresponding to their personal account) and then becomes root using the `su` command.

Unfortunately, the root password used by the `su` command will be transmitted unencrypted, but unless an outsider has both the root password and a user password, they will be unable to compromise the root account on the system. The use of an encryption channel, such as using SSH as described before, decreases this last risk.

- Under Solaris, root logins are restricted by editing the `/etc/default/login` file and by uncommenting the following line:

  `CONSOLE=/dev/console`

- Under HPUX, root access restrictions are done by editing the file `/etc/securetty` and by listing the terminals where direct root accesses are allowed. To enforce the policy described here, this file must contain only the following line:

```
console
```

- Because Linux uses PAM as a global management authentication scheme, the `pam_securetty` module is used to control direct root access. This module reads the file `/etc/securetty`, which lists the terminals (ttys) the root user is allowed to log into directly.
- Under AIX, this restriction is activated by editing the file `/etc/security/user` and setting the following configuration:

```
root:
login = false
su = true
```

Another safety precaution is prohibiting unauthenticated remote access; i.e., preventing the use of `.rhosts` configuration files by the `rlogin` and `rsh` daemons. Under Solaris, this is done by removing the following line from the `/etc/pam.conf` file:

```
#
rlogin   auth sufficient
/usr/lib/security/pam_rhosts_auth.so.1
```

Under Linux, this is achieved by editing the files `/etc/pam.d/rlogin`, `/etc/pam.d/rsh` and `/etc/pam.d/rexec`, and by replacing the line:

```
auth          required      /lib/security/pam_rhosts_auth.so
```

with

```
auth          required      /lib/security/pam_rhosts_auth.so
no_rhosts no_hosts_equiv
```

The option `no_rhosts` prevents the `rlogin` and `rsh` commands from reading `.rhosts` files located in home directories. The option `no_hosts_equiv` disables the `/etc/hosts.equiv` function, which acts as a global `.rhosts` file.

In the ideal case where the use of the `rsh/rlogin/rexec` services can be prohibited, the best way to disable these services is by commenting them out of `/etc/inetd.conf`, as will be explained later.

It is generally a good idea to restrict user access to windows of time, if this fits the model of your infrastructure. Should a system administrator expect a user to be connected to its host on a Saturday morning at 3:00 am? If your users can be profiled such that they only need access during certain time windows, this greatly reduces the possibility of an intruder accessing your infrastructure, even if they have all the authentication tokens they need.

Time restrictions are possible on:

- Linux, by editing the file `/etc/security/time.conf` and by adding the PAM module `pam_time` into the configuration file of the service to be restricted (in the case of the login service, the file `/etc/pam.d/login` needs to be edited).
- Windows 2000, by editing the user properties.

Securing Files

Aside from the standard file permissions built into the base operating system, there are two additional ways you can protect your files. These methods are through the use of Access Control Lists (ACLs) and by using file encryption.

Good host control starts with controlling which files can be accessed by specific users as follows:

- To protect the server itself. No one wants an uneducated user to be able to execute the command `rm -rf /` under UNIX or to delete the `winnt` directory under Windows 2000.
- To preserve the authenticity, integrity, and confidentiality of the data being manipulated on the server.

These levels of protection are achieved by managing which users can access which files or directories as well as managing access rights to those resources. Under UNIX, this is achieved (or was achieved initially, as will be demonstrated later) by managing three level of permissions (read, write, and execute) for three classes of users:

- The owner of the file or directory (the user who created it). Only the owner or root can assign or modify the permissions on a file or directory.
- A group (a set of users defined by the system administrator). Groups are either defined locally to the host by editing the file `/etc/group` or through NIS.
- The world (all other users on the system who are not the owner of the file, root, or part of a group with access to the file).

This technique presents a definitive lack of flexibility. Suppose that we had a file owned by `user1` and the system administrator needed to assign read and write access, but not execute access, to `user2`. This could be achieved with standard UNIX permissions by first creating a group, named guser2 for example, of which user2 was the only member, changing the group associated to the file to guser2, and giving read and write group access on this file.

Now, what if we wanted to assign read and execute rights, but no write access, to another user, for example user3. The default access to the file is set to read-only. It was in order to solve such a problem that work was started on the standard POSIX IEEE 1003 in 1997. This work was supposed to be a standard regarding Access Control Lists (ACLs) on files. ACLs are sometimes called extended ACLs to differentiate them from the original UNIX file access control system. However, this work has stopped and the standard drafts have been withdrawn. Sun has pursued this work to develop their own ACL mechanisms. A summary of this work can be found at http://www.sunworld.com/swol-06-1998/swol-06-insidesolaris.html

The mechanism of the ACL is implemented in Solaris 2.7, 2.6, and 2.5.1. ACLs can only be used under the UFS filesystem type. For example, a file copied from /etc to /tmp will lose its ACL since /tmp is generally mounted as the tempfs filesystem.

Let's use our initial example to demonstrate how to work with ACL under Solaris:

```
>ls -l junk.txt
-rwxr-r-   1 user1    gusers          1090 Nov  9 18:10
junk.txt
```

In the initial state, user1 has all rights on the file junk.txt, and the group gusers has read-only access. The default access given to everybody is read-only. We now need to give read and write access to user2 and read and execute access to user3, an action which is performed by using the command setfacl:

```
>setfacl -m user:user2:rw- junk.txt
>setfacl -m user:user3:r-x junk.txt
```

The command setfacl, used with the switch -m, adds an ACL entry on the file junk.txt. The block user:user2:rw- means the new entry is related to one user, user2, and read and write access is granted to user2 as well. The way to check the ACL settings we have made is to use the command getfacl on the file junk.txt:

```
>getfacl junk.txt
# file: junk.txt
# owner: user1
# group: gusers
user::rwx
user:user2:rw-          #effective:r—
user:user3:r-x          #effective:r—
```

```
group:r—
mask:r—
other:r—
```

This output shows us that we have a problem. Whereas `user2` has been given read and write access and `user3` read and execute access, the effective rights are still read for both users. This is due to the definition of the mask for the ACL of this file. The mask defines the maximum permissions that can be granted to users other than the owner. To fix this, we need to redefine the maximum for the ACL of this file to read, write, and execute, which is done by `>setfacl -m mask:rwx junk.txt`.

An equivalent mechanism is under development for Linux. Information about this can be found at `http://major.rithus.co.at/acl`. The Linux implementation has attempted to follow the initial drafts of the POSIX standard. However, this is an ongoing project that has yet to guarantee 100% stability and that requires a custom patch to the Linux kernel, as well as the installation of other packages (dealing with file manipulation).

Another project that needs to be mentioned is `http://www.braysystems.com/linux/trustees.html`.

 `/usr/bin/getfacl`—Displays ACL entries on a file.

`/usr/bin/setfacl`—Is used to set, modify, and delete an ACL entry on a file.

ACLs are implemented in AIX 4.3. They are managed via the following commands:

`Aclget`—Shows the ACL information on a file or directory.

`Aclput`—Sets up ACLs on a file or directory

`Acledit`—Edits an ACL on a file or directory.

Under HPUX 10.20 and 11.x, ACLs are managed using:

`Chacl`—Adds / edits ACLs.

`Lsacl`—Lists ACLs.

The list of default ACL settings on a Windows 2000 host can be found in the following Microsoft document:

`http://www.microsoft.com/windows/server/Technical/security/`
`SecDefs.asp`

A second method for securing files is through the use of encryption. Encryption is the process of encoding information is such a way that a password or key is needed to decode the data. Encryption can be used in two different ways when securing data on servers: by encrypting individual files, or by encrypting the complete filesystem. Encrypting individual files is a useful tool that you can give to users.

However, if all of the data on a system is sensitive, it is more efficient to encrypt the complete filesystem. Not only does this save the user from decrypting every file individually, encrypting the filesystem defeats the possibility of the physical disk being stolen and read in another location. This can also help to defeat people using tools like `ntfsdos` or `ext2dos` to bypass the security of the operating system. For an example of Windows 2000-level security, see `http://www.sysinternals.com/ntfe30` `.htm`.

Three tools of interests based on the OpenPGP standard for encrypting files are:

- GNU Privacy Guard—Works under Linux, Solaris, and HPUX 10.x. (`http://www.gnupg.org`).
- The free version of the PGP tools—Works under Linux, Solaris, and Windows 2000 (`http://www.pgpi.com`).
- The commercial version of PGP (from Network Associates)—Works under Linux, Solaris, Windows 2000, AIX, and HPUX (`http://www` `.nai.com/asp_set/products/tns/pgpess_intro.asp`).

No integrated filesystem encryption mechanism exists by default under AIX 4.3, HPUX 11.x , Solaris, or Linux. A free project, CFS (source code available in the U.S. at `http://www.cryptography.org`), works under Solaris 2.x and Linux. However, the last release is from December 1997.

Under Linux, several projects exist regarding the implementation of a cryptographic filesystem. TCFS (Transparent Cryptographic Filesystem) is one of these projects, that implements a cryptographic filesystem in the Linux kernel. TCFS can be found at `http://tcfs.dia.unisa.it`. One of the best projects at this date seems to be StegFS (Steganographic Filesystem). The approach taken is very interesting in that not only does SteFS encrypt data, but it also attempts to "hide data". StegFS can be found at `http://ban.joh.ac.uk/~adm36/StegFS/`.

Limiting User Impact on a System

The ultimate step in the protection of a server, that has non-administrator users is to limit the impact a user can have on the system. The challenge here is to allow the user to have enough access to do their job, but place limitations so that they cannot consume all of the resources of the system, thereby denying other users access to the system. Limitations can include:

- How much disk space can be used by a regular user. A user who uses too much disk space can cause the entire filesystem to become full, preventing others from performing their jobs correctly. The use and setup of quotas under Windows 2000 and UNIX has been already discussed in Chapter 4, the "Filesystem".
- In the case of UNIX, how many processes a user can run concurrently. A classic example of a denial of service is the use of the "fork bomb", where a user creates a simple program that spawns itself exponentially. For instance:

```
(main()
{
for(;;)fork();
}
```

The fork bomb works by calling itself recursively and indefinitely using all the entries in the process table.

- By default, there is a limit under Solaris. This limit can be increased by editing the variable `maxuprc` in the `/etc/system` file. To see the default under Solaris, do a `sysdef -i` and search in the "tunable parameters" section for the lines `maximum processes per user id`.
- Under Linux that supports PAM, look in the file `/etc/security/limits.conf`. It should be noted that it is possible to restrict the maximum number of processes by user, group of users, or netgroup.

In the case of Windows 2000, it is possible for the system administrator to define a security policy (see `http://www.microsoft.com/Windows/server/deploy/security/entsecwt.asp`).

NETWORK CONTROL

Controlling the network and the way hosts access and are accessed through the network is not only an immediate step, but a necessary foundation for the correct protection of an IT system.

Firewalls

Firewalls go beyond the scope of this book and may not even fall under the job description of a system administrator. In general, this job falls to the network administrator. However, a brief discussion is warranted, as firewalls provide an efficient and very helpful layer of protection. The term "firewall" designates any tool or system that filters network traffic between two IP subnets. Firewall systems are generally located between the organization's network (intranet) and the Internet, or the networks of partners (extranet).

A firewall is helpful since it narrows or blocks the ability of an outsider to access or view the internals of an organization's network. For example, it is possible to protect a Web server in such a way that only the Web service, and no other pieces of the operating system, can be accessed from anywhere on the Internet. Therefore, for example, the risk of an outsider being able to access the Netbios service is greatly reduced (but not null). It is also possible to extend this policy by opening, for example, the FTP service on the Web server and limiting access from certain specific hosts on the Internet.

Finally, it may be worth emphasizing the fact that a firewall can also be used to add an additional layer of security inside the organization. The use of an internal firewall can help to narrow the trust relationship between systems from two different IP subnets. For example, the network of the R&D department does not need to have full network access to the Marketing department.

Internal firewalls may help to contain an internal intrusion and limit an outsider if the infrastructure is compromised. The appropriate use of several firewalls allows you to obtain a structure pretty much like the watertight compartments of a boat or a submarine.

Firewall Drawbacks and an Example of a Network Attack

Firewalls are not the ultimate solution in that they can be circumvented. In some cases, an intruder can guess some of the rules of the firewall, using tools or having some knowledge of the organization. For example, let's suppose there is a rule that allows FTP access through the firewall from the external machine `cliet.foo.com` to the internal server `earth.sniglets.com`. If the intruder can guess this rule (by using a program such as `fire-walk`, as described earlier), then they can attempt to send fake IP packets (a packet with an IP address different from the host address from which the IP was really sent) to `earth.sniglets.com` with the source address of `client.foo.com`. While the intruder will not see a response (since any response will be sent to the real `client.foo.com`), properly designed packets may enable the intruder to execute remote commands on `client.foo.com` (with the goal to grant access), or deny others access through a *denial of service* attack.

A denial of service attack is an attempt to disable a running system by exploiting a race condition, design flaw, or just by using all of the available resources of a system. A race condition or design flaw can be located in the program used for the network service or in the TCP/IP protocol stack of the operating system itself. In any case, where an IP packet's source or destination is falsified, this is called "spoofing." Spoofing can be effective against older operating systems or infrastructures where no firewall is in place. However, a properly configured firewall can block such an attack by not allowing packets into the network from the outside if the source address is equal to a system on the inside.

Packet Filtering at the System Level

In some cases, the use of an internal firewall to filter intranet traffic can be seen as using a chain saw for cutting a straw. In other cases, an internal firewall may not be adequate because the filtering of the network is limited to only a few subnets, and may not provide an enterprise solution. In cases such as these, the solution is to set up a packet filtering mechanism on the server to protect it from attacks.

Packet filtering takes place before IP packets arrive in the TCP/IP stack of the operating system. As such, the use of filtering rules allow the system to block access to some network services that cannot normally be controlled, like Netbios under Windows 2000. Indeed, in the case of a Windows 2000 server serving only as a Web server, it might be worth some extra work to block TCP and UDP ports 137 to 139 for an additional layer of security, thus preventing remote filesystem access/probes.

Linux and Windows 2000 include such built-in mechanisms. This is not the case with Solaris, as the use of a commercial firewall for protecting a single system is required. A free alternative is the ip-filter package, which can be found at `http://coombs.anu.edu.au/~avalon/ipfilter.html`.

The packet filtering mechanism for Linux is called ipchains. More information about it can be found at `http://www.linuxdoc.org/HOWTO/IPCHAINS-HOWTO.html`. A new, more flexible mechanism is under development and will be included in kernel 2.4 and higher. This package is called netfilter. Information on netfilter can be found at `http://netfilter.kernelnotes.org`.

Windows 2000 also includes a packet filtering mechanism, which is less flexible than its UNIX counterparts. It can be accessed under the advanced TCP/IP properties of the TCP/IP stack of a network LAN connection, under `Options`. It is not possible to organize filtering rules or to specify a source's addresses from this GUI. Better management of packet filtering can be done using the management console "Local Security Policy." Select "IP Security Policies on Local Machine" then right-click and select "Manage IP filter lists and filter actions."

Network Service Control

A different approach to packet filtering can be taken. Rather than filtering IP packets before they arrive at the TCP/IP stack, it is possible to filter information at the network service level. This approach has the advantage of being easiest to deploy, and includes systems where no built-in packet filtering mechanisms exist. However, such systems are only available in the UNIX world. The name of the tool is TCP Wrapper, and it can be found at `ftp://ftp.porcupine.org/pub/security/index.html`.

Under UNIX, network services can be run in two ways:

- As a standalone daemon, started at the command line or at boot time.
- Started by a super daemon, `inetd`, the Internet service daemon. `inetd` listens on different TCP or UDP ports, according to the configuration in `/etc/inetd.conf`. Whenever an incoming request is received on one of these ports, `inetd` calls the corresponding service associated with that port number. The advantage of `inetd` is that the initial startup cost of a service is much less than the combined cost of having all possible network services running, even if there are no requests to use those services. Network services such as telnet, FTP, and rsh are generally started by the `inetd` daemon.

When using the TCP Wrapper program, the `tcpd` program will be called by `inetd` instead of the program in charge of providing the network service called. Then, based on the setting in the configuration file (`/etc/hosts.allow` and `/etc/hosts.deny`), the `tcpd` program will decide to call (if permitted) the network daemon, if that access is allowed, or drop the request (and log the attempt).

The two main drawbacks of TCP Wrapper are:

- It does not work with UDP-based service.
- It does not work in cases where the network service has to be run as a standalone daemon.

The second point tends to be less of an issue at present since more and more daemons developed in the open source world have the possibility to be linked against the TCP Wrapper library. This allows the administrator to control their access through a single mechanism. For example, the SSH service can be compiled in such a way. By default, in the Red Hat 6.1 Linux distribution, the `ypserv` and `portmap` daemons are compiled with support for TCP Wrapper.

Below is part of `/etc/inetd.conf` under Solaris 2.7. The commented lines (prefaced with the `#` character) are the original file before the introduction of `tcpd`. Below each commented line is the modified version when using TCP Wrapper.

```
# Ftp and telnet are standard Internet services.
#
#ftp     stream  tcp     nowait  root    /usr/sbin/in.ftpd      in.ftpd
ftp      stream  tcp     nowait  root    /usr/sbin/tcpd         in.ftpd
#telnet  stream  tcp     nowait  root    /usr/sbin/in.telnetd   in.telnetd
telnet   stream  tcp     nowait  root    /usr/sbin/tcpd         in.telnetd
```

Using TCP Wrapper requires the configuration of two files: `/etc/hosts.allow` and `/etc/hosts.deny`.

```
#
# tcp_wrapper /etc/hosts.allow file.
#
#
# We allow any hosts from .sniglets.com to do access ftp and telnet
#
in.telnetd:              .sniglets.com
in.ftpd:                 .sniglets.com
#
# Restrict rsh & rlogin to the system administrator workstation.
#
in.rshd, in.rlogind:     192.168.2.3

#
# tcp_wrapper /etc/hosts.deny file.
#
ALL: ALL
```

IPSec

Firewalls, host-based packet filtering, and tools like TCP Wrapper are very useful at limiting TCP/IP traffic, but they cannot fix the basic problem that, by design, the TCP/IP protocol is very trusting. Commonly, the three main security issues resulting from the current design of TCP/IP are:

- Sniffing—A machine connected to an IP subnet can be set up in such a way that it can listen to all the IP communications on the segment of the network that the system is connected to. In general, all IP traffic on a subnet is visible to the attached network devices, and by placing the network hardware in the proper state, all network traffic can be read by that host.
- Spoofing—A system sends an IP packet with an address that is different from that read from the IP source address of the system with the intent of confusing the destination system.
- Session hijacking—An intruder can take over an existing communication, such as telnet or FTP, and communicate as if they were an authorized user.

A mechanism to address these problems has recently been developed by the IETF. It is called IPSec, or the IP Security protocol suite. IPSec is a set of extensions to the IP protocol that brings security features such as integrity, confidentiality, and authentication to the network level. The underlying idea is to encrypt and authenticate the traffic that travels between two systems. The most important feature is not only being able to encrypt data between two systems, but to have two systems able to authenticate each other. The authentication scheme used can be a PKI (public key infrastructure). Basically, each time two systems try to communicate in a secure way, they exchange their certificates. The certificates are then verified against a CA (certificate authority, one of the main components of the PKI infrastructure).

The study of IPSec goes beyond the scope of this book. However, the reader is strongly encouraged to explore this path in the quest of protecting their infrastructure. At the time this book was written, IPSec had been implemented or was planned for implementation on the following platforms:

- Future-Solaris 8.0: `http://www.sun.com/solaris/ea`
- Windows 2000:
  `http://www.microsoft.com/Windows/server/technical/security/ip_security.asp` or `http://www.microsoft.com/windows/server/Deploy/security/ipsec.asp`
- Linux: `http://www.xs4all.nl/~freeswan`

Prevention

Whereas protection is the act of applying technology to prevent an intruder from accessing your systems, *prevention* is the application of knowledge and social engineering to help build an environment that is less susceptible to the actions of those seeking to compromise your organization. While prevention and protection are very similar, prevention extends to those situations where the administrator may or may not be able to control an environment or process. These processes include social engineering practices such as choosing good passwords and training users what not to share with others. This section will explore areas that when coupled with technology designed to protect the organization, should create a secure computing environment for your user community.

KNOWLEDGE IS POWER

The first weapon in the battle of prevention is knowledge. If a system administrator has more knowledge than an opponent, they will be successful in preventing the opponent from compromising the infrastructure. Everyday, new security bugs or weaknesses are found by crackers, hackers, and code writers and system administrators. So, how can the administrator, who has many duties, including security, stay ahead of those that may spend all of their time trying to find a way to their favorite server? On the Internet, there are thousands of resources that you, and your opponent, can take advantage of to learn the latest about security. There are also mailing lists available to anyone with an email account. New security holes, bugs, issues, and patches are discussed and announced in this forum. Some of the more prominent lists are:

- `bugtraq@netspace.org`
- `alert@iss.net`
- NTBugTraq: `http://www.ntbugtraq.com/ntbugfaq.htm`
- Computer Emergency Response Team (CERT) advisories: `http://www.cert.org/contact_cert/certmaillist.html`

A complete list of security-related mailing lists can be found at `http://xforce.iss.net/maillists/otherlists.php3`.

If you use Linux, there are several lists; most of them are dedicated to the security bugs that exist in many different releases of Linux:

- Red Hat: `http://www.redhat.com/community/list_subscribe.html`

- SuSe: `http://www.suse.de/de/support/security/`
- Debian: `http://www.debian.org/MailingLists/subscribe`

For Windows, it is possible to receive automatic security bulletins from Microsoft at `http://www.microsoft.com/security/services/bulletin.asp`.

CERT maintains a Web site that specializes in the reporting of security incidents. Every administrator should become familiar with the following:

- `http://www.cert.org/`
- `http://ciac.llnl.gov/`

The reader is also strongly encouraged to spend time learning about the latest security technologies and strategies under development. Some useful sites are:

- `http://www.cerias.purdue.edu/coast/hotlist/`
- `http://www.icsa.net/`
- `http://packetstorm.securify.com/`
- `http://www.opensec.net`
- The FreeFire project:
  `http://sites.inka.de/sites/lina/freefire-1/tools.html`
- `http://www.cerias.purdue.edu/coast/hotlist`

USER AND ADMINISTRATOR EDUCATION

Before attempting to apply technology and intricate processes to secure an organization against intruders, administrators should first work to educate themselves, as well as their user community. Without a solid foundation for security, the most elaborate security plans will fail. A security plan is only as strong as its weakest link. As stated in the beginning of this chapter, the advanced intruder starts by collecting information about the systems in an organization. The most popular way to accomplish this is to try and exploit weaknesses of individuals within the organization, including the system administrator. This includes:

- Giving the intruder information such as internal procedures or passwords.
- Obtaining passwords by guessing or using password-cracking tools.

Prevent Social Engineering Attacks

The term "social engineering," when used in reference to computer security, is using an understanding of human nature to gain access to an organization's infrastructure and systems. A good starting point for understanding what social engineering is can be found by visiting `http://packetstorm.securify.com/docs/social-engineering/socialen.txt`.

By applying social engineering techniques, an intruder will attempt to trick users and administrators by:

- Pretending to be a user in need of help.
- Pretending to be a contractor or employee who needs access to a certain system.
- Pretending to be a member of the computer support team, interacting with a user.

A skilled hacker will have more than just technological knowledge. Acting ability, coupled with charisma, will allow an intruder not only to fool users into giving them information, but will make the users feel at ease during the transaction. A common ruse is when a hacker contacts an unsuspecting user claiming to be an administrator. The hacker will tell the user there is a system problem and they need the user's login name and password to solve the problem.

It won't take long before the hacker will find some trusting user to divulge this information, and now the hacker has almost undetectable access to the infrastructure.

The prevention of socially engineered attacks starts by educating users. Basically, a responsible user should never:

- Give passwords over the phone to anyone, unless they can authenticate the person on the other end.
- Let someone access their desktop, even if:
  - The user knows the person, but the person states they need access for five minutes because they have forgotten to do an important job. Remember that potential intruders can come from inside the organization also. The real need for the intruder in this "five minutes' access" might be to use any special privileges the trusting user may have.
  - The person pretends to be the system administrator, possibly a new member of the administration team, or a contractor who has to perform some preventive maintenance on the desktop. The

user should first verify the identity of any person who claims to be a system administrator, or claims to work for that organization, by asking for proof of ID and by calling the IT department for confirmation. If the operation was not scheduled or does not correspond to an incident opened by the user, the user should check with someone they know from the computer support team.

- Give someone access to a place they do not have access to. This is especially true for janitors. Janitors, or other maintenance facility people, must be instructed to never let people without keys access rooms where servers, telecommunications , and network equipment is installed. Remember that an insider does not need special James Bond gadgets to cause damage. A laptop running Linux loaded with the correct tools is far more efficient. Even worse, two floppies can allow the intruder to do the job (check `http://www.trinux` `.org`).

This training, however, should not be limited to users. It should also extend to system administrators and their teams. Since intruders can come from inside or outside the organization, system administrators should:

- Be careful while performing maintenance on a desktop. The user does not need to watch over your shoulder, even if they are really interested. Good security requires keeping your system-level passwords and procedures secret. In other words, the less knowledge an intruder has of procedures, the topology of systems, and what tools are employed in your infrastructure, the more difficult it will be for them to break into the system.
- Be careful while working with temporary people, contractors, and partners. In practice, system administrators tend to be more open with people who have the same background and perform the same tasks. Therefore, they tend to share information more easily or try to make the job of a contractor easier by giving them special access. Only give contractors the access they need, and if you choose to give them a high level of access, make sure that you have documentation in place that holds them responsible for any damage they may inflict on your organization.

Protecting Passwords

Passwords are the Holy Grail of the intruder. Access to passwords that are tied to accounts with high levels of access is every intruder's goal. For this reason, the most tightly secured passwords should be those tied to administrative accounts. Access to administrator passwords in almost all cases gives an intruder access to all users' information and data. For this reason, a strong password, one that is difficult to guess, should be used for all administrative accounts. A strong password is a password that contains some random combination of letters, numbers, and non-alphanumeric characters. Passwords should never be names, places, dates, or anything else that an intruder may be able to guess if they have information about the user of the password. If possible, try to find a combination that you can type quickly as you do not want a user to be able to view your keystrokes while you enter the password.

In practice, administrators find themselves managing more than just one administration password. It is not unusual to have to manage 50 or 100 different passwords that allow access to distinct pieces of the infrastructure. If a system administrator has to manage a large number of passwords, rather than writing a list on a piece of paper hidden below a keyboard, they should try to store them in an encrypted database that requires a single encryption key. The key then is the only password the administrator has to remember. For UNIX, you can visit `http://gpasman.nl.linux.org`. A review of Windows techniques can be found at `http://www.zdnet.com/products/stories/reviews/0,4161,410473,00.html`.

It should be noted that even this system is not perfect. What happens if an intruder gains access to the encryption key? If the password database is on an accessible system, the intruder now has access to all the keys to your palace. An additional step you can take is to store your password database on media like a floppy and place it in a secure location. Now there are no copies on hard drives or backup systems.

If you are the lucky owner of a PalmOS-based device (like PalmPilot), an alternative is to store the password database on it using dedicated programs (which also make use of strong encryption). Such a program is GNU Keyring, and it can be found at `http://gnukeyring.sourceforge.net`.

Today, most passwords under UNIX are stored using the shadow system. The shadow system puts the user's encrypted password in a file that is separate from the `/etc/passwd` file.

The `/etc/passwd` file must be readable by programs to perform UID-to-username translation. In the past, the encrypted password was also stored in this file. However, with the use of the shadow password file, `/etc/shadow`, passwords can be stored in such a way that only the root user, or root-owned processes, can access the encrypted password. By denying access to the encrypted password, you attempt to deny hackers the ability to run password-guessing tools.

Under Linux, if NIS is not used, the local password can be encrypted using the MD5 function rather than DES `crypt()`, which is the UNIX standard. Passwords can then be 256 characters long instead of the standard 8 under DES.

While doing all you can to secure passwords is necessary and prudent, even in the best-controlled environments, hackers gain access to encrypted passwords. Once they have access, they will attempt to guess, or *crack*, encrypted information by trying all combinations of characters, encrypting each one, and comparing their encrypted strings with the encrypted passwords they have stolen. A match means that a password has been guessed. All passwords can be cracked given enough time.

The goal is to design passwords that cannot be cracked too quickly. To do so, it is recommended that the system administrator run the same tools used by hackers on a regular basis. By using these tools, administrators can expose weak passwords in their infrastructure and work with users to design stronger passwords. There are a number of tools that can perform this function, and a few are:

- Crack: `http://www.users.dircon.co.uk/~crypto/`.
- John the Ripper: `http://www.openwall.com/john`.
- L0phtCrack, which specializes in cracking Windows-based passwords: `http://www.10pht.com/10phtcrack`.

As stated on the Web site of L0phtCrack, as of November 1999, it takes approximately 20 days on a quad processor Xeon 400Mhz system to check an entire password space using a brute force method. The immediate answer to this is to force users to change their passwords every 20 days. However, success rate of forcing users to change passwords frequently is low, as users will then have to write down their passwords just to remember them. Changing passwords on a regular basis is a good idea; however, limit it to every 60-90 days to allow users the ability to keep up with all the changes.

A better answer is a technology under development that uses certificates, authentication mechanisms that have a specific lifetime, instead of passwords, for authenticating users. Windows 2000 has this feature implemented. For more information, visit `http://www.microsoft.com/windows/server/Deploy/security/MapCerts/default.asp`.

Efficient User Management System

One final aspect of user management is what to do when a user, or administrator, leaves the organization, or no longer requires a specific access level. As employees move from job to job, even in the organization, it is important for the computer support group to be aware of these changes so they can make sure to disable accounts of ex-employees, and change access for users that change jobs internally. However, even in small organizations, it is difficult to communicate every change to the computer operations team.

Inactive or unused accounts are a prime target for hackers. Administrators should periodically scan accounts and determine which accounts have been inactive for a period of time, say 60-90 days. If a user hasn't accessed their account in this timeframe, the administrator can generally feel comfortable in disabling access for that user. If a user hasn't accessed an account in, say, 180 days, that account should be backed up and removed. This type of process gives the administrator the ability to reinstate accounts if a user has been away for a long period of time, but reduces the risk of an attacker finding an unused account, where the owner may not notice unusual activity.

 In some highly secure sites, like military organizations, accounts may never be removed or UIDs recycled to preserve the audit trail.

OTHER PREVENTATIVE MEASURES TO USE

While knowledge and user education are two major factors in preventing break-ins at your organization, there are numerous other places where preventative measures can help to bring strength to your security infrastructure.

The Security of a System Begins at Installation

Computer systems are complex, and thereby offer an intruder a vast array of different possibilities when attempting to access those systems. The more services and users that are running on your systems, the more likely there is a security hole, and the more likely an intruder will target that system to compromise. Two things you can do to limit access at the time of installation are:

- Grant a minimum of network and user access from the beginning. It is always easier to grant additional access than it is to restrict access once users have already begun working on the system. Restrict access through the use of firewalls, TCP Wrapper and by scrutinizing who receives an account on the system.
- Limit the service, or daemons running on the system. For example, if the system is not a Web server, then disable any Web services that may be installed by default. The fewer services that are running, the less chance that a security hole exists on your system. Also, by running fewer services, the system looks less important to a potential intruder, and may be passed over as a potential target.

Under UNIX, it is generally recommended to disable the following services from the `/etc/inetd.conf` file:

- echo.
- chargen.
- daytime.
- discard.
- time.
- uucp.

And, depending on the function of the system:

- shell.
- login.
- exec.
- bootp.

Finally, the system administrator is urged to pay extra attention to the default settings of network services. A common mistake, for example, is not to check the settings of the SNMP client. Intruders will start by probing this service to determine if it is using a default value, or in our many cases, default community names (public and private). If default values are found, then the intruder potentially has access to a tremendous amount of system information. Worse, by using the RW access of SNMP (corresponding to the private community name), the intruder may be able to modify some settings on the host.

PATCHING SECURITY HOLES

As has already been stated, security is a race between the system administrator and the intruder. Just being aware of the latest vulnerabilities on different operating systems does nothing to block an attack on those systems. It is important that once an administrator knows of a security hole in their infrastructure, that they work to plug that hole before an intruder can exploit it. Firewalls and TCP Wrapper can keep some intruders at bay, but fixing or patching the hole is the only way to guarantee that it can't be exploited.

If you have multiple platforms, you may need to visit each system and deploy the patch that is relevant for each operating system.

DO NOT TRUST PRE-COMPILED BINARIES

A system administrator must check the integrity and authenticity of the pre-compiled binaries installed. Pre-installed binaries are software programs and packages that come ready to run on your system. Such precautions must be taken to avoid the installation of binaries that have and may contain Trojan horses. This applies equally to UNIX and Windows, especially when the binaries are downloaded from the Internet. It is also a good idea to educate Windows users to not execute binaries they receive as attachments. Indeed, most of the time, beyond the immediate risk of viruses, there is a risk of installing Trojan horses and other exploits targeted at weaknesses in the operating system and installed applications.

LIMIT USER PRIVILEGE

One issue that a system administrator has to face during day-to-day activities is granting users the correct privileges. For example, a common issue is giving users sufficient access to printing resources. It is quite common that a printer queue will become blocked due to a file or printer error. However, it usually takes administrator privilege to clear the problem. If the user had administrator access, they could fix it themselves, but giving them administrator access is not a good idea. So, how can you help the user without compromising your security?

Under UNIX, a happy medium is to install a package called `sudo`. `sudo` allows the system administrator to grant a user or group of users the rights to use a specific list of commands as if they were the administrator on a specified host. The `sudo` package is available for just about every UNIX operating system, and can be found at `http://www.courtesan.com/sudo`.

A list of platforms under which the `sudo` package has been tested is available at `http://www.courtesan.com/sudo/RUNSON`.

The installation of this package is easy, but it is strongly recommended that the system administrator pay some extra attention to the many options available. It is generally a good idea to set up the logging option to use `syslog` and to configure the `syslog` facility and priority to specific values to include `sudo` logs in with your other centralized logs. For example, when using the `./configure` script:

```
—with-logging=syslog —with-logging=local4 —with-
logging=alert
```

Then the `/etc/syslog.conf` file can be edited to add the following lines:

```
# Log successful and failed sudo attempts to the file
/var/log/sudo
local2.debug                                        /var/log/sudo
# All the logs which goes to /var/su/log are also sent to a
remote machine,
# where "loghost" is the name of the remote machine.
local2.debug                                        @loghost
```

The —with-mailto option is also strongly recommended so that each time a user attempts to access a command for which they don't have the proper authority, an email is sent to alert the system administrator. To configure the user functionality of sudo, you'll need to edit the file called sudoers. Note that this file needs to be edited by using the visudo program which comes with the sudo package, as using less secure, standard editing programs may introduce problems that could be used to exploit sudo. A simple example of the sudoers file is:

```
###
# Host alias specification
###
Host_Alias LABHOSTS = host1, host2, host3

###
# User alias specification
###
User_Alias     LABUSERS = user1, user2

###
# Cmnd alias specification
###
Cmnd_Alias     CLEARQUEUE = /usr/ucb/lprm
LABUSERS LABHOSTS = CLEARQUEUE
```

In this case, user1 and user2 are granted the right to clear the printing queue on host1, host2, and host3.

Under Windows 2000, by using the Security Configuration Toolset, it is possible to grant some limited administrative privileges to regular users such as:

- Increasing quotas.
- Performing backups and restores.
- Initiating the shutdown of remote systems.

For printers, two privilege rights can be given to users by editing the properties of the printer:

- Manage printers.
- Manage documents.

PERFORM A VULNERABILITY AUDIT

The final system to account for in the prevention component of security is the use of vulnerability auditing tools, which can perform a strict analysis of a specific part of the infrastructure. The purpose of this category of tools is to determine weaknesses that may be exploited by an intruder. These tools can employ two strategies:

- Passive—An assessment tool performs a host inspection by looking at the configuration for inappropriate settings or vulnerable programs.
- Active—Active assessment tools simulate possible intrusion attacks, without damaging your systems.

Using your Firewall

The starting point in a vulnerability assessment audit should be your firewalls. It is important that the configuration of every firewall be checked by the security officer or network engineer in charge of the system, as a firewall vulnerability exposes your entire infrastructure to intrusion.

A good firewall review will include:

- An extensive review of firewall rules.
- A test of the firewall against misconfiguration using active assessment tools like a network scanner or a specialized tool such as Firewalk. Firewalk can be found at `http://www.packetfactory.net/firewalk`.

Network Scanners

Network intrusion scanners represent the most common form of active vulnerability assessment tool. A system administrator has a number of choices between free and commercial high-quality network scanning tools. Free tools are:

- Nessus, which perfoms almost 300 different security checks (`http://www.nessus.org`).
- SARA, Security Auditor's Research Assistant (`http://home.arc.com/sara/index.html`).
- Saint, the successor of the famous SATAN (`http://www.wwdsi.com/saint/index.html`).

Among the commercial network intrusion scanners, it is possible to find:

- Internet Security Scanner from ISS (`http://www.iss.net/prod/isb.php3`).
- CyberCop scanner from Network Associates (`http://www.nai.com/asp_set/products/tns/ccscanner_intro.asp`).

Installing a network scanner like Nessus has become a very simple process. In fact, it is so easy that anyone with a system running Linux and an Internet connection can use it. This makes it both a simple tool for the administrator, as well as an easy-to-use weapon for the intruder. Pre-compiled binaries for UNIX are available on `ftp.nessus.org`. To install, use the following:

```
# rpm -Uvh nessus*.rpm
```

The next step is to start the `nessusd` daemon by running the following command:

```
#/etc/rc.d/init.d/nessus start
```

The last step is to edit the Nessus user file, `/etc/nessus/nessusd.users`, which restricts access to users of the scanner. While the scanner is non-destructive in that it won't exploit security holes, if an intruder can gain access, they can probe your network in a more efficient manner.

The following network scan was performed on a PC running Red Hat 6.1 with most of the network services activated. The network scanner used was Nessus v0.99.1. Figure 11.1 shows the Nessus host configuration screen, where you are authenticated before you launch your scan.

Before you begin your scan, you need to identify the system, or target, you wish to scan for security holes. As shown in Figure 11.2, you can choose a single host, a list of hosts, or read a file that contains a pre-configured list of hosts.

Once you have chosen a target, you'll need to decide what type of scan you wish to perform. Figure 11.3 shows possible scans you can run against a host. In many cases, it may not be necessary to run all possible scans, especially if the host is not vulnerable to certain attacks. This will save time, especially if you have a large number of hosts to scan.

Once you have configured your scan, return to the report screen and initiate your scan. Nessus will keep you informed of its progress, as seen in Figure 11.4.

Finally, once the scan is complete, you will be given a report that documents the results of the scan, and gives you information as to the number of possible vulnerabilities and the relative risk associated with each, as seen in Figure 11.5.

Figure 11.1
Nessus Setup
window.

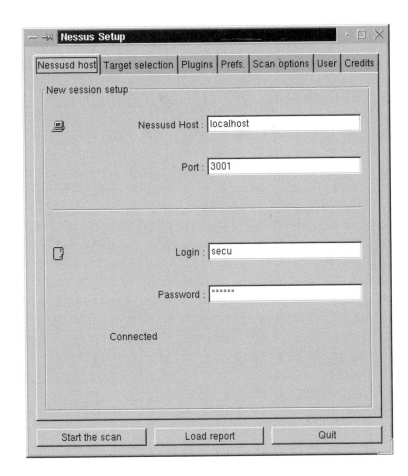

Knowing not only the possible vulnerabilities, but the number of possible risks, is very useful in planning a strategy to plug these holes. Also, you can use these numbers to justify additional resources to the boss, including additional manpower or security-related software.

Host Intrusion Scanner, or Find the Holes before the Intruder

Host intrusion scanners check for the appropriate setting of file permissions. For UNIX, this type of scanner searches for world-writeable files or directory permissions, as well as `setuid` or `setgid` files owned by root. More advanced commercial scanners check for missing security patches or known vulnerabilities of system-installed components.

Most of the freely available host intrusion scanners are somewhat obsolete, but can provide a good initial check, especially for older networks. These tools include:

Figure 11.2
Nessus target
configuration.

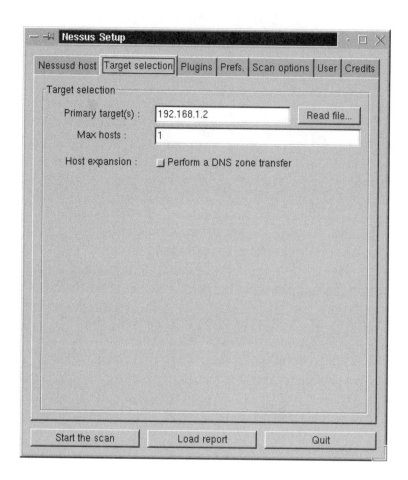

- COPS, which was originally distributed by CERT and last updated in 1993 (`http://www.fish.com/cops/`).
- Tiger: (`ftp://net.tamu.edu/pub/security/TAMU`).

Some more recent, freely available tools are:

- Sherpa (`http://www.nbank.net/~rick/sherpa`).
- Titan (`http://www.fish.com/~brad/titan/Titan-Docs/TITAN_documentation.html`).

Solaris 2.7 comes with a tool called the Automated Security Enhancement Tool (ASET), which has been designed to help the system administrator monitor and control the security level in an automated way. Finally, one of the most complete commercial host intrusion scanners is System Scanner from ISS (works under the most common UNIX versions, and a version for

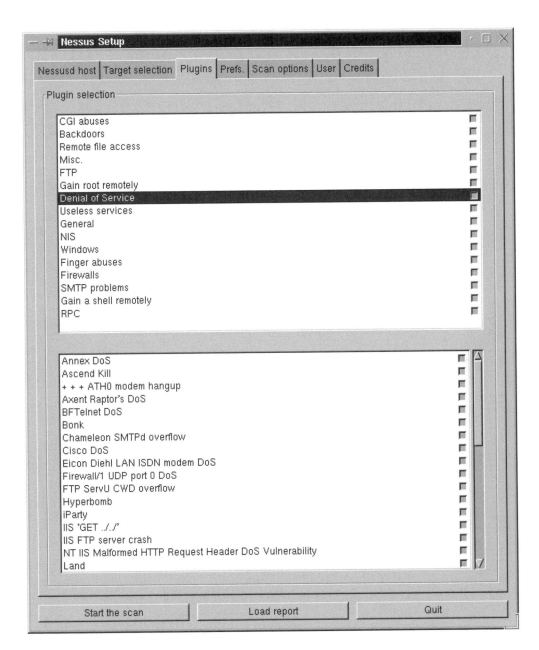

Figure 11.3 Nessus probe selection.

Figure 11.4
Nessus progress
screen.

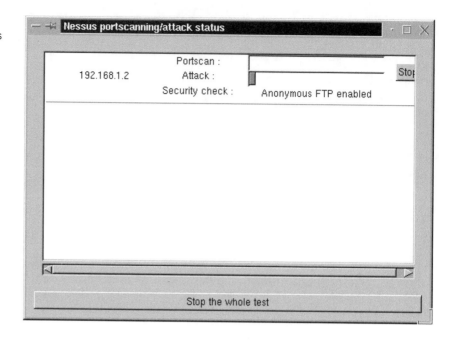

Windows 2000 is under development). More information on this scanner
can be found at `http://www.iss.net/prod/ss.php3`.

Other commercial system scanners or useful tools are:

- Inspector Scan (`http://www.shavlik.com/products/
  inspect/20103.htm`).
- Webtrends security analyzer (`http://www.webtrends.com/
  products/wsa/intro.htm`).
- DumpACL, a utility that dumps the permissions (DACLs) and audit
  settings (SACLs) for filesystems, registries, printers and shares:
  (`http://www.systemtools.com/somarsoft/`).

MODEMS

Even the best protection and prevention scheme can be ruined by a single modem installed improperly in your infrastructure. Modems, which require strong authentication and are managed by the computer group, are no
different than the login screen of a computer. However, a modem connected
to a random workstation or server by a user can present a simple point of attack for an intruder. Make removing improperly installed modems a high
priority in your security policy.

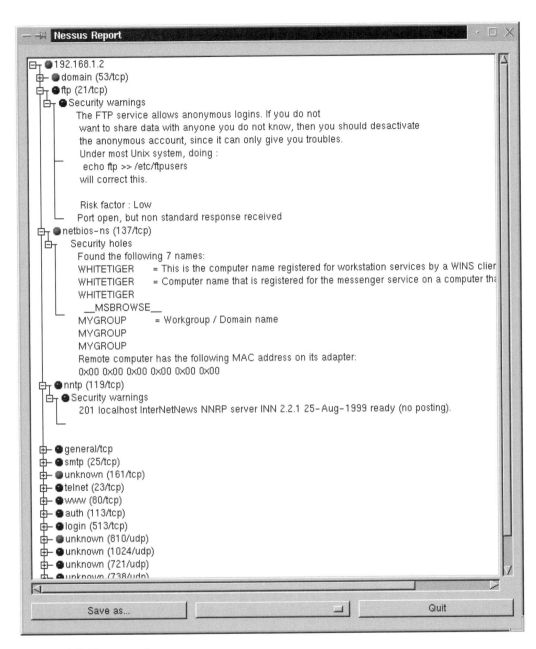

Figure 11.5 Nessus probe report.

A modem is only secure when a competent system administrator manages it, or when it is disconnected from the computer and unplugged from the wall.

A good portion of your security policy should be to prohibit users from connecting a modem to any device that is connected to your organization's network. Do not forget that the same rules apply to contractors and partners. If they need access to a server for maintenance or development, they should be directed to the organization's computer group to discuss their needs and possible solutions. While this at times may be a controversial issue, especially with partners, it is important to stress that the time spent in using modems correctly far outweighs the consequences of a break-in.

Another problem with modems is that they are hard to find. Modems are small, cheap, and easy to install, and can easily be overlooked, especially in large organizations with hundreds or thousands of computers. However, you do have some options that can be used to protect your infrastructure from improperly installed modems available to you:

- Running a war-dialer program, which scans all phone numbers in your organization looking for modem responses.
  - At the time of this printing, ISS had a commercial tool under development called telephony scanner (`http://xforce.iss.net/protoworx`).
  - Another commercial tool can be found at `http://www.verttex.com`.
  - There are many DOS-based programs that were developed during the hacking days of the 1980's.
- Another option is to have your telecommunications staff block modem access from your PBX. While this only benefits those organizations with PBXs, in those cases, the administrator can rest assured that even if modems are connected to network-attached systems, the phone system will provide the necessary level of security.

Detection

What is left when protection and prevention fail to keep an intruder from entering your infrastructure? Given that an intruder has penetrated your defenses, you will want to know what systems are under attack and what the intruder is doing on those systems. Your goal is to detect that an intruder has attacked and to expel them as soon as possible. Technology and processes that help to determine that your security has been breached are called intrusion detection system (IDS) tools. IDS tools function by gathering data from within your infrastructure, and then they perform an analysis to determine if there is a security breach. This analysis can function in two ways:

- **Post-mortem**—These tools assume that an intrusion has occurred and the system administrator wants to determine what damage has occurred.
- **Real-time**—The IDS tool attempts to detect an intrusion while it is occurring. When an intrusion is detected, the IDS tool sends an alarm to the system administrator and possibly launches a counter-attack. Such counter-attacks can be a firewall reconfiguration, the blocking of a user account, or of a system shutdown.

An IDS tool can perform its analysis by:

- Ongoing monitoring of user and system activity.
- Checking the integrity of critical components (such as binaries and configuration files or data).
- Trying to recognize a known attack by using pattern recognition.
- Performing a statistical analysis of user and system activity and generating alerts on suspicious readings.
- Checking the activity of users to determine policy violations.

The various IDS tools can be classified into the following categories:

- Network intrusion detection system (NIDS)—A NIDS act like a network sniffer. It captures all network traffic and analyzes it for network-based attacks, such as denials of service. Because of its design, a NIDS can monitor many machines for remote intrusion.
- Host-based IDS—A host-based IDS is different from a NIDS in that it monitors a single host by gathering logs, process information, and user activity. A host-based IDS can try to detect an intrusion by either performing attack recognition or statistical recognition (any unusual activity is detected). Among the different host-based IDS tools, the most common are:
  - Log monitors, whose role is to analyze logs produced on hosts and look for patterns that may suggest that a host is under attack.
  - Deception systems (also known as decoys or honeypots), which simulate a well-known security hole that can be exploited. They are used to entrap an intruder, study their activity, and give the administrator time to determine the identity of the intruder.

- File or system integrity verifier (SIV). This tool takes an initial snapshot of a system and stores this information in a database. Whenever a file is modified without a snapshot updated in the database, the SIV will alert the administrator that there may be a problem.

- Multiple or distributed host-based IDS—Designated systems where host-based IDS tools are implemented on multiple systems and each local IDS reports to a central management console. The console attempts to correlate the various suspicious activities occurring on the monitored systems and detect a widespread intrusion.

- Integrated IDS—This is considered the "ultimate" intrusion system. Its theoretical design mixes host-based IDS with NIDS. All monitoring systems report to one or several management stations, which together try to detect widespread attacks.

For more details on the various advantages and disadvantages of the different IDS categories, study the *Introduction to Intrusion Detection and Assessments,* published by ICSA (`http://www.icsa.net/services/consortia/intrusion/educational_material.shtml`).

The main problem with detection is false alarms. A false alarm is any event that causes the IDS to alert the administrator, but the event that caused the alarm does not correspond to a real intrusion or risk. Another problem is the absence of an alarm when a real intrusion is occurring, as this highlights a weakness in the IDS. One of the main difficulties in using an IDS is to manage false-alarm problems while providing enough information to detect real intrusions. An extensive time period is generally needed to properly configure the IDS and tune its sensitivity to appropriate user and activity.

NIDS AND INTEGRATED IDS PACKAGES

Due to the scope and complex nature of IDS packages, it is beyond the scope of this book to cover them in-depth; however, there is a plethora of information available on the Web at `http://www.cerias.purdue.edu/coast/ids/`.

Section 4 of the following FAQ on NIDS may also be helpful: `http://www.robertgraham.com/pubs/network-intrusion-detection.html`.

You may also be interested in reading this article, which compares some well-known NDIS systems: `http://www.nwc.com/1023/1023f1.html`.

One of the more well-known integrated IDS producers is RealSecure from ISS, which provides the functionality of a NIDS as well as a host-based

IDS with a management console that has limited correlation abilities
(http://www.issx.com/prod/rs.php3).

LOG MANAGEMENT AND
USER MONITORING

The first step in setting up a basic IDS is to make sure that you obtain as
much information about the activity on a monitored system. The more data
that is collected, the better and more accurate the analysis will be. Two types
of data can be obtained:

- Information on system status and activity. These data generally refer
  to the operating system logging of UNIX (syslog) or the event
  manager of NT.
- Audit or accounting data, which pertains to the activities of system
  daemons and user processes.

To use these tools effectively, it is important to have a basic understanding of how the system logs function, as well as how user processes are
monitored.

Log Management and Analysis

The logging mechanism under UNIX is managed by the syslogd daemon
(under Linux, this daemon is complemented by the klogd daemon, which
provides logging capability for the Linux kernel). The syslog mechanism can
be seen as a centralization point for system-level logging. Any programs or
daemons that want to send a log message can interface with the syslogd
daemon. Based on the configuration in /etc/syslog.conf, the syslogd
daemon dispatches messages to the host console or to the appropriate file. Another option allows for the forwarding of log information to a centralized host.

A good strategy for managing log files is to prevent regular users from
viewing log information. While passwords or other sensitive information is
never written to log files, an intruder could gather data, such as program
version information or daemon status, and use the information to their advantage. Under UNIX, hiding logged information is easily achieved by removing the read access privilege to the following directories (this may vary
depending on the flavor of UNIX used):

- /var/adm.
- /var/log.
- /usr/adm.

By default under Windows 2000, only the group administrator can have access to the Event Viewer, so further restrictions are not necessary.

At this point, the system administrator may want to check the integrity of the system logging mechanism they are using. With the popularity of open source operating systems and the use of the Internet, if you have any suspicions about the integrity of your logging binaries, you may wish to download a new copy, or recompile using a known valid source tree. System logging mechanisms also allow you the option of modifying your logging program to support other logging mechanisms. For example, you may wish to modify your log to send your Sendmail, Web, and kernel messages into different log files for easier administration.

Another step to increase the integrity of your log files is to store them on a central machine, ideally a system that does not allow user access. Remember, when an intruder successfully breaks into a system, their next goal is to hide themselves and to remove any traces of their intrusion. One of the first ways to hide their deeds is to remove all log files from the system, thereby removing any trace of their activities. Under UNIX, avoiding this can be achieved by defining an alias called `loghost` either locally in `/etc/hosts` or in `DNS`. This points to the machine that will be the centralized log management system. In the case of Windows 2000, there is no mechanism that allows centralized management of the Event Viewer.

The default `syslog` mechanism is seen by many administrators as inherently insecure. Indeed, it is very difficult to detect that a local log file (generated by `syslog`) has been tampered with. Also, an intruder can attempt to shut down the communication link between a loghost and a system This is made easier since the communication protocol used is UDP, which does not guarantee that a message sent by a system will be received by the loghost. Another intruder weapon is to write a program that attempts to overflow the loghost with junk messages, thereby causing important messages to be lost or overlooked. To solve some of these issues, two projects that propose a replacement to the default `syslogd` daemon in UNIX are under development:

- Syslog-ng (`http://www.balabit.hu/products/syslog-ng`).
- Nsyslogd (`http://coombs.anu.edu.au/~avalon/nsyslog.html`).

Syslog-ng seems to have some very promising aspects. This project allows the filtering of messages by regular expression, in addition to the default scheme. They also use a TCP connection to guarantee that the loghost receives logging messages, and they use a hashing mechanism to protect logs from direct editing.

Having logs is useless unless the administrator can use them to provide value in the infrastructure. There is no real cookbook for this kind of task since the information to extract depends on the security policy of the organization and what kinds of attacks or problems the administrator is looking for. For UNIX, there are a number of different tools available that can help you gather useful information from your log files:

- Advanced color logs (`http://spyjurenet.com/linuxrc .org/projects/acl`).
- A fast and reliable general UNIX log file auditing tool (`http:// www.psionic.com/abacus/logcheck`).
- LogWatch (`ftp://ftp.kaybee.org/pub/linux/ logwatch.lsm`).
- Swatch (`ftp://ftp.stanford.edu/general/security- tools/swatch`).

In addition, it is possible to find log analysis tools that specialize in a specific type of log file analysis. One example is the `firesoft` package (`http://www.unix.gr`), which includes some Perl scripts to analyze logs produced by the Linux filtering mechanism `ipchains`.

A final word regarding the risk of log file tampering. It may not be a bad idea to set up a system on the centralized log management host which performs a backup of the data every X minutes on WORM media (write once/ read many) or some other non-volatile media. This prevents an intruder from erasing their tracks by making it impossible to delete log information. While this can be expensive, if you have need for a high level of security, the system will pay for itself after your first intrusion.

User Monitoring

In many cases, your intruder will be an insider, or an outsider using a stolen user account. Because of this, it can be useful to track the processes and resources used by users, and in the event of suspicious activity, the administrator can be contacted. This is similar to the way credit card companies monitor your credit activity, and if they see charges that don't fit your account history, they may contact you, or even disable the card itself.

Under Linux, the package `psacct` performs user accounting. The command `accton`, when called with the name of a log file, activates the accounting process. The commands `sa` and `ac` are used for exploring accounting data.

Under Solaris, accounting is activated by using the `/etc/init.d/ acct` script. By default, the accounting package does not come on Sun workstations that have Solaris pre-installed, so you may need to find your installation CD to add this package. The `admcrontab` must be edited to run the `ckpacct`, `runacct`, and `monacct` programs automatically, as seen here:

```
#
# Sample admcrontab file
0 * * * * /usr/lib/acct/ckpacct
30 2 * * * /usr/lib/acct/runacct 2>
/var/adm/acct/nite/fd2log
30 7 1 * * /usr/lib/acct/monacct
```

The `runacct` shell script is the main script used in the accounting reporting task. It processes the different files used for accounting and prepares daily and cumulative summaries used by other scripts such as `prdaily` and `monacc`. These reports are highly useful for billing purposes, especially if you wish to charge your users by their resource usage. By itself, the `runacct` script generates four daily reports:

- Daily Report—Shows line utilization by tty number.
- Daily Usage Report—Indicates usage of system resources by users.
- Daily Command Summary—Summarizes the usage of system resources by specific commands.
- Last Login—Gives the last time each user logged in and the amount of time they stayed on-line.

Under Windows 2000, the audit function can be activated from:

- The Local Security Policy Editor for managing the auditing on a single host.
- The Security Configuration Toolset enables you to define Enterprise-wide security policy when the audit needs to be enabled on all domain controllers. This is achieved through the use of a Group Policy Object applied to the domain or the organizational unit scope in Active Directory.

SYSTEM INTEGRITY VERIFIER

There are several free and commercial system integrity verifiers (SIVs) available. The most famous one is certainly Tripwire, which was originally developed under UNIX as a free product in 1992 by Gene Kim and Dr. Eugene Spafford (from the COAST Laboratory at Purdue University). Currently, Tripwire has become a commercial product and has been ported to Windows. This latest port not only monitors files and directories, but also the Windows Registry. More information about Tripwire can be found at `http://www.tripwiresecurity.com`. The old source code for UNIX (v1.3) is still available for free at `http://www.tripwiresecurity.com/products/ASR1_3.html`.

Other free alternatives exist for UNIX. While their functionality is similar, their differences lie in the algorithms used for creating a fingerprint. A sampling of these include:

- ViperDB (`http://www.resentment.org/projects/viperdb`).
- AIDE (`http://www.cs.tut.fi/~rammer/aide.html`).
- L5 (`ftp://avian.org/src/hacks`).
- Gog security monitor (`http://www.multimania.com/cparisel/gog`).

The use of such tools is generally a good way to detect if a rootkit (a suite of Trojan horse programs that help hide an intruder from detection) has been employed on your systems. To learn more about rootkits under UNIX, visit `http://packetstorm.securify.com/UNIX/penetration/rootkits`.

Under Windows, the only rootkit known at the date of this book's printing can be found at: `http://www.rootkit.com`. This rootkit has been designed for Windows NT 4.0, and it is reasonable to assume that it will be modified to work under Windows 2000.

To complement SIV tools, a system administrator may wish to keep track of what files are being edited on their systems, especially for critical infrastructure servers that should have little activity. Such tools for UNIX can be found at `ftp://vic.cc.purdue.edu/pub/tools/unix/lsof`.

HOST-BASED INTRUSION DETECTION

The most advanced and complete host-based intrusion detection systems are commercial products. Below is a sampling of host-based intrusion detection packages:

- RealSecure Agent, which is part of the RealSecure suite (`http://www.iss.net`).
- Kane Security Monitor for Windows NT 4.0 (`http://www.intrusion.com/security/products/ksm.shtml`).
- CMDS, which is multi-platform (`http://www.intrusion.com/security/products/cmds.shtml`).

Free, mature, host-based intrusion detection does not currently exist. However, the reader may want to check the following tools:

- Host-based login anomaly detection and response tool (Linux and OpenBSD) (`http://www.psionic.com/abacus/hostsentry`).
- Port scan detection and active defense system (`http://www.psionic.com/abacus/portsentry`).

DECEPTION TOOLKIT

A deception system is a final approach in the goal of trying to detect an intrusion or attempted intrusion. Its use can be approached from two perspectives:

- The general use of a deception toolkit by an IT organization can increase the workload of the intruder in their study of the infrastructure. In addition, deception systems can give wrong or incorrect information about the network topology or system architecture of your network. The underlying idea is to cause the intruder enough headache that they will move on and attack someone else's network.
- At the same time, a deception system helps in the study of potential intruders as well as provides a collection of evidence to track the intruder. This may be especially useful when the system administrator or security officer attempts to prosecute an intruder.

The first commercial deception system is CyberCop Sting from NAI (`http://www.nai.com/asp_set/products/tns/ccsting_intro.asp`). Some freely available deception tools are:

- Deception Toolkit (`http://all.net/dtk/`).
- FakeBO (http://yi.com/home/KosturjakVlatko/fakebo.htm).

When It Is Too Late

Dispute your best efforts, there is no guarantee that your security measures will keep every intruder out or prevent your users from violating your security policy. Accidents happen, operating systems and applications have bugs, and users can be malicious. Knowing that security problems will happen, even to you, it is important to prepare for that day, just in case. Being prepared is more a matter of having the right procedures prepared and knowing what to do rather than deploying some technology. This is especially important, because in many cases, a successful intrusion can lead to an incredible state of confusion.

There is no "cookbook" on how to be prepared. However, guidelines have been established by the CERT, the Computer Emergency Response Team, on how to detect a break-in and report successful break-ins. These guidelines can be found at `ftp://ftp.cert.org/pub/tech_tips/intruder_detection_checklist`.

A group of the IETF is currently doing some similar work (`http://www.ietf.org/html.charters/grip-charter.html`).

And, there are documents available on how to recover from an intrusion at `ftp://info.cert.org/pub/tech_tips/root_compromise`.

Finally, a recommended lecture on how to handle and identify network probes can be found at `http://www.network-defense.com/papers/probes.html`.

Some sound advice is to prepare in advance, which should include identifying an incident response team in your organization to be responsible for responding to possible intrusions into your infrastructure. This team will verify intrusions, track problems, implement counter-measures, and communicate with your users and CERT. If you discover an intrusion, be sure to communicate your findings to both:

- CERT—The Computer Emergency Response Team (`http://www.cert.org`).
- FIRST—The Forum of Incident Response and Security Teams (`http://www.first.org/team-info`).

Communicating this information is important, because if your break-in is the first of its kind, the information you give to CERT and FIRST may help prevent the break-in from occurring in other places or help to track and apprehend the intruder.

Summary

This chapter tried to give a background on security from an IT point of view. You should spend some time "surfing" the several URLs listed in this chapter. You also need to be aware that despite all the technologies that have been developed so far for protecting, preventing, and detecting, the war is just starting.

Initially, the opponent was an individual or small group using mainly a sequence of commands based on their knowledge and guesses to probe and penetrate. These same people have now developed tools (like `nmap`) to help them by automating some tasks like probing vulnerable hosts.

Unfortunately, what we are witnessing today is the emergence of a new generation of tools alowing an opponent to launch distributed denials of service (DDOS) using hundreds of machines (most of the time which have been compromised) in a coordinated way. More information on this new topic can be found at the following sites:

- `http://www.fbi.gov/nipc/trinoo.htm.`
- `http://www.cert.org/advisories/CA-2000-01.html.`

Even worse, it is the strong assumption that tools have been developed (and closely held by their authors) for automating the tasks of remotely compromising dozens of machines, exploiting security holes, and installing components of DDOS tools. However, there are currently no tools that allow a site to defend itself efficiently against DDOS attacks. Patching security holes in an IT system becomes a nightmare, since during the time a security bug is discovered, it becomes public knowledge and hundreds or thousands of machines can be compromised. Obviously, the risk is out there, and system administrators are in need of new tools—more intelligent tools that can be used for collaboration. And, above it all, there is a need more than ever to have CERT track opponents quickly and from an international perspective.

USER ADMINISTRATION

UNIX

Creating UNIX User Accounts

passwd and group files

Startup Files and Home Directories

Removing Accounts

UNIX and Windows 2000 Account Integration

WINDOWS 2000

Creating Windows 2000 Accounts and Groups

User Account Properties

User Profiles and Home Folders

User Environment

UNIX and Windows 2000 Account Integration

A system without users is like a racecar without a road. It looks nice, can go real fast, but really doesn't serve much of a purpose, unless of course you like off-roading. From the previous chapters, you learned the techniques necessary to design, build, and maintain your computer infrastructure. However, while you're probably proud of what you've created, and confident that the systems are stable and secure, eventually you will have to let the users take the system for a ride.

However, now that your shiny new racecar is prepared, you just do not want to hand over the keys and walk away, for if you do, you'll turn around and find your car dented and scratched, and if you're really unlucky, up on blocks with the hood open! Before you hand over the keys to your users, you'll have to have a plan in place for granting access. Access to systems consists of providing an access ID and password, as well as defining other characteristics that form a *user account*.

Each account is special and identifies a unique entity on your computing system. Planning your account creation strategy in advance will help you manage both the users as well as the resources they access. Here are a few recommendations for an account creation strategy:

■ Standard login names—Though every user will want to create their login, you should have some rules. First initial and last name is a common scheme. This helps you identify to whom an account belongs.

■ Home directory/folder location—You should have a specified location for home directories. This can often be segmented based on the type of account you are building. Different divisions of your organization may have different locations for their home directories/folders.

■ Password requirements—In Chapter 11, "Security," we discussed password policies. Be sure that your users understand these rules before you give them their accounts.

■ Startup files/profile—Create a standard startup file or profile for your organization. Make sure that all user resources, programs, printing, etc. work with this configuration.

■ Email accounts—Be sure that the user's email account is created, configured properly, and secure.

Creating UNIX User Accounts

This section will introduce you to user and group management under UNIX. We will give you an overview of how users and groups are structured, the different properties associated with users and groups, and how to create users and groups. By the end of this section, you should have a fundamental understanding of how to create and manage users and groups under UNIX.

We will cover two variations of UNIX account creation: Solaris and AIX. Each flavor has its own GUI tools, but these two are representative of what you will find. The /etc/passwd file is the same in all flavors of UNIX, though various versions have other files associated with it for security reasons. Likewise, all of the UNIX variants have a group file. We will begin our explanation of account creation there.

Defining Users Using the /etc/passwd File

For UNIX, the /etc/passwd file defines a set of attributes that define a user. A user's definition is referred to as their *username*, and all the user definition components associated with that username define the user's *account*. In UNIX, almost all users are created equal. What makes UNIX accounts unique are the permissions and file ownerships (using ACLs) that are associated with each account. A unique number, which is known as the User Identification Number (UID), is attached to each unique username. It is through the UID that the operating system delineates who each user is and to what access levels that user is authorized.

The one exception is the root account, which is the most powerful account, as it can access all files. With a UID of 0, the operating system recognizes this account as special, and grants access to all functions. For this reason, the root account needs to be treated with respect, and a great deal of caution!

UNIX user definitions begin with the `/etc/passwd` file. In this file, the user's username, UID, and other account information is defined. A standard Solaris `/etc/passwd` file might look like the following:

```
root:x:0:1:mars superuser:/:/sbin/sh
daemon:x:1:1::/:
bin:x:2:2::/usr/bin:
sys:x:3:3::/:
adm:x:4:4:Admin:/var/adm:
lp:x:71:8:Line Printer Admin:/usr/spool/lp:
smtp:x:0:0:Mail Daemon User:/:
uucp:x:5:5:uucp Admin:/usr/lib/uucp:
nuucp:x:9:9:uucp
Admin:/var/spool/uucppublic:/usr/lib/uucp/uucico
listen:x:37:4:Network Admin:/usr/net/nls:
nobody:x:60001:60001:Nobody:/:
noaccess:x:60002:60002:No Access User:/:
nobody4:x:65534:65534:SunOS 4.x Nobody:/:
```

As you can see, the standard Solaris `/etc/passwd` file contains a list of administrative accounts, but out of the box, there are no user accounts. The administrative account handles system-level functions such as printing (`lp`) and email (SMTP). The reason that these files exist is to allow these services, or portions of these services, to run as a user other than the root account. While running all administrative functions as root will work, having all of your operating system running everything under the root account increases the chance for someone gaining root access through a system bug or misconfiguration.

A typical user password entry in Solaris will look like:

```
jsmith:x:1001:10:Smith, John:/users/jsmith:/bin/csh
```

An `/etc/passwd` entry is a colon-separated list of seven different parameters. These values are defined in Table 12.1.

The `/etc/passwd` file rarely changes over time, unless a user requests to have their default shell or default group modified. For this reason, administrators rarely interact with the `/etc/passwd` file, except at the time of account creation. While this may seem like a simple file to modify, common problems that can occur in creating an `/etc/passwd` entry include:

- Misspelling of the username.
- Duplicate UIDs.

Table 12.1	**Solaris** /etc/passwd **Entry Description**
Field (in order)	Description
User Name	An eight character string consisting of only alphanumeric (numbers or letters) characters. A username must begin with an alphabetic character, and all characters are case-insensitive.
Password Field	An"x"in this field specifies that the user's encrypted password is located in the /etc/shadow file.
User ID (UID)	User ID for the user. The range is from 0 to 2147483647, but it is recommended you keep this number below 60000 if you plan to interact with other operating systems.
Default Group ID (GID)	Users may have multiple group IDs, but this entry identifies the group ID that the user will be associated with at login.
User Information	This is a text-based field that is generally used to display the user's real name.
Home Directory	The file directory where the users will be placed at login and where all configuration files should be stored.
Default Shell	The user's default login shell.

■ Incorrect home directory.
■ Incorrect default shell.

Be most concerned about creating duplicate UIDs, as this mistake can allow one or more users to view the files of the original user with that UID. If you are in an environment where information is sensitive, take care not to commit this blunder.

 A user's UID is the single most important value that delineates them from all of the other users of the system. Mistakes or duplications in a user's UID can cause catastrophic results. Any account with UID 0 has root privileges.

/etc/shadow File

The /etc/passwd file define a user's password attributes. A standard Solaris /etc/shadow file might look like the following:

```
root:gH5517yJ6stOa:10899::::::
daemon:NP:6445::::::
bin:NP:6445::::::
sys:NP:6445::::::
adm:NP:6445::::::
lp:NP::::::
smtp:NP:6445::::::
uucp:NP:6445::::::
nuucp:NP:6445::::::
listen:*LK*:::::::
nobody:*NP*:6445::::::
noaccess:NP:6445::::::
nobody4:NP:6445::::::
```

It is important to note that the entries in the /etc/shadow file mimic the entries in the password file, both in username and in the order in which they appear in the file. This will make management of the file simpler, and will help reduce administrative errors.

A typical /etc/shadow user entry will look as follows:

```
jsmith:ptnTxOprtH4K6:10957::::::
```

Table 12.2 explains the different files attached to each username in the /etc/shadow file.

In this entry, jsmith only has information in the first three fields. This is the default for Solaris, as the remaining fields pertain to password and account aging policies. Aging refers to the amount of time a password will remain active. For example, if you wanted to have a policy that required these bulleted items,

- No more than one password change per week.
- Password expiration in 60 days.
- Password expiration warning 14 days before expiration.
- No more than six months of inactivity.
- All accounts expire on 1/1/2001.

then the /etc/shadow entry for jsmith would look like the entry that follows, where 11323 is the number of days from 1/1/2000 (10957 days from 1/1/1970):

```
jsmith:ptnTxOprtH4K6:10957:7:60:14:180:11323:
```

Password and account expiration policies can be useful in more secure environments. Be aware that implementing this policy will increase an administrator's workload as users will forget to change their passwords and will come to you to reset their password because they are locked out of the system.

Table 12.2	Solaris /etc/shadow **Entry Description**
Field (in order)	Description
User Name	An eight-character username that must match the appropriate entry in the /etc/passwd file.
Encrypted Password	A 13-character encrypted password string. An entry of NP indicates that that user account cannot be logged into using a password (only through the use of su). A null/empty entry means that there is no password for the account.
Last Change	This field indicates the last time the password was changed. The entry is a count of days from January 1, 1970.
Password Change Minimum	The minimum number of days allowed between password changes.
Password Duration	The length of time, in days, that the password is valid.
Password Expiration Warning	The time, in days, before the user is warned that their password is about to expire.
Inactivity Duration	The number of days the account can be inactive.
Account Expiration Date	The date the account expires.
Not Used	This field is not used and is available for future enhancements.

Adding Solaris Users

Adding and modifying entries in the /etc/passwd and /etc/shadow files can be done two ways: at the command line, or by using the GUI tool admintool. While either method will work, your choice of tool may vary based on your experience and the number of entries you need to modify. admintool is an easy-to-use GUI interface that allows the administrator to easily add new users, groups, and other system administration information. While simple to use, the more experienced administrator may choose to edit system files directly in order to make large groups of changes, or make changes more quickly.

Adding Users at the Command Line Adding a new user at the command line is relatively easy, but be careful, as typographical errors can cause user accounts to be inaccessible, or even disable the system. You may also want to employ a software version control system if more than one person has access to modify password files. Nothing is more frustrating than losing two hours of user changes because another administrator decided to make a quick account change and overwrote all of your changes. Information on using version control is discussed in Chapter 15, "Software Administration."

If you are uncomfortable with editing the files directly, go to the next section and use `admintool`. However, if you're up to command-line editing, a checklist for adding user accounts follows. Remember that all of these steps must be run as the root user.

1. Edit the `/etc/passwd` file—Make sure to choose a unique username and UID. Also, double-check all spellings, default group assignments, and the user's real name, for typographical errors will cause you problems later.

2. Edit the `/etc/shadow` file—Create an entry with the username. It is usually a good idea to copy an existing entry, change the username, and then delete the encrypted password. If you want to leave the password field blank, the user will be prompted to enter a password the first time they access the account. To set the password, save the `/etc/shadow` file, run the command `passwd username`, and you will be prompted to set the password.

3. Edit the `/etc/group` file to include the user in any supplemental groups—This is the best time to add the user to any other groups that they need to be a part of. Edit the `/etc/group` file and add the username to all appropriate groups.

4. Create the user's home directory—Using the command `mkdir`, create the home directory that you defined in the sixth field of the new user's `/etc/password` definition. For example, `mkdir /users/jsmith`.

5. `chown` and `chgrp` home directory—Finally, make sure you give proper ownership to the new directory, for example, `chown joeuser /users/joeuser`. Using `mkdir` as root will give ownership to root, not the new user. Also, be sure to set the default group permissions on the directory.

Once you've completed these five steps, you have done the necessary work to add a new user to your system. Depending on the frequency with which you add new users, performing these tasks manually may be sufficient. However, if you have an environment that adds many users on a frequent basis, you may investigate automating the above steps using your favorite method of scripting.

Adding Solaris Users Using admintool If you are hesitant to edit files manually, or if you are a weak typist, Solaris provides a simple and easy way to add and modify user definitions through the `admintool` program. As root, type `admintool`, and you will see the screen shown in Figure 12.1. While `admintool` can be used to do more than just add/modify users, `admintool` defaults to showing the `/etc/passwd` file.

To begin adding new users, choose `Add` from the `Edit` menu, and you will see the screen shown in Figure 12.2. From this screen, you can define all the relevant attributes needed to define our new user, `joeuser`. Once you have enter all of the information, choose `Apply` or `OK`, and the account will be created. If you choose `OK`, you will be taken back to the entry screen.

One thing you'll notice is that by default, `admintool` creates an account with a nonexistent password, that is, the password is null, and the user will be prompted to enter a password the first time they, or someone else, accesses the account. While this may not be a problem in your environment, it is generally a good rule to give the account an initial password, and pass this information on to the user. To set the initial password, under `Account Security`, click the box with `Cleared until first login`, choose `Normal Password...`, and you will see the screen shown in Figure 12.3.

Enter the new password twice, choose `Apply` or `OK`, and you're done. `admintool` takes care of the five steps shown in the previous section.

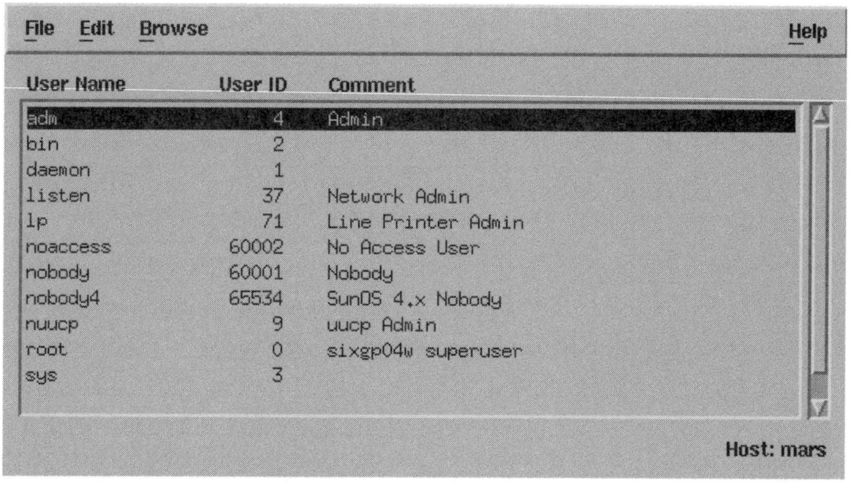

Figure 12.1 Solaris admintool.

Figure 12.2
admintool add
user information
screen.

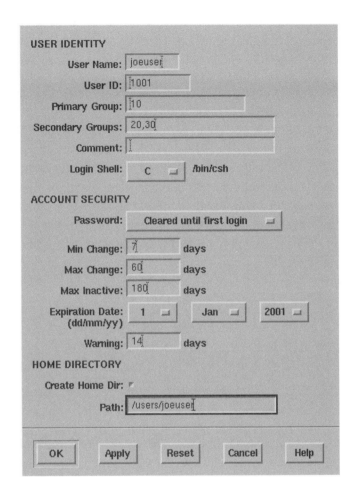

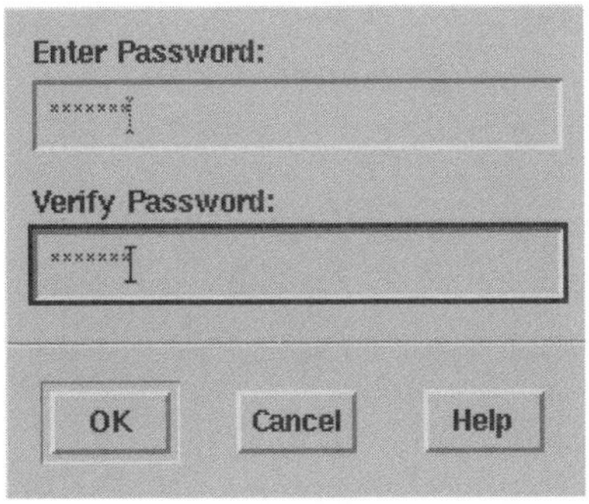

Figure 12.3
Add user
password screen.

AIX

AIX provides the system administrator with a choice of interfaces in managing local user accounts. AIX provides the traditional UNIX interface of managing and maintaining accounts via the command line. The System Management Interface Tool (SMIT) and Web-based System Manager (WSM) are the GUI interfaces for managing and maintaining user accounts. The next few sections will cover the command-line and GUI interfaces. This section pertains to local accounts only.

AIX Command Line The command-line interface is the traditional approach to managing accounts on an AIX system. The commands for adding, changing, and deleting users on an AIX system are contained in Table 12.3.

Creating a new user account in AIX updates the text files contained in Table 12.4.

The final step in creating a user account is assigning a password. The password can be set with either the `passwd` or `pwdadm` command. AIX uses a shadow password file. The encrypted password for each user is placed in the `/etc/security/passwd` file, and the `/etc/passwd` file will contain an exclamation point in the password field.

Group identifiers (GIDs) are maintained with the commands in Table 12.5. The file `/etc/group` contains the name, number, and list of group members. The `/etc/security/group` file contains extended attributes for each group.

The command-line interface is the quickest way to modify configuration files. The modification of a large amount of repetitive information can be accomplished quickly by developing scripts utilizing user account commands. The following simple example adds users contained in the file `/tmp/sales` (a text file with one user per line) to the existing `sales` group, and illustrates the ease of automating with commands:

Table 12.3	AIX User Account Management
Command	Definition
`mkuser`	Creates a new user account
`chuser`	Changes user attributes
`lsuser`	Displays user account attributes
`rmuser`	Removes a user account

```
#!/bin/sh

for file in 'cat /tmp/sales'
do
```

```
        chgrpmem -m + $file sales
done
```

Table 12.4	User Account Files in AIX
File	Information stored
/etc/passwd	User information
/etc/security/user	Extended attributes by user
/etc/security/limits	Process resource limits by user
/etc/security/environ	Environment attributes by user
/etc/group	Group names, numbers, and lists
/etc/security/group	Extended attributes of groups

It should be noted that this simple script will work for other flavors of UNIX. Just replace chgrpmem with the appropriate group attribute change command, and you're on your way.

Solaris provides the commands useradd, usermod, and userdel, which perform similar functions as the AIX commands described in this section. Most UNIX flavors have non-GUI commands for account management.

passwd or pwdadm—Sets the user password.

Table 12.5	AIX Group Commands
Command	Definition
mkgroup	Creates a new group
chgroup	Changes attributes for groups
lsgroup	Displays group attributes
chgrpmem	Changes administrators or members of a group
setgroups	Resets a session's process group set
newgrp	Changes a users's real GID

AIX GUIs AIX provides two GUI methods of managing user accounts under the X Windows System. The System Management Interface Tool (SMIT) is invoked with the `smit` command. The first screen in SMIT provides a list of all the system management categories available to configure the local system. Click `security and users` to manage user accounts. The Security & Users screen (Figure 12.4) gives you the choice of configuring users, groups, passwords, roles, and login controls. Subsequent screens guide you through the processes of editing, adding, and deleting properties associated with user accounts.

The other GUI provided by AIX is the Web-based System Manager (WSM). WSM is Java-based and platform-independent. Type in the command `wsm` to invoke WSM. The first screen contains icons for all system management categories supported under WSM. Click the Users icon and the screen in Figure 12.5 appears. All user accounts and groups are listed in the main portion of the window. Double-clicking on any user/group allows you to edit the properties associated with that user/group. WSM provides the system administrator with the functions available in SMIT or from the command line.

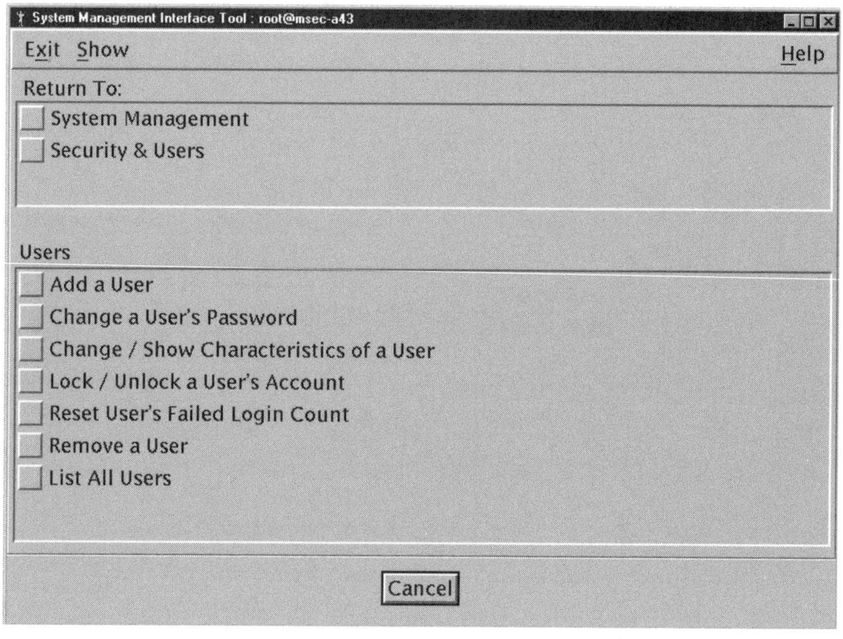

Figure 12.4 SMIT security and users screen.

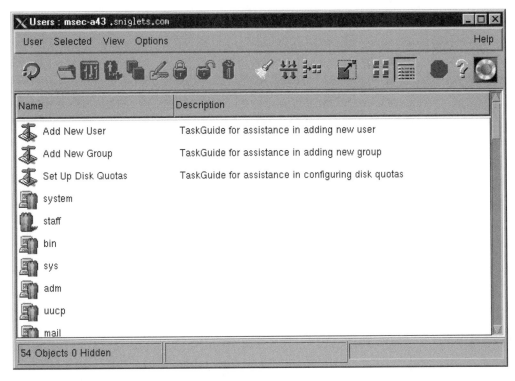

Figure 12.5 WSM users.

UNIX GROUPS

One of the founding principles of UNIX was the ability to easily share files between users. As was discussed in Chapter 11, each file in UNIX has the ability to allow access to a user, group, or other. While user-level access allows only one user access to a file, group access allows members of a group to have that privilege. With the use of group permissions, a file owner can grant read, write, and/or execute access to any file to a subset of all users that are part of a given UNIX group. Following is a standard Solaris /etc/group file:

```
root::0:root
other::1:
bin::2:root,bin,daemon
sys::3:root,bin,sys,adm
adm::4:root,adm,daemon
uucp::5:root,uucp
mail::6:root
tty::7:root,tty,adm
lp::8:root,lp,adm
```

```
nuucp::9:root,nuucp
staff::10:
daemon::12:root,daemon
sysadmin::14:
nobody::60001:
noaccess::60002:
nogroup::65534:
```

Each line in the /etc/group file represents a different group, with each element identified in Table 12.6.

A typical group entry will look something like this:

```
math101::150:jsmith,rjones,mbrown,bwhite
```

The group math101 has four users, with no password. Each user in this group has the ability to read, write, or execute any file that they can access that has group permissions. For example:

```
-rw-r----   1 jsmith  math101    810 Aug 18 20:29 answerkey
```

the file answerkey, while owned by joeuser, would be readable by group math101, but not by the world. Changing the permissions to:

```
-rw-rw-r----   1 jsmith  math101  810 Aug 18 20:29 answerkey
```

would allow users in group math101 to edit the file, while all users could read the file. To assign group ownership to a file, the chgrp program is used:

```
chgrp math101 answerkey
```

Table 12.6	Group Entry Description
Field (in order)	Description
Group Name	An eight-character string consisting of only alphanumeric (numbers or letters) characters. A group must begin with an alphabetic character, and all characters are case-insensitive.
Password Field	An empty field represents no password for group use. If a password exists, a user will be prompted for a password to change to that group.
Group ID (GID)	Group ID for the group. The range is from 0 to 2147483647, but it is recommended you keep this number below 60000 if you plan to interact with other operating systems.
List of Group Members	A comma-separated list of usernames that are members of the group.

To determine a user's group members, as root, or as the user, run the `groups` command:

```
# groups jsmith
students math101
```

This indicates that `jsmith` is a member of the groups `students` and `math101`.

Default Group

Each user has a default group that will be assigned to each file they create. Since users can be members of any number of UNIX groups, files are only created with ownership assigned to the default group. To determine the default group of a user, run the `id` command:

```
# id -a jsmith
uid=1001(jsmith) gid=14(students) groups=100(students),150(math101)
```

In this example, the `gid` identifies the default group to which user `jsmith` belongs. Upon login, `jsmith` can only create group files in the group `students`. However, `jsmith` can interact with any files that have `math101` ownership, given the proper permissions. It is convenient to be able to create files with the appropriate group, especially if you have a number of files to create. While using the `chgrp` command is an option, using the `newgrp` command as user `jsmith`:

```
#newgrp math101
```

will set `jsmith` is default group for that shell instance to the new group:

```
# id -a jsmith
uid=1001(jsmith) gid=150(math101) groups=100(students),150(math101)
```

To return to the default group, type `newgrp  students`, or exit the current login shell.

`groups`—Lists the groups of which the supplied user is a member.

USER STARTUP FILES AND THE HOME DIRECTORY

The shell specified in the password file is loaded when a user logs in. The shell (and a few other UNIX utilities) can be configured with the *startup* file associated with that shell or utility. Table 12.7 lists the startup files associated

Table 12.7	Common Shells and Startup Files
`Shell`	Startup File
Bourne	`.profile`
Korn	`.profile`
	`.kshrc`
C-Shell/csh	`.login`
	`.cshrc`
	`.logout`
tcsh	`.login`
	`.cshrc`
	`.logout`

with the most commonly used shells. Startup files are found in the user's home directory and are usually proceeded by a dot (.). The shell startup files control:

- Environment variables like `TERM`, the terminal type.
- Command aliases.
- Command search paths.
- Shell variables.

The Korn shell is an extension of the Bourne shell. The command `ksh` is added to the `.profile` in the Bourne shell to launch the Korn shell. The environment variable assignment, `ENV=.kshrc`, is also added to identify the startup file for the Korn shell (.kshrc is a convention, the file can be named anything).

Common Desktop Environment

While there are many flavors of UNIX, there are even more ways to connect to a UNIX system. Telnet, serail-attached terminals, modems, GUI-based terminals, and the console itself are just some of the ways to log on to a UNIX system. The most common way to connect to UNIX is through a GUI-based system, either through the console of the system, or by using X Windows, either from a dedicated X-terminal, or by using an X-emulation package on a personal computer. Unlike Windows, using X presents a user with hundreds, if not thousands, of different windowing environments for them to interact with when they connect.

However, in recent years, many of the largest UNIX vendors have worked together to create a similar (but not quite identical) window-based user interface. In compliance with the Common Open Systems Environment (COSE) standard, the Common Desktop Environment emerged. A broad consortium of UNIX providers including Sun, HP, IBM, SCO, and others developed CDE. CDE is built on top of the X Windows System originally created by MIT. In essence, CDE provides a collection of manager applications that handle many of the shell-based activities, as well as provide a common user *desktop*, which in Windows is pretty much taken for granted. These managers include:

- Login managers—Provide a standard entry interface into the system.
- Session manager—Saves the current session and desktop attributes, similar to profiles in Windows.
- File manager—Provides drag-and-drop-style direct manipulation tools similar to the Windows Explorer function.

Since CDE is X Windows-based, all of the programs written for that platform are also available. CDE comes with a standard configuration, which meets most user's needs. The man pages provide some guidelines for editing these settings. Regretfully, the names of files and some of the specific variables are where the UNIX variants differ.

 CDE and Motif: A Practical Primer by Antonino Mione is an excellent reference for CDE and the related Motif window manager.

MANAGING USERS ON MULTIPLE SYSTEMS

The previous three sections have given you the tools to create a user account by creating password and group entries, as well as a home directory and startup files on a single system. While using these techniques works great if you only have one system, you must repeat this process for every system on which the user needs access. Also, group additions, password changes, or home directory information will need to be replicated across all systems when a user's needs change. Managing this can be difficult, if not impossible!

If you have more than one or two systems on your network, you should consider using the tools NIS and NFS as presented in Chapters 7 and *8. Through the use of these tools, adding a new user to multiple systems is as simple as modifying the appropriate files on the NIS server and creating a user account on an NFS shared filesystem.

DELETING UNIX USER ACCOUNTS

Eventually, you will have to remove a user. This is not as easy as some may think. The entire paradigm of the UNIX filesystem often creates a situation in which a user has files on multiple partitions and machines. Likewise, those files are often in use by other users. An account also has associated mail files, possible `crontab` entries, group file entries, and quota file entries. Considerate removal of an account is a multi-step process.

1. First, disable the account by placing asterisk (*) in the password field in the `passwd` file.
2. Disable all `crontab` entries.
3. Be sure the user is not running any programs.
4. Locate and archive all user files. If you know of shared files, move them; otherwise, you may have to return them from the archives. (The `find` command is excellent for this!)
5. Remove the user from any groups in the `group` file.
6. Remove the user's disk quota entries.
7. Provide an email alias to forward all email, if that is your policy.
8. Remove the account from `passwd` and `shadow` files. If you are running accounting, you must wait until that has completed before removing the account

It is a good security policy to avoid recycling UIDs. That is not always possible, however. Remember that if a UID is reused, any remaining files, groups, or privileges from the old account will now be attributed to the new user of the UID.

Windows 2000 Users and Groups

This section will introduce you to user and group management under Windows 2000. We will give you an overview of how users and groups are structured, the different properties associated with users and groups, and how to create users and groups. By the end of this section, you should have a fundamental understanding of how to create and manage users and groups under Windows 2000.

WINDOWS 2000 USER ACCOUNTS

Windows 2000 identifies each user with a user account. The user account contains information that describes the user and is the user's identity on the network. The account allows the user to log on to network computers and access network resources. This section will provide an overview of user accounts and walk you through the account creation process.

Overview of User Accounts

Not all user accounts are created equal. In fact, there are three distinct types of user accounts in Windows 2000. Table 12.8 describes the three account types.

Table 12.8	Windows 2000 User Account Types
User Account Type	Description
Built-in User Accounts	These are accounts that are automatically created by Windows 2000. The two most commonly used built-in user accounts are: ■ Administrator—The Administrator account should only be used for system administration purposes, such as managing users, groups, and resources. The Administrator account password is set during the initial setup of the system. You should rename the Administrator account to enhance security. ■ Guest—The Guest account is useful for providing occasional users access to systems and network resources. The Guest account is disabled by default, but can be enabled by an Administrator. You should only use the Guest account in low-security networks, and it should always have a password assigned. As an added security precaution, you can rename the Guest account.
Local User Accounts	Local user accounts can be created on any Windows 2000 system. However, local user accounts will only work on the system on which they were created. Local user accounts will not allow users to access domain resources, so you should not create local user accounts on systems that are part of a domain.
Domain User Accounts	Domain user accounts can be created only on Windows 2000 domain controllers. Domain user accounts will allow users to access any systems and resources that are part of the Windows 2000 domain, provided the account has the appropriate access permissions. Domain user accounts are centrally managed and no configuration is necessary on local systems.

In addition to the three types of accounts, there are some key points that you must be aware of when working with user accounts:

- User logon names for domain user accounts must be unique throughout the Active Directory.
- User login names may be up to 20 characters in length and are not case-sensitive.
- Passwords are case-sensitive and can be up to 128 characters in length. You should require passwords to be at least 6-8 characters long and consist of mixed-case letters, numbers, and symbols.

Now that you understand the basics, we'll move on to creating a user account in our domain.

Creating User Accounts

Creating a user account is quite simple. We will walk through creating a domain user account on a Windows 2000 domain controller. The following steps describe how to accomplish this:

1. Log on to your Windows 2000 domain controller as Administrator.
2. Open the Active Directory Users and Computers MMC snap-in using the following sequence: from the Start menu → Programs → Administrative Tools → Active Directory Users and Computers. You will see a window similar to the one in Figure 12.6 appear.
3. Make sure the Users folder in the left pane is selected.
4. From the Action menu, select New and then User to display the new user properties window in Figure 12.7.
5. Fill in the fields appropriately and click Next to continue. The new user password options window in Figure 12.8 will be displayed.
6. Enter a password in the appropriate fields and select the password options you desire; the password options are detailed in Table 12.9. When you are finished, click Next to continue.
7. Review the summary screen, and then click Finish to create the account.
8. You will see the new account appear (alphabetically) in the list in the right pane.

Now that you have created a domain account, we can move on to discussing account properties in more detail.

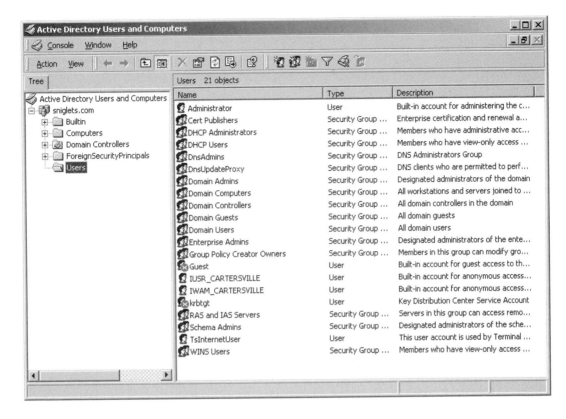

Figure 12.6
Active Directory Users and Computers MMC snap-in.

Figure 12.7
New user
properties
window.

Figure 12.8
New user password options window.

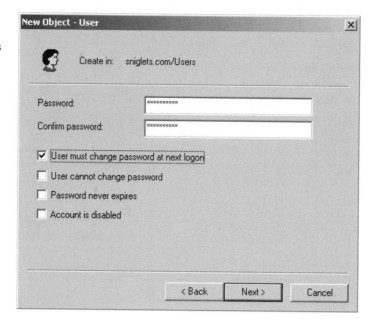

Table 12.9	**User Password Options**
Option	Description
`User must change password at next logon`	Setting this option forces the user to change their password the next time they log on to the Windows 2000 domain. It is recommended that you make new users change their default passwords.
`User cannot change password`	Setting this option prevents a user from changing their password. This option is rarely used for regular users, but you may find it useful for service accounts.
`Password never expires`	Setting this option prevents the password from expiring, despite the system default settings. This option is useful for Administrator and service accounts.
`Account is disabled`	Setting this option prevents the account from being used on the Windows 2000 domain. This option is useful in preventing old user accounts from being used before they are permanently removed from the domain.

Understanding User Account Properties

Up to now, you have seen a limited set of properties associated with the user account. This section will describe in detail the different properties you can configure for user accounts in Windows 2000 domains. To begin, double-click the account we just created to display the user `Properties` window in Figure 12.9.

As you can see, there are several tabs available. Each tab provides access to a different set of properties, which are described in Table 12.10.

In addition to the `properties` pages available for the user account, the `Action` menu provides several options when a user account is selected in the right pane. Table 12.11 describes these options.

This section has provided you with the necessary background to understand user accounts in Windows 2000. The next section will provide you with an overview of Windows 2000 groups.

Figure 12.9
User Properties window.

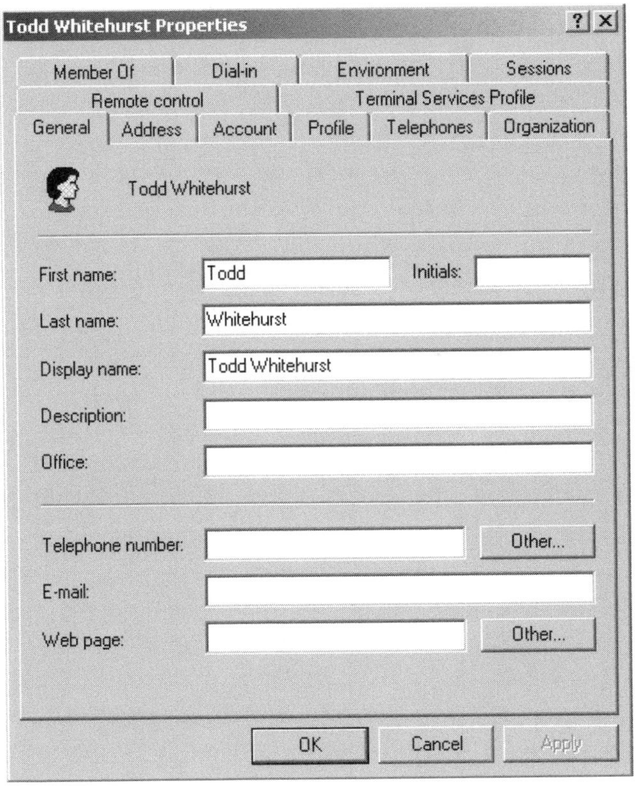

Table 12.10	User Account Properties
Property Tab	Description
General	Allows you to specify general user account information, including: ■ Name. ■ Description. ■ Office location. ■ Telephone number. ■ Email address. ■ Web page URL.
Address	Allows you to specify the user's address.
Account	Allows you to specify account-specific options, including: ■ Logon name. ■ Allowed logon hours (default is all hours). ■ Allowed workstations (default is all workstations). ■ Miscellaneous account options. ■ Account expiration.
Profile	Allows you to specify the location of the user's roaming profile, logon script, and home folder.
Telephones	Allows you to specify numbers for the following telephone types: ■ Home. ■ Pager. ■ Mobile. ■ Fax. ■ IP phone.
Organization	Allows you to specify the following organization-specific options: ■ Title. ■ Department. ■ Company name. ■ Manager. Using this property page can help you to keep track of your organization's structure.
Remote control	Allows you to configure remote-control options that are applicable during a Terminal Services session.

(continued)

Table 12.10	User Account Properties (continued)
Property Tab	Description
Terminal Services Profile	Allows you to specify the location of a user's roaming profile and home directory when logged on to a Terminal Services session. This page also allows you to enable/disable Terminal Services access.
Member Of	Allows you to specify the groups to which the user belongs.
Dial-in	Allows you to enable/disable dial-in permission and the available callback options.
Environment	Allows you to configure Terminal Services startup options, including: ■ Which program, if any, to start after logon. ■ Connections to network resources.
Sessions	Allows you to configure Terminal Services timeout and reconnection settings.

Table 12.11	Action Menu Options for User Accounts
Action Menu Options	Description
Copy	Allows you to create a new account based on the settings in the currently selected account. Some of the settings copied include the profile and account options.
Add members to a group	Allows you to add the selected account to a group.
Disable Account	Allows you to disable the user account, preventing users from using the account to log on to workstations or access network resources.
Reset Password	Allows you to reset the account's password, without having to know the old password.
Move	Allows you to move the account to a different container.
Open home page	Allows you to open the user's home page, if it has been specified in the account properties.
Send mail	Allows you to send email to the user, if their email address has been configured in the account properties.

WINDOWS 2000 GROUPS

Windows 2000 also provides the ability to organize users into groups. You can use these groups to grant/deny access to resources and to create an organizational structure. This section will provide you with an overview of groups in Windows 2000 and describe how to create a group on your Windows 2000 domain controller.

Overview of Groups

Simply put, a group is a collection of users, or rather, user accounts. You can use groups to assign permissions to groups of users instead of individual users. When working with groups, keep the following in mind:

- Users can be members of multiple groups.
- Each user account is assigned a "primary" group (the default is `Domain Users`).
- Members inherit group permissions.
- Groups themselves can be members of other groups.

You must also understand two things about groups: type and scope. Table 12.12 describes the different types of groups, and Table 12.13 describes the different group scopes.

By properly organizing your users into groups, you can make system administration much easier. Instead of assigning permissions to users, you can assign permissions to groups, thus reducing the administrative overhead required when user accounts are added and removed from the domain. Now that you understand the different types of groups and the scopes they cover, we can discuss creating groups.

Table 12.12	Windows 2000 Group Types
Group Type	Description
Security Group	Windows 2000 uses security groups to assign permissions to groups of users. Security groups can also be used as distribution groups.
Distribution Group	Distribution groups are used by applications for non-security-related functions, such as sending mail. You cannot use distribution groups for assigning permissions.

Table 12.13	Windows 2000 Group Scopes
Group Scope	Description
Global Group	Global groups can contain user accounts and other global groups from the same domain. Global groups can be used to assign permissions in any domain. Global groups are most commonly used for organizing users who require similar access to the network.
Domain Local Group	Domain local groups can contain user accounts, universal groups, and global groups from any domain, and other domain local groups from the same domain. Domain local groups can be used to assign permissions only in the same domain. Domain local groups are most commonly used for assigning permissions to resources.
Universal Group	Universal groups can contain user accounts, global groups, and other universal groups from any domain. Universal groups can be used to assign permissions in any domain. Universal groups are only available in Windows 2000 domains operating in native mode.

Creating Groups

Creating groups is very similar to creating user accounts. When creating groups, keep the following in mind:

- Use functional/intuitive names for your groups.
- Create groups in the Users container, or a container you have created specifically for groups.

For our purposes, we are going to walk through creating a Global group, and then describe how to add users to the new group. Refer to the following steps to complete this task:

1. Log on to your Windows 2000 domain controller as Administrator.
2. Open the Active Directory Users and Computers MMC snap-in as follows: from the Start menu → Programs → Administrative Tools → Active Directory Users and Computers. You will see a window similar to the one in Figure 12.6.
3. Make sure the Users folder in the left pane is selected.
4. From the Action menu, select New and then Group to display the New Object-Group properties window in Figure 12.10.

Figure 12.10
New Object-
Group properties
window.

5. Complete the fields in the window, being sure to select the Global scope and Security type.
6. Click OK to create the group. The new group will appear at the bottom of the list in the right pane.
7. Now, we need to "populate" the group with users. Double-click on the new group. The group Properties window will be displayed.
8. Select the Members tab and the window in Figure 12.11 will be displayed.
9. Click the Add button to select the users you wish to add to the group. When you are finished, select the Member Of tab to display the window in Figure 12.12.
10. Click the Add button and select the groups you wish to make this group a member of. When you are finished, click OK to close the group Properties window.

You can now use this group to assign permissions on files, folders, and resources.

This covers the basics of Windows 2000 groups. To learn more advanced group concepts, obtain a copy of the Windows 2000 Resource Kit.

Figure 12.11
Group Members
properties
window.

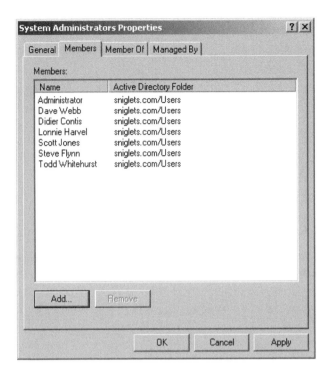

Figure 12.12
Group
membership
properties
window.

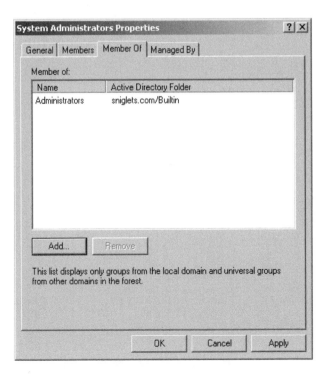

Windows 2000 User Profiles and Home Folders

One particularly significant part of the user account is the user profile. Along with the profile, we must include logon scripts and home folders. Configuring these settings can be accomplished on the `Profile tab` of the user `Properties` window in the Active Directory Users and Computers MMC snap-in. An example of a user profile configuration is shown in Figure 12.13.

This section will provide an overview of user profiles, logon scripts, and home folders. It is solely up to you if and how you use these features in your network.

PROFILES

Profiles store information about the user's environment, including Windows Desktop and Internet Explorer settings. Configuration information for other software packages may also be included in the user profile. Other settings stored in the user profile include:

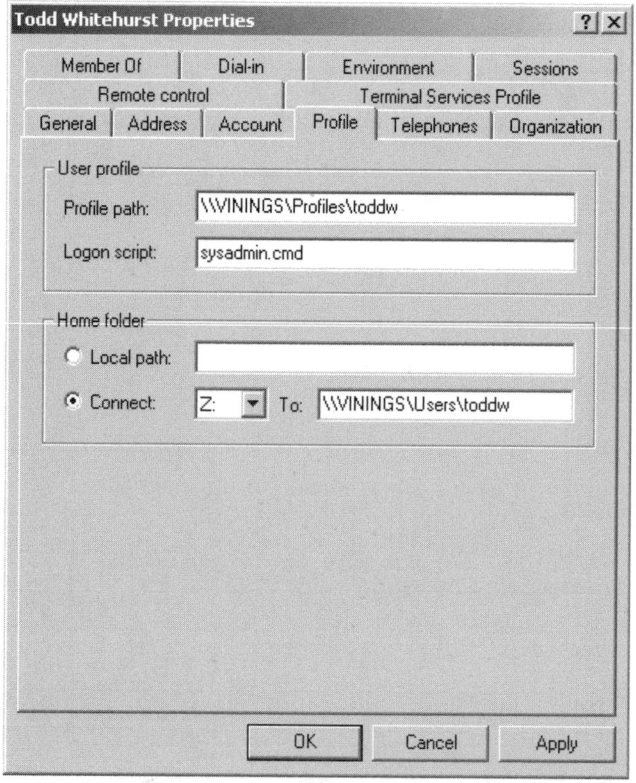

Figure 12.13
User profile
settings.

- Desktop shortcuts.
- `Start` menu shortcuts.
- Internet Explorer settings.
- Network connections.
- System settings, such as colors and backgrounds.
- The `My Documents` folder, discussed later.

Perhaps the most important obstacle in understanding Windows 2000 profiles is understanding the difference between local and roaming profiles.

Local vs. Roaming Profiles

Assuming a roaming profile is not specified in the user's properties (see Figure 12.8), the first time a user logs on to a system, Windows 2000 will create a profile for that user and store it in `%SystemDrive%\Documents and Settings\username` (typically `C:\Documents and Settings\username`). The profile does not follow the user from computer to computer, so any settings they make will have to be duplicated at each computer the user plans to use. The local profile will also contain a `My Documents` folder, which is the default location for storing the user's files and folders. If your users tend to use only one system, then local profiles will work for you; otherwise, you should look into using roaming profiles.

If you have configured a roaming profile for a user (as we have done in Figure 12.8), then it will be stored on a network server. It is available to the user regardless of where they log on. When a user with a roaming profile first logs on, a local copy is made of that profile and from then on, only changes are replicated between the server copy and the local copy. Roaming profiles are, in every way, identical in function to local profiles, except they are stored on a network server. If your users plan to work at multiple computers, you should implement roaming profiles.

The `My Documents` Folder

The `My Documents` folder is the default location Windows 2000 uses to store a user's files and folders. By default, the `My Documents` folder is a sub-folder of the user's local or roaming profile. While there is no problem in leaving the `My Documents` folder set as the default, we have found that it may be advantageous to change where the `My Documents` folder points. Fortunately, this is a built-in function supported by Windows 2000. Use the following steps to change where the `My Documents` folder points:

Figure 12.14
My Documents
Properties
window.

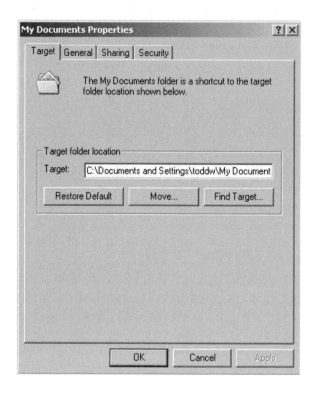

1. Right-click the My Documents desktop folder. The My Documents Properties window in Figure 12.14 will be displayed.
2. To change the location, click the Move button and select the new folder.
3. Once you have made your selection, click OK to apply the changes.
4. If you are prompted to move the current contents to the new location, select Yes.

The My Documents folder serves as a pointer to whatever folder you wish to set as the default for your users' files and folders.

LOGON SCRIPTS

Logon scripts allow you to accomplish many tasks during the user logon process. Most commonly, you will want to use a logon script to restore connections to network shares or printers. A logon script is typically a simple batch file (with a *.bat or *.cmd extension). The script below is a good example of a simple logon script:

```
@echo off

net use R: \\SMYRNA\ZipDisk /persistent:NO
net use S: \\SMYRNA\Software /persistent:NO

@echo on
```

Any command that can be used on the command line can be executed in the logon script; you can even launch standard executable programs from the logon script, if you so desire. To assign a logon script to a user account, you must do three things: create the script, save it in the *NETLOGON* share of your domain controllers, and configure the user profile to execute the logon script.

Fortunately, it is very easy to accomplish the above tasks. You can use Notepad to create the file itself, just remember to save the file as a `*.bat` or `*.cmd` file. You should save the file in the *NETLOGON* share of every domain controller in your domain. This share is actually located under `\\<domain_controller_name>\SysVol\<domain_name>\ scripts`. For example, on our system, the *NETLOGON* share is `\\VININGS\SysVol\sniglets.com\scripts`. Once you have created the file and stored it in the *NETLOGON* share, you need to configure the user profile. This, of course, is accomplished on the `Profile` tab of the user `Properties` page, as shown in Figure 12.8. The next time your user logs on, the script will be executed automatically.

HOME FOLDERS

A user's home folder in Windows 2000 is analogous to a user's home directory in UNIX systems. However, a home folder is not required in Windows 2000. While UNIX home directories contain essential configuration information pertaining to the user's account, the home folder in Windows 2000 is nothing more than a network share where a user can store their data.

There are two steps to providing a home folder for a user. The first step is to create the actual folder, and the second step is to configure the user account to connect to that folder. The best way to share home folders is to provide a single network share for all of your users, such as `\\VININGS\ Users`, as we have done. The actual folder can reside on any disk partition you wish, provided there is enough space to store your users' data. Once you have created the root share, you should make sure the NTFS permissions are set to allow the following:

- Administrators have full control.
- SYSTEM has full control.
- Everyone has read and execute access.

You should then make sure the share permissions are set to allow the following:

- Administrators have full control.
- SYSTEM has full control.
- Everyone has full control.

This will allow users unfettered access to their home directories, but not allow them to read other users' home directories. Creating a user's home directory and configuring their profile can be completed in a single operation. You should configure the user's profile, as we have done in Figure 12.8, to point to the appropriate network resource. Once you configure the profile properties and close the user `Properties` window, Windows 2000 will automatically create the home directory and set the following NTFS permissions:

- Administrators have full control.
- The user has full control.
- The user is given ownership of the folder.

As we said above, home folders are not required by Windows 2000. However, storage management and backup operations are greatly simplified by having users store their data in a home folder instead of on their local machine. The decision is ultimately up to you, but we definitely recommend providing home folders for your users.

 You can unify your users' UNIX home directories and Windows 2000 home folders by installing SAMBA on your UNIX servers and sharing your UNIX filesystems. SAMBA will allow your Windows 2000 users to utilize their UNIX home directory as their home folder.

Windows 2000 User Environment

Unlike UNIX, Windows 2000 users have only one possible user environment. This environment consists of two major parts: the Desktop and the Explorer. This section will briefly describe the major parts of the Windows 2000 user environment.

THE WINDOWS DESKTOP

When a user logs on to Windows 2000, the first thing they see is the Windows Desktop. The standard Windows 2000 Desktop is shown in Figure 12.15.

Figure 12.15 Standard Windows 2000 Desktop.

The Desktop itself contains several components. Included on the desktop is the `Start` menu, the taskbar, the System Tray, and the standard icons. This section will describe these Desktop components in greater detail.

The Start Menu

The `Start` menu is basically the one-stop shop for starting any program installed on your Windows 2000 system. A typical `Start` menu is shown in Figure 12.16.

Most every program you install will create shortcuts in the `Start` menu. You can then navigate through the `Start` menu to locate and run those programs. You can also customize the `Start` menu; that is, you can re-arrange the folders and shortcuts to meet your personal preferences. By right-clicking on the `Start` menu and selecting `Open`, you can easily

Figure 12.16
Example Start
menu.

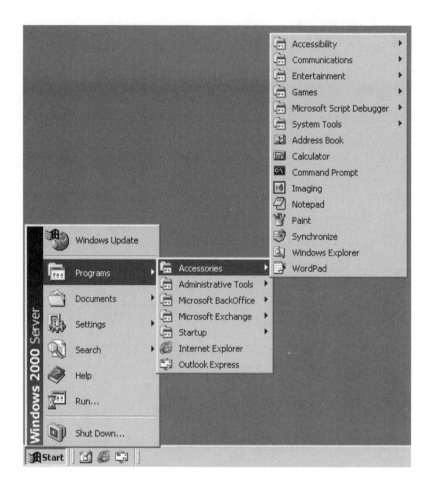

perform these customizations. Administrators will also see an `Open All Users` option, which allows you to edit the folders and shortcuts that are available to every user.

The Taskbar

The taskbar, shown in Figure 12.17, is located between the `Start` menu and System Tray.

You can also think of the taskbar as containing the `Start` menu and System Tray. In either case, we are concerned with two parts of the taskbar in this section. The first is the embedded toolbar, which is located directly to the right of the `Start` menu. The toolbar, by default, contains shortcuts for

Figure 12.17 Windows 2000 taskbar.

the Active Desktop, Internet Explorer, and Outlook Express. You can add and remove shortcuts by dragging and dropping existing shortcuts into or out of the toolbar. The second part of the toolbar is the task area, which is located between the toolbar and System Tray. The task area contains a button representing each running application. You can maximize a minimized application window simply by clicking on the appropriate button in the task area.

The System Tray

The System Tray is located at the right side of the taskbar, as shown in Figure 12.17. The System Tray always displays the current time on the right, and on the left, various programs and services may place an icon. You can click these icons to control some features of the associated programs and services. One common icon you will find there is the volume control, which allows you to adjust speaker volume using the mouse. The software vendor specifies the functions available for the icons placed in the System Tray.

Standard Desktop Icons

As you can see in Figure 12.11, there are a few icons available directly on the Desktop. These default icons are created by Windows 2000 and you should not remove them. Table 12.14 describes each of the standard icons.

Table 12.14	Standard Windows 2000 Desktop Icons
Icon	Description
My Documents	The My Documents icon is a link to the `My Documents` folder discussed earlier in this chapter.
My Computer	The My Computer icon is a link that provides access to all of the disk partitions and mounted network shares on your system. From My Computer, you can browse through all local and remote-mounted filesystems.
My Network Places	The My Network Places icon is a link to the Windows 2000 network. From My Network Places, you can browse the servers and workstations on the Windows 2000 network. You can also create direct links to your favorite network resources inside My Network Places.
Recycle Bin	The Recycle Bin contains all deleted files and folders. Once you "empty" the Recycle Bin, you lose all ability to recover a deleted file or folder.
Internet Explorer	This will launch the Internet Explorer Web browser.

In addition to the standard icons, you can create your own shortcuts directly on the Desktop. You can also place files and folders directly on the Desktop for quick access.

 Instead of placing files and folders directly on the Desktop, store them in your home folder or `My Documents` folder and place shortcuts to frequently used files and folders on the Desktop.

THE WINDOWS EXPLORER

The Windows Explorer allows you browse through the `My Documents` folder, the Desktop, local filesystems, and any network shares that you have mounted on your system, the Control Panel, and My Network Places. You can launch the Windows Explorer using one of two methods:

1. Open it from the `Start` menu via `Programs` → `Accessories` → `Windows Explorer`.
2. Type `explorer` after choosing `Run` from the `Start` menu or at a command prompt.

An example of the standard Windows Explorer is shown in Figure 12.18. The Windows Explorer allows you to do the following:

- Add and remove files and folders.
- Add and remove shortcuts.
- Search for files and folders.
- Modify file and folder permissions.
- Launch applications.
- Add and remove network connections.
- Search for network resources.
- Create and modify network shares.

You will inevitably spend a lot of time using Windows Explorer. Over time you will discover the methods that work best for you. The `Options` command from the `Tools` menu allows you to customize virtually any aspect of the Windows Explorer.

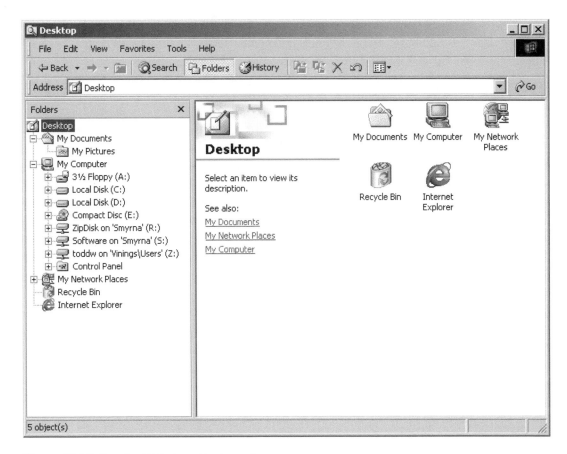

Figure 12.18 Standard Windows Explorer view.

UNIX and Windows 2000 Account Integration

By now, you are probably wondering how we can tie all of this together. It may be surprising to know that we have been giving you the tools and information you needed all along. Here is where we will try to bring it all together, basically by pointing you in the right direction and letting you run with it how you see fit. Remember, you are the system administrator, so what works for us may not necessarily work for you.

In an ideal world, you would have a single login for all of your users, across both your UNIX and Windows 2000 platforms. Regretfully, we do not live in an ideal world. Presently, there is no viable unified login available. We discussed LDAP in Chapter 7, "Directory Services," and we saw that as the "light at the end of the tunnel" for integrating UNIX and Windows 2000 logins. LDAP is an industry standard directory access protocol and is supported in both Windows 2000 and UNIX. In the near future, you should be able to use LDAP for your login authentication, thus requiring a single user account for both UNIX and Windows 2000 systems.

The real question is what to do until you are able to employ LDAP. Presently, there are two options for cross-platform access. The first is SAMBA, which was discussed in Chapter 8, "Distributed Filesystem." SAMBA will allow your Windows 2000 users to access resources on your UNIX systems and your UNIX users to access resources on your Windows 2000 systems. SAMBA runs on your UNIX systems and provides Windows 2000-compatible SMB services. The second option is Microsoft Services for UNIX, which was also discussed in Chapter 8. Services for UNIX provides the same functionality as SAMBA, but it runs on Windows 2000 systems. Services for UNIX emulates UNIX file and directory services for cross-platform access. In either case, you still must provide separate user accounts on both your UNIX and Windows 2000 systems. It is best to use the same username for each account, which will allow an easy mapping from a Windows 2000 account to a UNIX account, and vice versa. However, if it is necessary to have accounts of different names mapped to one another, both SAMBA and Services for UNIX support explicit mappings.

In short, the future holds great things for a single-login environment. However, the present still leaves us with a multi-login environment in which we must deploy additional services to enable cross-platform computing. For now, SAMBA and Microsoft Services for UNIX bridge the gap between UNIX and Windows 2000 systems. We look onward to LDAP for a more complete and integrated solution.

Summary

User accounts are an essential (if obvious) service on any computing system. Distributed infrastructures change the simple process of creating an account into a complicated one. A heterogeneous, distributed infrastructure further complicates the process. In this chapter, we explained how to create and manage accounts, and discussed strategies for interaction between the two platforms. This chapter is built on the knowledge gained in the previous 11 chapters.

UNIX USER ACCOUNTS AND GROUPS

In this chapter, we covered two variations of UNIX account creation: Solaris and AIX. The `/etc/passwd` file is the same in all flavors of UNIX, though various versions have other files associated with it for security reasons. Likewise, all of the UNIX variants have a `group` file. UNIX has the ability to easily share files between users. With the use of group permissions, a file owner can grant read, write, and/or execute access to any file to a subset of all users that are part of a given UNIX group.

WINDOWS 2000 USER ACCOUNTS AND GROUPS

We discussed how users and groups are structured, the different properties associated with users and groups, and how to create users and groups. The user account contains information that describes the user and is the user's identity on the network. The account allows the user to log on to network computers and access network resources. Windows 2000 also provides the ability to organize users into groups, to grant or deny access to resources, and to provide structure.

UNIX AND WINDOWS 2000 ACCOUNT INTEGRATION

The final section of this chapter discussed two strategies for integrating user accounts: SAMBA and Microsoft Services for UNIX. Combined with techniques discussed in Chapters 6-11, these tools can be used to share files and resources across the UNIX and Windows 2000 platforms. However, there is still a need for two separate accounts. LDAP, as discussed in Chapter 7, will eventually be available and make it possible to have one account for both platforms. The strategies discussed throughout this book will help to bridge the gap while we all wait.

BACKUPS

UNIX

Building a Backup Schedule

Native UNIX Backup Programs

Backing up UNIX from a Windows System

Cross-platform Backups with Amanda

WINDOWS 2000

Building a Backup Schedule

Windows 2000 Backup Utilities

Backing up Windows from a UNIX System

" **O**ops!" is possibly the most dreaded word in the system administrator's vocabulary. While the tips, techniques, and procedures presented in the previous chapters should help you to become an excellent administrator, everyone makes mistakes. In some environments, making that first big mistake is a rite of initiation that brings you into the inner circle of system administration. Common mistakes include overwriting a system file, installing a new operating system without saving critical information, or typing the infamous UNIX command in the wrong directory (and subsequently deleting everything in that directory):

```
# rm -r
```

Mistakes are not limited just to system administrators, as users will often lose information or require access to files that were archived months ago. System failure can corrupt data and require filesystems to be rebuilt. Finally, disasters can happen that can destroy a single system, or a complete data center.

So, what can an administrator do to survive the "oops" that will happen in their computing environment? Administrators need to make copies of, or *back up*, their user and system data in such a way that it can be retrieved in total, or *restored*, at some later date. This chapter will discuss the processes that should be employed to manage backups and restores. These topics will be split into two areas, the first being the methodology needed to provide a solid backup infrastructure.

Second, you will be presented with backup and recovery tools that you can use in your UNIX and Windows 2000 environments, including methods that merge UNIX and Windows 2000 into a single backup space.

Backup Methodology

The best backup systems are not only built on technology. Good backups require good procedures and constant care to provide the best possible system for your infrastructure. In this section, you will be presented with how to develop your backup process, as well as how to plan for catastrophic failures that hopefully will never strike your organization

SCHEDULING BACKUPS

Your backup schedule should not only identify what systems to back up, but should also specify at what time backups should occur as well as what data should be included. It is important to understand that backups are more complicated than just copying data to a tape or another media. With the proliferation of large, inexpensive disks, users can now store large quantities of data, and require quick and easy access to their data when they need it.

Making sure this data is available during regular circumstances , and most important, recoverable in the event of disaster, will drive your strategy for building a backup infrastructure.

Understanding the key elements of backups will help you achieve a strategy that will provide maximum protection for your systems and data. When developing your backup strategy, you can build an effective strategy if you employ the following four rules:

- Determine what data needs to be backed up, including user data, application files, and operating systems.
- Understand the differences between full backups and incremental backups, and applying them in the proper manner.
- Determine the impact of backups on your infrastructure and create appropriate backup windows to minimize the impact to your users.
- Build a backup schedule that incorporates the previous three elements and provides maximum data protection with a minimum of user impact.

Determining What to Backup

So, what data in your environment should you archive? At first glance, this may seem like a simple question with the answer being, "Back up everything." If you only have two or three computers with limited data, this may indeed be the correct answer. However, as your infrastructure grows, the amount of data you have increases, which affects the backup resources required. A standard DLT IV tape stores 70GB of compressed data. Let's assume that your data compresses at a 2:1 ratio; for every 140GB of data, you'll need at least one DLT tape, and possibly a tape drive. As you can see, as your environment grows, you will spend a significant amount of money purchasing tapes and tape drives to perform backups.

While you can't eliminate the need for backup resources, you can work to reduce the amount of data you need to archive without impacting the reliability or integrity of your infrastructure. As the administrator, you need to look at your systems and find places where data is redundant, or easily reproducible, and eliminate this data from your backup process. There are many places to look to reduce the amount of data you back up, including:

- Operating systems—Binaries and libraries exist on every system in your infrastructure and backing up multiple copes of each is inefficient. Only backing up one copy of your operating system will greatly reduce the amount of data on your backup media. If you use a default installation, or installation server, you can greatly reduce backup data by not backing up the operating system at all. Reinstalling an operating system from scratch is generally faster than attempting to rebuild the operating system from a backup device.

- Off-the-shelf-software—If your backup resources are limited, you may decide not to back up off-the-shelf-software, such as Office 2000. Off-the-shelf programs that may be installed on many systems will lead to duplication in your backups. Of course, this is only possible if your off-the-shelf program is easy to install and requires little custom configuration for each system.

- Replicated data—Look at your environment and try to find data that is duplicated, such as DNS, NIS, and /usr/local configurations. If you have built a centralized /usr/local structure, then it is not necessary to back up each copy, just the master. If there is a failure, you can either redistribute from the master, or if the master is the problem, pull the master copy from tape, or from another system. For more information on building a master /usr/local infrastructure, see Chapter 15, "Software Administration."

- Sensitive data—In many environments, sensitive data exists that should never be backed up. For example, in some organizations, administrators choose not to archive email messages that exist in users' inboxes. Many organizations are concerned about the legal issues of privacy with respect to email. If a user receives a sensitive email and deletes it, it should no longer exist. However, if the organization regularly backs up the inbox directory, then the organization may be pressed, or even ordered by a court, to produce the backup tape that contains the email inboxes. Before you employ this technique, be sure you have policies in place that spell out this process, and that the highest levels of management in your organization understand and sign off on such a practice.

While you may not be able to employ all of these techniques, reducing the amount of data backed up will improve your backup process, and make managing your data a simpler and less expensive operation.

Full Backups vs. Incremental Backups

Once you know what you need to back up, knowing how to back it up is very important. For example, say you have a 10GB data directory that stores relatively static information such as digitized pictures of every person in your organization. Backing up this information every night for a week requires 70GB of archive resources. While this may be effective if this is the only directory you are backing up, if this is just part of your back up structure, is it necessary to completely back up this directory every day if it changes only occasionally? Performing a backup every three days would reduce your archive resources by at least half, but how do you know what three days to choose? What if data changes every day; can you risk losing yesterday's work?

Answering the previous questions is difficult if your strategy for backups only employs full backups at some regular interval. However, if you only back up three times a week, you have large windows where a loss of data may not be recoverable because the last backup was run two days ago. In almost every situation, your backup strategy can't expose your users to a large window where they can lose data.

To overcome this, you can employ a strategy of *incremental backup*. Incremental backup is the process by which you choose a subset of your disk data to back up based on information available from previous backups. By reducing the amount of data you back up, you can better utilize your existing resources and back up more often, thereby reducing the window where data can be lost. While this window can never be reduced to zero (unless you do a backup every time a file changes on your system), you can provide a reasonable level of assurance for your users that their work is safe.

The best way to explain incremental backup is by example (Table 13.1).

Table 13.1	**Comparison of Full vs. Incremental Backups**	
Date	Full Backups Only	Full + Incremental Backups
Monday	A,B,C	A,B,C
Tuesday	A,B1,C	B1

On Sunday, we perform a full backup of files A, B, and C. On Monday, only file B changes, say to file B1. If we do a full backup again on Monday, the only file that has changed is B (to B1), but we use backup resources to store A and C again, even though exactly the same A and C are on Sunday's tape. This is shown in the second column of the table.

If we perform an incremental backup on Tuesday, only the files that changed since Monday's full backup are part of Tuesday's backup. In this case, only file B1 would be on Tuesday's tape, thereby saving the time and space to back up A and C.

This process can be extended to *levels*. To do this, define a full backup as level 0. The first incremental backup would then be level 1. Level 1 would signify backing up all files that have changed since the last level 0. For example, if you do a full backup on Sunday, and then a level 1 on Monday and Tuesday, on Monday, all files that changed on Monday would be backed up. On Tuesday, all files that changed on either Monday *or* Tuesday would be backed up. If you change Tuesday's backup to a level 2, then on Tuesday, only files that changed since Monday's level 1 backup would be saved. Now let's extend our example and say on Tuesday, file C changes to file C1. The files on each tape are shown in Table 13.2.

You should notice that on Tuesday, file B1 is again on your backup tape. Since B1 is already on Monday's tape, this process is wasting space. To help combat this problem, you can add another backup level, level 2, and use the backup process that is shown in Table 13.3.

Table 13.2	**Using Backup Levels**	
Date	Backup Level	Files on Backup Media
Sunday	0	A,B,C
Monday	1	B1
Tuesday	1	B1,C1

Table 13.3	**Using Multiple Backup Levels**	
Date	Backup Level	Files on Backup Media
Sunday	0	A,B,C
Monday	1	B1
Tuesday	2	C1

This process can be continued in any number of configurations that is only limited by the functionality of your backup program. However, it should be noted that restoring the data requires you to first restore the latest level 0 backup, then the latest level 1, latest level 2, and so on without going backward in time. In other words, if backup levels 0, 1, 5 and 2 were used, we would restore 0, 1, and 2.

While incremental backup is a useful and necessary mechanism for managing the amount of data you archive, there are two possible drawbacks to using it that need to be understood before you complete your backup plan. First, performing too many incremental backups in a row will, over time, grow your incremental backup to the size of a full backup. If you only perform one level 0 backup per month, then by the 28th or 29th level 1, the size of your level 1 could be almost as large as a full level 0. If the level 1 and level 0 tapes contain about the same amount of data, then you'll end up doubling the amount of time needed to complete a full restore of this data. That is, you'll restore the level 0 tape, and then have to restore the level 1 tape. If you had a more current level 0, you would have less data to restore.

A second problem with incremental backup can occur if you use too many levels in your backup strategy. For each level you employ, that is one more restore you'll need to run if you have to completely restore a directory or filesystem. For example, if you have 6 levels of backup (levels 0–5) on a filesystem and the filesystem fails, then you'll need to restore files from 6 different tapes, in order from the level 0 backup to the level 5, which will take a significant amount of time. Of course, the amount of time you'll spend doing restores depends on your backup medium, hardware, and program, but in general, the fewer the number of tapes, the faster you'll have the data to your users. Determining your incremental backup strategy is a function of history and the design of your infrastructure, as well as the technology you employ to archive your data. As you develop your backup strategy, you can adjust your level schedule to best utilize your backup resources, as well as reduce the amount of time it takes you to restore files.

Backup Windows

Another factor that is important is the amount of time it takes to perform a backup of your data. The time in which you want to perform your backup is called a *backup window*. Backup windows are very important, as the process of backups will impact the performance of the system being backed up, and can impact network performance if you back up your systems over the network. Your goal as the administrator is to make sure that users can perform their work, and if the system is bogged down doing backups, then your users will not be happy. You should also be aware that in some instances you may need to take a program or system off-line to perform a backup. If this is needed, make sure your users understand this well in advance, or be sure to provide redundant resources so they can continue to do their work.

A typical backup window during the week is from 9pm to 6am. These times are chosen because, in general, during these times, your systems and users will be working less. However, if your organization is a 24-hour operation, then you may need to narrow your window, or find other times during the day when user activity is less. On the weekends, you can extend your backup window if your users and systems are not as active on Saturday and Sunday. A typical backup window on the weekend can stretch from Friday at 8pm until Monday morning at 6am.

Using what you know about your systems and users should define your backup windows. Your goal is to complete every backup during these times, so as to lessen the impact on your users. If you find that your backup windows are not large enough, then you'll need to change your incremental strategy, or acquire more efficient backup resources to help complete your backups on time. With an understanding of backup windows, you now have all the tools to complete your backup strategy.

Backup Strategy

With backup terminology in hand, you can now build your *backup schedule*. A backup schedule combines what you plan to back up, what dump levels you plan to employ, and when you have scheduled your backup windows. Table 13.4 shows a simple backup schedule. It should be noted that you could develop a single backup schedule for your entire infrastructure, or a different backup structure for each system, or even each filesystem. However, if you employ multiple backup schedules, try to keep it simple!

Full backups will begin Saturday evening at 8pm and complete by Monday at 6am. The Monday level 1 will begin at 8pm and finish by Tuesday at 6am. A level 2 backup will begin Tuesday evening at 8pm and continue until Wednesday 8am. This continues until the next Sunday, at which time the cycle repeats.

Table 13.4	Simple Backup Schedule					
Sunday	Monday	Tuesday	Wednesday	Thursday	Friday	Saturday
Level 0	Level 1	Level 2	Level 3	Level 4	Level 5	Level 6

As you can see, this schedule employs an increasing level for each day of the week. This scheme will provide a high level of data integrity, while utilizing the least amount of archive resources. On each day except Sunday, only the previous day's changes will be archived. For some backup processes, this is called differential backup, as you are only archiving the difference between the current data and yesterday's data. While this is a resource-efficient backup process, the restoration process may be inefficient. Should an entire filesystem become corrupted after the level 6 dump, but before the next level 0, you would need to restore files from each tape, starting with the last level 0, then level 1, and so on. If restoring data quickly is a requirement of your infrastructure, this may not be the most efficient model to follow.

Table 13.5 shows a different backup schedule that provides a mechanism for quicker backups, but requires more archiving resources.

In this schedule, level 0 backups are performed over the weekend, providing a backup window from 8pm Friday night until 6am Monday morning. This is useful if you have a great deal of data to back up and a 10- or 12-hour window is insufficient to archive all the data. Also, this schedule is built to only require two tapes to restore any file or filesystem. In the event of a failure, the latest weekend backup tape, along with the most current level 1 tape, will allow the administrator to reproduce the most up-to-date version of the data.

The downsides of this schedule are threefold. First, with backups running over the weekend, any data that changes won't be archived until the Monday evening backup. If your environment is 24 × 7, this may not provide the level of data integrity your users require. Second, if a great deal of data changes over the week, the Wednesday and Thursday backups will become large and may not fit into the designated backup windows. Finally, you will notice that our backup strategy creates a 24-hour window where data can be lost. With every backup strategy, there will always be a window of risk of losing data, and your job as an administrator is to limit this risk to be as small a window as possible.

Table 13.5	Backup Schedule with Large Weekend Backup Window					
Sunday	Monday	Tuesday	Wednesday	Thursday	Friday	Saturday
None	Level 1	Level 1	Level 1	Level 1	Level 0	None

Hopefully these examples have illustrated some of the techniques and issues you will face when you design your backup strategy. Remember that there is no single strategy that works for everyone. You should also be aware that a strategy that works today might not work tomorrow. As you add additional data, you may find that your backup windows are no longer sufficient, and you'll need to adjust your levels to fit into new windows. Remember that backups cost money also, and backup media will need to be evaulated for wear and replaced over time. Be aware of the resources your backups consume and plan accordingly, so you don't get caught without enough backup media to do an evening's backup. (Murphy's Law dictates that the night you run out of tapes will be the night your boss loses a file.) Additionally, new technology or additional resources may allow you to reduce your backup windows or decrease the number of levels you use. Your backup schedule should be a living entity, with at least quarterly reviews to evaluate new options and changes to your infrastructure.

DISASTER RECOVERY

Backups are an effective tool to counter hardware failures and user error. However, what happens when a disaster strikes and your backup medium, or even your data center, is destroyed. Fires, floods, and other catastrophes can happen to you. As an administrator, it is part of your job to plan for the worst and develop a strategy when the unthinkable happens. The implementation of this strategy provides your organization a method for *disaster recovery*.

Disaster recovery in itself is a topic that could span a number of chapters. Having additional computer resources, or even duplicate networks and data centers, goes beyond the scope of this book, as well as the average administrator. However, disaster recovery is important with respect to the survivability of your backup resources. Accidents will happen, and if your backups are damaged or destroyed, you and your users may lose valuable time and irreplaceable data.

Building disaster recovery into your backup routine does not need to be an expensive and complicated undertaking. Even an administrator with only one system to back up can help to provide disaster recovery by learning these three key ideas:

- Store backup media in a safe, secure place—Once you've performed your backups, make sure you save them in a safe and secure place. This is especially true for tape resources, which can be sensitive to heat, humidity, and light. The number of people that leave tapes lying around right next to their favorite beverage, or store tapes on a windowsill in direct sunlight, would surprise you.

- Physically separate backup media from the backup server—Once you've completed your backup, you should move your backup media to a physically distant location from your backup server. Fires and floods are two of the most common disasters that can happen to your equipment. If you keep your tapes in the same room as your server, a fire can destroy both your most current backups and your archived data as well. Always try to keep at least one week's backup media in a physically distant location to minimize the chance of a disaster destroying your data.

- Follow an off-site storage and rotation schedule for maximum security—If you have very sensitive or important data, archive this data outside of the organization, ideally with a company that specializes in the archiving and maintenance of backup media. Many companies specialize in storing your backup media in an environmentally controlled, secured area.

Table 13.6 shows a backup schedule that repeats weekly, but has a four-week cycle. After completing a week's worth of backups, and after the next week's level 0, the previous week's backups are moved off-site to a secure location.

This continues for the first four weeks. During week 5, week 1's media can be brought back on-site and recycled. However, the level 0 backup that was performed has special significance. The week 4 backup will be placed off-site and archived, effectively removing it from the backup process, or *rotation*. By removing this media from the rotation and storing it, you provide your organization the reassurance of at least one snapshot of your infra-

Table 13.6 Monthly Backup Schedule With Off-site Disaster Recovery

Week	Sunday	Monday	Tuesday	Wednesday	Thursday	Friday	Saturday	Notes
1	Level 0	Level 1	Level 1	Level 1	Level 1	Level 1	Level 2	
2	Level 0	Level 1	Level 1	Level 1	Level 1	Level 1	Level 2	Week 1 off-site
3	Level 0	Level 1	Level 1	Level 1	Level 1	Level 1	Level 2	Week 2 off-site
4	Level 0	Level 1	Level 1	Level 1	Level 1	Level 0	Level 2	Week 3 off-site
5	Level 0	Level 1	Level 1	Level 1	Level 1	Level 0	Level 2	Week 4 level 0 archived

structure for each month. How many months you choose is up to you, but this provides at least a starting point should you suffer a major disaster.

Backup Methods

With a foundation now in place, you can look at different methods for backing up your infrastructure. One of the most difficult problems faced by the administrator is building a functional, yet simple backup structure when an infrastructure consists of different types of systems, such as multiple UNIX platforms or Windows systems. This section will investigate some of the tools available to the administrator in the quest to provide an environment where a user's data is safe and secure.

UNIX BACKUP TOOLS

UNIX provides a number of different methods for archiving data. Many of these tools grew out of methods that were originally written to archive on a single system. As networks became more popular, these tools grew and adapted to meet the ever-increasing number of systems and data. In this section, you will be introduced to some of the methods available on UNIX systems, as well as a cross-platform backup method that has grown out of university research.

Using `tar` to Back Up Information

For administrators that have only a small number of systems, or who need a quick way to archive a single filesystem or directory, complex backup software and procedures are not necessary. Just about every UNIX variant will provide you with the `tar` command to help in archiving files from one disk to another disk, tape, or other type of external media. Using `tar` as your only backup mechanism can be difficult if you have more than a few systems to back up as `tar` only works on a single directory or filesystem at a time, and was not designed as a tool for backing up large numbers of systems simultaneously. However, for single systems, or specific purposes, `tar` is a very quick and effective way to copy files from one place to another.

A simple `tar` command will take the form:

```
#tar -cvf /dev/rmt0 .   //period is required//
```

This command will create a `tar` file on the device `/dev/rmt0` and include all files that are in the current directory. The `-v` option will give you verbose output of all files as they are copied to the tape. Once you have the data on the tape, you can restore it using:

Table 13.7	tar **Options**
Option	Description
-c	Creates a new tar file
-x	Extracts from a tar file
-f *filename*	Specifies the file on which to perform an operation
-v	Specifies verbose output
-p	Retains file modes and ACLs
-t	Shows table of contents of specified tar file

```
#tar -xvf /dev/rmt0 /home/restoredir
```

This command will extract the files from the tape and place them in the directory /home/restoredir. It should be noted that by default, tar does not restore files with the ownership and permissions on the original files unless you use the -p option:

```
#tar -xvpf /dev/rmt0 /home/restoredir
```

Table 13.7 shows a list of common tar options that can be used as part of your backup procedures.

 tar—Creates an archive of UNIX directories or small filesystems.

Platform-specific Backup Utilities

There was once a time when almost every UNIX platform used the commands dump and restore to back up files from disk to a specified tape medium. As UNIX evolved and matured, each flavor of UNIX migrated to its own variant of the dump and restore commands. Table 13.8 shows some of the different commands you can use to back up your UNIX platforms. Note that for all but Linux, each program works at the filesystem level. Before you run the commands below, make sure to read the man page thoroughly for any additional commands, or to determine if it is recommended to unmount a filesystem or bring the system to single-user mode.

Table 13.9 gives examples of the same commands that need to be used when restoring data from backup media. Something that is common to all of these commands is the -i option, which allows for interactive restores. If

Table 13.8	**Platform-specific Backup Commands**	
Platform	Backup Method	Backup Command Example
AIX	`backup`	`backup -0 -u -f /dev/rmt0 /`
HPUX	`dump`	`dump 0df 6250 /dev/rmt/c0t0d0BEST /export/home`
	`vxdump` (Veritas filesystem)	`vxdump 0Bf 2097152 /dev/rmt/0m /mnt`
Linux	BRU-2000	BRU is actually GUI-driven
Solaris	`ufsdump`	`ufsdump 5fuv /dev/rmt/1 /dev/rdsk/c0t3d0s6`

you only need to capture a few files from the backup tape, the `-i` option allows you to navigate the directory structure on the tape and mark the files you wish to restore.

Using these commands is effective for a single system with an attached backup media device, or when backing up multiple systems to a single server. However, these commands fall short when you have a multi-vendor UNIX installation, or when you have to mange multiple backup servers to provide enough backup resources to effectively back up your environment. It should also be noted that almost all native UNIX backup utilities need to be configured in `cron` to run your backup schedule. Use `cron`, coupled with changes to the command line of each command, to provide you with your backup schedule for each day of the week.

While there are a number of vendor backup packages that can help you manage large amounts of data and multi-vendor UNIX platforms, they can be very expensive to install on all of your UNIX systems. One alternative is the freeware package *Amanda,* which provides multi-platform backups and support for a wide array of backup media devices.

Table 13.9	**Platform-specific Restore Commands**	
Platform	Restore Method	Restore Command Example
AIX	`restore`	`restore -i -f/dev/rmt0`
HPUX	`restore`	`restore -i /dev/rmt/c0t0d0`
	`vxrestore`	`vxrestore -i /dev/rmt/0m`
Linux	BRU-2000	BRU is GUI-driven
Solaris	`ufsrestore`	`ufsrestore -i /dev/rmt/1`

Multi-platform Backups Using Amanda

A very robust and powerful multi-vendor UNIX backup platform is the Advanced Maryland Automated Network Disk Archiver (known as Amanda), a project at the University of Maryland. Amanda will also support Windows platforms if you have SAMBA installed in your infrastructure. Information about this software package can be found at `http://www` `.cs.umd.edu/projects/amanda/amanda.html`. The latest distribution of the Amanda software can be downloaded from `ftp://ftp` `.amanda.org/pub/amanda`.

Once you've downloaded the distribution, you will need to compile and distribute the binaries for each UNIX platform you wish to back up, as well as install the software on the server(s) to which your backup media is attached. Amanda uses a combination of the `tar` command with `gzip` compression to perform backups. A central server is configured and remotely manages a list of servers that you define. You will need to create a trust relationship between the Amanda clients and the server for the UID that is responsible for running the backups. In almost every case, you will use the user `operator` to run the backups, and you will need to create an `.rhosts` file in `/home/operator` that contains the following:

```
#
#sample .rhosts file
#
backup.sniglets.com      operator
```

This will allow Amanda to use `rsh` to initiate the backup process on each remote system. Once the `operator` user is configured, you are ready to begin configuring and using Amanda. Some of the more frequently used Amanda programs are shown in Table 13.10.

Once you've installed the program, you will need to configure the `amanda.conf` file to reflect your infrastructure. While each line of

Table 13.10	Commonly Used Amanda Commands
Command	Purpose
`amdump`	Performs a backup using Amanda
`amlabel`	Writes valid label to backup media so it can be catalogued by Amanda
`amrestore`	Extracts files from an Amanda tape
`amcheck`	Verifies the correct media is mounted and available
`amadmin`	Administers interface to Amanda

amanda.conf is well-commented, there are a few lines to pay special attention to. Please note that for clarity, we've assigned line numbers to the right of the amanda.conf file. You can define, using mailto, either a list of users or an email alias for users who are to receive Amanda reports and error messages.

```
#                                                              Line 0
# amanda.conf - sample Amanda configuration file.  This is the actual config
#              file in use at CS.UMD.EDU.
#
# If your configuration is called, say, "csd", then this file normally goes
# in /etc/amanda/csd/amanda.conf.
#

org "Sniglets Support (EE)"  # your organization name for reports
mailto "amanda"              # the mailing list for operators at your site
Line 10
dumpuser "operator"     # the user to run dumps under

inparallel 15           # maximum dumpers that will run in parallel
netusage  900           # maximum net bandwidth for Amanda, in KB per sec

dumpcycle 58 days # weeks     # the number of days in the normal dump
cycle
tapecycle 58 # tapes    # the number of tapes in rotation
```

The dumpcycle and tapecycle variables allow you to define your backup schedule and how you rotate your tapes. The physical tapes used in your rotation will be defined in the tapelist file, which will be discussed later.

```
bumpsize 10 MB          # minimum savings (threshold) to bump level 1 -> 2
bumpdays     2          # minimum days at each level
bumpmult     2          # threshold = bumpsize * (level-1)**bumpmult
etimeout -10800         # estimated timeout - 3 hours - for gtrep
# maxdumps     2

#tapedev "0"            #                                      Line 20
#tpchanger "chg-scsi" # the tape-changer glue script
#changerfile "/usr/local/amanda/sniglets/hpsurestore"
```

Be sure that you change the tapedev variable at line 23 to reflect the backup hardware that is attached to your server. You will also need to define the tapetype, on line 24, which is the media used in your hardware. The amlabel command requires you to label each media you use, and the labelstr variable, line 25, defines the range of valid strings (here, SNIG0—SNIG99). You should also take time to configure the holdingdisk variable, as Amanda has the ability to temporarily store backups on disk should there be a problem with your backup hardware. This helps prevent lost backups, and provides additional security for your users' files.

```
tapedev "/dev/rmt/1un"  # or use the (no-rewind!) tape device directly

tapetype DLT    # what kind of tape it is (see tapetypes below)
labelstr "^SNIG[0-9][0-9]*$"    # label constraint regex: all tapes must
match

holdingdisk hd1 {
        comment "main holding disk"
        directory "/home/backup/sniglets"
        use 8000 Mb
        chunksize 2Gb                        #                           Line 30
        }
```

Amanda allows you to configure the location of your logs, using the `in-fofile`, `logfile`, and `indexdir` variables, found on lines 31–33.

```
# Amanda needs a few MB of disk space for the log and debug files,
# as well as a database.  This stuff can grow large, so the conf directory
# isn't usually appropriate.  We use /usr/adm.  Create an amanda directory
# under there.  You need a separate infofile and logfile for each
# configuration, so create subdirectories for each conf and put the files
# there.  Specify the filenames below.

infofile "/var/amanda/logs/sniglets/curinfo"     # database filename
logfile  "/var/amanda/logs/sniglets/log"  # log filename
indexdir "/var/amanda/logs/sniglets/index"
```

Next you will need to define all the media types you have attached to your backup server, which begin after line 40. Amanda comes configured with a wide array of standard media types, and our `amanda.conf` file has been edited for brevity. As you can see, for the type DLT, Amanda understands a great deal about each media. Amanda uses this information when planning backups so as to optimize time and available media resources.

```
# tapetypes                                            Line 40
#
# Define the type of tape you use here, and use it in "tapetype" above.
# Some typical types of tapes are included here.  The tapetype tells amanda
# how many MB will fit on the tape, how big the filemarks are, and how
# fast the tape device is.
#
# For completeness Amanda should calculate the inter-record gaps too, but it
# doesn't.  For EXABYTE and DAT tapes, this is ok.  Anyone using 9 tracks
# for amanda and need IRG calculations?  Drop me a note if so.
```

```
define tapetype DLT {                      #                       Line 50
    comment "DLT tape drives"
    length 35000 mbytes          # 40 Gig tapes
    filemark 2000 kbytes         # I don't know what this means
    speed 2 mbytes
}
```

Finally, you can define the parameters of each backup by defining a dumptype (line 56), for each type of disk partition you have in your infrastructure. In this example, a different dumptype has been defined for root filesystems, line 91, and user filesystems, line 86. As you can see, the only difference is in the priority, with user filesystems being given higher priority.

Amanda will attempt to complete high-priority jobs first so that in the event of a lack of resources, or other problems, the most important files will be completed first.

```
# dumptypes
#
# These are referred to by the disklist file.  The dumptype specifies
# certain "options" for dumping including:
#                                                              Line 60
#       compress-fast  - (default) compress on the client using fast algorithm
#       compress-best  - compress using the best (and slowest) algorithm
#       no-compress    - don't compress the dump output
#       record         - (default) record the dump in /etc/dumpdates
#       no-record      - don't record the dump, for testing
#       no-hold        - don't go to the holding disk, good for dumping
#                        the holding disk partition itself
#       skip-full      - skip the disk when a level 0 is due, to allow
#                        full backups outside amanda, eg when the machine
#
#
#                        is in single-user mode
#       skip-incr      - skip the disk when the level 0 is NOT due (This
#                        is used in archive configurations, where only full
#                        dumps are done and the tapes saved.)
#       no-full        - do a level 1 every night (This can be used, for
#                        example, for small root filesystems that only change
#                        slightly relative to a site-wide prototype.  Amanda
#                        then backs up just the changes.)
#                                                              Line 80
# Also, the dumptype specifies the priority level, where "low", "medium," and
# "high" are the allowed levels.  These are only really used when Amanda has
# no tape to write to because of some error.  In that "degraded mode", as
# many incrementals as will fit on the holding disk are done, higher
# priority first, to insure the important disks are dumped first.
```

```
define dumptype user {
    comment "User partitions on slow machines"
    options no-compress
    priority high
}                                              #                              Line 90
define dumptype root {
    comment "Root partitions without compression"
    options no-compress
    priority low
}
```

With your `amanda.conf` file complete, you can now turn to defining which systems should be included in your backup schedule. Defining systems and disk partitions to include in your backups is very simple, as shown in the example `disklist` file.

```
#
# disklist for Amanda on the Sniglets machines.
#
#
earth.sniglets.com               /                          root
earch.sniglets.com               /usr                       root
earth.sniglets.com               /export/home1              user

mars.sniglets.com                /export/home2              user
```

All that needs to be defined is the system, the filesystem to be backed up, and the type of backup to be performed as defined by the `dumptype`. With your `amanda.conf` and `disklist` complete, you can now schedule the `amdump` command and Amanda will manage your backups for you.

 Amanda is a cross-platform backup/restore utility that is freely available. It has more capabilities than the backup/restore tools included with most UNIX variants.

USING THE WINDOWS 2000 BACKUP UTILITY

The Windows 2000 backup utility was custom developed for Windows 2000 by Veritas Software. You can launch the Windows 2000 backup utility using the following sequence: from the `Start` menu → `Programs` → `Accessories` → `System Tools` → `Backup`; or, you can run `ntbackup` from the `Start` menu's → `Run` dialog box or a command prompt. The Windows 2000 backup utility is shown in Figure 13.1.

Windows 2000 backup can be used to perform enterprise-wide backups. Administrators usually perform backups, but you should keep the following in mind when planning your backups:

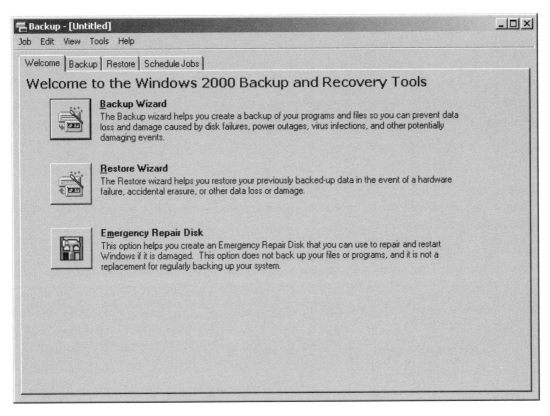

Figure 13.1 Windows 2000 backup utility.

- Users that are members of the `Administrators,` `Server Op-erators,` and `Backup Operators` groups can perform backup and restore operations on all files and folders.
- Users are permitted to back up and restore their own files and folders, as well as files and folders to which they are explicitly granted access in the file or folder permissions.

Every network environment is different. There is no single solution that will work for everyone. Depending on your company's needs, the resources available, and the size of your network, the backup strategies will differ. We hope that you will use this section to decide what will work best for you, and to plan an effective backup strategy for your network. This section will describe the different backup types and strategies, backup media, backup schedules, and how to perform a simple backup and restore.

Backup Types and Strategies

The first thing you need to understand is the different backup types that Windows 2000 supports. Table 13.11 details the five backup types available.

 Whenever a file or folder is modified, the archive attribute is set. The Windows 2000 backup utility examines the archive attribute to determine the backup state of a file or folder.

Now that you know what types of backups are available, you should decide what files and folders you want to back up. You should, obviously, back

Table 13.11	Windows 2000 Backup Types
Backup Type	Description
Copy	Copies all selected files and folders, but does not mark the file or folder as having been backed up (the archive attribute is not cleared). Copy backups are useful if you want to get a snapshot of data between regular backups because the archive attribute is not modified.
Daily	Copies all selected files and folders that were modified the same day the daily backup is performed. The files and folders are not marked as having been backed up.
Differential	Copies all selected files and folders that were modified since the last normal or incremental backup was performed. Differential backups do not mark the files or folders as having been backed up. Differential backups are useful in combination with normal backups because it is only necessary to restore the most recent normal backup and the most recent differential backup to get a complete restore.
Incremental	Copies all selected files and folders that have been modified since the last normal or incremental backup, and the files and folders are marked as having been backed up (the archive attribute is cleared). Incremental backups typically require less space than differential backups, but when used in combination with normal backups, it is necessary to restore the most recent normal backup, as well as all subsequent incremental backups, to get a complete restore.
Normal	Copies all selected files and folders and marks the file or folder as having been backed up. Normal backups can consume vast amounts of storage space.

up those files and folders that contain critical data. You should also back up the Registry of each workstation and the Active Directory database. In addition to your critical data, you could also back up your users' data stored on servers and their workstations.

 To make backing up data stored on individual workstations easier, you can implement a policy that specifies a single location on those workstations that is backed up, such as C:\Data. Whatever location you choose should be shared to the network using an appropriate share name, such as Backup.

A final consideration is choosing between network or local backup jobs. Table 13.12 details the differences between network backups and local backups.

You should consider the above information when deciding how to back up your data. Sometimes a hybrid of local and network backups is preferable; other times it is desirable to rely only on one or the other. One suggestion is to schedule local backups that create files on a network share, and then back up that data to tape from your backup server. The decision is ultimately up to you, as only you know what will work best in your environment.

Table 13.12	Network vs. Local Backups
Backup Type	Description
Network Backup	Network backups can consolidate data from multiple computers into a single backup job. This allows the administrator to back up multiple workstations from a single system using a single backup device. This is useful when your local systems do not have a backup device and you wish to consolidate your clients' data into a single job. You cannot, however, back up the Registry or Active Directory database over the network. Network backups will also generate a lot of network traffic, so they should be performed when demand for network bandwidth is low.
Local Backup	Local backups are much more difficult to administer than network backups. Often you will need to visit each machine you wish to perform a local backup on. However, local backup jobs can back up the Registry and Active Directory database and will not congest your network.

Selecting Backup Media

Windows 2000 backup provides two options for backup media, tape and files. Each media type has specific characteristics that may make it more desirable than the other for different backup jobs. Table 13.13 describes the two media types in detail.

It is your decision as to which type of backup media to employ. Tape, however, is the most widely accepted medium at this time.

Performing a Simple Backup

Now that you have the necessary background information, we can perform a simple backup. We are going to back up some local and network data to an attached tape device. You should make sure the device is included on the Windows 2000 hardware compatibility list, installed in the system, and that the driver is loaded. Also ensure that there is a blank tape in the drive. Refer to the following steps to complete the backup:

1. Launch the Windows 2000 backup utility from the `Start` menu by choosing `Programs` → `Accessories` → `System Tools` → `Backup`. You can also execute `ntbackup` from the `Start` menu's → `Run` dialog or from a command prompt. You will see the screen in Figure 13.1.
2. Click the `Backup Wizard` to start the backup process. Click `Next` on the welcome screen to display the `What to Back Up` selection screen.

Table 13.13	Windows 2000 Backup Media Types
Media Type	Description
Tape	Tape is less expensive than most other removable media types. Tape also provides a very high capacity, often as high as 80GB per tape (using compression). However, since tape is a magnetic medium, it has a limited lifespan and can deteriorate over time, plus it is susceptible to environmental factors such as humidity and temperature.
Files	You can back up your data directly to a file, and that file(s) can be stored on any type of removable media you desire, such as CD-ROMs or ZIP disks. Windows 2000 places a `*.bkf` extension on files that are created. As mentioned earlier, local backups can be stored as files on a network server and then transferred to removable media by an administrator.

Figure 13.2
Items to Back Up
selection screen.

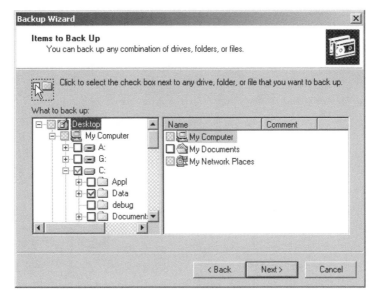

3. We are going to select specific files and folders to back up. Click the middle choice, `Back up selected files, drives, or network data`, and click `Next` to continue. The `Items to Back Up` selection screen in Figure 13.2 is displayed.

4. Select a specific folder on your local machine and one from the network and click `Next` to continue. The `Where to Store the Backup` selection screen will be displayed.

5. We are going to select our tape device, a `4mm DDS` drive. Make your selection and click `Next` to continue. The confirmation screen in Figure 13.3 will be displayed.

Figure 13.3
Backup
confirmation
screen.

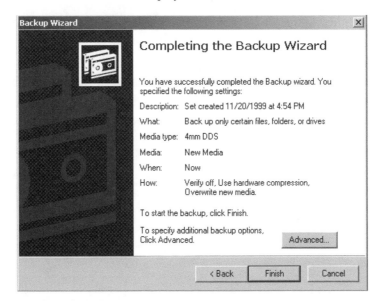

Figure 13.4
Type of Backup
selection screen.

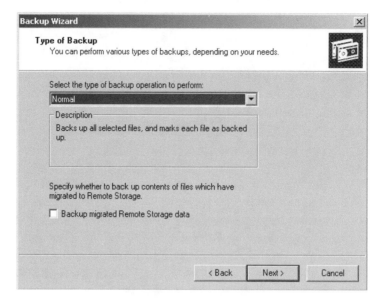

6. We are now going to configure the advanced options. Click the Advanced button to configure the advanced options. The Type of Backup selection screen in Figure 13.4 will be displayed.

7. We are going to select a Normal backup. Make your selection and click Next to continue. The How to Back Up selection screen in Figure 13.5 will be displayed.

8. We are going to stick with the defaults. Make your selections and click Next to continue. The Media Options configuration screen in Figure 13.6 will be displayed.

Figure 13.5
How to Back Up
selection screen.

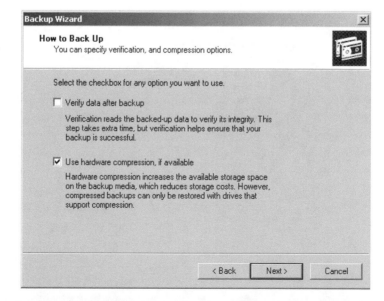

Figure 13.6
Media Options
configuration
screen.

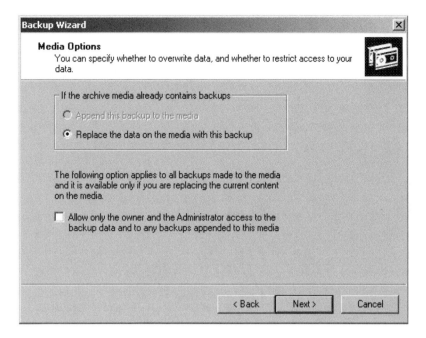

9. Again, we are going to keep the defaults. Make any changes you wish and click `Next` to continue. The `Backup Label` configuration screen will be displayed.

10. Enter the label names you desire and click `Next` to continue. The `When to Back Up` configuration screen will be displayed.

11. You can run the job now or select a later date and/or time. We are going to run the job now. Make any changes you wish and click `Next` to continue. The final confirmation screen is displayed.

12. Review the information and click `Finish` when you are ready.

13. If the tape in the drive is new, you will be prompted to prepare the new media for use. Click `Yes` to do so. Windows 2000 backup will take a few minutes to prepare the tape.

14. Once the new tape is prepared, the backup job will begin. You will see the `Backup Progress` window shown in Figure 13.7 while the backup is running.

15. Once the backup job is finished, you will see the report window in Figure 13.8.

16. To view a detailed summary of the backup job, click the `Report` button; otherwise, click `Close` to complete the job.

Now that you have prepared and executed a single job, we can move on to scheduling a recurring job. The next section will detail scheduling backups using the Windows 2000 backup utility.

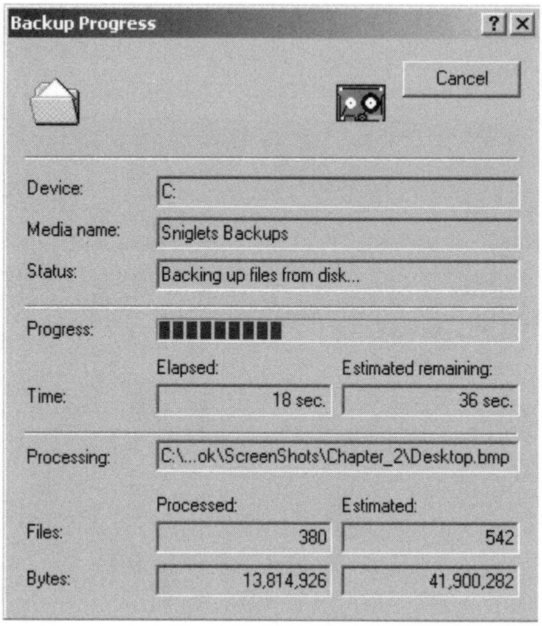

Figure 13.7
Windows 2000
Backup Progress
window.

Scheduling Backups

Windows 2000 backup integrates with the Task Scheduler so that you can create backup jobs that will run automatically, on a schedule that you set. This is very beneficial, as you can configure your backups to run unattended at times when system and network demand is minimal. This section will walk you through scheduling a weekly backup of the same data we backed up in the previous section. The steps below detail this process:

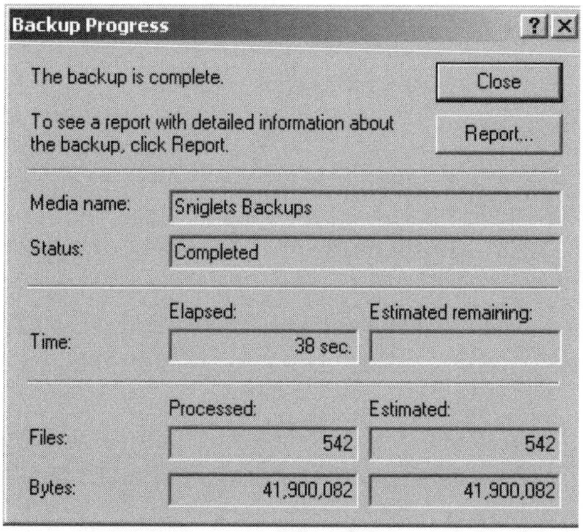

Figure 13.8
Windows 2000
backup
completion
window.

1. Launch the Windows 2000 backup utility as follows: from the `Start` menu → `Programs` → `Accessories` → `System Tools` → `Backup`. You can also execute `ntbackup` from the `Start` menu's Run dialog or from a command prompt. You will see the screen in Figure 13.1.

2. Click the `Schedule Jobs` tab and you will see a screen similar to the one in Figure 13.11.

3. Click the `Add Job` button to start the `Backup Wizard`.

4. Click `Next` on the welcome screen to continue. You will be presented with the `What to Back Up` selection screen.

5. Make your choice and click `Next` to continue. We are going to select specific files and folders, so choose the middle option. You will see the `Items to Back Up` selection screen from Figure 13.2.

6. As before, make your selections and click `Next` to continue. You will be presented with the `Where to Store the Backup` selection screen.

7. Select your media type and which media to use and click `Next` to continue. Choose to use the media we created earlier. You will see the `Type of Backup` selection screen from Figure 13.4.

8. As before, we are selecting a `Normal` backup. Make your selection and click Next to continue. You will see the `How to Back Up` selection screen from Figure 13.5.

9. As before, we will stick with the defaults. Make any changes you wish and click `Next` to continue. The `Media Options` selection screen from Figure 13.6 will be displayed.

10. This time we will select to `Append this backup to the media`, since we already have one backup job stored on it. Click `Next` to continue. The `Backup Label` configuration screen will be displayed.

11. Set the labels however you desire and click `Next` to continue. You will be presented with the `Set Account Information` configuration screen.

12. Enter a username with backup rights (`Administrator`, `Server Operator`, or `Backup Operator`) and the appropriate password (twice). Click `OK` when you are ready to continue. The `When to Back Up` configuration screen in Figure 13.9 will be displayed.

13. Enter a name for your backup job and click the `Set Schedule` button to choose when to run the job. The `Schedule Job` configuration screen in Figure 13.10 will be displayed.

14. Choose the dates and times to run the job. We selected to run the job every `Sun`(day) at `11:00 PM`. When you are done, click `OK` to return to the `When to Back Up` configuration screen.

Figure 13.9
When to Back Up
configuration
screen.

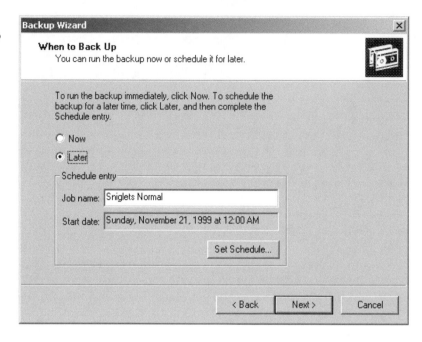

Figure 13.10
Schedule Job
configuration
screen.

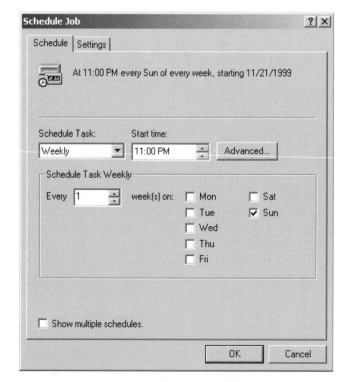

15. Click `Next` to continue. The confirmation screen will be displayed.

16. Review the information and click `Finish` when you are done. You will be returned to the `Schedule Jobs` screen, and the backup jobs will be shown on the appropriate days, as you can see in Figure 13.11.

You can now create more jobs, such as incremental backups, to round out your automated backup plan. We will next move on to performing a simple restore of the data we backed up earlier.

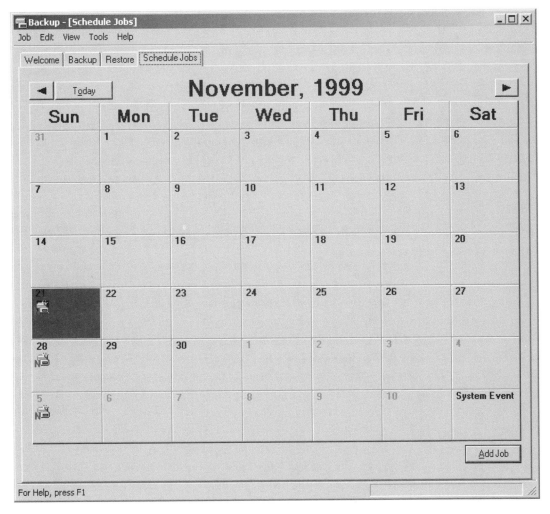

Figure 13.11 Schedule jobs screen with new backup jobs shown.

Performing a Simple Restore

The final task to master is restoring data. In this section, we will assume that the data we backed up earlier has been lost (you might want to delete the data to "enhance" the experience) and we will restore it from the tape we created previously. Follow the steps below to complete the restore:

1. Launch the Windows 2000 backup utility as follows: from the `Start` menu → `Programs` → `Accessories` → `System Tools` → `Backup`. You can also execute `ntbackup` from `Start` menu's Run dialog or from a command prompt. You will see the screen in Figure 13.1.

2. Click the `Restore Wizard` to start the restore process. Click `Next` on the welcome screen to display the `What to Restore` selection screen in Figure 13.12.

3. Select the tape we created earlier, and then the data sets from the tape. When you are done, click `Next` to continue. The confirmation screen in Figure 13.13 will be displayed.

4. We are now going to configure the advanced options. Click the `Advanced` button to configure the advanced options. The `Where to Restore` selection screen will be displayed.

5. We are going to restore our files to their original locations, but you can also choose to restore the files to an alternate location or to a

Figure 13.12
What to Restore
selection screen.

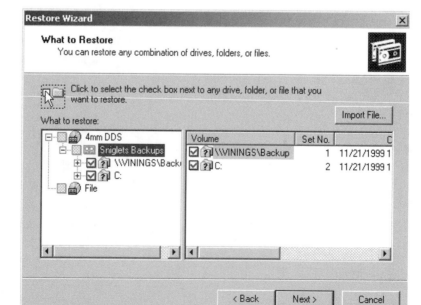

Figure 13.13
Restore
confirmation
screen.

single folder. Choose your destination and click `Next` to continue. The `How to Restore` selection screen in Figure 13.14 will be displayed.

6. Choose how you want to restore the files and click `Next` to continue. We are going to use the default selection to not overwrite files. The

Figure 13.14
How to Restore
selection screen.

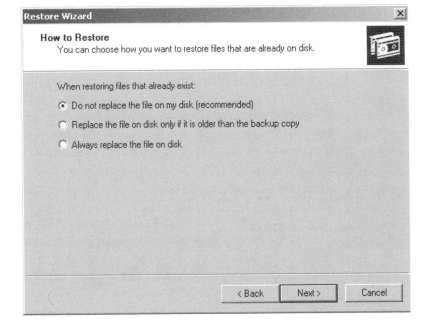

Figure 13.15
Advanced
Restore Options
selection screen.

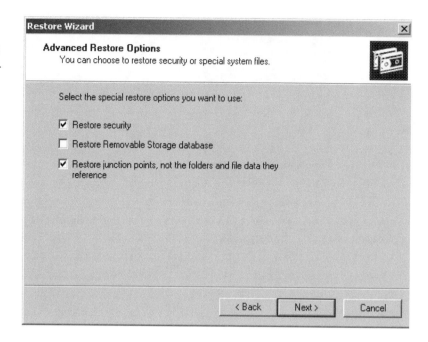

Advanced Restore Options selection screen in Figure 13.15 will be displayed.

7. We are going to leave the defaults selected. If you wish to make changes, do so, and click Next to continue. The final confirmation screen is displayed.

8. Review the information on the confirmation screen and click Finish to continue.

9. The restore job will run just like the backup job and will display a report window when it is finished. When the job is done, you can close the report window.

This should provide you with everything you need to get started with backups. For more detailed information, you should read the Windows 2000 help files, or obtain a copy of the Windows 2000 Resource Kit.

USING WINDOWS 2000 TO BACK UP UNIX

There are two basic methods to back up your UNIX systems from a Windows 2000 system. The first method involves purchasing a third-party backup utility, which includes a client that will allow the UNIX system to be backed up from a Windows 2000 server. Veritas BackupExec includes such a client, and other vendors offer similar solutions. The third-party solution, of course, requires the purchase of server and client software and, depending on the size of your network, can become very costly. The second, and much more economical, solution is to install and configure SAMBA on your UNIX systems. Using SAMBA, you can create shares on your UNIX systems that the Windows 2000 server can connect to. You should refer to Chapter 8, "Distributed Filesystem," for instructions on how to install and configure SAMBA shares on your UNIX systems. Once you have installed SAMBA and created shares for the data you wish to back up, you can complete the backups from your Windows 2000 server using the instructions provided earlier in this chapter.

USING UNIX TO BACK UP WINDOWS 2000

You can back up your Windows 2000 systems from a UNIX system. This also involves using SAMBA, and can be more complicated than backing up UNIX systems from Windows 2000. However, this section will provide the framework necessary for you to get started. First, you should refer to Chapter 8 to get SAMBA installed and configured on the UNIX system from which you wish to run backups. Once SAMBA is running, you can use the smbtar command to back up Windows 2000 shares from your UNIX system. Please keep in mind that you should use a backup system, such as Amanda, to manage the backup jobs on the UNIX system. The syntax for the smbtar command is detailed here:

```
smbtar -s server [-p password] [-x service] [-X] [-d
directory] [-u user] [-b blocksize] [-N filename] [-i]
[-r] [-l log_level] [-v] filenames
```

Table 13.14 describes the smbtar options discussed above.

You can integrate the use of smbtar into whatever UNIX backup solution you decide to implement. While this is not a catchall solution, it should be sufficient for most organizations and provide you with the background information necessary to develop an efficient backup strategy.

smbtar—SAMBA command to create tar files from Windows 2000 systems.

USING THIRD-PARTY BACKUP UTILITIES

In addition to the Windows 2000 backup utility, there are also third-party solutions available. Veritas Software provides a commercial package, BackupExec, which provides many features that the Windows 2000 backup utility does not. One particularly significant advantage of BackupExec is its ability to use a tape library/autoloader instead of a single drive. By providing library

Table 13.14	`smbtar` **Options**
Option	Description
`-s server`	Specifies the SMB/CIFS server from which the desired share is served. This is the machine you are backing up.
`-p password`	Specifies the password used to access the share.
`-x service`	Specifies the share to connect to on the specified server. The default is `backup`.
`-X`	Enables Exclude mode. Used to exclude a file from `tar` `create` or `restore`.
`-d directory`	Specifies a directory to change to before beginning a backup or restore operation.
`-u user`	Specifies the user ID to connect to the share with. The default is the current UNIX login name.
`-b blocksize`	Specifies the `tar` file block size. The default is 20. You should refer to the `tar(1)` man page for more details.
`-N filename`	Specifies that only files newer than `filename` should be backed up. This can be used with a log file to implement incremental backups.
`-i`	Enables Incremental mode. Files are backed up only if the archive bit is set. The archive bit is reset after each file is backed up.
`-r`	Enables Restore mode. Files will be restored to the share from the `tar` file.
`-l log_level`	Specifies the log/debug level to be used. This corresponds to the `-d` flag of `smbclient(1)`; you should refer to the `smbclient` man page for more details.
`-v`	Enables Verbose mode.
`filenames`	Specifies the files and folders to be backed up.

support, a truly unattended backup solution and rotation schedule can be developed. Unfortunately, the current release of BackupExec runs only under Windows NT 4.0, but there is a Windows 2000 version scheduled for release sometime next year. We were unable to obtain an evaluation copy of the new product; hence, we cannot provide a great deal of detail on its operation.

Aside from providing greater functionality and capabilities, most third-party backup utilities also allow you to back up Windows, Macintosh, and UNIX systems from your Windows 2000 system. This added benefit will allow you to deploy a single backup solution. Other software vendors, such as Computer Associates and Hewlett Packard, also provide effective third-party backup utilities.

Summary

Backup and restore operations are essential parts of good system administration. Though time-consuming, if done correctly, they will certainly save time in the long run. In this chapter, we discussed the creation and implementation of a backup/restore system.

BUILDING A BACKUP SCHEDULE

Determining what you should include in your backup strategy, and when you should back up, can be difficult. Infinite storage space (and time) would make it possible to back up everything, everyday. However, most of us have to rely on selective backups on incremental schedules. When selecting what to back up, you need to consider the following categories of data:

- System files.
- Off-the-shelf software.
- Replicated data.
- Sensitive data.

Incremental backups are necessary to balance backup needs with available storage space. Remember that a restore may require multiple volumes to perform.

UNIX BACKUPS

The simplest backup tool in UNIX is the `tar` command. Though not designed for large backup routines, it is excellent for quickly creating portable archives of directories or even partitions. Each UNIX variant comes with some form of backup utility. Tables 13.8 and 13.9 list the variant-dependent backup routines. In this chapter, we focused on the cross-platform Amanda utility, a very robust and powerful multi-vendor UNIX backup system, and a project at the University of Maryland. Amanda will also support Windows platforms if you have SAMBA installed in your infrastructure.

WINDOWS 2000 BACKUPS

The Windows 2000 backup utility was custom developed for Windows 2000 by Veritas Software. Windows 2000 backup can be used to perform enterprise-wide backups. Table 13.11 lists the different types of backups available. Depending on your company's needs, the resources available, and the size of your network, the backup strategies will differ. Windows 2000 backup integrates with the Task Scheduler so that you can create backup jobs that will run automatically. This is very beneficial, as you can configure your backups to run unattended at times when system and network demand is minimal.

PERFORMANCE MONITORING

UNIX

Key Components

UNIX Performance Tools

`vmstat`

`netstat`

Performance Tuning

WINDOWS 2000

Key Components

Windows 2000 Performance Tools

Performance Logs and Alerts

Performance Monitoring

Let's face it, our society is consumed by performance. We have turbo cars, mega bass sound, ultra SCSI, and Gigahertz chips. There is a constant struggle to get the last bit of performance from all of our appliances. As much as we would like to provide performance-monitoring advice on all of your needs, this chapter will be limited to Windows 2000 and UNIX workstations/servers. We'll first cover the key components/tools of all Windows 2000 and UNIX systems that most affect performance. The discussion then will switch to UNIX and Windows 2000 tools.

Performance monitoring and tuning are essential parts of system administration. They are as difficult as they are important. This chapter requires a solid understanding of the material covered in previous chapters. The assessment of system performance is an ongoing effort. Remember, however, that performance monitoring *must* be part of the workstation/server installation process. It is very important to identify trends and potential bottlenecks before they become a painful reality for you and your customers. UNIX and Windows 2000 provide multiple tools that allow real-time and remote logging of performance statistics. The time expended in installing and configuring these tools will greatly aid in providing systems that perform to the expectations of everyone.

Key Components

The performance of all systems can be traced to the following four main components:

- Processor.
- Memory.
- Disk.
- Network interface.

The failure of any one of these components can bring a system to a grinding halt. This section examines each component and provides suggestions on make changes to hardware or procedures that may impact performance.

 It is good practice to schedule jobs to maximize system resources, eliminate jobs not required (screen savers, browsers, etc.), and increase or decrease a job's priority.

PROCESSOR

The processor is the brain of a system. The more MHz the better to provoke "MHz envy" in your system administrator peers. Upgrading to a faster processor is the "knee jerk" reaction to a slow machine. Performance problems attributed to a slow processor will be a small minority of all performance problems. Most applications (word processors, email clients, spreadsheets, Web browsers) utilized in a corporate setting can be easily handled by modern processors. Applications that are computationally intensive (graphics and modeling) are the types of programs that benefit from a faster processor. If the processor is the problem, then the following actions can be taken to increase performance:

- Upgrade to a faster processor.
- Add additional processors (workstation must support additional processors).

MEMORY

Random access memory (RAM) is usually what most people think about when you mention memory. Advanced operating systems like Window 2000 and UNIX also utilize Level 1 and 2 caches and a paging/swap file. The memory manager is responsible for moving programs and data between memory components. The memory manager is beyond the scope of this book.

RAM

You can never have enough of it. RAM is relatively cheap, so always buy as much as you can afford. A single user workstation should have a minimum of 128MB. Servers should have at least 256MB. Insufficient RAM will be one of the biggest performance bottlenecks of the four components covered.

Cache

There are two levels of cache associated with modern processors (Level 1 and Level 2). Level 1 cache is contained on the processor, is very fast, and is usually split between data and instructions. Level 1 cache is loaded from Level 2 cache. Level 2 cache is attached to the processor via a dedicated bus and is loaded from RAM. Level 2 cache is faster than RAM and varies in size from 128KB to 4MB. Both operating systems are optimized to take advantage of cache memory.

Virtual Memory

Virtual memory consists of a special file on disk that is used by the memory manager to increase the amount of memory available to the system to run programs larger than the physical amount of RAM contained in the system. The memory manager breaks memory into pages and loads only those parts of the program currently required. When physical memory is exhausted, the memory manager will transfer the least recently accessed pages to the paging (Windows 2000) or swap (UNIX) file. The memory manager keeps track of all memory pages and transparently moves programs/data between disk and RAM.

If virtual memory utilization is continually greater than 95 percent on a workstation/server, then the following actions can be taken to increase performance:

- Increase the size of the paging or swap file.
- Upgrade Level 2 cache to a larger size. Level 2 cache should be as large as possible for database servers.
- Add additional RAM.
- Add additional disks with paging/swap file space.

DISK

The disk system is one of the most important parts of the system. It stores the operating system, applications, and data. It must be able to transfer this information from disk to memory quickly and reliably. The disk system is made up of a disk controller and hard drive. The most popular controllers are EIDE/ATA, Ultra DMA, and different levels of SCSI. EIDE/ATA and Ultra DMA are limited to a maximum of four internal devices. SCSI supports from 8 to 16 devices that can be a mixture of internal or external drives. Make sure the controller and hard drive are compatible.

Redundant Array of Inexpensive Disks (RAID) is a technology that increases the fault tolerance and speed of storing data to disk. There are multiple levels of RAID that provide different fault tolerances for your data. Disks are going to fail sooner rather than later. RAID is a solution that will not lose data or make a filesystem unavailable when a disk fails. RAID can be implemented in software or via dedicated hardware. RAID is implemented in SCSI storage arrays.

Storage Area Networks (SANs) disconnect the storage array from a server. SANs are private, high-speed networks between servers and storage arrays. Fibre Channel is the protocol utilized in a SAN. SANs provide transfer performance of up to 200MB/s and can have cable lengths up to 10 kilometers. SANs allow multiple servers to access the same storage array without putting traffic on the local area network (LAN).

 Servers that host email, Web servers, DNS, directory services, user files, or applications require RAID to preserve the integrity of that data.

If the disk system is the problem, then the following actions can be taken to increase performance:

- Upgrade the controller.
- Upgrade to faster disks.
- Defragment the disks.
- Stripe the disks.
- Distribute the load among the current disks.

NETWORK INTERFACE

The network interface card (NIC) is the hardware that allows your machine to access all the resources contained on your local network, intranet, and the Internet. It is important to have a fast and reliable connection to the network. Token ring, FDDI, ATM, and all the different speeds of Ethernet make up the majority of networks. If the NIC is the problem, then the following actions can be taken to increase performance:

- Upgrade the NIC.
- Add additional NICs and load-balancing software.
- Add a hardware load-balancing NIC.
- Upgrade the network.

UNIX Performance Tools

UNIX performance tools can be split into monitoring and tuning categories. The monitoring category includes commands that allow the system administrator to capture data on the performance of a workstation to a log file or to interactively monitor a workstation. Monitoring tools allow you to determine the "health" of a UNIX workstation and to pinpoint problems. Diagnosing performance problems on a UNIX workstation are never easy and not always obvious. Problem identification requires a logical examination of performance data for all major components of the workstation.

The tuning category provides commands that allow the system administrator or user to specify the priority of a job and to schedule jobs during off-peak hours. The tuning commands are useful in maintaining a "healthy" UNIX workstation. These commands can also be utilized to solve some performance problems.

This section is composed of two subsections. The first subsection reviews performance-monitoring commands available in UNIX. The second subsection will highlight tools provided with UNIX that allow system administrators to maximize the performance of workstations and servers.

UNIX MONITORING COMMANDS

This subsection contains UNIX commands to monitor the four major performance components outlined previously in this chapter. The commands covered in this subsection allow a system administrator to interactively monitor the utilization and performance of a UNIX workstation. The commands can be utilized in simple scripts to capture data to log files. It is important to take advantage of all the commands in this subsection to monitor the performance of a UNIX workstation. Successful performance monitoring requires a logical approach and an examination of all aspects of the affected system.

vmstat

vmstat provides statistics on processes, virtual memory, disk, interrupts, and CPU activity. CPU utilization and virtual memory monitoring are the primary uses for this command. Figure 14.1 is the output of the vmstat command on a Solaris 2.6 machine with one argument. vmstat will summarize activity every five seconds until the program is terminated. Make sure you check the man pages to determine at what rate the information for each column is being reported. The first line of output is a summary of activity since the system was booted. Ignore the first line. We will review the procs, memory, page, and cpu headings. Do not focus on a particular column of information and make a quick judgement. Consider all the data; things are not always what they first appear to be.

The procs area reports the number of processes in the run queue (r column), blocked for resources (b column), and runnable but swapped (w column). The run queue (r column) is a good indicator of whether your processor is fast enough to handle the system load or not. Run queues that exceed the number of processors by a factor of three or more for sustained intervals indicate that a faster processor is required. The blocked for resources column (b) is a good indicator of a slow disk subsystem. When the

```
duchess> vmstat 5
 procs      memory            page            disk          faults      cpu
 r b w   swap  free  re  mf pi po fr de sr s0 s2 s4 --   in   sy   cs us sy id
 0 0 0  13760  1232   0  41  9  1  1  0  0  1  1  2  0  186  972  295  3  5 92
 1 0 0 389608 43888   0  15  0  0  0  0  0  0  0  0  0  183  259  220 97  3  0
 1 0 0 389608 43920   0   0  0  0  0  0  0  0  0  0  0  140  114  122 99  1  0
 1 0 0 389608 43912   0   0  1  0  0  0  0  0  0  0  0  249  145  340 95  5  0
 1 0 0 389608 43904   0   0  0  0  0  0  0  0  0  0  0  141  146  132 98  2  0
 1 0 0 389608 43816   0  15  6  0  0  0  0  0  0  0  0  167  207  157 98  2  0
 1 0 0 389608 43752   0   0  0  0  0  0  0  5  0  2  0  176  146   98 98  2  0
 0 0 0 399120 53224   0   0  0  0  0  0  0  0  0  0  0  125  129   88 98  2  0
 0 0 0 401504 55600   0  44  0  3  3  0  0  1  0  0  0  128  865   85 96  4  0
 0 0 0 406256 60344   0  11  0  0  0  0  0  0  0  0  0  125  131   72 69  2 29
 0 0 0 413400 67456   0  15  0  0  0  0  0  0  0  0  0  125  103   69  0  1 99
 0 0 0 413400 67456   0   0  0  0  0  0  0  0  4  0  0  149  103   68  0  2 98
 0 0 0 413400 67456   0   0  0  0  0  0  0  0  0  0  0  122  100   56  0  1 99
 0 0 0 413400 67456   0   0  0  0  0  0 10  0  0  0  0  210  260   60  1  2 97
 0 0 0 413400 67464   0  15  0  0  0  0  0  0  1  0  0  126  129   59  0  1 99
 0 0 0 413400 67464   0  11  0  0  0  0  0  0  0  0  0  119  106   50  0  1 99
 0 0 0 413400 67464   0  32  0  0  0  0  0  0  0  0  0  136  192   88  1  1 98
^C
duchess>
```

Figure 14.1 vmstat on Solaris 2.6.

blocked number is equal to or greater than the number in the run queue for sustained intervals, the disk subsystem is a bottleneck and needs to be tuned, upgraded, or replaced. The runnable but swapped column (w) should remain at zero.

The memory heading reports the amount of free swap space (swap) and the size of the free list (free). The swap column gives you a good idea, of how much swap space is being utilized. The free column can be ignored. The memory heading for AIX, HPUX and BSD contains an active virtual pages (avm) column instead of a swap column. The avm column contains the number of pages that belong to a current process or a process that has run in the last 20 seconds. Multiply this number by the page size and you will have a good approximation of how much physical memory the system is utilizing.

The page heading has seven columns. You only need to concern yourself with page reclaims (re), kilobytes paged in (pi), kilobytes paged out (po), and pages scanned by the clock algorithm (sr). The page reclaims counter is the number of pages placed on the free list that were later required by a process and the data on the page was still valid for that process. The pi column reports the number of kilobytes paged in. All processes must be paged in when they start up, so this column is not vital. The po column reports on kilobytes paged out. When the value of po has sustained values of zero, life is good and your system has sufficient physical memory. The sr column reports the number of pages scanned by the clock algorithm. The pages have not been accessed recently by the owning process and are being evaluated for use by a different process or for different data for a running process. When the sr column has sustained periods of values in the hundreds, you are probably short of physical memory and need to add more.

Figure 14.2 shows the Red Hat Linux 6.0 output for vmstat with two arguments. All versions of vmstat interpret a single or dual argument in the same manner. The first argument is the reporting interval in seconds and the second argument is the number of intervals to be sampled. Our example has an interval of five seconds and will sample data for 15 intervals. The procs and cpu headings contain the same information as the previous examples of vmstat. The memory heading has four columns. You only need to concern yourself with the swpd column. This displays the amount of virtual memory used. A sustained level of twice the amount of physical memory in the system indicates that additional memory is required. The so column under the swap heading displays the amount of memory swapped to disk in kilobytes per second (KB/s). Values over 1000 KB/s sustained over long periods are indicative of a physical memory shortage (add RAM).

The cpu heading consists of the user time (us), system time (sy), and idle time (id). These columns are self-explanatory and should be used in conjunction with the previous information to pinpoint insufficient processor

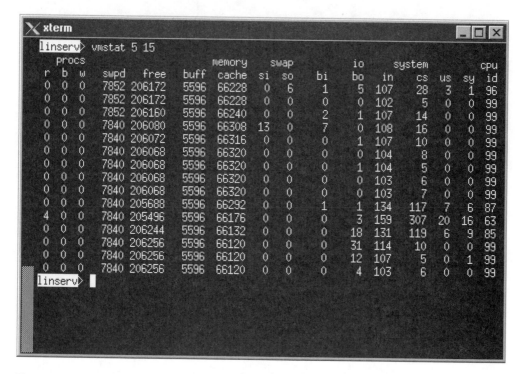

Figure 14.2 vmstat with two options on Red Hat Linux 6.0.

speed or physical memory. The `cpu` heading is standard on all versions of UNIX for `vmstat`.

`vmstat`—Provides statistics on processes, virtual memory, disk, interrupts, and CPU activity. CPU utilization and virtual memory monitoring are the primary uses for this command.

iostat

`iostat` provides statistics on disk, terminal, and CPU activity. This command should be utilized to monitor your disk subsystem. Figure 14.3 is the output of the `iostat` command on an HPUX machine with two arguments. `iostat` will summarize activity 10 times at five-second intervals. The columns report on kilobytes transferred per second (`bps`), number of seeks per second (`sps`), and milliseconds per average seek (`msps`). The important columns are `bps` and `msps`. Make sure the disk with the fastest `msps` has the most accessed data on it. On systems with identical disks, try to spread the load over all of the disks so the `bps` for each disk are close.

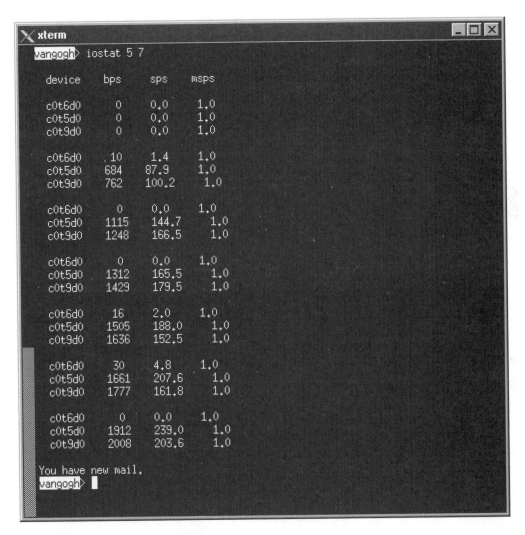

```
X xterm                                                    _ □ X
vangogh> iostat 5 7

     device    bps     sps     msps

     c0t6d0      0     0.0     1.0
     c0t5d0      0     0.0     1.0
     c0t9d0      0     0.0     1.0

     c0t6d0     10     1.4     1.0
     c0t5d0    684    87.9     1.0
     c0t9d0    762   100.2     1.0

     c0t6d0      0     0.0     1.0
     c0t5d0   1115   144.7     1.0
     c0t9d0   1248   166.5     1.0

     c0t6d0      0     0.0     1.0
     c0t5d0   1312   165.5     1.0
     c0t9d0   1429   179.5     1.0

     c0t6d0     16     2.0     1.0
     c0t5d0   1505   188.0     1.0
     c0t9d0   1636   152.5     1.0

     c0t6d0     30     4.8     1.0
     c0t5d0   1661   207.6     1.0
     c0t9d0   1777   161.8     1.0

     c0t6d0      0     0.0     1.0
     c0t5d0   1912   239.0     1.0
     c0t9d0   2008   203.6     1.0

You have new mail.
vangogh> █
```

Figure 14.3 iostat on HPUX 10.20.

`iostat`—Provides statistics on disk, terminal, and CPU activity. This command should be utilized to monitor your disk subsystem.

netstat

`netstat` provides information on network counters and parameters. We will only cover the switches to `netstat` that provide information on network performance.

The `netstat -i` command will show all configured interfaces and a total column for all interfaces. `netstat -I le0` will produce output for network interface card `le0`.

Figure 14.4 is the output produced on a Solaris 2.6 workstation with the `-i` switch and an interval of five seconds. The output contains a column for each interface and a total column combining all interface statistics. The first row contains the values since the machine was booted. Each succeeding row contains the activity that has taken place during the interval indicated on the command line. The output is very easy to understand. The `input` column shows incoming packets and the `output` column shows outbound packets. You can determine the percentage of collisions by substituting the values into the simple equation *colls * 100/ packets* for the `output` column.

Collisions occur when workstations are trying to transmit packets at the same time. Sustained collision percentages above seven percent indicate an overloaded network. You can also determine the percentage of error packets by substituting values into *errs * 100/ packets*. Values greater than one percent indicate a network problem. Call a professional to investigate.

```
duchess> netstat -i 5
       input       be0      output           input  (Total)    output
   packets errs  packets errs  colls   packets errs  packets errs  colls
   110012281 1   123712189 0   805968  114166013 1   127865921 0          805968
   62      0    58      0    0      94       0    90      0    0
   29      0    26      0    0      53       0    50      0    0
   138     0    1148    0    66     154      0    1164    0    66
   621     0    945     0    0      629      0    953     0    0
   174     0    295     0    0      182      0    303     0    0
   441     0    428     0    0      449      0    436     0    0
   43      0    29      0    0      51       0    37      0    0
   36      0    33      0    0      36       0    33      0    0
   73      0    70      0    0      97       0    94      0    0
   58      0    61      0    0      66       0    69      0    0
   83      0    84      0    0      83       0    84      0    0
   103     0    164     0    0      103      0    164     0    0
   80      0    81      0    0      104      0    105     0    0
   52      0    57      0    0      68       0    73      0    0
   69      0    52      0    0      77       0    60      0    0
   49      0    175     0    0      49       0    175     0    0
   701     0    1912    0    167    717      0    1928    0    167
   17      0    13      0    0      33       0    29      0    0
^C
duchess>
```

Figure 14.4 netstat with two options on Solaris 2.6.

```
X xterm                                                      _ □ X
linserv> netstat -ic
Kernel Interface table
Iface   MTU Met    RX-OK RX-ERR RX-DRP RX-OVR    TX-OK TX-ERR TX-DRP TX-OVR Flg
eth0    1500   0   361456      0      0      0   279128      0      0      0 BRU
lo      3924   0   197251      0      0      0   197251      0      0      0 LRU
Kernel Interface table
Iface   MTU Met    RX-OK RX-ERR RX-DRP RX-OVR    TX-OK TX-ERR TX-DRP TX-OVR Flg
eth0    1500   0   361458      0      0      0   279130      0      0      0 BRU
lo      3924   0   197251      0      0      0   197251      0      0      0 LRU
Kernel Interface table
Iface   MTU Met    RX-OK RX-ERR RX-DRP RX-OVR    TX-OK TX-ERR TX-DRP TX-OVR Flg
eth0    1500   0   361460      0      0      0   279132      0      0      0 BRU
lo      3924   0   197251      0      0      0   197251      0      0      0 LRU
Kernel Interface table
Iface   MTU Met    RX-OK RX-ERR RX-DRP RX-OVR    TX-OK TX-ERR TX-DRP TX-OVR Flg
eth0    1500   0   361464      0      0      0   279134      0      0      0 BRU
lo      3924   0   197251      0      0      0   197251      0      0      0 LRU
Kernel Interface table
Iface   MTU Met    RX-OK RX-ERR RX-DRP RX-OVR    TX-OK TX-ERR TX-DRP TX-OVR Flg
eth0    1500   0   361466      0      0      0   279136      0      0      0 BRU
lo      3924   0.  197251      0      0      0   197251      0      0      0 LRU
linserv> █
```

Figure 14.5 netstat on Red Hat Linux 6.0.

netstat is quite different under Linux. Executing netstat -ic outputs cumulative counters every second for all interfaces on the workstation until an interrupt is received. This version does not include collisions. Figure 14.5 contains sample output.

Table 14.1 contains the definition of each column in Figure 14.5. You can determine the percentage of errors, drops, or overruns for an interface by substituting values into *TX-ERR * 100 / TX-OK*. The same can be computed for packets received. To determine the collision rate, you will have to use the ifconfig command. ifconfig provides all the counters reported by netstat, as well as additional information, including collisions. Figure 14.6 is the output from the ifconfig -e command.

---

netstat—Provides information on network counters and parameters. The netstat -i command will show all configured interfaces and a total column for all interfaces. netstat -I le0 will produce output for network interface card le0.

Table 14.1	`netstat` Column Heading Definitions
Heading	Definition
`Iface`	Interface
`MTU`	Maximum Transmission Unit Number is in bytes and default for Ethernet is 1500
`Met`	Metric Default is zero Utilized by routing information protocol
`RX-OK/TX-OK`	Packets received/transmitted error-free
`RX-ERR/TX-ERR`	Packets received/transmitted with errors
`RX-DRP/TX-DRP`	Packets received/transmitted/dropped
`RX-OVR/TX-OVR`	Packets received/transmitted/lost due to overrun
`Flg`	Flags set for interface

Figure 14.6 ifconfig on Red Hat Linux 6.0.

ps

This is the UNIX equivalent of the `pmon` command in Windows 2000. `ps` provides a snapshot of processes currently running on the system, and is probably one of the most utilized commands on UNIX systems. Figure 14.7 is the output of `ps` with the `-e` (every process now running) and `-l` (generate long listing) switches.

Column `S` indicates the state of the process (definitions in Table 14.2). Column `UID` contains the effective user ID of the process and is how you identify the guilty party. Column `PID` contains the process ID of the process and is required to `kill` or `renice` the process. Column `NI` contains the nice value. Column `SZ` contains the size in pages of the process' image in memory. Column `TIME` is the cumulative execution time of the process and column `CMD` is the command name up to 80 characters. The other columns can be ignored with respect to performance monitoring.

 `ps`—Provides a snapshot of processes currently running on the system, and is probably one of the most utilized commands on UNIX systems. This is the UNIX equivalent of the `pmon` command in Windows 2000.

```
X xterm                                                                    _ □ X
duchess> /usr/bin/ps -el | more
 F S   UID   PID  PPID  C PRI NI    ADDR     SZ    WCHAN TTY        TIME CMD
19 T     0     0     0  0   0  0 SY 10416f88    0           ?       0:00 sched
 8 S     0     1     0  0  41 20 60579608   84 60579800 ?      13:24 init
19 S     0     2     0  0   0  0 SY 60578f48    0 10434c34 ?       0:00 pageout
19 S     0     3     0  1   0  0 SY 60578888    0 10437cdc ?     138:01 fsflush
 8 S     0   600     1  0  41 20 60a68da0  200 600b82a6 ?       0:21 nfsd
 8 S     0   144     1  0  41 20 60576008  561 600b8d96 ?      32:38 in.named
 8 S     0   637     1  0  41 20 60577b08  186 60047d38 ?       0:00 sac
 8 S     0   114     1  0  41 20 60719610  267 600b8f26 ?       2:12 rpcbind
 8 S     1    79     1  0  99 20 605781c8  468 600b8f4e ?      46:24 lpd
 8 S     0   116     1  0  49 20 60718f50  251 600b8e86 ?       0:00 keyserv
 8 S     0   155     1  0  41 20 60718890  259 600b8d1e ?       1:26 inetd
 8 S     0   127     1  0  41 20 607181d0  275 600b8ed6 ?      11:20 ypserv
 8 S     0   160     1  0  41 20 60717b10  465 61bd686e ?       0:01 statd
 8 S     0   134     1  0  41 20 60717450  229 600b8efe ?       0:00 ypbind
 8 S     0   162     1  0  41 20 60716d90  220 600b8d6e ?       0:01 lockd
 8 S     0   206     1  0  41 20 607166d0  207 60047eb8 ?       0:51 cron
 8 S     0   181     1  0  41 20 60716010  312 600b8b8e ?     368:12 amd-2.6
 8 S     0   215     1  0  41 20 608c3618  218 600b8706 ?      17:45 atalkd
 8 S     0   644   572  0  40 20 608c2f58 1139 60bb1f3e ?       0:08 Xsun
 8 S     0   216     1  0  40  8 608c2898  278 608c2a90 ?       6:51 xntpd
 8 S     0   191     1  0  41 20 608c21d8  568 600b8de6 console 23:45 syslogd
--More--
```

Figure 14.7 ps piped to more on Solaris 2.6.

Table 14.2	Process States
Codes	Meaning
D	Uninterruptible sleep
O	Running
R	Runnable: on run queue
S	Sleeping
T	Stopped or traced
Z	Zombie or defunct process

sar

The system activity reporter is available on Solaris, HPUX, and AIX systems. `sar` is the best utility to log performance statistics for these UNIX operating systems. Table 14.3 contains a list of switches that will produce performance statistics for the four main components covered in this chapter. Figure 14.8 is an interactive session that will report statistics every 5 seconds for 10 iterations. The default for iterations is one. To save statistics to a binary file, execute `sar -o filename`.

`sar`—Is the best utility to log performance statistics for UNIX operating systems. The system activity reporter is available on Solaris, HPUX, and AIX systems.

Table 14.3	sar options	
Switch	Information Reported	Important Columns
-d	Disk activity	`%busy, avque, write/s, blks/s, avseek`
-q	Queue length	`runq-sz, %runocc`
-u	CPU utilization	`%user, %sys, %wio, %idle`
-w	System swapping	`swpot/s, bswot/s`

```
 X xterm                                                      _ □ X

 vangogh> sar -d 5 10

 HP-UX vangogh B.10.20 A 9000/770     06/28/99

 17:52:24   device   %busy   avque   r+w/s   blks/s   avwait   avserv
 17:52:29   c0t6d0   0.60    0.50      1      15       7.39     17.34
 17:52:34   c0t6d0   0.60    0.50      1       6       4.65      9.01
            c0t9d0   0.80    0.50      1      16       4.76     14.47
 17:52:39   c0t6d0   0.40    0.50      0       6       0.94     12.12
 17:52:44
 17:52:49
 17:52:54
 17:52:59   c0t6d0   0.20    0.50      0       3       8.92      4.33
 17:53:04
 17:53:09   c0t6d0   3.20    0.50      3      34       6.18     11.89
            c0t5d0  12.60    0.50     22     265       4.73      6.95
 17:53:14   c0t6d0   0.80    0.50      1      13       1.71     17.05
            c0t5d0  78.00    0.50    112    1051       5.07      7.15

 Average    c0t6d0   0.58    0.50      1       8       5.35     12.83
 Average    c0t9d0   0.08    0.50      0       2       4.76     14.47
 Average    c0t5d0   9.06    0.50     13     132       5.01      7.11
 vangogh>
```

Figure 14.8 sar interactive session on HPUX 10.20.

Free

The `free` command is included in the Red Hat Linux 6.0 distribution. The `free` command displays the amount of memory in a system. It provides you with a breakdown of total, used, and free memory statistics for physical and swap memory. The command `free -o -t` produces:

```
         total      used      free      shared    buffers   cached
Mem:     289976     25976     264000    5780      4892      12528
Swap:    265032     8992      256040
Total:   555008     34968     520040
```

`free` can be run continuously with the `-s` switch.

 free–Displays the amount of memory. It is available in Red Hat Linux 6.0.

top

`top` is a great utility to identify processes consuming large percentages of processor time. Figure 14.9 depicts the output from an HPUX 10.20 system. The header gives you an overview of the number of processes run-

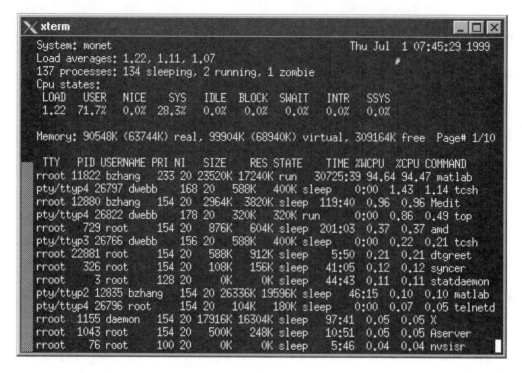

Figure 14.9 `top` output on HPUX 10.20

ning, CPU activity, and memory utilization. The remainder of the output gives you detailed information (similar to `ps`) on the processes currently running. The process detail is sorted in descending order by CPU utilization. This command allows you to quickly identify the biggest CPU hogs on a system.

PERFORMANCE TUNING OF UNIX SYSTEMS

This subsection contains UNIX performance-tuning commands common to AIX, HPUX, Red Hat Linux, and Solaris. The commands covered in this subsection fall into two categories. The first category consists of commands (`nice` and `renice`) that allow the system administrator or user to alter the priority of processes/jobs. The second category consists of commands (`crontab`, `at`, `batch`) that allow scheduling of jobs at non-peak times. Both categories can aid you in extracting the best performance from your UNIX workstations.

Table 14.4	`nice` Values	
Operating System	Range	Default
Solaris	−20 to 20	0
HPUX	0 to 39	20
Linux	−20 to 20	0
AIX	0 to 39	10

nice

The `nice` command allows you to invoke a command with a different system scheduling priority. This command is useful in decreasing or increasing the priority of a process at invocation. Each UNIX system has a range of `nice` values (Table 14.4). The lower the number, the higher the priority. Only the superuser can increase the priority of a process with the `nice` command. Users are limited to assigning lower priorities to commands. To decrease the priority of a command:

```
%/bin/nice -8 myjob
```

The above command will assign a `nice` value of *default - 8* to `myjob`. To increase the priority of a command:

```
#/bin/nice -5 importantjob
```

The command `importantjob` will be assigned a `nice` value of *default - 5*.

`nice`—Allows you to invoke a command with a different system scheduling priority. This command is useful in decreasing or increasing the priority of a process at invocation.

renice

`renice` allows you to alter the priority of running processes. This command allows you to lower the priority of resource-hogging programs to allow interactive jobs better response time. Conversely, it allows you to raise the priority of jobs to the detriment of all other processes. The superuser can alter the priority of a process. Users can only decrease the priority of their own processes. Table 14.5 summarizes the switches that can be used with `renice` to increase or decrease a running process' priority.

`renice`—Allows you to raise or lower the priority of a process that is already running.

Table 14.5	`renice` **Switches**
Switch	Definition
`-g ID....`	ID is a process group ID. Members of a process group have their system `nice` value altered.
`-n newoffset`	Add `newoffset` to current `nice` value.
`-p ID...`	ID is process ID.
`-u ID...`	ID is a user ID. All processes owned by the user ID will have their `nice` values altered.

crontab

`crontab` schedules recurring jobs or processes, and is very similar to the Task Scheduler in Windows 2000. The `cron` daemon is the process that activates commands scheduled via `crontab`. `cron` utilizes the `cron.allow` and `cron.deny` files to determine who is permitted to submit jobs. Table 14.6 contains a matrix to determine access or denial of `crontab` privileges.

If you execute `crontab` without options, it will copy the specified file or standard input to the directory containing all user `crontab` files. `crontab` supports three basic options. The `-l` option will list your current `crontab`, the `-r` option will remove your `crontab`, and the `-e` option will allow you to edit your current `crontab` file.

Figure 14.10 depicts a typical `crontab` file. The `crontab` file consists of six different fields separated by tabs or spaces. The first five fields are explained in Table 14.7.

Table 14.6	`cron` **Permissions Matrix**	
`Cron.allow` file	`Cron.deny` file	Permission
Name in file		Yes
Does not exist	Name not in file	Yes
Does not exist	Does not exist	Root only
Name not in file		No
Does not exist	Name in file	No

Figure 14.10 crontab on Solaris 2.6.

Table 14.7	`crontab` **Fields**	
Field	Description	Valid Values
1	Minutes	0-59
2	Hours	0-23
3	Day of month	1-31
4	Month of year	1-12
5	Day of week	0-6
		0 = Sunday
First five fields	Valid notation	* = All values
		1,3,5
		10-30 inclusive
		5-8,12,15-30

The sixth field is a string that will be executed by `sh` at the time specified. `cron` supplies a default environment consisting of `HOME`, `LOGNAME`, `SHELL`, `TZ`, and `PATH` (`/usr/sbin:/usr/bin` for root and `/usr/bin` for users).

`crontab`—Schedules recurring jobs or processes and is very similar to the Task Scheduler in Windows 2000.

at/batch

Both of these commands are best suited to run a command once at a later time. Environment variables, the current working directory, and the file creation mask will be saved at the invocation of the command and used later when the command is executed. Permission to run `at` or `batch` is governed by `at.allow` and `at.deny`, utilizing the same rules as `cron` in Table 14.7.

`at/batch`—Are the UNIX equivalents of the Windows 2000 `at` command. They are used to run a command at a later time.

Windows 2000 Performance Tools

Windows 2000 performance tools can be split into monitoring and tuning categories. The monitoring category includes tools that allow the system administrator to capture data on the performance of a workstation to a log file, interactively monitor a workstation, and set alerts when performance thresholds are exceeded. These monitoring tools allow you to determine the "health" of a Windows 2000 workstation and aid in pinpointing problems. Diagnosing performance problems on a Windows 2000 workstation is never easy, and problems not always obvious. Problem identification requires a logical examination of performance data for all major components of the workstation.

The tuning category provides tools and commands that allow the system administrator or user to specify the priority of a job, terminate a job, and schedule jobs to run at different times. These tuning tools and commands are useful in maintaining a "healthy" Windows 2000 workstation. These commands can also be utilized to solve some performance problems.

This section is composed of two subsections. The first subsection outlines the steps required to enable logging and alerts. It also covers interactive performance monitoring and reviews performance logging files. The second subsection highlights tools and commands that allow the system administrator to tune the performance of a Windows 2000 workstation or server.

WINDOWS 2000 PERFORMANCE-MONITORING COMMANDS

This subsection contains Windows 2000 tools that monitor the four major performance components described previously in this chapter. The tools covered in this subsection allow a system administrator to interactively monitor the utilization and performance of a Windows 2000 workstation. The tools can also be utilized to capture data to log files or send alerts when performance thresholds are exceeded. It is important to take advantage of all the tools in this subsection to monitor the performance of a Windows 2000 workstation.

Performance Logs and Alerts

Configuring logging and alerts should be part of the installation procedure for all systems. It is important that performance statistics be captured on all Windows 2000 workstations and servers. Table 14.8 contains counters that should be logged as a minimum for a server. A server will include additional counters that pertain to specific services it is providing. Keep in mind that these logging and alert processes consume system resources. Items logged from Table 14.8 will create a binary file of approximately 200KB in a 24-hour period, with samples taken every 15 seconds. Try to keep counters to a minimum and the sampling rate at a reasonable level or your disks will be filled with log files. Let's go through the procedures to set up logging and alerts for the counters in Table 14.8.

1. Open the Control Panel using the following sequence: `Start→ Settings→Control Panel`.
2. Double-click `Administrative Tools`.
3. Double-click `Performance` (see Figure 14.11).
4. Double-click `Performance Logs and Alerts`.
5. Click `Counter Logs` or `Alerts`.
6. Right-click in the right side of the window. Next, highlight `New`, and then select `Create New Log Settings`.
7. Specify a meaningful log file name. For this example, we used `MinWrkStat`. You are then presented with the screen in Figure 14.12. The next four sections will cover each tab page in Figure 14.12.

Table 14.8	Counters to be Logged	
Performance Object	Performance Counter	Definition
Memory	Available Bytes	Physical memory available in bytes
Memory	%Committed Bytes in Use	Ratio of committed bytes to memory
Network Interface	Bytes Total/Sec	Bytes input and output on the network interface
PhysicalDisk	%Disk Time	Percentage of time disk is busy reading or writing
PhysicalDisk	Disk Bytes/sec	Bytes transferred to disk during read or write operations
Processor	%Processor Time	Percentage of time processor is executing a non-idle thread
System	Processor Queue Length	Threads in queue ready to run

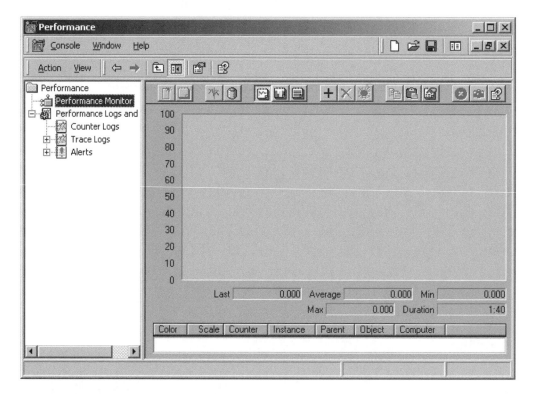

Figure 14.11 Performance Monitor main screen.

Figure 14.12
New log creation
screen.

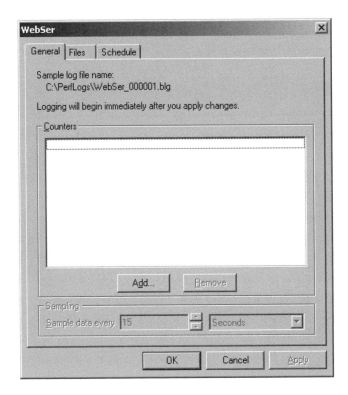

The General and Schedule tabs are similar for counter logs and alerts, except the Counter Logs menu contains a Log Files tab and the Alerts menu has an Action tab.

General Tab (Counter Logs and Alerts) The first page in setting up counterlogs and alerts is the General page. The General page allows you to add counters and set the sampling rate. You must select at least one counter or alert on this page to access the other tabs on this screen. This configuration page is reached via the steps outlined in the "Logging and Alert" section. Execute the following steps to add the counters from Table 14.8:

1. Click Add (Figure 14.13)
2. Select Use local computer counters. This allows you to save these settings and use them on other Windows 2000 workstations.
3. Select a Performance object, then highlight the associated counter from the table. Clicking the Explain button will display a definition for each Performance counter highlighted.
4. Highlight the associated counter.
5. Highlight the instance. For multiple processors or disk drives, you have the option of selecting an individual item or selecting all instances.

Figure 14.13
Counter selection
page.

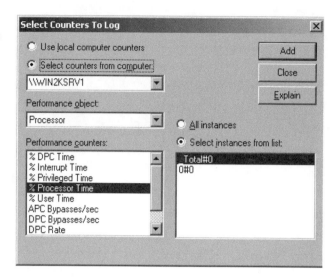

6. Click Add. Repeat steps 3 through 6 until complete.

7. Alerts only: Set the Alerts when value is value. This must be set for each counter.

8. Select the sampling rate. For logging, select 15 seconds. For alerts, select 60 seconds.

Figure 14.14
Log file page.

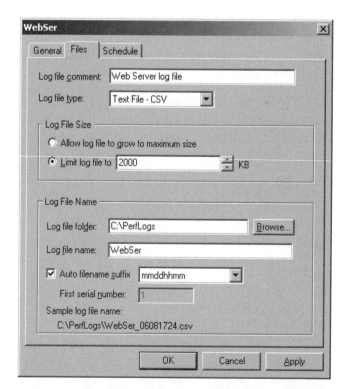

Log Files Page (Counter Logs) The `Files` page is reached via the steps outlined in "Logging and Alerts." Selecting the `Files` tab (Figure 14.14) allows you to specify the type, size, location, and suffix of the log file. The location of the log file should be in a standard folder on all machines. This folder must be shared and accessible to the administrator account. Log file size should always be limited for servers and user workstations. You never want to "lock up" a production machine due to logging. The suffix should include the month, date, and hour at a minimum. This suffix will aid you in identifying the time the logging information was captured.

 Any type of log file can be saved as an HTML file. This provides a mechanism for sharing performance data via the network and facilitates printing of logged data.

The log file on a user workstation should be limited to 1MB. This will give you approximately 30 days of statistics sampled every 10 minutes for the 7 counters in Table 14.8. The binary circular type of file is the best selection for a user workstation. When a binary circular file fills, logging statistics will overwrite the oldest data first in the file and continue to the end of the file. This allows you to set up and forget the logging process on a user workstation.

The size and type of log file for a server is much more complicated. Servers require much more in-depth analysis than user workstations. Organizations that use spreadsheets for analysis will probably benefit most from utilizing the Text File—CSV (comma-separated text file) or Text File—TSV (tab-separated text file) format. The binary circular file introduces the possibility of losing data and is not an appropriate selection for servers. Logging file size should approximate a 24-hour period of sampling data for the selected counters. Limit the size of the log files and move inactive log files to a central repository for logging statistics.

Action Page (Alerts) The `Action` page is reached by following the steps outlined in "Logging and Alerts." Selecting the `Action` tab allows you to specify the action taken when the threshold for a counter is exceeded. Multiple actions can be specified for each event. Actions consist of logging to the event log, sending a network message, or executing a command file. It is even possible to activate counter logs that were previously defined.

Schedule Page The `Schedule` page is reached by following the steps outlined in the "Logging and Alerts." Selecting the `Schedule` tab allows you to specify starting and stopping parameters. The user workstation parameters consist of manually starting and stopping using the `Context` menu (Figure 14.15). Server workstation parameters consist of manually starting using the

Figure 14.15
Schedule page.

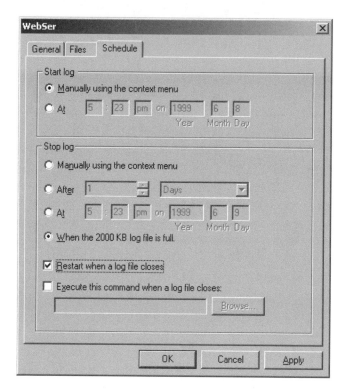

`Context` menu and stopping when the log file is full. The following server parameters should also be checked: `Restart when a log file closes` and `Execute this command when a log file closes`. The command to be executed can consist of a simple command script (batch file), or a Perl script that will copy the recently closed log file to the logging central repository.

The `Schedule` tab window for alerts allows you to start either manually or on a particular date. Stopping can be accomplished manually, for a particular length of time or on a particular date. For continuous monitoring, select any start procedure, select `After` in the `Stop log` section and check `Restart when an alert scan ends`.

Performance Monitoring

Windows 2000 provides an outstanding performance-monitoring tool. It can provide statistics on almost every conceivable object that is part of the Windows 2000 system. This performance-monitoring tool allows you to monitor local or remote systems in real time or load files created with Performance Logs and Alerts.

Perform the following steps to open the Performance Monitor:

1. Open the Control Panel with the following progression: `Start→Settings→Control Panel`. Next, double-click

Administrative Tools, and then double-click the Performance icon. (See Figure 14.11).

2. The default system monitor displays the current activity on the local machine. To view log files previously created, click the View Log File Data icon at the top of the right pane.

3. Right-click and highlight Add Counters, or click the + icon. (See Figure 14.13).

4. Select the local or remote computer on which you want to monitor performance activity.

5. Select a Performance object and then select the required performance counter from the menu. Windows 2000 highlights the most important counter for the object. Select the instance if required.

6. Click Add.

7. Repeat Steps 4 through 7 until all required counters are selected (seven items is about the limit for display purposes).

8. Click Close.

Right-clicking in the right pane allows you to add counters, save as an HTML file, or change the properties of Performance Monitor.

pmon

pmon.exe is part of the Windows 2000 Resource Kit. pmon.exe is a command-line tool that monitors memory and processor usage (see Figure 14.16). The up/down arrow keys are used to move around the screen, and

CPU	CpuTime	Mem Usage	Mem Diff	Page Faults	Flts Diff	Commit Charge	Usage NonP	Pri Page	Hnd Cnt	Thd Cnt	Image Name
		36376	-52	547070	4						File Cache
97	258:19:52	16	0	1	0	0	0	0 0	0	1	Idle Process
0	0:17:02	248	0	49040	0	88	0	0 8	189	49	System
0	0:00:02	300	0	708	0	416	1	6 11	49	6	smss.exe
0	0:00:41	1616	8	3983	2	1228	8	44 13	615	11	csrss.exe
0	0:06:13	5040	0	441695	0	11676	64	38 13	470	20	winlogon.exe
0	0:22:17	7620	0	6358167	0	3084	865	38 9	714	39	services.exe
0	0:27:27	9644	0	1097332	12	9836	5146	52 13	812	38	lsass.exe
0	0:00:07	1928	0	3285	0	1516	1549	27 8	363	11	svchost.exe
0	0:00:42	4176	0	27522	0	4984	54	30 8	214	13	spoolsv.exe
0	0:00:02	552	0	1273	0	1648	1770	24 8	176	19	msdtc.exe
0	0:01:51	236	0	1251134	0	1800	12	28 8	317	16	cisvc.exe
0	0:00:01	1356	0	1167	0	1436	48	19 8	135	7	dfssvc.exe
0	0:01:47	2196	0	49896	0	2464	1569	29 8	262	17	tcpsvcs.exe
0	0:00:01	2132	0	5168	0	1292	5	23 8	190	12	svchost.exe
0	0:00:03	1084	0	8652	0	1680	254	29 8	266	14	ismserv.exe
0	0:00:56	2184	0	85005	0	1548	28	16 9	109	11	llssrv.exe
0	0:00:00	556	0	374	0	484	14	11 8	68	7	sfmsvc.exe
0	0:00:00	400	0	326	0	496	167	11 8	58	4	sfmprint.exe

Figure 14.16 pmon output.

the <q> key terminates the program. This is a good tool for identifying memory problems or processor hogs.

 `pmon.exe`—Is a ommand-line tool that monitors memory and processor usage.

PERFORMANCE-TUNING TOOLS FOR WINDOWS 2000

This subsection contains Windows 2000 performance-tuning commands. Some of these commands also provide a performance-monitoring capability. The tools covered in this subsection fall into two categories. The first category consists of tools/commands (`at` and the Task Scheduler) that allow job scheduling. The second category consists of tools (Task Manager and Process Viewer) that allow you to monitor the performance of the Windows 2000 workstation and to kill or change the priority of running processes. Both categories aid in extracting the best performance from your Window 2000 workstations or servers.

at

The `at` command is a console-mode command that allows the scheduling of programs and commands on a local or a remote system. Figure 14.17

```
C:\Documents and Settings\Administrator>at 23:50 /next:F,S f:\perl\eg\done.pl
Added a new job with job ID = 4

C:\Documents and Settings\Administrator>at
Status ID   Day                      Time            Command Line
--------------------------------------------------------------------------
        1   Next 8                   11:30 PM        f:\perl\eg\example.pl
        3   Each 5 10 15 20 25 30    11:45 PM        f:\perl\eg\clean.pl
        4   Next F S                 11:50 PM        f:\perl\eg\done.pl

C:\Documents and Settings\Administrator>at 05:15 /every:Su f:\perl\eg\cleantmp.p
l
Added a new job with job ID = 5

C:\Documents and Settings\Administrator>at
Status ID   Day                      Time            Command Line
--------------------------------------------------------------------------
        1   Next 8                   11:30 PM        f:\perl\eg\example.pl
        3   Each 5 10 15 20 25 30    11:45 PM        f:\perl\eg\clean.pl
        4   Next F S                 11:50 PM        f:\perl\eg\done.pl
        5   Each Su                  5:15 AM         f:\perl\eg\cleantmp.pl

C:\Documents and Settings\Administrator>
```

Figure 14.17 at command with no switches.

is the output of executing the `at` command without arguments. The status ID is required to delete the scheduled command. Under the `Day` column there are `Next` or `Each` entries, followed by a number or abbreviation for the day of the week. The `Next` entries will execute once. The `Each` entries will execute every month on the designated day. The `Time` and `Command` columns are obvious. The `at` command does not validate your command line, so check for typos!

at—Is a console-mode command that allows the scheduling of programs and commands on a local or remote system.

Task Scheduler

Task Scheduler is another new graphical management tool included in the Windows 2000 operating system. Adding tasks is accomplished by executing the following commands:

1. Click `Start→Settings→Control Panel`, and then double-click on the Scheduled Task icon.
2. Click the Add Scheduled Task icon, which activates a wizard that guides you through the steps of scheduling new programs or processes.

The Task Scheduler allows programs to be assigned to a specific user, but requires the correct password for that user account for the task to complete successfully. Scheduling a task as a specific user requires the correct password for the account as well. The scheduling of processor-intensive tasks, or memory hogs, during slack periods of system usage is much easier to manage with this tool. Scheduled tasks are stored in folder `tasks` under the `WINNT` directory. `schedLog.txt`, located in the `WINNT` directory, contains logging information for the Task Scheduler. You can administer tasks on remote systems by executing the following commands:

1. Double-click `My Network Places`.
2. Double-click the remote machine name.
3. Double-click the `Scheduled Tasks` folder.

Programs scheduled to run via the `at` command will appear in the `Scheduled Tasks` folder. Task Scheduler can modify settings in a job submitted with the `at` command, but the ability to modify the task via the `at` command is lost.

Task Manager

The Task Manager provides continuous data on performance, processes, and applications that are currently running on a local machine. The Task Manager can be used to end processes/programs, change the priority of a running process, and start new programs. It provides a graphical representation of CPU and memory usage. The Task Manager can be started by right-clicking in an empty space on the taskbar or by pressing <CTRL> + <ALT> + <DELETE> and selecting Task Manager. Figure 14.18 shows the Task Manager with the Processes tab highlighted.

Figure 14.18
Task Manager
Processes page.

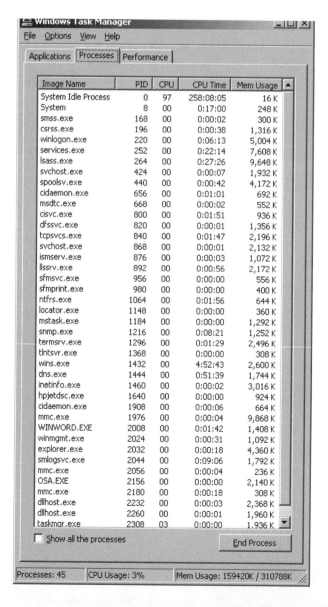

Process Viewer

Process Viewer (`pviewer.exe`) is part of the Windows 2000 Resource Kit. It allows you to monitor running processes on a local or remote system. It is a Windows-based tool very similar to `pview.exe`. This is a great tool to kill a non-essential process or change a process' priority. Figure 14.19 shows you the Process Viewer screen. The process, processor time, process memory used, and priority of the process are the important fields.

 `pviewer.exe`—Is part of the Windows 2000 Resource Kit and allows you to monitor running processes on a local or remote system.

Summary

Performance monitoring is an essential but difficult part of system administration. It begins with the installation of a system and continues as long as the system is in use. In most cases, however, systems are not monitored until they exhibit some difficulty. Performance monitoring requires a thorough understanding of all areas of system administration.

Figure 14.19
Process Viewer main page.

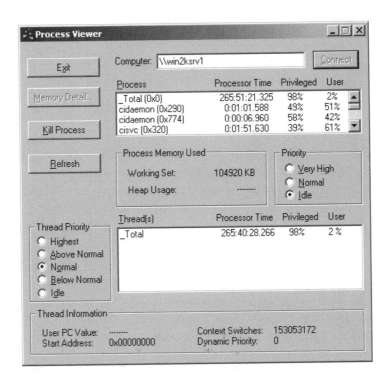

UNIX PERFORMANCE TOOLS

UNIX performance tools can be split into monitoring and tuning categories. Monitoring tools allow you to determine the "health" of a UNIX workstation and to pinpoint problems. Diagnosing performance problems on a UNIX workstation is never easy and not always obvious. Problem identification requires a logical examination of performance data for all major components of the workstation. Tuning provides commands that allow the system administrator or user to specify the priority of a job and to schedule jobs during off-peak hours. These commands can also be utilized to solve some performance problems.

WINDOWS 2000 PERFORMANCE TOOLS

The tools covered in this section allow the system administrator to interactively monitor the utilization and performance of a Windows 2000 workstation. The tools can also be utilized to capture data to log files or send alerts when performance thresholds are exceeded. It is important to take advantage of all the tools in monitoring the performance of a Windows 2000 workstation.

SOFTWARE ADMINISTRATION

UNIX

Building a /usr/local Repository

Managing a Multi-vendor /usr/local Structure

Utilizing File Version Control

Software Distribution Methods

WINDOWS 2000

Installing Applications

Microsoft Systems Management Server

The Windows 2000 Registry

As your infrastructure grows in size, one of the tasks that you will find yourself increasingly called upon to do is to install software and move files from one system to another. With the trend by vendors to send out multiple releases of an application per year, coupled with patches and mid-release updates, the task of keeping all of your computers systems up-to-date with the latest software versions can be daunting. To complicate matters, just keeping up-to-date isn't enough, as it is often very important to make sure that all of your systems have access to the same software versions at approximately the same time. If it takes three weeks to update all of your systems to the latest release, the continuity of your infrastructure is in flux, and can cause problems for your users who expect consistent access to the software they use everyday.

These programs include system utilities such as compilers, editors, and shell programming tools that are constantly being updated and will always be in demand by your users. Added to all the software applications, both vendor and utility, is the daunting number of user-generated files, which from time to time need to be relocated to take better advantage of your infrastructure's disk resources. This chapter will give you the tools, as well as some practical advice, for managing software and user files, helping you make your infrastructure both stable and productive.

Managing UNIX Applications

In UNIX environments, managing software can become a significant drain on your personnel resources if you don't have a strong structure in place. From utility software to vendor packages, almost every day you'll be asked to investigate some new version, or add patches to an existing installation. If you install your software in a random, "just fix the fire" mentality, at some time down the road, you'll find yourself with an infrastructure of systems where no two are alike. Users will not be able to configure their environments, and even if they can, they'll find drastically different versions of software depending on where they log in.

ORGANIZING UTILITY APPLICATIONS

Utility applications have been part of UNIX for its many generations. UNIX itself is, in essence, a collection of applications wrapped around a core kernel. UNIX provides many programs that aid the user in manipulating their computer environment, such as `telnet`, `ftp`, `vi`, `cat`, `sh`, and `csh`. Having access to these tried and true UNIX utilities gives the user a minimum toolbox with which to manipulate their UNIX environment and be more efficient.

UNIX itself is, in essence, a collection of applications wrapped around a core kernel.

While these core applications provide the basics for users, over time, thousands of additional programs have been created to provide additional functionality to the user above and beyond what the installed operating system offers by default. These utilities run the gamut from editors and browsers, to network and performance enhancements, to programming languages and tools. Table 15.1 gives some examples of common UNIX utilities that are generally not considered part of the core operating system, but you will commonly find installed by the local system administrator.

Almost all of these utility programs are easily available on the Internet, on a supplemental CD that ships with your operating system, or as part of a CD that is included with a specific OS reference purchase. However, it is highly inefficient for each user to download, compile, and/or configure each utility for which they may have a need. It is more efficient for the system administrator to provide a shared area in which utility programs can be made available to the user.

Table 15.1	OS-independent User and System Utilities
Type	Brand
Text Editors	`emacs`, `pico`, `xedit`
Programming and Scripting Languages	GNU C, C++, FORTRAN, Java, Perl
Browsers	Internet Explorer, Netscape, Mosaic
GUI Tools and Libraries	X11R6, Motif
User Utilities	`gzip`, `less`, `more`, `traceroute`, `top`

The `/usr/local` structure

While any user-accessible directory can provide a repository for utility programs, choosing customized locations for different systems can be confusing. The most widely used location for storing utility programs is in `/usr/local`. Using `/usr/local` as a repository for administrator-compiled programs grew out of the existing structure, where operating system utilities were stored in `/usr/bin`. Using `/usr/local` signified that programs stored in `/usr/local` were local to that system, or to all the systems in that infrastructure. Having local and system utilities separate ensures sure that system upgrades don't affect local files, as well as ensures that administrator-installed utilities don't overwrite or interfere with operating system programs.

Building Your `/usr/local` When designing a new `/usr/local` structure, there are five subdirectories that are essential to provide maximum functionality, both for the users and the administrator. The vast majority of software packages you download from the Internet and compile to use on your systems will expect the `/usr/local` structure as shown in Table 15.2.

Once you've created the basic `/usr/local` subdirectory tree, you can begin the process of installing software. If you adhere to the following process, your `/usr/local` should provide a useful toolkit for your users without creating a management nightmare for the administrator:

1. For all utility packages, create a directory `/usr/local/lib/package.version`, where `package` is the name of the software, and `version` is the software version release, if applicable. By creating a directory for each distinct utility, as well as for the specific release number of that utility, you help organize and track what

Table 15.2	Standard Subdirectory Structure for `/usr/local`	
Directory	Function
`/usr/local/bin`	Utility binaries or links to binaries
`/usr/local/etc`	Utility and package configuration files
`/usr/local/include`	Package `include` files
`/usr/local/lib`	Package installations, including source code and binaries
`/usr/local/man`	Man page files

versions of software are installed. This also provides your users access to older versions of a package should they need to continue to use older software.

2. Once a package is installed and tested, create a symbolic link, `/usr/local/lib/package`, which points to the new `/usr/local/lib/package.version`. While in the initial process of building your `/usr/local`, this step is not a requirement; however following this procedure creates a mechanism to easily install newer versions. This creates a fixed point that users can use as a reference to the currently supported release. If multiple versions of a package are installed, only a symbolic link change is needed to reflect this change.

3. Create a link from `/usr/local/lib/package.version/bin/command` to `/usr/local/bin/command`, where *command* is the utility command that users will use to invoke the software. Once the software package is installed in `/usr/local/lib/package`, installing a symbolic link in `/usr/local/bin` gives your users access to the command, without having to copy the binary program physically into the directory. This serves two important purposes. First, it saves hard drive space by not replicating files that are located in `/usr/local/lib`. Second, and more important, it provides a fixed program name and location for your users to incorporate into their environment and scripts. Changing to the latest new version of a program will be accomplished in Step 2 when the package link is updated.

4. Install all man pages in `/usr/local/man`. Finally, once the installation is complete, add the man pages, if available, into the `/usr/local/man` directory. This also provides a fixed point of reference for users to incorporate into their user environments for man pages.

Additions of man pages will be instantaneously available to users, with no actions necessary on their part.

For example, assume that your users request you to install the program `foo` on your system. You find that the latest version of fooware is version 3.5. You should create a directory `/usr/local/lib/fooware.3.5`, and install and compile `foo` version 3.5 there. Once that is complete, create a set of symbolic links in `/usr/local` using:

```
#mkdir /usr/local/lib/fooware.3.5
#ln -s /usr/local/lib/fooware /usr/local/lib/fooware.3.5
#<install fooware 3.5 software>
#ln -s /usr/local/lib/fooware.3.5 /usr/local/lib/fooware
#ln -s /usr/local/lib/fooware.3.5/bin/foo /usr/local/bin/foo
#<install manual pages>
```

Finally, install the man pages in `/usr/local/man`.

As usual, fooware version 3.6 is released only a moment after you tell your users that `foo` version 3.5 is available. When you download the latest version of fooware, you should create the directory `/usr/local/lib/fooware.3.6`. Then when you've tested `foo` version 3.6, all that is required to make `foo` version 3.6 the supported version is to change the links in `/usr/local/lib` as follows:

```
#mkdir /usr/local/lib/fooware.3.6
#<install fooware 3.6 software>
#rm /usr/local/lib/fooware
#ln -s /usr/local/lib/fooware /usr/local/lib/fooware.3.6
#<install manual pages>
```

The symbolic link in `/usr/local/bin` does not need to be modified, and your users won't know the difference.

If you choose to be a benevolent administrator, you can give your users easy access to fooware version 3.5 by creating the following symbolic link in `/usr/local/bin`:

```
#ln -s  /usr/local/lib/fooware.3.5/bin/foo
/usr/local/bin/foo-3.5
```

This is a simple way to continue to support older software versions without affecting the majority of your user base.

Designing a Single-vendor `/usr/local` Infrastructure The number of applications you choose to install in your `/usr/local` will directly impact the amount of time you spend managing your `/usr/local` repository. While managing a `/usr/local` on a single system can be a full-time job for an administrator, what happens when you have a distributed infrastructure with many systems, all of which require access to `/usr/local`?

Having to install every new package on every system is neither a good use of your time or of system resources. Through the use of file sharing using NFS and software distribution techniques, you'll need to develop a /usr/local infrastructure to serve your users' needs.

Designing your /usr/local infrastructure should follow the same logic as the design of your DNS and NIS infrastructure with a few modifications. The following four key elements should be kept in mind when developing a /usr/local strategy:

- Identify a central machine to be the master /usr/local server and install all new software packages on that system only to maintain consistency.

- Identify other systems throughout your infrastructure that can function as additional /usr/local servers. The file server resources that serve /usr/local are different from those serving DNS or NIS. Acting as a file server increases the processing and I/O on the server, as well as consumes disk resources to maintain a copy of /usr/local.

- On large time-sharing systems with numerous users, have a copy of /usr/local on a local disk if there are resources available. Running programs across the network from an NFS-mounted /usr/local can add significant traffic to your network, as well as impact performance for the users on the local system.

- Replicate /usr/local files nightly to assure that files stay synchronized. As you make changes to your master /usr/local server, make sure you put a process in place to keep all of your /usr/local copies the same. This helps to provide a stable environment for your users, and they'll thank you for it.

Identifying a central system to be your master repository is very important. This is the system on which you'll perform all of your installations and testing. If at all possible, choose a system that has no, or a minimum of, users. Changing your symbolic links while users are attempting to do work is not the best way to keep users on your good side. Also, when choosing additional /usr/local servers, make sure they have ample resources to not only handle your current /usr/local, but additional growth.

Having to change /usr/local servers down the line because they run out of disk space can be a painful process, especially if you have a number of systems using that /usr/local server that need to be reconfigured to point to another server.

Once you've set up your secondary /usr/local servers, be aware of what systems are using them. If you have servers that have high user load, or make overly frequent use of programs in /usr/local, you may want to consider installing a local copy of /usr/local on those systems. While there is nothing wrong with running programs out of /usr/local over the network, you'll find that users get better response with a local /usr/local, and you'll see less load on your network. The only penalties you'll pay for having local /usr/locals are the disk space you'll consume and the incremental work needed to manage an additional /usr/local. If you have the disk space available on the local machine, don't be afraid to install /usr/local.

Finally, designing your /usr/local infrastructure is very similar to designing your DNS and NFS infrastructure, but there is one major difference. Unlike DNS and NFS, there are no automated functions built into the operating system to manage the replication of your /usr/local information. However, there are operating system tools that you can use to automate this process. For more information on how to keep your /usr/local copies synchronized, see the section titled "UNIX File Management Tool," presented later in this chapter.

Organizing a Multi-vendor /usr/local **Structure** While trying to keep up with a single /usr/local is a task in itself, what happens when you have a mixed environment that contains systems from multiple UNIX vendors? Providing a common cross-platform environment to your users, one in which all the tools they're used to are available on every platform, is well worth the investment of your time. Constructing a multi-vendor /usr/local is not as difficult as it may seem. You'll still need to follow the key concepts presented in the previous section, but you will have to wrap some additional design and process around those concepts to be successful.

The additional design piece involves identifying multiple systems to be your /usr/local masters. For each UNIX vendor in your environment, you'll need to identify a system to provide resources for building, testing, and storing your master /usr/local for that UNIX vendor. Once that is in place, you can identify additional servers, similar to a single-vendor environment. However, if you have sufficient resources, namely disk space, you may consider housing your entire multi-vendor /usr/local directory structure on one system. While this may seem a strange concept since you can't compile and test other operating system types on this system, there are two very good reasons to manage your /usr/local in this way:

■ This allows you to identify a single system as your /usr/local master, helping to avoid confusion. You still need other vendor systems identified to compile and test your /usr/local programs.

Use NFS mounts to mount /usr/local from the master system to the compile and test systems.

■ Distributing /usr/local to secondary servers is much simpler, as the process you put in place to distribute updates to secondary /usr/locals can be managed from a single machine. This will help you keep your entire vendor /usr/local directory structure synchronized, providing your users with a consistent cross-platform environment.

ORGANIZING VENDOR APPLICATIONS

While utilities and programs stored in /usr/local will be used by the vast majority of your users, there will be times when software packages will only be needed by subsets of your user communities. In many of these cases, the software is a specialized vendor application that only needs to be installed on a limited number of systems and used by a small group of users. In these cases, installing these packages in /usr/local most likely is not the best option, for if you install every software package in /usr/local, you'll quickly run out of disk resources before you run out of applications you'll want to put there.

There are a few key factors to consider when planning and installing vendor applications:

■ Keep them separate from the operating system's disk and directory structure. Vendor applications can be very complex and consume ample amounts of disk resources. Keep them separate from your operating system, and they won't impact your procedures for upgrading and maintaining your operating system.

■ Install vendor applications with portability in mind. As applications age, new releases tend to consume more disk resources than pervious releases. Try to install your applications in locations that have ample resources to handle growth over time. However, if this is not possible, you'll need to plan for the time when you'll need to move the application to a new filesystem, or even a new computer system that has added resources.

■ Use symbolic links for version and location management. Employ the same process as installing utilities in /usr/local when you install vendor applications. Use symbolic links to make version management transparent to users, as well as to minimize the impact if you have to move the application to another location.

Avoid installing vendor applications on your operating system disk whenever resources permit. Over time, new vendor releases will need to be installed, and very rarely does a new vendor application require fewer resources than its previous version. You don't want to get into the situation where your vendor application drains all of the available resources on your operating system disk, thereby making upgrades, patching, and log retention more difficult. Also, if you are able to install your application to a physically distinct disk, your installation will not be affected if you need to complete re-install your operating system.

Another advantage of installing vendor applications on distinct disk resources is that those resources can be moved to different systems. As new technology arrives into your infrastructure, if your vendor application is portable, you can move the disk resources to the new, faster system, allowing your users to see increased performance on the application. Another advantage of portability is when vendor applications have to live in the same disk resource space as user home directories. As the disk resources are filled, you'll find yourself moving the application from one filesystem to another.

Moving applications, and installing new versions of applications, are good motivations to use symbolic links for both version management and to attempt to make the location of the application transparent to the user. For version management, use the same technique you would use for `/usr/local`. For transparent locations, you can use either symbolic links or symbolic links with automounting to provide consistency of location to your users.

For example, say you install acmeware version 1.1 on `mars.sniglets.com` in `/export/home`. Users will need to add `/export/home/acmeware-1.1` to their user environment, and then log into `mars` to use it. For these users, acmeware is now tied to `mars`, and only one `/export/home`. However, if you make `/export/home` an NFS filesystem, and use automount to share it, and then make a link `/export/home/acmeware` that points to `/export/home/acmeware-1.1`, you now have a portable system. The symbolic link provides version management control, and the use of NFS and automounting allow you to move acmeware to a different filesystem or even another machine. As far as the users are concerned, the software is always located in `/home/acmeware`. This level of portability and consistency will be appreciated in even the smallest UNIX infrastructures.

This can be easily extended to a multi-vendor environment by replicating this operation for each version of UNIX you support. You can choose to install acmeware in two different ways. First, you can install the Solaris version of acmeware on a Solaris system, the HP version on an HP system, and so on. You can then use NFS to share each version with systems of similar type. This is the simplest way, but it does require you to keep track of four different servers of acmeware.

A second method is to choose a single server to support acmeware, say `mars.sniglets.com`. Let's assume we have a Linux system called `jupiter.sniglets.com`. On the Solaris server `mars`, export `/export/home` to `jupiter`, and allow `jupiter` read and write access to `/export/home`. Then on `jupiter`, mount `mars:/export/home`, say as `/export/mars`. Create a directory `/home/mars/Linux` and install acmeware under `/home/mars/Linux/acmeware`. Now, `mars` is a server to both Solaris and Linux, and by using automounts, the management of this is simple.

TRACKING SOFTWARE CHANGES

Another important software management technique is the ability to track changes made to files. Both administrators and users can benefit from having all changes to files archived and stored, so that in the event of problems, they can refer to previous copies. This is highly useful when a number of users, or administrators, have access to change files, but may not have a method to communicate when they are going to make changes. If two users edit a file at the same time, only the changes saved by the last person to write the changes will be saved. While this can be frustrating when developing software, having two administrators edit a system file at the same time can create problems, or even crash a running system. Controls need to be put in place to make sure two administrators are never editing critical files at the same time.

For users, one simple method is to manually make copies of each file they want to change, and store all of these copies in another place for safekeeping. However, as the number of files, or the number of changes, grows, this method takes up a great deal of both time and disk resources. This also isn't effective for administrators, who need to edit a specific file. And, copies won't keep multiple administrators from editing at the same time. To overcome these problems, version control software was created. Version control software automates the process of tracking changes and limits multi-user access to files. In essence, version control places a layer between the user and the actual file, which archives changes, manages access, and automates recovery of previous versions of the file.

Version control software comes in many flavors. Sometimes it is installed with the operating system, like SCCS in Solaris; it is also available free on the Internet, like GNU Revision Control System (RCS). For this section, we will focus on GNU RCS, which is a simple, yet powerful tool in managing version control. Creating a version control system is a relatively simple process if you follow a few simple steps.

1. Prepare for RCS in your directory structure. Create a directory named `RCS` in the directory in which you want to track changes.

2. Insert new files into the RCS system. Using the `ci` command, check files into your `RCS` directory.

3. Be sure to "check out" a file before editing it. Use the `co` command before you begin to edit the file.

4. Use "check in" after changes are complete. Once you have completed your modifications, be sure to check in your changes, or they will be lost the next time someone edits the file.

5. When needed, enable previous versions of the modified file. You have the option of choosing any previous version to retrieve, using the `-r` option to `co`.

Once you've downloaded and installed GNU RCS, developing the human processes for using RCS is much more difficult than using the software itself. To begin using RCS in a directory, say `/etc`, you'll need to create the subdirectory `/etc/RCS`. This subdirectory will store all the changes you check in to specified files. To activate RCS, you must initially check in each file you wish to track. For example, to begin tracking changes to your `/etc/hosts` file, in the `/etc/` directory, type:

```
#ci hosts
```

This will create revision 1.0 of `/etc/hosts` in the `/etc/RCS` directory. However, don't edit any files in the `RCS` directory! To begin editing a file, you should check it out and lock the file. The process of *locking* a file gives ownership to the user with the lock, and prevents other users from overwriting any changes. For system files, or when multiple users will interact with a file, locking is essential. Failure to lock a file can cause multiple users to overwrite each other's changes if they are working on that file at the same time. To check out a file, type:

```
#co -l hosts
```

The `-l` option locks the file and gives ownership to the user checking it out. The file you should now edit is `/etc/hosts`. Anyone else editing the `/etc/hosts` file without using RCS will have their changes lost once you check in `/etc/hosts` using:

```
#ci -u hosts
```

The `-u` option unlocks the file so that others can now edit the file. Failure to use the `-u` option will keep `/etc/hosts` locked and only editable by the user who checkd it out.

In time, you'll want to bring back earlier versions of a file to correct some problems, or retrieve some information that was previously deleted. To check out the most recent version, type:

```
# co -r  hosts
```

and this will recover to the last `/etc/hosts` version that was checked in. To recover to previous versions, you can give a version number such as:

```
#co -r1.12 hosts
```

This will restore version 1.12 of `/etc/hosts` for editing. If you choose to keep version 1.12 as your current version, just check it in again, and it will become your current version.

RCS, like other version control software, is very powerful and offers more options and tools than can be discussed here. However, the most important point you should take from this section is that you have to buy into using version control 100% of the time, or it becomes ineffective. The most common problem is the failure to check out a file in the first place, where an administrator edits a file as root, saves it, and then someone else, or the same administrator, then uses RCS to manage the file. All the changes that were input during the non-RCS sessions will be lost, with no hope of recovery. Once you've lost an hour's worth of changes the first time, you'll better understand the rigor needed to use RCS. However, good practices started early can save you hours of replicating work later.

 `ci, co`—Check in and check out, respectively. These are part of the suite of commands that make up the RCS version control system.

Distributing Files and Applications

Moving files from one place to another can be a tedious task. Before the introduction of the Internet and local networks, moving files from one system to another required copying data to a transportable device such as a tape or floppy disk. This method was quite effective for small amounts of data, but not very useful for large amounts of data, or in situations where you needed information transferred quickly. In this section, you will be presented with some tools and processes that take advantage of system utilities, as well as the network, to keep your files moving freely and make your users more productive.

UNIX FILE MANAGEMENT TOOLS

Managing UNIX files can be simple or complex, depending on the functionality you choose to build into your process. In the following sections, you will be presented with a few of the simpler, yet more powerful tools for managing UNIX files. These tools can be broken into two categories: those that work over NFS or on the local system, and those that work with remote systems where NFS file sharing is not an option. For NFS or local systems, the `cp` command is a powerful and useful way to replicate and copy files. For remote systems, both the File Transfer Protocol (FTP) and Remote File Distribution program (`rdist`) are simple and useful tools when applied to different software management problems.

MOVING FILE STRUCTURES ACROSS FILESYSTEMS USING CP

One of the more mundane, but surprisingly frequent tasks that a UNIX administrator needs to perform is moving files and directories from one place to another. As disks fill up, or new systems are put in place, it becomes necessary to move packages and user files to new filesystems. If only one user or a single package needs to migrate, the task is rather simple, as in the following simple copy command:

```
#cp -r /home/userdir /home/newuserdir
```

This will copy all of the files and directories from `/home/userdir` to `/home/newuserdir`, keeping the current file structure. The `-r` option to `cp` tells the copy command to perform a recursive copy. A recursive copy starts copying in the directory defined by the first argument to the command (`/home/userdir`) and copies all files and directories in the directory tree under this directory to the directory specified by the second argument (`/home/newuserdir`). Using `cp` is very effective in copying files, however, `cp -r` alone is not enough in many situations. Whenever `cp` copies the existing file and creates a new file or directory, the new file or directory has its access and creation times set to the current time, as well as its owner and group set to the user performing the copy. If you are moving a user's home directory, all files in the directory will be set to the current time, and the files will be owned by root, not the user. Times on files are critical, as some programs look at the time a file was created or accessed and use that information; and of course, ownership is very important, especially for the user!

Preserving file times and ownership is simple if you use the `-p` option to `cp`:

```
#cp -rp /home/userdir /home/newuserdir
```

The `-p` option preserves the file owner, group owner, access time, and creation time. It is always good practice to use the `-p` option so that you don't accidentally leave files owned by the wrong user, and don't lose creation and access time information.

`cp`—Copies files or directories in UNIX systems.

MANAGING PACKAGE INSTALLATIONS AND TRANSFERS

While the `cp` command is very useful for moving files and directories across local filesystems or NFS-mounted filesystems, what methods are available when you have to move files from one system to another, and NFS is not available? Copying files to a tape or floppy disk is always an option, but that channel, commonly called "sneaker net," while once the only way, is very inefficient by today's standards. The administrator has a number of options to move files from one system to another. This section will compare two different methods for moving files between UNIX systems: File Transfer Protocol (FTP) and Remote File Distribution (`rdist`).

File Transfer Protocol

The FTP program, `ftp`, is one of the most widely used programs by UNIX administrators and users. FTP provides a mechanism to transfer files from one system to another where a direct filesystem copy is not an option. FTP is widely used to transfer software packages, image files, and user data between geographically distinct systems, as well as side-by-side computers where NFS is not being used. Figure 15.1 shows a simple FTP connection that downloads a single file from the remote system `earth` to the local system `mars`.

The command line that is part of the FTP program functions very similar to the command-line shells users are accustomed to when interacting with the UNIX environment. The commands `cd` and `ls` can be used to navigate the directory and file structure of the remote system. The `get` command will initiate the transfer of a file, such as `foo.c`, shown in Figure 15.1. While retrieving files from remote systems is very useful for downloading utility or vendor packages from the Internet, FTP can also be useful when distributing software throughout your local infrastructure. By using the FTP command `put`, you can transfer files to remote systems, given that you have write permission to the directory.

A very important feature of FTP is the *binary* command. By default, FTP transfers files in ASCII mode. While this is okay for plain text or simple programming files, if you don't use the *binary* command when downloading compressed or binary program files, the files will become corrupted. In ASCII mode, the FTP program will interpret some characters as carriage returns or line feeds, and insert improper codes into your binary files. When in doubt, always use the *binary* command.

When transferring *binary* programs or compressed packages, always use the *binary* command in FTP or your files will be corrupted.

Figure 15.1
Using FTP to
transfer files from
a remote system.

```
Window  Edit  Options                                            Help

mars# ftp earth
Connected to earth.sniglets.com.
220 earth.sniglets.com FTP server (Version wu-2.6.0(2) Thu Oct 21 10:23:31 EDT 1
999) ready.
Name (earth:sflynn):
331 Password required for sflynn.
Password:
230 User sflynn logged in.
ftp> cd ftp
250 CWD command successful.
ftp> ls
200 PORT command successful.
150 Opening ASCII mode data connection for file list.
foo.c
foo.h
foo.jpeg
typescript
226 Transfer complete.
36 bytes received in 0.025 seconds (1.42 Kbytes/s)
ftp> get foo.h
200 PORT command successful.
150 Opening ASCII mode data connection for foo.h (1135 bytes).
226 Transfer complete.
ftp> quit
221-You have transferred 1131 bytes in 1 files.
221-Total traffic for this session was 1171 bytes in 3 transfers.
221-Thank you for using the FTP service on earth.sniglets.com.
221 Goodbye.
mars#
```

Another useful feature of FTP is the ability to send a group of files at one time through the use of the `mput` and `mget` commands. These commands allow you to give a single file name, a wildcard file name, or no file name at all. Through the use of `mput` and `mget`, you can quickly transfer an entire directory as shown in Figure 15.2; and, by using the `prompt` command, you can bypass the interactive questioning that is on by default in FTP. Figure 15.3 shows the advantage of using the `mget` command with the functionality of the `prompt` command.

Table 15.3 highlights some of the pros and cons of using FTP for software management. On the plus side, FTP provides a secure, password-protected method that provides a simple mechanism for transferring files between two distinct systems. However, if you need to distribute files to a large number of systems, the process is highly manual and very time-intensive. You are also limited to transferring files only from the current directories, so if you have a large directory tree to transfer, you'll spend a great deal of type typing the `cd` command.

FTP provides a mechanism to transfer files from one system to another where a direct filesystem copy is not an option. FTP is used to transfer software packages, image files, and user data.

Figure 15.2
Using mget to speed file transfer.

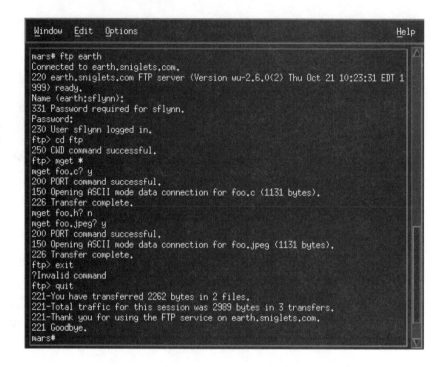

Figure 15.3
Using mget and prompt to automate transfers.

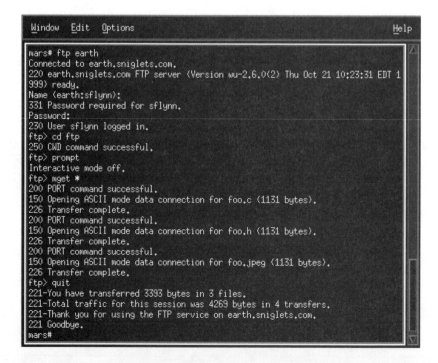

Table 15.3	Pros and Cons of FTP Usage for Software Management	
Pros	Cons
Simple Machine-to-machine Transfer	Highly manual
Password Protected	Does not scale well
	Limited to a single directory; no recursion

Remote File Distribution

Since FTP is not an acceptable solution for managing a large volume of files and packages, another utility you should employ is the Remote File Distribution program rdist. The rdist program is designed to automatically replicate a directory structure from one system to another, without manual intervention. The rdist utility is highly effective at making replicas of existing file structures, like /usr/local, or archiving a copy of a file structure for redundancy. Figure 15.4 shows the file structure we wish to replicate from mars.sniglets.com/home/local to [earth.snigets.com], into /export/local. As you can see in Figure 15.5, [earth.sniglets.com] has nothing in /export/local. If we run rdist from mars, the complete file structure from mars is transferred to earth in /export/local.

In the example in Figure 15.5, we only added files to an existing file structure. Over time, if you continue to run rdist in this manner, you'll eventually fill up the disk on earth, since by default, rdist only copies additions to the remote system, and does not remove files that have been deleted

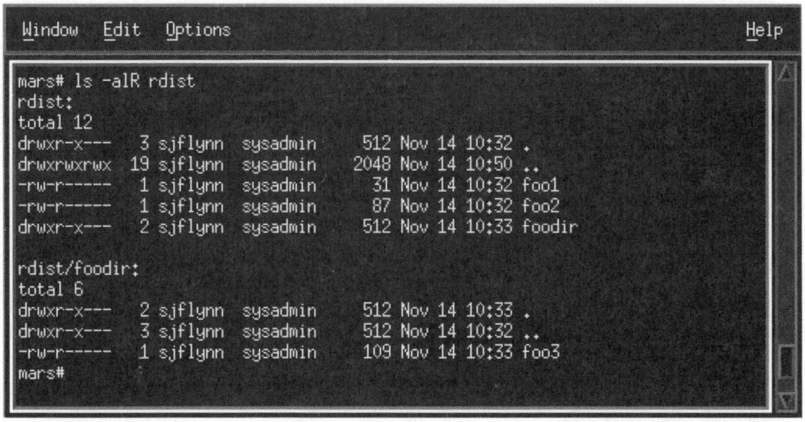

Figure 15.4
Example directory structure to replicate using rdist.

```
Window  Edit  Options                                          Help

mars# ls -alR rdist
rdist:
total 12
drwxr-x---    3 sjflynn  sysadmin     512 Nov 14 10:32 .
drwxrwxrwx   19 sjflynn  sysadmin    2048 Nov 14 10:50 ..
-rw-r-----    1 sjflynn  sysadmin      31 Nov 14 10:32 foo1
-rw-r-----    1 sjflynn  sysadmin      87 Nov 14 10:32 foo2
drwxr-x---    2 sjflynn  sysadmin     512 Nov 14 10:33 foodir

rdist/foodir:
total 6
drwxr-x---    2 sjflynn  sysadmin     512 Nov 14 10:33 .
drwxr-x---    3 sjflynn  sysadmin     512 Nov 14 10:32 ..
-rw-r-----    1 sjflynn  sysadmin     109 Nov 14 10:33 foo3
mars#
```

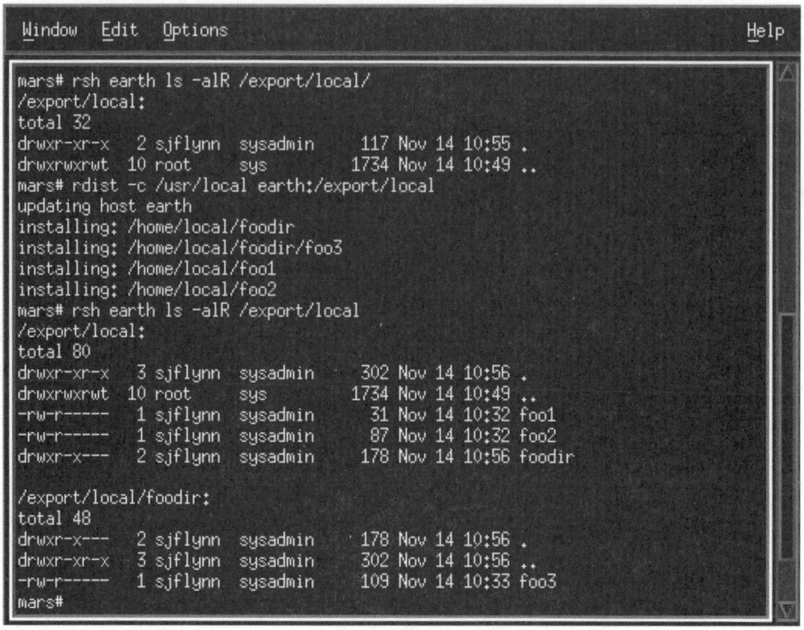

Figure 15.5
Using rdist to distribute files to a remote system.

```
 Window   Edit   Options                                              Help

 mars# rsh earth ls -alR /export/local/
 /export/local:
 total 32
 drwxr-xr-x    2 sjflynn   sysadmin      117 Nov 14 10:55 .
 drwxrwxrwt  10 root      sys          1734 Nov 14 10:49 ..
 mars# rdist -c /usr/local earth:/export/local
 updating host earth
 installing: /home/local/foodir
 installing: /home/local/foodir/foo3
 installing: /home/local/foo1
 installing: /home/local/foo2
 mars# rsh earth ls -alR /export/local
 /export/local:
 total 80
 drwxr-xr-x    3 sjflynn   sysadmin      302 Nov 14 10:56 .
 drwxrwxrwt  10 root      sys          1734 Nov 14 10:49 ..
 -rw-r-----    1 sjflynn   sysadmin       31 Nov 14 10:32 foo1
 -rw-r-----    1 sjflynn   sysadmin       87 Nov 14 10:32 foo2
 drwxr-x---    2 sjflynn   sysadmin      178 Nov 14 10:56 foodir

 /export/local/foodir:
 total 48
 drwxr-x---    2 sjflynn   sysadmin      178 Nov 14 10:56 .
 drwxr-xr-x    3 sjflynn   sysadmin      302 Nov 14 10:56 ..
 -rw-r-----    1 sjflynn   sysadmin      109 Nov 14 10:33 foo3
 mars#
```

from the local system. Figure 15.6 shows a directory on `mars` that has a new file, `foo4`. `foodir` has been deleted, but it still exists on `earth`. By using the `-R` option, which deletes files from the remote system that no longer exist on the local system, after `rdist` has completed, the directories will be exactly the same, as shown in Figure 15.7.

Using `rdist` is a simple and powerful way to manage directory structures that you want to replicate and keep synchronized. Table 15.4 shows the pros and cons of using `rdist`. The `rdist` program is highly configurable, keeps files perfectly synchronized, maintains ownership and access times, and doesn't send passwords over the network like FTP. The only downside

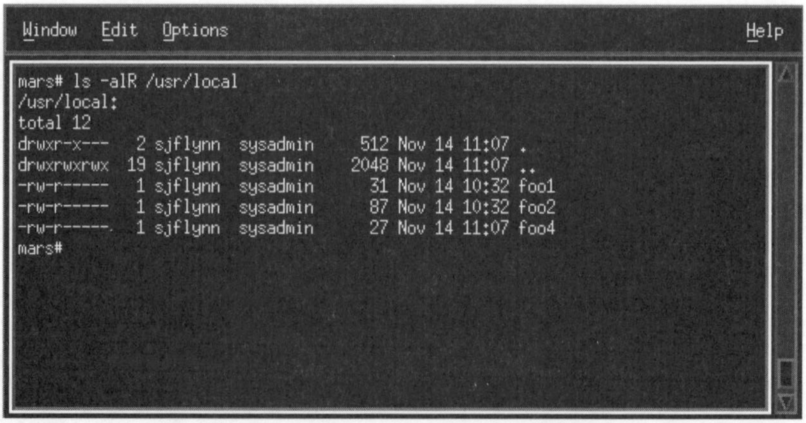

Figure 15.6
New directory structure, with a directory deleted and a new file added.

```
 Window   Edit   Options                                              Help

 mars# ls -alR /usr/local
 /usr/local:
 total 12
 drwxr-x---    2 sjflynn   sysadmin      512 Nov 14 11:07 .
 drwxrwxrwx  19 sjflynn   sysadmin     2048 Nov 14 11:07 ..
 -rw-r-----    1 sjflynn   sysadmin       31 Nov 14 10:32 foo1
 -rw-r-----    1 sjflynn   sysadmin       87 Nov 14 10:32 foo2
 -rw-r-----.   1 sjflynn   sysadmin       27 Nov 14 11:07 foo4
 mars#
```

Figure 15.7
Using rdist to
synchronize a
remote directory
structure to a
local directory
structure.

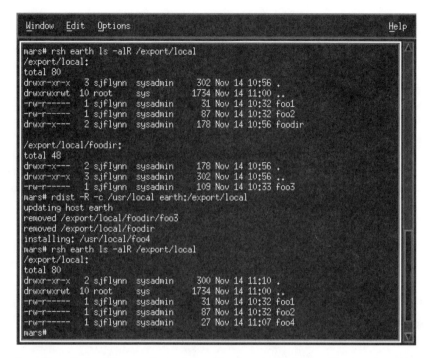

```
Window  Edit  Options                                              Help

mars# rsh earth ls -alR /export/local
/export/local:
total 80
drwxr-xr-x   3 sjflynn  sysadmin     302 Nov 14 10:56 .
drwxrwxrwt  10 root     sys         1734 Nov 14 11:00 ..
-rw-r-----   1 sjflynn  sysadmin      31 Nov 14 10:32 foo1
-rw-r-----   1 sjflynn  sysadmin      87 Nov 14 10:32 foo2
drwxr-x---   2 sjflynn  sysadmin     178 Nov 14 10:56 foodir

/export/local/foodir:
total 48
drwxr-x---   2 sjflynn  sysadmin     178 Nov 14 10:56 .
drwxr-xr-x   3 sjflynn  sysadmin     302 Nov 14 10:56 ..
-rw-r-----   1 sjflynn  sysadmin     109 Nov 14 10:33 foo3
mars# rdist -R -c /usr/local earth:/export/local
updating host earth
removed /export/local/foodir/foo3
removed /export/local/foodir
installing: /usr/local/foo4
mars# rsh earth ls -alR /export/local
/export/local:
total 80
drwxr-xr-x   2 sjflynn  sysadmin     300 Nov 14 11:10 .
drwxrwxrwt  10 root     sys         1734 Nov 14 11:00 ..
-rw-r-----   1 sjflynn  sysadmin      31 Nov 14 10:32 foo1
-rw-r-----   1 sjflynn  sysadmin      87 Nov 14 10:32 foo2
-rw-r-----   1 sjflynn  sysadmin      27 Nov 14 11:07 foo4
mars#
```

to `rdist` is that it uses the `rsh` protocol and requires a client system trust relationship between the client and servers through the use of `.rhosts` files. While using `.rhosts` files is generally not a security issue, in some highly secure operations, `.rhosts` files may be discouraged because if `mars.singlets.com` allows `rhost` access from [`jupiter.sniglets.com`], a security breach on `jupiter.sniglets.com` now allows access to `mars.sniglets.com`.

`rdist`–Designed to automatically replicate the directory structure from one system to another, without manual intervention.

Table 15.4	**Pros and Cons of Using `rdist` for Software Management**
Pros	Cons
Highly Configurable	Requires machine-to-machine trust relationship
Provides for File Addition and Deletion	
Maintains Ownership and Creation Times	
No Clear Text Passwords	

Windows 2000 Software Administration

Unlike UNIX systems, Windows 2000 does not have a native means of centralizing software installations. In fact, Windows 2000 typically requires that software be installed locally. This, as you might have guessed, makes software administration on Windows 2000 systems very difficult. It is inevitable that you will be forced to manage systems that have the same applications installed in different locations on each system. In time, this will begin to drive you insane, and you will spend most of your time just trying to figure out where a particular application is installed on different systems. Fortunately, hope is not completely lost. We will offer some guidelines for both local and network application installation. In addition, we will briefly discuss server-based software administration with Microsoft Systems Management Server. We will conclude this section with an overview of the Windows 2000 Registry.

Keep in mind that there is no one "best" solution for Windows 2000 software administration. This section offers what we believe to be constructive guidelines for managing your installed software.

INSTALLING APPLICATIONS

You will find that most Windows 2000 applications include their own setup or installation utility. This utility is usually named `setup.exe`, and occasionally `install.exe`. You can run an application's setup utility directly from the Explorer or a command prompt, or by using the Add/Remove Programs Control Panel applet shown in Figure 15.8. Any way, your biggest concern is *where* the application will actually be installed. This is not a simple question to answer by any means. In this section, we will discuss application installation, both locally and on the network. We hope to give you a basis for developing your own "policy" for software installation.

Local Installation

It is by far the most common practice to install Windows 2000 applications locally on each user's system. While there is nothing wrong with this, you should decide up-front where you want to install applications. By default, most Windows 2000 applications will install in a vendor-specified directory under *%SystemDrive%\Program Files*, which is typically `C:\Program Files`. If this is acceptable to you, then you can usually use the default installation path provided during setup. However, some older applications do not handle long filenames very well and may need to be

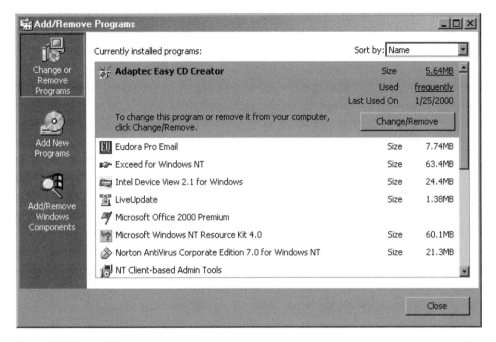

Figure 15.8 Add/Remove Programs.

installed under a directory whose path does not include a long filename. This scenario would require that some applications be installed in one directory, while others are installed in another. You may be comfortable with this, but our solution has been to create an application-only directory, such as C:\Appl, for all applications. This makes it easy to determine which applications have been installed on the system, simply by looking at a single directory listing. This is very similar to the /usr/local infrastructure discussed earlier in this chapter.

When you install applications locally, you should do so with an Administrator-level account. A good way to ensure that your user will not have problems running the application is to (temporarily) make their account a member of the local Administrators group and install the application while logged on with their username. When you are done installing the application(s), you can remove their account from the local Administrators group. It is, however, an accepted practice for a user to be a member of the local Administrators group on their own machine.

Network Installation

Unfortunately, most Windows 2000 applications do not support network-based installation. Now, when we say network-based, we do not mean running setup from the network, but rather actually installing the application to a network share and running it over the network. Because applications depend on the Windows 2000 Registry to function, a local installation is usually recommended. Even those applications that support a network-based installation (such as Microsoft Office), also require a minimal local installation for Registry settings and some library files. Unfortunately, there is no easy solution to this problem. The closest we can get to managing software over the network is to use a server-based management utility, such as Microsoft Systems Management Server.

MICROSOFT SYSTEMS MANAGEMENT SERVER

Now that you think that all hope is lost, we're going to tell you it isn't. Microsoft Systems Management Server (SMS) is a server-based system management package that can centrally manage your servers and workstations. SMS provides centralized hardware and software inventory, software distribution, installation, metering, and remote troubleshooting tools. SMS uses industry-standard network protocols, such as SNMP, to provide server-based configuration management for your networked workstations and servers. While this book can hardly begin to touch on configuring and using SMS itself, we will provide you with two things: what you need to deploy SMS, and the features in SMS that will benefit you. For a more thorough overview of SMS, as well as pricing and purchasing information, we suggest you take a look at `http://www.microsoft.com/backoffice`.

System Requirements

You will need to install SMS on a system running Windows NT Server 4.0 SP4 or later. Additionally, you will need another Windows NT 4.0 server running Microsoft SQL Server 6.5 SP4 or later. You should consider the following a minimum set of requirements for your server hardware:

- Pentium 133 or higher CPU.
- 128MB of RAM.
- 1GB available disk space.
- CD-ROM drive.

As we said earlier, these requirements are the bare minimum. You should decide, based on the size of your organization, what hardware will best fulfill your needs; the more workstations and servers you intend to support, the more you should spend on hardware. It is not unreasonable to purchase a

Pentium III-class system with more RAM and available disk space than we mentioned earlier.

SMS Features

One question you have to ask yourself before deciding on deploying SMS is if it will provide the services and functionality you need. Table 15.5 details the important features of Microsoft Systems Management Server 2.0.

Hopefully this section has provided enough information for you to decide if SMS can benefit your network environment.

THE WINDOWS 2000 REGISTRY

The Windows 2000 Registry stores information on virtually every aspect of the operating system. Software packages also use the Registry to store application-specific configuration data. The Registry itself is not a new concept. In fact, Microsoft replaced the familiar `ini` files with the Registry in Windows 95. You can view and edit data in the Registry using `regedt32.exe`, which can be executed from the `Start` menu's `Run` dialog, or from a command prompt. Figure 15.9 shows the `Registry Editor`.

The Windows 2000 Registry is hierarchical, meaning it has a parent-child structure, much like the files and folders on a disk. The Registry consists of subtrees, which themselves contain keys and values. The actual data is stored on disk in Registry hives, in `%SystemRoot%\system32\config`. Table 15.6 details the different subtrees contained in the Registry.

Each subtree can contain multiple keys, and those keys can themselves contain keys and values. Table 15.7 details the different components of the subtrees.

You can use the Registry Editor to search for specific keys and values, edit existing keys and values, and create new keys and values. The Registry Editor will also allow you to modify the security settings on subtrees and their components. We caution you to be very careful when manipulating the Windows 2000 Registry as it is very easy to leave a software application and/or your system in an unstable state. You should only directly modify the Registry when it is absolutely necessary to do so. However, searching the Registry is a very convenient method of determining application and system settings.

Summary

As your infrastructure grows, managing user data as well as application files can become a full-time job. Users outgrow their disk resources and application software changes almost daily. In this chapter, we discussed some of the possible ways to manage the software in your environment.

Table 15.5	Microsoft Systems Management Server 2.0 Features Overview
Feature	Description
Hardware Inventory	Gathers details about your client systems, without the need to sit down at the workstation or server. This allows administrators to plan for hardware and software upgrades.
Software Inventory	Gathers information about every application installed on your client systems. This will help administrators plan for software upgrades, as well as identify software that is being used without permission.
Software Distribution	Software can be distributed directly to the client systems without ever visiting the workstation or server. Software can be added or removed based on a set of administrator-defined rules and without any user intervention.
Software Installation	Provides the ability to repackage any Windows application for unattended distribution.
Software Metering	Tracks and controls software use to help administrators manage software licenses and plan future purchases.
Operating System Deployment	SMS can effectively deploy Windows 98, Windows NT 4.0, and Service Packs.
Network Discovery	Gathers information about network topology and helps administrators understand their network layout, as well as plan for future growth.
Network Monitoring	SMS can identify network problems, such as rogue protocols or IP address conflicts.
Remote Diagnostics	Allows an administrator to troubleshoot client systems without having to visit the workstation or server (assuming the network is up, of course).
Reporting Tools	Crystal informational reports are included to help create understandable reports of the data SMS gathers.

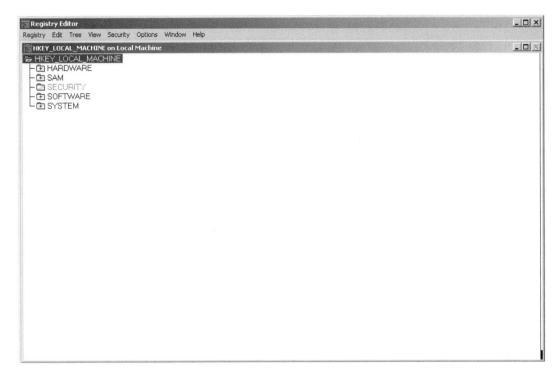

Figure 15.9 Windows 2000 Registry Editor.

MANAGING `/usr/local`

Building a UNIX `/usr/local` structure is a must for almost every system in your infrastructure. Unless your UNIX system has a sharply defined function and needs nothing other than operating system utilities, you'll probably want to invest in the time to build a `/usr/local`. Building a `/usr/local` from scratch involves first defining your subdirectory structure, and then identifying one system to be the master `/usr/local` repository. Once these initial steps have been completed, look into your infrastructure and determine where secondary `/usr/local` servers will provide the best flexibility and performance increases for your systems.

VERSION CONTROL

Use version control to manage all critical files that may change over time. Version control provides change tracking, which is useful to identify when changes were made, who made a change, and what information was changed. Version control is a highly effective tool for managing files that are modified by multiple users, as well as for tracking changes to system and

Table 15.6	Windows 2000 Registry Subtrees
Subtree	Description
HKEY_LOCAL_MACHINE	Contains all of the configuration data for the local system. This includes device driver information, service information, and hardware information. This subtree also includes system-wide software settings. During boot, Windows 2000 accesses this subtree to determine which drivers and services must be loaded.
HKEY_CLASSES_ROOT	This subtree is a shortcut to HKEY_LOCAL_MACHINE\Software\Classes. It contains software configuration data, such as OLE and file associations.
HKEY_CURRENT_CONFIG	This subtree contains information on the current hardware configuration loaded from the SYSTEM and SOFTWARE hives during boot.
HKEY_USERS	Contains information about the system's user accounts. The .DEFAULT key specifies default settings for all users, and can be overridden by the current user's profile. The HKEY_CURRENT_USER key is discussed below.
HKEY_CURRENT_USER	Contains information about the currently logged-on user. This subtree is a child key of HKEY_USERS. This information is loaded from and stored in the ntuser.dat file, which is part of the user's profile. Data contained in this subtree will override duplicate data contained in the HKEY_LOCAL_MACHINE subtree.

application configuration files. By locking file access and tracking changes, multiple users can work together to write code or modify the system while retaining the integrity of the files.

DISTRIBUTING FILES AND APPLICATIONS

Using tools such as cp, FTP, and rdist, you can move and distribute data to large numbers of systems with less effort than servicing each system individually. Coupled with techniques for managing application software using /usr/local structuring, providing your users an up-to-date and consistent environment doesn't have to monopolize your time.

Table 15.7	Windows 2000 Registry Components
Component	Description
Key	Corresponds to hardware or software objects and is similar to folders and subfolders. Keys can contain values and sub-keys.
Value	A value is a data element stored in a key. Windows 2000 applications can read the values from the Registry for configuration information.
Data Type	Specifies the type of data a value holds. Valid data types are: • `REG_BINARY` – This is a string of 1s and 0s that represent some binary number. • `REG_DWORD` – A string of 1-8 hexadecimal numbers. • `REG_SZ` ◊ a simple string. • `REG_EXPAND_SZ` – Same as `REG_SZ`, except the string can contain environment variables which will be expanded. • `REG_MULTI_SZ` – Same as `REG_SZ`, except it can contain multiple strings.
Data	The actual information contained in the value.

WINDOWS 2000 SOFTWARE ADMINISTRATION

Windows 2000 typically requires that software be installed locally. You will find that most Windows 2000 applications include their own setup or installation utility. This utility is usually named `setup.exe`, and occasionally `install.exe`. You can run an application's setup utility directly from the Explorer or a command prompt, or by using the Add/Remove Programs Control Panel applet.

The Windows 2000 Registry stores information on virtually every aspect of the operating system. Software packages also use the Registry to store application-specific configuration data. The complexity of Windows software administration requires the administrator to keep good records of what packages are loaded, and where they are.

Web Servers

UNIX

Installing Apache Web Server

Configuring Apache Web Server

Apache and SSL

WINDOWS

Apache Web Server for Windows 2000

Internet Information Server 5.0

FTP Services in IIS 5.0

We live in the .com age. As we come to the end of this book, it would not be complete without discussing Web servers. In a few short years, the Internet has become a part of everyday life. Until recently, universities, government agencies, and large companies were the primary users of the Internet. Today, everyone from elementary students to the elderly use the Internet. Among the many tools and resources in use, Web servers are by far the most prevalent. Windows 2000 includes Internet Information Server 5.0 for providing Internet services. There are also third-party Web servers available for Windows 2000 and UNIX. In this chapter, we will discuss IIS 5.0 and the Apache Web Server for Windows 2000 and UNIX.

631

Apache Web Server

The Apache Web Server is the most widely used Web server on UNIX platforms. The Apache Web Server has been ported to all major UNIX platforms. The following sections cover the Apache Web Server included with Red Hat Linux 6.1, a source installation of the Apache Web Server on a Solaris 2.6 server, installation of the Apache Web Server on a Windows 2000 workstation, and a review of the configuration files for the Apache Web Server. The Apache Software Foundation provides organizational, legal, and financial support for the Apache Web Server open source software project. Source and binary distributions can be downloaded from [http://www.apache.org].

RED HAT LINUX 6.1

Red Hat Linux distributions include the Standard, Deluxe, and Professional editions. All of the editions include the latest Apache Web Server. The Professional edition includes a secure Web server, software for e-commerce, and 30 days of Apache configuration support. It is the best selection if your company plans on conducting e-commerce. The next sections will cover the installation of the Apache Web Server package on Red Hat Linux 6.1.

Installation

Chapter 2, "System Planning, Installation, and Configuration", included the steps required to install Red Hat Linux. Selection of the `Server` install type during initial installation automatically loads the Apache Web Server package. The `Custom` install type allows selection of the Web server package during the initial installation process. To confirm that the Apache Web Server is installed on your system, enter the following command on your Red Hat Linux server:

```
#rpm -q apache
apache-1.3.9-4
```

The result of this query indicates that version 1.3.9 of the Apache Web Server is loaded on this server. The installation process modifies the workstation startup scripts to automatically start the Apache Web Server during the boot process. `rpm` will return the following if Apache is not installed:

```
#rpm -q apache
package apache is not installed
```

See Chapter 5, "Upgrades, Patches, Service Packs, and Hot Fixes", for instructions on installing packages with `rpm` or `GNOrpm` on a Red Hat Linux workstation.

Apache Configuration

The Apache configuration files are located under the `/etc/httpd` directory. The `conf` directory contains the main configuration files for the Web server. Table 16.1 contains the name and content of each file.

The `logs` directory contains the error logging file (`error_logs`) and the access logging file (`access_log`). The error logging level is set to `warn`. The `warn` level logs information on emergencies, alerts, critical conditions, errors, and warning conditions. The access logging file logs all requests to the Web server. The access log is written in the Common Log Format (CLF). The CLF writes a separate line of information for each request to the log file in the following format (each field is separated by spaces):

```
Host ident authuser date request status bytes
```

The `modules` directory contains shared object module files. The Apache Web Server package includes Dynamic Shared Object (DSO) support. DSOs are loaded at runtime and are not compiled into the Web server executable, thereby saving memory. All of the standard modules are implemented as DSOs in Red Hat.

The Apache Web Server serves pages from the `/home/httpd/html` directory. This is specified in the `/etc/httpd/conf/httpd.conf` file. The `cgi-bin` directory is located at `/home/httpd/cgi-bin`. The `cgi-bin` is important in maintaining a secure Web site. The system administrator or webmaster can exercise greater control over this directory to ensure scripts do not have an adverse effect on the rest of the Web directories.

Table 16.1	Apache Web Server Configuration Files
File	Content
`httpd.conf`	Contains directives controlling operation of Web server daemon (`httpd`)
`srm.conf`	Contains directives controlling specification of documents Web server can provide
`access.conf`	Contains directives controlling access to documents

Testing the Apache Web Server

The final step is testing the Apache Web Server. Open your favorite browser and type in:

```
http://192.168.3.11
```

Substitute the IP address of your workstation for `192.168.3.11` above. Your browser should resemble Figure 16.1.

SOLARIS 2.6 SOURCE INSTALLATION OF APACHE WEB SERVER

The next few sections will describe a source code installation of the Apache Web Server on a Solaris 2.6 workstation. The Apache Autoconf-style

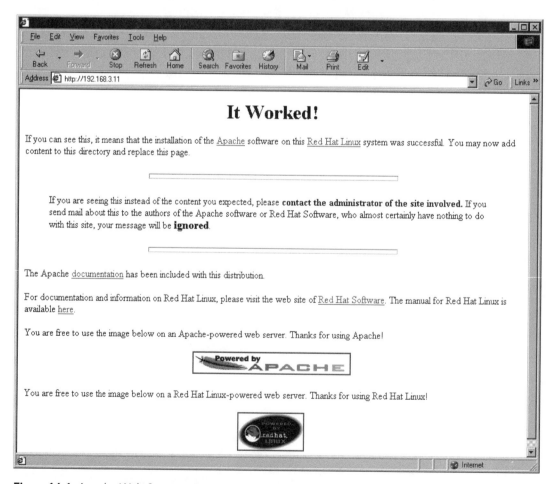

Figure16.1 Apache Web Serve main page.

Interface (APACI) greatly simplifies the compilation and installation process. The APACI generates the correct configuration files for the operating system. The following Solaris installation procedures would be the same for any AIX, HPUX, or Red Hat Linux workstation.

Downloading the Packages

There are two requirements for installing a source distribution of the Apache Web Server. The first requirement is a directory that has approximately 30MB of free disk space to download, unpack, and compile the sources. The second requirement is an ANSI-C compiler. Enter the following command to determine if your Solaris system contains an ANSI-C compiler:

```
#pkginfo SPROcc
application SPROcc        SPARCompiler C 3.0.1
```

The above indicates that the SunSoft ANSI-C compiler is installed. If you do not have the SunSoft compiler installed (`ERROR: information for SPROcc was not found`), `www.gnu.org` contains links to binary distributions of the GNC C compiler for Solaris, AIX, and HPUX. This package can be downloaded, uncompressed, and added to your Solaris system with the `pkgadd` command. The GNU C compiler package will be installed under the `/usr/local` directory.

Now that we have all the required pieces, we need to download the Apache Web Server sources. The latest stable version of the Apache Web Server can be downloaded from `http://www.apache.org.`. The distribution we downloaded is `apache_1.3.9.tar.gz`. The `gz` suffix indicates that this file is compressed. To uncompress it, execute the following command:

```
#gunzip apache_1.3.9.tar.gz
```

We are left with the file `apache_1.3.9.tar`. Now we must process this file with the following command:

```
#tar -xvf apache_1.3.9.tar
```

The result of this command is a new directory called `apache_1.3.9`. We are now ready to configure, compile, and install the Apache Web Server.

Apache Web Server Installation

First, change directory (`cd`) into the top-level directory (`apache_1.3.9`) of the Apache server distribution. Configuration of the server, compilation, and installation will require only three commands using APACI. We are building a server that will include support for DSOs and add a few modules that are not included in the default server.

The first command, `configure`, executed under APACI, is the most important. The command `configure` accepts approximately 40 options. To obtain a listing of all options that `configure` supports, execute the following command:

`#configure —help`

The following listing contains only the `Configuration options:` portion of the `configure -1` command:

```
Configuration options:
 —enable-rule=NAME        enable  a particular Rule named 'NAME'
 —disable-rule=NAME       disable a particular Rule named 'NAME'
                          [DEV_RANDOM=default EXPAT=default    IRIXN32=yes ]
                          [IRIXNIS=no        PARANOID=no       SHARED_CHAIN=de]
                          [SHARED_CORE=default SOCKS4=no        SOCKS5=no   ]
                          [WANTHSREGEX=default                               ]
 —add-module=FILE         on-the-fly copy & activate a 3rd-party Module
 —activate-module=FILE    on-the-fly activate existing 3rd-party Module
 —permute-module=N1:N2    on-the-fly permute module 'N1' with module 'N2'
 —enable-module=NAME      enable  a particular Module named 'NAME'
 —disable-module=NAME     disable a particular Module named 'NAME'
                          [access=yes       actions=yes     alias=yes    ]
                          [asis=yes         auth_anon=no    auth_dbm=no  ]
                          [auth_db=no       auth_digest=no  auth=yes     ]
                          [autoindex=yes    cern_meta=no    cgi=yes      ]
                          [digest=no        dir=yes         env=yes      ]
                          [example=no       expires=no      headers=no   ]
                          [imap=yes         include=yes     info=no      ]
                          [log_agent=no     log_config=yes  log_referer=no ]
                          [mime_magic=no    mime=yes        mmap_static=no ]
                          [negotiation=yes proxy=no         rewrite=no   ]
                          [setenvif=yes     so=no           speling=no   ]
                          [status=yes       unique_id=no    userdir=yes  ]
                          [usertrack=no     vhost_alias=no               ]
 —enable-shared=NAME      enable  build of Module named 'NAME' as a DSO
 —disable-shared=NAME     disable build of Module named 'NAME' as a DSO
 —with-perl=FILE          path to the optional Perl interpreter
 —without-support         disable the build and installation of support tools
 —without-confadjust      disable the user/situation adjustments in config
 —without-execstrip       disable the stripping of executables on installation
```

Under the `- -disable-module=NAME` heading is a listing of the standard modules included in the Apache Web Server distribution. Modules that are assigned a value of `yes` (`access=yes`, `mime=yes`...) are included by default. Modules assigned a value of `no` (`mime_magic=no, so=no,...`) are not included by default. The modules `mime_magic` and `rewrite` will be added for this Web server. Each module added will require a separate `- -enable-module` (`--enable-module=mime_magic`) option on the configuration command line. We have also decided that the `rewrite` module will be a DSO. This will require an additional option of `--enable-shared`.

The final option we need to specify is where the Apache Web Server is going to be installed. This server will be installed under the `/usr/local/apache` directory. The option for the Apache Web Server installation directory is `--prefix=/usr/local/apache`.

We are now ready to configure our server. The following command will generate our configuration:

```
#./configure —prefix=/usr/local/apache \

               --enable-module=so \ --enable-module=mime_magic
\
         --enable-module=rewrite \
         --enable-shared=rewrite \
```

Next, execute the command:

```
# make
```

This command will take approximately 10 to 30 minutes to complete. A large amount of information will scroll by on the screen, showing the progress of the compilation. Successful completion requires one more step.

Install the Apache Web Server by executing the following:

```
#make install
```

The Apache Web Server binaries (`bin` directory), configuration files (`conf` directory), and Web site files (`htdocs` directory) are installed in the `/usr/local/apache` directory.

Starting Apache

The Apache installation program builds a script, `/usr/local/apache/bin/apachectl`, that provides an easy way to start and stop the Apache Web Server.

```
#/usr/local/apache/bin/apachectl start
```

Do not start the server yet! The configuration file for the Web server must be reviewed and configured. Review the "Apache Web Server Configuration File" section of this chapter before starting your Apache Web Server.

The final step is to copy the `/usr/local/apache/bin/apachectl` file to the `/etc/init.d` directory. Chapter 3, "System Boot and Shutdown", contains the steps required to enable the Apache Web Server at boot. The script can also be utilized to manually start and stop the Apache Web Server. The Apache Web Server binary is located at `/usr/local/apache/bin/httpd`. The `httpd` binary accepts the command-line options contained in Table 16.2.

Table 16.2	**Command-line Options for** `httpd`
Option	Action
`-D name`	Defines a name for use in `<IfDefine name>` directives
`-d directory`	Specifies an alternate initial `ServerRoot`
`-f file`	Specifies an alternate `ServerConfigFile`
`-C "directive"`	Processes directive before reading `config` files
`-c "directive:`	Processes directive after reading `config` files
`-v`	Shows version number
`-V`	Shows compile settings
`-h`	Lists available command-line options
`-l`	Lists compiled-in modules
`-L`	Lists available configuration directives
`-S`	Shows parsed settings (currently on `vhost` settings)
`-t`	Runs syntax check for `config` files (with `docroot` check)

APACHE WEB SERVER CONFIGURATION

All platforms (UNIX and Windows 2000) utilize the same configuration files. The directives that control the Web server are the same for all platforms (Windows 2000 contains a few additional directives that are covered in the "Windows 2000 Installation" section). The following sections highlight the main configuration files, directives contained in configuration files, and guidelines on securing a Web server.

Configuration Files

The configuration files for the Apache Web Server are text files, and are located in the `conf` directory under the top-level directory specified by the `--prefix` option to `configure`. There are three configuration files. The `httpd.conf` file is processed first by the `httpd` daemon. The other two configuration files, `srm.conf` and `access.conf`, are processed in order after the `httpd.conf` file. It is recommended that the `srm.conf` and access.conf files remain empty and that all configuration directives be placed in the httpd.conf file. The httpd.conf file is divided into three sections.

The first section of httpd.conf contains the directives that control the operation of the Apache Web Server. Values in this section include the number of servers to start initially, maximum number of clients allowed, server root directory, timeout values, and keep-alive values. The values set in this section apply to the operation of the Apache server. The following listing is a condensed version of the first section of the httpd.conf file:

```
### httpd.conf — Apache HTTP server configuration file
# Based upon the NCSA server configuration files originally by Rob McCool.
# This is the main Apache server configuration file.  It contains the
# configuration directives that give the server its instructions.
# See <URL:http://www.apache.org/docs/> for detailed information about
# the directives.
# Do NOT simply read the instructions in here without understanding
# what they do.  They're here only as hints or reminders.  If you are unsure
# consult the online docs. You have been warned.
# After this file is processed, the server will look for and process
# /usr/local/apache/conf/srm.conf and then
# /usr/local/apache/conf/access.conf
# unless you have overridden these with ResourceConfig and/or
# AccessConfig directives here.
### Section 1: Global Environment
#
# The directives in this section affect the overall operation of Apache,
# such as the number of concurrent requests it can handle or where it
# can find its configuration files.
# ServerType is either inetd, or standalone.  Inetd mode is only supported on
# Unix platforms.
ServerType standalone
# ServerRoot: The top of the directory tree under which the server's
# configuration, error, and log files are kept.
ServerRoot "/usr/local/apache"
MinSpareServers 5
MaxSpareServers 10
#
# Number of servers to start initially -- should be a reasonable ballpark
# figure.
#
StartServers 5

#
# Limit on total number of servers running, i.e., limit on the number
# of clients who can simultaneously connect -- if this limit is ever
# reached, clients will be LOCKED OUT, so it should NOT BE SET TOO LOW.
# It is intended mainly as a brake to keep a runaway server from taking
# the system with it as it spirals down...
```

```
#
MaxClients 150
# Dynamic Shared Object (DSO) Support
# Example:
# LoadModule foo_module libexec/mod_foo.so
LoadModule rewrite_module      libexec/mod_rewrite.so

#  Reconstruction of the complete module list from all available modules
#  (static and shared ones) to achieve correct module execution order.
#  [WHENEVER YOU CHANGE THE LOADMODULE SECTION ABOVE UPDATE THIS, TOO]
ClearModuleList
AddModule mod_env.c
AddModule mod_log_config.c
AddModule mod_mime_magic.c
AddModule mod_mime.c
AddModule mod_negotiation.c
AddModule mod_status.c
AddModule mod_include.c
AddModule mod_autoindex.c
AddModule mod_dir.c
AddModule mod_cgi.c
AddModule mod_asis.c
AddModule mod_imap.c
AddModule mod_actions.c
AddModule mod_userdir.c
AddModule mod_alias.c
AddModule mod_rewrite.c
AddModule mod_access.c
AddModule mod_auth.c
AddModule mod_so.c
AddModule mod_setenvif.c
```

The second section defines settings for the "default" or "main" server. The main server responds to all requests that are not handled by a virtual host. Default settings for all virtual hosts are set in this section of the `httpd`
`.conf` file. The following listing is a condensed version of the second section of the `httpd.conf` file:

```
### Section 2: 'Main' server configuration
#
# The directives in this section set up the values used by the 'main'
# server, which responds to any requests that aren't handled by a
# <VirtualHost> definition.  These values also provide defaults for
# any <VirtualHost> containers you may define later in the file.
#
# All of these directives may appear inside <VirtualHost> containers,
# in which case these default settings will be overridden for the
# virtual host being defined.
#
# Port: The port to which the standalone server listens.  For
```

```
# ports < 1023, you will need httpd to be run as root initially.
#
Port 8080
# If you wish httpd to run as a different user or group, you must run
# httpd as root initially and it will switch.
  #
User nobody
Group nobody
# DocumentRoot: The directory out of which you will serve your
# documents. By default, all requests are taken from this directory, but
# symbolic links and aliases may be used to point to other locations.
#
DocumentRoot "/usr/local/apache/htdocs"

# Each directory to which Apache has access, can be configured with respect
# to which services and features are allowed and/or disabled in that
# directory (and its subdirectories).
#
# First, we configure the "default" to be a very restrictive set of
# permissions.
#
<Directory />
    Options FollowSymLinks
    AllowOverride None
</Directory># Note that from this point forward you must specifically allow
# particular features to be enabled - so if something's not working as
# you might expect, make sure that you have specifically enabled it
# below.
<Directory "/usr/local/apache/htdocs">
# This may also be "None", "All", or any combination of "Indexes",
# "Includes", "FollowSymLinks", "ExecCGI", or "MultiViews".
#
# Note that "MultiViews" must be named *explicitly* --- "Options All"
# doesn't give it to you.
    Options Indexes FollowSymLinks
# This controls which options the .htaccess files in directories can
# override. Can also be "All", or any combination of "Options", "FileInfo",
# "AuthConfig", and "Limit"
    AllowOverride None
# Controls who can get stuff from this server.
    Order allow,deny
    Allow from all
</Directory>
# UserDir: The name of the directory which is appended onto a user's home
# directory if a ~user request is received.
UserDir public_html
# Control access to UserDir directories.  The following is an example
# for a site where these directories are restricted to read-only.
#
#<Directory /home/*/public_html>
```

```
#       AllowOverride FileInfo AuthConfig Limit
#       Options MultiViews Indexes SymLinksIfOwnerMatch IncludesNoExec
#       <Limit GET POST OPTIONS PROPFIND>
#           Order allow,deny
#           Allow from all
#       </Limit>
#       <Limit PUT DELETE PATCH PROPPATCH MKCOL COPY MOVE LOCK UNLOCK>
#           Order deny,allow
#           Deny from all
#       </Limit>
#</Directory>
DirectoryIndex index.html
# AccessFileName: The name of the file to look for in each directory
# for access control information.
AccessFileName .htaccess
# The following lines prevent .htaccess files from being viewed by
# Web clients.  Since .htaccess files often contain authorization
# information, access is disallowed for security reasons.  Comment
# these lines out if you want Web visitors to see the contents of
# .htaccess files.  If you change the AccessFileName directive above,
# be sure to make the corresponding changes here.
# Also, folks tend to use names such as .htpasswd for password
# files, so this will protect those as well.
#
<Files ~ "^\.ht">
    Order allow,deny
    Deny from all
</Files>
```

The final section contains settings for virtual hosts. Virtual hosting allows a single Apache Web Server process to process requests for different IP addresses or hostnames. Settings in this section will override settings contained in the second section. The following listing is the third section of the `httpd.conf` file:

```
### Section 3: Virtual Hosts
#
# VirtualHost: If you want to maintain multiple domains/hostnames on your
# machine you can setup VirtualHost containers for them.
# Please see the documentation at <URL:http://www.apache.org/docs/vhosts/>
# for further details before you try to setup virtual hosts.
# You may use the command line option '-S' to verify your virtual host
# configuration.
#
# If you want to use name-based virtual hosts you need to define at
# least one IP address (and port number) for them.
#
#NameVirtualHost 12.34.56.78:80
#NameVirtualHost 12.34.56.78
#
```

```
# VirtualHost example:
# Almost any Apache directive may go into a VirtualHost container.
#
#<VirtualHost ip.address.of.host.some_domain.com>
#    ServerAdmin webmaster@host.some_domain.com
#    DocumentRoot /www/docs/host.some_domain.com
#    ServerName host.some_domain.com
#    ErrorLog logs/host.some_domain.com-error_log
#    CustomLog logs/host.some_domain.com-access_log common
#</VirtualHost>
#<VirtualHost _default_:*>
#</VirtualHost>
```

The Apache Web Server distribution includes a user's guide. It is located in the `htdocs/manual` directory. The user's guide includes an extensive section on all valid runtime configuration directives and should be consulted for the latest changes and updates. The following sections provide a brief overview of some of the more important Apache Web Server directives.

Server Directives

Server directives configure the Apache server and are found in the first section of the `httpd.conf` file. These directives set values for the root location, process identifier, and connection characteristics. Table 16.3 contains the most frequently used server directives.

Block Directives

Block directives allow the specification of directives that apply to only specified directories, files, or URLs. Table 16.4 contains a listing of the directives, their meanings, and the order in which they are applied. `Directives` are placed on lines between the beginning of the block `<Directory>` and the end of the block `</Directory>`. Regular expressions can also be specified in `Directory`, `Files`, and `Location` block directives, but must be preceded with a ~. `DirectoryMatch`, `FilesMatch`, and `Location-Match` require a regular expression in the argument field.

The merger order determines which directives have the highest priority. For instance, `Location` and `LocationMatch` are processed last, have the highest priority, and will override directives set in levels 1,2, or 3. Block directives processed last will override previous block directives with the same merger order.

Virtual Hosts

The `VirtualHost` block directive contains directives that apply to only that host. The `VirtualHost` directive allows your Apache Web Server to service requests for multiple hostnames. A simple example is setting up

Table 16.3	Server Directives
Directive	**Value**
`User UNIX-userid`	UNIX-userid under which server will answer requests Default is –1
`Group UNIX-groupid`	UNIX group under which server will answer requests Default is –1
`DocumentRoot directory-filename`	Server serves documents from `directory-filename` Default is `/usr/local/apache`
`PidFile file`	Places PID of `httpd` in `file`
`KeepAlive number`	Keeps connection open for number of requests Default is 5
`TimeOut seconds`	Server will wait for receipt of request and then completion block by block for seconds Default is 1200
`MaxClients number`	Limits simultaneous request to `number` Default is 150
`StartServers number`	Number of servers started initially Default is 5
`MaxSpareServers number`	No more than number of servers left running and unused Default is 10
`MinSpareServers number`	Server keeps at least this number of servers running Default is 5

virtual hosts for the Sales department, `www.sales.sniglets.com`, and the Accounting department, `www.accounting.sniglets.com`. The user only needs to know the main address (`www.accounting.sniglets.com`) to get to their required information.

Virtual hosts are supported as IP-based or name-based. IP-based virtual hosts require a different IP address for each virtual host. This can be accomplished on machines with multiple network interface cards or by assigning

Table 16.4	Block Directives		
Block Directive	Action	Merger Order	

`<Directory dir>`
`</Directory>`
`<DirectoryMatch dir>`
`</DirectoryMatch>`
	Applies directives to `dir` and directories below `dir`	1 without regular expressions, with `.htaccess` overriding 2 and `Directory` with regular expressions	

`<Files file>`
`</Files>`
`<FilesMatch file>`
`</FilesMatch>`
	Applies directives to `file`	3
		3	

`<Location URL>`
`</Location>`
`<LocationMatch URL>`
`</LocationMatch>`
	Applies directives to URL	4
		4	

`<IfDefine name>` `</IfDefine>`	Applies directives if the `-Dname` option is specified on Apache start	NA	
`<IfModule module-name>` `</IfModule>`	Applies directives if `module-name` was compiled in or is dynamically loaded	NA	
`<VirtualHost host>` `</VirtualHost>`	Applies directives to `host`	NA	

virtual interfaces (multiple IP addresses) to a single network interface card (check the `ifconfig` command for your operating system). The easier method of using virtual hosts is name-based. Name-based virtual hosts allow unlimited servers, easy configuration, and do not depend on the host operating system supporting virtual interfaces. The following contains the directives for two virtual hosts on the Apache Web Server `www.sniglets.com`:

```
Port 80

NameVirtualHost 192.168.33.44

<VirtualHost www.sniglets.com:80>
ServerAdmin webmaster@sniglets.com
DocumentRoot /export/www/virtual/main
```

```
ServerName www.sniglets.com
...
</VirtualHost>


<VirtualHost www.accounting.sniglets.com:80>
ServerAdmin accounting@sniglets.com
DocumentRoot /export/www/virtual/accounting
ServerName www.accounting.sniglets.com
...
</VirtualHost>

<VirtualHost www.sales.sniglets.com:80>
ServerAdmin sales@sniglets.com
DocumentRoot /export/www/virtual/sales
ServerName www.sales.sniglets.com
...
</VirtualHost>
```

The directives must be entered in the `httpd.conf` file. The `Port` directive is placed in the main server section of the `httpd.conf` file, and instructs the Web server to listen for requests on `Port 80`. The `Name-VirtualHost` directive is required to configure name-based virtual hosts, and utilization of the IP address of the Web server is recommended. The final three entries consist of the `VirtualHost` block directives. Notice that the default server (`www.sniglets.com`) is also treated as a virtual host.

.htaccess

The `.htaccess` file allows you to change directives in a directory without restarting Apache, and `.htaccess` is the default filename for file access directives. This file allows users to control their own Web pages without the assistance of the webmaster. These files must be parsed on each request and impose a small performance penalty. The `AccessFileName` directive can specify the name of files to check for file access directives. `AccessFileName` is a global directive. The `AllowOverride` directive tells the server which directives in the `.htaccess` file can override directives previously set. For the latest options for the `AllowOverride` directive, check the Apache documentation.

Common Gateway Interface (CGI)

CGI is a standard for interfacing Web servers with external applications. Plain HTML documents are static; they are files that do not change. A CGI program allows execution of a program in real time, allowing users to query databases or enter information on forms on a Web page. Apache calls an interpreter every time a CGI program is called. It is important to maintain a separate directory for CGI scripts (`/usr/local/apache/cgi-bin`). The system administrator or webmaster can exercise greater control over this directory to ensure scripts do not have an adverse effect on the rest of the Web directories

Executing scripts can wreak havoc with the security and stability of a Web server. It is very important to maintain a non-production Web server that can be a test-bed for new scripts and programs. Once the scripts/programs have been tested on the non-production server, they can be moved to the production server.

Logging

The Apache Web Server can give a webmaster an extensive amount of information through its logging module (`mod_log_config.c`). Table 16.5 contains the main logging directives in Apache. The `LogFormat` directive uses the standard CLF, which is supported by most commercial log analyzers. The `LogLevel` directive should be set to at least the level of `error`.

Apache and SSL

The Apache-SSL and Apache Interface to OpenSSL (`mod_ssl`) packages provide cryptography for the Apache Web Server. Apache-SSL implements the SSL as a set of patches to the Apache source code. The Apache Interface to OpenSSL is a source extension and a set of patches for the Apache source code. The Apache Interface to OpenSSL implements SSL and transport-layer

Table 16.5	Logging Directives
Directive	Action
`LogLevel` *level*	Sets the amount of information recorded in the error logs, where *level* can be `emerg`, `alert`, `crit`, `error`, `warn`, `notice`, `info`, or `debug`.
`LogFormat format` `[nickname]`	Sets the format of the default log file set by the `TransferLog` directive.
`ErrorLog filename|` `syslog[:facility]`	Sets the name of the file to which the server will log any errors. `syslog` enables logging via `syslogd`, if the system supports it. *Facility* can be a documented name in `syslog`.
`TransferLog`	Adds a log file in the format defined by the `LogFormat` directive.

security protocols. These packages are free and can be utilized outside of the U.S. and Canada for non-commercial and commercial purposes.

Both of these packages can be utilized in the U.S. and Canada by obtaining a license from RSA Security Inc. (`www.rsa.com`). As an alternative, commercial packages are available that provide Apache with SSL. Red Hat Linux Professional (`www.redhat.com`) includes a secure Web server with the Red Hat Linux distribution. Covalent Raven SSL [(`www.covalent.net`)] and Stronghold (`www.c2.net`) are modules that provide Apache with SSL.

Security

Security cannot be ignored when setting up an Apache Web Server. The permissions on the configuration and executable directories should only allow write permission by root. The `httpd` binary should be owned by root and executable by all users.

The following actions should be followed in securing your Web server:

- Use the `ScriptAlias` directive to force all CGIs to a separate directory. This gives the system administrator control over what is allowed in this directory.
- Run a non-production Apache Web Server. Require all CGI programs to be thoroughly tested on this machine before moving them to the production Web server.
- Do not allow `.htaccess` files to override security to protect the Web server.
- Lock down the `ServerRoot` and allow access only on a directory or virtual host basis.
- Access to directories by default is allowed. Use the `order` directive to protect the `ServerRoot`, and enable access by specific directory.
- Do not ignore the merge order of block directives. `Files` and `Location` block directives can override directives in `Directory` blocks.

WIN32 BINARY INSTALLATION

The Apache Web Server binaries are available at [`http://www.apache.org`]. The Apache Web Server was originally designed for UNIX. It is still considered beta-quality code for Windows (NT and 2000), as of version 1.3.9.

During the installation of the Apache server, you will be reminded that it is beta-quality code and that there are known bugs and security concerns. Taking these warnings into consideration, you should probably utilize this version of Apache Web Server on Windows 2000 as an internal Web server behind your company's firewall. Of course, once the Apache Web Server is no longer considered a beta release, you will have to make the decision on whether to deploy it as a primary Web server.

Windows 2000 Installation

The Windows 2000 Apache distribution binary is an executable file. Executing the binary requires you to select an installation directory, the `Start` menu name, and installation type. Table 16.6 outlines the different selections available and packages that will be installed.

The installation program will configure the Apache server in the `conf` directory under the selected installation directory. If configuration files already exist, the installation program will not overwrite the current files, but place a copy of the configuration file containing a `*.default` extension. Upon completion of the installation, check the `*.default` configuration file for changes that may be required in your original configuration files.

The Apache Web Server serves files from the `htdocs` directory under the installation directory. It will not overwrite an existing `index.html` file in the `htdocs` directory. This allows upgrading the server without losing the existing Web site.

The Apache Web Server binary is placed in the top level of the installation directory. The server binary is `apache.exe`.

Windows 2000 Configuration

The Apache Web Server configuration files are installed in the `conf` directory. The main configuration file is `httpd.conf`. The configuration files were described in the *"Apache Web Server Configuration"* section. The next few paragraphs will highlight the major differences in configuring Windows 2000.

Table 16.6	Apache Web Server Installation Options on Windows 2000
Option	Packages
Minimum	Application files
Typical	Application files Manuals
Custom	Application files Manuals Source code

The Apache server uses UNIX filenames internally. This requires the use of forward slashes (/) instead of backward slashes (\). Configuration files (`httpd.conf`, `srm.conf`, and `access.conf`) and Web page files (`htdocs` directory) must use forward slashes. Drive letters can be included, with the default drive being the drive containing the Apache executable. However, directives that accept filenames as arguments must utilize the backward slash or Windows-style filenames. The following is an example of a directive utilizing Windows-style filenames:

```
E:\program files\Apache Group\Apache>apache -f "c:\
mywebsite\conf\web.conf"
```

The DSO module is compiled into the Apache Web Server binary. This allows the server to load modules at runtime. DSO modules included with the distribution, but not compiled into the Web server binary, are located under the directory modules. Activating a DSO module at runtime requires the addition of the `LoadModule` directive in the `httpd.conf` file. The following line would be the correct entry to add the `rewrite` module (note the use of forward slashes):

```
LoadModule rewrite_module modules/ApacheModuleRewrite.dll
```

The Internet Server Applications Programming Interface (ISAPI) extensions module is compiled into the Apache binary. This allows ISAPI to be used with Apache on Windows 2000. To enable ISAPI, copy the ISAPI `.dll` files into the document root, and then add the following line to the `httpd.conf` file:

```
AddHandler isapi-isa dll
```

Process management under Windows 2000 utilizes multi-threading. The Apache Web Server under Windows 2000 will not generate separate processes to handle each request like UNIX versions. Apache will run with two processes-consisting of the controlling parent process and the child process. The child process does most of the work and handles each request by a separate thread. The `MaxRequestPerChild` sets the number of requests a process will handle before terminating. Under Windows 2000, one process handles all requests. Setting the `MaxRequestPerChild` to 0 lets the process run until the machine is rebooted. The `ThreadsPerChild` directive is only valid under Windows 2000, and it controls the number of threads the child process utilizes to service requests. The default setting is 50. If you have a very busy site, you may need to increase this number.

Starting Apache in Windows 2000

The Apache Web Server can be started two different ways under Windows 2000. It can be configured as a service, allowing the server to start automatically at boot and continuing to run after you log out. It can also be run from a console window.

Installation of Apache as a Windows 2000 service is accomplished with the `-i` option. The following command will add the Apache Web Server as service `apache` on Windows 2000:

```
E:\program files\Apache Group\Apache>apache -I
```

Renaming the service to `Apache Web Server` requires two steps. First, remove the apache service with:

```
E:\program files\Apache Group\Apache>apache -u
```

Next, install the service with its new name:

```
E:\program files\Apache Group\Apache>apache -I -n "Apache
Web Server"
```

To specify a configuration file, enter the following:

```
E:\program files\Apache Group\Apache>apache -I -n "Apache
Web Server" -f "\myweb\conf\web.conf"
```

Once installed, the service can be manipulated with the Windows 2000 Control Panel's `Administrative Services->Services` interface.

Running Apache from the command line can be as simple as typing in `Apache`. Once Apache is running in a console window, you can stop it two different ways. The ungraceful way is to execute a <CTRL-C> in the console window. This will stop the Apache server and kill all requests currently being processed. To shut down gracefully, which will complete requests currently running, open a different console window and execute:

```
apache -k shutdown
```

Command-line options supported under Windows 2000 are included in Tables 16.2 and 16.7:

Table 16.7	**Windows 2000 Command-Line Options**
Option	Result
`-n name`	Sets service name and uses it
`-k shutdown`	Tells running Apache to shut down
`-k restart`	Tells running Apache to do a graceful restart
`-k start`	Tells Apache to start
`-I`	Installs an Apache service
`-u`	Uninstalls an Apache service

Internet Information Server 5.0

Microsoft's Internet Information Server (IIS) has quickly become a popular Web server platform. IIS 5.0 builds on previous releases of Internet Information Server with new features and capabilities. IIS 5.0 is integrated into Windows 2000 Server and can be installed during the initial system setup or afterward using the Add/Remove Programs Control Panel applet. IIS 5.0 provides the following key features:

- World Wide Web (WWW) services.
- File Transfer Protocol (FTP) services.
- News (NNTP) services.
- Mail (SMTP) services.

As you can see, IIS 5.0 is much more than just a Web server. In this chapter, we will describe the steps necessary to install a basic IIS 5.0 system, the basic configuration of default WWW services, and the basic configuration of default FTP services. While there is much more to IIS than what this chapter will describe, we cannot possibly cover everything here. For advanced configuration options and features, you should consult the IIS 5.0 documentation or the Internet Information Server Resource Kit.

Installing IIS 5.0

You can install IIS 5.0 during the initial setup of Windows 2000 Server, or afterward using the Add/Remove Programs Control Panel applet. In both cases, you must select which IIS options you intend to install. If you are using the Add/Remove Programs Control Panel applet, you should select the Add/Remove Windows Components option to select the IIS options you wish to install. The options selection screen for IIS is shown in Figure 16.2.

For the basic IIS installation we will discuss in this chapter, we suggest you select the following IIS components:

- `Common Files`
- `Documentation`
- `File Transfer Protocol (FTP) Server`
- `FrontPage 2000 Server Extensions`
- `Internet Information Services Snap-In`
- `Internet Services Manager (HTML)`
- `World Wide Web Server`

Once you have completed copying files, IIS 5.0 will be ready to begin processing WWW and FTP requests. By default, IIS 5.0 uses `C:\InetPub`

Figure 16.2
IIS installation
options.

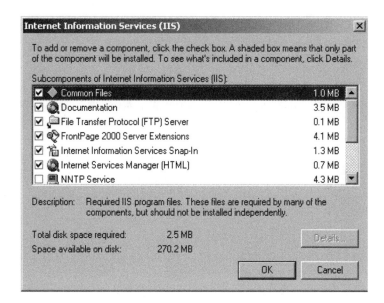

for WWW and FTP document storage. Table 16.8 describes the default locations for document storage.

You have the ability to change the location of the default folders and/or to create virtual links to folders stored on other local and network drives. For our purposes, however, we will utilize the default settings. The next sections will describe the basic configuration options for WWW and FTP services.

WWW Services

IIS 5.0 provides basic and advanced Web server functions such as Active Server Pages (ASPs) and Common Gateway Interface (CGI) scripting. This section will describe the configuration options available for the default Web site configured when IIS 5.0 is installed. The options are configured using

Table 16.8	Default IIS 5.0 Document Locations
Document Type	Description
Web Documents (`*.html`, `*.htm`) and Folders	Should be stored in or under `C:\ InetPub\wwwroot`
FTP Documents and Folders	Should be stored in or under `C:\ InetPub\ftproot`
Scripts	Should be stored in or under C:\ InetPub\scripts

the Internet Services Manager MMC snap-in, which can be launched as follows: from the `Start` menu → `Administrative Tools` → `Internet Services Manager`. The Internet Services Manager is shown in Figure 16.3.

To configure the options for the default Web site, select `the Default Web Site` from the list of IIS sites on your system, and select `Properties` from the `Action` menu. The `Default Web Site Properties` window in Figure 16.4 will be displayed.

As you can see, there are several option tabs available. The following sections will describe the different option tabs and the options available.

Web Site This page allows you to configure the identification parameters for your entire Web site. Here you can configure the IP address and TCP ports for the site, connection limitations, and logging options. The default settings found on this page are acceptable for most sites. To host multiple sites from a single machine, or to create virtual sites, you should refer to the on-line documentation or to the IIS Resource Kit.

Operators This page allows you to specify which Windows 2000 user accounts are granted operator privileges on the Web site. Operators have the ability to change Web site settings, and to start and stop the Web site.

Performance This page allows you to configure memory, processor, and bandwidth usage parameters. Table 16.9 describes the properties available.

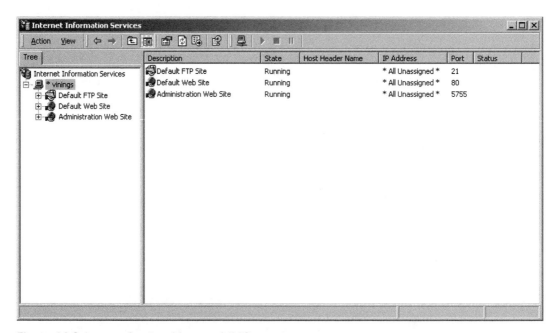

Figure 16.3 Internet Services Manager MMC snap-in.

Figure 16.4
Default Web Site
Properties.

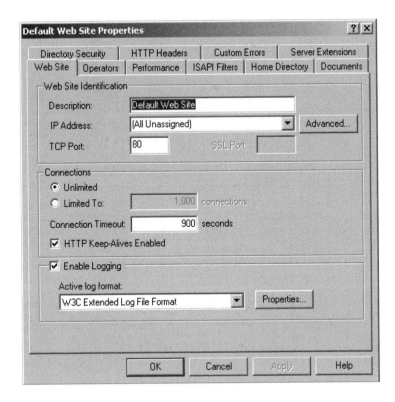

ISAPI Filters This page allows you to add, remove, and configure ISAPI filters, which are programs that are invoked in response to HTTP-generated events.

Home Directory This page allows you to configure the location of the Web site's home directory. By default, the location is `C:\Inetpub\wwwroot`. There are three types of directories:

Table 16.9	Web Site Performance Properties
Property	Description
Performance Tuning	Allows you to configure the site for an expected number of daily connections. By properly configuring this setting, memory will be optimally used by the Web server service.
Bandwidth Throttling	Allows you to limit how much of the available network bandwidth is utilized by the Web site.
Process Throttling	Allows you to limit how much of the Web server's processor time can be utilized by this Web site.

■ A directory located on this computer is physically located on the same server that the WWW service runs on.

■ A share located on another computer is physically located on another server and shared over the network with the appropriate permissions.

■ A redirection to a URL will send connections to another Web site, which can be hosted from the same server or another server on the network.

As part of the home directory configuration, you are also presented with options for configuring access permissions, browsing, and logging.

Documents This page allows you to configure the default document and document footer for your Web site. Default documents are automatically sent to clients when they connect to your Web site. Document footers are appended to every HTML document sent to clients when they connect.

Directory Security This page allows you to configure directory and file security for your Web site. NTFS permissions can be utilized to protect sensitive content on your Web site. This page allows you to tailor how security is implemented. Table 16.10 describes the different configuration options available.

HTTP Headers This page allows you to configure and add HTTP headers that will be returned to the client browser. This page includes configuration options for content expiration, custom HTTP headers, and MIME (Multipurpose Internet Mail Extensions) mappings.

Table 16.10	Web Site Directory and File Security Configuration Options
Option	Description
Anonymous Access and Authentication Control	Allows you to configure how users will be authenticated, when required, during a connection. Users that do not connect anonymously must have a valid Windows 2000 user account and have been granted permission to the files and directories via NTFS permissions.
IP Address and Domain Name Restrictions	Allows you to allow/deny access based on IP addresses and domain names.
Secure Communications	Allows you to install and configure Secure Sockets Layer (SSL) certificates to enable encrypted communications.

Custom Errors This page allows you to customize the error messages sent to clients when errors occur during requests.

Server Extensions This page allows you to configure the options required for enabling publishing to your Web site using Microsoft FrontPage.

FTP Services

In addition to the built-in WWW services, IIS 5.0 also provides FTP services for your Windows 2000 Server. This section will describe the configuration options available for the default FTP site configured during IIS 5.0 installation. As with the WWW service, the FTP service options are configured using the Internet Services Manager MMC snap-in shown previously in Figure 16.2. Again, to refresh your memory, you can launch the Internet Services Manager as follows: from the `Start` menu → `Administrative Tools` → `Internet Services Manager`.

FTP Site This page, Figure 16.5, allows you to configure the identification, connection, and logging options for your FTP server. Table 16.11 describes the different options available on the FTP site `Properties` page.

Figure 16.5
Properties for the
default FTP site.

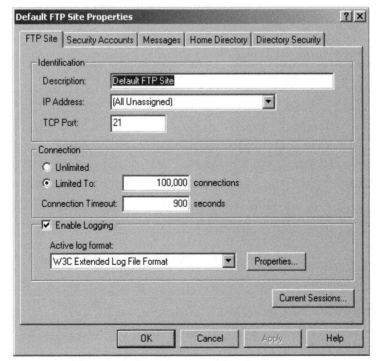

Table 16.11	FTP Site Identification Options
Option	Description
Identification	This section allows you to enter a description for your FTP site, configure the IP address(es) for your FTP site, and determine which TCP port your FTP service will operate on. In most cases, the default settings are sufficient.
Connection	This section allows you to determine the number of simultaneous connections to support on your server, and how long a connection can remain idle before a user is disconnected. The default settings are normally sufficient.
Enable Logging	This section allows you to enable or disable logging of FTP site activity, as well as choose a log file format.

Security Accounts This page allows you to configure anonymous access to the FTP site, as well as define the operators of the FTP site. You can enable or disable anonymous FTP access and assign a Windows 2000 user account for anonymous access purposes. FTP site operators are granted limited administrative control over the FTP site.

Messages This page allows you to configure the messages returned by the FTP server when a user logs on, logs off, and when the maximum number of connections has been reached. The messages are blank by default.

Home Directory This page, much like its WWW service counterpart, allows you to configure the location of the FTP site's home directory. By default, the location is C:\Inetpub\ftproot. There are two types of directories:

- A directory located on this computer is physically located on the same server that the WWW service runs on.
- A share located on another computer is physically located on another server and shared over the network with the appropriate permissions.

As part of home directory configuration, you are also presented with options for configuring access permissions and logging. In addition, you are also allowed to configure the directory listing style:

- UNIX directory listing style displays a four-digit year for file dates when the date of the file is different from the year of the FTP server. When the file date is the same as the year of the FTP server, no year is returned in the directory listing.
- MS-DOS directory listing style displays a two-digit year when displaying file dates.

Directory Security This page, like its WWW service counterpart, allows you to specify which computers are granted or denied access to your FTP server. You can specify computer systems by using an IP address, subnet mask, or domain name. By default, all computers are granted access.

Summary

This chapter has been a brief description of installing and configuring the Apache Web Server and Internet Information Server 5.0. In many cases, Web server installation is now an option when installing the operating system. However, it is still important to understand this process and know how to configure the server.

APACHE WEB SERVER

The Apache Web Server is the most widely used Web server on UNIX platforms. The Apache Autoconf-style Interface (APACI) greatly simplifies the compilation and installation processes. The APACI generates the correct configuration files for your operating system. Most UNIX variants are supported. All platforms (UNIX and Windows 2000) utilize the same configuration files. The directives that control the Web server are also the same for all platforms. The Apache-SSL and Apache Interface to OpenSSL (`mod_ssl`) packages provide cryptography for the Apache Web Server.

INTERNET INFORMATION SERVER

IIS 5.0 is integrated into Windows 2000 Server and can be installed during the initial system setup or afterward using the Add/Remove Programs Control Panel applet. IIS 5.0 provides basic and advanced Web server functions such as Active Server Pages (ASPs) and Common Gateway Interface (CGI) scripting. ISS 5.0 also provides advanced FTP support for Windows 2000. In addition to the two services covered in this chapter, IIS 5.0 offers news (NTTP) and mail (SMTP) support.

COMMAND SUMMARY

- `Acledit`—Edits an ACL on a file or directory.
- `Aclget`—Shows the ACL information on a file or directory.
- `Aclput`—Sets up ACLs on a file or directory
- Amanda is a cross-platform backup/restore utility that is freely available. It has more capabilities than the backup/restore tools included with most UNIX variants.
- `at/batch`—Are the UNIX equivalents of the Windows 2000 `at` command. They are used to run a command at a later time.
- `at`—Is a console-mode command that allows the scheduling of programs and commands on a local or remote system.
- `Chacl`—Adds / edits ACLs.
- `chgroup`—Changes attributes for groups
- `chgrpmem`—Changes administrators or members of a group
- `chuser`—Changes user attributes
- `ci, co`—Check in and check out, respectively. These are part of the suite of commands that make up the RCS version control system.
- `cp`—Copies files or directories in UNIX systems.
- `crontab`—Schedules recurring jobs or processes and is very similar to the Task Scheduler in Windows 2000.
- `domainname`—displays the domain name for the system. Generally this is used to determine the NIS+ domain to which the system is attached.
- `domainname`—used without an argument will display the domain name of the system. If an argument is used, the domain name is set to that. `ypinit`—initializes a system to be an NIS server.
- `enq`—can start and stop queues and printers. It can also change the priority of a job, remove a job from a queue, and list the status of a printer's queue.
- `exportfs`—(BSD) used export file systems to remote machines. `share` (SysV) similar to `exportfs`, used for SysV based systems.
- `format`—is a disk partitioning and maintenance utility. Options vary throughout the UNIX family. Linux uses the `fdisk` command.

- `Format`—is used to partition, label, and prepare a new or existing disk to be recognized by the system. Once a disk device is selected, use the `print` option to display the current partition table. The **partition** command is used to subdivide a disk into multiple sections. For standardization, always use `partition a` (slice 0) for root and `partition b` (slice 1) for swap.

- free—Displays the amount of memory. It is available in Red Hat Linux 6.0.

- FTP provides a mechanism to transfer files from one system to another where a direct filesystem copy is not an option. FTP is used to transfer software packages, image files, and user data.

- `fuser`—will show processes which are using a mounted filesystem.

- `getfacl`—Displays ACL entries on a file.

- `groups`—Lists the groups of which the supplied user is a member.

- `halt`—(SysV and BSD) halts the system. If given the `-q` option, it will do so without any attempt at a graceful shutdown. With the `-n` option, it prevents the `sync` command. Use caution with this command; if used unwisely, it could result in damage to the filesystems and loss of data. On some systems, it is linked to `poweroff`.

- `hostname`—determines the hostname of a given system. This command gives the true name (not aliases) and can be useful in scripting. Licensed software may also use this command to unlock the software.

- `init`—(SysV and BSD) is a BSD command but it is only called by the system and should not be called by users. The SysV version of the command allows the super-user to change the run level of the `init` process.

- `iostat`—Provides statistics on disk, terminal, and CPU activity. This command should be utilized to monitor your disk subsystem.

- `job#`—Removes the job number listed.

- `ln`—creates a hard link to a file

- `ln -s`—creates a symbolic link to a file

- `loadkeys` and `dumpkeys`—(SysV and BSD) load and dump keyboard translation tables, respectively.

- The `lp` command is the command-line interface for submitting print jobs. Multiple options can be entered with the `lp` command to specify destination, number of copies, and other options. `lpadmin` configures spooling systems to describe printers, classes, and set the default printer.

- The `lpc` command enables the system administrator to control the actions of the printer system.

- `lpr`—is the command-line interface for sending jobs to a printer. Some of the options are listed here.
- `lprm`—Removes a job(s) from the queue.
- `Lsacl`—Lists ACLs.
- `lsgroup`—Displays group attributes
- `lsuser`—Displays user account attributes
- `mailq`—Provides a listing of all messages in the mail queue.
- `mailstats`—Provides current mail statistics for the local machine.
- `mkgroup`—Creates a new group
- `mkuser`—Creates a new user account
- `mount`—used to mount local or remote filesystems into the directory structure.
- `netstat`—Provides information on network counters and parameters. The `netstat -i` command will show all configured interfaces and a total column for all interfaces. `netstat -I le0` will produce output for network interface card `le0`.
- `net`—There are several commands beginning with `net` that provide command-line control on NT networking. `net./?` will provide a listing of the commands available.
- `newfs` constructs a new UNIX filesystem. It is a friendly front-end to the `mkfs` program.
- `newgrp` Changes a users's real GID
- `nfsstat` provides statistical data on NFS and RPC activity.
- `nice`—Allows you to invoke a command with a different system scheduling priority. This command is useful in decreasing or increasing the priority of a process at invocation.
- `niscat` similar to `ypcat` in NIS, it provides a listing of an NIS+ map.
- `nisping` provides information on the NIS+ root master you are using.
- `nisserver` initiates a system to be an NIS+ server. `nispopulate` populates the database of an NIS+ server.
- `passwd` or `pwdadm`—Sets the user password.
- `pmon.exe`—Is a command-line tool that monitors memory and processor usage.
- `ps`—Provides a snapshot of processes currently running on the system, and is probably one of the most utilized commands on UNIX systems. This is the UNIX equivalent of the `pmon` command in Windows 2000.

- `pviewer.exe`—Is part of the Windows 2000 Resource Kit and allows you to monitor running processes on a local or remote system.

- `rdist`—Designed to automatically replicate the directory structure from one system to another, without manual intervention.

- `reboot`—(SysV and BSD) performs a shutdown and then a restart of the operating system. You can pass boot arguments to the system with this command. It does not warn users of its actions.

- `renice`—Allows you to raise or lower the priority of a process that is already running.

- `rmuser`—Removes a user account

- `rpm`—is a powerful utility that can be used to install, uninstall, query, and verify software.

- `sar`—Is the best utility to log performance statistics for UNIX operating systems. The system activity reporter is available on Solaris, HPUX, and AIX systems.

- `sendmail`—Is the email server in UNIX. `sendmail` does inter-network forwarding as necessary to deliver a message to its correct place. `sendmail` is commonly launched with `-bd -q30m` which puts the server in the background and processes the queue every 30 minutes.

- `setfacl`—Is used to set, modify, and delete an ACL entry on a file.

- `setgroups`—Resets a session's process group set

- `shutdown`—(SysV and BSD) is used to halt or reboot the system. It has options (many unique to individual versions of UNIX) that allow a grace period to be provided, user warnings to be broadcast, and boot options to be provided.

- `smbtar`—SAMBA command to create `tar` files from Windows 2000 systems.

- `smit`—menu-driven system administration and management tool for AIX

- `smitty`—character based version of *smit*

- `sync`—(SysV and BSD) updates the super-block and writes all system buffers to disk. This is necessary for filesystem integrity. `Shutdown`, `reboot`, and `init` call the `sync` primitive.

- `tar`—Creates an archive of UNIX directories or small filesystems.

- `umount` used to remove mounted filesystems.

- `User`—Removes all jobs for the user if a username is specified (superuser only).

- `vmstat`—Provides statistics on processes, virtual memory, disk, interrupts, and CPU activity. CPU utilization and virtual memory monitoring are the primary uses for this command.
- `ypcat`—provides a listing of an NIS map.
- `ypmatch`—returns the match of a search key within a map, if any exist.
- `yppush`—is used only on the server to transfer files to a slave.
- `ypwhich`—returns the name of the server to which a client is bound. The -m option provides a listing of available maps.
- `ypxfr`—transfers NIS maps from the master server to one slave.

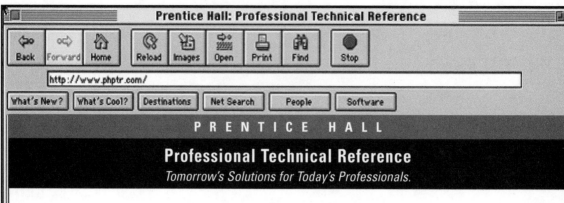